MW01277163

Introduction to Programming Using Ada

Dennis Volper
California State University, Long Beach
Martin D. Katz
California State University, Fullerton

PRENTICE HALL
Englewood Cliffs, New Jersey 07632

Library of Congress Cataloging-in-Publication Data

Volper, Dennis J.
Introduction to programming using ADA / Dennis Volper, Martin D. Katz.
p. cm.
ISBN 0-13-493529-2
1. Ada (Computer program language) I. Katz, Martin D. II. Title.
QA76.73.A53V65 1990
005.13'3--dc20 89-23153
CIP

Editorial/production supervision: Joanne Jimenez
Cover design: Ben Santora
Manufacturing buyer: Lori Bulwin

Printed in the United States of America
10 9 8 7 6 5 4 3 2 1

ISBN 0-13-493529-2

PRENTICE-HALL INTERNATIONAL (UK) LIMITED, LONDON
PRENTICE-HALL OF AUSTRALIA PTY. LIMITED, SYDNEY
PRENTICE-HALL CANADA INC., TORONTO
PRENTICE-HALL HISPANOAMERICANA, S.A., MEXICO
PRENTICE-HALL OF INDIA PRIVATE LIMITED, NEW DELHI
PRENTICE-HALL OF JAPAN, INC., TOKYO
SIMON & SCHUSTER ASIA PTE. LTD., SINGAPORE
EDITORA PRENTICE-HALL DO BRASIL, LTDA., RIO DE JANEIRO

Contents

Preface

This book is designed for an introductory course in computer science. We hope that the book is not just another Ada text, but rather an introduction to computer science which happens to use Ada as its language. We have taken care to make the material in the text accessible to students who have no previous programming background. On the other hand, the book also provides sufficient depth to satisfy experienced students learning Ada for the first time.

The growing availability of Ada offers an opportunity for the instructional use of a programming language which reflects previous experience and experimentation with structured languages. Specifically, Ada supplies the means to write modularized programs in a standardized language. We believe that it is never too early to teach the fundamental principles of programming that are embodied in the structuring and modularization capabilities of Ada. Mastery of these principles is essential for anyone who will be involved with a large-scale programming project. Particularly for computer science majors, practice of the principles should begin with the very first course and not be delayed until late in the curriculum, as is all too common.

Since we believe practice to be essential to the grasp of concepts and the acquisition of knowledge, we have designed this book so that the student begins applying concepts in the very first chapters. The presentation methodology we use is often called the *spiral approach.* According to this technique, the first time a topic is presented, the simplest concepts of that topic are covered. Later the topic will be revisited, possibly several times, with additional details covered each time. Indeed, the interaction among Ada language features is such that if the traditional approach of exhaustive coverage of topics in order is insisted on, most of the language would have to be covered before the student could write a program.

Each chapter is designed to advance the student to a new level of problem-solving capabilities. Each begins with a list of objectives and a motivational discussion. Each emphasizes correct programming practices, especially for the topics introduced in that chapter. Finally, each includes programming exercises which emphasize the application of ideas introduced in the chapter.

Several aspects of the book provide a motivation and foundation for later courses. For example, the book builds an appreciation for data structures and algorithms and includes advanced language topics, such as concurrent programming. The intent is not to provide exhaustive coverage, but to introduce such topics in a way that encourages further study.

We supply a number of packages. Some of these provide problem domains, allowing the student to solve problems in an interesting and yet conceptually simple context. For example, we introduce input and output with a package that is easy to use, because the input and output support provided by Ada is quite complex. Full input and output support is covered in later chapters. The supplied packages serve to illustrate to the student the great convenience of modularization, particularly as expressed in the provision of tools.

Since we have designed the course as a series of topics and chapters in a spiral approach, the student needs to master early material in order to have the background for later material. To assist in providing and checking this mastery, a computerized quiz system is available which is coordinated with the chapters. If these quizzes are used, the student should approach each chapter by (1) studying the material, (2) using the quizzes, and (3) doing the homework by designing, writing, and testing packages or procedures. The factual quizzes may be used both for drill and practice and for testing. In addition, there is a series of programming quizzes designed to test the student's problem-solving abilities.

The first chapter of the book is an overview of computers and programming, intended as an easy introduction into the realm of computer programming. Advanced students may skip sections 1.3 through 1.5. Chapters 2 through 8 cover data structures, types, and control structures; generics, access types, and concurrency are not included. Coverage of the topics in Chapters 2 through 8 excludes some details and uses packages to hide some of the complexity of the language.

Chapter 9 discusses scope, naming, and visibility in detail. This is the beginning of tying up the details missing from earlier chapters. It is in this chapter that recursion is first introduced as a separate concept (earlier examples make use of it implicitly). Chapter 10 discusses exception handling in detail. Chapter 11 introduces concurrency, leaving details to Chapters 18 and 19.

Chapters 12 through 16 explore the powerful data structures available in Ada. Chapters 12 and 13 discuss abstract data types and how these are represented in Ada. Chapter 14 discusses the details of numbers in Ada. Chapter 15 presents an extensive coverage of access types (pointers). Finally, Chapter 16 covers generics, Ada's method of representing collection of data structures and algorithms in a somewhat type-independent manner.

Chapter 17 wraps up the special rules in Ada reguarding libraries, compilation order, and other details left out earlier to avoid confusion. The chapter also includes a discussion (although not details) of Ada's support for system-dependent programming. Finally, Chapters 18 and 19 provide a complete discussion of tasks, Ada's construct for support of concurrent programming.

USING THE TEXT

This book may be used with either a one-semester (or quarter) course or a two-semester (or quarter) sequence. If it is to be used in a one-semester course, Chapters 1 through 8 will provide a basic background in both Ada and programming (about equivalent to introducing programming using Pascal, but excluding pointers). Should time permit, Chapters 9, 10, and/or 11 can be used to augment Ada coverage, depending on the concentration desired by the instructor.

The text is designed to complement a two-semester introductory course. The Ada language is too complex to be covered in detail in a one-semester course for students who do not have an extensive programming background. In most curricula, the second semester is an introduction to data structures. Almost all of the material normally covered in such a course is covered in the examples and exercises in this book. Thus, the book may be used in conjunction with a two-semester sequence in which the second semester introduces data structures.

As a prelude to, or at the start of, an introductory course in data structures, we recommend covering Chapters 12, 13, and 15 in the text. Chapter 15 (on access types) can be covered immediately after Chapter 9 if section 15.3.4 is omitted. Chapter 11 (on tasking) is required only by Chapters 18 and 19. Chapter 14 (real numbers) is not required for any later chapter.

ACKNOWLEDGMENTS

Over the past five years, numerous people have assisted our development of this book. They have read and criticized our documents and our approaches to teaching the topics. They have provided new examples, uncovered flaws in existing examples, pointed out topics not covered, and discovered mistakes in those covered. We hope that we have not omitted anyone in our acknowledgments, but the list is extremely long.

Our special thanks go to two persons for extensive cooperation in our effort. Steve Franklin has participated in every aspect of development and has been enthusiastic in discussing the what and why of Ada. Cindy Tittle not only helped develop the manuscript, but also developed portions of the software and some of the exercises and supervised our other student workers.

The manuscript has benefited from the detailed examination of Steve Hampson and Cathryn Tallman-Evans and from the development of the syntax diagrams by Ching-Chi Kaw. We appreciate the excellent suggestions of the reviewers, including Lance B. Elliot of the University of Southern California, Anthony Gargaro of the Computer Science

Corporation, J. L. Diaz-Herrara of George Mason University, and Stephen Wampler of Northern Arizona University. Their work has resulted in many improvements in this book.

We wish to express our thanks to the students who struggled through various versions of the homework problems to discover which ones worked and which ones did not. We particularly wish to thank Steve Huberty, Byon Garrabrant, and Dave O'Shea, who helped our students and us through the assignments.

We offer our thanks to the five years' worth of special-projects students and student employees who participated in developing the Ada components we used in the course: Jack Ahn, Penelope Auyang, Jung (Jaime) Bae, Frank Bielsik, Nanette Bloom, Timo Bruck, Mary Cameron, Grace Chang, Carol Cisar, Chia-Wei Chow, Donald Duffin, Jennifer-Ann Durand, Byon Garrabrant, Michele Goddard, Dave Godwin, Maurice Hermeyer, Steve Huberty, Ray Hwang, Becky Jones, Cheryl Kaneko, Glen Kauffman, Joseph Kim, Samuel Kim, Sang Kim, Nils Kollandsrud, David Kolson, Glen Kosaka, Stephanie Leif, Debra Leisge, April Lovell, Lee Marvin, Jeffry Miller, Alistair Milne, Wayne Mintz, Pamela Moore, Lisa Nakama, Cuong Nguyen, Kari Nies, Kevin Packard, Richard Parker, Gary Petersen, Rob Retter, Lynn Reynolds, Roger Ritchie, Cynthia Rohrig, Thomas Ryono, Wayne Sameshima, Jay Sierzchula, Scott Simpson, Mark Torres, Terri Tracey, Dung Trieu, Maryann Wall, Nangnang Widjaja, Sharon Winn, David Wolverton, Winnie Woo, Grace Wu, Jeanette Yang, and Harry Yessayan.

Especially, we would like to thank our editor, Marcia Horton. She was particularly helpful in determining the target audience and helping us to know how to interpret the reviews. Without her patience and support, the book would probably not have been completed. In addition, we would like to thank our production editors at Prentice Hall, Joanne Jimenez and Cheryl Adelmann Hadley.

Finally, our thanks to Dr. John King and the Department of Information and Computer Science at the University of California, Irvine, for their continued support of this project.

Dennis Volper
California State University, Long Beach

Martin D. Katz
California State University, Fullerton

1

Building Procedures and Using Packages

1.1 OBJECTIVES

In this chapter, you will learn to construct simple Ada programs. By the end of the chapter, you should be able to write and run an Ada program that makes use of some predefined tools.

There are three principal topics in the chapter: a brief explanation of the computer from the programmer's standpoint (sections 3–5), a description of how to put together a simple Ada program (sections 6–14), and a description of some predefined tools that can be used to build interesting programs (sections 15–16).

A crucial technique in Ada is to define a set of tools that can be used for constructing programs. In this chapter, we introduce the use of existing Ada tools; in the next chapter, we show how to construct such tools.

CONCEPTS:

- A computer follows instructions.
- A program is a set of instructions to be followed.
- A computer language is a means of communicating with a computer.
- A program should be a document that is readable by a human.
- Predefined tools are an important problem-solving technique.

GOALS:

- Understand the use of syntax notation.
- Learn the syntax of some fundamental Ada constructs.

- Run a stored program.
- Use a translator (compiler), editor, file-handling system, and other standard computer programming tools.
- Write a program that uses predefined tools from some prepared packages.

1.2 MOTIVATION

A computer is a machine that follows instructions. In computer terminology, a set of instructions is called a *program.* Giving instructions to the computer is called *programming.* Programs are written in special languages called *programming languages.* One of these programming languages is called Ada. When a computer is following the instructions in a program, we say that the computer is *executing* the program.

In Ada, a program is often made up of smaller parts. These smaller parts can be complete programs themselves, but when the *main* program is executed, the parts perform their particular duties as requested by the main program. We can view these parts as *tools.* Ada contains features that facilitate the construction and use of tools. These features encourage the decomposition of a program into parts which can be written or changed independently, without serious effects on the rest of the program.

In this chapter, we introduce two concepts for decomposing programs; the *procedure*, one of the important types of tools, and the *package*, a construct for collecting related tools. Initially, we will use a procedure as the main program and packages as a means of accessing the tools we need.

A computer program is built from many different pieces. One common method of referring these pieces is to *name* them. In Ada, one kind of name is the *identifier.* The identifier provides a method of naming that is convenient for the programmer. In Ada, each procedure, each package, each tool within a package, and each of many other things yet to be introduced has associated with it an identifier by which the programmer can refer to it.

It is convenient to have a formal way of describing what is "legal" in a given computer language. In English, *syntax* (grammar) describes the way words are put together into sentences. Correct syntax is necessary to make the sentences you construct understandable. For a computer language, syntax describes how the "words" of the language may legally be put together into programs. Note that although correct syntax is needed to correctly communicate a program to the computer, correct syntax does not guarantee that you have correctly stated what you intended to communicate. That is, having correct syntax is a necessary, but not sufficient condition for communicating a program to the computer.

1.3 COMPUTER HARDWARE

There is an enormous variety of computers. In general, computers can be viewed as collections of two types of components: *hardware* and *software.* Hardware is the physical part of the computer, while software is the programs that command or control the hardware. In describing the principal components of a computer in the rest of this and the next section, we expect that you will be receiving some additional instruction about your particular computer and some hands-on experience.

The computer must provide a means of communication between itself and a person. Traditionally, a *video display* allows the computer to communicate to the human, and a *keyboard* allows the human to communicate to the computer. Additional communication to the human sometimes comes in the form of audible messages ranging from a simple beep to voice generators that emulate human speech. Additional communication to the computer sometimes comes through devices such as light pens, touch screens, and mice.

Each computer has a component called the *processor*. The processor follows instructions. In computer terminology we say that the processor *executes* instructions. Processors differ considerably in the nature of their instructions; however, Ada hides these differences.

Information is stored in a part of the hardware called *memory*. Memory usually comes in two varieties. *Main memory* is usually a temporary working area, containing information that is forgotten after you are finished using the computer. *Secondary memory* is long-term storage. Here, information can be stored for future use. Main memory usually uses a technology called *random access memory*, often called *RAM*. Secondary memory usually uses a storage device called a *disk*.

1.4 COMPUTER SOFTWARE

A set of instructions to the computer is called a *program*. Most computers are to some extent *programmable*, that is, capable of being given new instructions. Most computer systems have software components that support programming and the execution of programs. These components are part of what is called the computer's *operating system*.

Programs are often reused. In fact, they are very often modified and used to achieve some slightly different result. In reusing or modifying a program, you do not wish to retype the whole thing. Thus, software systems usually supply facilities to save, modify, and reuse programs. Some of these facilities are the following:

1. *File Utilities*. File utilities provide a means of controlling what is in secondary memory. A file is an association of stored material similar to a loose-leaf notebook. A single file may contain a variety of information — for example, a program, a phone list, and/or statistics on students.

   File utilities allow you to store, duplicate, and remove programs and other information. For convenience, files are given names so that the user can easily communicate to the computer which stored information is wanted.

2. *Editor*. The editor is a principal means of creating and/or modifying files containing the text of a program. The editor allows you to insert information into a file, remove information from a file, or move information around within a file. If the file contains a program, the editor is the software component you use to modify that program.

3. *Translator*. The computer's processor uses a language that is generally very tedious for a human to deal with. This language is different for different computers. Thus, most programming is done in other languages, one of which is Ada.

   The Ada translator takes an Ada language program and converts it into the language of the computer's processor. Usually, it takes a file containing the Ada language program and produces a file containing the program translated into the language of the computer's processor. Two common language classifications are *low-level languages* and *high-level languages*. Low-level languages are closer to the language of the computer's processor and hence are relatively simple to translate. High-level languages are designed for the computer programmer. Ada is a high-level language. As with many other high-level language programs, an Ada program is translated by a *compiler*.

   Since the processor is a hardware component, its language is often called a *machine language*. Because programming is usually done in high-level languages like Ada, they are often called *programming languages*.

4. *Command Language*. An operating system must have a method for the user to access the editor, file utilities, and translator, and a way to execute the user's programs. Traditionally, this method has been called the command language because it was used to command the computer. The command language is different for different computers. Recently, command languages have been replaced on some computers by other methods of issuing commands, such as mice and menus.

With the foregoing components, the following process is often used. First, you use the editor to build or modify a program which you then store in a file. Next, you use the translator to convert the stored program into the form understood by the computer's processor, and you store that converted program in another file. Finally, you command the computer to follow the instructions found in the file in which you stored the converted program.

1.5 COMPUTER PROGRAMMING

A computer executes instructions. If you fail to give the correct instruction in the correct manner, the computer will not be able to translate your instruction into an action. Remember, the computer does what you *say*, not what you *intend*.

To illustrate this consider a noncomputer example. We could be told to "go back from forward of room." Although all the words in this phrase are "legal," it is very difficult to determine what the phrase instructs us to do. The guiding principle for both human and computer languages is that *instructions must be intelligible*.

For example, in Ada, if there is a spelling error, such as using "**`Moove`**" instead of "**`Move`**", the compiler will issue an error message. The compiler doesn't understand the misspelled command, and *it will not guess* what you are trying to instruct the computer to do. Or if the compiler expects "**`Turn(Right)`**" or "**`Turn(Left)`**", but gets "**`Turn(Off)`**", again, it will issue an error message. Of course, the instruction must be something within the capabilities of the computer to perform. For example, the computer might not have the capability to execute an instruction such as "**`Fly`**".

The computer often needs to be supplied with details that a human may be able to figure out. If we say, "Leave the room," additional information such as "Exit through a door (not a wall)" may be necessary for the computer.

The conclusions you should draw are as follows:

1. You must use a programming or machine language to be understood by the computer.
2. The computer follows the instructions you give, not the instructions you intended to give.
3. The instructions you give must be complete.

1.6 SYNTAX AND SYNTAX NOTATION

Syntax is the term used for the rules that organize communication. Humans use syntax in their language to govern the formation of words into sentences. The Ada language also has a syntax.

In English, when the syntax of a sentence is poor, we are often able to guess what was meant. However, even in English, it is easy to misunderstand the meaning of a poorly constructed sentence. In Ada, the correct syntax is enforced by the compiler. If the program does not conform precisely to the syntax, the compiler will issue a message and will not guess a meaning. Consequently, unless a program's syntax is correct, a form of the program executable by the computer's processor will not be prepared.

Syntax notation provides a formal way of describing what may be legal in the Ada language. We say *may be legal* because constructs can satisfy all the requirements of the notation, yet be illegal because of considerations beyond the scope of the notation. We shall see some examples of such considerations in section 14.

A common and easily understood type of syntax notation is the *syntax diagram.* Figure 1–1 shows such a diagram.

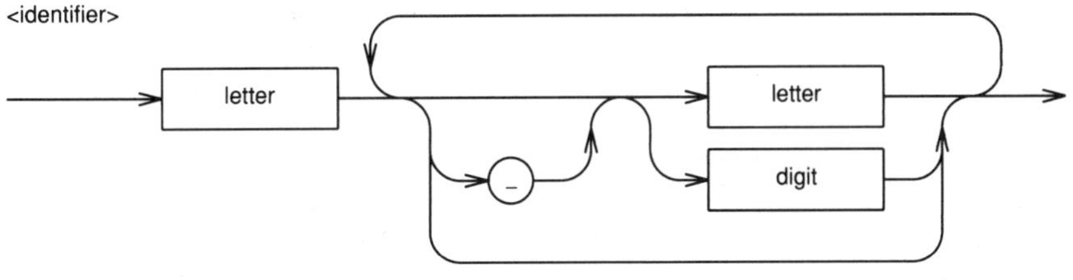

Figure 1–1

The label at the upper left of the figure indicates that this particular diagram describes the legal way to write an identifier. To have a legal identifier, you must enter the syntax diagram from the left and follow the arrows through the diagram, until you exit to the right. When you reach a branch in any arrow, you may choose to go either way, even if you loop back to somewhere you have already been.

Items you pass along the path of the arrow must appear in the Ada construct. If these items appear in a circle or oval, they appear exactly as shown. Items occurring in rectangles need further explanation. Usually, this means that these items are described by other syntax diagrams. For example, *letter* needs further explanation; that is, we need to know what letters are. (Remember, we must be complete and literal.) Again, some information is not captured in the diagrams, and thus, a program that satisfies the diagrams can still be illegal.

Finally, even if a program uses completely correct syntax, this does not mean that the program is *semantically* correct. *Semantics* refers to the meaning or behavior of the program, whereas syntax refers to the structure of the program. As a noncomputer example, consider the goal of computing the square of a variable X. The formula $2X$ is syntactically correct as a mathematical expression. However, it is semantically wrong because it computes 2 times X instead of the square of X. In Ada, just because the compiler finds no errors and you are able to run the program does not mean that the program will do what you intended.

1.7 A SAMPLE PROGRAM

```
with Robot;
procedure Paint_Box is
   -- Purpose: Draw a box in the following order:
   --  top, right side, bottom, left side.
   -- Leave the robot exactly where it started
   --  and facing in its original direction.
begin
  Robot.Set_Paint('+');       -- Prepare the paint
  Robot.Paint_On;
  Robot.Move(10);             -- Draw top of box
  Robot.Turn(Robot.Right);    -- Draw right side of box
  Robot.Move(10);
  Robot.Turn(Robot.Right);    -- Draw bottom of box
  Robot.Move(10);
  Robot.Turn(Robot.Right);    -- Draw left side of box
  Robot.Move(10);
  Robot.Turn(Robot.Right);    -- Face the original direction
  Robot.Exit_World;           -- Return control of the screen
end Paint_Box;
```

Program 1–1

Consider the program **Paint_Box** in Program 1–1. Provided that the predefined group of tools named **Robot** is available, this is a legal Ada program. The program causes the robot to walk around the edge of a square leaving a trail which draws a box.

Lines 8–18 contain the actual instructions to the computer. For example, lines 8 and 9 instruct the **Robot** tools to draw by placing **+** characters on the screen. Line 10 instructs the computer to use a tool named **Move** found in the group of tools named **Robot**, to draw a line forming the top of the box. Lines 11 and 12 tell the **Robot** tools to turn to the right and draw another line. To the right of several of the lines listed are *comments*, messages for the human reader which describe what the program is doing.

The program draws the following figure:

```
+++++++++++
+         +
+         +
+         +
+         +
+         +
+         +
+         +
+         +
+         +
+++++++++++
```

Many of our examples, including **Paint_Box**, have numbers at the start of each line. These numbers and the colons that follow them never appear in the actual program; they are there so that we can refer to parts of the program in the text.

The program **Paint_Box** illustrates the Ada concepts of identifiers, comments, accessing packages, statements, and compilation units. These will all be discussed in detail in the sections that follow.

1.8 IDENTIFIERS

It is convenient to identify objects, qualities, actions, and conditions by giving them names. In the sentences "Go to the house" and "Open the book" the words "house" and "book" name objects and the words "open" and "go" name actions. In Ada and many other programming languages, many objects are named, and one form of a name is the *identifier*.

The syntax diagram for an identifier in Figure 1–1 says that an identifier is a combination of letters, underscores, and digits. Since the "in" arrow points directly at a box marked "letter," an identifier always starts with a letter. Likewise, each underscore is followed by a letter or digit because a path out of the circle containing the underscore must go through either the box marked "letter" or the box marked "digit."

In Ada, capital **A** through **Z** and lower case **a** through **z** of the English alphabet are considered letters, and **0**, **1**, **2**, **3**, **4**, **5**, **6**, **7**, **8**, and **9** are considered digits. Even though this seems obvious, a moment's thought shows that languages other than English have other symbols that are considered letters. These, however, are not legal letters within the Ada language.

Some identifiers that have special meaning in Ada language are called *reserved words*. We shall be introducing reserved words throughout this book. A list of all the reserved words in Ada is found in Appendix B. Because reserved words have special meanings, their use by the programmer is restricted to those situations in which their special meanings apply.

A fact which is not reflected in the syntax diagram is that identifiers are *independent* of capitalization. That is, upper case letters and lower case letters are considered equivalent. Thus, **AnIdentifier**, **ANIDENTIFIER**, and **anidentifier** are all the same identifier under the rules of Ada.

The following are legal Ada identifiers:

```
A              cost_of_living
X15            OvertimeHours
xUdwO3i        Chapter_4_Section_2
```

The following are not legal Ada identifiers, for the reasons given:

15thfloor	— does not start with a letter
Flight#45	— contains the illegal character **#**
tx__y	— underscore not followed by letter or digit
tx_y_	— underscore not followed by letter or digit

Although there are many identifiers which are legal, your choice of identifiers is very important. Appropriately chosen identifiers help you (and other people) to read and understand the program, so care should be taken in choosing them.

Examples of humanly readable identifiers we have used thus far are:

```
Move     Turn     Robot     Paint_On     Set_Paint
```

Each of these identifiers reflects the action or object associated with it.

The following two identifiers are poor because it is not clear what action or object they represent:

```
X        JGOSGJWEI
```

To maximize the understandability of our programs, we shall use the convention that reserved words are in lower case, identifiers that are predefined in the package "**STANDARD**" are in upper case (more about these later), and other identifiers are in mixed case.

1.9 COMMENTS: READABLE PROGRAMS

In the sample program **Paint_Box** there is a construct called the *comment*. A comment begins with a double dash (--) and includes everything until the end of the line. Sequences of commands can become too complex for a human to understand them unless there is additional information. Comments assist people in understanding what a program is intended to accomplish. Comments are ignored by the computer, so computer programs work very well without them. However, humans work much better if good comments are found within the program. The moral is, if you expect your program to be used and understood by humans, make sure that it is well commented.

Notice the style we encourage in comments: Good comments explain the goals behind the programming construct. For example, in

```
Robot.Move(Right);    -- turn right
Robot.Move(10);       -- move 10
```

the comment merely repeats the actual command. This does not supply the person reading the program with any additional information to assist in understanding the program. A better comment style is

```
Robot.Move(Right);    -- Draw bottom of box
Robot.Move(10);
```

This comment describes the *purpose* involved in executing the commands.

A good style of commenting is illustrated by the comments in lines 3–6 of **Paint_Box**. These comments *outline* the steps to be taken in order to draw the box. Such and outline helps the reader visualize how the **Move** and **Turn** commands are used by **Paint_Box** to build the box.

A good programmer should think of programming as communicating with people. Remember, the object is that a person unfamiliar with the program should be able to understand it *easily*. Comments should assist this process of understanding.

1.10 PACKAGES (1): COLLECTIONS OF TOOLS

Ada calls a collection of tools a *package*. A package contains tools that may be used by other programs, yet knowledge of how these tools work is hidden from the user. In Program 1–1 we use tools from a package called "**Robot**". This package includes the tools "**Move**", "**Turn**", "**Set_Paint**", and others. The package allows the user's program to command a robot. You have not been told, nor do you need to be told, the details of how the package carries out the foregoing commands. It is sufficient to know what tasks these tools accomplish.

In conjunction with packages, we introduce two terms commonly used in computer science that are also used in other situations. The *specification* says what is to be accomplished. For example, the specification for using a car brake pedal is, the harder you push on the pedal, the faster the car stops. The *implementation* states how the specification is to be accomplished. In terms of the car brake pedal, it says how the push on the pedal is transmitted though levers, rods, fluid, and pads into an action that slows down the car.

If you do not have to change an implementation, it is sufficient to know the specification. That is, you do need not to understand the implementation, as long as it accomplishes the goals stated in the specification. In programming, this has the same advantage as in driving. You do not want to have to know all the details of the brake pedal implementation in order to drive the car. You leave that to the experts who build and repair brakes. What you do is use brakes that function properly in order to accomplish your goals.

For each of the tools in **Robot** there is a specification. For the purposes of this chapter, the description in section 16 will suffice to specify these tools. Ada provides methods for giving specifications which we shall discuss beginning in Chapter 2.

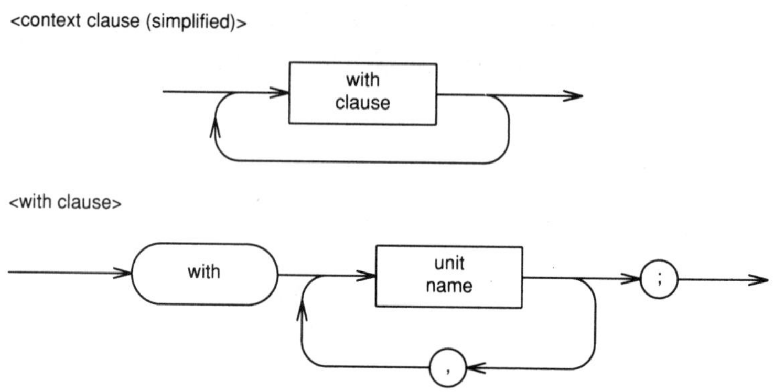

Figure 1–2

To access packages that are already defined, Ada uses the *context clause*. A simplified syntax for the context clause is given in Figure 1–2. Line 1 of **Paint_Box** is a context clause. As shown by the syntax diagram, a context clause can contain several with-clauses. Each with-clause consists of the reserved word **with** followed by a list of unit names. A **with** followed by the name of a package indicates that the tools in that package are to be made available. The programmer can then use these tools. The line

```
with Robot;
```

indicates that the tools in the **Robot** package are to be made available. More specifically, the reserved word **with** indicates that certain tools are to be placed within the context of the program. Thus, the line "**with Robot;**" says that the tools of the package **Robot** are to be added to the context of the program. This enables the program to use those tools. If this line is omitted, the program does not have access to the tools in the package and will complain that it does not recognize identifiers such as **Turn**, **Move**, and **Robot**.

As shown in Figure 1–2, a program can request access to several collections of tools. An example of a context clause that does this is

```
with Weather_Tools, Math_Tools, Calculus_Tools;
```

This clause allows the program to access tools in any or all of the three packages named. An examination of the syntax diagram reveals that

```
with Weather_Tools;
with Math_Tools;
with Calculus_Tools;
```

is also legal. In fact, the two context clauses are equivalent.

In the **Paint_Box** program, the first line indicates that the program can use the tools from **Robot**. Within **Paint_Box**, these tools are accessed by the syntax

```
<package identifier>.<identifier>
```

where the first identifier is the name of the package and the second identifier is the name of the tool. For example,

```
Robot.Move
```

and the other commands in lines 8–18 of **Paint_Box** have this format. In this way, the computer is told to use the tool named "**Move**" found in the collection of tools called "**Robot**".

A good programmer uses prepared tools rather than building the entire program from scratch each time. Certain tools and concepts that are used by most programs are often provided directly by the hardware of the computer. Included among these are arithmetic operators such as addition and concepts such as numbers.

In Ada, there is a package whose tools are always available to any program. This package includes some very commonly used tools and is called "**STANDARD**". It is never named in a context clause because its tools are automatically available to every compilation. Throughout the rest of the book, we shall be introducing tools from the package **STANDARD**.

1.11 STATEMENT LISTS

As shown in the syntax diagram of Figure 1–3, a *statement list* contains one or more statements. One thing you will discover when we look at the various statements is that the last character in each statement is a semicolon. A common programming mistake is to omit the semicolon. The compiler will detect this syntax error, but the error message

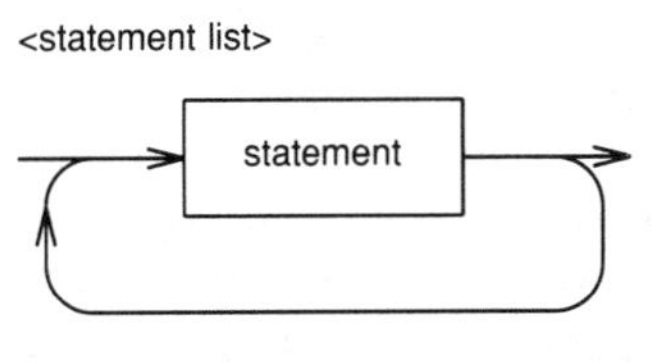

Figure 1–3

may be obscure because the omission causes the compiler to attempt to combine that statement and the following statement into a single statement.

Ada has a large variety of statements which we shall discuss throughout this book. In **Paint_Box**, lines 8–18 each contain a statement. These 11 statements are the definition of the actions that **Paint_Box** performs. Put another way, they are the implementation of the operations of **Paint_Box**. The program **Paint_Box** achieves its goal by a series of turns and moves. In addition, certain other details, such as preparing the paint, must be handled before moving around the box. To correctly achieve its goal, the program must ensure that all these operations are performed in the correct order. Within a statement list, Ada will perform the statements in the order in which they are listed.

In **Paint_Box**, every statement refers to a tool from the package **Robot**. Later in this chapter, we shall see statements that refer to tools in another package and in subsequent chapters we shall introduce many other statements.

1.12 PROCEDURES (1)

The main component of an Ada program is a *procedure*. A simplified description of the syntax for a procedure is found in Figure 1–4. The procedure body starts with the reserved word **procedure**, followed by an identifier (the procedure name) and then the reserved word **is**. For example, line 2 in procedure **Paint_Box** starts the declaration of the procedure with the reserved word **procedure**, the identifier **Paint_Box**, and the reserved word **is**.

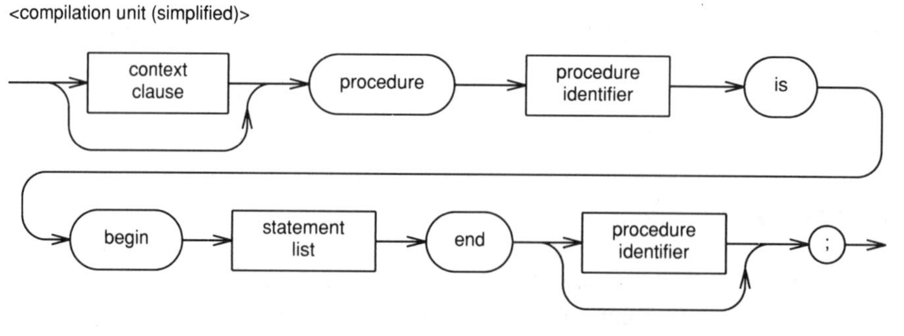

Figure 1–4

What follows next is the procedure's executable part. The executable part includes the details of the procedure's implementation. The reserved words **begin** and **end** followed by a semicolon indicate the beginning and ending of the executable part. The actual operations are in the statement list. The final identifier must be the name of the procedure. Although the syntax permits the omission of the final procedure identifier, its use is highly recommended. The declaration of **Paint_Box** is finished at the semicolon of line 19.

When a procedure is to be compiled separately, as would be the case if it were to be the main program, it qualifies as a *compilation unit.* This means that the procedure is preceded by a context clause (which may be empty). Since **Paint_Box** is being separately compiled, it is allowed to have a context clause. This context clause is in line 1. As mentioned before, the context clause of **Paint_Box** names the package **Robot** so that the program may use the tools in that package.

1.13 CHARACTERS, STRINGS, AND INTEGERS

Paint_Box contains commands that require different kinds of information. For example, **Move** takes a distance, **Turn** takes a direction, and **Set_Paint** takes a character. Many different kinds of information are predefined in Ada. We shall deal with just three kinds of information in this section — characters, strings, and integers, all of which are defined in the **package STANDARD**.

In the **Robot** package, both characters and integers are used to convey information to procedures. The Ada terminology for the type of information we have seen conveyed is "literal." We will show how to construct character, string, and integer literals.

An *integer literal* is a simple numeral; for example, **34**, **2**, and **195** are integer literals. Note a subtle distinction here: We know that a phrase like **2+3** yields an integer; however, **2+3** is not an integer literal, because it contains an operation symbol (the plus sign) and is thus a computation. This and other distinctions will be considered in later chapters. Also of particular interest here is the fact that **-1** is not an integer literal because the minus sign is an operation.

Each integer literal has a value. We are so used to this that we don't think about the fact that the value of the integer literal "**2**" is the integer two. To emphasize the distinction, suppose we had chosen to represent integer literals as Roman numerals instead of Arabic numerals. In that case, the Roman numeral literal "**II**" would have the integer value two. The integer value two can be represented by a variety of literals. In Ada, integer literals are represented by Arabic numerals.

A *character literal* is a single letter, digit or other symbol enclosed in apostrophes. For example, **'a'**, **'C'**, **'5'**, and **'$'** are character literals. The apostrophes serve to designate the single enclosed character as a character literal. You can even write an apostrophe as a character literal as **'''**.

The apostrophes make a difference. For example, **5** is an integer literal and **'5'** is a character literal. This distinction is important: The value of the character literal is really the single character inside the apostrophes.

A *string literal* is a series of characters between quotation marks. For example, the following are string literals:

```
"Hi There"
"495"
"X"
"6 a.m. Tuesday"
"This account pays 5.5% interest"
```

The value of a string literal is the sequence of characters between the quotation marks. The quotation marks serve to designate this sequence as a string literal. In Ada, the entire string literal must be on the same line.

One special consideration is a string literal that contains a quotation mark. Since we don't know how long a string is, things aren't as simple as for a character literal. The rule is that you must use two quotation marks to represent a single quotation mark. For example, the string literal **`"ABC""DE"`**, contains six characters: five letters and a quotation mark. The value of this string literal is **`ABC"DE`**. The pair of adjacent quotation marks inside the string represent a single quotation mark in the string literal's value. Note that if adjacent dashes occur in a string literal, as in **`"To be -- Not to be"`**, the dashes do not start a comment. Rather, we just have a string that happens to contain two dashes.

The difference between apostrophes and quotation marks is significant. Thus **`'A'`** is a character literal (character literals contain only a single character), while **`"A"`** is a string literal that happens to contain a single character. Each procedure is defined to take information of a particular type. You must supply the correct type of literal or the compiler will tell you that you made an error.

The following examples will help clarify the apostrophe–quotation mark convention:

`'"'` — is a character literal containing a quotation mark.
`"'"` — is a string literal containing one character which is an apostrophe.
`""""` — is a string literal containing one character which is a quotation mark.
`" "` — is a string literal containing a single space.
`""` — is a string literal containing no characters.

1.14 SYNTAX ERRORS

The procedure **`Paint_Box_With_Errors`** in Program 1–2 illustrates some common syntax errors.

```
with Paint_It;                  -- No such package
procedure Paint_Box_With_Errors is
begin
   Robot.Paint_On               -- No semicolon
   Robot.Moove(10);             -- Misspelled
   Robot.Move(10);
   Robot.Move(Robot.Left);      -- Not an integer amount
   Turn(Robot.Right);           -- No package name
   Robot.Turn(Off);             -- Bad parameter
   Robot.Fly;                   -- Not a Robot tool
end Boxed;                      -- Wrong procedure identifier
```

Program 1–2

Line 1 contains an error because a package must exist before you request use of the procedures within it. This type of error is often due to a misspelled identifier. Line 4 illustrates the requirement that each statement end with a semicolon. Line 5 contains a misspelling that will cause the compiler to search for a tool (**Moove**) that does not exist. Line 7 contains an error in communicating how far to move, and line 9 contains an error in communicating which way to turn. The compiler will complain about mismatched parameters, this will be explained in Chapter 2. Line 8 shows that even though the only **Turn(Robot.Right)** that is available is from **Robot**, it is still illegal to omit the package name. Line 10 is incorrect because **Fly** is not defined in the package **Robot**.

The compiler will not correct any of these errors. Only when the program has been corrected will the compiler prepare a translation into the language of the machine.

1.15 THE SIMPLE_IO PACKAGE (1): OUTPUT

The interface between the computer and the human is one of the more complicated parts of the Ada language. To avoid this complexity in the early chapters, we supply a package, **Simple_IO**, which provides communication to and from the computer. In this chapter, we introduce only those tools which allow a program to send information to the display. In Chapter 2 we introduce the tools which accept information from the human user, and in Chapter 7 we discuss the details of the packages provided as part of the Ada language environment.

The package **Simple_IO** includes the tools **Write** and **New_Line**. The tool **Write** takes information and writes it to the screen. Each **Write** starts exactly where the previous **Write** or **New_Line** finished. **Write** is designed so that you may use integers, characters, or strings.

The tool **New_Line** begins a new line. The next thing that is written will start at the left side of this next line.

The procedure **Print_Demo** shown in Program 1–3 writes literals of all three of the types we have introduced.

```
with Simple_IO;
procedure Print_Demo is
begin
  Simple_IO.Write("It's September");    -- String literal
  Simple_IO.Write(25);                  -- Integer literal
  Simple_IO.Write("th.");               -- String literal
  Simple_IO.New_Line;
  Simple_IO.Write("This is section ");  -- String literal
  Simple_IO.Write('C');                 -- Character literal
  Simple_IO.New_Line;
end Print_Demo;
```

Program 1–3

Print_Demo produces the following output:

```
It's September 25th.
This is section C
```

Each **Write** starts exactly where the previous write finishes. **New_Line** causes a new line to be begun. Furthermore, the apostrophes and quotation marks designating the character and string literals in the procedure are not printed because they are not part of the value of those literals. The space that follows **section** in the **Write** statement produces the space between **September** and **C** in the output. The space that follows **September** in the output is produced by the **Write(25)** because numbers are printed with either a leading blank or a minus sign.

1.16 THE ROBOT PACKAGE (1): MOVEMENT

The package **Robot** supplies simple tools for examples and exercises. In this section, we shall introduce some of the tools available in this package. The robot commands we introduce will supply the capabilities for the robot to move, turn, and leave a trail of paint. Later in the book, we shall introduce other tools available in **Robot**.

The robot normally starts at the upper left corner of its world, facing to the right. The robot's world is 20 squares in each direction and is surrounded by walls. You must keep the robot within its world when you move: An error occurs if the robot bumps into something, including one of the walls.

The following are some tools supplied by the package **Robot**:

Robot.Paint_On; Turn the paint on. When the paint is on, the robot leaves paint behind whenever it leaves a location. Painting a new symbol over an old hides the old symbol.

Robot.Paint_Off; Turn the paint off. When the paint is off, the robot does not leave any trail when it leaves a location. If the paint is off and the robot crosses a location that has already been painted, the old paint will remain at that location.

Robot.Set_Paint('.'); Set the paint. As shown, this command will leave a trail of periods when painting. The paint can be set to any of five characters: **+,-./**. When the robot leaves a trail, it will be of whatever character was last specified as the paint regardless of how many times the paint is turned on and off.

Robot.Turn(Robot.Right); Turn the robot to the right 90 degrees. For example, if the robot is facing toward the bottom of the screen, this command will cause it to face toward the left of the screen.

Robot.Turn(Robot.Left); Turn the robot to the left 90 degrees.

Robot.Move(5); Move the robot the specified number of squares in the direction it is currently facing. As shown, this command will move the robot five squares forward in the current direction. If a negative number of squares is specified, the robot backs up. Moving backwards does not cause the robot to turn around, so moving −5 is the same as turning around, moving 5 squares, and turning around again.

Robot.Exit_World; Discontinue use of the robot. When in use, the package **Robot** takes control of the screen. This command restores the screen to the normal control mode.

1.17 PROGRAMMING PRACTICES

We have discussed the convenience of using packages written by other programmers. It is almost always preferable to use well-designed packages than to write your own. A programmer should determine what tools are already available and use those tools which are appropriate, rather than building programs from scratch. Taking advantage of work already completed, the programmer can produce better programs more quickly than would otherwise be possible.

A programmer should always use features of the language that help the human reader understand the goal of the program and how the program attempts to achieve that goal. In Ada, comments and meaningful identifiers assist in understanding a program. The program should be kept as easily readable by humans as possible. Any good program will be used by others, and the best programs almost always are enhanced to include new capabilities. Readability makes a program easy to use and easy to enhance.

The programmer should worry about the side effects of each procedure. Side effects are changes made by a tool which are not part of the central goal of the tool. The fewer side effects, the better a procedure is. For example, when we built **Paint_Box**, we were very careful to leave the robot exactly as it was before the procedure started. **Paint_Box** thus paints a box and does not have the side effect of leaving the robot in a different position or facing a different direction from its position and direction at the start of the procedure.

1.17.1 Problem Solving

One of the major skills of a good programmer is the ability to solve problems in an organized manner. Good computer programming requires that the programmer be able to explain to another person how the program solves the problem. Many chapters in this book will contain a section such as this one to focus on the problem-solving aspects of computer programming.

We shall introduce several problem-solving techniques by showing examples. This method is often called an *operational definition* because the definitions are informal and based on how the techniques are used.

There is a large collection of problem-solving techniques called *divide and conquer*. Basically, these are techniques for *dividing* the problem into smaller parts, and then solving (*conquering*) the smaller problems. As an example, suppose that we are given the following problem:

Write a program that moves a robot to a given position and faces it in a given direction. Then the robot draws a diagonal line three squares long, beginning at the current position. The line is drawn by painting the three squares that the line passes over. Each square in the line will be filled with the current paint character. The robot should end in the square three boxes ahead and three boxes to the left with respect to its initial position and direction. The robot will end up facing in the original direction. For example, if the robot is initially facing toward the bottom of the screen, the diagonal line will be toward the lower right, and the robot will be one square beyond the end of the line.

We start by reading the problem carefully. The first thing we notice is that the line is three squares long. Since we do the same thing for each square, we determine that each square can be handled in the same manner. The fact that the problem consists of several identical parts indicates that we can try the technique called *do one and repeat* (one of the divide-and-conquer approaches). As the name of the technique implies, at first we shall only try to solve the problem for the first square. In this subproblem, we paint the current square and move the robot one square forward and one square to the left. After we have solved the first square, we shall use the same approach to deal with the remainder of the problem.

One important technique that must almost always be applied is often called *avoidance of side effects*. This is not a divide-and-conquer technique; rather, it is an aid to organized problem solving. A side effect is a change made to the environment (e.g., the position or direction of the robot) which is not part of the direct purpose of the procedure. Side effects are one of the major causes of errors in computer programming.

In making the robot take a diagonal step, we are required to move the robot on the screen (this is part of the direct purpose imposed by taking the step). But we want the robot to be facing the same direction after taking the step as it faced before taking the step. If the robot were not facing the same direction after the step as before the step, this would be an unintentional action and would require that the programmer remember this change when solving the rest of the problem.

Now we examine the work to be performed in taking the step. We also apply divide-and-conquer here. We divide the problem into painting the current square and moving one square beyond the end of the line.

First, we must paint the current square. Since a square is painted as the robot leaves it, we shall turn on the paint and move one square. Then, in order to avoid a side effect, we turn the paint off and move back to the original square. This part of the problem is small enough that we can write the following Ada statements to solve it:

```
Robot.Paint_On;
Robot.Move(1);
Robot.Paint_Off;
Robot.Move(-1);
```

Next, we shall move the robot one square forward and one square to the left. We must make sure that the robot is facing the same direction after the step as before the step.

We have:

```
Robot.Move(1);
Robot.Turn(Robot.Left);
Robot.Move(1);
Robot.Turn(Robot.Right);
```

Now we put the two parts together. These are the instructions to the robot to paint the current step and then to move one step along the diagonal:

```
    -- Paint the current square and take one step along the diagonal.
1: Robot.Paint_On;
2: Robot.Move(1);
3: Robot.Paint_Off;
4: Robot.Move(-1);
5: Robot.Move(1);          -- This line undoes the previous line.
6: Robot.Turn(Robot.Left);
7: Robot.Move(1);
8: Robot.Turn(Robot.Right);
```

Notice that we have two **Robot.Move** commands in a row (lines 4 and 5). This is not efficient. We wrote the **Robot.Move** in line 4 to avoid a side effect in painting a square. We wrote the **Robot.Move** in line 5 as part of the direct effect of the task we were trying to perform (stepping one square along the diagonal).

Sometimes when we solve parts of the problem independently, we add extra work that could be avoided if the problem were solved all at once. Unfortunately, trying to solve even such a simple problem all at once, rather than solving the problem in parts, often leads to an incorrect program. As a general rule, it is better to have a slow but correct program than to have a fast program with errors.

When we assemble the parts together (sometimes called by the fancy name, *integration*), we look for any extra work and determine how to remove it. In this case, since the effect of the commands in lines 4 and 5 is to exactly cancel each other, we can remove both lines. The result is the following:

```
-- Paint the current square and take one step along the diagonal.
Robot.Paint_On;
Robot.Move(1);
Robot.Paint_Off;
Robot.Turn(Robot.Left);
Robot.Move(1);
Robot.Turn(Robot.Right);
```

It is very important to keep track of which parts of the problem have been solved and which remain to be completed. If you have been keeping track, you will remember that we have completed only the first step of the three required. We can now apply another problem-solving technique, *reuse of previous work.* That is, we can just use a copy of the first step to perform each of the remaining two steps.

Another type of reuse is the use of a *program skeleton.* This involves taking a working program and removing those parts which are not needed for the current problem. Then, the work needed for the current problem is inserted into the skeleton in the appropriate place. Here is a skeleton derived from the **Paint_Box** program:

```
with Robot;
procedure ... is
-- Purpose:   ...
begin
  Robot.Set_Paint('.');
  ...          -- do the work here
  ...
end ... ;
```

We shall insert an additional line after **Robot.Set_Paint('.')** to make the robot face downward initially. We shall then fill in the name and purpose of the program. Finally, we shall insert the lines required to solve the problem which we have just programmed. We end up with the following code:

```
with Robot;
procedure Draw_Diagonal is
-- Purpose: Draw a diagonal line three squares long,
--    beginning in the upper left corner,
--    aimed down and to the right.
begin
  Robot.Set_Paint('.');
  Robot.Turn(Robot.Right);          -- Face downward initially
  -- Paint the current square and take one step along the diagonal.
  Robot.Paint_On;
  Robot.Move(1);
  Robot.Paint_Off;
  Robot.Turn(Robot.Left);
  Robot.Move(1);
  Robot.Turn(Robot.Right);
  -- Paint the second square and take one step along the diagonal.
  Robot.Paint_On;
  Robot.Move(1);
  Robot.Paint_Off;
  Robot.Turn(Robot.Left);
  Robot.Move(1);
  Robot.Turn(Robot.Right);
  -- Paint the third square and take one step along the diagonal.
  Robot.Paint_On;
  Robot.Move(1);
  Robot.Paint_Off;
```

```
    Robot.Turn(Robot.Left);
    Robot.Move(1);
    Robot.Turn(Robot.Right);
    -- Return control of the screen
    Robot.Exit_World;
  end Draw_Diagonal;
```

In writing this procedure, we have used and discussed the following problem-solving techniques:

- Divide and conquer
- Do one and repeat
- Avoidance of side effects
- Reuse of previous work
- Use of a program skeleton

These are the basic problem-solving techniques of the computer programmer. We shall introduce more techniques and more examples in later chapters. Eventually, you will have acquired a toolbox full of techniques and the experience needed to choose the appropriate techniques for each problem.

As you write programs, it is often helpful to keep in mind the problem-solving techniques you are using. Programs written using explicit problem-solving techniques tend to have fewer errors and be easier to read than those that do not employ such techniques.

1.18 ADA SUMMARY

In this chapter, we have introduced the complete syntax for *identifiers*, and we have shown how these identifiers are used for naming *procedures*. We have shown how to include *comments* in a *program* and how such comments can make the program easier to understand.

We have introduced the idea of the procedure as a list of instructions to be followed to achieve a goal. We have taken a first look at *compilation units*. We have used the *context clause* to make available *packages* which others have already built for our use. We have seen several different types of *statements* and how *statement lists* are used to form a sequence of instructions.

Finally, we have introduced *character*, *integer*, and *string literals*.

EXERCISES

1.1. (a) Examine the procedure **`Paint_Box`** (Program 1–1). Why aren't there comments on every line? (b) Which lines would have to be changed to make the box produced twice as wide? By reading the comments in the program, you can answer this question without knowing much about Ada.

1.2. Identify how each part of **`Paint_Box`** is associated with the syntax diagrams in this chapter.

1.3. Modify the procedure **`Paint_Box`** so that it produces one of the following outputs:

```
   A              B              C
-------       .........          .
.     .       .   .   .          .
.     .       .   .   .          .
-------       .........      ---------
.     .       .   .   .          .
.     .       .   .   .          .
.     .       .........          .
```

Since it will no longer paint a box, you should also change the procedure's name.

1.4. Modify the procedure **`Print_Demo`** (Program 1–3) so that it produces the following output:

```
Good Morning, it's nice to see you.
This is section 12.
```

(Note: There are several ways to accomplish this.)

1.5. In the procedure **`Draw_Diagonal`**, set out in section 1.17.1, suppose that you wanted to draw the diagonal line in the center of the robot's world. You already have a program to draw the line at the upper left corner of the robot's world. Use the problem-solving techniques described to determine what change needs to be made to the program. Describe the exact steps you use to make the changes, write the new program, and try it.

1.6. In **`Draw_Diagonal`**, suppose that you wanted to draw the diagonal line four squares long instead of three. Use the problem-solving techniques described to determine what change needs to be made to the program. Describe the exact steps you use to make the changes, write the new program, and try it.

2

Defining and Using Simple Tools

2.1 OBJECTIVES

Encapsulating or grouping related items is one of the most powerful programming techniques. In Ada, the package greatly assists the construction of large programs by providing a mechanism to encapsulate a group of tools. The package is one of the most important constructs which distinguishes Ada from other programming languages. In this chapter, we define and use packages (section 5). In addition, we expand the coverage of procedures (sections 3 and 4), we discuss compilation (section 6), we briefly introduce arithmetic (section 7), and we consider the storage of information (sections 8 and 9). Finally, we introduce additional capabilities in the package **`Simple_IO`** that allow us to communicate information to the program (section 10).

CONCEPTS:

- Packages are a tool for systematically building large programs.
- Related tools should be encapsulated (grouped).
- Reusing tools saves work and avoids errors.
- Limiting communication between tools makes modifying programs and locating errors simpler.
- Parameters can be used to modify the behavior of a procedure.
- Storing information is necessary to solve many problems.
- Automatic checks for consistency avoid many common errors.

GOALS:

- Write procedures that communicate using parameters and store information using variables.
- Write and use simple packages.
- Do simple arithmetic.
- Use various types of data.

2.2 MOTIVATION

In Ada, the *package* provides the basis for collecting tools into tool kits. Computer scientists have observed that the best way to design and construct large programs is to build them in convenient parts. For this reason, it is a good practice to build programs by building tools and then using those tools. The larger the program, the more important it is to construct it systematically by building and using tools. Large numbers of tools can be cumbersome and confusing, so it is important to separate tools into related groups. Packages serve to encapsulate these groups. Thus, packages are a critical construct for the programmer to use.

Parameters are a means of communicating information to procedures. As an analogy, we can liken a parameter to the gas pedal of a car. The gas pedal is a means of communicating information to the engine. By varying how much you depress the pedal, you can vary the behavior of the car. Further, it is far safer to vary the car's speed by using the gas pedal than by adjusting the various rods, levers, and valves within the engine. Similarly, using parameters as the method of communicating information to procedures makes procedures safer and more flexible.

Most computer programs use and store information. An important safety concept is that information should only be used or stored in a consistent manner. Many home appliances are designed to contain automatic consistency checks to ensure safety. For example, on a video cassette recorder (VCR), different plugs are shaped differently so that you cannot accidentally plug them into dangerous locations. Thus, the cable that carries the picture to the television cannot be plugged into the wall socket because it physically will not fit there. In programming, extensive automatic checking of consistency serves to eliminate many "trivial" errors because it allows the compiler to detect and report these errors. Such errors could become serious if they went undetected.

2.3 PROCEDURES (2)

A procedure is a group of instructions which accomplish a goal. For example, in Chapter 1, the procedure **`Paint_Box`** (Program 1–1) drew a rectangle. If we had a job that required a number of rectangles to be drawn, it would be very convenient to be able to reuse this procedure.

```
 1:with Robot;
 2:procedure Row_of_Boxes is
 3:  procedure Paint_Box is                          -- Declaration
 4:  -- Purpose: Draw a square.
 5:  --   The robot is left at the original position
 6:  --   and facing the original direction.
 7:  begin    -- Actions performed by Paint_Box (body) start here
 8:    Robot.Paint_On;
 9:    Robot.Move(5);
10:    Robot.Turn(Robot.Right);
11:    Robot.Move(5);
12:    Robot.Turn(Robot.Right);
13:    Robot.Move(5);
14:    Robot.Turn(Robot.Right);
15:    Robot.Move(5);
16:    Robot.Turn(Robot.Right);
17:    Robot.Paint_Off;
18:  end Paint_Box;
19:begin   -- Actions performed by Row_of_Boxes (body) start here
20:  Robot.Set_Paint('.');
21:  Paint_Box;              -- First invocation
22:  Robot.Move(8);
23:  Paint_Box;              -- Second invocation
24:  Robot.Move(8);
25:  Paint_Box;              -- Third invocation
26:  Robot.Move(-16);        -- Put the robot back where it started.
27:  Robot.Exit_World;       -- Return control of the screen.
28:end Row_of_Boxes;
```

Program 2–1

Most programming languages, including Ada, provide a method that permits one procedure to make use of another procedure. This is illustrated in Program 2–1, **Row_of_Boxes**. In this program, the procedure **Paint_Box** is used as a component to help create a row of boxes.

In conjunction with using a procedure as a tool, we introduce several new words in the Ada terminology. An *invocation* is a request to a procedure to perform its job. In the procedure **Row_of_Boxes**, the procedure **Paint_Box** is invoked three times, once on each of the lines 21, 23, and 25. A synonym of "invocation" is the term *call*. The procedure **Row_of_Boxes** is said to call or *invoke* the procedure **Paint_Box**, while the procedure **Paint_Box** is said to be *invoked* or *called* by **Row_of_Boxes**.

Since we are going to call a procedure for the purpose of having it perform a set of actions, we must indicate how to call it and what it does when it is called. The *declaration* tells Ada how the procedure may be called. Lines 3–18 of **Row_of_Boxes** contain the declaration of the procedure **Paint_Box**.

The definition of what a procedure does and how it does it is contained in the declaration of the procedure *body*. Not surprisingly, "body" is the same term used for the definition of what a program is and how it does its job.

The declaration of the procedure **`Paint_Box`** is familiar; whenever the procedure is called, it performs its sequence of actions which draw a box. Thus, the call on line 21 causes a box to be drawn, as do the calls on lines 23 and 25. The result is a row of three boxes.

The actions which **`Row_of_Boxes`** performs begin at line 20. The first action performed (line 20) is to set the paint to a period. Next, **`Row_of_Boxes`** calls **`Paint_Box`** at line 21. **`Row_of_Boxes`** will then wait at line 21 until **`Paint_Box`** has finished its actions.

The procedure **`Paint_Box`** turns the paint on (line 8), draws the box (lines 9–16), and turns the paint off (line 17). **`Paint_Box`** is now done. This means that **`Row_of_Boxes`** has finished its wait at line 21 and may proceed. **`Row_of_Boxes`** now performs line 22, moving the robot to the right. At line 23, **`Row_of_Boxes`** again calls **`Paint_Box`** and waits until **`Paint_Box`** has finished drawing the second box. **`Row_of_Boxes`** is then done waiting at line 23 and proceeds to line 24, moving the robot to the right again. Then **`Row_of_Boxes`** calls **`Paint_Box`** a third time at line 25 and waits until the third box is drawn. When **`Paint_Box`** is done this time, **`Row_of_Boxes`** moves back to the original position (to avoid a side effect). **`Row_of_Boxes`** has now finished its statement list, and so the program is done.

Some of the advantages of using a procedure are immediately obvious. Instead of having to type lines 8 to 17 three times, we typed them once and utilized procedure calls to use them three times. This saved us considerable work.

Another savings in work occurs whenever we have to fix a mistake. If we misunderstood how to draw the box and we typed the lines three times, we would have to fix the mistake three times. Using the procedure, we only have to fix the mistake once. Procedures not only make mistakes easier to fix, but help keep the program short and simple. Short and simple procedures usually have fewer mistakes to fix than procedures that are long and complex.

2.4 PARAMETERS (1): MODE IN

In previous examples, we have seen the benefits of communicating information to a procedure. Most of the tools in the package **`Robot`** are procedures — for example, the **`Move`** procedure. The **`Move`** command, that accomplishes the goal of moving the robot, takes a parameter. In "**`Move(5);`**", the "**`5`**" communicates information to the **`Move`** procedure. In this case, the parameter indicates how far to move. We have also seen that **`Turn`** has a parameter indicating direction and **`Set_Paint`** has a parameter indicating what character should be used if the robot is painting its trail. In these procedures, parameters are used to communicate information to the procedure. Because these parameters communicate information "into" the procedure, Ada terminology describes them as parameters of *mode* "**in**." Parameters of other modes will be covered in subsequent chapters.

By using parameters, we can adjust or adapt the job that a procedure performs. Thus, instead of having separate procedures for each specific job, we can concentrate on a single procedure which adapts itself according to the information supplied by its parameters. For example, the **Move** procedure adapts itself according to a parameter that tells it how far to move.

The concept of a parameter is applied to things other than computers. For example, the kitchen oven has a parameter that is set with the temperature control knob. Rather than having multiple ovens, such as a high-temperature oven, medium-temperature oven, and low-temperature oven, it is much more practical to have a single oven with a "parameterized" temperature.

<procedure call>

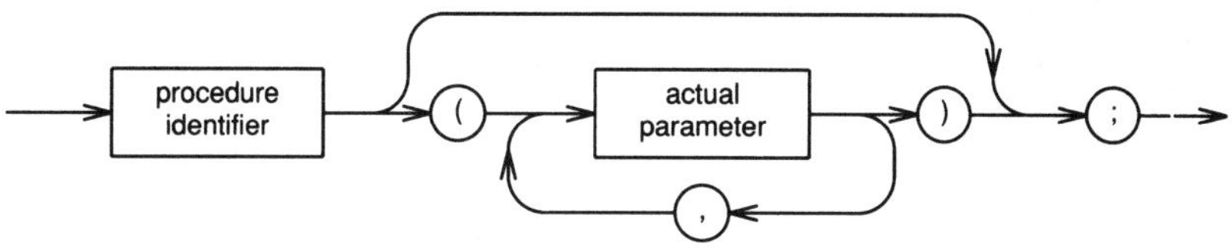

Figure 2–1

The calling procedure hands a value to the procedure that is called. This value is said to be *passed* to the procedure that is called, and the action as a whole is called *parameter passing*. As with a telephone conversation, there are two ends to parameter passing: the caller and the one who is called. The calling procedure passes (sends) a value to the procedure that is called, this value is called the *actual parameter*. The syntax for a procedure call with an actual parameter is given in Figure 2–1. For example, in the call

```
Move(50);
```

the actual parameter to the procedure **Move** is the integer value **50**. This value is derived from the integer literal **50**. That is, the literal is evaluated, and the value is passed to the procedure. In the call

```
Set_Paint('.');
```

the actual parameter to the procedure **Set_Paint** is the character value **'.'**. This value is derived from the character literal **'.'**. Parameters do not have to be literals. For example, if the call

```
Move(10 + 20);
```

is made, the actual parameter has the value 30.

The general rule for parameters is that the value of the actual parameter is *evaluated* before it is passed to the procedure. In other words, the value of the parameter is computed before the procedure is called.

At the other end of parameter passing is the procedure that receives the value. Once a value has been received, the procedure must have a way to use it. Each value received is associated with an identifier called the *formal parameter*. By using the formal parameter, a procedure uses the value received through that parameter.

The syntax for declaring a procedure with parameters is given in Figure 2–2. In Ada, not only does a procedure have to say that it is expecting information by declaring its parameters, but it also must say what type of information it expects to receive in those parameters. Thus, **Move** declares that it requires an integer, while **Set_Paint** declares that it requires a character. This helps prevent the common error of sending the wrong type of information to a procedure.

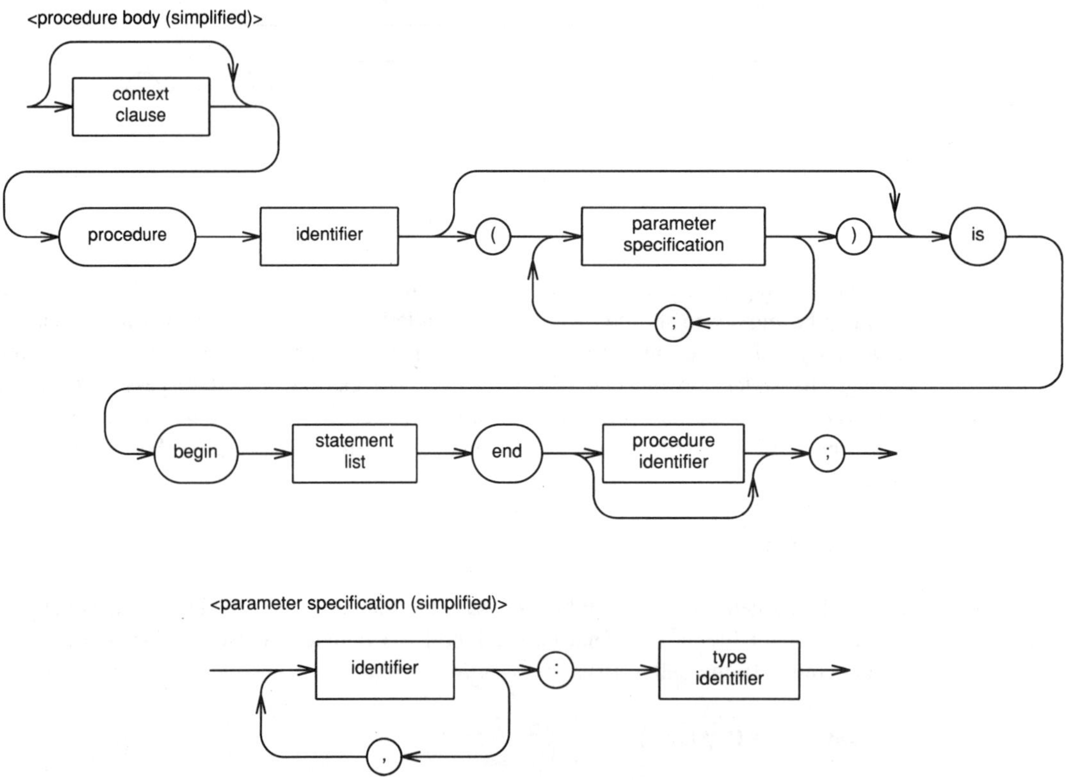

Figure 2–2

As an example, the declaration of the procedure **Paint_Sized_Box** in the program **Tunnel** (see Program 2–2, line 4) says that the procedure expects *one* parameter and that that parameter must be an *integer*. This means that the actual parameter supplied in a call to **Paint_Sized_Box** must be an integer. An example of a legal call is

```
 1:with Robot;
 2:procedure Tunnel is
 3:-- Purpose: Draw boxes of decreasing size.
 4:   procedure Paint_Sized_Box(Box_Size: INTEGER) is
 5:   -- Purpose: Draw a box moving clockwise
 6:   --   around the sides. The current direction
 7:   --   is the direction we start in.
 8:   -- Leave the robot exactly where it started
 9:   --   and facing in its original direction.
10:   begin
11:     Robot.Paint_On;
12:     Robot.Move(Box_Size);
13:     Robot.Turn(Robot.Right);
14:     Robot.Move(Box_Size);
15:     Robot.Turn(Robot.Right);
16:     Robot.Move(Box_Size);
17:     Robot.Turn(Robot.Right);
18:     Robot.Move(Box_Size);
19:     Robot.Turn(Robot.Right);
20:     Robot.Paint_Off;
21:   end Paint_Sized_Box;
22:begin  -- Tunnel
23:   Robot.Set_Paint('.');
24:   Paint_Sized_Box(10);
25:   Paint_Sized_Box(6);
26:   Paint_Sized_Box(4);
27:   Robot.Exit_World;
28:end Tunnel;
```

Program 2–2

```
Paint_Sized_Box(4);
```

The value of the actual parameter is accessed through the formal parameter **Box_Size**. In this case, **Box_Size** obtains the value **4**. To use the value of the parameter, the procedure **Paint_Sized_Box** uses the identifier **Box_Size** (see lines 12, 14, 16, and 18).

When **Paint_Sized_Box** is called on line 24, the parameter **Box_Size** receives the value 10. The call is legal because the formal parameter requires an integer and the actual parameter is an integer. The main program (**procedure Tunnel**) waits at line 24 while **Paint_Sized_Box** performs its actions. When **Paint_Sized_Box** reaches line 12, the formal parameter **Box_Size** is used in the call to **Move**. Since **Box_Size** received the value 10, this is the value that is passed to **Move**, and the robot moves 10 squares. Thus, the formal parameter **Box_Size** of **Paint_Sized_Box** is used as the actual parameter to **Move**.

The second time **Paint_Sized_Box** is called, the parameter **Box_Size** receives the value 6, and the moves are of size 6. The third time, **Box_Size** receives the value 4, and the moves are of size 4.

As implied by the syntax diagram in Figure 2–2, several parameters can be passed to a procedure. This is illustrated in the procedure **Pattern** (Program 2–3). In this example, the procedure **Sized_Box** requires three parameters — two integers and one character. In the case of several parameters, we have an additional task: We must indicate which actual parameter belongs to which formal parameter. There are two methods of doing this.

```
 1:with Robot;
 2:procedure Pattern is
 3:-- Purpose: Draw boxes of different shapes.
 4:   procedure Sized_Box(Height, Width: INTEGER; Color: CHARACTER) is
 5:   -- Purpose: Draw a box, where Height and Width specify the size
 6:   --   and Color specifies the character to be used.
 7:   begin
 8:      Robot.Set_Paint(Color);
 9:      Robot.Paint_On;
10:      Robot.Move(Width);           -- Draw top
11:      Robot.Turn(Robot.Right);
12:      Robot.Move(Height);          -- Draw right side
13:      Robot.Turn(Robot.Right);
14:      Robot.Move(Width);           -- Draw bottom
15:      Robot.Turn(Robot.Right);
16:      Robot.Move(Height);          -- Draw left side
17:      Robot.Turn(Robot.Right);  -- Restore direction
18:      Robot.Paint_Off;
19:   end Sized_Box;
20:begin  -- Pattern
21:   Sized_Box(10,  2, '.');         -- Tall
22:   Sized_Box( 3, 14, ',');         -- Wide
23:   Sized_Box( 4,  4, '+');         -- Square
24:   Sized_Box(Height=>3,  Width=>4, Color=>'/');
25:   Sized_Box(Color=>'-', Width=>6, Height=>5);
26:   Robot.Exit_World;
27:end Pattern;
```

Program 2–3

The first method is called *positional association*. In positional association, the first actual parameter is associated with the first formal parameter, the second actual parameter is associated with the second formal parameter, and so on. The procedure call at line 21 of **Pattern** uses positional association. Thus, the actual parameter **10** is associated with the formal parameter **Height**, the actual parameter **2** is associated with the formal parameter **Width**, and the actual parameter **'.'** is associated with the formal parameter **Color**. The result is a tall, thin rectangle made of periods. The calls in lines 22 and 23 also use positional association.

The second method of indicating which actual parameter is associated with which formal parameter is called *named association*. Using named association, it is possible to specify the parameter associations using the formal parameter identifiers. If parameters are associated by names, the order of the actual parameters does not matter. Lines 24 and 25 of the procedure **Pattern** use named association. In line 24, the actual parameter **3** is explicitly associated with the formal parameter **Height**, the actual parameter **4** is explicitly associated with the formal parameter **Width**, and the actual parameter **'/'** is explicitly associated with the formal parameter **Color**. The syntax for named association is given in Figure 2–3. It is simply the identifier for the formal parameter followed by the symbol **=>** (called an *arrow*) and then by the actual parameter.

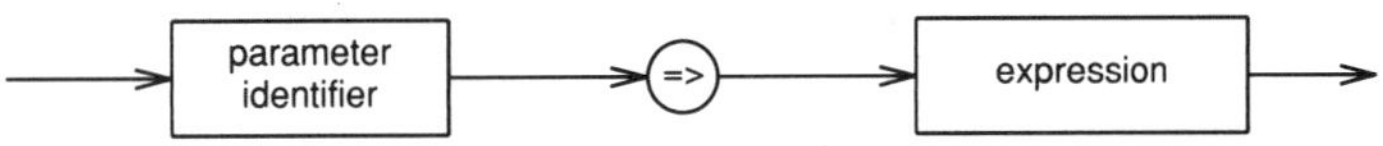

Figure 2–3

Named and positional association may be mixed in a single procedure call, but this is not recommended as a programming practice. When it is performed, all positional associations must precede all named associations. The following are legal calls to the procedure **Sized_Box**:

```
Sized_Box(3, Width=>4, Color=>'/');
Sized_Box(3, Color=>'/', Width=>4);
Sized_Box(3, 4, Color=>'/');
Sized_Box(3, 4, '/');
```

Each of these calls passes the same parameter values as the call on line 24 of Program 2–3.

The following are samples of the most common mistakes which occur with parameters:

`Sized_Box(3, '/');   -- illegal`
This call contains the wrong number of parameters. The procedure requires three parameters, but only two are supplied.

`Sized_Box(3, 4, Color=>6);   -- illegal`
The formal parameter **Color** is of type **CHARACTER**. The actual parameter is the wrong type because it is an integer literal.

`Sized_Box(Height=>3, 4, Color=>'/'); -- illegal`
In this call, a positional association follows a named association. By the syntax of Ada, any positional association must precede all named association.

```
Sized_Box(Hite=>3, Color=>'/', Width=>4); -- illegal
```

In this call, the first identifier is misspelled. It does not match any formal parameter identifier.

Because the parameters of a procedure may be used outside the procedure through named association, special care should be taken to use meaningful identifiers for formal parameters.

To summarize, communication with a procedure must be defined. The procedure states what parameters it expects and what identifiers are used to access those parameters. The procedure must be called in the prescribed manner.

2.5 PACKAGES (2): DECLARATION

The capability to group tools provides the programmer with a powerful method for organizing a program into coherent sections. In Ada, one or more tools can be placed within a group. Since these groups serve to "package" the tools, Ada calls them *packages*.

Some packages (including **STANDARD**) are defined in all implementations of Ada, while others have been defined for you by other programmers. But most importantly, Ada permits you to define your own packages.

There are two parts to a package: The first is the *package declaration*, which states what tools (procedures) are available in the package and how to communicate with them. The second is the *package body*, which specifies how the tools do their work. The syntax for both of these parts is given in Figure 2–4. When you use a package, you only need to know about the package declaration — that is, the kind of communication that is expected and what is accomplished by means of such communication.

To return to the analogy with a car, when you drive a car, you need to know the means of communicating with the car (steering wheel, brake pedal) and what they accomplish. You do not need to know the details about how they work. In fact, the details of how steering wheels and brakes work differ from car to car, but you can still drive the cars because the basic means of communication (wheel and pedal) are the same.

In a package declaration, the means of communication and capabilities of the tools are specified precisely. The package declaration gives the identifier by which the package is accessed (often called the package name), and it outlines what is available in the package. In effect, the package declaration tells you how to access the tools which are in the package. For tools which are procedures, the package declaration gives the declaration of the procedure, including the parameter list.

Ada uses the term *declaration* in several ways. The procedure name and parameter list followed by a semicolon is what Ada calls the *procedure declaration* (see Figure 2–4). The procedure declaration establishes the existence of the procedure and provides the information needed to call it. The procedure body is also declared, and, as is the case with the procedure **Paint_Sized_Box** in the package **Boxes** (see Program 2–4), the declaration of the body of the procedure can be separated from the procedure declaration. We shall use the term *procedure body* when referring specifically to the procedure body

<package declaration (simplified)>

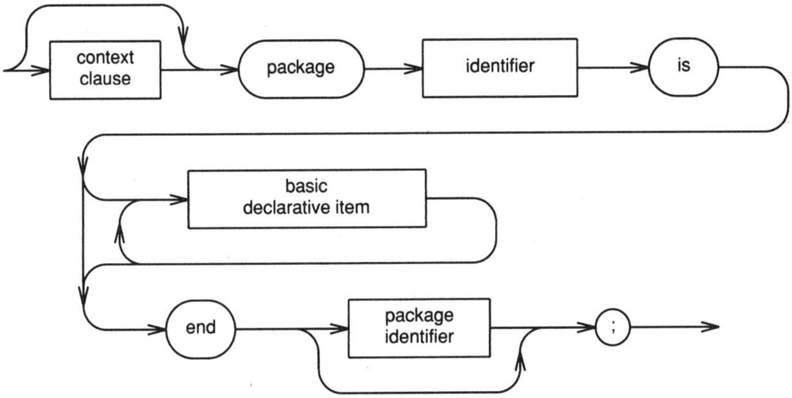

<package body (simplified)>

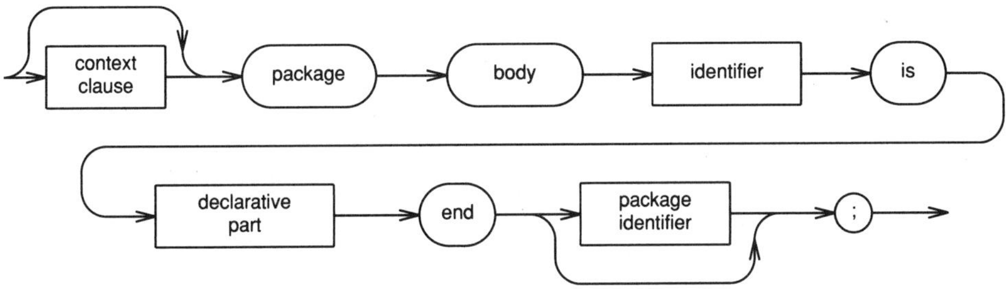

<procedure declaration> (a basic declarative item)

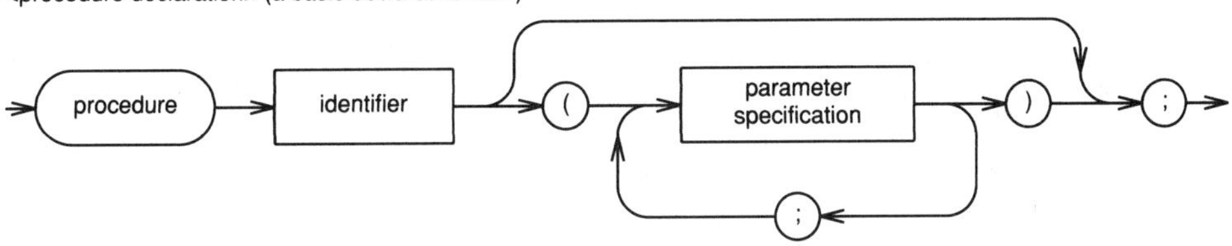

Figure 2–4

```
package Boxes is
  procedure Paint_Sized_Box(Box_Size: INTEGER);
  -- Purpose: draw a rectangle, of size Box_Size on each side.
  procedure Done;
  -- Purpose: Restore screen control.
end Boxes;
```

Program 2–4

and the term *procedure declaration* when referring to the declaration which establishes the existence of the procedure.

The complication in using this terminology is illustrated by the procedure **Paint_Side** within the body of the package **Boxes** (Program 2–5) and the procedure **Paint_Sized_Box** within the procedure **Tunnel** (Program 2–2). In both cases, there is *no* separate procedure declaration. Instead, the procedure body also acts as the procedure declaration, establishing the existence of the procedure, the manner in which it is called, and the actions it performs. Again, when talking of establishing the existence of a procedure or the existence of the tools in a package, we shall use the terms *procedure declaration* and *package declaration.* When discussing the body of a procedure or package, we shall use the terms *procedure body* and *package body.*

```
with Robot;
package body Boxes is
  procedure Paint_Side(Side_Size: INTEGER) is
  -- Paint a side and turn to line up
  --  for the next side.
  begin
    Robot.Move(Side_Size);
    Robot.Turn(Robot.Right);
  end Paint_Side;
  procedure Paint_Sized_Box(Box_Size: INTEGER) is
  -- Draw a box moving clockwise
  --  around the sides.
  -- Leave the robot exactly where it started
  --  and facing in its original direction.
  begin
    Robot.Set_Paint('.');
    Robot.Paint_On;
    Paint_Side(Box_Size);
    Paint_Side(Box_Size);
    Paint_Side(Box_Size);
    Paint_Side(Box_Size);
    Robot.Paint_Off;
  end Paint_Sized_Box;
  procedure Done is
  -- Have the Robot package restore normal screen control
  begin
    Robot.Exit_World;
  end Done;
end Boxes;
```

Program 2–5

Now consider the package **Boxes**. The package declaration says that **Boxes** contains a tool for drawing rectangles. This tool is a procedure that is associated with the identifier **Paint_Sized_Box**. It also contains a tool associated with the identifier **Done**. Since the declaration of each procedure given in the package declaration always includes any parameter list, the package declaration contains all we need to know about how to call a procedure in the package.

Once you declare the package, you must state how the procedures in the package work. This is done in the package body. The package body for **Boxes** illustrates how this is done. Since the package declaration guarantees that the procedure **Paint_Sized_Box** exists, procedure bodies for **Paint_Sized_Box** and **Done** must be declared in the package body. In addition, other procedures, such as **Paint_Side**, may be declared. The procedure **Paint_Side** is not accessible outside the package body because it is not found in the package declaration. The sole purpose of **Paint_Side** is to be used in implementing **Paint_Sized_Box**.

Once the package **Boxes** is declared, we can use it to build other procedures. As with "predefined" packages, if you wish a program to have access to a package you have declared, you must use a context clause in that program. The context clause says that the specified package is to be available to the current compilation. Because the procedure **Tunnel** in the package **Boxes_2** (see Program 2–6) needs access to the procedure in the package **Boxes**, **Boxes_2** contains a context clause (line 4) that makes the package **Boxes** available.

```
 1:package Boxes_2 is
 2:  procedure Tunnel;
 3:end Boxes_2;

 4:with Boxes;
 5:package body Boxes_2 is
 6:  procedure Tunnel is
 7:  -- Purpose: draw boxes of decreasing size.
 8:  begin
 9:    Boxes.Paint_Sized_Box(10);
10:    Boxes.Paint_Sized_Box(6);
11:    Boxes.Paint_Sized_Box(4);
12:    Boxes.Done;
13:  end Tunnel;
14:end Boxes_2;
```

Program 2–6

Notice that the context clause of **Boxes_2** names only **Boxes**. It does not name **Robot**, nor does it need to know that **Boxes** uses **Robot**. How the package **Boxes** accomplishes its task is of no concern to **Boxes_2**. In Ada, you need not care how the job gets done, as long as it is done right. Also, notice that the context clause that names **Boxes** is associated with the body of **Boxes_2**. We could have associated the context clause with the declaration of **Boxes_2**, but the association with the body is legal because there is nothing in the declaration (lines 1–3) which requires **Boxes**.

We could, of course, declare **Tunnel** as a compilation unit (i.e., a unit that can be compiled on its own — see section 2.6), but here we have chosen to declare it as a tool in the package **Boxes_2**. The package **Boxes_2** can now be used to perform even more complex actions by creating procedures with multiple calls to **Tunnel**.

We see, then, that each package has a package declaration and a package body (actually, the package body is also called a package body declaration). Whereas the package declaration contains the information on how to use a tool, the package body contains the information on how the tool is implemented. The situation is similar with procedures. The procedure declaration contains the information on how to use the procedure, and the procedure body contains the information on how the procedure is implemented. In the package **Boxes_2**, the procedure declaration for **Tunnel** is found in the package's declaration, and the declaration of the procedure body is found in the package's body. The declaration of the procedure body *must* contain a repetition of the parameter list, which in turn *must* match the parameter list of the procedure declaration.

A general rule in Ada is that tools must be defined before they are used. In the case of packages, package declarations must be compiled before you can use them. The package declaration contains the information about what components are in a package and how they are to be accessed. This must be correct before anything depending on the package can successfully use it.

2.6 COMPILATION UNITS (1)

In Ada, a *compilation unit* is something that can be compiled separately. Thus far, we have seen three kinds of compilation units: package declarations, package bodies, and procedure bodies.

We have seen packages named in context clauses. We can also name procedures in context clauses. Doing so makes the procedure available in the compilation unit that names it.

For example, in a different version of **Tunnel** (Program 2–7), the procedure **Paint_Sized_Box** is named in the context clause. Moving **Paint_Sized_Box** outside of the package makes the procedure a compilation unit (a tool that stands on its own). When this is done, **Paint_Sized_Box** can be named in a context clause of another compilation unit, as is done in line 1 of **Tunnel**. The naming of **Paint_Sized_Box** within the context clause makes the procedure available within **Tunnel**. It can be called, as in lines 6–8 of **Tunnel**. In this situation, a package name does not precede the procedure name because the procedure is not declared within a package. Because this new version of **Tunnel** directly sets the paint, it must name the **Robot** package in its context clause.

When a compilation unit is successfully compiled, it becomes part of a *library*. Units in the library may be used (named in a context clause) by other units. Thus, after they are successfully compiled, **Robot**, **Paint_Sized_Box** (as found in Program 2–7), and even **Tunnel** will be in the library and may be named by other compilation

```
with Robot;
procedure Paint_Sized_Box(Box_Size: INTEGER) is
-- Purpose: Draw a box moving clockwise
--  around the sides.
-- Leave the robot exactly where it started
--  and facing in its original direction.
begin
  Robot.Paint_On;
  Robot.Move(Box_Size);
  Robot.Turn(Robot.Right);
  Robot.Move(Box_Size);
  Robot.Turn(Robot.Right);
  Robot.Move(Box_Size);
  Robot.Turn(Robot.Right);
  Robot.Move(Box_Size);
  Robot.Turn(Robot.Right);
  Robot.Paint_Off;
end Paint_Sized_Box;

-- Separate compilation unit
with Robot, Paint_Sized_Box;
procedure Tunnel is
-- Draw boxes of decreasing size.
begin
  Robot.Set_Paint('.');
  Paint_Sized_Box(10);
  Paint_Sized_Box(6);
  Paint_Sized_Box(4);
  Robot.Exit_World;
end Tunnel;
```

Program 2–7

units. If a unit in the library is changed, that unit must be compiled again before the new version becomes available. After compilation, this new version now becomes the one that is used in compiling other units. In changing a library unit, in addition to compiling that unit, you will need to recompile any unit that you want to use the new version of the library unit.

2.7 ARITHMETIC

Computers can do arithmetic. The details of computer arithmetic can be quite complicated, but for simple programs you can get along without this complexity. In this chapter, we introduce just enough arithmetic to enable you to build a few packages. The key arithmetic symbols we introduce now are

```
+ - * /
```

corresponding to addition, subtraction, multiplication, and division, respectively. As examples, **6+2** corresponds to the sum of **6** and **2**, which is 8; **6-2** corresponds to the difference of **6** and **2**, which is 4; **6*2** corresponds to the product of **6** and **2**, which is 12; and **6/2** corresponds to the quotient of **6** and **2**, which is 3.

We can use arithmetic in Ada statements. For example, the command **Move(3+4);** moves the robot 7 units. It is a rule in Ada that arithmetic with integers produces integers. This is obvious for addition, subtraction, and multiplication, but it is also true for division. Integer division discards any remainder, so the expression **11/4** yields 2.

Simple arithmetic is useful for many things. In the procedure **Rectangle** given in Program 2–8, it is used to form a short, wide rectangle from a single parameter.

```
with Robot;
procedure Rectangle(Rectangle_Size: INTEGER) is
-- Purpose: Draw a short, wide box moving clockwise
--   around the sides.
-- Leave the robot exactly where it started
--   and facing in its original direction.
begin
  Robot.Set_Paint('.');
  Robot.Paint_On;
  Robot.Move(2 * Rectangle_Size);
  Robot.Turn(Robot.Right);
  Robot.Move(Rectangle_Size);
  Robot.Turn(Robot.Right);
  Robot.Move(2 * Rectangle_Size);
  Robot.Turn(Robot.Right);
  Robot.Move(Rectangle_Size);
  Robot.Turn(Robot.Right);
  Robot.Paint_Off;
  Robot.Exit_World;
end Rectangle;
```

Program 2–8

2.8 TYPES

A *type* is a set of values and a set of operations on those values. For each type, different operations may be defined. Thus far, we have seen three types in Ada:

1. **INTEGER** — a (signed) number (no fractions or decimal point).
2. **CHARACTER** — a letter, digit, or other single symbol.
3. **STRING** — a sequence of characters.

Some examples of legal values in the type **INTEGER** are as follows:

```
12      +37      0      -17
```

The operations allowed on integers include **+**, **-**, *****, and **/** (addition, subtraction, multiplication, and division).

Some examples of legal values in the type **CHARACTER** are:

```
'A'      '+'      '3'
```

We have not yet seen any operations that we can use with characters. However, we have used characters as parameters to the **Set_Paint** and **Sized_Box** procedure.

Some examples of legal values in the type **STRING** are the following:

```
"Hi There"     "Good Bye"
```

So far, we have used strings only as actual parameters to the **Write** procedure of the **Simple_IO** package.

In the case of characters and strings, apostrophes and quotation marks are required and serve to delimit the literal. That is, they indicate where the literal starts and stops, as well as the type of the literal. These delimiters are not printed by the **Write** procedure.

In the preceding examples, each type has its own set of possible values which is distinct from the set of possible values of the other types. We have used types in parameter declarations to specify what kind of information is acceptable to a procedure. Types, however, are more pervasive than this in Ada: All literals have a type, all parameters have a type, and many other things yet to be introduced use the concept of a type.

Note the difference between the character literal **'3'**, the integer literal **3**, and the string literal **"3"**. Each has a different meaning and is appropriate under different circumstances. For example, given the declaration of the procedure **Rectangle** in Program 2–8 the call

```
Rectangle(3);     -- legal
```

is legal, while the calls

```
Rectangle('3');   -- illegal
Rectangle("3");   -- illegal
```

are illegal because the parameter of **Rectangle** is declared to be an integer and the literals in these last two calls are not integer literals.

2.9 VARIABLES

In many situations, saving information is useful. This is particularly true in computer programs. Ada's method for saving and retrieving information is called the *variable*.

A variable is an association between an identifier and a container that stores a single value of the designated type. That is, a variable that is of the type **INTEGER** can only store integers and not characters.

A variable must be declared. Declaring a variable specifies (1) an identifier that will be used to refer to the variable and (2) the type of the information allowed to be stored in the variable. The syntax for declaring a variable is given in Figure 2–5. Variables may be declared either in procedures or in packages.

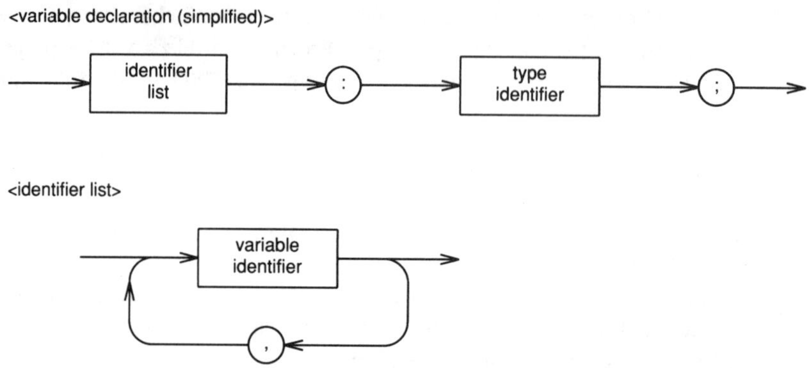

Figure 2–5

A number of identifiers may be listed, separated by commas, and followed by a colon and then an identifier associated with a type. This structure declares a number of variables of the same type. Several variable declarations may be given within the program.

We say that a variable *holds a value*. It only holds one value at a time, but the value it holds can change.

Ada assists the programmer in avoiding errors by limiting the type of the value a variable can hold. For example, if you are trying to put oranges into an egg carton, you are probably making a mistake. In Ada, when you store a value into a variable or pass a parameter, the types must match. Thus, an integer, and only an integer, can be stored in a variable of type integer; and a character, and only a character, can be passed to a formal parameter of type character.

Every value has a type, and every variable has a type, and every parameter has a type. The compiler checks to make sure that types match. In the declaration

```
Count: INTEGER;
```

the identifier **Count** is associated with the ability to store an integer. Hence, only an integer value can be stored in this variable.

To retrieve a value that has been stored in a variable, you simply use the identifier associated with the variable. For example, to use a value that has been stored in the variable associated with the identifier **Count**, the identifier is used in a statement, such as

```
Robot.Move(Count * 2);
```

This statement means, "Take the value that is stored in the container associated with the identifier **Count**, and multiply that value by 2." The result of this multiplication determines how far the robot will move. Thus, if **Count** contained the value 3, the multiplication would yield the value 6. As mentioned, one way in which a value may be used is as a parameter to a procedure. We have already used formal parameters in this way in the procedure **Rectangle**. Note that when an operation uses the value of a variable, it does not modify that variable. For example, after the multiply operation in the preceding call to the **Move** procedure, **Count** will still contain the value 3.

The value stored in a variable can change (vary) within a procedure, but the value associated with a formal parameter of mode **in** cannot. Formal parameters (as we have defined them so far) are only for communication, retaining the same value throughout each procedure invocation.

2.10 SIMPLE_IO (2): INPUT

One method of storing a value into a variable is to use the **Read** procedure from the package **Simple_IO**. A call to the **Read** procedure is given by

```
Read(Count);
```

The call to the **Read** procedure is a request for a value to be read from the keyboard and then placed into the variable. The type of value to be read depends on the type of the variable. Type checking requires that the user enter a value that is of the type associated with the variable identifier. If the variable is of type integer, **Read** ensures that an integer value is obtained from the user. If the user fails to enter an integer, the user is given another try.

Remember that a procedure can only accept parameters of the specific type declared. The procedure **Read** appears to be able to have parameters of type **INTEGER** or **CHARACTER**. Actually there are multiple procedures named **Read**. In a subsequent chapter we will explain how this is done. For now, just notice that we can use **Read** in a similar way for several types.

The procedure **Double_It** in Program 2–9 prompts the user (line 7) to type in a number to be doubled. At line 8, it reads the value the user types at the keyboard and places that value in the variable **The_Number**. It then uses that variable to print twice the number (line 11).

```
with Simple_IO;
procedure Double_It is
-- Purpose: Double a number.
   The_Number: INTEGER;
begin
   -- The number is up to the user.
   Simple_IO.Write("Double what number? ");
   Simple_IO.Read(The_Number);
   Simple_IO.New_Line;
   Simple_IO.Write("Double that number is ");
   Simple_IO.Write(2 * The_Number);
end Double_It;
```

Program 2–9

When reading integers, **Simple_IO** expects each integer to be on a separate line. It will read the first integer on the line and discard the rest. Note that a program can contain more than one **Read**.

Another procedure in the package **Simple_IO** is called **Await_User**. **Await_User** ignores everything that is typed until the user enters a carriage return, that is; it causes the program to wait until a return is keyed.

```
 1:with Boxes, Robot;
 2:procedure Paint_Any_Sized_Box is
 3:-- Purpose: Draw a box of any size the user wants.
 4:   Actual_Size: INTEGER;
 5:begin
 6:   -- The size of the box is up to the user.
 7:   Robot.Write("What box size? ");
 8:   Robot.Read(Actual_Size);
 9:   Boxes.Paint_Sized_Box(Actual_Size);
10:end Paint_Any_Sized_Box;
```

Program 2–10

Because it takes control of the screen, the **Robot** package contains its own routines for reading and writing. These are identical to those we have introduced in **Simple_IO** except that they carefully read and write to the right of the robot's world. The procedure **Paint_Any_Sized_Box** in Program 2–10 prompts the user (line 7) to type in the size of the box that should be drawn. At line 8, it reads the value the user types at the keyboard and places that value in the variable **Actual_Size**. It then uses that variable to draw the box of the correct size.

2.11 PROGRAMMING PRACTICES

The programming practices we now present are intended as guidelines that will, in general, make a program more readable, more likely to be correct, and easier to correct or enhance. They are not strict rules, because in some cases alternative structures or practices are necessary. When applying programming practices, always remember that the goals they are intended to achieve are more important than the practices themselves.

Packages provide us the capability to declare collections of tools which can be reused later. It is worth the effort to design packages well. The comments in the package declaration should state clearly what capabilities each tool in the package supplies and what its options are. These comments are necessary to make the package truly easy to use. Everything that does not need to be visible should be hidden within the package body. This way, no one can use these things in ways they were not intended to be used.

Variables, parameters, and procedures also need descriptive names so that they can be easily understood. Good programs can be read, rather than merely puzzled out. Generally, only one variable should be defined per line so that it can be properly described with a comment. All the available information should be divided so that as much of it as possible is hidden from other procedures. This technique, called "information hiding," prevents inappropriate changes and simplifies the writing of correct programs.

Calling procedures with parameters should be done as uniformly as possible: Mixing named and positional association within a single call can confuse the reader; so it is good practice not to mix the two methods of parameter association. Also, calls to a particular procedure should be similar; that is, either use named association or use positional association for all the calls. When using named association, the parameters should be kept in the same order in all calls to a procedure. In general, named association is more readable and more easily maintainable for procedures having more than two parameters.

2.11.1 Problem Solving

As mentioned earlier, the use of procedures permits sequences of statements, and thus work, to be reused. In the diagonal-line example of Chapter 1, we repeated a sequence of statements three times, once for each square drawn. It is easy to see that if we used procedures, the program would have been shorter and simpler.

As each chapter presents new tools, you will acquire new, more elegant techniques for approaching the same problems. For instance, the procedure and the package are tools for supporting the reuse of software: Procedures are useful for grouping statements that may be used more than once, while packages create tool kits that can be reused later. Most important, the procedure and the package are structures that can be used to group items for easier problem solving and for producing a solution that is more readable.

2.11.2 Testing

Testing is one of the most important activities in computer programming. To demonstrate that a program works correctly, one should execute the program several times with different typical input values. You should also try the program with some nonsensical input values to make sure that it behaves in a reasonable way. We shall discuss this further in later chapters.

2.12 ADA SUMMARY

In this chapter, we have seen how to *declare* packages. We have discussed procedures and how to use *parameters* to vary the behavior of procedures. We have introduced the concept of *type* and discussed the types **INTEGER**, **CHARACTER**, and **STRING**. Finally, we have discussed the *variable* as a storage mechanism for a value of a specific type and the **Read** statement as a mechanism for storing a value in a variable.

EXERCISES

2.1. Modify procedure **Pattern** in Program 2–3 to call **Sized_Box**: (a) only with positional association and (b) only with named association. The displayed boxes should remain the same.

2.2. Use the package **Boxes** in Program 2–4 to build a procedure **Row_of_Boxes** that draws the following:

```
.....   .....   .....
.   .   .   .   .   .
.   .   .   .   .   .
.   .   .   .   .   .
.....   .....   .....
```

(The beginning of this chapter gives a version of **Row_of_Boxes** built as a procedure.)

2.3. Modify the procedure **Rectangle** in Program 2–8 so that, instead of using parameters, it asks the user for the height and width of the rectangle and the character to use for paint.

2.4. Rewrite the program **Draw_Diagonal** from Chapter 1, using the tools (procedure and package) introduced in this chapter.

2.5. In Program 2–2 we presented the procedure **Tunnel** without showing the problem solving involved because we were using it to present tools. Show how we could have developed **Tunnel** (from **Boxes_2**; see program 2–6) if we were using problem solving techniques.

2.6. Complete the package **Graph_Tools** (given below) which uses the tools in the package **Robot** and provides the utilities described in it. The procedure **Box_At** has two parameters which represent the upper left hand corner of the box to be drawn. The size of the box is found in the variables **Height** and **Width** which are declared in the package body. These variables are set by the procedure **Read_Box_Size** which writes a message to the user requesting that the information be typed and then reads the user's answer. The procedure **Box_At** should move the robot to the appropriate location, use the procedure **Sized_Rectangle** to draw the box, and then return the robot to its starting position. Be careful to maintain the direction of the robot, and don't forget to put appropriate comments into the procedures you build.

To test your package, write a procedure that calls **Read_Box_Size** and then makes two calls to **Box_At** with different parameters.

```
package Graph_Tools is
  procedure Box_At(Bx, By: INTEGER);
  -- Purpose: Draw a box at Bx, By.
  procedure Read_Box_Size;
  -- Purpose: Read the Height and Width for a box from the user.
  procedure Done;
  -- Purpose: Restore screen control.
end Graph_Tools;

with Robot;
package body Graph_Tools is
  Height, Width: INTEGER;
  -- The horizontal and vertical size of box.
  -- You fill in any additional variable declarations.
  procedure Sized_Rectangle(Height, Width: INTEGER) is
  begin
    Robot.Paint_On;
    Robot.Move(Width);          -- Draw top
    Robot.Turn(Robot.Right);
    Robot.Move(Height);         -- Draw right side
    Robot.Turn(Robot.Right);
    Robot.Move(Width);          -- Draw bottom
    Robot.Turn(Robot.Right);
    Robot.Move(Height);         -- Draw left side
    Robot.Turn(Robot.Right); -- Restore original direction
    Robot.Paint_Off;
  end Sized_Rectangle;
  procedure Box_At(Bx, By: INTEGER) is
  begin
    -- You fill in
  end Box_At;
  procedure Read_Box_Size is
  begin
    -- You fill in
  end Read_Box_Size;
  procedure Done is
  -- Have the Robot package restore normal screen control
  begin
    Robot.Exit_World;
  end Done;
end Graph_Tools;
```

3

Types and Objects

3.1 OBJECTIVES

Storage of information in variables is a common action in computer programs. In this chapter, a second method of storing information is introduced (section 3). Safety features exist to ensure that the programmer uses variables correctly. We discuss key safety features including restrictions on the type of information stored (sections 3 and 7), storage that does not change (section 4), and limiting where variables can be used or changed (sections 5 and 6). We introduce additional capabilities for communicating with subprograms (sections 9 and 10). Most large programs undergo several adaptations during their lifetime. We introduce some of the Ada facilities that encourage adaptability by place restrictions upon and by providing information about types (section 7). We subsequently introduce a new package that is both a useful tool and a rich source of examples (section 11). Finally, we develop a simple example (section 12).

CONCEPTS:

- Strong typing provides valuable error detection early in the development of programs.
- Hiding information and capabilities simplifies using procedures and packages while increasing program safety.
- You can communicate both to and from subprograms.
- Types have attributes that can be determined and used by the programmer.
- Restricting the contents of a variable assists in error detection and understanding a program.

GOALS:

- Use types and subtypes as a safety device.
- Use parameters for communication into and out of a procedure.
- Use scope rules to hide information.
- Use constants and range restrictions.

3.2 MOTIVATION

Although the ideal practice is to avoid mistakes, one of the principle tasks of programming is to discover and correct errors. The more complete the set of tools for detecting errors, the better is the programming environment. Because the programming language is central to the process of constructing solutions, a well-designed language can greatly assist in the detection of errors. The philosophy of the Ada language is that it is better to detect an error than to run an incorrect program.

Several key concepts in this chapter: types, constants, and range constraints, are means of detecting many common programming mistakes. Once they are discovered, many errors can be corrected easily. The Ada language assists the programmer in producing a correct program by providing for the detection of several classes of errors.

Another set of concepts: scope, parameters, packages, and functions, are directed at the detection of a more difficult type of error. Ada is constructed so that the programmer can partition each problem into smaller pieces. Each piece is assigned a particular responsibility and has a particular method of communicating with other pieces. When you know which piece is responsible for what, you can avoid errors by testing each piece to assure that it performs its job properly. Partitioning is not guaranteed to detect all mistakes, but it does limit them. In an appropriately structured program, when a mistake is discovered in later phases, the piece of the program responsible for the mistake is easier to pinpoint, making errors easier to fix.

3.3 ASSIGNMENT STATEMENT

In Chapter 2, we introduced **`Read`** as a method of storing a value in a variable. *Assignment* is another method of storing a value in a variable. The syntax for the assignment statement is given in Figure 3–1. The symbol "`:=`" represents the assignment and divides the assignment statement into a right- and a left-hand side. The value of the expression on the right-hand side of the assignment is computed and stored in the variable indicated on the left-hand side. The procedure **`Paint_Picture`** in Program 3–1 uses several assignment statements. This program computes the actual size of the box, based upon a parameter.

The simplest form of assignment is shown in line 5 of **`Paint_Picture`**. In this line, the value 4 is stored in the variable associated with the identifier **`Actual_Size`**. In computer programming terminology, we often say that the value 4 is *assigned* to the variable **`Actual_Size`**.

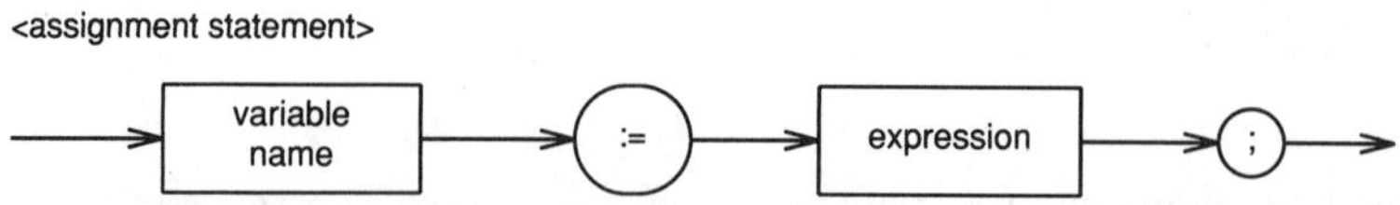

Figure 3–1

The literal **4** on line 5 is one of the simplest forms of an expression. More complicated expressions may be used in an assignment statement. For example, suppose **Paint_Picture** is called with an actual parameter of 2. Then in line 6, the expression on the right-hand side of the assignment becomes **2*2+3**, or 7. The assignment statement stores the value 7 in the variable **Actual_Size**.

In line 7, when the expression **Actual_Size+1** is evaluated, the value of **Actual_Size** is 7, so the value of the expression is 8. The assignment statement now stores the value 8 in the variable **Actual_Size**.

```
 1:with Boxes;
 2:procedure Paint_Picture(Box_Size: INTEGER) is
 3:   Actual_Size: INTEGER;
 4:begin
 5:   Actual_Size := 4;
 6:   Actual_Size := 2 * Box_Size + 3;
 7:   Actual_Size := Actual_Size + 1;
 8:   Boxes.Paint_Sized_Box(Actual_Size);
 9:   Boxes.Paint_Sized_Box(Actual_Size + 3);
10:   Boxes.Done;
11:end Paint_Picture;
```

Program 3–1

The consequence of an assignment statement is obvious if you remember the rules that (1) statements are performed in a given order and (2) the value of the expression (the right-hand side of the assignment) is computed and then stored. These mean that the value stored by an assignment statement can be affected by previous assignment statements. Note that failure to correctly order assignment statements is a major cause of errors, and the Ada compiler cannot detect this kind of situation at all! For example, if we swapped lines 6 and 7 in **Paint_Picture**, the program would remain completely legal, but the boxes drawn would be quite different.

We have already seen that parameters can receive only a certain type of information. The same is true of variables: The value to be stored must be of the same type as the variable into which it is stored. If the programmer inadvertently violates this restriction, the compiler detects the mistake. In Ada terminology, the type of the value must *match* the type of the variable.

Given the variables

```
Letter: CHARACTER;
Number: INTEGER;
```

the assignment statements

```
Letter := 'A';
Letter := '2';
Number := 2;
```

are legal because the type of the expression on the right matches the type of the variable on the left. In the first two assignments, the type of both sides is **CHARACTER**, a **CHARACTER** variable on the left and a **CHARACTER** literal on the right. Notice the distinction between the character **'2'** and the number **2**. In the third assignment, we have an **INTEGER** variable on the left and an **INTEGER** literal on the right.

Both of the statements

```
Number := 'A';      -- illegal
Number := '2';      -- illegal
```

are illegal because the expression on the right is of type **CHARACTER** and the variable is of type **INTEGER**. This is true even though the character in the second line is a digit. Numeric literals are not surrounded by apostrophes; thus, **'2'** can only be interpreted as a character literal. Detecting a mismatch of types is quite easy. Similarly,

```
Letter := 2;        -- illegal
```

is illegal because the literal on the right is an integer and the variable can only store a character.

In the procedure **Paint_Picture**, the variable **Actual_Size** can only store integers. Therefore, **Actual_Size** may be freely used in integer expressions and other places where integers are required. This occurs in the expression on line 7 and in the procedure calls on lines 8 and 9.

As a word of warning, consider what would happen if we switched lines 5 and 7. Such a switch causes the program to try to get a value from **Actual_Size** before **Actual_Size** has been given a value. Any number of things may then happen. Ada does not specify exactly what should happen, but the program clearly would not be correct. So, be sure that a variable has been given a value before that value is used.

3.4 VARIABLE AND CONSTANT OBJECTS

The syntax for another method of supplying a value to a variable is shown in Figure 3–2. The diagram indicates that an initial value can be supplied for a variable in its declaration.

This is demonstrated in line 2 of the procedure **Variables_and_Constants** in Program 3–2. When the procedure starts, the variable comes into existence and receives its initial value. This initial value is assigned before execution of the statements in the procedure begins.

When execution of the statements in **Variables_and_Constants** begins, the value of the variable **Initialized** is 7 because that was the initial value specified in line 2. Since **Initialized** is a variable, it can be given a new value, as shown in line 8. The initial value is precisely that — a value with which a variable starts when execution of a procedure begins. If an initial value is supplied, type checking is performed just as if an assignment statement were being used to store the value.

```
1:procedure Variables_and_Constants is
2:   Initialized: INTEGER := 7;
3:   Maximum_Occupancy: constant INTEGER := 432;
4:   Little_Prime: constant INTEGER := 3;
5:   First_Capital_Letter: constant CHARACTER := 'A';
6:   Last_Capital_Letter: constant CHARACTER := 'Z';
7:begin
8:   Initialized := 4;
9:end Variables_and_Constants;
```

Program 3–2

This capability helps avoid the common error of using a variable before it has been given a value. Many languages, including Ada, do not always detect this error, and the result is that some undefined value is found in the variable. This undefined value is often called "garbage" because there is no telling what the value might be.

One advantage of giving a variable an initial value in its declaration is that you know that the variable does not contain garbage. For those variables which are not given explicit initial values, you need to ask yourself, "Where is this variable given its value?" Of course, the initial value you supply must be an appropriate one. For example, initializing all variables of type **INTEGER** to 0 could mean that many of these variables contain a meaningless value.

In Ada terminology, a variable is one kind of *object*. We shall introduce another kind of object shortly. The process of bringing an object into existence is one instance of an action which Ada calls *elaboration*. If an initial value is specified for an object, that value will be assigned to the object as part of the object's elaboration. The elaboration of the variable **Initialized** on line 2 initializes the value of that variable to 7.

A second kind of object in Ada is the *constant object*. Constant objects are often referred to simply as *constants*. The syntax for declaring a constant is given in Figure 3–2. The syntax is quite similar to the syntax for declaring a variable with an initial value, except the reserved word **constant** appears in front of the type. Examples of

<object declaration (simplified)>

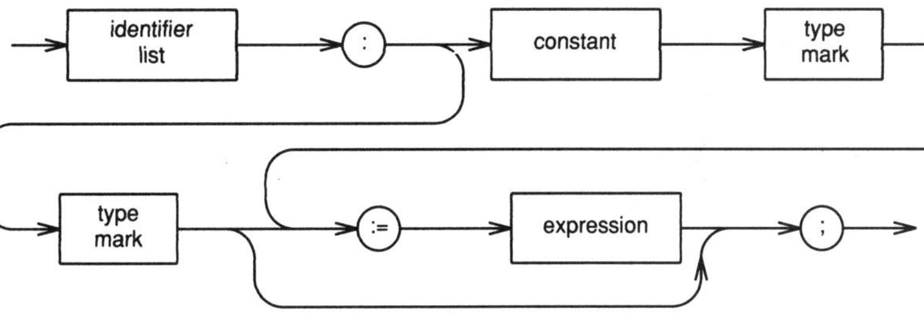

Figure 3–2

declarations of constants are found on lines 4–6 of **`Variables_and_Constants`** in Program 3–2.

A constant object is an object whose value cannot be changed after elaboration. Although constants, like variables, can be initialized, they cannot be assigned different values in the body of the procedure. A constant can only receive a value when it is elaborated. Furthermore, constants must always be initialized at elaboration.

Too often, programmers use literals instead of constants. But constants are preferred for a number of reasons. The first is readability: A meaningful identifier such as **`Days_In_Week`** is far more understandable than a literal such as 7, because the identifier makes the intent of the constant clear. The second reason is reliability: A variable could be used instead of a constant, but a programming mistake could cause the variable to assume a different value. This cannot occur with constants, since such an error will be detected by the compiler. The third reason is flexibility: A constant such as **`Maximum_Number_of_Students`** defines a limit on a particular implementation. Modification of that limit requires a change in a single place in the program — the place where the constant is declared. With literals, we would have to carefully find and modify each occurrence of the literal, a time-consuming and error-prone process.

The use of named constants is an example of what we refer to as *readability* in the section on programming practices.

3.5 SCOPE

If information is kept hidden, it cannot be seen or changed by anyone; therefore, it cannot be corrupted or misused by anyone. Ada allows objects to be declared as accessible only in a local setting. Limiting the amount of access to data helps locate errors. Suppose you were managing a bank and some of the accounts came up with the wrong balance. The more people who have authorization to modify the accounts, the harder it will be to trace the mistake. Further, if there are twice as many people modifying accounts, there are twice as many opportunities for errors. The same is true in writing programs: The wider the access to an object, the more likely it is that an error will be made in correctly maintaining the integrity of the value in that object, and the more difficult it will be to find the error when it occurs.

A more subtle problem occurs quite frequently. Successful programs are often modified in response to requests for additional features. When you perform a modification that affects the value of a variable, you must analyze the impact of the change on all other uses of that variable. The more uses of a variable, the more difficult it is to correctly make the modification.

For the moment, we shall only consider variables declared in procedures. These variables are protected in the sense that they can only be used within the procedure in which they are declared. A variable is re-created each time its procedure is called, and it ceases to exist each time the procedure finishes.

Ada and many other modern programming languages express part of what the preceding discussion is driving at with the term *scope*. The scope of a variable is the portion of the program in which the identifier associated with the variable can be used to refer to the variable. Thus, the scope of a variable is (approximately) the procedure in which it is declared. More precisely, the (immediate) scope of a variable is from the beginning of its declaration to the end of the declarative region. The *declarative regions* we have seen thus far are procedures and packages. We next give examples of immediate and extended regions of scope for procedures and then discuss scope as it applies to packages.

The procedure **Scope_Demo** in Program 3–3 illustrates the principle of scope. The variable **Global_Var** is declared within **Scope_Demo**. By the scope rule, the scope of **Global_Var** begins at its declaration (line 2) and ends at the end of procedure **Scope_Demo** (line 24). The variable **Local_to_First** is declared in the procedure **First_Global_Proc**, so the scope of **Local_to_First** begins at its declaration (line 4) and ends at the end of **First_Global_Proc** (line 13). The variable **Local_to_First** cannot be accessed in **Second_Global_Proc** because this procedure is outside of its scope. The only variables available in procedure **Second_Global_Proc** are **Local_to_Second** and **Global_Var**. In Ada terminology, these variables are *visible* in **Second_Global_Proc**. Similarly, the variable **Very_Local** can only be accessed within procedure **Local_Procedure** (lines 6–9).

Since the scope of **Local_to_First** begins at its declaration (line 4), in addition to being visible in the body of **First_Global_Proc** (line 11), **Local_to_First** is also visible in **Local_Procedure** (lines 5–9). An example of usage of **Local_to_First** in **Local_Procedure** is shown in line 8. Used here, **Local_to_First** refers to a variable that is not declared in **Local_Procedure**. Such a use is called a *nonlocal* reference to the variable. Nonlocal variables are called *global* if they are defined in the outermost procedure. Use of nonlocal variables often leads to errors; as a general rule, variables should be declared as locally as possible.

The scope rules that apply to variable declarations also apply to procedure declarations. If access to subprograms is kept local, then only authorized users can call the subprograms; therefore, they cannot be misused by anyone except those users. As is illustrated by the declaration of **Local_Procedure**, Ada allows procedures to be

```
1:procedure Scope_Demo is
2:  Global_Var: INTEGER;

3:  procedure First_Global_Proc is
4:    Local_to_First: INTEGER;

5:    procedure Local_Procedure is
6:      Very_Local: INTEGER;
7:    begin
8:      Very_Local := Global_Var + Local_to_First;
9:    end Local_Procedure;

10:  begin
11:    Local_to_First := 5;
12:    Local_Procedure;
13:  end First_Global_Proc;

14:  procedure Second_Global_Proc is
15:    Local_to_Second: INTEGER;
16:  begin
17:    Local_to_Second := Global_Var
18:    First_Global_Proc;
19:  end Second_Global_Proc;

20:begin
21:  Global_Var := 3;
22:  First_Global_Proc;
23:  Second_Global_Proc;
24:end Scope_Demo;
```

Program 3–3

declared in a local setting. Since **Local_Procedure** is declared within **First_Global_Proc**, it can only be used within **First_Global_Proc**.

Since a procedure is visible immediately after its declaration to the end of the declarative region, **Local_Procedure** can be called in lines 6–13. By the same reasoning, **First_Global_Proc** can be called in lines 4–24 and can be called within **Second_Global_Proc** as illustrated by the call on line 18. However, **Second_Global_Proc** cannot be called in **First_Global_Proc**, because its declaration begins (line 14) after the end of **First_Global_Proc** (line 13). Of course, the visibility of both **First_Global_Proc** and **Second_Global_Proc** ends at the end of procedure **Scope_Demo** (line 24). So **Second_Global_Proc** can be called in the main program, as is done on line 23.

Like variables, constants can be declared locally. A constant that is local to a procedure has its value recomputed *each* time it is elaborated. Recall that it is elaborated *each* time the procedure is entered. While it is constant from the time it is created, each time it is created it can be given a different value.

```
 1:with Simple_IO;
 2:procedure Recreate_Constant is
 3:   X: INTEGER := 2;
 4:   procedure Use_Const is
 5:     C: constant INTEGER := X;
 6:   begin
 7:     Simple_IO.Write(C);
 8:   end Use_Const;
 9:begin  -- Recreate_Constant
10:   Use_Const;   -- C will be set to 2
11:   X := 4;
12:   Use_Const;   -- C will be set to 4
13:end Recreate_Constant;
```

Program 3–4

Recomputation of constants is illustrated in the procedure **Recreate_Constant** in Program 3–4. In **Recreate_Constant**, the global variable **X** declared on line 3 is used to determine the value of the local constant **C** declared on line 5. The first time the procedure **Use_Const** is called (line 10), **X** has the value 2. Thus, the constant **C** receives the value 2, and this value cannot be changed during execution of **Use_Const**. When the procedure **Use_Const** is exited, the constant **C** ceases to exist.

On the next call to **Use_Const** from line 12, **C** is recreated. However, this time **X** has the value 4, so that when **C** is elaborated, it is given the value 4. Again, this value cannot be changed while **C** remains in existence.

It is legal and useful to use constants or variables in defining initial values for variables and in defining other constants. For example, if we have the declaration

```
Little_Prime: constant INTEGER := 3;
```

then the declaration

```
Twice_Little_Prime: constant INTEGER := Little_Prime * 2;
```

is preferable to

```
Twice_Little_Prime: constant INTEGER := 6;
```

because if **Little_Prime** is changed and the program is recompiled, the first declaration automatically contains the correct value for **Twice_Little_Prime** while the second does not. A change in the definition of **Little_Prime** could introduce an error if the second declaration were used and we forgot to change the literal associated with **Twice_Little_Prime**.

We have already seen that the identifiers associated with formal parameters may be used to pass parameters by name. This use of these identifiers outside the procedure declaration is an instance of *extended scope*. For example, given the procedure declaration

```
procedure Sized_Box(Height, Width: INTEGER; Color: CHARACTER);
```

from Chapter 2, we used the identifiers in the call

```
Sized_Box(Height=>3, Width=>4, Color=>'/');
```

which was in the main program. Since this procedure call does not occur inside **Sized_Box**, this use of identifiers is outside the declarative region of that procedure. In Ada terminology, the declarative region (of **Sized_Box**) is the immediate scope of the identifiers. However, in Ada, identifiers associated with formal parameters have an extended scope. For parameters, the allowable extended scope is within the parameter list of calls to the procedure. This is why **Height**, **Width**, and **Color** may be used in the actual parameter list of any call to **Sized_Box**.

3.6 PACKAGES (3): SCOPE AND VISIBILITY

A variable declared in a package body has some of the advantages of both local and nonlocal variables. Being local to the package body, it is visible only within the package body. However, it is permanent with respect to the duration of the package.

To make the contrast clear, variables in a procedure are elaborated upon entry into the procedure and cease to exist upon exit from the procedure. Variables in a package are elaborated upon elaboration of the package and exist throughout the existence of the package. Packages named in the context clause exist during the entire program; thus, so do the objects declared in those packages. Variables may be declared in the declaration or the body of a package, the difference being that declarations that occur within the declaration part of a package have an extended scope. Such variables are always visible within the package. In addition, they may be made visible outside the package by naming the package in the context clause of a compilation unit. In Ada terminology, the compilation unit naming the package becomes an extended scope for the variables declared in the package declarations.

The package **Box_Tools** in Program 3–5 is a modification of an exercise from Chapter 2. The goal of **Box_Tools** is to produce more efficient movement of the robot. Specifically, there is no need for the robot always to return to its corner. But in order to avoid this, it is necessary to record where the robot was left after the last call to **Draw_Box_At**. This requires some variables within the package. Not only does **Draw_Box_At** need to move the robot, but it must compute and record where it leaves

```
 1:package Box_Tools is
 2:  procedure Draw_Box_At(X, Y: INTEGER);
 3:  -- Purpose: Draw a box at X, Y.
 4:  Vertical_Size, Horizontal_Size: INTEGER := 5;
 5:   -- The size of the boxes to draw.
 6:end Box_Tools;

 7:with Robot, Sized_Box;
 8:package body Box_Tools is
 9:  -- The current horizontal and vertical position of the robot.
10:  Horizontal_Position, Vertical_Position: INTEGER := 0;
11:  procedure Draw_Box_At(X, Y: INTEGER) is
12:  begin
13:    Robot.Move(X-Horizontal_Position);
14:    Robot.Turn(Robot.Right); -- Turn to face down
15:    Robot.Move(Y-Vertical_Position);
16:    Robot.Turn(Robot.Left);  -- Turn to face left
17:    Sized_Box(Vertical_Size, Horizontal_Size, '.');
18:    Horizontal_Position := X;
19:    Vertical_Position := Y;
20:  end Draw_Box_At;
21:end Box_Tools;
```

Program 3–5

the robot after the final move. Thus, **Draw_Box_At** will move the robot 4 or more times, but it only has to record the position of the robot after the last of these moves.

As we have seen before, the procedure **Draw_Box_At** may be used outside of the package **Box_Tools** because it occurs in the package declaration. The same is true of variables in the package declaration. The variables **Vertical_Size** and **Horizontal_Size** may be accessed outside the package. The syntax for accessing a variable from the package is similar to that for accessing a procedure. For example,

```
Box_Tools.Horizontal_Size := 10;
```

can be used to access the variable **Horizontal_Size**. In all respects, such variables behave as do all other variables. In particular, the statement shown stores the value 10 into the variable **Horizontal_Size**.

The variables **Vertical_Position** and **Horizontal_Position** cannot be accessed outside of the package **Box_Tools** because they are declared in the package body. It is intended that they be used by the procedures of the package for recording the position at which the robot is left between drawing boxes. As lines 13 and 15 indicate, they are used for computing how far the robot must move from its current position to the position it must be at when starting to draw the new box. In lines 18 and 19, the latter position is recorded.

Although we have declared **Vertical_Size** and **Horizontal_Size** for the purpose of illustrating the allowable syntax, this is not the best method for achieving the goal of package **Box_Tools**. It would be better to declare these variables within the package body and declare a procedure **Set_Box_Size** in the package declaration. We would then still be able to set the box size, but the procedure could also do other useful items, like refuse to make the change for negative box sizes or box sizes that are too large. In general, it is better to protect variables and access them only through procedure or function calls.

So far, in every access to a component declared in a package, we have used what is called *visibility by selection*. That is, we have had to supply the package name in front of the component, as in

```
Robot.Move(5);
```

In some cases this becomes very repetitive, so Ada supplies what is called *direct* visibility. Direct visibility can be achieved through the *use clause*. With direct visibility, you do not need to supply the package name in front of the component. The procedure **Paint_Box** is shown rewritten with a use clause in Program 3–6.

```
with Robot;     -- "use Robot;" could go here
procedure Paint_Box is
   use Robot;
   Box_Size: constant INTEGER := 10;
   -- Purpose: draw a box in the following order:
   --   top, right side, bottom, left side.
   -- Leave the Robot exactly where it started
   --   and facing in its original direction.
begin
   Set_Paint('.');
   Paint_On;
   Move(Box_Size);        -- Draw top of box
   Turn(Right);
   Move(Box_Size);        -- Draw right side of box
   Turn(Right);
   Move(Box_Size);        -- Draw bottom of box
   Turn(Right);
   Move(Box_Size);        -- Draw left side of box
   Turn(Right);           -- Restore the original direction
   Exit_World;            -- Return control of the screen
end Paint_Box;
```

Program 3–6

Notice that all references to **Robot**, except those in the use and with clauses, have been removed. It is not required to have the use clause present. If the use clause is not present, direct visibility is not achieved; however, visibility by selection is still available.

The use clause can be either in the context clause or in any declaration part. If the use clause is part of a declaration, then direct visibility of items in the package declaration holds until the end of the declarative region. As with other capabilities, the rule is to keep the use clause as local as possible. Therefore, in the procedure **Paint_Box**, we have put the use clause within the procedure declaration as recommended, and indicated in the comment on line 1 where it would be if it were in the context clause. If the use clause occurs in the context clause, then the package components are directly visible through the entire compilation unit. In the case of **Paint_Box**, either position achieves the same effect. However, in choosing to place the use clause in line 3, we are applying the principle of keeping visibility as localized as possible.

All of the packages we have declared thus far have been compilation units. They thus became part of the library and could be named by other compilation units. Ada allows the declaration of local packages. For example, suppose that instead of making the package **Box_Tools** publicly available, we did not want it used outside of the procedure **Protect_Tools** indicated in Program 3–7. This can be accomplished by declaring **Box_Tools** within **Protect_Tools**. The components of **Box_Tools** would then be visible within **Protect_Tools**, as well as in local procedures declared in **Protect_Tools**.

```
procedure Protect_Tools is
     ...
   package Box_Tools is
       ...
   end Box_Tools;
     ...
   package body Box_Tools is
       ...
   end Box_Tools;
     ...
end Protect_Tools;
```

Program 3–7

Of course, the standard scope rules apply. First, **Box_Tools** need not be the first item in the declaration of **Protect_Tools**. As with other declarations, **Box_Tools** does not become available until its declaration; thus, procedures declared before **Box_Tools** is declared would not be able to use its components. Second, unless there is a use clause, visibility is by selection, in which case the use clause must occur after the declaration of the package.

Notice the absence of a context clause. The purpose of a context clause is to cause a previously compiled package to become visible. The compiler would have no idea that we wanted one of these previously compiled packages unless we told it so. Since a locally declared package is declared within the procedure, it is found during the compilation, and it is immediately made available, but not directly visible. A reference to the variable **Horizontal_Size** would still have the form

```
Box_Tools.Horizontal_Size
```

Since the declaration of the package **Box_Tools** is in the declarative region of **Protect_Tools**, the package is elaborated when **Protect_Tools** is called and ceases to exist upon exit from **Protect_Tools**. Consequently, the variables in the package (**Horizontal_Size** and **Vertical_Size**) are created on each call to **Protect_Tools** and cease to exist upon exit from **Protect_Tools**.

We have now introduced sufficiently diverse kinds of declarations (packages, variables, constants, and procedures) so that we must indicate a restriction that applies to the order of declarations. The general rule is that small items must precede large items. In particular, variables and constants must precede the bodies of packages and procedures. In the **Protect_Tools** example, variable declarations could occur from lines 1 to 5, but not between 5 and 6 because there they would follow the body of a package. This same rule applies within the body of **Box_Tools**, requiring us to place the declaration of the variables **Horizontal_Size** and **Vertical_Size** before the declaration of the body of the procedure **Draw_Box_At**.

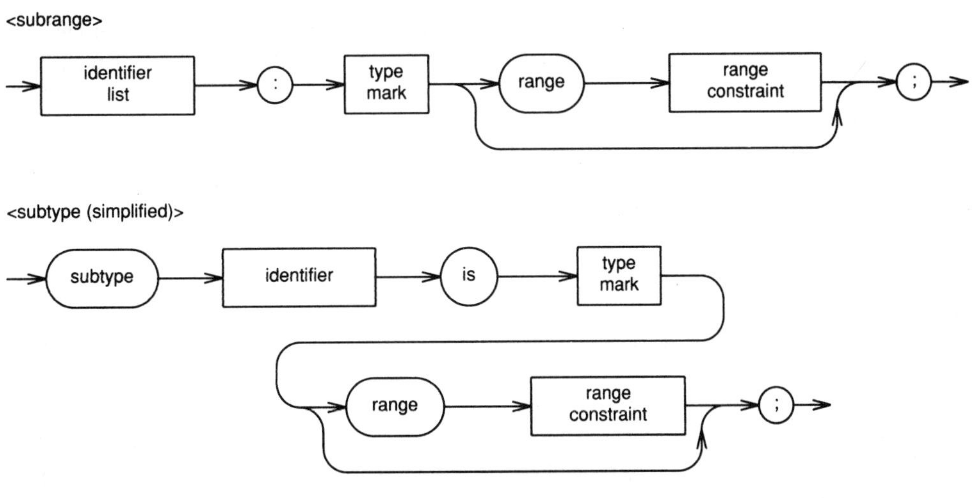

Figure 3–3

3.7 SUBRANGES

A *subrange* is a limited and contiguous set of values of a previously declared *scalar* type. The scalar types we have so far introduced are integers and characters. We have also introduced string literals and will subsequently introduce the type **Normal_Line**, but neither of these is a scalar type.

```
1:procedure Subrange_Demo
2:   Age: INTEGER range 7..105;
3:   Temperature: INTEGER range -70..140;
4:   Capital_Letter: CHARACTER range 'A'..'Z';
5:   subtype Small_Number is INTEGER range 0..15;
6:   subtype Small_Letter is CHARACTER range 'a'..'z';
7:   Chapter_Number: Small_Number;
8:   Lower_Case: Small_Letter := 'c';
9:   subtype Really_Small is INTEGER range 0..2;
10:  Low_Unit: Really_Small;
11:  Standard_Integer: INTEGER;
12:begin
13:  Standard_Integer := 5;
14:  Chapter_Number := Standard_Integer;
15:  Low_Unit := Chapter_Number;     -- CONSTRAINT_ERROR
16:  Capital_Letter := Lower_Case; -- CONSTRAINT_ERROR
17:end Subrange_Demo;
```

Program 3–8

Examples of variable declarations with subrange limitations are found in lines 2 through 4 of procedure **Subrange_Demo** in Program 3–8. The syntax for these declarations is shown in Figure 3–3. In line 2 of the program, the variable **Age** is declared to have a subrange limitation of **7..105**. This defines a variable which can store only integers between 7 and 105, inclusive. In line 3, **Temperature** is declared to have a subrange limitation of **-70..140**, and in line 4, **Capital_Letter** is declared to have a subrange limitation of **'A'..'Z'**.

The purpose of having subranges is simple: to limit the values that are allowed to be stored in variables. Declaring a subrange limitation means that the implementation will automatically check to make sure that a variable is assigned a value within the correct range. Ada uses the term *constraint* for these limitations. In technical terms, the implementation is responsible for detecting any violation of the constraint. If the value is not within the range, a **CONSTRAINT_ERROR** will occur. In some implementations, **CONSTRAINT_ERROR** will be detected and reported by the compiler. Most implementations will report any **CONSTRAINT_ERROR** that occurs when you run a program. When a **CONSTRAINT_ERROR** occurs while a program is running, the program immediately stops. In Ada terminology, execution of the main program is *abandoned.*

With a subrange, the implementation assures that a constraint is enforced. Thus, the programmer is protected from having an unexpected value go undetected.

Accordingly, the constraint on the variable **Age** might reflect a reasonable assumption about the age of persons enrolled in college, while the constraint on **Temperature** would reflect a reasonable assumption about weather, and the constraint on **Capital_Letter** reflects a very reasonable assumption about the alphabet. No longer will a program using **Capital_Letter** have to explicitly check the variable before each use, because the implementation is responsible for enforcing this constraint.

As shown in Figure 3–3, subranges can also be applied to types. A type with a range constraint forms a *subtype*. Any subrange can be declared as a subtype. Examples of subtypes are found in lines 5, 6, and 9 of **Subrange_Demo**. The "type" used in the declaration of a variable may be a type or a subtype.

A variable of a subtype is a variable of the type from which it was formed with a constraint. For example, a variable of type **Small_Number**, is a variable of type **INTEGER** with a range constraint of **0..15**, and a variable of type **Small_Letter** is a variable of type **CHARACTER** with a range constraint of **'a'..'z'**. The variables **Chapter_Number** and **Lower_Case** in lines 7 and 8 are constrained because their type is a subtype.

Variables of the types **INTEGER**, **Small_Number** and **Really_Small** are all of type **INTEGER** with various constraints and are compatible. This allows the assignments shown in lines 13–15 of **Subrange_Demo**. All these assignments are syntactically legal. However, the assignment in line 15 results in a **CONSTRAINT_ERROR** because it attempts to assign the value **5** to the variable **Low_Unit**, which has a range constraint of **0..2**.

The bounds on a subrange or subtype may be given by an expression. In the declaration

```
procedure Guess_Number(Low, High: INTEGER) is
  subtype Number_Range is INTEGER range Low..High;
  Guess: Number_Range;
  Short_Guess: INTEGER range 2 * Low..High - 2;
  ...
```

the range constraints on the subtype **Number_Range** and the variable **Short_Guess** are computed from expressions involving parameters. Variables could also appear in these expressions. When using variables, be sure to give them values before using them in any expression.

When **Guess_Number** is called, the range constraints of its subtypes and variables are computed. Thus, suppose that we call

```
Guess_Number(1, 6);
```

For this call, the constraint of **Number_Range** is computed as **1..6**. Any of the six values in this range can be stored in **Guess**. Attempts to store any other value will result in a **CONSTRAINT_ERROR**. For this call, the constraint on the variable **Short_Guess** is **2..4** because **2*Low** is **2** and **High-2** is **4**.

An interesting case is illustrated by the call

```
Guess_Number(4, 2);
```

When this call occurs, the constraint of **Number_Range** is computed as **4..2**. But there are no numbers which are at least **4** and at most **2**. This is an illustration of what is called the *null* range. Sometimes it is also called the *empty* range. The null range is legal; however, an attempt to store any value into the variable **Guess** will result in a **CONSTRAINT_ERROR**.

If we have a number of variables that have the same constraint, using a subtype is both convenient and makes the program more readable. In addition, having a different identifier for their types shows that the objects are not identical. This helps avoid errors such as adding your age to the temperature. A more effective way of doing this will be introduced in a later chapter.

Two subtypes of the type **INTEGER**, **POSITIVE** and **NATURAL**, are defined in **package STANDARD**. The subtype **POSITIVE** contains the numbers from 1 through the largest integer and the subtype **NATURAL** contains the numbers from 0 through the largest integer.

3.8 ATTRIBUTES

Attributes are a way to obtain information about a type. Ada has many attributes, but because different kinds of information are meaningful with respect to different types, the attributes that are available to a given type vary. Here, we introduce the two attributes at this time, **PRED** and **SUCC**.

PRED stands for *predecessor*. This attribute tells you the predecessor of a value; that is, the value immediately "in front of a value." For example,

```
CHARACTER'PRED('B')
```

yields the character **A** because **A** is immediately in front of **B** in the type **CHARACTER**.

The attribute **PRED** only applies to types that are discrete; that is, types in which each value has a discernible predecessor. The discrete types we have seen so far are **CHARACTER** and **INTEGER**. A string is an example of a nondiscrete type. Predecessors are not applicable to strings. For example, what string is the immediately in front of **SDFWE**?

The identifier **SUCC** stands for *successor*. This attribute tells you the successor of a value — that is, the value immediately following a value. For example,

```
CHARACTER'SUCC('A')
```

yields the character **B**, and

```
INTEGER'SUCC(4)
```

yields the integer **5**. Like **PRED**, **SUCC** only applies to discrete types.

Although thus far values have been derived from literals, they can also result from variables or expressions. At line 4 of the procedure **Attribute_Demo** in Program 3–9, the variable **First_Letter** is assigned the character **C** since **C** is after **B** in type **CHARACTER**. At line 5, **First_Letter** contains the character **C**, so its successor, **D**, is

```
1:procedure Attribute_Demo is
2:  First_Letter, Second_Letter: CHARACTER;
3:begin
4:  First_Letter := CHARACTER'SUCC('B');
5:  Second_Letter := CHARACTER'SUCC(First_Letter);
6:  First_Letter := CHARACTER'PRED(First_Letter);
7:end Attribute_Demo;
```

Program 3–9

assigned to **Second_Letter**. At line 6, **First_Letter** still contains a **C**, so its predecessor, **B**, is the value that **First_Letter** receives. Just before **Attribute_Demo** finishes, **First_Letter** contains **B** and **Second_Letter** contains **D**.

Note that the last value in a type has no successor and the first value has no predecessor. Asking for a successor or predecessor when there is none results in a **CONSTRAINT_ERROR**.

3.9 PARAMETERS (2): MODES IN AND OUT

A parameter of *mode* **in** allows information to enter a procedure. All the parameters we have used thus far have been of mode **in**. As we have seen, an **in** parameter behaves like a constant object: It receives a value at entry into a procedure, and this value cannot be changed within the procedure.

If no mode is specified, then the mode of a parameter is **in**. This is said to be the default mode. However, the parameter mode **in** may be explicitly specified. The syntax for this is given in Figure 3–4. The following two procedure declarations achieve the same result.

```
procedure Sized_Spiral(Size:    INTEGER);
procedure Sized_Spiral(Size: in INTEGER);
```

In the second of these the mode is explicitly declared to be **in** while in the first the mode is **in** by default.

Although the two declarations of **Sized_Spiral** achieve the same results, they are distinct according to the rules of the Ada language. In particular, they are sufficiently distinct so that the following code is illegal:

```
package X is
  procedure Sized_Spiral(Size: INTEGER);
end X;

package body X is
  procedure Sized_Spiral(Size: in INTEGER) is ... -- illegal
end X;
```

The particular illegality is that the two declarations of **Sized_Spiral** are not identical. In this situation Ada requires that either both or neither of the declarations explicitly declare mode **in**. In Ada terminology, the procedure declaration in the package body fails to *conform* to the procedure declaration in the package declaration.

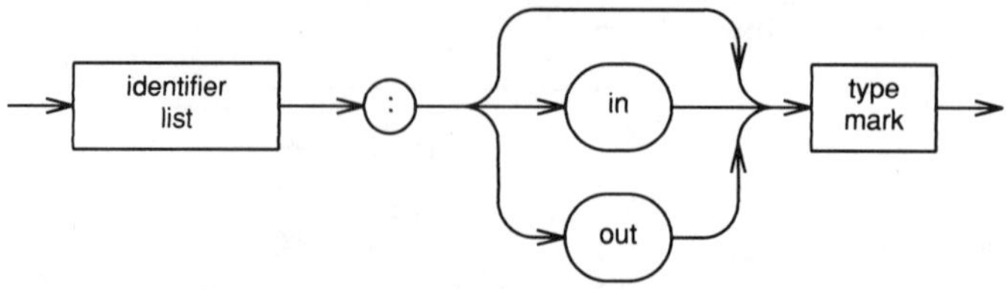

Figure 3–4

Often, you wish to get information out of a procedure. Consider the **Read** procedure from the package **Simple_IO** discussed in Chapter 2. We pass this procedure a variable as the actual parameter. A value is then stored in that variable by the procedure. In Ada, a parameter of mode **out** is one of the methods by which a procedure can pass information out to another portion of the program.

Since a parameter of mode **out** is going to put a value somewhere, the associated actual parameter must be capable of storing a value. This means that if the formal parameter is of mode **out**, the actual parameter must be either a variable or a parameter of another procedure which can receive a value. For example, the actual parameter could be a formal parameter of mode **out**.

```
procedure Triple(Input: in INTEGER; Output: out INTEGER) is
begin
   Output := 3 * Input;
end Triple;
```

Program 3–10

The procedure **Triple** in Program 3–10 illustrates the use of parameters of mode **out**. If we have an integer variable **A**, the call

```
Triple(6, A);
```

is allowed and the variable **A** receives the value 18. However, the call

```
Triple(6, 8);     -- illegal
```

is illegal because the integer literal 8 is not a variable and cannot be changed to become

18. In fact

```
Triple(6, 18);    -- illegal
```

is also illegal even though the literal has the correct value.

Parameters of mode **out** are designed for the purpose of getting information out of a procedure. To ensure that they are used only in this way, certain restrictions apply. The most important restriction is that you can never obtain a value from a parameter of mode **out** within the procedure. For example, if we attempted to add the line

```
Output := 2 * Output;    -- illegal
```

to **Triple** just after line 3 to negate the result, we would have a syntax error. This line uses **Output** on the right-hand side of the assignment, which means that we are asking what value **Output** contains. Parameters of mode **out** are not designed for this kind of duty. The analogy is that of a laundry chute: You can put things in at the top, and someone else can take them out at the bottom, but once you have put something in at the top, you cannot get it back out of the top. Similarly, a procedure can put values into a parameter of mode out, but it cannot get values out.

The preceding restriction has an number of consequences, one of which is that the attributes **PRED** and **SUCC** cannot be applied to parameters of mode **out**. Suppose that within the procedure **Triple** we had the statement

```
INTEGER'PRED(Output);    -- illegal
```

In order to figure out the predecessor of **Output**, we would need to obtain the value of **Output**, which Ada does not allow us to do.

```
procedure Six_Times(Six_In: in INTEGER; Six_Out: out INTEGER) is
begin
  Triple(2 * Six_In, Six_Out);
end Six_Times;
```

Program 3–11

We stated that the actual parameter could be a parameter of another procedure which can receive a value. This situation is illustrated by the procedure **Six_Times** in Program 3–11. The actual parameter to the procedure **Triple** is a formal parameter of the procedure **Six_Times**. This parameter association is legal because the formal parameter **Six_Out** is of mode **out** and, therefore, may receive a value.

Be sure that each **out** parameter is given a value before exit from a procedure. If an **out** parameter is not given a value, the variable that receives the value will contain an arbitrary value. For example, if **Triple** did not assign a value to **Output**, then the call **Triple(6, A)** could leave any value in **A**.

3.10 FUNCTIONS (1): HOW TO CALL FUNCTIONS

Functions are a familiar idea we have seen before in other circumstances. In mathematics we see many functions, for example, the square root function. We know that $\sqrt{4}$ returns the integer value 2, and you may remember from trigonometry that $\cos(\pi/4)$ returns the real value $\sqrt{2}/2$. Another thing you may be familiar with is that functions are often used in expressions, such as $A + \sqrt{B}$. Since many problems of a mathematical nature require functions, it is only natural to allow functions in a programming language. It is also natural to allow functions to be used in expressions.

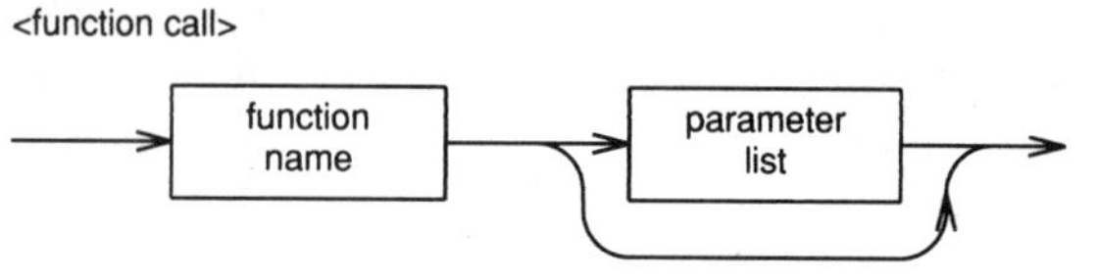

Figure 3–5

In this section we discuss how functions can be called (used) by the programmer. The syntax for allowing the programmer to declare a function will be discussed in Chapter 5. Like procedures, functions are a kind of subprogram. One important difference is that a function returns a value while a procedure does not. A number of functions are defined for our use in previously introduced packages.

A function is called by using its name and supplying any necessary parameters. The syntax for a function call is given in Figure 3–5. As with procedures, the number of parameters a function expects must match the number supplied, and the types of the formal parameters must match the types of the actual parameters. Also as with procedures, named or positional notation may be used.

As mentioned, one difference between a function and a procedure is that a function always returns a single value. Since this is for the purpose of doing something with that value, it leads to the following simple rule which handles most cases we shall encounter in the first part of this book: "You can call a function anywhere that you could use a literal." Technically, we can consider a literal as "returning" a value, so there is a similarity between a function and a literal.

Suppose we have a function **Fn** which takes an **INTEGER** parameter and returns an **INTEGER**. If **X** is an integer variable, then the following are legal:

```
X := Fn(3);
X := Fn(3) * 3 + Fn(1);
```

In the first line, the value returned by **Fn** is stored in the variable **X**. In the second line, the values returned, **Fn(3)** and **Fn(1)**, are used in an expression to compute the value stored in **X**.

Observe that a statement such as

```
Fn(-7) := 4;
```

is illegal because an assignment stores a value and the function call **Fn(-7)** does *not* designate a place to store a value.

3.11 THE LINES PACKAGE (1): PROCEDURES AND FUNCTIONS

We shall use a package called **Lines** in many examples. Also, many of the homework exercises of this and later chapters will be built around the capabilities of this package. At this point, the description of **Lines** we give is a simplification (see Program 3–12). The internal structure of the package and the types it contains are hidden using techniques which you will learn later. For now, we provide a specification and description which give enough information for this chapter. As we cover additional Ada techniques, we shall expand our explanation of the capabilities of **Lines** and finally will describe how the package is built. A copy of the actual package declaration is found in Appendix D. The values and variables of **Lines** are accessed (used) by means of procedures and functions.

Defined within the **Lines** package is a type called **Normal_Line**. A variable of type **Normal_Line** contains between 0 and 96 characters. The details of how **Normal_Line** is implemented are hidden for now. The functions and procedures of the **Lines** package use the type **Normal_Line**. We have arranged the package so that string literals behave in most cases as though they were constants of type **Normal_Line**. In the examples that follow, we shall assume that the variable **Demo_Line** is defined as

```
Demo_Line: Normal_Line;
```

The function **Length** returns the length of the line, that is, how many characters are actually in the line. For example, if **Demo_Line** contained the string **"Message"**, the function call

```
Length(Demo_Line)
```

would return 7 because the variable currently contains 7 characters.

The function **Location** looks for an occurrence of some fragment within the string. It returns an integer that indicates where in the **Normal_Line** the fragment is located. Zero is returned if the fragment is not found. For example, if **Demo_Line** contains **"ABCDEF"**, then

```
Location("CD", Demo_Line)
```

```
package Lines is
  subtype Line_Size is NATURAL;
  type Normal_Line is ... -- hidden
  subtype Index is NATURAL;
  function Length(Source: Normal_Line) return Line_Size;
  -- Purpose: Determine how many characters are currently in the line.
  function Location(Fragment: in Normal_Line; Source: in Normal_Line)
                   return Index;
  -- Purpose: Returns the location (index) of the first occurrence of Fragment
  --  in Source. Returns 0 if the Fragment is not found in Source.
  procedure Change(Source: in out Normal_Line; Position: Index;
                  Alteration: CHARACTER);
  -- Purpose: Changes the character at the indicated Position to the character
  --  given in Alteration.
  procedure Delete(A_Line: in out Normal_Line; Start: Index;
                  Amount_Removed: Line_Size);
  -- Purpose: Deletes Amount_Removed characters from A_Line starting at Start.
  procedure Insert(Destination: in out Normal_Line; Insertion: Normal_Line;
                  Location: Line_Size);
  -- Purpose: Inserts the given Insertion into Destination starting at the
  --  position given by Location.
  procedure Assign(Destination: out Normal_Line; Source: Normal_Line);
  -- Purpose: Assigns the value in Source to the variable associated with
  --  Destination.
  function A_Character(Source: Normal_Line;  Position: Index) return CHARACTER;
  -- Purpose: Returns the character found at the indicated Position of Source.
  function Extract(Source: Normal_Line; Start: Index; Count: Line_Size)
                  return Normal_Line;
  -- Purpose: Returns the fragment of Source that starts at Start and
  --  continues for Count characters.
end Lines;
```

Program 3–12

returns the value 3 because the fragment **CD** occurs starting at position 3 in the value of **Demo_Line**. The call

```
Location("CDF", Demo_Line)
```

returns the value 0, because the fragment **CDF** does not occur in **Demo_Line**.

The procedure **Change** is used to replace the character at the indicated location with the indicated alteration. Note that the mode of the parameter **Source** has not yet been discussed. The details of this mode will be explained in Chapter 6. For now, we say simply that we use a variable for the actual parameter. This means that the actual parameter associated with **Source** must be a variable. Further, the actual parameter will be changed. For example,

```
Change(Demo_Line, 3, 'X');
```

will change the third character in **Demo_Line** to an **X**.

The procedure **Delete** removes the indicated characters from **Normal_Line**. The parameter **Start** indicates where to start removing characters, and the parameter **Amount_Removed** indicates how many characters to remove. Again, the actual parameter **Demo_Line** will be changed. Suppose that **Demo_Line** contains **"ABCDEF"**. Then the call

```
Delete(Demo_Line, 3, 2);
```

will remove two characters starting with the third character. Hence, after the deletion, **Demo_Line** will contain **"ABEF"**, with the **C** and **D** having been deleted.

The procedure **Insert** puts the indicated characters (in **Insertion**) into the line at the indicated location (**Location**). Again, if **Demo_Line** contains **"ABCDEF"**, then

```
Insert(Demo_Line, "XYZ",3);
```

changes **Demo_Line** so that it contains **"ABXYZCDEF"**. The **XYZ** has been inserted starting at location 3, and the rest of the line has been moved back.

The procedure **Assign** puts a value into a variable of type **Normal_Line**. The value of the second parameter is assigned to the first. For example,

```
Assign(Demo_Line, "ABCDEF");
```

assigns the value **"ABCDEF"** to the variable **Demo_Line**. Because string literals are not truly of type **Normal_Line**, the standard assignment (**:=**) will not work.

The function **A_Character** returns the value of the character at a specified position in the **Normal_Line**. For instance,

```
Ch := A_Character("ABCDEF", 3);
```

sets **Ch** to **C** because **C** is the third letter in the line.

The function **Extract** returns a copy of a portion of a line. For example, if **Demo_Line** contains **"LongLine"**, then

```
Extract(Demo_Line, 3, 4)
```

returns the value **"ngLi"**, that is, 4 characters starting at the third location. Since **Extract** is a function returning a **Normal_Line**, you must be sure to use its value in a manner which is appropriate for a **Normal_Line**.

To summarize the preceding capabilities, we present the procedure **Use_Lines** in Program 3–13. In **Use_Lines**, a **Normal_Line** is read (using **Simple_IO**) and the last 4 characters are extracted and reported. The only tricky part is the extraction at line 10. The expression **Length(Demo_Line)-3** is the position in the line 4 characters

```
1:with Lines, Simple_IO;
2:procedure Use_Lines is
3:   use Lines;
4:   Demo_Line, Second_Line: Normal_Line;
5:begin
6:   Simple_IO.Read(Demo_Line);
7:   Simple_IO.Write("I have received a line of length ");
8:   Simple_IO.Write(Length(Demo_Line));
9:   Simple_IO.Write(" and the last four characters are ");
10:   Assign(Second_Line, Extract(Demo_Line, Length(Demo_Line) - 3, 4));
11:   Simple_IO.Write(Second_Line, 4));
12:end Use_Lines;
```

Program 3–13

from the end. Starting at this position, **Extract** returns the next 4 characters. Because of the starting position, these are the last 4 characters in the line. The value returned is immediately passed as a parameter to the **Assign** procedure. Thus, **Second_Line** will be assigned the 4 characters that were extracted. Be careful to note that if **Demo_Line** is less than 4 characters long, the **Extract** operation cannot be performed, and an error will result.

If one tries to access a character after the end of a **Normal_Line**, an error will occur. This error is called **Illegal_Lines_Index**. Some Ada implementations will report another error message instead; for example, "user defined exception."

In a number of the diagrams in this section, we have used the term *type mark* instead of type identifier because a type can be expressed by things other than simple identifiers. For example, if the procedure **Use_Lines** did not have the use clause at line 3, then the declaration of line 4 would have to become

```
Demo_Line, Second_Line: Lines.Normal_Line;
```

The type mark **Lines.Normal_Line** indicates that the variables are of the type **Normal_Line** which is defined in the package **Lines**. Of course, all other references to entities from this package have to be prefixed by the package name unless direct visibility is achieved through a use clause.

3.12 THE BANK ACCOUNT PACKAGE

To illustrate some of the points we have introduced in the previous sections, we shall now develop an example. Suppose you wish to use a computer to maintain a balance in a bank account. You need to perform four operations: You may deposit money, withdraw money, request to know the current balance, and open an account.

The package **Bank_Account** in Program 3–14 allows the user to make three types of request. The user may make a deposit, increasing the value of the bank account;

```
package Bank_Account is
   procedure Deposit(Amount_of_Deposit: INTEGER);
   procedure Withdraw(Amount_of_Withdrawal: INTEGER);
   procedure Account_Balance;
end Bank_Account;
```

```
with Simple_IO;
package body Bank_Account is
   Balance: INTEGER := 0;
   procedure Deposit(Amount_of_Deposit: INTEGER) is
   -- Increase the account balance by the amount deposited
   begin
      Balance := Balance + Amount_of_Deposit;
   end Deposit;
   procedure Withdraw(Amount_of_Withdrawal: INTEGER) is
   -- Decrease the account balance by the amount withdrawn
   begin
      Balance := Balance - Amount_of_Withdrawal;
   end Withdraw;
   procedure Account_Balance is
   -- Report the balance in the account
   begin
      Simple_IO.Write(Balance);
   end Account_Balance;
end Bank_Account;
```

```
with Bank_Account;
procedure Transactions is
begin
   Bank_Account.Deposit(30);
   Bank_Account.Withdraw(20);
   Bank_Account.Deposit(10);
   Bank_Account.Account_Balance;
end Transactions;
```

Program 3–14

make a withdrawal, decreasing the value of the bank account; or request to know the bank account's balance, leaving the value of the bank account undisturbed. The account is automatically opened.

The procedures **Deposit** and **Withdraw** modify the variable **Balance** by the amount deposited or withdrawn. Since **Balance** is declared in the package body, it remains active as long as the package exists. Furthermore, **Balance** can be accessed only from within the body of the package. This means that **Balance** cannot be modified except by invoking the procedures which are made visible by the package declaration. This arrangement protects the balance from being modified by anything other than deposits and withdrawals.

The procedure **Transactions** uses the procedures from **Bank_Account** to perform a series of operations on the account. Because **Bank_Account** is named in the context clause of **Transactions**, the package is elaborated before execution of the statements in **Transactions**. As part of this elaboration, the variable **Balance** is elaborated and receives its initial value of 0 as specified in line 3 of the package body (thus opening the account). When **Transactions** is run, the final balance reported by the call to **Account_Balance** in line 7 should be 20.

3.13 PROGRAMMING PRACTICES

An important programming concept chapter is *readability*. Good programming practice, including documentation, results in a program that is easily understandable. That is, we can understand the program by reading it rather than by spending a long time studying it. Language features such as constants, subranges, attributes, and parameters should be used because they enhance understandability by making restrictions explicit.

We shall continue to stress the importance of matching the appearance of the solution to the solution being used. For example, associating the identifier **Two** with the value 3 would be a poor match.

Some language features should be used because they help avoid many errors and help locate those errors which do occur. For example, a constant cannot be assigned a new value. Errors are avoided because the compiler detects an accidental attempt to change a constant. Furthermore, errors can be more rapidly located because you are guaranteed that the constant has not changed since elaboration, so you can more easily determine its value. When searching for an error, eliminating one possibility gets you closer to finding out what went wrong.

Subranges are another example. Many programs run but do not do what you wanted. The problem then is finding out what is wrong. Usually, after you have found the problem, it is easy to fix. If you used subranges and did not get a constraint error, there are fewer places to look for what went wrong.

Direct visibility can increase readability by eliminating the clutter of repeating the package name. However, one very common programming fault is the overuse of direct visibility. We recommend that no more than one package be directly visible at a time. The reason is simple: It is important that the program be easily understood by someone not familiar with it. If a program has seven or eight packages directly visible, it is extremely time consuming for someone else to understand the program. The reader sees a reference to a component and cannot tell whether it is locally declared or from which package it comes. With visibility by selection, it is easy to tell which package the components belong to. Even when you have direct visibility, it is still permissible to use visibility by selection and it is often good style to do so. For instance, the package name often helps to clarify the meaning of a procedure identifier.

As mentioned earlier, a good technique for programming is "divide and conquer." In this technique, the problem is broken down into small, easily understood chunks. If the problem is large or complex, the chunks initially obtained may have to be broken into even smaller chunks. The programmer should build and test a solution for each chunk and then put the chunks together to solve the problem. Packages, functions, and procedures are usually the chunks, so the problem may be broken into subprogram calls. The subprograms (grouped appropriately in packages) should be built and tested and then put the subprograms together to form a solution.

The division of a problem into subproblems has many advantages. One such advantage is that protection and division are related in programming. In the bank account program, the procedure **Transactions**, which was the interface to the user to set up the transactions, was separated from the package which contained the variable that stored the account balance. Because of this, the account balance was protected from change by outsiders; that is, it could not be changed from outside the package. This meant that all modifications to the balance had to go through the deposit and withdrawal procedures.

These techniques combine to allow the Ada programmer to build a program that can be easily understood and that has protective mechanisms which both avoid errors and provide for the early detection of errors.

3.13.1 Documentation of Subprograms

During the life of a program or package, it is likely to be modified several times. Statistically, around 90 percent of the programming time spent on a program is spent fixing errors, installing enhancements, making new versions, and performing other modifications that occur after the program has been completed. The programmer performing the modification will need to be able to determine what a tool does — both when reusing it and when modifying it. Part of a software developer's job is to supply sufficient information so that later programmers can make needed modifications more easily. Information about a program is called *documentation.*

It helps the reader if the documentation is in a form that is consistent across the entire program. This makes it easier to quickly scan the program for the desired information. As with most programming practices, experts disagree about the best way to document subprograms.

If you are in a course and your instructor requires a different documentation standard from that to be given here, you should use your instructor's standard. The same is true of private companies: each will have a different documentation style. However, all these styles have the same purpose. Accordingly, most styles will have similar content and will differ primarily in details such as the order of presentation of information and its exact format. We propose the documentation standard demonstrated by the package **Commented_Box_Tools** in Program 3–15. Because of space limitations, the examples in the text often lack the comments they would otherwise have if they were "real-world" programs. However, the detailed explanations of these examples in the text serve the purpose of supplying sufficient information to the programmer.

The declaration of **Commented_Box_Tools** is almost the same as that of **Box_Tools** in Program 3–5, but is extended and adjusted for the purposes of demon-

```
1:package Commented_Box_Tools is
2:-- Purpose: Package for demonstration of commenting techniques.

3:   procedure Draw_Box_At(X, Y: INTEGER);
4:   -- Purpose: Draw a box whose upper left corner is at (X,Y).
5:   --   X: Horizontal position for upper left corner.
6:   --   Y: Vertical position for upper left corner.
7:   -- Affects: screen and robot position on screen.
8:   -- Description: This procedure moves the robot to a position
9:   --   suitable for drawing a box at position (X,Y) and draws
10:  --   the box.  The box size is defined by Vertical_Size and
11:  --   Horizontal_Size.  After drawing the box, the robot is
12:  --   left at the upper left corner of the box.

13:  Vertical_Size, Horizontal_Size: INTEGER := 5;
14:  --   Vertical_Size: Top to bottom size to draw a box,
15:  --    including the top line.
16:  --   Horizontal_Size: Left to right size to draw a box,
17:  --    including the left line.
18:  end Commented_Box_Tools;
```

Program 3–15

stration of good documentation. The most important change is that the package declaration has been rewritten to reflect the addition of comments.

Line 2 is a comment that defines the purpose of the package. This should usually be a single sentence which gives an overview of the package. If the package is complicated, a section of comments with the heading "Description" should follow the "Purpose" comment. Every package, subprogram, or object should have its purpose defined for the reader.

Lines 5 and 6 provide documentation for the parameters of the procedure. They are indented further than "`Purpose`" to set them off from the main headings of the comments. Usually, the only documentation needed for a parameter is its declaration and a single sentence describing its purpose.

Line 7 lists the things changed by the procedure. Every subprogram should list all of the changes it makes to things with which the person modifying the program must be concerned. Neither the parameters of the subprogram nor the returned value of a function are listed here. If the comment is in the declaration of a package, only changes to things outside of the package are listed; otherwise, all changes to things outside the subprogram itself are listed.

Lines 8 through 12 are a more complete description of the subprogram. Since the comments are in a package declaration, only information needed to use the subprogram is provided. In the body of the package, the description would provide this information plus a paragraph giving an overview of how the subprogram works. Notice how lines 9 to 12 are indented so that it is obvious that they are a continuation of the description.

Lines 13 through 18 declare and document variables in the package. Plainly, objects and parameters should have similar-style comments. Notice that we have deliberately avoided repeating information in the comments which is given in the declaration. These variables are declared here as an example; as mentioned earlier, variables should usually be kept local.

For easier reading, spacing occurs between lines 2 and 3, and between 12 and 13. In the actual program, we leave blank lines for emphasis.

In general, documentation in a package declaration should discuss things only from the user's point of view. Documentation in a package body should discuss implementation strategy. If a subprogram is declared separately from its body, the same rules hold. Even if a subprogram is declared by its body, the two types of comments should be separated.

As a final note, remember that part of good documentation is choosing appropriate identifiers.

3.13.2 Problem Solving

One problem-solving technique we have not yet discussed may quite possibly be the most important: *analyze* the problem thoroughly. This means getting a full understanding of the problem by breaking it into smaller pieces and determining what each piece requires. Notice that there is a parallel between the technique of divide and conquer for finding a solution to a problem and that of analysis for understanding the problem.

Much of the work performed by a computer program involves data (information). Part of the task of the programmer is to determine what information is necessary for a program to perform its task and how to derive that information. In addition to writing the necessary statements to derive the information, one must keep track of what information is available and how long it must be kept. This *information tracking* can serve as a problem-solving technique.

We shall discuss analyzing a problem and information tracking by applying these techniques to a specific task. Suppose we have received the following request to write a program:

> The Last City Bank has a large list of names of clients. Unfortunately, the names are recorded in a different format than is required for the new data base program.
>
> The old format is LASTNAME, FIRSTNAME I.
>
> The new format is FIRSTNAME I. LASTNAME
>
> (I. means an optional middle initial.) Each name is on its own line in the input.
>
> Only one name will be processed. In Chapter 4, we consider processing multiple names, with the end signaled by a blank line.
>
> The bank has engaged our consulting firm to convert the names in its list. The firm will receive one cent for each character converted. Therefore, the program must keep track of the number of characters. As a consistency check, we also wish to know the total number of names (say, one, for now).

The first step in approaching a problem like this is to analyze the problem thoroughly. Technically, the word "analyze" means to break apart. In analyzing a problem, we usually break the problem into pieces, determine the meaning of each piece, and then check to make sure that our understanding of each piece is both unambiguous (that is, there is only one way to interpret that part of the assigned task) and consistent with all other pieces. If any piece is ambiguous, we may be able to arrive at a single meaning if the other meanings are not consistent, but more likely, we need to obtain more information.

What are the pieces of this problem? The following is a typical decomposition of an information-processing problem:

1. Understand the input data, the meaning of each datum, and the format in which it is stored.
2. Understand the output data, the meaning of each datum, and the format in which it is stored.
3. Examine the input and output data, and determine whether they both contain the same information, except in a different format. Make sure that information is not lost or gained.
4. Determine what summary information must be kept, the source of the information being summarized, and the format in which the summary will be reported.
5. Determine what, if any, interaction with an operator (person controlling the program) is required, other than entering the input information.
6. Determine how the end of the input is indicated.

The analysis that follows is more detailed than that which is commonly applied. But in this example we present all of the details so that you can see them and how they can be obtained. The analysis uses the foregoing framework.

1. The input data are strings of characters that can be separated into seven sections:
   - **a.** LASTNAME
   - **b.** comma
   - **c.** space
   - **d.** FIRSTNAME
   - **e.** space
   - **f.** middle initial
   - **g.** period

Each section is a string whose meaning is unimportant, except insofar as it is assigned the appropriate character(s).

2. The output data are strings of characters that can be separated into six sections:
   - **a.** FIRSTNAME
   - **b.** space
   - **c.** middle initial
   - **d.** period

e. space
f. LASTNAME

Each section is a string whose meaning is unimportant, except insofar as it is assigned the appropriate character(s).

3. Each input datum contains a comma, and each output datum does not. Otherwise, each output datum contains the same sections as the corresponding input datum, with each corresponding section containing the same characters. The change is in the removal of the comma and the rearrangement of the sections.
4. Two summaries are required:
   a. The total number of characters converted.
   b. The total number of names converted.
5. No interaction with an operator is required. The only inputs and outputs are the explicit input of names, output of names, and output of summaries.
6. Only one line will be processed.

The next step is to evaluate the preceding pieces of the problem to determine whether each is unambiguous. In particular, we must ask whether we understand the definition of each item previously mentioned. Notice that we have used the technique of *itemization* (listing) as an analysis tool. So we list the items resulting from the analysis and attempt to define them as follows:

1. LASTNAME	a string of letters
2. comma	a particular character
3. space	a particular character
4. FIRSTNAME	a string of letters
5. I.	a letter followed by a period
6. section	(of a datum) one of the preceding
7. rearrangement	(of the sections) the arrangement of the sections into the defined (explicit) format
8. The total number of characters converted	WAIT!...Is this the total number of characters of input, or the total number of characters of output?
9. The total number of names converted	One, but we shall keep track.

There is one term that is not precisely defined. We next check to see whether there are any conflicts between the different pieces of the problem (as we understand them). Such conflicts could arise from several sources, for example,

a. Output data that cannot be determined from the input
b. Input data that are neither represented in the output nor accounted for as discarded
c. The same item having conflicting definitions (e.g., two pieces of the problem statement requiring different input formats)

To be thorough in checking for consistency, we need to compare every item with every other item and each definition with each other definition. This process is not possible with a large problem. Fortunately, by dividing the problem into pieces in accordance with a framework and by listing all definitions, we can usually catch such inconsistencies even though we have not been as thorough as we might like. In some cases the written statement of the problem is several hundred pages long, so that the technique presented here will not work because it becomes too difficult to ensure that we are being consistent in our assignment of names to the different pieces of the problem.

In the miniscule problem we are concerned with, we find that there are no inconsistencies, regardless of which definition we choose for the total number of characters converted. This is both good news and bad news: The good news is that there is no consistency problem; the bad news is that the problem statement is ambiguous.

Regardless of whether the difficulty is an ambiguity or an inconsistency, the proper solution is a renegotiation of the problem statement with the client (or the person assigning the problem). In this case, the president of our consulting firm must negotiate with the bank and determine exactly which characters we are to be paid to convert. It may even be that the bank president has in mind the number of letters in the names alone as the total number of characters converted (a totally different definition from either of those we listed in determining our definitions). The final agreement would then be to charge for each character in the names which are output.

We now have a consistent, unambiguous problem statement. This is required for the proper solution of any problem (unless you just happen to implement exactly what is needed, even though it is not defined by the problem statement).

One of the advantages of using a predefined framework for a particular class of problems is that this framework is the result of analyzing that class of problems and represents a great deal of work that is already done. In particular, if the problem fits the framework well, then the program can follow the framework.

The solution framework corresponding to the preceding analysis is as follows:

1. Perform any initial setups (initializations) needed.
2. Set all summaries (variables summarizing information) to zero.
3. Repeat the following for each input datum:
    a. Read the input datum.
    b. Determine whether the end of input has been reached. If so, leave the series of repetitions and go on to the next step.
    c. Transform the input datum to the output datum.
    d. Update the summaries.
    e. Output the output datum.
    f. Output any intermediate summary information (e.g., subtotals).
4. Output the summary information.
5. Perform any cleanups needed.

The close correspondence between this solution framework and the analysis framework means that once the pieces of the problem statement are assigned to the pieces of the analysis framework, it is easy to plug them into the pieces of the solution framework. With sufficient programming experience, it is then relatively easy to write a program from such a framework.

Now consider the information-tracking aspect of the problem. As part of the analysis, we determined that the information in this problem consists of input data (which we divided into sections), output data (which we again divided into sections), and summary information. For each of these informational entities, we need to identify those sections of the solution framework in which the datum becomes available, is used, and becomes obsolete. In addition, we need to know what information is necessary to determine the value of the particular datum.

In this manner, we track the information as if flows through the program. Tracking values through the program is sometimes called *live-dead analysis*, because we determine the useful lifetime of a piece of information. The reason for performing such an analysis is to ensure that the information will be available when it is needed and to permit values to be stored in the most local variables.

To implement our information-tracking ideas, we copy the framework and add notes describing what information is associated with each step and what happens to it. In particular, we even show parts of the framework which might not be used in our particular problem. Here is the annotated framework:

1. Perform any initial setups (initializations) needed.

2. Set all summaries to zero.
Set the number of words read and number of characters output to zero.

3. Repeat the following for each input datum:
  a. Read the input datum.
  Makes the input datum available for processing.
  b. Determine whether the end of input has been reached. If so, leave the series of repetitions and go on to the next step.
  There is nothing to do here.
  c. Transform the input datum to the output datum.
  Divide the input datum into sections, and put the sections together to form the output datum. The input datum is not needed after this step.
  d. Update the summaries.
  Changes the summary values. (Requires the output datum.)
  e. Output the output datum.
  The output datum is not needed after this.
  f. Output any intermediate summary information (e.g., subtotals).
  There is none in this problem.

4. Output the summary information.
The summary information is not needed after this step.

5. Perform any cleanups needed.

This analysis shows that the input and output values can be local to the particular name being processed, but the summary information must last almost the entire length of the program. This means that if the processing of a single name is a procedure, then the input and output data can be stored in variables local to that procedure. Since the summary information must last the entire length of the processing, it would be best to declare the variables that hold the summary information in the body of a package (to avoid erroneous reference to nonlocal variables).

The package for Last City Bank could appear as shown in Program 3–16 (the numbers and letters in parentheses refer to the steps in the solution framework).

3.13.3 Testing

Once procedure **`Put_First_Name_First`** has been constructed, it should be tested with normal names, names with multiple commas, names with no comma, names that begin with a comma and names that end with a comma. In this manner, you can test all the likely combinations that could cause the program not to work correctly.

If the program doesn't work, how do you find out what is wrong and fix it? The processing of fixing a program is called *debugging*. There are three important debugging techniques. The first is to try many input values in order to determine which part of the program may be wrong. This becomes more successful if it is used in conjunction with the second technique, printing messages at various locations in the program. These messages should indicate where in the program they are being written and what the values in the variables and parameters are at that point. Thus, if an error occurs, you can find out where it does by looking at the information that the program prints. Sometimes you will only put in a few messages at first, and after you have found the general area containing the error, you will add more messages to that area. Placement of print statements at the start and end of the statement list of a procedure can be particularly useful; at the start of the procedure, it is often useful to print the values of any parameters. The third debugging technique is to analyze the actions that the program should perform. In effect, you perform, with pencil and paper, the instructions that the computer should perform. When you compare your analysis of what should be printed with what the computer actually prints, many errors will become obvious.

3.14 ADA SUMMARY

In this chapter, we have expanded our knowledge of *types* and *objects*. We have introduced *elaboration* as the point at which types and objects are built, *assignment* as the second method of storing a value in a variable, and *constants* as objects which cannot be changed after elaboration.

With respect to both objects and procedures, we have introduced the concepts of *scope* and *visibility*. We have seen that the *immediate* scope of an identifier is within a declarative region and that in certain cases, such as procedure parameters and identifiers in package declarations, there is an *extended* scope. Related to scope is visibility: In their extended scope, identifiers from a package declaration can have direct visibility or visibility by selection.

We have considered the concept of an *attribute* and have discussed two attributes, **`SUCC`** and **`PRED`**, related to the values of a type. We have examined *subranges* as a safety feature that restricts the values a subtype or a variable.

```
with Lines;
package Fix_Name is
-- Purpose: Reverse the order of lines.  Also perform accounting.
  procedure Put_First_Name_First(Original: in  Lines.Normal_Line;
                                 Reversed: out Lines.Normal_Line);
  -- Purpose: Change the format of the name.
  --  Original: input name.  Format:  LAST, FIRST I.
  --  Reversed: output name. Format:  FIRST I. LAST
  -- Description: Divide Original into parts, and reassemble the
  --   parts into the Reversed parameter.
  --   Also keep track of the number of characters output and the
  --   number of calls made.
  procedure Summarize(Chars_Output, Calls_Made: out INTEGER);
  -- Purpose: Returns the summary information in the appropriate
  --   parameters.
  --  Chars_Output: Total number of characters in Reversed in
  --   all calls to Put_First_Name_First.
  --  Calls_Made: Total number of calls to Put_First_Name_First.
end Fix_Name;

package body Fix_Name is
-- Purpose: Reverse the order of lines.  Also perform accounting.
  Total_Chars: INTEGER := 0;
  -- Total number of characters returned in Reversed in all calls
  --  to Put_First_Name_First (2).
  Total_Calls: INTEGER := 0;
  -- Total number of calls to Put_First_Name_First (3).
  procedure Put_First_Name_First(Original: in  Lines.Normal_Line;
                                 Reversed: out Lines.Normal_Line) is
  -- Purpose: Change the format of the name.
  --  Original: input name.  Format:  LAST, FIRST I.    (3a)
  --  Reversed: output name. Format:  FIRST I. LAST     (3e)
  -- Description: Divide Original into parts and reassemble the
  --   parts into the Reversed parameter. (3c)
  --   Also keep track of the number of characters output and the
  --   number of calls made. (3d)
    use Lines;
    Comma_Pos: INTEGER;
    -- Position of comma in Original.
    Before_Comma: Normal_Line;
    -- First part of Original line (LAST)
    After_Comma: Normal_Line;
    -- Last part of Original line, after comma and space. (FIRST I.)
    Working_line: Normal_Line;
    -- Build output line here.
```

Program 3–16

```
  begin
    -- Calculate the sections of the name and reorder them (3c).
    Comma_Pos := Location('','' Original);
    Assign(Before_Comma, Extract(Original, 1, Comma_Pos - 1));
    Assign(After_Comma, Extract(Original, Comma_Pos + 2,
                                  Length(Original) - Comma_Pos - 1));
    Assign(Working_Line, Before_Comma);
    Insert(Working_Line, '' '', 1);
    Insert(Working_Line, After_Comma, 1);
    -- Calculate summaries (3d)
    Total_Chars := Total_Chars + Length(Working_Line);
    Total_Calls := Total_Calls + 1;
    Assign(Reversed, Working_Line);    -- (3e)
  end Put_First_Name_First;
  procedure Summarize(Chars_Output, Calls_Made: out INTEGER) is
  -- Purpose: Returns the summary information in the appropriate
  --   parameters (4).
  --  Chars_Output: Total number of characters in Reversed in
  --   all calls to Put_First_Name_First.
  --  Calls_Made: Total number of calls to Put_First_Name_First.
  begin
    Chars_Output := Total_Chars;
    Calls_Made := Total_Calls;
  end Summarize;
end Fix_Name;
```

Program 3–16 Continued

For communication between components, we have introduced the notion of getting information out of a subprogram. We can use either *out parameters* or *functions* (subprograms that return values).

EXERCISES

3.1. Add a procedure **Interest** to the package **Bank_Account** in Program 3–14. When this procedure is called, it should add interest to the bank account using the formula

```
Balance := Balance + Balance / 20;
```

Also, add a local variable to **Transactions** so that, instead of using integer literals in the procedure calls, the program uses this variable. Use **Simple_IO** to print a prompt, and then read a value into the variable. This value will be the amount of the deposit or withdrawal.

3.2. Write a program that asks the user for a name in the input format, calls **Put_First_Name_First** of Program 3–16, outputs the reversed name, calls procedure **Summarize**, and outputs the summary information.

3.3. Add a procedure to package **Fix_Name** of Program 3–16 which does the opposite of **Put_First_Name_First**. Call this procedure **Put_Last_Name_First**. The input format is the same as the output format for **Put_First_Name_First**, and the output format is the same as the input format for **Put_First_Name_First**. Charge for conversions in either direction. Be sure to make appropriate changes in the comments.

3.4. Build a package that breaks a sentence into words. The procedures in the package are as follows:

```
with Lines;
package Break_Words is
  use Lines;
  procedure Next_Sentence(New_Sentence: in Normal_Line);
  -- Purpose: Accept a new sentence for processing.
  --  New_Sentence: the new sentence to be processed.
  procedure Next_Word(Word: out Normal_Line);
  -- Purpose: Return the next word in the sentence.
  --  Word: The next word.
  procedure Words_So_Far(Count: out INTEGER);
  -- Purpose: Accounting procedure for the package.
  --  Count: The total number times Next_Word has been called so far.
end Break_Words;
```

Next_Sentence allows the user to put in a new sentence, **Next_Word** returns the next word in the sentence, and **Words_So_Far** returns how many words have been extracted from all sentences processed so far. Words in a sentence will always be separated by a single space, and there will be no spaces at the beginning or end of the sentence. If there is no next word, **Next_Word** should return a line of length 0. Use the following program to test your package:

```
with Break_Words, Simple_IO, Lines;
procedure Test_Break_Words is
  use Lines;
  Sentence, Word: Normal_Line;
  Word_Count: INTEGER;
begin
  Simple_IO.Write("Type a sentence:");
  Simple_IO.Read(Sentence);
  Break_Words.Next_Sentence(Sentence);
  Break_Words.Next_Word(Word);
  Simple_IO.Write(Word);  Simple_IO.New_Line;
  Break_Words.Next_Word(Word);
  Simple_IO.Write(Word);  Simple_IO.New_Line;
  Break_Words.Words_So_Far(Word_Count);
  Simple_IO.Write(Word_Count);  Simple_IO.New_Line;
end Test_Break_Words;
```

If the sentence

```
A test of Break Words.
```

is input into the program, the words "**A**" and "**test**" would be printed followed by the number 2. Make sure your program is well documented.

3.5. Modify the procedure **Draw_Box_At** in the package **Box_Tools** of Program 3–5 so that instead of drawing a simple box, it draws one of the figures found in exercise 1.5. Test your modification with a procedure which names **Box_Tools** in its context clause and draws several figures in different locations.

3.6. Modify the package **Box_Tools** so that the procedure **Draw_Box_At** has four formal parameters: height, width, horizontal position, and vertical position.

Test your modification by writing a procedure **House** which names the package **Box_Tools**, but not the package **Robots**. **House** should have three calls to **Draw_Box_At**, which builds the following display:

```
. . . . . . . . . . . .
.                     .
.             . . .   .
.             . . .   .
.     . . .           .
.     .   .           .
.     .   .           .
. . . . . . . . . . . .
```

3.7. Write a package **Scaled_Robot** that has the ability to scale the size of the robot's movements. The package contains the following procedures:

```
procedure Set_Scale(New_Scale: INTEGER);
procedure Scaled_Move(Distance: INTEGER);
```

Set_Scale sets the scale factor by which the robot's movement is multiplied. **Scaled_Move** moves the robot, but the distance moved is adjusted by the scale factor.

Test the package by building a main program which sets the scale to 1, calls **Scaled_Move** with 10, sets scale to 2, and then calls **Scaled_Move** with 4. The total distance moved should be 18.

3.8. Write a procedure **Replace** that takes four parameters of type **Normal_Line**: **In_Line**, **Out_Line**, **Pattern**, and **Replacement**. The procedure finds the first occurrence of the substring **Pattern** within **In_Line**, replaces that substring with **Replacement**, and puts the result in **Out_Line**. The parameter **Out_Line** must be of mode **out**, and all other parameters must be of mode **in**. Embed the procedure within the following main procedure at the indicated location:

```
with Simple_IO, Lines;
procedure Test_Replace is
  use Lines;
```

```
    Original, Modified, Pat, New_Text: Normal_Line;
    procedure Replace(In_Line, Pattern, Replacement: in Normal_Line;
                     Out_Line: out Normal_Line) is
    --Place any local variable declarations here.
    begin
      null; --Place the instructions for procedure Replace here
    end;
  begin
    Simple_IO.Write("In_Line? ");
    Simple_IO.Read(Original);
    Simple_IO.Write("Pattern? ");
    Simple_IO.Read(Pat);
    Simple_IO.Write("Replacement? ");
    Simple_IO.Read(New_Text);
    Replace(Original, Pat, New_Text, Modified);
    Simple_IO.Write(Modified);
    Simple_IO.New_Line;
  end Test_Replace;
```

4

Controlling Program Execution

4.1 OBJECTIVES

In this chapter, we examine variables and expressions in more detail. We present new techniques that allow more complex information handling. We cover the complexities of integer expressions (section 3). We introduce the important type **BOOLEAN** (sections 5 and 6) and several operators associated with this type.

We introduce two simple constructs to control program execution. The if statement (section 4) allows decisions to be made during execution, and the while schema (section 7) allows repetition of groups of instructions. Both constructs make use of the capabilities of the type **BOOLEAN**.

CONCEPTS:

- Arithmetic expressions are for mathematical computation.
- A program can select an action on the basis of some conditions.
- Ada provides Boolean values and Boolean operators.
- A program can iterate (repeat) of a sequence of actions to achieve a goal.

GOALS:

- Solve a problem using selection and iteration.
- Solve a problem requiring arithmetic expressions.

4.2 MOTIVATION

Solutions to many problems use the techniques of decision and repetition. Like many machines, a computer is adept at repetition, or, as it is called in computer jargon, *iteration*. All modern computers include decision-making capabilities. Ada contains extensive constructs for both iteration and decision making. Because these techniques are so extensive, we spread their introduction over several chapters. However, even with what we cover in this chapter, it is easy to write programs to solve much more complex problems than before.

Both iteration and decisions often depend on a condition. A condition is said to be *true* or *false*. Boolean algebra is the mathematics of statements which evaluate to true or false. Boolean algebra has long been used by mathematicians and has found some use in other sciences. In solving problems, decisions are naturally expressed by making a choice on the basis of a condition being true or false. By providing both Boolean values and Boolean expressions, Ada allows you to formally write the conditions on which you wish to base decisions.

Traditional problem-solving areas such as mathematics and science have used formulas for a long time. Because of this, they have established techniques of expressing formulas. One of the first uses of computers was in mathematics and science, so from the beginning, programs have had to express formulas in order to solve problems. Consequently, methods of expressing complex formulas are found in programming languages. These methods of expression are similar to those found in mathematics and science.

4.3 INTEGER EXPRESSIONS

In Chapter 2, we introduced the simplest integer expressions. Here, we discuss integer expressions fully. The syntax for integer expressions is given in Figure 4–1. We illustrate the effect of this diagram with several examples. The expression "**6**" qualifies as an **<integer literal>**. By a close examination of Figure 4–1 we will see that "**6**" is also a legal integer expression. To see that this is so, we note that one of the options of **<primary>** is **<integer literal>**. This means that "**6**", in addition to being an **<integer literal>**, is a legal **<primary>**. Now, if we examine the diagram for **<factor>**, we find that a single **<primary>** is a legal **<factor>**. Thus, "**6**" qualifies as a legal **<factor>**. Next, we examine the diagram for **<term>** and see that a single **<factor>** is a legal **<term>**. This means that "**6**" qualifies as a legal **<term>**. Finally, examining the diagram for **<integer expression>**, we see that a single **<term>** is a legal **<integer expression>**. Thus, "**6**" is a legal **<integer expression>**.

Now consider the expression "**-15**". By the same reduction as in the preceding paragraph, "**15**" is an **<integer literal>**, which is a **<primary>**, which is a **<factor>**, which is a **<term>**. Examining the diagram for **<integer expression>**, we see that a **<term>** preceded by a minus sign is an **<integer expression>**. Thus, "**-15**" is a legal **<integer expression>**.

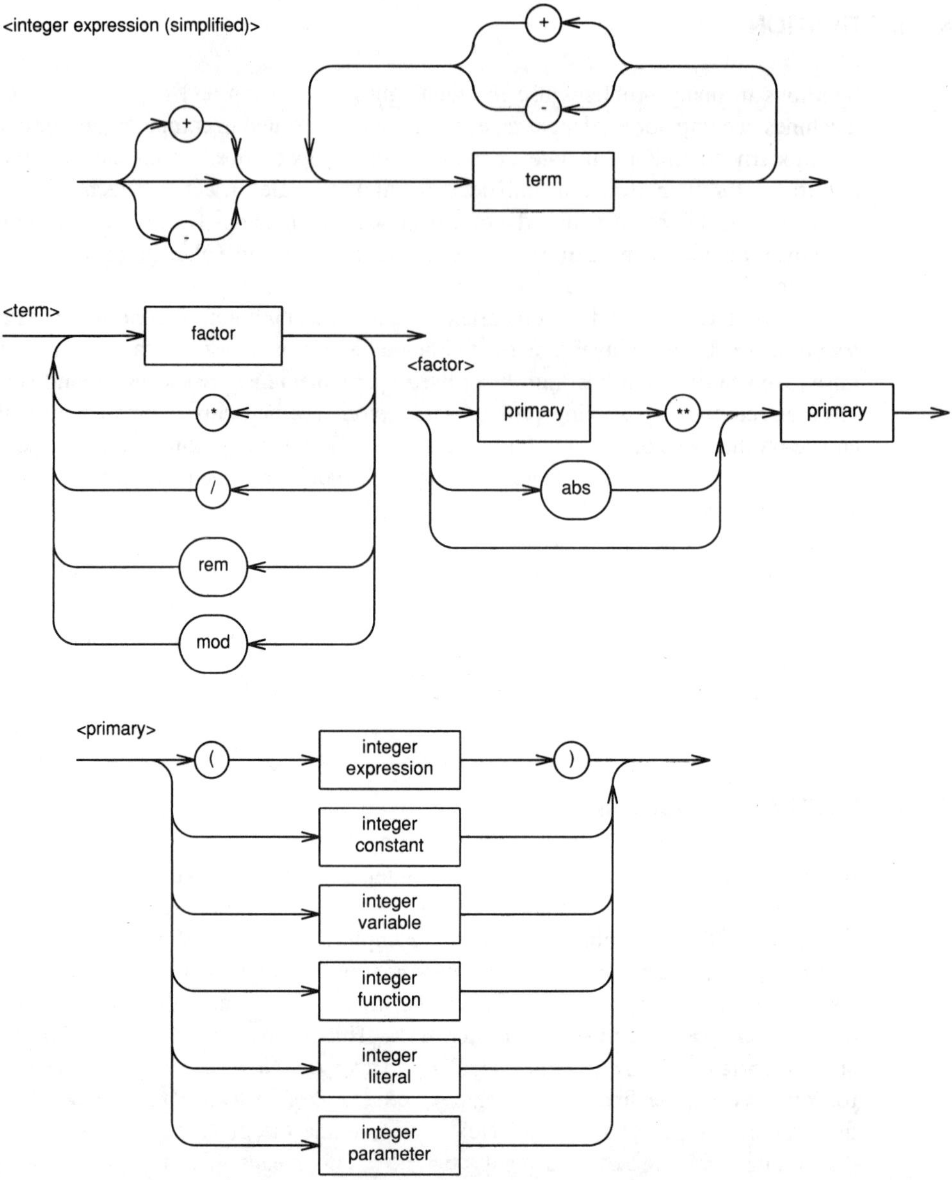

Figure 4–1

If we next examine the diagram for **<integer expression>**, we see that the formula "**6+5**" qualifies as a legal **<integer expression>** because it is two **<term>**s separated by a **+**. (Recall that **6** and **5** are **<integer literal>**s which qualify as **<term>**s.)

A formula for a product, such as "**2*3**", qualifies as a **<term>** because it is the product of two **<factor>**s. Of course, the **<term>** "**2*3**" also qualifies as an **<integer expression>**.

A more complex formula such as "**(2+3)*5**" can be seen to be an **<integer expression>** for the following reason. The expression "**(2+3)**" qualifies as a **<primary>** because it is an **<integer expression>** surrounded by parentheses. As a **<primary>** it also qualifies as a **<factor>**. Now plainly, "**5**" qualifies as a **<factor>** also. But then, the **<factor>** "**(2+3)**" multiplied by the **<factor>** "**5**" is a legal **<term>**, and a **<term>** is a legal **<integer expression>**.

In addition to literals, an integer variable, an integer constant and a call to a function that returns an integer also qualify as **<primary>**s.

These examples illustrate how the syntax shown in Figure 4–1 is used to define legal integer expressions. The figure also shows the operators that are available to perform operations on integers. Certain operations are performed before others. This ordering is called the *precedence* of the operations. This precedence is implied in the syntax diagram: Because **<primary>** is a component of **<factor>**, a **<primary>** must be evaluated before any **<factor>** that includes it is evaluated. A detailed examination of the diagram reveals that the operations are performed in the order that we normally perform arithmetic operations.

The arithmetic operators of highest precedence form the **<primary>**s. Primaries include variables, constants, and literals, all of which have intrinsic values. They also include functions, which obviously must be called before they can return a value to be used in an expression. Primaries also include operations within parentheses. This means that operations within parentheses are performed before other operations in an expression are performed.

The arithmetic operators of second highest precedence form the **<factor>**s. These operations raise a number to some power or take the absolute value of a number. They will be covered in detail later.

The arithmetic operators of third highest precedence form the **<term>**s. These include multiplication and division ("*****" and "**/**"), among others. These operations are performed after factors, but before addition and subtraction.

The arithmetic operators of lowest precedence are addition and subtraction, which form the **<integer expression>**s.

When several operators of the same precedence occur in an expression, they are evaluated from left to right. The following two examples illustrate these points. First, in the expression

```
9 - 2 * 4 + 2
```

there are no parentheses, so the operation of highest precedence is the multiplication **2*4**. It is thus evaluated first, yielding the expression

```
9 -   8   + 2
```

Now, only addition and subtraction are left. Since they are of the same precedence, they are performed from left to right. This left-to-right rule is not reflected in the syntax diagram, but because of it, the subtraction, **9-8**, is performed first, yielding

```
1         + 2
```

Finally, the addition is performed to obtain

```
3
```

In the second example, there are parentheses in the expression:

```
1  +  (4  +  7)  *  (5  -  2)
```

Either of the two expressions within the parentheses may be evaluated first. If the left one is, the result is

```
1  +     11      *  (5  -  2)
```

Next, the other expression in parentheses is evaluated, yielding

```
1  +     11      *    3
```

Now there are no more parentheses. So because multiplication has precedence over addition, multiplication is performed next. We obtain

```
1  +             33
```

With just the single addition operator remaining, we apply it to get the answer

```
34
```

```
procedure Expression_Demo is
  A, B, C, D: INTEGER;
begin
  A := 5;                             -- 5
  B := 6 + 5;                         -- 11
  C := B - 6;                         -- 5 (gets 11 from B)
  D := C * A;                         -- 5 * 5 =  25
  D := 1 + (A + 1) * (C + 2);         -- = 43
  A := B / A;                         -- 11 / 5 = 2
end Expression_Demo;
```

Program 4–1

Very often, an assignment statement is used to store the result of evaluating an expression. This is illustrated in the procedure **Expression_Demo** in Program 4–1. What happens in this procedure is well defined and easy to understand, as long as you remember the fundamental principle that *statements (assignments) are performed one at a time and in order*. When the program begins, the variables are elaborated (created), but not assigned initial values. The first instruction in this procedure, at line 4, assigns the value 5 to **A**. The variable **A** will contain the value 5 until **A** is supplied a new value by a subsequent statement (such as is done in line 9).

Line 5 illustrates how the value computed by an expression may be stored. The expression **6+5** evaluates to 11, so this is the value that is assigned to **B**.

A more complex evaluation occurs in line 6. Here, the expression contains the identifier **B**. Since, by the previous step, **B** contains the value 11, the subtraction evaluates to 5, and this value is stored in **C**. Lines 7 and 8 are similar in that they both use more than one variable. The only difference is that line 8 is a more complex expression. Since both **A** and **C** contain the value 5, line 7 evaluates to 25, while line 8 evaluates to 43.

An interesting example occurs in line 9. It involves the principle that *the expression is evaluated before the assignment is performed*. Thus, in evaluating **B/A**, we use the values that are currently in **A** and **B**, compute the value of the expression, and then assign the result to **A**. Since **A** is 5 and **B** is 11, the expression evaluates to 2. (Remember that integer division throws the remainder away.) Thus the value in **A** is changed to 2. To confirm that our demonstration program works as claimed, just add a **Simple_IO.Write** after each of the lines to write out the value of the variable that was assigned a new value.

Both the principle "one at a time and in order" and the principle "the expression is evaluated before the assignment is performed" apply to all assignment statements.

Integer expressions may also be used as parameters. We have previously seen such a use in the statement

```
Robot.Move(2 * Size);
```

In this case also, the value of the expression is determined, and that value is passed as the parameter. Remember, that integer expressions may only supply values for integer parameters of mode **in**.

We will next introduce some additional arithmetic operators. The arithmetic operator **rem** computes the remainder that is left when the left-hand operand is divided by the right-hand operand. For example, **14 rem 4** returns **2** because 14 divided by 4 has a remainder of 2. The operator **mod** computes the modulus. In the case of positive numbers, this is the same as the remainder. Additional cases that arise when using these operators with negative numbers will be covered in Chapter 13.

The operator **abs** computes the absolute value of a number. As examples, **abs (3*(-2))** returns **6**, and **abs A** returns the value **3** if **A** is an integer variable that contains the value **-3**. Remember that **abs** has a high precedence, so **abs 3*(-2)** evaluates to **-6** because first **abs** is applied to **3**, and then the multiplication occurs.

The exponentiation operator **`**`** computes a number raised to a power. For example, **`2**3`** computes the value of 2^3, which is 8.

Sometimes an arithmetic operation cannot be successfully performed; for example, if the program attempts to divide by zero. In these cases the operation is not completed, and a **`NUMERIC_ERROR`** occurs. If a program has such an error, check its operations to determine which one it was not able to perform.

4.4 DECISIONS (1): THE IF STATEMENT

Decision making is important in everyday life. For instance, a very common decision is what to have for dinner. This decision may be based on what is available, what we have not had in a while, what sort of a mood we are in, and so on. As another example, if it is raining, we take an umbrella to work; otherwise, we skip work and go to the beach. Decision making is also necessary in computer programming, so computer languages supply decision-making mechanisms.

One language construct that supports decision making in Ada is the *if statement.* The purpose of an if statement is to make a decision and select a course of action. A simplified syntax for the if statement is shown in Figure 4–2.

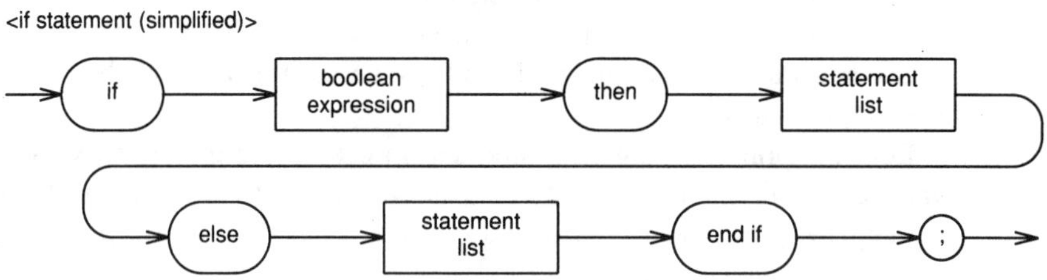

Figure 4–2

Three reserved words and one reserved word-pair that are associated with the if statement are "**`if`**", "**`then`**", "**`else`**", and "**`end if`**". Between the reserved words **`if`** and **`then`** is a *Boolean expression.* We shall consider Boolean expressions in the next section. For an if statement, the Boolean expression is the condition on which the decision will be based. On the basis of the Boolean expression, one of two courses of action is taken: Either the statement list following the **`then`** is performed, or the statement list following the **`else`** is performed.

In the previous example, the Boolean expression was "it is raining." If this was true, we took an umbrella; if this was false, we went to the beach. In an if statement, one course of action is performed, never both. We could say, "If it is raining, we take an umbrella, else we go to the beach." We would do one or the other, but not both.

Consider the procedure **`Test_Number`** in Program 4–2. In the if statement on lines 6–10, the truth of the Boolean expression depends on the value of an integer variable that has been read. If the integer is greater than zero (**`I>0`**), the message "**`Positive`**" is written; otherwise (else) the message "**`At most, nothing`**" is written.

```
 1:with Simple_IO;
 2:procedure Test_Number is
 3:  I: INTEGER;
 4:begin
 5:  Simple_IO.Read(I);
 6:  if I > 0 then
 7:    Simple_IO.Write("Positive");
 8:  else
 9:    Simple_IO.Write("At most, nothing");
10:  end if;
11:  if I < 0 then
12:    if I < -3 then
13:      Simple_IO.Write("very negative");
14:    else
15:      Simple_IO.Write("slightly negative");
16:    end if;
17:  else
18:    Simple_IO.Write("not negative");
19:  end if;
20:end Test_Number;
```

Program 4–2

The syntax of an if statement allows the type of nesting seen in lines 11–19. The statement list for the "else" part of this statement is in line 18. The statement list for the "then" part is in lines 12–16. These lines are an if statement *nested* inside the if statement of lines 11–19.

In line 11, if it is discovered that **I** is less than (<) zero, then we must decide whether it is "very negative" or only "slightly negative." If it is discovered that **I** is not less than zero, then our only action is to print "not negative." in the first instance (**I<0**), a second decision must be made, whereas in the second instance no further decision is required. Of course, we could construct programs in which second decisions are needed in both cases or in which even more deeply nested decisions are made.

4.5 BOOLEAN EXPRESSIONS (1): OBJECTS AND OPERATORS

In procedure **Test_Number** in Program 4–2, we saw some simple Boolean expressions. In many cases, decisions need to be made on the basis of quite complex conditions. Because decision making is so important, many programming languages have a wide range of Boolean capabilities. In this section, we examine Boolean expressions in Ada.

A Boolean expression is something that is either true or false. Accordingly, there are two Boolean values: *true* and *false*. A Boolean expression always evaluates to one of these two values. The type **BOOLEAN** and the literals **TRUE** and **FALSE** are predefined in **package STANDARD**.

The simplest Boolean expression is, of course, a Boolean literal. The literal **TRUE** evaluates to true and the literal **FALSE** evaluates to false.

A more complex form of expression is the relation. Lines 6, 11 and 12 of procedure **Test_Number** give three different uses of relational operators. The motivation for using relations is that we need a way to make decisions based on the relationship between values. There are six types of relational operators in Ada. The syntax for their use is given in Figure 4–3. These, together with the membership tests **in** and **not in** constitute the relations in Ada.

<relation>

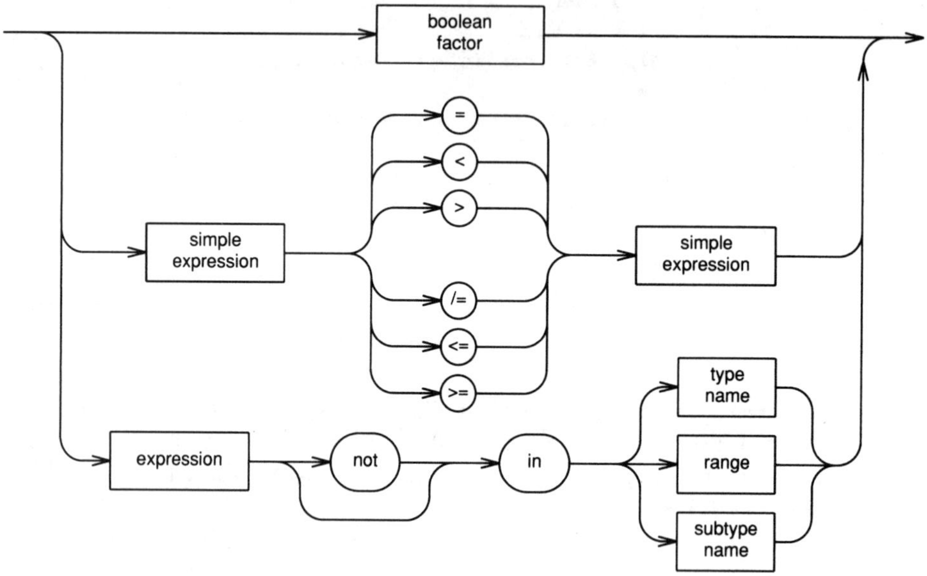

Figure 4–3

The relational operator "**>**", used on line 6 of **Test_Number** evaluates to true if the quantity to its left is greater than quantity to its right. Thus, the Boolean expression on line 6 evaluates to true if **I** is greater than zero. In particular, the "simple expressions" in Figure 4–3 can be arithmetic expressions, but there are other allowable expressions.

In a similar fashion, the relational operator "**<**" evaluates to true if the quantity to its left is less than the one to its right. The syntax calls for both of these quantities to be simple expressions. In line 12 of **Test_Number**, "**-3**" is an example of simple expression. Any integer expression qualifies as a simple expression, but many other expressions do also.

The relational operator "**=**" evaluates to true if the quantities to its left and right are equal. For example, "**I=3**" evaluates to true if the variable **I** contains the value **3**. The relational operator "**/=**" is the negation of "**=**"; that is, it evaluates to true if the quantities to its left and right are *not* equal.

The two remaining relational operators are those for less than or equal to "**<=**" and for greater than or equal to "**>=**".

Following are some examples of the evaluation of relational operators:

`2 < 3`	true
`3 <= 2`	false
`4 = 5`	false
`4 = (5-1)`	true (the parentheses are not required because subtraction has higher precedence than comparison)
`X >= 5`	depends on the value of **X**

Like the assignment statement, relational operators can be applied to types other than **INTEGER**. Also like the assignment statement, type checking is performed on relations. We may compare two integers or two characters, but we may not compare a character to an integer. The type-checking rule for relations is that the simple expressions on the two sides of the relational operator must have the same type. Thus, in the following examples both sides are of type **CHARACTER** while in the preceding examples both were of type **INTEGER**.

`'Y' = 'Y'`	true, characters can be compared
`'Y' = 'y'`	false, case is significant in characters
`'N' /= 'Y'`	true
`'A' > 'B'`	false, order is alphabetic
`'X' = '5'`	false, we are comparing two different characters

There is also a method for checking whether a value belongs to a given range, type or subtype. This is supplied by a relation called the *membership test*. The membership test uses the reserved word **in**. Given the declarations

```
subtype Small is INTEGER range 1..5;
X: INTEGER;
```

we can test to see whether **X** is in a given subrange by an expression of the type

```
X in INTEGER range 4..8
```

The membership test "**in**" evaluates to true if the checked value is in the range; otherwise it evaluates to false. We can also check to see whether **X** is in the range of a given type or subtype with an expression, such as

```
X in Small
```

Because the subtype **Small** has the range **1..5**, this expression evaluates to true if the value stored in **X** is in the range **1..5**.

To test for nonmembership, we use the reserved word **not**, as in

```
X not in Small
```

The preceding constructs provide us with considerable power in making decisions within a program. Four Boolean operators supply additional capabilities and make the

<boolean expression (partial)>

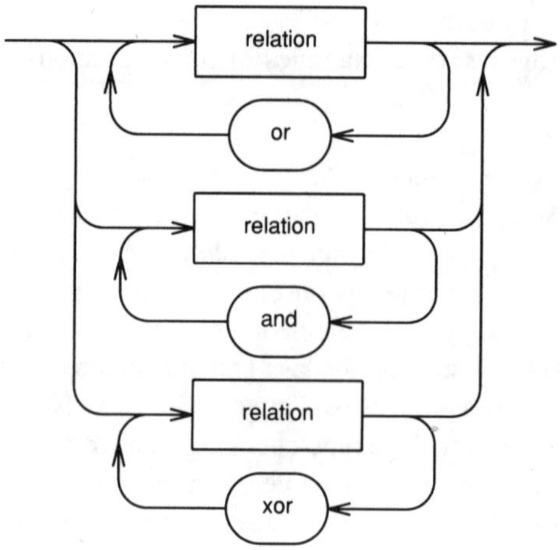

Figure 4–4

use of Boolean values generally more convenient. Figure 4–4 shows the syntax for three of these operators. We will introduce additional Boolean operations in Chapter 5.

The operator **or** can be used to link two relations, as, for example, in

```
I <= 2  or  J > 3
```

This particular Boolean expression evaluates to true if either **I** is less than or equal to 2 or **J** is greater than 3. In general, the **or** operator evaluates to true when either or both of its operands evaluate to true. Another example of the use of **or** is

```
FALSE or TRUE
```

Here, each of the "relations" is a trivial **<simple boolean expression>**; that is, they are Boolean literals.

What we are beginning to see with Boolean expressions is something we have already seen with integer expressions, namely, that the syntax implies a precedence. Plainly, the precedence of the **or** operator is lower than that of the relational operators. This is why, in our example, the two relationals **I<=2** and **J>3** were evaluated before the operator **or** was.

The operator **and** evaluates to true only if *both* the operands evaluate to true. Thus, the expression

```
2 < X and Y > 0
```

requires that both **2 < X** and **Y > 0**. As before, the expression

```
TRUE and FALSE
```

is a legal use of the **and** operator in which the relations are Boolean literals. Like **or**, the precedence of the **and** operator is lower than that of relations.

An expression may contain more than one **and** operator (and hence, more than two relations). Thus, the expression

```
2 < X and X <= 9 and Y > 0
```

is true if and only if all three relations in it evaluate to true. As with the addition operator, it does not matter in which order the **and**'s are performed: The same Boolean value will result. And since the syntax for **or** is the same, as that for **and**, a similar construction is possible with **and**s replaced by **or**s, except that here the expression evaluates to true if at least one of the relations is true.

Another Boolean operator is the *exclusive or*. For this operator Ada uses the reserved word **xor**. The **xor** operator evaluates to true if exactly one of the operands is true. If both operands evaluate to true or both evaluate to false, the **xor** operator evaluates to false. The four possibilities are as follows:

FALSE xor FALSE	false
FALSE xor TRUE	true
TRUE xor FALSE	true
TRUE xor TRUE	false

As the syntax indicates, several **xor** operators can be used in a single expression. Thus, we may have

```
2 < X xor X <= 9 xor Y > 0
```

It isn't as easy to see as for **or** and **and**, but the order in which the **xor**'s are evaluated does not matter. The general rule is that an expression with more than one **xor** relations evaluates to true if an odd number of the relations in the expression evaluate to true, and the expression evaluates to false if an even number of its relations evaluate to true. Thus, for an expression with two relations and one **xor**; if none or two of the relations evaluate to true, the operator evaluates to false, and if one of the relations evaluates to true, the operator evaluates to true.

Two additional Boolean constructs, those of **<boolean factor>** and **<boolean primary>**, serve the same purpose as integer factors; that is, they define a precedence for the various Boolean operators. The syntax for these constructs is given in Figure 4–5. In the diagram, we also find the unary Boolean operator **not**. This operator inverts the value of an Boolean expression. More specifically it inverts the value of a Boolean primary, which is a somewhat more restricted form of a Boolean expression, in the same way that an integer factor is a restricted form of an integer expression. Boolean primaries include Boolean literals and Boolean objects (constants and variables). An example of the usage of **not** is

```
not (X > 3)
```

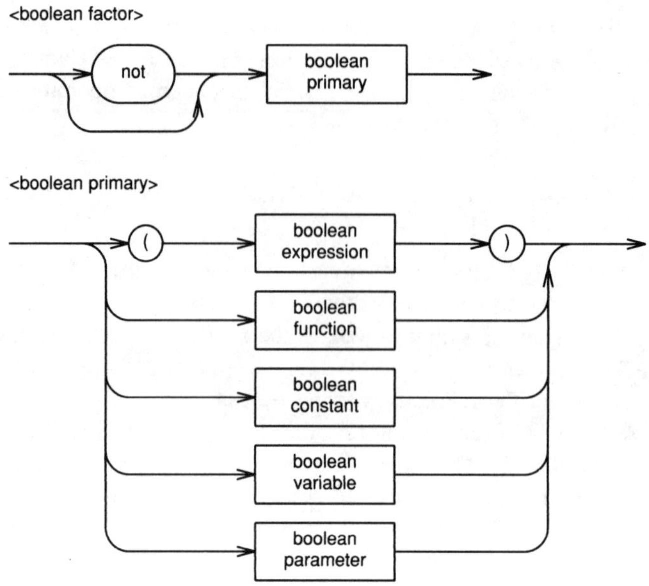

Figure 4–5

This Boolean expression evaluates to true whenever **X > 3** evaluates to false, and it evaluates to false whenever **X > 3** evaluates to true.

The syntax implies that **not** has higher priority than other operations, such as relations, addition, and multiplication. This means that you will often need to use parentheses with **not**, as in the expression

```
not ( 2 < 3 and 3 <= X )
```

Without parentheses, there would be a syntax error because the precedence would require that the **not** apply to the integer literal **2**. Obviously, you can only apply **not** to Boolean values.

In the expression

```
not (2 < 3) or (3 > 1)
```

first **(2<3)** yields the value true. The **not** is then applied to this value and yields the value false. The **or** operator is then applied to this value and the result of the relation **(3>1)**, yielding the value of true for the entire expression.

The syntax of Boolean operators also implies that the mixing of **and**, **or**, and **xor** is not allowed without explicitly using parentheses to indicate the order of evaluation. Thus,

```
2 < 3 and 2 <= X or Y > 5  -- illegal
```

is syntactically illegal. Parentheses are required to indicate that either the **and** or the **or** are evaluated first. The first case is accomplished by

```
(2 < 3 and 2 <= X) or Y > 5
```

the second by

```
2 < 3 and (2 <= X or Y > 5)
```

The identifiers **and**, **or**, **xor**, and **not** are reserved words, but in addition, these reserved words are operators that are defined for the type **BOOLEAN** in the package **STANDARD**. Boolean operators are treated the same as other operators defined in package **STANDARD**, such as the arithmetic operators.

Like other types of values (integers, characters, strings), Boolean values (**FALSE**, **TRUE**) can be stored in variables. Storing Boolean values is valuable for the same reasons as storing values of other types. First, it saves repeatedly recomputing a value, and second, the computation may have depended on conditions that have subsequently changed. An example of a declaration of a Boolean variable is

```
Big: BOOLEAN;
```

The variable **Big** can now contain either the value **TRUE** or the value **FALSE**.

Because Booleans are relatively unfamiliar to many beginning programmers, it is very common to find bad style in programming Boolean expressions. One of the more common mistakes in style is found in the following if statement:

```
if J > 5 then
  Big := TRUE;
else
  Big := FALSE;
end if;
```

At first glance, it appears that a choice is being made. However, this is deceptive because what is really happening is that a condition is being evaluated and the result is being stored. A better way to achieve this is with the single assignment statement

```
Big := J > 5;
```

In this version, the Boolean expression is evaluated and the result is stored directly into the Boolean variable, just as we have done with integer expressions and variables.

Another common mistake is to use a complicated Boolean expression where a simpler one would suffice. In the simplest version of this mistake, the programmer uses the construct

```
if Big = TRUE then ...
```

instead of the simpler

```
if Big then ...
```

Remember that Boolean expressions return Boolean values. Use this fact to make your programs more readable and understandable.

4.6 OPERATOR PRECEDENCE

Precedence can be very confusing to new programmers. Figuring out the precedence of operators from syntax diagrams takes time and practice. To make things easier, we present a precedence table for the Ada operators we have discussed. The operators and membership tests we have seen fall into six precedence levels as follows

```
1:  ()
2:  not   **   abs
3:  *     /    rem    mod
4:  +     -
5:  <     >    >=     <=     /=     =    in    not in
6:  and   or   xor
```

Because parentheses are at the highest precedence level, they can be used to force a certain order of evaluation. When they are nested, as in

```
2 ** (3 * (4 + 5))
```

the innermost expression, which in this example is **(4+5)**, is evaluated first. Without the parentheses, the expression yield a value of 37; with the parenthesis as shown, it yields 134,217,728.

In the following example, we use operators from all the precedence levels and discuss the order of evaluation in detail. In this example, several orders of evaluation are possible but equivalent.

```
1: 3 * 2**3 < 37 + 1 xor 'A' /= 'B' xor not (3 < 5)
2: 3 * 2**3 < 37 + 1 xor 'A' /= 'B' xor not  TRUE
3: 3 * 2**3 < 37 + 1 xor 'A' /= 'B' xor  FALSE
4: 3 *    8 < 37 + 1 xor 'A' /= 'B' xor  FALSE
5:  24      < 37 + 1 xor 'A' /= 'B' xor  FALSE
6:  24      <    38  xor 'A' /= 'B' xor  FALSE
7:        TRUE       xor 'A' /= 'B' xor  FALSE
8:        TRUE       xor   TRUE     xor  FALSE
9:                 FALSE            xor  FALSE
10:                               FALSE
```

In line 1, the highest precedence belongs to the parentheses. Therefore, the comparison within the parentheses is done first. This comparison evaluates to true, and starting with line 2, that value is used in subsequent evaluations. At line 2, the remaining operators of highest precedence are **not** and `**`. Since they are of equal precedence, they may be evaluated in either order. Let us evaluate **not** first. The **not** is applied to the true which resulted from line 1 and produces the value false we see in line 3. In line 3, the operator of highest precedence is now `**`, and `2**3` evaluates to `8`. In line 4, the product of `3` and `8` is `24`. In line 5, the operator of highest precedence is now + which, applied to `37` and `1`, results in a `38`. In line 6, there are two relational operators of equal precedence, < and /=. These may be evaluated in either order. Let us evaluate the < in line 6 and /= in line 7. In line 8, there are two **xor** operators. Again, although they may be evaluated in either order, both orders of evaluation yield the value false.

Note that relational operators of equal precedence are not a problem because they are never adjacent. The syntax makes expressions such as

```
2 > 5 /= 8    -- illegal
```

illegal. Relational operators are always separated by Boolean operators of lower priority, such as **and**, **or**, and **xor**. Boolean operators are not a problem for two reasons. First, different operators cannot be mixed without parentheses because the syntax makes expressions like

```
TRUE and FALSE or FALSE   -- illegal
```

illegal. Second, if all the operators are the same, as in

```
TRUE and FALSE and TRUE
```

any order in which they are performed yields the same answer. (An exception to this is when the operands are Boolean functions with side effects. However, using an expression whose evaluation can be changed by side effects is bad programming style.)

With addition and subtraction, order of evaluation matters: The expression `3-2+1` evaluates to 2 if the subtraction is performed first and to 0 if the addition is performed first. To conform to standard mathematics, Ada adopted the rule that different arithmetic operators of equal precedence are evaluated from left to right. This forces the subtraction to be performed first, so that the value 2 results. The same is true for the class of operators that includes multiplication and division.

Sometimes, even when operands of different precedence are present, the order of evaluation may vary, but not the end result. For example, in

```
2 + 3 < 3 * 5
```

although the multiplication operator has higher precedence than the addition operator, Ada allows the evaluation to be performed in either order since the relation "<" is always applied last.

Whenever you are unsure of the precedence of an expression, you can use parentheses to force the desired precedence. Of course, using too many parentheses can make an expression difficult to read, so overuse of parentheses should be avoided. But you often can make an expression easier to read through judicious use of spaces and parentheses.

4.7 ITERATION (1): THE WHILE SCHEMA

Iteration is the repetition of an action or object. In the current discussion, iteration will be the repetition of an action toward a purpose. For example, walking can be described as iteration of the process of taking a single step.

Many problems are solved by repeating an action several times. A common example is building a brick wall. This is achieved by repeatedly laying a brick. A traffic signal repeats an action that achieves a purpose, and so does a sewing machine. Much of the machinery used in industrial production uses iteration.

Iteration is very common in computer programming. As in other instances of iteration, we seek to repeat an action which brings us closer to achieving some goal. Programming languages in general supply a number of forms of iteration, and Ada contains several of these. Here, we consider the *while schema*, the syntax of which is given in Figure 4–6.

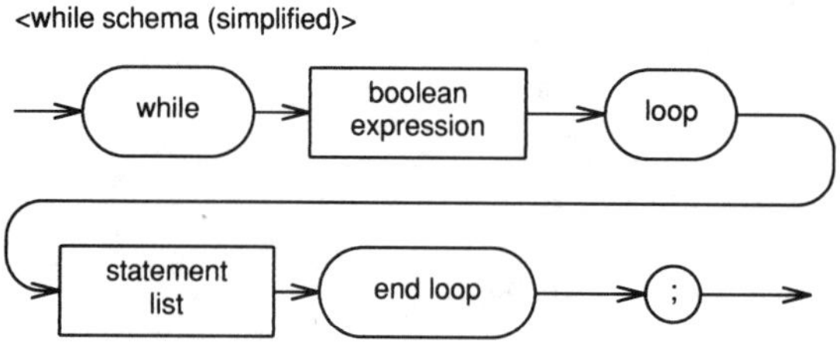

Figure 4–6

The purpose of the while schema is to continue performing a sequence of statements while a condition holds. For example, while not yet home, step. If we are pointed in the right direction, this use of the schema gets us closer to our goal.

The while schema introduces two new reserved words, **`while`** and **`loop`**, and a reserved word pair, **`end loop`**. In the while schema the test of the condition is made at the top of the loop. This test is given by a Boolean expression occurring between the reserved words **`while`** and **`loop`**. The actions to be repeated are placed between the reserved word **`loop`** and the reserved word pair **`end loop`**. Any sequence of statements can be repeated.

An example of how the while schema may be used with a loop is given in the procedure **`Spiral`** in Program 4–3. This procedure causes the robot to spiral in toward a center point. The repeated action achieves a goal of painting a spiral. When line 6 is reached for the first time, the test is performed. Because 13 is greater than 0, the loop is performed. The robot moves (line 7), 4 is subtracted from **`Distance`** (line 8), and finally the robot turns (line 9). Execution now returns to the top of the loop, and the test is repeated.

```
 1:with Robot;
 2:procedure Spiral is
 3:   use Robot;
 4:   Distance: INTEGER := 13;
 5:begin
 6:   while Distance > 0 loop
 7:      Move(Distance);
 8:      Distance := Distance - 4;
 9:      Turn(Right);
10:   end loop;
11:   Exit_World;
12:end Spiral;
```

Program 4–3

At this point, **Distance** is 9, which is still greater than 0, so the move, decrement of **Distance** and turn are repeated. Again execution returns to the top of the loop. This time, **Distance** is 5, which is still greater than 0, so the loop is repeated again. After this repetition, **Distance** is 1, so yet another repetition begins. During this repetition, **Distance** becomes −3 upon execution of line 8. However, because the test is performed at the top of the loop, the turn at line 9 is still executed.

Only after the turn does execution return to the top of the loop, and the test now indicates that the value in **Distance** is less than zero. Accordingly, the test returns a value of false, the loop is skipped, and execution resumes at the instruction after **end loop**, that is, at **Exit_World** at line 11.

Program 4–4 contains nested while loops. The object of the procedure **Remove_Blanks** is to remove all blanks from a sentence. This is achieved by the inner loop of lines 10–12. As long as the condition on line 10 detects a blank, that blank is deleted by line 11. When all blanks have been removed, the modified sentence is printed (lines 13–15). At lines 16–17, the user can direct the procedure to accept another sentence. After the user responds at line 17, execution loops back to line 7, and the Boolean expression is reevaluated. If the user has entered a capital **Y**, another sentence is read. If the user has entered any other character, the loop condition will evaluate to false, and the statement following the loop (line 20) will be executed next. In this manner, the outer loop allows us to process multiple sentences.

4.8 THE NULL STATEMENT

Sometimes, the right thing to do at a certain point of a program is to do nothing, or a certain portion of the program may not yet be finished. Some languages allow the programmer to leave these portions of the program blank. In Ada, however, the programmer must explicitly declare that a piece of the program has knowingly been left blank or unfinished.

```
with Simple_IO, Lines;
procedure Remove_Blanks is
-- Purpose: Remove blanks from sentences.
  Sentence: Lines.Normal_Line;
  Answer: CHARACTER := 'Y';
begin
  while Answer = 'Y' loop
    Simple_IO.Write("Enter a sentence:");
    Simple_IO.Read(Sentence);
    while Lines.Location(" ", Sentence) /= 0 loop
      Lines.Delete(Sentence, Lines.Location(" ", Sentence), 1);
    end loop;
    Simple_IO.New_Line;
    Simple_IO.Write(Sentence);
    Simple_IO.New_Line;
    Simple_IO.Write("Y to continue");
    Simple_IO.Read(Answer);
    Simple_IO.Await_User;     -- Get rid of the carriage return.
  end loop;
  Simple_IO.Write("Bye");
end Remove_Blanks;
```

Program 4–4

The identifier **null** is a reserved word that Ada provides for this purpose. When it appears in the program, it is immediately obvious that a statement list or a portion of a declaration has been omitted. Forcing the use of **null** allows the compiler to report such errors as loops unintentionally left blank.

An example of the use of the *null statement* is as follows:

```
procedure Not_Done_Yet is
begin
  null;
end Not_Done_Yet;
```

The presence of the null statement satisfies the requirement that there be a statement list, yet indicates clearly that something is deliberately not there.

4.9 THE ROBOT PACKAGE (2): HANDLING OBJECTS

In this section, we introduce some additional tools of the **Robot** package which can be used with decisions and iteration. Each of these tools is a procedure that may be called.

The first such procedure is **Initialize_World**. A prepared robot world may be stored as a file. **Initialize_World** has one parameter which indicates the name of that file. The file indicates where the robot starts in the world and where any additional items are placed in the world. These include items the robot can carry, as well as additional walls. Walls look the same as the boundary of the robot's world. Items the robot can carry are indicated by lower case letters.

The robot can carry one item at a time. To handle that item, two procedures are supplied, **Pick_Up** and **Put_Down**. Items are picked up or put down from directly beneath the robot.

Finally, there is the function **Look**. **Look (Here)** returns a character describing the item in the location directly beneath the robot. **Look (Ahead)** returns a character describing the item in the location directly in front of the robot. The robot can see paint, items, and walls. The items in a square form a stack, and **Look** reveals what item is on top of the stack. A stack of items sits on top of any paint in the square, so the robot cannot see the paint unless the square is empty of items. **Look** may be used as follows:

```
if Robot.Look(Robot.Here) = 'a' then
  Robot.Pick_Up;
else
  Robot.Move(10);
end if;
```

Or it may be used as in

```
while Robot.Look(Robot.Here) = 'a' loop ...
```

In each of these, **Look** is used in a Boolean expression to ascertain something about the robot's world. An alternative use is

```
Item_Seen := Robot.Look(Robot.Here);
```

where **Item_Seen** is a variable of type **CHARACTER**. This assignment could be used to remember exactly what character was seen.

As an example of how the preceding commands might be used, suppose the file **World.txt** initializes the robot's world so that the robot is standing on a stack of items. The procedure **Move_Stack** in Program 4–5 moves these items five spaces to the right. After the robot's world has been initialized at line 10, execution continues at line 11. The first thing the robot does is to look to see whether there is an item beneath it. If there is no item, execution skips to line 19, and the robot has done its job. If there are one or more items in the location, the robot picks up the top item (line 12), carries it to the new location (line 13), puts it down (line 14), turns around (line 15), and goes back to its original position (line 16) and direction (line 17). Execution then goes back to the top of the loop (line 11) and the test to see whether there is at least one item left beneath the robot is repeated. Restoration of the robot to its original position and direction at the end of the loop is important: In that manner, all changes except for that which is explicitly the goal of the procedure (i.e., moving items) are undone. This elimination of side effects makes it easier to see that the loop does exactly what it is supposed to do and makes construction of a program using the **Move_Stack** procedure

```
 1:with Robot;
 2:procedure Move_Stack is
 3:   use Robot;
 4:   procedure Turn_Around is
 5:   begin
 6:      Turn(Right);
 7:      Turn(Right);
 8:   end Turn_Around;
 9:begin
10:   Initialize_World("World.txt");
11:   while Look(Here) in 'a'..'z' loop -- Move a stack.
12:      Pick_Up;                       -- Get another item.
13:      Move(5);
14:      Put_Down;                      -- Drop it in the new location.
15:      Turn_Around;                   -- Go back where we started.
16:      Move(5);
17:      Turn_Around;                   -- Face our original direction.
18:   end loop;
19:   Exit_World;                       -- Restore control of the screen.
20:end Move_Stack;
```

Program 4–5

much easier. The loop on lines 11–18 terminates when all items in the stack have been moved.

A better form of the test on line 11 is

```
11:   while Look(Here) in Item_Range loop
```

where **Item_Range** is a subtype declared as

```
subtype Item_Range is CHARACTER range 'a'..'z';
```

in the declaration of the package **Robot**. Since it occurs in the declaration of **Robot**, this subtype is available to any compilation unit naming **Robot**.

As mentioned before, the **Robot** package has its own read and write procedures. These procedures use the area to the right of the robot's world and avoid disrupting the robot's display. **Robot.Read** will read values of type **CHARACTER**, **INTEGER**, or **Normal_Line**. **Robot.Write** will write values of type **CHARACTER**, **INTEGER**, or **Normal_Line**, or string literals. There is also a **Next_Line** command which causes the next input or output to begin at the start of the next line. With **Robot**, the start of the next line is actually the leftmost portion of the area reserved for output. If a long message is printed, it will be displayed on several lines.

4.10 THE LINES PACKAGE (2): RELATIONAL OPERATIONS

The package **Lines** includes the capability to compare two variables of type **Normal_Line**. In the examples that follow, we use the variables

```
Left, Right: Normal_Line;
```

The relations available for the type **Normal_Line** include the operators **<**, **>**, **<=**, and **>=**. Consider the first of these (the less than operator). It can be used to compare two variables of type **Normal_Line**. For example, if we have

```
Assign(Left,  "ark");
Assign(Right, "art");
```

then

```
Left < Right
```

is a Boolean expression that evaluates to true. The comparison is lexicographical; that is, the order is that in which the words would appear in the dictionary. Thus, since "ark" appears before "art" in the dictionary, "ark" is less than "art." Similarly, "art" would be less than "artist," because "art" occurs before "artist" in the dictionary. The one thing about these kinds of comparisons that is not like the dictionary is that *capitalization matters*. Capital letters are in front of lower case letters. For example, capital **Z** is in front of lower case **a**. This means that "Zebra" is before "aardvark" in this kind of comparison. Comparisons using the other relations obey the same rules. Note that the relation

```
"15" < "2"
```

evaluates to true because the character **1** is lexicographically before the character **2**. The point is that here we are comparing two string literals, not two integers.

A **Normal_Line** can be compared to a string literal. For example,

```
Left <= "maple"
```

tests to see whether the value in **Left** comes before the literal "maple". Note that in order to use the preceding relations in the manner shown, it is necessary to name **Lines** in a use clause.

One function defined in **Lines** allows testing for equality. The function

```
Equals(Left, Right)
```

returns a Boolean value and so, like the relational operators, must be used in a Boolean expression. Again, in testing variables of type **Normal_Line**, the case of letters is important; thus a **Normal_Line** containing the value "**Zebra**" is not equal to a **Normal_Line** containing the value "**zebra**".

As with the relational operators, string literals may be used with **Equals**. Supposing **Left** still contains the value "**ark**", the call

```
Equals(Left, "ark")
```

would yield the value true.

```
 1:with Robot, Lines;
 2:procedure Random_Robot is
 3:   use Lines;
 4:   Command: Normal_Line;
 5:begin
 6:   Robot.Read(Command);
 7:   Robot.Initialize_World(Robot.Empty_World);
 8:   while Length(Command) > 0 loop
 9:     if A_Character(Command, 1) >= 'A' and
10:        A_Character(Command, 1) <= 'Z' then
11:       Robot.Turn(Robot.Left);
12:     else
13:       Robot.Turn(Robot.Right);
14:     end if;
15:     Delete(Command, 1, 1);
16:     Robot.Move(1);
17:   end loop;
18:end Random_Robot;
```

Program 4–6

The procedure **Random_Robot** in Program 4–6 illustrates both the while schema and Boolean expressions. The program moves the robot according to a **Normal_Line** typed in by the user. For each character typed, the robot turns and moves one square. The direction the robot turns depends on the character. If the character is an upper case letter, the robot turns left; otherwise it turns right.

Actually, the entire **Normal_Line** is typed before the robot begins to move. The value typed is stored in the variable **Command**. The loop on lines 8–17 uses one letter at a time from this variable to direct the movement of the robot. Once a letter has been used, it is deleted in line 15.

The Boolean expression in line 8 controls the while loop. Letters are deleted from **Command** as they are used. **Command** will have no letters left, that is, it will have length 0, when all letters have been used.

Within the body of the while loop, the first letter of **Command** is examined using the Boolean expression in lines 9 and 10. The value of this Boolean expression controls which **Turn** command is executed, that at line 11 or that at line 13.

4.11 PROGRAMMING PRACTICES

Iteration and decision capabilities allows the programmer to build more complicated programs. Much of the power of these constructs lies in the ability to nest them within each other. You might have a while statement which includes an if statement which determines whether another while statement is to be executed. This nesting is powerful, but it can be confusing. You should be able to describe a clear purpose for each while and if statement in your program. These descriptions should be put into the program as comments. If things are still confusing, the problem needs to be broken into smaller subprograms.

Each part of a program should be easy to understand. If you cannot understand or follow your program, it probably is incorrect. If someone else is unable to understand your program, you need to improve the program's style. So when writing a program, first make sure you can explain it to yourself, and then write that explanation into the documentation for others to read. The explanation should be in the form of comments explaining the purpose of each section of the program. Next, write the Ada (if's, while's, procedures, etc.) that matches your explanation. Finally, write the comments that explain how the program achieves the goal of each section, and write the statements inside each section.

Whenever you do something subtle in a program, or even something that is just potentially confusing, comment what you are doing.

Many of the programming practices we shall introduce in this text are part of the general area of software engineering. Software engineering is the art of designing software. Just as civil engineers study how to design buildings, software engineers study how to design software. In addition, software engineers study techniques for building new software and enhancing existing software. The study of enhancing software is particularly important because most of the work done on a program is done after the program has been "completed." This work involves correcting errors, adding new capabilities, and converting the program so that it can run on another computer system. Because of the high cost of such work, programs should be designed so that they are easy to work on after they have been "completed." Some ways to do this are by careful documentation, by writing programs that are easy to read, and by defensive programming. Defensive programming is programming in such a way as to help prevent errors. Constants, subranges, and attributes are some of the tools Ada provides to simplify defensive programming.

Software engineers often talk about the programming *life cycle*. This is the cycle of analyzing the problem to be solved, designing the program, producing the program, testing the program and correcting (debugging) the program. This cycle is repeated several times in the life of a program, first for the initial development and then each time the program is modified. Good programs result from paying attention to each part of the life cycle.

4.11.1 Structure Charts

Structure charts are a tool for both writing and documenting a program. They provide a graphical representation of the relationship between various parts of the program, showing especially what parts are used by what other parts.

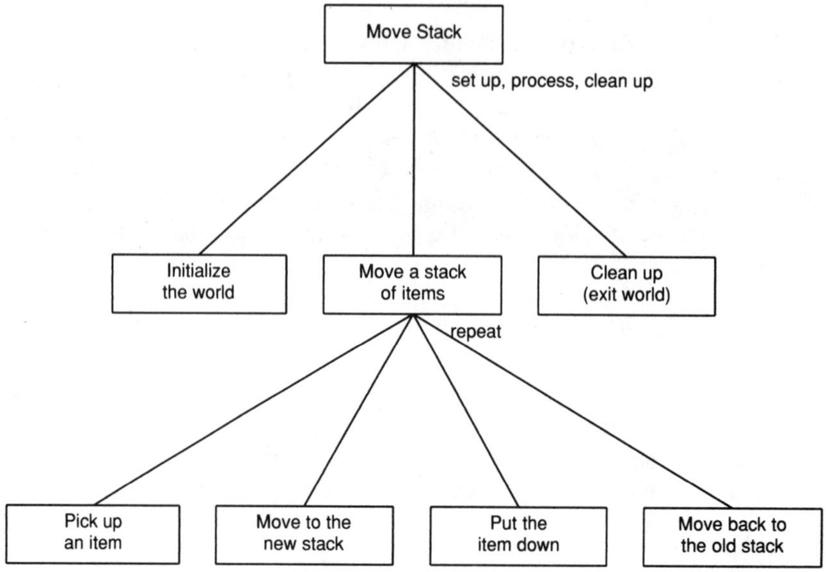

Figure 4–7

Figure 4–7 shows a structure chart for a simple program, **`Move_Stack`**. The top box in the chart is always the name of the program. Each box can have boxes connected to its bottom. Boxes can be thought of as solutions to parts of the problem the program is designed to solve.

If the action of a box is simple, it is enough to list the name of the box on its own (e.g., pick up an item). If the action of a box is complicated (e.g., move a stack of items), we draw boxes below for each of the actions that the complicated box uses, and draw lines to connect the complicated box to the boxes underneath it. Each box represents a "major idea" in the solution of the problem.

Labels below boxes describe how the box relates to the boxes below it in terms of solving the problem at hand.

Normally, you begin with a problem and divide it into smaller problems until the problems are small enough to solve easily. Since we begin with the top of the structure chart, this is called "top-down program design." Designing programs this way usually leads to higher quality programs than most other approaches.

There are many general frameworks available in solving a problem top down. The top level of a program usually requires one to "set up, process, clean up." Most programs require some initializations (set ups) to be performed. Some of these initializations are done automatically by object elaboration, while others must be performed in the statements of the program. After the program is finished, there is usually some cleaning up to do (e.g., move the robot back to the starting position). In many subprograms, the top level also has this structure. Sometimes, we include a box for a part of a problem-solving technique, even if the box is empty (e.g., clean up) to assure the reader that we have considered a particular aspect of the problem.

A program or subprogram that is interactive usually contains an example of "read, evaluate, write." Reading involves getting input from the user or from a parameter, as well as related problems (e.g., prompting and checking for validity). Evaluation is doing the work. Writing refers to outputting the results to the user, a variable, or a parameter.

Some problem-solving structures correspond to structures in Ada. For instance, "option" is a generalized term signifying a choice of boxes, and it corresponds to the if statement (as well as to some other statements). There is also a problem-solving technique called "loop" which means to repeatedly use the boxes.

It is not common in computer science to actually mark the problem-solving technique used on the lines in the structure diagram, as we have done in Figure 4–7, but it is sometimes found to be helpful if these labels are included. As you develop a program, you should try to identify what problem-solving technique you are using and include an appropriate label in your structure chart.

If the structure chart for an entire problem is too large to fit on one page, any box that has not yet been subdivided may be treated as a separate problem. A structure chart may then be drawn for this smaller problem, beginning on another page. If a problem is separately charted, it should be indicated on the primary chart where that separate chart can be found. This may be done by putting the page number of the separate chart under the corresponding box in the main chart.

Structure charts can be used for several purposes. The most common is as documentation of a program. This use of a structure chart makes future modifications of the program easier by making the program easier to understand. The use of a structure chart as a problem-solving tool is just as important. When used as documentation, the structure chart should exactly match the final version of the program. When used as a problem-solving tool, the structure chart is only a preliminary design, so the program produced may not exactly match the chart. It is not unusual in this case to have to redraw the chart after completing the program.

4.11.2 Problem Solving

In Chapter 3, we examined the problem of converting a name from the last-name-first format to the first-name-first format. We solved the problem just for a single name there because we did not have the capability to perform a loop. In addition, because we did not have the capability to perform different statements depending on a condition, we could not ensure that the name was in the correct format.

In this section, we discuss an expansion of the problem from Chapter 3 in which some of the names are already in first-name-first order and in which the user may enter more than one name. Our revised problem statement reads as follows:

> The Last City Bank has a large list of names of clients. Unfortunately, many of the names are recorded in a different format than is required for the new data base program. The old format is
>
> **`LASTNAME, FIRSTNAME I.`**
>
> The new format is
>
> **`FIRSTNAME I. LASTNAME`**
>
> where **`I.`** is an optional middle initial.
>
> Some of the names are already in the new format. Each name is on its own line in the input. After all names are entered, the user will enter a blank line to indicate the end of the input list.

According to the preceding description, there are two changes in the problem definition: how the end of the input is signaled, and the existence of some names that are already in the new format and may not need to be processed. These changes do not require any change to the package **`Fix_Names`** in Program 3–16, and we can just continue using the procedure **`Put_First_Name_First`** as it stands. We merely have to change the program that calls this procedure.

We shall use the same problem solution framework as we used in Chapter 3, but alter the analysis of the framework to correspond to the new problem. This adaptability to new problems is one of the major virtues of frameworks. Newly set up, the problem solution framework is as follows:

1. Perform any setups needed.
2. Set all summaries to zero.
   Set the number of words read and number of characters output to zero.
3. Repeat the following for each input datum:
   a. Read the input datum.
      Make the input datum available for processing.
   b. Determine whether the end of input has been reached. If so, leave the series of repetitions and go on to the next step.
      Check whether the line that was read is empty. If it is, indicate that it is time to exit the loop.
   c. Transform the input datum to the output datum.
      Make sure that the input datum contains a comma, and if it does, divide the input datum to get its sections, and put the sections together to form the output datum. The input datum is not needed after this step.
   d. Update the summaries.
      Change the summary values. This requires the output datum.
   e. Output the output datum.
      The output datum is not needed after this step.
   f. Output any intermediate summary information (e.g., subtotals).
      There is none in this problem.
4. Output the summary information.
   The summary information is not needed after this step.
5. Perform any cleanups needed.

Plainly, the changes to the framework are easy. We next discuss the changes needed in the program. Note that the **`Put_First_Name_First`** procedure corresponds to steps 3c (excluding the check for the comma) and 3d. Writing the actual program is left as an exercise.

One change in the program arises because not all names are in the last-name-first order. For those names, we do not wish to call **`Put_First_Name_First`**. Accordingly, we need a simple way to determine whether names are already in the output format. We can use the fact that names which are already in first-name-first order do not contain a comma.

Another change is that we have to be careful to exit the loop correctly when an empty line is read. Moreover, we do not wish to reverse a name that does not contain any letters. Fortunately, names that are empty do not contain a comma. Thus, the test to ensure that the names are in last-name-first order will also stop us from calling **`Put_First_Name_First`** if the name is empty. On the other hand, all names should be written to the screen, but the empty line should not, so you must check for this condition.

Finally, the comments in the program must indicate clearly the way in which processing of the empty line is handled. Because the check for a comma serves more than one purpose, a programmer attempting to understand the program could become confused unless the program has good comments.

Remember, using frameworks is an important part of programming. They make a program easier to write, modify, and understand. But you must carefully identify the steps of the framework and what decisions have been made as to how to implement those steps. In documenting the program, make sure that comments are phrased in terms of both the problem and the framework. It is more important to include comments that discuss the solution strategy than comments that discuss the statements you have written.

4.11.3 Testing

Programs containing an if statement or a loop are said to have *multiple paths*. Each part of an if statement (signaled by **`then`** or **`else`**) is a separate path through the program. You should test the program with data that exercise each part of every if statement. Each different number of times through a loop can be considered a different path. Because this results in an unlimited number of paths, we usually test each loop for 0 repetitions, 1 repetition, 2 repetitions and several repetitions. Ideally, we would like to test all combinations of paths through all if statements and all loops, but this is usually not practical, so we settle for making sure we exercise each if statement and each loop individually in our tests.

Testing is supposed to detect errors in the program. When an error is discovered it must be located and fixed. One method of locating an error is to write critical information from different points in the program. Knowing the values of variables often helps locate an error. Sometimes, writing the value is even sufficient to reveal the nature of the error; for example, the program makes mistakes only when handling a sentence of length 1. When you write information, you have to examine it to determine whether what was written is what you would expect to be written if the program were functioning correctly. Sometimes the information written only serves to indicate where the problem is *not* located. In this case, additional output statements will need to be added to other portions of the program.

Applying this thinking to the Last City Bank program, we should ensure that once it is built, it correctly performs along each path. We should test names with the last name first and with the first name first. We should test both of these cases with and without the middle initial.

4.12 ADA SUMMARY

In this chapter, we have introduced the *while schema* for iteration and the *if statement* for decision making. Further discussion of these topics will occur in later chapters. We also extended our coverage of integer expressions to include detailed discussions of *precedence rules* and what they do and do not imply.

We also introduced the concepts of *Boolean* values, objects, and expressions and their use in iteration.

EXERCISES

4.1. Modify the procedure **Put_First_Name_First** of Program 3–16 so that the middle initial is optional. Your modified procedure should correctly handle names with and without a middle initial. This will require the use of an if statement.

4.2. Modify procedure **Remove_Blanks** in Program 4–4 so that it removes extra blanks. All blanks at the start or end of a sentence are extra. If two or more blanks are adjacent inside a sentence, only one of them is necessary. For example, the sentence

```
" This is a test  of        blank removal   "
```

should become

```
"This is a test of blank removal"
```

Here, the delimiting quotation marks are not part of the sentence, but are present to make leading and trailing blanks visible. Of course, you should change the name of the procedure to reflect the fact that what it now does is **Remove_Extra_Blanks**.

4.3. Build the **Remove_Extra_Blanks** procedure described in the previous exercise to match the following declaration:

```
with Lines; use Lines;
procedure Remove_Extra_Blanks(Sentence: in Normal_Line;
                    Sentence_Without_Extra_Blanks: out Normal_Line);
```

```
-- Purpose: Remove extra blanks from a line.
--   Sentence: A line with (possible) extra blanks.
--   Sentence_Without_Extra_Blanks: The same line with the extra
--    blanks removed.
```

This form of the procedure is more flexible than the one in the previous exercise because, by doing input and output through parameters, it can be used in a variety of situations other than those that take input from the keyboard and send output to the terminal. To test **Remove_Extra_Blanks**, compile the procedure as a library unit, and name it in the context clause of a test program that you design. Your test program should read a line from the keyboard and echo the line with the blanks removed. As with **Remove_Blanks**, the test program calling **Remove_Extra_Blanks** should contain a loop allowing the user to enter as many sentences as desired.

4.4. Modify procedure **Move_Stack** of Program 4–5 so that it moves multiple stacks. The world will be initialized so that the robot is standing on the first stack, and there will be a number of other stacks directly below the robot as in the following diagram:

```
 Before                          After
********** ... **               ********** ... **
*A             *                *    a           *
*a             *                *    a           *
*a             *                *    a           *
*a             *                *    a           *
*a             *                *    a           *
*              *                *A               *
```

Move each of these stacks five spaces to the right. Because we do not tell you how many items per stack, or even how many stacks there are, we suggest that you use nested **while** loops. After you have moved a stack, move down to the start of the next line to move the next stack. You will know you are out of stacks when you move down and find nothing.

4.5. Modify the **Bank_Account** package and the **Transactions** procedure from Program 3–14. In the body of **Bank_Account**, modify the procedure **Withdraw** so that it keeps the customer from withdrawing more money than is in the account. If there is enough money in the customer's account, the balance should be decreased; but if there is not, the balance should remain the same and the message "Insufficient funds" should be printed.

In **Transactions**, add a loop similar to that in **Remove_Blanks** so that transactions are performed as long as the user signals a desire to continue. Within this loop, add statements that allow the user to choose either to deposit or to withdraw. Whenever a transaction has been completed, print the account balance.

4.6. Modify the procedure **Replace** from exercise 3.8 so that it replaces all occurrences of a given word.

4.7. Write a structure chart corresponding to the framework used in the development of **Put_First_Name_First** in the Problem Solving section of Chapter 3.

4.8. Using the package **Fix_Name** from Program 3–16, develop a program that reads a list of names from the user, prints each name with the first name first, and then prints summary information at the end. The user will enter an empty **Normal_Line** to indicate the end of the list. Prompt the user for each name in the list, and tell the user how to end the list at the beginning of the program.

4.9. Write a procedure **Searcher** that causes a robot to search a maze until it finds an **'a'**. The robot's world should be initialized to contain such a maze by a call to the **Initialize_World** procedure.
You should use the *left-hand-on-the-wall* algorithm of maze searching. One way of describing this algorithm is to say that the robot puts its left hand on the wall and never removes it while moving. A different way of describing it is that the robots tries to turn left and move one square. If it cannot do this, it tries to move forward (with respect to the original direction) one square. If it cannot do this, it tries to turn right and move one square. If none of these are possible it turns around (from its original direction) and moves one square (essentially retracing its path).

5

Iteration

5.1 OBJECTIVES

This chapter extends our coverage of the decision making constructs in Ada by introducing additional forms of the if statement (section 3). It also extends our coverage of iteration by introducing an additional construct for the iteration of instructions (section 4) and introducing a construct for the iteration of data (section 6). Because iterating data involves types, the chapter examines several aspects of types (sections 5, 7, 8). The iteration and decision capabilities presented in this chapter permit you to write some complex programs.

CONCEPTS:

- Iteration is a useful tool, and the special case of iteration over a range is so common that it deserves its own constructs.
- Iteration can be used for both control and data.
- Since the use of types is a valuable programming feature, the programmer should be allowed to declare the types appropriate to the problem.

GOALS:

- Solve a problem that requires both data and control to be iterated over a fixed range.
- Solve a problem that requires complex decision making.

5.2 MOTIVATION

With what we have learned thus far, we are able to choose between two actions based on some condition. Many problems, however, require a more complex decision-making capability. Sometimes, we wish to do something if a condition holds, and do nothing otherwise. At other times we wish to choose from among more than two alternatives. We complete our presentation of the if statement by introducing the forms designed to allow the programmer to decide among any number of statements.

Iteration is very common in our experience. We have seen iteration of instructions, but iteration sometimes involves data. For example, every term, a university iterates the process of updating its data for each student. This assumes that the information about each student is similarly organized. The library card catalogue is another example. Each card in the catalogue is similarly organized. We thus have a repetition or iteration of cards with similar data.

Obviously, a programming language that hopes to deal with a wide class of problems must provide powerful iteration constructs. We have already examined the iteration capability of the while schema. In this chapter, we extend our coverage of iteration to include another schema and to introduce the capability to iterate data.

5.3 DECISIONS (2): COMPLEX IF STATEMENTS

The *if statement* as presented in Chapter 4 enabled us to choose between two sets of actions. In this section, we introduce additional forms of the if statement for more extensive kinds of decision making. Two special cases of making a decision are very common: (1) we wish to do something if a condition holds, but if the condition does not hold, we wish to do nothing. (2) There is a series of cascading decisions; that is, we go down a list of conditions, looking for the first one that holds and perform the action associated with that condition. Ada supplies constructs for both of these situations. The full syntax for the if statement is given in Figure 5–1.

As the figure shows, the else and elsif alternatives of the if statement are optional. Thus, the construct:

```
if B1 or I < 3 then
  Robot.Move(10);
end if;
```

will move the robot if the condition holds. Otherwise, nothing will be done.

Also shown in the figure is the construct for cascading decisions using the reserved word **elsif**. In a cascaded situation, at most one of the statement lists is performed. If an **else** clause is associated with the if statement, exactly one of the statement lists is performed.

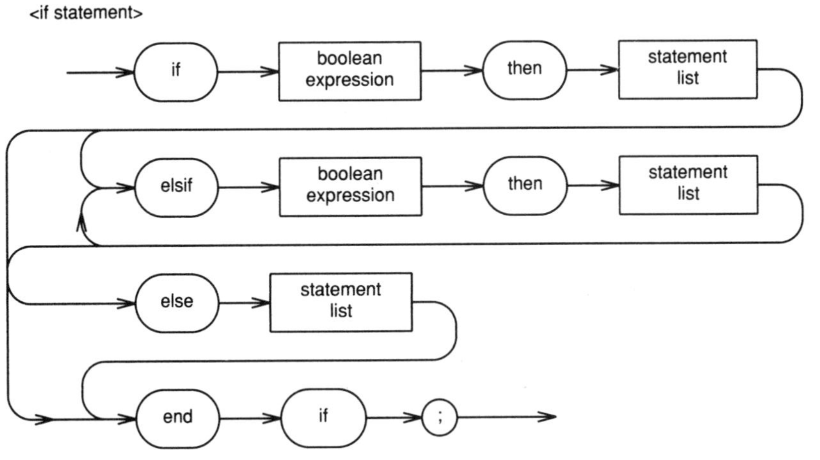

Figure 5–1

One situation in which cascaded decisions are useful is in determining to which range a value belongs. This is illustrated in the following if statement:

```
if I < 0 then
  Write("Negative");
elsif I < 5 then
  Write("Small");
elsif I <= 100 then
  Write("Medium");
else
  Write("Large");
end if;
```

The objective of this statement is to decide on the relative size of a number. Numbers less than 0 are negative, numbers from 0 through 4 are small, numbers from 5 through 100 are medium, and numbers over 100 are large. The number **`I`** is tested. If it is found to be less than 0, the message **`Negative`** is printed. If the **`Negative`** message is printed, the if statement is complete and execution continues at the statement following the if statement. On the other hand, if the number is not negative, then it is tested again to see whether it is less than 5. If at this second testing **`I`** is determined to be less than 5, **`Small`** is printed and the if statement is complete. If the second test determines instead that the number is greater than or equal to 5, then the number is tested a third time to see whether it is less than or equal to 100. If it is less than or equal to 100, **`Medium`** is printed and the if statement is complete. If the number is not less than or equal to 100, **`Large`** is printed.

No matter what value **`I`** has, exactly one message will be printed. That message will be the first one for which the Boolean expression evaluates to true. The **`elsif`** construct is natural in a situation where the actual concept is one of several choices. As in any if statement, in an if statement with a series of **elsif**'s the else clause is optional and, if present, occurs last.

The indentation illustrated for the **elsif** construct reflects the intent of the structure. Within such an if statement, we are selecting one statement list from among several choices. In this sense, all the statement lists are equally important. That is why they are all at an equal level of indentation. Of course, with this construct, there is a preference for a choice occurring earlier in the list, but this is of secondary importance to the fact that the statement is selecting an option.

5.4 ITERATION (2): THE FOR SCHEMA

The previously introduced while schema provides a powerful tool for controlling iteration. However, the while schema is a fairly general construct. The schema introduced next is designed for a more specific situation that is so common that it deserves special consideration.

In many problems, the natural solution is to step through a task one item at a time. In these cases, you usually know how many items there are and hence, how many steps to take. The *for schema* is designed specifically for this kind of situation. It permits a loop to be iterated a precomputed number of times.

The syntax for the for schema, as well as how to attach it to a loop, is found in Figure 5–2. The syntactical difference from the while schema is that a "for condition" instead of a "while condition" precedes the loop. For a given loop you may only use one schema; that is, you cannot attach both a while and a for schema to the same loop.

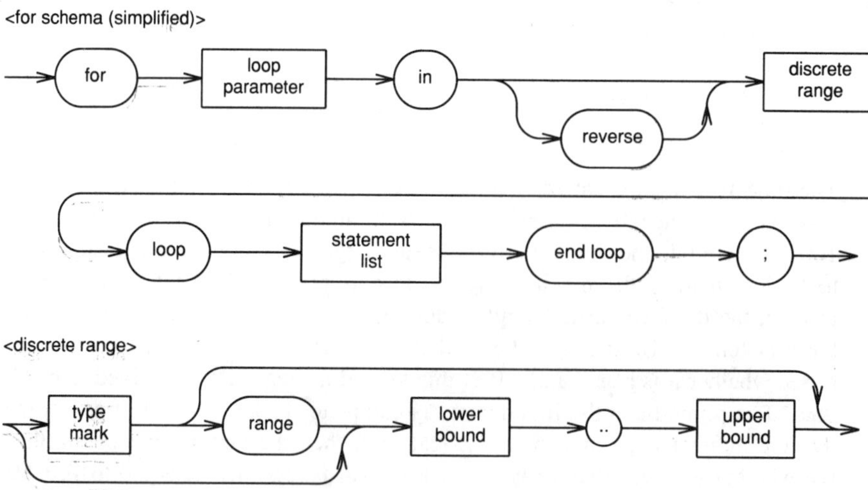

Figure 5–2

The for schema involves two principal parts: the definition of a *loop parameter* and the definition of the range of the iteration. The loop parameter is similar to a procedure parameter of mode **in**. It receives its value on entering the loop body and cannot be changed within the loop body. Since the loop body is entered once for each iteration, the loop parameter receives a new value each time it enters. The values the loop parameter assumes are defined by the range portion of the schema.

In the simplest case, the first value the parameter assumes is the first element in the range. Each successive time through the loop, the parameter is incremented to its next value. For example, in the loop

```
for Letter in CHARACTER range 'A'..'F' loop
  Simple_IO.Write(Letter);
end loop;
```

Letter is the loop parameter. The first value that **Letter** assumes is **'A'**, the first element of the range. Therefore, on the first iteration through the loop, the character "**A**" is printed. On the second iteration through the loop, **Letter** assumes the value **'B'**, which is then printed; on the third iteration, the value **'C'** is printed, and so forth. This continues until the sixth time through the loop, when **Letter** assumes the value **'F'** and an "**F**" is printed. After this iteration, the loop is completed and execution continues at the statement following the loop. During execution of the loop, six iterations occur and the loop parameter **Letter** assumes each of the six values in the range, one value for each iteration.

Since counting down is a common practice, Ada allows the loop parameter to be decremented as well as incremented. The parameter is incremented if the reserved word "**in**" occurs by itself and is decremented if the reserved word pair "**in reverse**" occurs. Thus, the loop

```
for Distance in reverse INTEGER range 1..10 loop
  Robot.Move(Distance);
  Robot.Turn(Robot.Left);
end loop;
```

causes the loop parameter **Distance** to begin at 10 and to be decremented each of the 10 iterations through the loop until, during the last iteration, **Distance** assumes the value 1. The loop causes the robot to spiral toward a point.

One additional form of the discrete range should be mentioned because it is used often. If we had the subtype definition

```
subtype Small_Number is INTEGER range 1..10;
```

then the for schema of the previous loop could have been written as

```
for Distance in reverse Small_Number loop ...
```

This form is preferred because it is more adaptable. If all references are to a subtype such as **Small_Number** and that subtype needs to be modified, this form would automatically adjust all loops, whereas the previous one would require the programmer to find and adjust all loops individually.

Notice that the loop parameter is not declared in the same manner as are variables. Instead, it is declared automatically by the for schema. The scope of the loop parameter is entirely within the loop, it does not exist outside the loop. In the previous example, the identifier **Distance** is visible only between the **loop** and **end loop** associated with the for schema. Thus, this particular **Distance** cannot be referred to outside the loop. If some other **Distance** is declared, it may not be directly visible within the loop.

```
 1:with Simple_IO;
 2:procedure Loop_Parameter is
 3:   K: CHARACTER:
 4:begin
 5:   K := 'Z';
 6:   for K in CHARACTER range 'B'..'E' loop
 7:     Simple_IO.Write(K);       -- loop parameter K
 8:   end loop;
 9:   Simple_IO.Write(K);         -- variable K
10:end Loop_Parameter;
```

Program 5–1

This is illustrated in the procedure **Loop_Parameter** in Program 5–1. In this procedure there are two objects named **K**. The first is a character variable declared in line 3, and the second is a loop parameter declared in line 6. The scope of the loop parameter is only within the loop. Thus, we use the loop parameter at line 7, but it does not exist at lines 5 and 9. The variable declared in line 3 is not directly visible within the loop because the loop parameter has the same name. Since line 9 is outside the loop, the identifier **K** in that line refers to the variable declared in line 3.

The procedure **Loop_Parameter** prints **BCDEZ**. The first four letters (**BCDE**) are printed by the loop, and the last (**Z**) is printed by line 9. Notice that the value in the variable **K** declared in line 3 is not changed by the use of **K** as the loop parameter because the **K**'s refer to different entities. Note that, having two different objects of the same name is legal, and it illustrates a point, but it is not good programming style.

A loop parameter is similar to a procedure parameter of mode **in**, in that it cannot be changed within the loop. It can only be changed (incremented/decremented) by the for schema. This means that in the earlier loops, **Letter** and **Distance** act in the same fashion as parameters of mode **in** do within subprograms. A loop such as

```
for J in reverse INTEGER range 1..10 loop
  J := 7;  -- illegal
  ...
end loop;
```

would not be legal because it attempts to modify the loop parameter. Neither would the statement

```
J := 7;
```

be legal outside the loop, unless it referred to a **J** other than the loop parameter. Again, the loop parameter cannot be changed within the loop, and it does not exist outside the loop. It is defined by the for schema and incremented or decremented according to the schema.

Finally, the loop parameter has a type. This type is determined by the type of the range. Consequently, the type of the range must be determinable. In the earlier loop whose first line is

```
for Letter in CHARACTER range 'A'..'F' loop
```

the type of the loop parameter is explicitly declared to be **CHARACTER**. Explicit declaration is always available, however, the type of the loop parameter can be implicit in the bounds of the range. We could have said

```
for Letter in 'A'..'F' loop
```

for the previous loop. Because the loop parameter has a range from one character (**'A'**) to another character (**'F'**) the loop parameter is of type **CHARACTER**. Explicitly indicating the type is the better style.

In the loop whose first line is

```
for Distance in reverse INTEGER range 1..10 loop
```

Distance is of type **INTEGER**, and thus the command **Move(Distance)**, which requires an integer, is legal. We use the explicit method for giving the type in order to avoid problems that can arise from the existence of other integer types. In many cases, if no type is given, the type **INTEGER** is assumed. This point is discussed in more detail in Chapter 13.

We have mentioned that a type must be determinable. The simplest illustration we have of this is

```
for Letter in 'A'..5  --  illegal
```

where the type of the first value is **CHARACTER** and the type of the second is not. The type of **Letter** is not determinable because no single type makes sense here. More complex situations can occur in which the type cannot be determined, and these will be covered as they arise in conjunction with the presentation of other features of the language.

A restriction applies on the types that can be used for the range of the for schema. Because the for schema steps through the range, the loop parameter must be of a *discrete* type. As we saw in Chapter 3, **INTEGER**, **CHARACTER**, and **BOOLEAN** are discrete types, so loop parameters can have these types. We also saw that **Normal_Line** is *not* a discrete type, so loop parameters cannot have that type.

The range of a for schema can be computed during execution. The following loop illustrates this:

```
for Which_Letter in INTEGER range 1..Lines.Length(Sentence) loop
  if Lines.A_Character(Sentence, Which_Letter) = 'A' then
    Simple_IO.Write("Found another A at position ");
    Simple_IO.Write(Which_Letter);
    Simple_IO.New_Line;
  end if;
end loop;
```

Assuming that **Sentence** is of type **Normal_Line**, this loop reports the position of each "**A**" in **Sentence**. The number of times through the loop depends on the length of **Sentence**. If the value of **Sentence** is read from the user, it is only during execution that the program knows how long **Sentence** is.

Several details about the for schema require careful consideration. The range of a for schema is computed *before* execution of the loop. For instance, in the loop

```
for I in INTEGER range 10..1 loop
  Write("OOPS");
end loop;
```

10 is greater than 1, so we have what is called a *null range*. That is, there are no valid values for the loop parameter to assume if it starts at 10 and never exceeds 1. Because the range is computed before execution of the loop, the body of this loop will never execute. A common mistake is to assume that such a loop would count down, but it will not. If we want to count down, we would say

```
for I in reverse INTEGER range 1..10
```

Notice that even when we use **in reverse**, the range is still given in increasing order. Thus, the loop

```
for I in reverse INTEGER range 10..1
```

has a null range and its body will never be executed. Furthermore, in

```
for I in INTEGER range 1..Lines.Length(Sentence) loop
```

if the length of **Sentence** is 0, the loop has a null range and the body will not be executed. However, if the length of **Sentence** is 1, the range (1..1) contains a single value (obviously, 1) and the loop will be executed once.

The starting and ending values of a for schema are evaluated only once, at *loop entry*. Specifically, they are evaluated when the for schema is encountered and before any iterations occur. They are not reevaluated after each iteration. This becomes important in the case where the range over which the loop is to iterate is determined by the values of variables, as in the following example:

```
X := 5;
Y := 10;
for I in X..Y loop
  X := X + Y;
  Y := X - Y;
end loop;
```

The number of times this loop is iterated and the values **I** assumes during those iterations are determined by the variables **X** and **Y**. These values are changed during the iteration of the loop. However, the range of values that **I** assumes is determined at the point of loop entry and is *not* recomputed after each iteration. Thus, when the loop is entered, the range for **I** is computed to be **5..10**. During the first iteration of the loop, the values of **X** and **Y** are changed; however, the range for **I** remains **5..10**. No matter what new values **X** and **Y** assume within the loop, the loop is executed six times.

Programmers often make the mistake of thinking that the range of values in a for schema is recomputed after iteration, but usually in a more subtle manner. Consider the following loop.

```
for I in INTEGER range 1..Lines.Length(Sentence) loop
  ...
  Lines.Delete(Sentence, 1, 1);
end loop;
```

The number of times the loop is iterated is determined by the original size of the line **Sentence**. This number is not recomputed, even though the size of **Sentence** changes. Because of this, the loop may iterate right "off the back end" of **Sentence**, resulting in an error.

During execution of a program, a loop can be entered several times. The procedure **A_Report** shown in Program 5–2 enters the loop that searches a line for the character **A** ten times. Each time it enters, **Sentence** has a different value. Thus, if the first line typed is "**XYZ**" the value of **Which_Char** will range from 1 to 3. The loop is iterated three times, and no **A**'s are found. The program then exits the inner loop.

Exiting the inner loop leaves the program at the **end loop** of the outer loop, the program then loops back, reads another line, and reenters the inner loop to search that new line for **A**'s. Because it is reentering the inner loop (as opposed to iterating within the loop), the program recomputes the value of the range.

```
with Lines, Simple_IO;
procedure A_Report is
-- Purpose: to show the position of A's in a sentence
  Sentence: Lines.Normal_Line;
begin
  for Which_Line in INTEGER range 1 .. 10 loop
    -- We do 10 lines just to use a for schema.
    Simple_IO.Read(Sentence);
    -- Examine each line for A's
    for Which_Char in INTEGER range 1..Lines.Length(Sentence) loop
      if Lines.A_Character(Sentence, Which_Char) = 'A' then
        Simple_IO.Write("Found another A at position ");
        Simple_IO.Write(Which_Char);
      end if;
    end loop;
  end loop;
end A_Report;
```

Program 5–2

Suppose now that the second line typed is "**ABCD**". Then length of **Sentence** is 4 when the inner loop begins. This time, the loop is iterated 4 times and an **A** is found at position 1. The value of the range is computed once when the loop starts. However, the loop will start 10 times because it is nested inside an outer loop.

An example of the convenience of the for schema can be found by rewriting the body of procedure **Paint_Box** of Program 1–1. In that procedure, each of the four sides of the box was drawn by its own two lines of instructions. By placing these two lines within a for loop as follows

```
for Side in INTEGER range 1..4 loop
  Robot.More(10);             -- Draw a side of the box
  Robot.Turn(Robot.Right); -- Set up for next side
end loop;
```

we can substantially decrease the amount of code in the procedure. The substitution makes sense because we easily conceive of drawing a box as iterating the action of drawing a side four times.

The procedure **Count_Vowels** in Program 5–3 uses nested loops. The procedure counts the upper case vowels in 10 sentences typed in by the user. The outer loop starts at line 9 and ends at line 23. Each iteration through the outer loop handles one sentence. Lines 10 and 11 get the sentence, and lines 21 and 22 report the vowel count for that sentence. Within the outer loop, an inner loop in lines 13–20 counts the vowels. This loop goes through the sentence one character at a time. The Boolean expression in lines 15–17 tests for a vowel. If this expression yields a value of true, the vowel count is incremented; otherwise nothing is done.

```
with Simple_IO, Lines;
procedure Count_Vowels is
-- Purpose: Count 10 lines of upper case vowels.
  use Lines;
  Sentence: Normal_Line;
  Letter: CHARACTER;
  Count: INTEGER;
begin
  for Line_Number in INTEGER range 1..10 loop
    Simple_IO.Write("Type a line>");
    Simple_IO.Read(Sentence);
    Count := 0;
    for Which_Letter in 1..Length(Sentence) loop
      Letter := A_Character(Sentence, Which_Letter);
      if Letter = 'A' or Letter = 'E' or
         Letter = 'I' or Letter = 'O' or
         Letter = 'U' then
        Count := Count + 1;
      end if;
    end loop;
    Simple_IO.Write("I counted ");
    Simple_IO.Write(Count);
  end loop;
end Count_Vowels;
```

Program 5–3

5.5 USER-DECLARED TYPES

The programmer knows how the data should be structured to achieve an elegant solution. So it makes sense for a programming language to let programmers declare and name their own types. Some types, of course, such as **INTEGER**, are predefined in the **package STANDARD**.

A *type* defines a set of possible values and a set of operations on those values. For integers, the values are represented by integer literals, and two of the many operators are addition and subtraction. For types that the user declares, the legal set of values must somehow be defined. In addition, a mechanism to define a set of operations must be supplied. The simplest mechanism to define an operation is to declare a procedure which has parameters that are of user-defined types.

The syntax for declaring a type is given in Figure 5–3. The key word in the declaration is the reserved word **type**. Types can be declared in any declarative part, just like variables and constants. In fact, type declarations and object declarations can be mixed in the same declarative region; subject of course, to visibility limitations. The same visibility rules apply to types that apply to variables. A type must be visible when used. In particular, a type must be declared before it can be used.

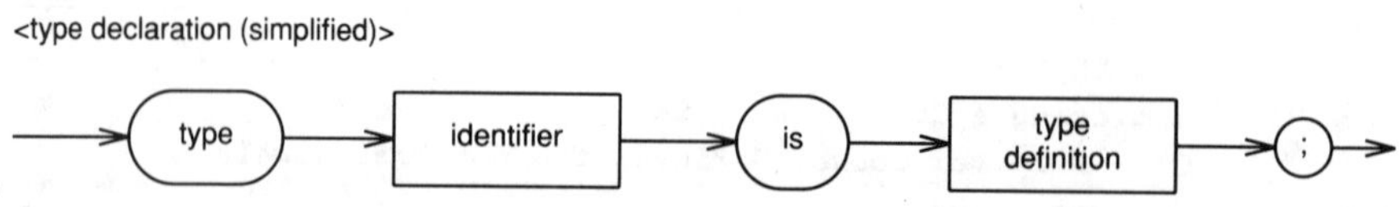

Figure 5–3

In Chapter 3, we introduced subtypes. The distinction between a type and a subtype is that a type is a new and distinct entity while a subtype is an existing type with a (possible) constraint. A subtype is compatible with the type from which it was formed and is consequently legal wherever that type is legal. Also, the original type is legal wherever the subtype is legal. A **CONSTRAINT_ERROR** will occur with a subtype if the constraint is violated. Different types are not compatible, so the use of one type where another is expected is illegal and will be detected by the compiler.

5.6 DATA ITERATION: ARRAYS

An *array* is an indexed collection of components that are all of the same subtype; that is, it is an iteration of variables of the same subtype. The array construct allows one identifier to represent many objects or *components*. These components are distinguished by an *index* (subscript). Some uses of arrays include keeping track of a group of objects, computing during execution which object in the group you want, storing and using tables, and representing vectors.

Mathematics defines the concept of a vector. For vectors, we use subscripts to designate components in an indexed collection (series) of objects of the same type. For example, a vector could be described as a set of six subscripted numbers

$$A_1 \quad A_2 \quad A_3 \quad A_4 \quad A_5 \quad A_6$$

Similarly, in printing, a book is a collection of the same "type", i.e., pages, that are indexed by page numbers. And in storing information about students, the records are usually all of the same "type"; that is, they contain the same kinds of information, and they are often indexed by a student number. In each of these cases, arrays are a natural way of handling the data.

The syntax for declaring an array type is given in Figure 5–4. The reserved word designating a type as an array type is the identifier **array**. In addition, we must supply information about how to index the components in an array and how many components there are. An example of a simple array declaration is

```
type Array_Demo is array (INTEGER range 1..10) of INTEGER;
X: Array_Demo;
```

Here, **Array_Demo** is an array type, each of whose components is an integer. The variable **X** is an object whose type is an array type. **X** contains 10 components, each of which is an integer. Here, the integers **1** and **10** are called the *bounds* of the array.

<array type declaration (simplified)>

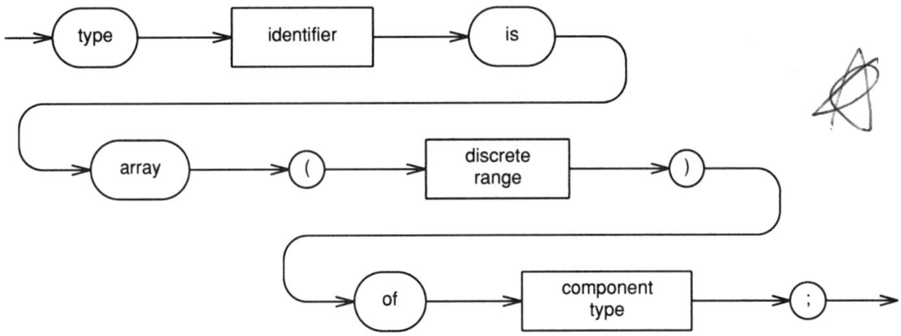

Figure 5–4

Accessing an array element differs only slightly from accessing a simple variable. As with any variable, the identifier associated with the array must be specified. In addition, you must specify which member of the array is to be accessed. This is done by specifying an index, the type of which must match the type of the bounds and the value of which must be within the range of the bounds.

Access to the third component in **X** is achieved by the notation **X(3)**. For example, we could give this component a value with the statement

```
X(3) := 4;
```

or we could get a value from this component (and print it) with the statement

```
Write(X(3));
```

In this example, a total of 10 integers can be stored in **X**, one per component. The assignment

```
X(3) := 10;
```

changes one of these integers, while the other 9 remain unchanged. This also means that if the other nine were previously uninitialized, they remain uninitialized; that is, they contain "garbage."

Any discrete range can be used as an index (subscript). The syntax for a discrete range was given in Figure 5–2. Recall that a for schema defines an iteration over a discrete range. Since **CHARACTER** is a discrete type, the following declarations are legal:

```
type Implicit_Index is array ('A'..'Z') of BOOLEAN;
type Explicit_Index is array (CHARACTER range 'a'..'m') of BOOLEAN;
type Subtype_Index is array (CHARACTER) of BOOLEAN;
```

Arrays of type **Implicit_Index** are indexed by characters. The variable **Seen** in the following declaration is such an array.

```
Seen: Implicit_Index;
Ch: CHARACTER range 'A'..'Z';
```

With the array **Seen**, indexing may be done by character literals, as in

```
Seen('C') := FALSE;
```

by character variables, as in

```
Seen(Ch) := TRUE;
```

by expressions evaluating to a character, or by an attribute that returns a character, as in

```
Seen(CHARACTER'SUCC(Ch)) := FALSE;
```

In general, indices of an array object may be constants, variables, or expressions of the appropriate discrete type. The type used to index an array variable must match (i.e., conform to) the index type in the declaration. Thus, **Seen**, being of type **Implicit_Index**, must be indexed by a **CHARACTER**. This means that

```
Seen(56)...    -- illegal
```

is a syntax error. In a similar manner, the array **X** of type **Array_Demo** must be indexed by an **INTEGER**.

Too often, programmers limit their use of indices or values stored in arrays to integers. The following declarations illustrate the variety of combinations that are available:

```
type Name is array (INTEGER range 1..15) of CHARACTER;
type Totals is array ('B'..'E') of INTEGER;
subtype Capital_Letter is CHARACTER range 'A' .. 'Z');
type Capital_Found is array (Capital_Letter) of BOOLEAN;
type Legal is array (BOOLEAN) of CHARACTER;
```

The array type **Name** has components of type **CHARACTER**, indices explicitly declared of type **INTEGER**, and bounds **1** and **15**. The array type **Totals** has components of type **INTEGER**, indices implicitly of type **CHARACTER**, and bounds **'B'** and **'E'**. The array type **Capital_Found** has components of type **BOOLEAN**, indices of the subtype **Capital_Letter** (type **CHARACTER**), and bounds of **'A'** and **'Z'**. The declaration of type **Legal** illustrates that it is possible to use a type name directly to indicate the bounds of the index. **Legal** has components of type **CHARACTER**, indices of type **BOOLEAN**, and bounds of **FALSE** and **TRUE**. **Legal** will contain a **CHARACTER** for each of the two values in the type **BOOLEAN**. The declarations of **Legal** and **Capital_Found** also illustrate the capability to use a subtype as the type of the index (often a good practice).

5.6.1 Array Bounds and Protections

The principle of both arrays and the for schema is a predefined number of iterations. With the for schema, the bounds of the iteration are computed before execution of the loop begins. Similarly, the bounds of an array type are computed when the type is elaborated. For example, if **A** and **B** are already defined objects of type **CHARACTER**, then the declaration

```
type Some_Totals is array (CHARACTER range A..B) of INTEGER;
```

is legal. The number of characters in objects of the type **Some_Totals** will depend on the values of **A** and **B**. In most declarations, **A** and **B** will be constants, but this is not required. Indeed, as with the for schema, any two expressions of the correct type could be used for the bounds of an array. For example, if **C** and **D** are of type **INTEGER**, then

```
type Some_Name is array (INTEGER range C - 1 .. 2 * D) of CHARACTER;
```

is legal. When used with expressions, the behavior of array bounds is similar to that of the bounds of a for schema. The bounds of an array type are evaluated at elaboration. For example, if value of **C** is 3 and the value of **D** is 4 at the point that **Some_Name** is elaborated, arrays of this type will have bounds 2 and 8, even if the values of **C** and **D** subsequently change.

Like the for schema, arrays are allowed to iterate zero times. For example, if before the declaration of **Some_Totals** we had set **A** to be **'Z'** and **B** to be **'A'**, there would be no indices that were at least **A** and at most **B**. In that case, arrays of type **Totals** would be able to store *no* (zero) integers. This is legal, and, as with the for schema, having zero iterations does occasionally occur in programs.

Ada provides protection for programs that use arrays. Suppose we have the following declarations:

```
X: INTEGER := 1;
Y: INTEGER := 6;
type Truth_Table is array (INTEGER range X..Y) of BOOLEAN;
Bounds_Check: Truth_Table;
Z: INTEGER;
```

Then there are six Booleans in **Bounds_Check** that are indexed by the integers 1 through 6. Now, if we had the statements

```
Z := 7;
Bounds_Check(Z) := TRUE;
```

then, because there is no component indexed by 7, there can be no assignment to a component with index 7. What has happened is that the components in **Bounds_Check** can only be indexed by the numbers 1 through 6, and this assignment violates that constraint. Not surprisingly, a **CONSTRAINT_ERROR** occurs. On every access to an array, the index is checked to ensure that it a legal index for that array. If it is not, there is a **CONSTRAINT_ERROR.**

A **CONSTRAINT_ERROR** can also occur in the declaration of an array. In the declarations

```
subtype Lower_Case is CHARACTER range 'a'..'z';
type Counts is array (Lower_Case range 'A'..'Z') of NATURAL;
```

there is a **CONSTRAINT_ERROR** because the range supplied (**'A' .. 'Z'**) is not in the subtype **Lower_Case**. We have seen this sort of error before with subtype declarations.

5.6.2 Array Attributes

To assist the programmer in the task of writing generalized procedures for arrays, Ada provides array attributes. Two such attributes are **FIRST**, which returns the value of the index for the first element in the array or array type, and **LAST**, which returns the value of the index for the last element in the array or array type.

Given the following declarations

```
type Vector is array (INTEGER range 3..10) of INTEGER;
subtype Capital_Letters is CHARACTER range 'A'..'Z';
type Counts is array (Capital_Letters) of INTEGER;
X: Vector;
Ch: CHARACTER;
Sentence_Count: Counts;
```

the attribute

```
X'FIRST
```

is of type **INTEGER** and has a value of 3. We can use array attributes wherever function calls would be appropriate, as, for example, in

```
if Ch /= Sentence_Count'FIRST ...
```

Here, **Sentence_Count'FIRST** is of type **CHARACTER** and has the value **'A'**, so the statement is equivalent to

```
if Ch /= 'A' ...
```

Note that we could have also written

```
if Ch /= Counts'FIRST ...
```

which, in this instance, has the same effect. **Sentence_Count'FIRST** is the same as **Counts'FIRST** because **Sentence_Count** is of type **Counts**.

A third attribute, **RANGE**, returns the range of values of an indices of an array or array type. Thus, for any array type **T**, **T'RANGE** is the same as **T'FIRST..T'LAST**.

We could use the **RANGE** attribute in the for schema as

```
for C in Counts'RANGE loop ...
```

or, more directly, as

```
for C in Sentence_Count'RANGE loop ...
```

Both these forms are extremely flexible. Using either would remove the dependence of the loops on the nature of the index of the array type **Counts**. This would be particularly important in a larger program where that array type might be declared in another package. Using attributes, if the range of **Counts** were to change, or even if its type were to change, say, from **CHARACTER** to **INTEGER**, we would not have to change the for schema. In general, whether you use array or subtype attributes should depend on whether the goal of your loop is to process an array or a type. When both have the same effect, it comes down to what you wish to stress to the reader. Additional capabilities of array attributes are introduced in subsequent chapters.

5.7 STRONG TYPING

Ada provides types to assist the programmer in preventing errors. In Ada, each object or value is of a specific type. Ada is a strongly typed language. In such a language, type compatibility depends on name and not structure. Variables (objects) are not of the same type (i.e., not type compatible) unless they are associated with the same type identifier.

Different identifiers are different types, even if they have the same structure. For example, in the declarations

```
type Vector1 is array (INTEGER range 1..10) of INTEGER;
X, Y: Vector1;
type Vector2 is array (INTEGER range 1..10) of INTEGER;
P, Q: Vector2;
```

X and **Y** are of the same type and **P** and **Q** are of the same type. But **P** and **Q** are of a different type than **X** and **Y**, even though the types **Vector1** and **Vector2** have identical structures. We shall discuss this topic further in Chapter 13.

We have now seen two constructs: subtypes and types. A subtype is used when you wish to retain type compatibility with the parent type. A type is used when you wish to specify a new type that is not compatible with an existing type.

5.8 TYPES AND EXTENDED SCOPES

Types and subtypes may have extended scopes. Most important, types declared in a package declaration may be used by compilation units that include the package name in their context clause. We have also made use of several types declared in **package STANDARD**, including **INTEGER**, **CHARACTER**, and **BOOLEAN**. We have also made use of the subtype **Normal_Line**, which is declared in the **Lines** package, and the subtype **Item_Range**, which is declared in the **Robot** package.

The following package declaration illustrates a type that is declared in a package declaration:

```
package Array_Utilities is
  type Letter_Count is array (CHARACTER range 'A'..'Z') of INTEGER;
end Array_Utilities;
```

The type **Letter_Count** has an extended scope. Any procedure that names **Array_Utilities** in its context clause has the type **Letter_Count** available. This type may be either directly visible (through a **use Array_Utilities;** clause) or visible by selection. If the type is visible by selection, variable declarations must use the selected name. An example is

```
X: Array_Utilities.Letter_Count;
```

In addition to the type declaration, the package may also supply procedures that make use of the type. For example, we have seen that the package **Lines** declares the type **Normal_Line** and also procedures (e.g., **Insert**, **Delete**, and **Append**) and relational operators (e.g., **<**, **>**) that make use of the type.

5.9 SAMPLE PROGRAM: COUNT_LETTERS_IN_SENTENCE

The goal of the procedure **Count_Letters_in_Sentence** presented in Program 5–4 is to count the number of each of the upper case letters found in a sentence and store those counts in an array. The program is a simple example of how arrays and the for schema may be used. Since we are associating counts (integers) with letters (characters), the appropriate data structure is an array of integers indexed by characters. This is reflected in the declarations of lines 9–12. The array component associated with

```
1:with Lines;
2:package Count_Letters_Utility is
3:  use Lines;
4:  procedure Count_Letters_in_Sentence(Sentence: Normal_Line);
5:  -- Purpose: Count the upper case letters in a sentence.
6:end Count_Letters_Utility;

7:with Simple_IO;
8:package body Count_Letters_Utility is
9:  subtype Capital_Letters is CHARACTER range 'A'..'Z';
10:  type Counters is array (Capital_Letters) of NATURAL;
11:  -- The counts of the various characters are stored in this array.
12:  Counts: Counters;
13:  procedure Count_Letters_in_Sentence(Sentence: Normal_Line) is
14:  -- Modify Counts to contain how many of each upper case letter there are in
15:  --  Sentence.
16:    Letter: CHARACTER;
17:  begin
18:    -- Initialize the counts to zero.
19:    for Which_Letter in Capital_Letters loop
20:      Counts(Which_Letter) := 0;
21:    end loop;
22:    -- Process the sentence a character at time
23:    for Which_Position in 1..Length(Sentence) loop
24:      Letter := A_Character(Sentence, Which_Position);
25:      -- Increment the count of the appropriate upper case letter.
26:      if Letter in Capital_Letters then
27:        Counts(Letter) := Counts(Letter) + 1;
28:      end if;
29:    end loop;
30:  end Count_Letters_in_Sentence;
31:end Count_Letters_Utility;
```

Program 5–4

a letter, say, `'C'`, will be an integer which contains the count of the number of C's seen thus far. Note the use of the subtypes **`Capital_Letters`** and **`NATURAL`**. These serve to convey the intent of the program to the reader, to ensure that unexpected occurrences (such as negative counts) will be detected, and to make the program easier to modify (such as to count characters other than upper case characters).

Before processing a sentence, the counts for all letters are set to zero (lines 19–21). When passed a sentence, the procedure updates the array **`Counts`**. The loop of lines 23–29 steps through the sentence one character at a time. The membership test in line 26 is applied to each character. If the character is an upper case letter, the appropriate count is incremented. As always, the program should be checked to ensure that the variables were initialized.

```
type Numbers is array (INTEGER range 1..10) of INTEGER;
  ...
 1:procedure Find_Largest(List: in Numbers; Largest, Where: out INTEGER) is
 2:-- Purpose: Find the largest number in an array.
 3:--   List: The array containing the numbers.
 4:--   Largest: The value of the largest number in List.
 5:--   Where: The index of the largest number in List.
 6:  Largest_So_Far, Where_So_Far: INTEGER;
 7:begin
 8:  -- Start with the first component, it is the largest seen so far.
 9:  Largest_So_Far := List(List'FIRST);
10:  Where_So_Far := List'FIRST;
11:  -- Scan the components in the array one at a time.
12:  for This_Number in INTEGER'SUCC(List'FIRST)..List'LAST loop
13:    -- Check to see if this component is the largest we've seen so far.
14:    if List(This_Number) > Largest_So_Far then
15:      -- It was the largest so far, update out information to reflect that
16:      --  fact.
17:      Largest_So_Far := List(This_Number);
18:      Where_So_Far := This_Number;
19:    end if;
20:  end loop;
21:  Largest := Largest_So_Far;
22:  Where := Where_So_Far;
23:end Find_Largest;
```

Program 5–5

5.10 SAMPLE PROGRAM: FIND_LARGEST

Program 5–5 searches for the largest value stored in an array. The procedure **Find _Largest** is passed an array and returns the value of the largest element in that array together with its location. The principle on which it operates is to remember the largest value seen so far. Initially, the largest value seen is the first element (lines 9 and 10). The loop in lines 12–20 steps through the remaining components of the array, examining each element. The if statement in lines 14–19, updates the largest value and location whenever the Boolean expression indicates that a larger value has been found.

Notice that by using attributes, no mention is ever made of any explicit bounds for the array, so that the procedure does not depend on the range of the array index.

5.11 PROGRAMMING PRACTICES

We have now examined the while and the for schemata. The while schema is a general construct, and the for schema specializes in iteration over a range. In programming, you should use the schema that best matches your problem. In particular, use the for schema whenever solving a problem where you need to loop for each item in a range (as in the do-one-and-repeat problem-solving technique). This is an application of a more general programming principle: select the control structure which matches your problem. The same principle should be applied when choosing how to organize your if statements.

The principle of matching the program structure to the problem you are solving also extends to data. For any problem, you should define types to match the way you want the reader of the program to think about the data. For example, if your program used one integer to store the age of a car and another to store the number of cars in a parking lot, it would be inappropriate to store these in an array of two integers. They are not a natural iteration. This is in contrast to the procedure **Count_Letters_in_Sentence**, where the similar treatment of all letters with respect to the goal of the program made data iteration (i.e., an array) the most natural way to store the data.

Language features should be used in a way that avoids confusion. For example, if the values used to specify the bounds of a loop could change inside the loop, a readable program would store the values in variables before entering the loop and carefully document (i.e., comment upon) this tricky situation. This is not necessary for the Ada compiler, because the compiler will not become confused, but a programmer assigned to modify a program might be.

It is often argued that certain constructs ought to be used because they are efficient. There is no objection to using efficient constructs, but efficiency should be secondary to having a well-structured and readable program. Great caution should be exercised when making use of obscure or confusing language details, even when those details are supposedly efficient. Such actions should be carefully localized and completely explained by the program's comments. In most cases, readability is more important over the lifetime of the program than any efficiency achieved by obscure procedures.

5.11.1 The Insertion Sort Algorithm

A method for solving a problem is called an *algorithm*. In this section we analyze a specific problem, supply an algorithm to solve that problem and construct a program which performs that algorithm.

Many times, you want to put things in order. Dictionaries, phone books, and catalogues all are easier to use if their contents have been ordered. The process of putting items in order is called *sorting*. In this section, we consider a simple method of sorting called *insertion sort*.

The principle of the insertion sort is to pick up an item and insert it at the correct place. This method is often used by people sorting playing cards. They pick up one card, place it where it belongs, then pick up the next card, place it, and so on. The only trick is that you may have to make space; that is, you may have to spread previous items apart to make room for the item you are inserting.

As an example of the insertion sort, suppose we have the following list of items to sort:

```
4 2 8 5 3 7
```

We set up a list of of sorted items and begin with that list being empty. We then pick up the first item, a 4, and insert it into the list of sorted items to obtain

```
4
```

Next, we pick up the second item, a 2. We want to insert the 2 in front of the 4, so we move the 4 back and put the 2 in front of it to obtain

```
2 4
```

Next we pick up an 8, and place it at the back of the list to obtain

```
2 4 8
```

Next we pick up a 5, which belongs in front of the 8, but behind the 4. We move the 8 to make space and insert the 5 to obtain

```
2 4 5 8
```

Then we pick up a 3, which belongs between the 2 and the 4. We need to move the 4, the 5, and the 8 back to make space before we insert the 3 to obtain

```
2 3 4 5 8
```

Finally, we pick up the 7, which belongs between the 5 and the 8. We move the 8 back and insert the 7 to obtain

```
2 3 4 5 7 8
```

Usually, the data to be sorted is stored in an array. Many times we need to sort the data using only the original array, that is, without using a lot of extra variables. This can be done in almost the same way as we have just done it. The principle involved is that the front of the array contains the part of the list that has already been sorted and the back of the array contains the part that remains to be sorted. As each value is inserted into the front of the array, this value is taken out of the back of the array. Thus, there is always enough room for all the values.

As a specific example, suppose the array contains

```
4 2 8 5 3 7
```

Initially, the entire array has yet to be sorted. We pick up the 4. A list with one item is always sorted, so we do nothing. The sorted portion of the list now contains a 4. Graphically, we show this by inserting a vertical bar between the sorted and unsorted portions of the list. Items to the left of the bar have been sorted, items to the right of the bar are yet to be inserted. We have

```
Array
4|2 8 5 3 7
```

Next we pick up the 2 and hold it. The array is now as follows:

```
Array                                 Hold
4|X 8 5 3 7                              2
```

Although a copy of the 2 remains in the array, we have replaced it with an **X** to indicate that vital information is no longer there. The 2 belongs in front of the 4. So we move the 4 back to get

```
Array                                 Hold
X|4 8 5 3 7                              2
```

Again, although a copy of the 4 remains in the first location of the array, we have replaced it with an **X** to indicate that vital information is no longer there. Now we place the 2 in the appropriate location. This gives us the following:

```
Array                                 Hold
2 4|8 5 3 7                              X
```

Here again, although a copy of the 2 remains in Hold, we have replaced it with an **X** to indicate that vital information is no longer there. The 2 and 4 are now the sorted part of the list. For the rest of the discussion, we shall not use the **X**, but show which value remains in each location.

Now we pick up the 8 and hold it:

```
Array                                 Hold
2 4|8 5 3 7                              8
```

It belongs after the 4, that is, exactly at the position from which we just picked it up. So place it back down in that same position. We now have:

```
Array                                 Hold
2 4 8|5 3 7                              8
```

We now pick up the 5 and hold it:

```
Array                                 Hold
2 4 8|5 3 7                              5
```

It belongs between the 4 and the 8, so we move the 8 back as follows:

```
Array                                          Hold
2 4 8|8 3 7                                       5
```

Then we place the 5 in the correct position:

```
Array                                          Hold
2 4 5 8|3 7                                       5
```

We now pick up the 3 and hold it:

```
Array                                          Hold
2 4 5 8|3 7                                       3
```

The 3 belongs between the 2 and the 4, so we move the 8, then the 5, and then the 4 back. This reverse order is important because once the 3 has been copied to **Hold**, we can move the 8 into the place from which the 3 came. Then we can move the 5 to where the 8 was because the 8 has already been copied into its new location. Then, since the 5 has now moved to its new location, we can copy the 4. Notice that attempting to move the 4 before the 5 would replace the 5 with a 4, and the value 5 would be lost. We put the 3 in the correct location:

```
Array                                          Hold
2 3 4 5 8|7                                       3
```

Finally, we pick up the 7:

```
Array                                          Hold
2 3 4 5 8|7                                       7
```

It belongs between the 5 and the 8, so we move the 8 back, getting

```
Array                                          Hold
2 3 4 5 8|8                                       7
```

Then we place the 7 in the correct location:

```
Array                                          Hold
2 3 4 5 7 8|                                      7
```

The array has now been sorted.

The procedure **Insertion_Sort** in Program 5–6 performs an insertion sort of the kind we have just done in an array. The outer loop in lines 6–20 picks up one item at a time. Note that it does not bother to pick up the first item, because, as we saw in our discussion, a list of size one is always sorted. The variable **Hold** contains the item we have picked up. The question is where to put it. The loop in lines 11–13 examines the sorted portion of the array to determine where the item goes. Although there is only

```
type Table is array (INTEGER range 1..6) of INTEGER;
List: Table;

 1:procedure Insertion_Sort is
 2:-- Purpose: Sort an array using insertion sort
 3:  Hold, Put_At: INTEGER;
 4:begin
 5:  -- Process the items in the list one at a time.
 6:  for Look_At in INTEGER range List'FIRST + 1..List'LAST loop
 7:    -- Save the value of the item currently being examined.
 8:    Hold := List(Look_At);
 9:    -- Find where it goes.
10:    Put_At := 1;
11:    while List(Put_At) < Hold loop
12:      Put_At := Put_At + 1;
13:    end loop;
14:    -- Move back the back of the array to make room to insert the item.
15:    for Open_Space in reverse Put_At + 1..Look_At loop
16:      List(Open_Space) := List(Open_Space - 1);
17:    end loop;
18:    -- Put the new item into the list.
19:    List(Put_At) := Hold;
20:  end loop;
21:end Insertion_Sort;
```

Program 5–6

one Boolean expression, this loop technically exits on one of two conditions: Either we have found where the item goes by finding an item in the sorted list which the item we are looking at belongs in front of, or we discover that the element should be the last item in the sorted list. If the item should be the last item, **Put_At** eventually becomes equal to **Look_At**, **List(Put_At)** equals **Hold** so the Boolean expression is false again. Now we know where the item goes, and lines 15–17 open a space for the item. Notice that, as before, the loop must move the items in reverse. When the items have been moved, line 19 places the item chosen in the space that has been opened.

Several things are worthy of notice in this insertion sort. First, we have used attributes so that nothing in the procedure needs to be changed to sort arrays with different bounds. Second, we have been very careful with the bounds on the loops. A common mistake is to be off by one on such bounds. In that case, you are too short, the last item might not be sorted, or if the item is large, it might not be placed in the sorted portion of the array. If the loop bounds are too large, a **CONSTRAINT_ERROR** will probably occur. Finally, the insertion sort is just one of a number of ways to sort. We shall introduce other, more efficient methods in later chapters.

Notice that the comments describe what each part of the program does, not how it does it. Like an algorithm the comments should be written before the program. The reason is that it is easier to build a program if you can describe how it is going to work.

5.11.2 Testing

Each program or subprogram has input either through parameters or from the user. A critical issue is how to choose test values for inputs. If the input is a discrete subrange, the ends of the range should be tested. One of the most common errors is the failure of a program to work correctly for the first or last values of such a subrange. In addition, values just inside (i.e., one away from) these bounds should be tested, as should a value somewhere in the middle of the range. Testing these five values will find most (but not necessarily all) the errors in a program. For example, if a program should accept integers in the range `0..100` we would test the values `0`, `1`, `50`, `99`, and `100`.

With values which are not discrete a similar technique should be applied. For example, when testing the procedure **`Remove_Extra_Blanks`** of exercise 4.3, lines with no blanks at all, lines with blanks at only one end or the other, a line consisting of a single blanks, and the empty line represent boundary cases. A value in the middle of the range is one with both letters and several removable blanks.

In sorting you should test arrays with values in reverse order, arrays with just the first two components out of order, arrays with just the last two components out of order, and arrays that are already in the correct order.

For programs that take input from the user, you should test to determine what happens when the user inputs illegal values. Good programs will detect illegal values and refuse to use them in a calculation. Good programs will also tell the user why a value is illegal. For a program accepting integers in the range `0..100`, we would test the values `-1` and `101`. Handling incorrect input is not always possible with the techniques shown thus far. Later we shall consider additional capabilities of Ada that assist us to do this.

5.12 ADA SUMMARY

In this chapter, we extended our coverage of control structures by completing coverage of the *if* statement for decisions and the *for schema* for iteration. We also extended our coverage of *types* by introducing the capability of the user to declare types. Scope rules make types declared in package declarations available outside the package. We considered how the protection provided by typing applies to user-declared types. Finally, we introduced the *array* type as an iteration of data, illustrating how arrays can be declared and used and indicating that the iteration of instructions provided by the for loop is similar to the iteration of data provided by the array.

EXERCISES

5.1. Write a program that reverses a **`Normal_Line`**. The program should use **`Simple.IO`** to read a line, reverse that line, then use **`Simple_IO`** to print the reversed line.

5.2. Write a program that uses nested for loops to produce one of the following patterns.

```
A               B                   C          D
AA             BBB                CCC        DDDDD
AAA           BBBBB              CCCCC     DDDDDDDDD
AAAA         BBBBBBB            CCCCCCC        D
AAAAA       BBBBBBBBB          CCCCCCCCC     DDDDD
AAAAAA                        CCCCCCCCCCC  DDDDDDDDD
AAAAAAA                                        D
AAAAAAAA                                     DDDDD
                                           DDDDDDDDD
                                        (3 deep nesting)
```

The emphasis is on doing this with loops; therefore, each **Simple_IO.Write** that you use should write only a single character.

5.3. In the package **Count_Letters_Utility** in Program 5–4, we omitted a means of reporting the counts accrued. Add a procedure **Report_Counts** to this package which does this. Modify the package so that it can accrue counts for several different sentences. Do this by adding a procedure **Reset_Counts** and moving the code that initializes the array **Counts** into that procedure. Build another procedure **Test_Counts** that tests the package. This procedure should have a loop that allows **Count_Letters_in_Sentence** to be called as often as the user wishes. After the user signals that no more sentences are desired, the test program should call **Report_Counts** and reset the counters. **Test_Counts** should allow the user to repeat the above test several times.

5.4. Write a procedure **Heap** that takes as its parameters **Number_Of_Lines**, **Length**, and **Character_To_Print** and builds (i.e., prints) a "heap" of letters. **Number_Of_Lines** is the number of lines to be printed. **Character_To_Print** is the letter (**CHARACTER**) used in printing. The first line printed should contain **Length** characters, the second line should contain **2*Length** characters, the third line **3*Length**, and so on until the last line, which should contain **Number_Of_Lines*Length** characters. The characters should be right justified as shown below. To right justify you need **(Number_Of_Lines-1)*Length** spaces at the front of the first line, **(Number_Of_Lines-2)*Length** spaces at the front of second line, and so on until the last line, which should not have any spaces at the front. For example, with the parameter list of

```
Heap(Number_Of_Lines => 5, Length => 4, Character_To_Print => 'A')
```

the procedure should print out

```
                AAAA
            AAAAAAAA
        AAAAAAAAAAAA
    AAAAAAAAAAAAAAAA
AAAAAAAAAAAAAAAAAAAA
```

There are 5 lines, 4 characters in the first line, 8 in the second line, and so on. The program should use for loops. Each write statement should print a single character. Be sure to write a main program that asks the user for the size, length, and character to be passed to the **Heap** procedure.

5.5. Write a procedure **Sorted_Subset** that returns a sorted subset of the components found in an array. The array should be of the type **Data_Type** which you should declare in your test program as follows:

```
subtype Data_Range is INTEGER range 1..10;
type Data_Type is array (Data_Range) of NATURAL;
```

The first of the four parameters the procedure uses is an array of type **Data_Type** of mode **in** which contains the data from which the procedure is to form the sorted subset. The second procedure parameter, also of mode **in**, defines the subset. This parameter will be an integer that should always be within the range 0 through 9. The components of the array will be nonnegative integers. The subset of the array that is of interest is those values in the array whose last digit matches the integer that is the second parameter. This is the same as saying that an array value belongs to the subset of interest if that value **mod 10** is equal to the integer parameter.

The third parameter is of mode **out** and indicates how many values were in the subset. The fourth parameter is also of mode **out** and is an array of **Data_Type**. The front of this array contains the subset sorted in order of largest to smallest. The back of the array contains zeros. For example, given an array containing the values

```
12 87 14 42 93 2 23 28 162 139
```

and the integer **2**, the out parameters are set to **4** and

```
162 42 12 2 0 0 0 0 0 0
```

Be sure to write a main program that asks the user for the integers to initialize the array with and the integer to search for before passing these two to your procedure.

5.6. Modify procedure **Insertion_Sort** of Program 5–6 to sort an array of **Normal_Line**s. Write a test program.

5.7. Modify **Insertion_Sort** to sort an array declared as

```
subtype Sort_Range is (CHARACTER range 'A'..'F');
type Table is array (Sort_Range) of INTEGER;
```

You will have to use attributes with the array index rather than arithmetic. Write a test program.

5.8. Write a program to solve the following problem. The input is up to 10 names, entered one per line. The user will enter an empty line to indicate the end of input if there are fewer than 10 names. Some of the names will be last name first, and some will be first name first. The formats of these names will be as described in the **Fix_Name** package. Convert all the names to last name first, sort them, and then convert them to first name first and print them. The name formats are described in the Problem Solving sections of Chapters 3 and 4. Start with a previously constructed version of **Fix_Name** (Program 3–16 or exercises 3.3, 4.1, 4.7, or 4.8).

5.9. Modify the **Bank_Account** program (Program 3–14, exercise 3.1, or exercise 4.5) Maintain an array of 10 bank accounts. Write a procedure **Teller** that prompts the teller and allows selection of deposits, and withdrawals, reporting the balance for any account. The procedure should also allow the teller to post interest. Use the following package declaration:

```
package Bank_Account is
  procedure Deposit(Amount_of_Deposit, Account: NATURAL);
  -- Purpose: Record a deposit to the specified account.
  procedure Withdraw(Amount_of_Withdrawal, Account: NATURAL);
  -- Purpose: Record a withdrawal from the specified account.
  procedure Get_Account_Balance(Account: NATURAL; Balance: out NATURAL);
  -- Purpose: Gives the balance in the specified account.
  procedure Post_Interest;
  -- Purpose: Post interest to all accounts.
  procedure Restart_Bank;
  -- Purpose: Starts the bank by setting all account balances to zero.
end Bank_Account;
```

5.10. Build a program that sorts an array using the exchange sort method. Exchange sort works as follows:

Find the smallest number in the array, and swap it with the number in the first position. The smallest number is now first.

For the remaining components in the array, find the smallest number and swap it with the number in the second position.

Repeat this process for each of the positions.

5.11. Write the procedure

```
type Table is array (INTEGER range 1..10) of POSITIVE;
procedure Where(Data: Table; What_Number, Which_Occurrence: POSITIVE;
                Here: out NATURAL);
```

which finds the **Which_Occurrence** occurrence of **What_Number** in the array **Data** and places that number in **Here**. If there is no such occurrence, it places a **0** in **Here**. For example, if the array **Numbers** contains the 10 values

```
2, 3, 2, 4, 2, 5, 2, 6, 2, 8
```

then the call

```
Where(Numbers, 2, 3, Location);
```

would place a 5 in the integer variable **Location** because the third occurrence of 2 is at index 5 of **Numbers**.

5.12. Write a line format package with the following declaration:

```
with Lines;
package Line_Format is
```

```
-- Purpose: Takes in words, organizes them into (i.e., prints them)
-- lines of the specified length.
  procedure Set_Line_Length(Length: POSITIVE);
  -- Purpose: This is the length of the line to print.
  --   The initial value of Length is 80.
  procedure Add_Word(Word: Lines.Normal_Line);
  -- Purpose: This is the next word in the sentence.
  --   When it puts the word into the line to be printed, the package
  --   will add a trailing blank.
  procedure End_Paragraph;
  -- Purpose: Prints out any partially filled line.
end Line_Format;
```

This package is designed to format the words in a paragraph into lines. Whenever adding a word would cause the length of the line to be exceeded, that line is printed and the word will appear at the start of the next line printed.

5.13. Write a procedure **Find_Lower_Case** that has two parameters, a **Normal_Line** and an integer variable. The procedure says where the first lower case letter is found in the line. It does this by placing a number into the integer variable that indicates the position of this first lower case letter. If there are no lower case letters in the line, a **0** should be placed in the integer variable.

5.14. Write a procedure **Find_Largest** that takes an array of integers and an integer variable. The procedure places the value of the largest integer in the array into the integer variable.

5.15. Write a postfix calculator package. "Postfix" means that the operands precede the operators. For example, the sequence "**2 3 + 4 ***" yields the value **20** because the **+** adds the operands **2** and **3** producing the operand value **5**. The ***** then multiplies the operand **5** and the operand **4**. In our calculator, a maximum of two operands are allowed to be stored pending an operation. Use the following declaration:

```
package Calculator is
  procedure Add_Operand(Operand: INTEGER);
  -- Purpose: This integer is the next operand.
  procedure Execute_Operator(Operator: CHARACTER);
  -- Purpose: Execute this operator. The four valid operands are:
  --   '+' '-' '*' which take two operands and produce one, and '=' which
  --   takes one operand, prints it and leaves nothing.
end Calculator;
```

The package will have to keep track of whether it currently has none, one or two operands. "**2 3 + 4 ***" is produced by sequence of calls:

```
Add_Operand(2);
 Add_Operand(3);
Execute_Operator('+');
Add_Operand(4);
Execute_Operator('*');
Execute_Operator('=');
```

The execution of `'*'` is what actually produces the value **20**, but it is the execution of `'='` that prints that value and removes it from the package, so that afterwards the package is not holding any operands.

5.16. Write a package with the following specification:

```
with Lines;
package Word_Buffer is
-- Purpose: This package stores a line of words. Its utilities may be
-- used to modify the contents of that line.
  subtype Word is Lines.Normal_Line;
  procedure Set_Line(Source: Word);
  -- Purpose: Sets the stored line to the given value.
  -- It erases whatever was previously stored.
  procedure Get_Word(Where: Word_Number; The_Word: Word);
  -- Purpose: Removes the specified word from the line. A copy of the word
  -- is placed in The_Word.
  procedure Insert_Word (Source: Word; Where: Word_Number);
  -- Purpose: Inserts the specified word into the line. Where indicates
  -- which word number this word will be. The value of Source followed by
  -- a single space is inserted.
  procedure Write_Buffer;
  -- Purpose: Writes a line containing what is currently stored.
end Word_Buffer;
```

Internally the package stores a line containing words. Calls to the package procedures modify this line as indicated in the declaration. A call to **Set_Line** must occur before any other calls to this package.

5.17. Build a page-formatting package with the following declaration:

```
package Page_Formatter is
--Purpose: Produce formatted pages with numbered lines.
  procedure Set_Page_Length(Length: Line_Count);
  -- Purpose: Set the length of a page.
  procedure Set_Page_Heading(Title: Normal_Line);
  -- Purpose: Set the heading printed at the top of each page.
  procedure Write(Next_Line: Normal_Line);
  -- Purpose: Add this line to the document.
end Page_Formatter;
```

The format of a page is a title line (not numbered) followed by a blank line. After this blank line, there is a page of lines numbered from 1 to the page length that has been set. After these lines there is a blank line, followed a line containing the page number, followed by another blank line. (This last symbolizes skipping to a new page.) Test the package with a program that sets the page length to a small number (such as 3) and writes about 9 lines (3 pages).

6

Intermediate Control Structures and Information Passing

6.1 OBJECTIVES

This chapter completes several of the topics developed in previous chapters. We complete the discussion of information passing by introducing additional capabilities for getting information into and out of subprograms (sections 3 and 4). The remaining loop capabilities are introduced which, together with previously examined loop constructs, allow great flexibility in loop construction (section 5). We summarize loops with a discussion on how to choose the most appropriate construct (section 6). For the sake of complete coverage of control structures, the chapter discusses the goto statement (section 7). We consider the two remaining Boolean operations (section 8). These operations provide special capabilities that simplify many common Boolean expressions.

In addition, we touch on one new subject: real numbers (section 9). Ada has extremely powerful and complex capabilities with fractional numbers, but for several chapters we shall limit our use to the simplest cases.

CONCEPTS:

- Loop constructs have great flexibility.
- In some cases of Boolean expressions, a test should be made only if a previous test was successful.
- Some subprograms can be called in order to get information back.
- Not all numbers are integers: some have fractional parts.

GOALS:

- Declare and use a function.
- Use a loop with an exit statement.
- Use short-circuit control forms.
- Use floating point numbers.

6.2 MOTIVATION

Information handling is critical to many programs, and incorrect information handling is a common source of errors. As programming languages have evolved, a good deal of attention has been paid to tools for limiting access to information as a means of reducing the number of errors in a program. Ada contains many constructs for limiting access to information. The capabilities for information hiding and passing introduced so far are extended further to support easy and effective limitation of information flow. One desirable feature is the capability of passing a variable into a procedure in a manner which permits the variable to be updated. Another is to provide the programmer the ability to declare *functions*.

Some problems are not appropriate for either of the two loop schemata we have examined thus far. To express these problems naturally, Ada provides some flexible loop constructs, including the *exit* statement. These constructs are quite powerful, and it is easy to write extremely unreadable code using them. However, carefully used, they may make a program simpler and more understandable. Another enhancement of control structure capabilities requires additional Boolean operations. We shall show how these *short-circuit* operations can simplify the structure of a program.

Toward the end of the chapter, we consider another class of numeric types, the *real types*. We limit our discussion to a single type from this class. Real types extend the numeric capabilities of Ada by providing the ability to handle numbers with fractional parts.

In general, the chapter takes useful capabilities we have already seen and extends them to make them even more useful.

6.3 FUNCTIONS (2): DECLARATIONS

In Ada, there are two kinds of subprograms, procedures and functions. Now, we review how to call functions and discuss how to declare them. Functions are similar to procedures, yet the differences between them are important. The most obvious difference is that a function *returns* a single value while a procedure does not. We have already seen some functions which were declared for us. A simple function from the **Lines** package is the function **Length**. **Length** is passed a **Normal_Line**, and the value it returns is the length of that **Normal_Line**. For example, if **Sentence** is a **Normal_Line** variable containing **"Tuesday"**, the call **Length(Sentence)** would return an integer whose value is 7. We have typically used functions like **Length** in situations such as

```
for I in INTEGER range 1..Length(Sentence) loop ...
```

where we wanted to examine every character in a line.

Notice that, like a procedure, a function is called (invoked) by using its name and supplying any necessary parameters. A function may be called anywhere an expression can be used. In the preceding for schema, an expression can be used to define the range of the schema, therefore a function can be used to define the range.

As mentioned in Chapter 3, the statement

```
Length(Sentence) := 4;   --illegal
```

is not legal. The function **Length** returns an **INTEGER**; it does not return a variable in which you can store the value 4.

Since a value may appear in expressions, such as the **4** and **5** in

```
4 * 3 + 5
```

you could use function calls in the same situation, as in:

```
Fn(3) * 3 + Fn(1);
```

The same restriction applies as for anything else that has a value in this position; the value must be of the appropriate type. Therefore, to be used in an integer expression, **Fn** must be a function that returns an integer.

Ada allows the programmer to declare functions. The syntax for a function declaration is shown in Figure 6–1. Notice that it is similar to the syntax for declaring a procedure. The two differences are that (1) the function declaration begins with the reserved word **function**, and (2) the function declaration specifies the type of the value returned. As with procedures, a function can have a declaration that is separate from its body. Indeed, the function declaration could occur in a package declaration, while the function body occurs in the corresponding package body.

Two other differences between function and procedure declarations are not shown in the syntax diagram. First, function parameters can only be of mode **in**, and second, a function must execute a return statement. These points are illustrated in the two programs which follow.

The function **Triple** in Program 6–1 has one integer parameter, and it *returns* an integer value. The type of the value returned must match the type the function specification claims you will return. Thus, the expression "**Number * 3**" in the return statement must be of type **INTEGER** to be legal.

Furthermore, the return statement is executed. The syntax for the return statement is found in Figure 6–2. Execution of the return statement consists of two parts. First,

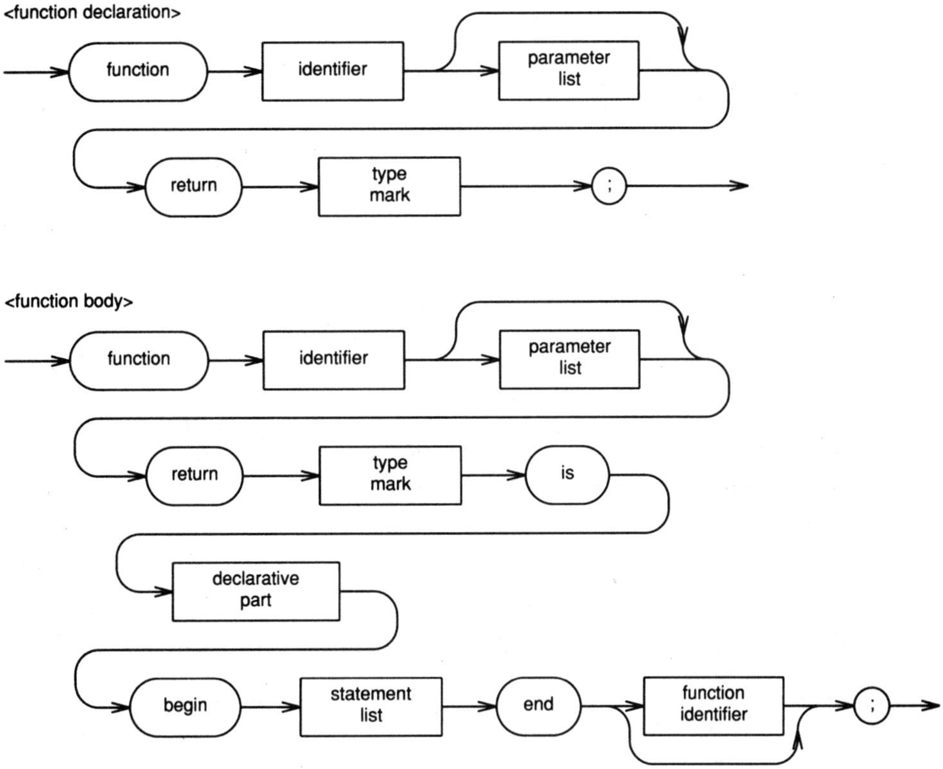

Figure 6–1

the return statement for a function contains an expression. The expression is evaluated, and the value computed is the value the function returns. Second, the return statement causes execution to switch from the function, which is now completed, to the point at which the function was called.

```
with Simple_IO;
procedure Function_Demo_1 is
  function Triple(Number: INTEGER) return INTEGER is
  begin
    return Number * 3;
  end Triple;
begin
  Simple_IO.Write(Triple(6));
end Function_Demo_1;
```

Program 6–1

In **Function_Demo_1** of Program 6–1, the call **Triple(6)** returns the value 18. Because this call is used to supply a parameter to the **Write** procedure, 18 becomes the value of the actual parameter to **Write** and, as a consequence, is printed.

<return statement>

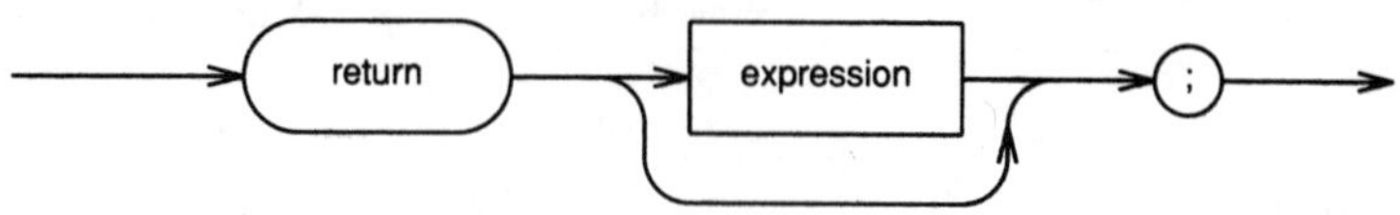

Figure 6–2

In Program 6–2, a more complex function is computed. The function **Has_Blank** (lines 5–13) has one parameter, of type **Normal_Line**, and returns a Boolean value. The function returns **TRUE** if the line contains a blank and **FALSE** if it does not contain a blank.

Remember that execution of a function is terminated when a return statement is executed. Thus, if a blank is found, the if statement in lines 8–10 will cause the return at line 9 to be executed. Because this return statement contains the simple Boolean expression **TRUE**, the value **TRUE** will be returned if this statement is executed.

```
 1:with Simple_IO, Lines;
 2:procedure Function_Demo_2 is
 3:   use Lines;
 4:   Sentence: Normal_Line;

 5:   function Has_Blank(Line: Normal_Line) return BOOLEAN is
 6:   begin
 7:     for I in INTEGER range 1..Length(Line) loop
 8:       if A_Character(Line, I) = ' ' then
 9:         return TRUE;
10:       end if;
11:     end loop;
12:     return FALSE;
13:   end Has_Blank;

14:begin
15:   Simple_IO.Read(Sentence);
16:   if Has_Blank(Sentence) then
17:     Simple_IO.Write("Has a blank");
18:   else
19:     Simple_IO.Write("Has no blanks");
20:   end if;
21:end Function_Demo_2;.
```

Program 6–2

The return statement causes execution of the function to terminate. This means that execution immediately shifts back to the point where the function was called. In Program 6–2, execution of the return at line 9 causes execution to shift back to line 16. Obviously, this means that execution of the loop in lines 7–11 immediately terminates.

If a blank is never encountered, the loop exits after examining all the characters in the line. In this case, the statement following the loop (line 12) is executed. This causes the value **FALSE** to be returned by the function. In either case, the value returned is used in the expression containing the function. Since the expression in line 16 contains only the function call, if the value **TRUE** is returned, line 17 will be executed. If the value **FALSE** is returned, line 19 will be executed.

```
with Simple_IO, Lines;
procedure Count_Characters is
  use Lines;
  Char: CHARACTER;
  Line: Normal_Line;

  function Count(Ch: CHARACTER; Str: Normal_Line) return INTEGER is
  -- Purpose: Count the number of times a character is found in
  -- a line. Ch: The character to find.
  --   Str: The line to search.
    Current_Count: INTEGER := 0; --Count thus far
  begin
    for I in INTEGER range 1..Length(Str) loop
      if A_Character(Str, I) = Ch then
        Current_Count := Current_Count + 1;
      end if;
    end loop;
    return Current_Count;
  end Count;

begin
  Simple_IO.Write("Character? ");  Simple_IO.Read(Char);
  Simple_IO.Write("String? ");     Simple_IO.Read(Line);
  Simple_IO.Write("Count = ");  Simple_IO.Write(Count(Char,Line));
end Count_Characters;
```

Program 6–3

The function **Count** shown in Program 6–3 has two parameters, one of type **CHARACTER** and one of type **Normal_Line**. It returns the number of occurrences of the character in the line. It computes this number in a local variable, then returns the value it has computed. Notice that **Count** calls the functions **Length** and **A_Character** from the package **Lines**.

Functions must execute a return statement in order to terminate normally. If a function reaches the end of its body without a return statement being executed, a **PRO-**

GRAM_ERROR occurs. Care should thus be taken to ensure that each function will execute a return statement.

Procedures may also contain return statements. However, since procedures do not return values, an expression is not allowed in such a return statement. As with functions, execution of a return statement in a procedure immediately causes execution to shift to the point at which the procedure was called. Recall that the other method of returning from a procedure is for execution to reach the end of its body. As far as the caller of the procedure is concerned, it makes no difference by which of these methods the procedure has completed its execution. The caller knows only that the procedure has finished its job and that it may now resume execution.

6.4 PARAMETERS (3): MODE IN OUT, DEFAULT VALUES

Two valuable aspects of parameters are a mode that allows a variable to be updated, and the ability to allow the omission of certain actual parameters. We now examine these aspects in detail.

6.4.1 Mode In Out

Before presenting the last of the parameter modes, **in out**, let us briefly review the parameter modes we have already examined. The full syntax for the specification of a subprogram parameter is given in Figure 6–3.

<subprogram parameter specification>

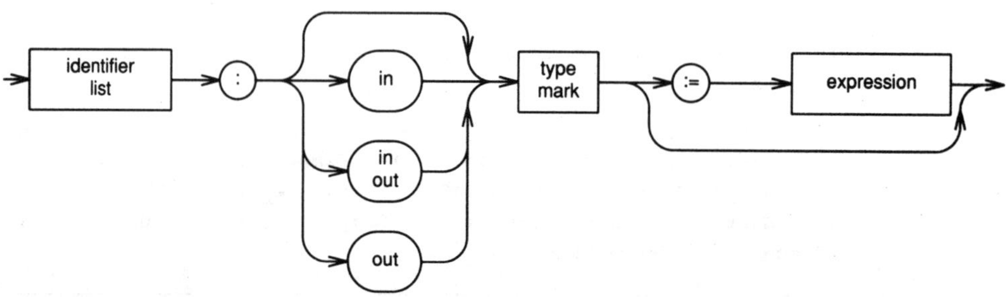

Figure 6–3

The parameter mode **in** is a method of communicating information into a procedure or function. In this mode, the formal parameter is *initialized* to the value of the actual parameter. Within the procedure, the formal parameter acts as a local constant.

The parameter mode **out** is a method of communicating information out of a procedure. The actual parameter associated with a parameter of mode **out** must be a variable (or a parameter of mode **in out** or **out**). Within the procedure, the formal parameter can be used in such a way as to give a value to the actual parameter. Because mode **out** supplies one-way communication out of a procedure, no value may be obtained from the parameter within the procedure.

The parameter mode **in out** allows two-way communication. Using this mode, the procedure can both receive and return values. As with mode **out**, the actual parameter must be a variable (or a parameter of mode **in out**) of the correct type. The effect of mode **in out** is to allow the procedure to read *and* change the value associated with the actual parameter. Thus, the principal use of **in out** parameters is to update the actual parameter.

As with the other modes, the mode **in out** is specified just in front of the type, as shown in the following examples:

```
procedure W(A: in out INTEGER);
procedure X(B: in INTEGER; C, D: in out INTEGER);
procedure Y(E, F: in out BOOLEAN; G: out CHARACTER);
procedure Z(H: out INTEGER; I: INTEGER);
```

If multiple parameters of the same type have different modes, their specifications must be separated. In the preceding examples, the parameter **B** of procedure **X** must be in a separate list from the parameters **C** and **D** because **B** is of mode **in** while **C** and **D** are of mode **in out**. Similarly, in procedure **Z**, the variables **H** and **I** must occur in separate lists because they are of different modes. Notice that **C** and **D** can occur in the same identifier list because they are of the same mode and the same type.

```
 1:with Simple_IO;
 2:procedure In_Out_Parameters is
 3:   Global_Var: INTEGER := 0;
 4:   Was_4: INTEGER := 4;

 5:   procedure Change_It(X: in out INTEGER) is
 6:   begin
 7:      X := X + 1;
 8:   end Change_It;

 9:begin
10:   Change_It(Global_Var);
11:   Simple_IO.Write(Global_Var);
12:   Change_It(Was_4);
13:   Simple_IO.Write(Was_4);
14:end In_Out_Parameters;
```

Program 6–4

The semantics of **in out** parameters is illustrated in the procedure **In_Out_Parameters** shown in Program 6–4. In this procedure, **Global_Var** is the actual parameter of the first call to **Change_It** (line 10). On entry into the procedure, **Global_Var** contains the value 0. At line 7, **Change_It** uses the value of its parameter to compute a new value. The old value (0) plus one yields the new value (1). After exit from the procedure, the value of **Global_Var** has become 1. At line 12, a second call to **Change_It** occurs. This time, the variable **Was_4** is the actual parameter. At line 7, **Change_It** again uses the value of its parameter to compute a new value. Since the parameter's value is 4, the result is a new value of 5. After exit from the procedure, the value of the **Was_4** has become 5. During this second call to **Change_It**, the value of **Global_Var** was *not* changed because it was not the actual parameter used in the call.

Note that, because the actual parameter must refer to a variable, the call

```
Change_It(3);   -- illegal
```

would be a syntax error.

```
 1:with Simple_IO;
 2:procedure When_Does_It_Change is
 3:   Global_Line: Normal_Line;

 4:   procedure Change_Line(X: in out Normal_Line) is
 5:   begin
 6:     Simple_IO.Read(X);
 7:     Simple_IO.Write(Global_Line);
 8:   end Change_Line;

 9:begin
10:   Simple_IO.Read(Global_Line);
11:   Change_Line(Global_Line);
12:   Simple_IO.Write(Global_Line);
13:end When_Does_It_Change;
```

Program 6–5

The fact that the variable used as the actual parameter is changed raises the question of exactly when the value of the actual parameter is updated. This becomes important if a variable serves as both an actual parameter and a variable whose value is used or changed in the procedure. For example, in the procedure **When_Does_It_Change** in Program 6–5, if changing the value of **X** immediately changes the actual parameter, the **Write** in line 7 will write the message just read. On the other hand, if the actual parameter is not changed until exit from the procedure, the original message will be printed.

For simple types, such as integers and characters, the value changes on exiting the procedure. Ada specifies that the initial value is copied in, and then the final value is copied out. For more complex types such as **Normal_Line**, the exact time of change is not specified. In procedure **When_Does_It_Change**, the value of **Global_Line** might be updated immediately, or it might be updated upon exit from the procedure. Ada does not define which one of these happens. Any program that depends on whether the change is immediate or at the end of the procedure is bad, but syntactically legal.

In Ada terminology such a program is *erroneous*. Ada allows (but does not require) an implementation to cause a **PROGRAM_ERROR** to occur if erroneous code is executed.

We have already used several procedures with parameters of mode **in out** from the **Lines** package. We introduced these procedures in Chapter 3, and we now repeat their declarations:

```
procedure Change(Source: in out Normal_Line; Position: Index;
                 Alteration: CHARACTER);
procedure Delete(A_Line: in out Normal_Line;  Start: Index;
                 Amount_Removed: Line_Size);
procedure Insert(Destination: in out Normal_Line; Insertion: Normal_Line;
                 Location: Line_Size);
```

Of course, the procedures do not reference any variables outside the **Lines** package. This means that they will never cause a program to be erroneous, although it is always possible to build an erroneous program that includes them. Note that each of the procedures modifies the **in out** parameter in a specific way.

6.4.2 Parameter Default Values

Parameters allow us to design flexible subprograms. Sometimes, however, this flexibility is only needed occasionally: Most of the time the programmer would prefer not to supply values for certain parameters, but instead, to allow the package to supply the appropriate values. For example, the **Location** function of the **Lines** package provides the capability to control the position in the line at which the search starts. Most of the time, the programmer wants the search to start at the beginning of the line. Being forced to always supply a parameter that nearly always has the value 1 would make **Location** more cumbersome to use.

We have seen that in Ada, you can supply an initial value to a variable at elaboration time. A related capability is available for parameters: Parameters of mode **in** may be supplied with a default value. The syntax is similar to supplying an initial value for variable or constant objects and is given in Figure 6–3. Consider the following procedure declaration:

```
procedure Default_Values(No_Default: INTEGER;
                         Default_Boolean: BOOLEAN := TRUE;
                         Default_A, Default_B: INTEGER := Initial_Value);
```

In the procedure **Default_Values**, there are four parameters, three of which are supplied default values. When we call the procedure, we may or may not supply values for these three parameters. For example, the call

```
Default_Values(4);
```

supplies the value 4 for the parameter **No_Default**, but gives no values for the other three parameters. When no value is supplied, a parameter assumes its default value.

So in the case of this call, **Default_Boolean** would assume the value **TRUE** while **Default_A** and **Default_B** would both assume the value **Initial_Value**. Here, **Initial_Value** could be any expression of type **INTEGER**. In fact, as with initial values for variables, any expression compatible with the type **INTEGER** (such as **2*Initial_Value+1**) could be used.

As in the case with variables,

```
Default_A, Default_B: INTEGER := Initial_Value
```

is a shorthand method for writing

```
Default_A: INTEGER := Initial_Value;
Default_B: INTEGER := Initial_Value;
```

Specifically, if **Initial_Value** is a function, the function is called twice. The rule is that the default expression is evaluated only if the parameter is omitted. Thus, if we supplied a value for **Default_A** but not for **Default_B**, the expression **Initial_Value** would be evaluated only once. This means that if **Initial_Value** were a function, it would only be called once.

In the call

```
Default_Values(5, FALSE);
```

both **No_Default** and **Default_Boolean** are explicitly supplied values, while **Default_A** and **Default_B** assume their default values. Because with positional association the association is in order, proceeding from left to right, you will usually want to place the parameters with defaults last in the parameter list. Furthermore, you will usually want to place the least used parameters last among those with defaults. However, with named association, any of the parameters may be supplied explicit values. For example:

```
Default_Values(5, Default_B => 9);
```

supplies an explicit value for **Default_B**, leaving **Default_Boolean** and **Default_A** to assume their default values.

One restriction on default expressions is that they cannot use formal parameters from the parameter list in which they occur. For example, the default expression for **Default_A** and **Default_B** could not contain **No_Default**. Thus,

```
procedure Z(No_Default: INTEGER;
            Default_A: INTEGER := No_Default); --illegal
```

is not legal.

In the case of the **Location** function from the **Lines** package, the declaration, including defaults, is

```
function Location(Fragment: in Normal_Line;  Source: in Normal_Line;
                  Start: in POSITIVE := 1;
                  Which_Occurrence: in POSITIVE := 1) return NATURAL;
```

Notice that there are two parameters which assume default values. The first parameter, **Start**, tells at what position in **Source** the search is to start. The default is to start at the first position. The second parameter, **Which_Occurrence**, permits us to specify which occurrence of **Fragment** the function is to report. If we ask for the location of the third occurrence and there are only two occurrences, the function will report the value 0, indicating that a third occurrence was not found. If we do not specify a particular occurrence, the location of the first occurrence will be returned.

There is an appropriate place to use each of the methods for passing information that Ada possesses. Mode **in out** should be used only when the procedure modifies the variable on the basis of its existing value. Mode **in** should be used when values are brought into the subprogram. Mode **out** and functions should be used to return values from the subprogram. Functions must be used when the value returned is expected to be used directly in an expression. In most other cases, mode **out** is easier for the reader of the program to understand.

6.5 ITERATION (3): LOOP AND EXIT

Suppose you are in a loop and have just discovered that conditions require that the iteration terminate at a place other than at the top of the loop. The exit statement provides a method for such termination. The syntax of the exit statement is given in Figure 6–4.

Execution of the exit statement terminates iteration of the loop and causes the statements following the loop to be executed. For example, in a loop, the if statement

```
if X > 5 then
  Simple_IO.Write("Good-bye");
  exit;
end if;
```

would cause the loop to terminate whenever it was executed with a value of **X** greater than 5.

The simple conditional exit is so common that a special form of the exit statement is provided. The conditional execution of the exit statement in the if statement

```
if J = 4 then
  exit;
end if;
```

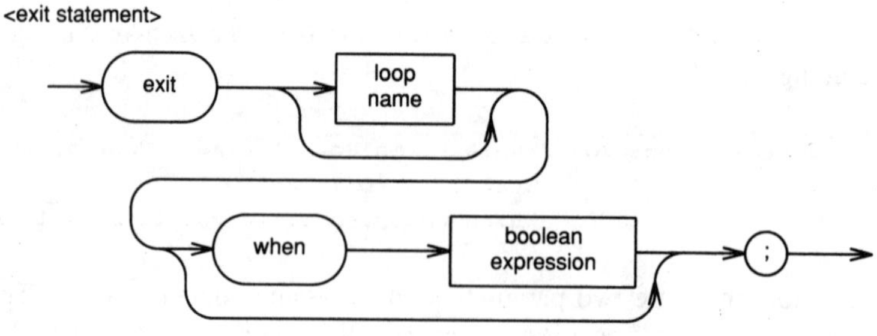

Figure 6–4

can also be written as

```
exit when J = 4;
```

Both of these statements cause exit of the loop when the condition **J=4** is satisfied. The second statement, however, is usually easier to understand when reading a program.

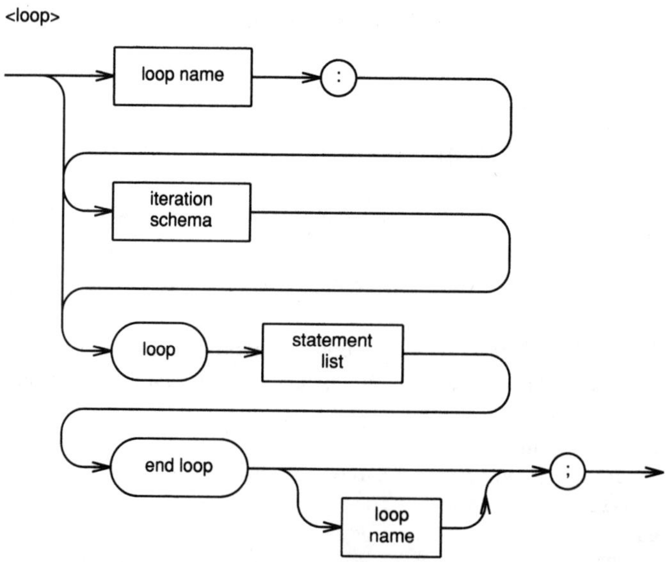

Figure 6–5

The full syntax for loop constructs is given in Figure 6–5. In previous chapters, we have always attached an iteration schema, either the for schema or the while schema, to the loop. Observe from the syntax diagram that an iteration schema is optional and there is also an optional loop name which will be discussed shortly. A schema is a plan. Loops with iteration schemata have a predefined plan for terminating iteration. Loops without such schemata have no predefined plan for terminating iteration, rather, they must rely on an exit statement, return statement, or error for such termination.

For some loops an iteration schema is not appropriate, particularly for loops in which the natural place to discover that the loop should be terminated is in the middle of the sequence of statements. We illustrate such a loop by considering the following problem: You wish to read a yes or no character and refuse all others. In order to do this, you must read characters until you have received either a yes or a no indication. This may be accomplished by the following loop:

```
loop
  Simple_IO.Read(Ch);
  exit when Ch = 'Y' or Ch = 'N';
  Simple_IO.New_Line;
  Simple_IO.Write("Sorry, Please answer Y or N");
end loop;
```

In this loop, a character is read. If it is an acceptable character, we leave the loop and continue execution at the statement immediately following "**end loop;**". If the character is not acceptable, we print an error message and read again. The error message should not occur before reading a character because the message may be unnecessary. This means that the natural place for the read is at the beginning of the loop, and the natural place for the exit is following the read, but before the error message.

When you use an exit in the preceding manner, the immediately enclosing loop is the one that is terminated. This rule is critical when loops are nested, as in the following example:

```
loop
  Simple_IO.Read(I);
  exit when I < 10;      -- Leave outer loop
  loop
    Simple_IO.Read(Ch);
    exit when Ch = 'Q'; -- Leave inner loop
  end loop;
  Simple_IO.New_Line; -- Comes after inner loop exits
end loop;
```

In these nested loops, the inner loop exit (**exit when Ch='Q';**) causes program execution to leave the inner loop and execute the **New_Line** call. Since execution is still within the outer loop, the program then goes back to **Read(I)**. The outer loop exit (**exit when I < 10;**) causes iteration of the outer loop to stop, and execution resumes immediately following the outer loop.

For some problems, an exit for an outer loop will need to be executed from within an inner loop. To achieve this, we need a way to identify which loop to exit. In Ada, it is possible to name a loop. As indicated by the syntax shown in Figure 6–4, the exit statement can refer to this name. If we want to modify the previous nested structure so that a **Q** results in an exit from the outer loop, we could rewrite these loops as follows:

```
Outer:
  loop
    Simple_IO.Read(I);
    exit when I < 10;
Inner:
    loop
      Simple_IO.Read(Ch);
      exit Outer when Ch = 'Q';
    end loop Inner;
    Simple_IO.New_Line; --can't get here
  end loop Outer;
```

Here, both loops have been given names, and one of the exit statements specifies one of those names. If an exit statement specifies a loop name, then the program exits the loop indicated by the name. Obviously, all loops nested inside the one you exit are also exited. In the preceding example, exiting of the loop labeled **Outer** also exits the loop labeled **Inner**. This reconstruction has a side effect: The exit which causes termination of the outer loop is the only way out of the inner loop. Thus, there is no way execution can reach the **New_Line** statement. Observe also that the label **Inner** is not used and could be removed. If the loop is labeled, the **end loop** *must* be followed by the loop label.

An exit statement may be used in conjunction with an iteration schema. When the exit statement is executed, iteration of the loop terminates immediately, regardless of the iteration schema. This is illustrated by the following example:

```
Outer:
  for I in INTEGER range 1..10 loop -- caution, exit used!
Inner:
    loop
      Simple_IO.Read(Ch);
      exit when Ch = 'Y' or Ch = 'N';
      exit Outer when Ch = 'Q';
    end loop Inner;
    Simple_IO.New_Line;
  end loop Outer;
```

Here, a **Y** or **N** exits the inner loop, but execution remains within the outer loop. The outer loop is controlled by a for schema and will terminate when it has performed 10 iterations. However, reading a **Q** within the inner loop terminates the outer loop regardless of the number of iterations performed thus far. A comment warning the reader should appear whenever an exit statement is used in a loop containing a schema.

A number of restrictions apply as to where a loop exit can be located. However, since all of these restrictions are related to what can be done with block statements, these are covered in Chapter 7, which discusses such statements. For now, an exit must be within the loop it causes an exit from.

A loop name can be used as a qualifier to reference a loop parameter. In the nested loops

```
Outer:
  for I in INTEGER range 1..10 loop
Inner:
    for I in INTEGER range 1..10 loop
      Simple_IO.Write(Outer.I);
    end loop Inner;
  end loop Outer;
```

an unqualified reference to **I** inside the inner loop would refer to the loop parameter of the inner loop. Using the capability in Ada that allows us to qualify the reference by the loop name, we have used **Outer.I** within the inner loop to refer to the loop parameter of the outer loop. In Ada terminology, loop parameters, like variables and procedures in package declarations, may be directly visible or may be visible by selection. Within the inner loop, the inner loop parameter is directly visible, while the outer loop parameter is visible by selection. Because such qualification makes it more difficult to read the program we suggest each loop parameter have a unique and meaningful identifier.

6.6 SUMMARY OF LOOPS

Each loop structure has its own peculiar advantages and disadvantages; consequently, each is appropriate in a certain set of circumstances.

The while schema conducts a potentially complex test at the top of a loop. Before each iteration, the test is performed before entering the loop. If the test evaluates to true, the iteration is performed. Because the test is before entry, there is the possibility that the loop body may not be entered at all.

The for schema defines a loop parameter. A range is determined, and then the loop is executed once for each value in the range. If the range is empty, the loop body is not executed. The loop parameter is a local constant within the loop. You can cause the loop parameter to run through the range in reverse.

In both the while schema and the for schema, an exit statement can be used to cause premature termination of the loop. If neither schema is specified, the loop continues iteration until an exit statement is executed. Any loop can be named. This name can also be used by the exit statement to specify which loop is exited, and it can also be used to qualify a reference to the loop parameter.

The general rules for choosing a loop construct are:

1. Choose the *for schema* when, upon loop entry, you can compute the number of repetitions that need to be performed.
2. Choose the *while schema* whenever you can terminate at the top of the loop and the for schema is inappropriate.
3. Choose the general *loop* construct only when the others are inappropriate.

6.7 THE GOTO STATEMENT

Some early programming languages supplied only the one control construct:

```
if condition goto label
```

This construct would test the condition and if the condition was true, execution would continue at (go to) the labeled statement. If the condition was false, execution would continue at the next statement.

It soon became apparent that programs written with statements such as for loops, while loops, and Ada's form of the if statement usually had fewer errors and were easier to understand. This began one of the earliest controversies of software engineering: the "go to controversy." Two interesting papers about this controversy are "Go To Statement Considered Harmful," by E. W. Dijkstra (*Communications of the ACM*, March 1968) and "Structured Programming with Go To Statements," by D. E. Knuth (*ACM Computing Surveys*, December 1974).

Currently, the consensus seems to be that programs written with goto's tend to jump all over the place and consequently lack an easily understandable structure.

Occasionally, there are subprograms that cannot be implemented easily or efficiently without a goto statement. Therefore, Ada supplies the **goto** statement which transfers execution to the label referred to by the statement. We shall not give any examples of programs that use goto statements because such statements are so rarely useful and all programs can be written without them anyway. For the syntax of the goto statement and the associated labels, see the Ada language reference manual.

6.8 BOOLEAN EXPRESSIONS (2): SHORT-CIRCUIT CONTROL FORMS

In Chapter 4, we introduced some of the operations used in Boolean expressions. We now consider the remaining operations.

Very often, you want to test a condition only if another condition holds. For example, only if there are at least *i* characters in a line do we want to check the *i*-th character of the line to see whether it is an **'A'**. In Ada, two constructs are provided for such checking. Since the evaluation of the second condition occurs only some of the time, the evaluation of the Boolean expression can be cut short as soon as it is known that the answer is true or false. Ada calls these constructs *short-circuit control forms*.

The first short-circuit form is **and then** whose syntax is given in Figure 6–6. The **and then** form declares that the program should check the second condition only if the first is true. Thus, this form allows us to replace the construct

```
if Boolean_Expression_1 then
  if Boolean_Expression_2 then
    ...
  end if;
end if;
```

<boolean expression (completed)>

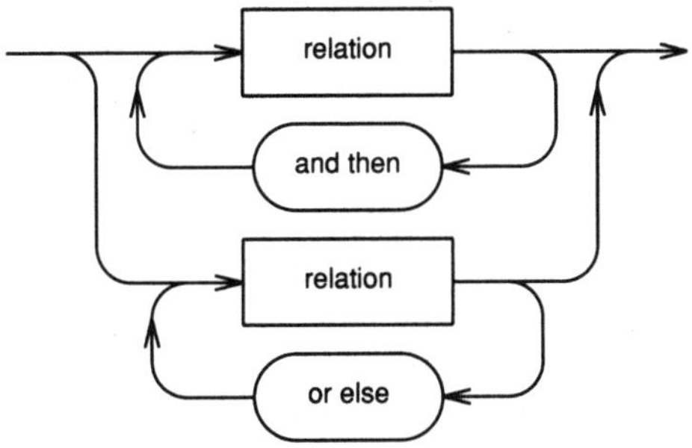

Figure 6–6

with the simpler construct

```
if Boolean_Expression_1 and then Boolean_Expression_2 then
  ...
end if;
```

Notice that the principal reason for the first construct is to prevent the second Boolean expression from being evaluated when the first Boolean expression is false. This goal is achieved much more simply by the second construct. How this is useful is illustrated by the following loop:

```
while Length(S) > 0 and then A_Character(S, 1) = ' ' loop
  Delete(S, 1, 1);
end loop;
```

This loop deletes all leading blanks from a **Normal_Line**. The algorithm is simple: If the leading character is a blank, delete it. However, if there are no characters in **S**, the test to see whether the first character is a blank would cause an error. So the loop condition specifies: First, check to make sure that there are some characters. If there are, check to see whether the first character is a blank. Running out of characters terminates the loop because the length of **S** becomes 0. Most importantly, if **S** has length 0, then the check on the first character is not performed. Of course, running out of leading blanks also terminates the loop.

To see how useful this idea is, try constructing the loop without the **and then** construct. In order to be safe, you do not want the character check to occur as part of the condition of the while schema. This forces you to use a program structure that is more complicated and harder to read.

The second short-circuit form is **or else**, whose syntax diagram is also found in Figure 6–6. The **or else** form checks the second condition only if the first condition is found to be false. For example, if we want a loop to terminate if either no command was given or the command to quit was given, this could be achieved by the statement

```
exit when Length(S) = 0 or else A_Character(S, 1) = 'Q';
```

The first check is for the absence of a command. If there is no command, then **Length(S)=0** and the Boolean expression will be true regardless of the value of the second operand. In this case, because a short-circuit form was used the second operand is not evaluated. The loop is exited either when no characters are found in **S** or when the first character in **S** is a **Q**, but the important accomplishment of the short-circuit control form is to avoid checking for a character when none exists.

As indicated by the syntax, and as is the case for logical operators, you can have multiple short-circuit control forms in a single Boolean expression provided that all the operations are of the same kind. Thus,

```
I > 0 and then 3 / I > 2 and then J < 0 and then 1 / J < -4
```

is a syntactically legal **and then** expression. In this multiple short-circuit control form, the first condition is evaluated, and then, only if it is true is the second condition evaluated. Only if the second condition also evaluates to true is the third condition evaluated, and so on.

The precedence of both **and then** and **or else** is the same as that of the logical operators **and**, **or**, and **xor**. The restrictions are also identical to those for logical operators. That is, **and then** and **or else** cannot be mixed with each other or with other Boolean operations without explicitly indicating the order of evaluation by means of parentheses.

6.9 REAL NUMBERS (1)

Many computations performed in the realm of science use numbers that are not integers. These numbers have fractional parts, as for example, in the number "3.14159". In noncomputer applications, there is a decimal point somewhere within these *real* numbers.

Ada allows a special kind of number with a fractional part. A predefined type associated with these numbers is the type **FLOAT**. In fact, **FLOAT** belongs to a particular class of real numbers called *floating point numbers*. In addition to the capabilities briefly described in this section there are many other capabilities and complexities of floating point numbers. Chapter 14 considers real numbers in more detail.

As is the case with many other types, there are real literals. Real literals must have decimal points such as, for example, in **1.5** or **3.14159**. The decimal point is required, so we must write **1.0** when we want a real value of one. There must be at least one digit before and after the decimal point.

Real literals may have exponents such as **2.0E3** or **6.023E23**. These exponents behave in the same way as exponents in scientific notation. The real literal **2.0E3** is the same as 2.0×10^3 in scientific notation, or 2000.0. As with scientific notation, negative exponents are also allowed. So **5.0E-2** is a real literal representing the value 5.0×10^{-2}, or 0.05.

The type **FLOAT** and its associated operations are predefined in the package **STANDARD**. You can declare variables of type **FLOAT**, as in

```
Radius, Circumference: FLOAT;
```

as well as constants of type **FLOAT**, as in

```
Pi: constant FLOAT := 3.14159;
Avagadro: constant FLOAT := 6.023E23;
Planck: constant FLOAT := 6.626E-27;
Gravity : constant FLOAT := 6.67E+8;
```

Real types are scalar types, so variables and subtypes of any real type, including **FLOAT**, may have range constraints. Constraints on the type **FLOAT** behave like constraints on any other scalar type, that is, any attempt to assign a value that is outside the range results in a **CONSTRAINT_ERROR**. Ranges for variables of type **FLOAT** may be specified using the full notation available for real literals:

```
Y: FLOAT range 0.0 .. 7.9;
subtype Tiny_Number is FLOAT range 0.0 .. 1.0E-13;
Z: Tiny_Number;
```

In addition, as with other types, the bounds on the range may be specified by any expression of type **FLOAT**.

Of course, there are floating point expressions and assignments, as in

```
Circumference := 2.0 * Pi * Radius;
```

Many of the normal arithmetic operators, including **+**, **-**, *****, and **/**, may also be used with **FLOAT**. However, **rem** and **mod** apply only to integers. The operator ****** also applies to floating point numbers, but the exponent must be an integer. Note that

```
2.0 + 2.0
```

returns the floating point value **4.0**, while

```
2 + 2
```

returns the integer value **4**.

From these last statements, we see that the **+** operator has two meanings. One of these takes two integer parameters and returns an integer value. The other takes two floating point parameters and returns a floating point value. In Ada, an operator with multiple meanings is said to be *overloaded*. The operators **+**, **-**, *****, **/**, and ******, are overloaded in the package **STANDARD** because multiple meanings are defined for each of them. Overloading is a complicated subject that will be discussed more fully in

Chapters 8 and 11. The point here is that

```
2 + 2.0
```

is a syntax error: There is no predefined overloading of the **+** operator in **package STANDARD** for mixtures of **FLOAT** and **INTEGER** types.

Since you occasionally need to convert between **INTEGER** and **FLOAT**, Ada provides a syntax for such a conversion. The instance of this syntax we introduce now is

```
FLOAT(2)
```

which converts the **INTEGER** value 2 to a **FLOAT** value. An example of how such a conversion could be used is

```
Circumference := FLOAT(2) * Pi * Radius;
```

As with other types, numbers of type **FLOAT** may be passed as parameters. They behave exactly as do other parameters, including requiring that a **FLOAT** formal parameter must be matched by a **FLOAT** actual parameter (and not an **INTEGER**). **FLOAT** is a simple type, so when it is used as the type of an **in out** parameter, the value of the actual parameter will be changed on exiting the procedure. The package **Simple_IO** handles values of type **FLOAT**.

```
with Simple_IO;
procedure Average is
  Total: FLOAT := 0.0;
  Next_Number: FLOAT;
  Count: NATURAL := 0;
  Continue: CHARACTER;
begin
  loop
    Simple_IO.Write("Enter a real number: ");
    Simple_IO.Read(Next_Number);
    Total := Total + Next_Number;
    Count:= Count + 1.0;
    Simple_IO.Write("Continue? (Y continues)");
    Simple_IO.Read(Continue);
    Simple_IO.New_Line;
    exit when Continue /= 'Y';
  end loop;
  Simple_IO.Write(Total / FLOAT(Count));
end Average;
```

Program 6–6

The type **FLOAT** is not discrete, a floating-point number does not have a discernible number that is its immediate successor (or predecessor). Therefore, type **FLOAT** cannot be used with the attributes **PRED** or **SUCC**, and neither can it be used as the type of a for loop parameter.

The procedure **Average** shown in Program 6–6 is an example of a computation using real numbers. This procedure computes the average of a series of real numbers. The average is computed in line 18 by dividing the total of all the numbers read (**Total**) by the number of numbers (**Count**). Each time a number is read, its value is added to **Total** and the **Count** is incremented by one. For example, if the user enters the numbers **2.0**, **2.5**, and **3.0**, the average will be approximately **2.5**. We say *approximately* because computations with real numbers round. As a result of this rounding, the answer may not be exact.

6.9.1 Numeric Literals

As with real literals, exponent notation can be used with integer literals. Exponents in integer literals cannot have a minus sign; otherwise they behave the same as real literals. For example, the following integer literals yield the same value:

```
1234000
12340E2
1234E3
```

Note that even when using an exponent, a decimal point is not allowed in an integer literal.

In noncomputer applications, reading large numbers is made easier by the use of a comma to separate sets of three digits. In Ada, the underscore is used. For example, the above number could be written:

```
1_234_000
```

In this form, it is much easier to see that the number is slightly over a million. The rules for placement of underscores in numeric literals are similar to those for placing them in identifiers, that is, they must be embedded and not adjacent. Unlike underscores in identifiers, underscores in numeric literals do not affect the value of the literal. For example, all of the following represent the same numeric value:

```
12_34_000
12_340_00
12340_0_0
```

Of course, we do not necessarily recommend these forms, but bank account numbers, social security numbers and phone numbers are examples where appropriately placed separators are added to make numbers more readable.

Further, the underscore can be embedded in the exponent as in:

```
1234E0_3
```

In a real literal, underscores can be embedded in the integer before (the whole part), after (the fractional part) the decimal point or in the exponent. They are not allowed to be adjacent to each other, to the decimal point, to the **E** or to any sign preceding the exponent. As with integers, underscores do not affect the value of the literal.

6.10 PROGRAMMING PRACTICES

Information hiding avoids errors and increases clarity by hiding unnecessary details. Thus, a good programming practice is to avoid directly changing nonlocal variables. Instead, use parameters and return values.

Use the most specific method; that is, the method that most closely matches the problem. For example, do not use a parameter of mode **in out** unless the variable to be passed is to receive a new value based upon its old value. If its value is not to be changed, use mode **in**. If its new value does not depend on its old value, use mode **out**. Using the correct mode will help avoid errors and make the program easier to read.

The constructs we have examined are flexible enough to allow a single variable to be accessed in multiple ways. This is called the "aliasing problem." An example is when a program accesses a nonlocal variable directly and with a parameter of mode **in out** which has been passed the same nonlocal variable as its actual parameter. Such programming is poor practice because it encourages mistakes. Even though Ada requires a certain "copy-in, copy-out" behavior with scalar parameters, it is bad practice to build a program that depends on this behavior.

Be consistent about loop labeling. Labels can be useful as documentation, but another approach is to only label loops that are referred to by exit statements. In any case, as with procedure names, if a loop is labeled, a meaningful identifier should be selected. In addition, the use of exit should be limited to the most local loop whenever feasible. Exiting out of nested loops makes a program hard to understand and debug.

6.10.1 Problem Solving

Suppose we wish to write the function

```
function Square_Root(Number: FLOAT) return FLOAT;
```

which, given a number, returns the square root of that number. The first thing we should do is examine the problem and attempt to understand it fully. We immediately determine that what is needed is not the calculation of the exact square root, but rather an approximation of the square root. This is because we are dealing with values of type **FLOAT** and we know that these values are only approximate.

One of the mathematical definitions of the square root is: Y is the square root of X if $X = Y * Y$. Since we cannot exactly represent real numbers, we shall have to test for an inequality instead of for an equality. We shall say that Y is the square root of X if $Y * Y$ differs from X by less than $Fuzzy$, where $Fuzzy$ is a small tolerance value which says how close Y must be to the square root of X before we consider it a good approximation.

To find the square root of a number, we shall use a search technique called *binary search*. (Other methods are used in "real" square root routines.) In binary search, we know that the value we need is between two bounds, and guess that the correct value is the middle. If the middle value is not the correct value, we can use the middle value as a new bound (we know that the correct value is either higher or lower than the guess) and try again.

We can state this as an algorithm:

```
-- Binary Search: We know that the value is between High and Low.
loop
  (guess that the answer (Middle) is halfway between High and Low)
  (stop if Middle is close enough to the answer)
  if (Middle is too high) then
    High := Middle;
  else   -- Middle is too low
    Low := Middle;
  end if;
end loop;
```

To check whether the guess is close enough, we shall compute the difference between the square of the guess and the number. If this error is small, we are done. Otherwise, the direction of the error indicates whether the guess was too high or too low. Thus, we can fill in the loop as follows:

```
-- Binary Search: We know that the value is between High and Low.
loop
  -- Guess that the answer (Middle) is halfway between High and Low.
  Middle := (High + Low) / 2.0;
  -- Stop if Middle is close enough to the answer.
  Error := Number - Middle * Middle;
  if abs(Error) <= Fuzzy then
    return Middle;
  end if;
  -- Adjust the bounds of the search.
  if Error < 0.0 then
    High := Middle;
  else   -- Middle is too low
    Low := Middle;
  end if;
end loop;
```

We know that the square root is always between 1.0 and the **Number** we are taking the square root of, so we can initialize the low and high values as follows:

```
if Number <= 1.0 then
  Low := Number;
  High := 1.0;
else
  Low := 1.0;
  High := Number;
end if;
```

Now, before we can write a program based on this algorithm, we need to decide how to deal with two matters. First, our algorithm assumes that **Number** is at least 0.0, so we need to use a subtype to ensure this condition holds. We do this by placing the square root function within a package which declares a subtype of **FLOAT** that allows only nonnegative numbers and use that subtype for the parameter to the function.

The second thing we need to deal with is what the value for **Fuzzy** should be. Because of the way that **FLOAT** approximates real numbers, we must use a value of **Fuzzy** that is proportional to the number we are taking the square root of. We shall discuss this in more detail when we consider how Ada approximates real numbers in Chapter 14. Here, we shall use a constant called **Tolerance** which defines the proportionality we desire. Thus, **Fuzzy** will be **Tolerance*Number**. We shall use the value **0.001** for **Tolerance**. Finally, if a number is 0.0, its square root will 0.0.

The entire package is given in Program 6–7. The function **Square_Root** has a declaration that is separate from its body. Notice that the comments on the body describe the implementation, while the comments on the declaration do not.

Of course, binary search is a much more general algorithm than we have seen here. From this example, you could easily extend the algorithm to searching for the answer to any function over a scalar type such that the values increase from one end of the range to the other. (Mathematicians call this a monotonic function.)

One such extension allows us to quickly search an array of items, if the items are in order. For instance, if one kept a list of names in an array of **Normal_Line**s and needed to be able to quickly find the location of any name in the array, you could use binary search. This application is an instance of an increasing (or decreasing) function, where we think of the index as the input to the function and the names in the array as the values of the function.

If we are searching for a **Normal_Line**, we need to keep guessing a value for the index (**Middle**), and we compare the value in the **Normal_Line** to determine whether we have found the name, are before the name, or are after the name in the list. You must be careful when searching and using an integer as the guess (**Middle**), as Ada will always round down and you have to make sure that you will try all values if that is needed. In addition, we must be careful to properly treat the situation in which the name is not in the array. If **Low=High** and the **Normal_Line** at this position does not contain the correct name, then the name is not in the array.

```
package Numeric_Utilities is
  subtype Non_Negative_Float is FLOAT range 0.0 .. FLOAT'LAST;
  function Square_Root(Number: Non_Negative_Float) return Non_Negative_Float;
  -- Purpose: Calculate the square root of Number.
  -- Description: Calculates the square root of any positive FLOAT number.
end Numeric_Utilities;
package body Numeric_Utilities is
  function Square_Root(Number: Non_Negative_Float) return Non_Negative_Float is
  -- Purpose: Calculate the square root of Number.
  -- Description: Use binary search to find the square root.
    Tolerance: constant Non_Negative_Float := 0.001;
    Fuzzy: constant Non_Negative_Float := Tolerance * Number;
    -- Tolerance within which the value must be found.
    Low, High: Non_Negative_Float;
    -- Bounds between which we know the correct value lies.
    Middle: Non_Negative_Float;
    -- Our current guess at the correct value.
    Error: FLOAT;
    -- For computing how close the guess was.
  begin
    -- Return 0 for the square root of 0.
    if Number = 0.0 then
      return 0.0;
    end if;
    -- Set the initial values of High and Low.
    if Number <= 1.0 then
      Low := Number;
      High := 1.0;
    else
      Low := 1.0;
      High := Number;
    end if;
    -- Binary Search: We know that the value is between High and Low.
    loop
      -- Guess that the answer (Middle) is half way between High and Low.
      Middle := (High + Low) / 2.0;
      -- Stop if Middle is close enough to the answer.
      Error := Number - Middle * Middle;
      if abs(Error) <= Fuzzy then
        return Middle;
      end if;
      -- Adjust the bounds of the search.
      if Error < 0.0 then
        High := Middle;    -- Guess is too high
      else
        Low := Middle;     -- Guess is too low
```

Program 6–7

```
      end if;
    end loop;
  end Square_Root;
end Numeric_Utilities;
```

Program 6–7 Continued

6.10.2 Testing

Programs that use real numbers can be difficult to test. In particular, values close to 0.0 and values close to other integers may cause the program to fail. This means that the testing strategy discussed in the previous chapter must be modified.

Suppose that a program should accept real values from −10.0 through 10.0. A set of values to test are −10.0, −9.9999, −9.0, −0.0001, 0.0, 0.0001, 9.0, 9.9999, and 10.0. Again, illegal values should also be tested.

For example, the function **Square_Root** should be tested with a negative value (i.e., an illegal value), **0.0**; a very small number (e.g., **1.0E-7**); several numbers less than 1 (e.g., **0.1, 0.5, 0.7**), 1 and a number on each side of it (e.g., **0.999**, **1.001**); a selection of numbers larger than 1 some of which are integers and others which are not (e.g., **1.2**, **9.0**, **9.1**, **64.0**); and some very large numbers (e.g., **1.0E6**, **1.0E12**). The square root function developed in this chapter has limitations. Try to discover what those limitations are.

Each new data type, or even each change in the nature of the problem, changes the values that should be tested. The particular problem must be studied carefully to determine which values should be chosen for testing. Many software engineers suggest choosing test values before beginning construction of the program. This avoids unintentionally biasing the tests toward values for which the program is expected to work. The use of values that are chosen without knowledge of the program structure is often called *black box* testing. In addition to these values, we should choose additional values to test each portion of the program.

6.11 ADA SUMMARY

This chapter has extended our coverage of control structures and information passing. We have shown how to declare functions that can be used in situations in which a value needs to be computed and returned. We have introduced the parameter mode **in out** which can be used when the purpose of a procedure is to update a variable. Remember, there are three methods of passing information into a subprogram: nonlocal variables, **in** parameters, and **in out** parameters. There are four methods of passing information out of a subprogram: nonlocal variables, **in out** parameters, **out** parameters, and function values.

We have examined the remaining loop constructs: a loop without a schema, the *exit statement*, and the *loop label*. These constructs can be used when the appropriate solution to a problem involves an exit from the middle of a loop. Remember, the for schema is used when the loop is to be executed a precomputed number of times, and the while schema is used when the loop has a natural test at the start of the loop.

We have introduced the *short-circuit* control forms and shown some practical cases in which they simplify the structure of a program. We have mentioned the *goto* statement. Finally, we have introduced a new type of numbers, **FLOAT**.

EXERCISES

6.1. Write a function with the following declaration:

```
function Remove_Extra_Blanks(Line: Normal_Line) return Normal_Line;
```

The value this function returns is its parameter **Line** with all extra blanks removed. Leading and trailing blanks are extra, and if there are several blanks in a row, all but one of them is extra. (Note: This is similar to exercise 4.2.)

6.2. Write a function

```
function Reverse_Line(Forward_Line: Normal_Line) return Normal_Line;
```

that returns a **Normal_Line** with the same characters as its parameter, but in reverse order. (Except for the function declaration, this is the same as exercise 5.1.)

6.3. Write a function

```
function Palindrome(Line: Normal_Line) return BOOLEAN;
```

that returns the value true when its argument is a palindrome. A palindrome is a line which reads the same forwards and backwards. For example, "**acxca**" is a palindrome.

6.4. Write a procedure

```
procedure Remove_Extra_Blanks(Line: in out Normal_Line);
```

that removes all extra blanks from a **Normal_Line**. Leading and trailing blanks are extra, and if there are several blanks in a row, all but one of them is extra. (This procedure should be similar to the function in exercise 6.1 and is similar to exercise 4.2.)

6.5. Implement and test the following function:

```
function Cube_Root(Number: FLOAT) return FLOAT;
-- Purpose: Calculate the cube root of Number.
-- Description: Calculates the number which when cubed equals Number.
--   If Number is less than 0.0, a negative value is returned.
```

Be careful to set **High** and **Low** to set correctly, even if **Number** is negative. This function is almost the same as the **Square_Root** function discussed in the text. Implement

Cube_Root by modifying the **Numeric_Utilities** package (i.e., by replacing the **Square_Root** function).

6.6. Implement and test the following procedure:

```
procedure Powers_Of_Two(First, Last: INTEGER);
-- Purpose: Print out all of the powers of two, starting from
--    2 ** First and continuing until 2 ** Last, one per line.
```

Test this procedure with several values for **First** and **Last** including **Powers_Of_Two(60, 64)** and **Powers_Of_Two(2, 1)**. Since your computer probably cannot represent 2^{64} as an **INTEGER**, you will have to perform the calculation with a **FLOAT**.

6.7. Implement and test the following function:

```
type Name_List is array (INTEGER range 1..100) of Normal_Line;
function Find_Name(Name: Normal_Line; List_Of_Names: Name_List;
                   Number: INTEGER) return INTEGER;
-- Purpose: Find the location of Name in List_Of_Names.
--    Name: Name to find in List_Of_Names.
--    List_Of_Names: Names to search through.
--    Number: Number of names actually in List_Of_Names.
--    Returns: Location of Name in List_Of_Names, or 0 if not found.
-- Description: Searches through the first Number elements of
--    List_Of_Names to find which element contains Name.
--   If Name is not found, returns 0.
```

Write a test program that reads in a sequence of names (the list is ended when a blank line is entered). The test program then sorts the names (see Problem Solving in Chapter 5), and prints the sorted list with the number of the entry for each name. Then the test program gets a name from the user, calls **Find_Name** to find where in the array the name is stored, and prints the element number (or a message if the name is not found). The program should continue reading names and reporting until the user enters an empty (blank) name. Use the binary search algorithm, as described in the text.

6.8. Write a function

```
function Capitalize(Original_Line: Normal_Line) return Normal_Line;
```

that returns a **Normal_Line** that is the same as its input, except that all the letters have been converted to upper case. Nonletters in the line should be left undisturbed. Use an array to contain the conversion (e.g., **To_Upper('a')** would contain the character **'A'**). Initialize this array in a loop in the main program. The main program should allow the user to enter as many lines as desired. The user will signal "no more lines" by entering a line of length 0. The main program should print each value returned by the function, but it should not print anything in response to the "no more lines" signal.

6.9. Do the preceding exercise using a procedure with an **in out** parameter instead of a function. The declaration of your procedure should be

```
procedure Capitalize(Line_To_Capitalize: in out Normal_Line);
```

6.10. Write a function:

```
function Find_Largest(Number_List: Integer_Array) return INTEGER;
```

that takes an array of integers and returns the largest integer it finds in the array. The type **Integer_Array** should be declared in the main program. Within the function, use attributes in such a way that if the declaration of **Integer_Array** is changed (i.e., a new range), the function does not have to be modified. Your function may assume that the array will always have at least one element. This is similar to the **Find_Largest** procedure of exercise 5.14.

6.11. Write a function

```
function Same_Up_To(Left, Right: Normal_Line) return INTEGER;
```

The number this function returns indicates that the lines **Left** and **Right** are the same up to the character position denoted by the number. The function never returns a number larger than the length of the shortest of the two lines. For example: "**ABCXABC**" and "**ABCYAB**" are the same up to the third character so a 3 would be returned.

6.12. The **Location** function in package **Lines** enables you to write some interesting programs. However, building location functions involves a number of problems that must be carefully solved. Write a **Location** function that locates a pattern in an array. The array should have the declaration

```
subtype Array_Range is INTEGER range 1..6;
type Source is array (Array_Range) of INTEGER;
```

The program will initialize this array to contain the values 2, 4, 6, 8, 10, and 12. It will then ask the user how long the pattern is and which numbers are in the pattern. After the pattern has been entered, the program will call the **Location** function and report where the pattern occurs in the array. If the pattern does not occur in the array, the function should return the value 0. The following examples show what values should be reported for several inputs:

how long	pattern	value returned
1	4	2
2	6 8	3
1	3	0
3	8 10 12	4
3	10 12 14	0

On the last pattern it is quite common for a program to get a **CONSTRAINT_ERROR**, so be careful that your program does not. Programs often contain a similar mistake that occurs if the pattern is too long. However, patterns over 6 numbers long cannot possibly be found in an array of size 6. Make sure the program handles this case also.

6.13. Write a package that computes statistics about lines. The package should contain the following subprograms:

`Clear`: Sets all appropriate package counters and frequencies to 0.

`Add_Line`: Takes a parameter of type **`Normal_Line`** and adjusts the statistics.

`Average_Length`: Returns (type **`FLOAT`**) the average length of the lines processed since the last **`Clear`**. The average length is computed from the total number of characters in each line.

`Average_Words`: Returns (type **`FLOAT`**) the average number of words in the lines processed since the last **`Clear`**.

A word is a sequence of nonblank characters separated from other sequences of nonblank characters by spaces (or by the end of the line). For example,

```
Clear;
loop
  Simple_IO.Read(A_Line):
  Add_Line(A_Line);
  Simple_IO.Write(Average_Length);
  Simple_IO.Write(Average_Words);
end loop;
```

will output 8.0 and 2.0 if the first line input was "**`hi there`**" and 8.5 and 2.5 if the second line input was "**`Got to go`**". (There were 8 letters and 2 words in the first input and 9 letters and 3 words in the second input which gave the above averages.)

7

Using Data Types

7.1 OBJECTIVES

This chapter extends the coverage of data types and control structures. The capability of the programmer to build data types is increased by the introduction of the syntax for declaring and using enumeration types (sections 3–5). The need to do input and output of enumeration values leads to the introduction of the package **TEXT_IO** (section 7). That a user can cause an error by mistyping a value leads to the introduction of block statements and exception handlers (section 8). Both topics are covered at an introductory level, with details in later chapters. In the coverage of **TEXT_IO**, we take the opportunity to introduce a method for using disk files. We also finish up the standard control structures by presenting a decision structure that is used in many special cases (section 6).

CONCEPTS:

- Enumerations of identifiers are more meaningful than encoding information with numbers.
- Many problems require a group of data items, all of which are alike.
- When something goes wrong, the program should have the option of fixing it.
- Using disk files allows the programmer to save and retrieve data between invocations of a program.

GOALS:

- Solve a problem by using an enumeration type.

- Build a program that protects itself from user errors.
- Build a program that uses disk files.

7.2 MOTIVATION

Not everything is appropriately represented as an integer. For example, we could have used integer encodings instead of character literals for strings and characters. But it was much easier to use character literals, such as `'C'`, instead of memorizing the encodings. Since the values (or concepts) that should be encoded depend on the nature of the program, Ada provides a mechanism that allows the programmer to declare encodings. These encodings are called *enumeration types*. For example, a program dealing with calendars may wish to represent the days of the week (Monday, Tuesday, etc.) as something more readable than the integers from 1 to 7. The reason the type **CHARACTER** is provided as part of Ada is that in the experience of programmers, this type is very commonly needed in programs. Ada provides some additional enumeration types because they are commonly used.

In considering enumeration types, we shall review and extend our coverage of attributes and subranges. As before, attributes strengthen our ability to write programs that are adaptable and readable, while subranges strengthen readability and the ability to detect and correct errors.

Previously, we have introduced specialized control structures. For example, the for schema was designed to handle a special kind of iteration that commonly occurs in programs. A specialized decision-making construct is the *case statement*. This construct is a convenient way to express the necessity of choosing exactly one of many options. Like the for schema, the case statement makes it easy to program a special situation that commonly occurs.

In the programs we have examined thus far, all information was temporary. It came into existence while the program was running and ceased to exist when the program finished. Many problems, however, require permanent storage of information; for example, a payroll system for a business. Ada provides this and other capabilities for the input and output of information. These input and output capabilities are extensive and complicated. This chapter introduces a few capabilities of the predefined package **TEXT_IO**.

In writing a program, the programmer would like to protect against unexpected occurrences. It is better that an error be detected than a wrong result be delivered. However, an error is not always sufficient cause to abort a program. If the programmer is able to handle errors, a program can be designed to recover from errors.

7.3 ENUMERATION TYPES

An enumeration is a listing. In Ada, an *enumeration type* is a type whose values are listed. The syntax for declaring an enumeration type is given in Figure 7–1.

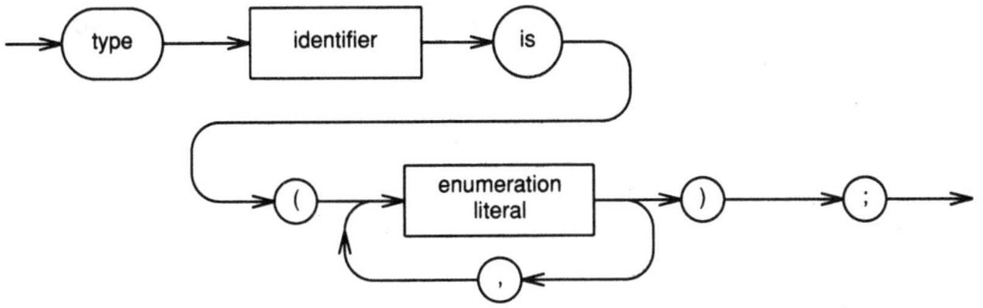

Figure 7–1

We have seen a special kind of enumeration type, **CHARACTER**, which is defined in the package **STANDARD**. In the type **CHARACTER**, the values in the "list" have a special form, most of them are single letters surrounded by apostrophes. These letters are the values the type can assume.

Another enumeration type we have seen is **BOOLEAN**. This type has only two values, **FALSE** and **TRUE**. According to the syntax, the declaration of the type **BOOLEAN** is

```
type BOOLEAN is (FALSE, TRUE);
```

Like that of the type **CHARACTER**, the type **BOOLEAN** is defined in the package **STANDARD**. Thus, the types **CHARACTER** and **BOOLEAN** are predefined in all Ada implementations.

In addition to having predefined enumeration types, Ada allows the user to define an enumeration type by listing the *enumeration literals* (or elements) in the type. Enumeration literals can be either identifiers or character literals. For the moment, we shall restrict ourselves to using identifiers; the use of character literals will be covered when we discuss the package **ASCII** in Chapter 10.

An enumeration type is declared in line 2 of the procedure **Type_Demo** in Program 7–1. This type is associated with the identifier **Days**. The elements in the list in line 2 are the values within the type. There are seven values in type **Days**. Unless we choose to modify the declaration in line 2, no other value or literal can be associated with that type.

As with the predefined types, variables can be declared that hold values of an enumeration type. A variable of an enumeration type can store one of the values listed for that type. For example, the variable **Today** declared in line 3 is of the type **Days** and may be assigned any one of the seven values in the enumeration list. It cannot be assigned values outside of the seven listed.

As with other types, the assignment statement can be used to place an enumeration value into a variable. This is done in line 7. Furthermore, parameters can be declared using enumeration types, and functions can return enumeration types, as shown in lines 4 and 5.

Enumeration values are ordered. Thus, we may compare two enumeration values, not only for equality, but also for order. In previous programs we have used the fact that

```
procedure Type_Demo is
   type Days is (Mon, Tue, Wed, Thur, Fri, Sat, Sun);
   Today: Days;
   function Work_Day(Day: Days) return BOOLEAN is ...
   function Which_Day(Date: INTEGER) return Days is ...
begin
   Today := Fri;
end Type_Demo;
```

Program 7–1

the values in type **CHARACTER** are ordered. We could compare two characters to see which came first. Although we have not previously mentioned it, Boolean values can be compared in this manner also (**FALSE** is less than **TRUE**). The order of the enumeration values is defined by the order of the values in the enumeration list.

The same is true for user-declared enumeration types. In the type **Days**, **Wed < Sat** is a legal Boolean expression that evaluates to true because **Wed** occurs before **Sat** in the enumeration list. As with other Boolean expressions, these comparisons can be used in decision making, as in the statement

```
if Tue < Today and Today <= Fri then ...
```

and in the Boolean expression of the while schema, as in

```
while Today <= Thursday loop
```

Enumerated types are discrete types. Therefore, they can be used in the for schema, as in

```
for A_Day in Days range Mon..Fri loop ...
```

and as array indices. The preceding for schema traverses the values between the bounds, in order. The order in the enumeration list is the order in which the loop parameter (**A_Day** in the example) assumes the values defined by the bounds.

7.3.1 Attributes of Discrete Types

As we have seen, data types have attributes. The particular attributes available depend on the nature of the data type. The following attributes can be applied with any discrete type.

The *successor* attribute is obtained by using the identifier **SUCC**. The successor of an enumeration value is the next item in the enumeration type. For example, in the type **Days**, the successor of **Mon** is **Tue**. This means that the value of **Days'SUCC(Mon)** is **Tue**. Similarly, the value of **Days'SUCC(Wed)** is **Thur**. A problem occurs with the last element in an enumeration. Because it has no successor, to request one results in a **CONSTRAINT_ERROR**. So if we ask for **Days'SUCC(Sun)**, we get a **CONSTRAINT_ERROR**. This means that we have violated the constraints of the enumeration by asking for a nonexistent element.

The *predecessor* attribute is obtained by using the identifier **PRED**. The predecessor of an enumeration value is the previous item in the enumeration. For example, in the type **Days**, the predecessor of **Sun** is **Sat**. Thus, the value of **Days'PRED(Sun)** is **Sat**. Again, asking for a nonexistent element results in a **CONSTRAINT_ERROR**. Thus, **Days'PRED(Mon)** causes a **CONSTRAINT_ERROR**.

Variables and expressions are allowed with both the successor and predecessor attributes. So if **Today** is a variable of type **Days**, then **Days'PRED(Today)** returns the predecessor of whatever value is stored in **Today**. Technically, any expression of type **Days** is allowed. For example,

```
Days'PRED(Days'SUCC(Wed))
```

evaluates to **Wed**.

The *position* attribute **POS** returns the position of the value in the enumeration list. The starting position is always position 0. In Ada, unless the programmer directs otherwise by using a representation clause (described in Chapter 17), this is the same as the integer that is used to encode an enumeration value. Thus, using the type **Days** as defined in the procedure **Type_Demo** in Program 7–1, **Days'POS(Mon)** returns the value 0, **Days'POS(Tue)** returns the value 1, **Days'POS(Wed)** returns the value 2, and so forth.

The *enumeration value* attribute **VAL** returns the enumeration value that is at the specified position in the enumeration list. **VAL** is the reverse of **POS**, that is, **Days'VAL(0)** returns the enumeration value **Mon**, **Days'VAL(1)** returns **Tue**, **Days'VAL(2)** returns **Wed**, and so forth. Supplying **Days'VAL** with an integer less than 0 or greater than 6 causes a **CONSTRAINT_ERROR**.

The combination of **VAL** and **POS** is useful for those rare occasions when it is appropriate to convert an enumeration to integers, apply some arithmetic operations, and then convert back. Calculating the day of the week from the date is an example of such an occasion. Again, **POS** or **VAL** may be applied to any expression that yields the appropriate type.

The *string image* attribute **IMAGE** returns the string that is equivalent to an enumeration identifier. The string returned is always in upper case, regardless of the case used in the enumeration list. For example, **Days'IMAGE(Mon)** returns **"MON"** (the quotation marks are delimiters and not part of the string's value), **Days'IMAGE(Tue)** returns **"TUE"**, **Days'IMAGE(Wed)** returns **"WED"**, and so forth. Note that **Days'IMAGE (TRUE)** is syntactically illegal because **TRUE** is not one of the legal values of the type **Days**.

The **VALUE** attribute returns an enumeration value that is equivalent to a string. In other words, **VALUE** is the reverse of **IMAGE**. The evaluation of **VALUE** ignores the case of the characters in the string, as well as any leading or trailing blanks. Both **Days'VALUE("Mon")** and **Days'VALUE("MON")** return the enumeration value **Mon**.

Remember that an enumeration value is an identifier and the case of its letters does not matter.

Converting a string to an enumeration value is not possible if there is no enumeration value that corresponds to the string. If a program attempts to do this a **CONSTRAINT_ERROR** occurs.

The **IMAGE** attribute provides a convenient method to perform output on enumeration types. For example,

```
Simple_IO.Write(Days'IMAGE(Today));
```

writes the enumeration value stored in the variable **Today**.

The *width* attribute **WIDTH** returns the width of the longest identifier in the enumeration type. For example, **Days'WIDTH** returns 4 because the longest identifier in the type **Days** is **Thur**, which has a length of 4. This attribute is particularly useful in controlling format when printing forms.

All the preceding attributes also apply to integers, since, like enumeration types, they are a discrete type. The **VAL** and **POS** of an **INTEGER** have the same values as the integer itself.

With integers, the attribute **IMAGE** returns the string that is equivalent to the integer. This string never contains underscores, leading zeros, exponent notation, or trailing spaces. Also, there is always a leading character that is either a blank for natural numbers or a negative sign for negative numbers. For example, **INTEGER'IMAGE(6)** returns the string **" 6"**, while **INTEGER'IMAGE(-2E2)** returns the string **"-200"**.

With integers, the attribute **VALUE** returns the integer value that is equivalent to the string. As with other discrete types, leading and trailing blanks are ignored. In addition, any string whose characters form a valid integer literal will be converted. Thus, **INTEGER'VALUE("-2_345E3")** returns the integer **-2345000**. With integers, a **CONSTRAINT_ERROR** can occur if the string would represent a number out of the range of the type **INTEGER**. Also, as with enumeration types, a **CONSTRAINT_ERROR** occurs if the string does not correspond to an integer.

7.3.2 Enumerated Types and Strong Typing

One of the capabilities provided by types is that the types of variables and expressions can be checked for compatibility at compilation time. Detecting an attempt to use an illegal or nonsensical operation, such as trying to add two characters, is far better than silently returning a meaningless result. Type checking does not prevent errors, but it changes the time and method of detection. Without type checking, the programmer who accidentally added two characters would be faced with a meaningless answer and be forced to analyze the program with little clue as to what went wrong. With type checking, the compiler provides a clear indication of the problem. Thus, type checking helps avoid having errors make their first appearance when a program is run.

Type checking is helpful when we use enumeration types. Consider the following declarations:

```
type Days is (Mon, Tue, Wed, Thur, Fri, Sat, Sun);
Today: Days;
type Fruits is (Apple, Banana, Pear, Orange);
Fruit: Fruits;
```

Since both **Fruit** and **Apple** are of type **Fruits**, the assignment

```
Fruit := Apple;
```

is legal. However, the statement

```
Today := Apple;
```

is illegal because a value of the type **Fruits** cannot be stored in a variable that can accommodate only values of type **Days**. Similarly, the Boolean expression in the if statement

```
if Today = Mon then ...
```

is legal, since the values being compared are both of the type **Days**. A comparison of values of different types, as in **Fruit=Mon** is illegal.

The same is true for other situations. In a for schema, we can iterate over enumeration values, as in

```
for Tomorrow in Thur..Sat loop
```

The loop parameter **Tomorrow** takes its value from the iteration range. Since both **Thur** and **Sat** are of type **Days**, **Tomorrow** is of type **Days**. But because in the for schema the type of the loop parameter must be determinable from the range,

```
for Fruit_Day in Pear..Sat loop    -- illegal
```

is illegal because the lower bound is of type **Fruits** and the upper bound is of type **Days**.

Note that the loop

```
for Fruit in Thur..Sat loop
```

is legal, but misleading. Inside the loop, the identifier **Fruit** refers to the loop parameter, which is of type **Days**. Using a more appropriate identifier would avoid confusing the person reading the program.

The procedure **Pay_Roll** in Program 7–2 illustrates some of the preceding points. In the procedure **Compute_Pay**, the first loop (lines 10–17) runs through the enumeration type, summing the hours worked and using the **IMAGE** attribute to print those hours. The second loop (lines 18–28) runs through the **Off** array (indexed by integers) and uses

```
 1:with Simple_IO;
 2:procedure Pay_Roll is
 3:  use Simple_IO;
 4:  type Days is (Mon, Tue, Wed, Thur, Fri, Sat, Sun);
 5:  type Time_Card is array (Days) of INTEGER;
 6:  type Days_Off is array (INTEGER range 1..2) of Days;

 7:  procedure Compute_Pay(Hours: Time_Card; Off: Days_Off) is
 8:    Total_Hours: NATURAL := 0;
 9:  begin
10:    for Which_Day in Days loop  -- Basic pay
11:      Total_Hours := Total_Hours + Hours(Which_Day);
12:      Write("Day: ");
13:      Write(Days'IMAGE(Which_Day));
14:      Write(" Hours: ");
15:      Write(INTEGER'IMAGE(Hours(Which_Day)));
16:      New_Line;
17:    end loop;
18:    for Holiday in Off'RANGE loop
19:      if Hours(Off(Holiday)) /= 0 then
20:          -- Double-time adjustment for working holidays
21:        Total_Hours := Total_Hours + Hours(Off(Holiday));
22:        Write("Holiday hours for: ");
23:        Write(Days'IMAGE(Off(Holiday)));
24:        Write(" are " );
25:        Write(INTEGER'IMAGE(Hours(Off(Holiday))));
26:        New_Line;
27:      end if;
28:    end loop;
29:    Write("Total Hours are ");
30:    Write(INTEGER'IMAGE(Total_Hours));
31:    New_Line;
32:  end Compute_Pay;

33:begin
34:  ...
35:end Pay_Roll;
```

Program 7–2

the value found in **Off** to locate any hours worked on a holiday. The enumeration type **Days** is the type of the loop parameter for the first loop (lines 10–17), which computes the basic pay. Lines 11, 13, and 15 use the loop parameter **Which_Day**, providing a direct association of the enumeration (printed in line 13) with the index of the array (lines 11 and 15).

The use of attributes in procedure **Computer_Pay** will assist us if we ever modify the program. For example, suppose we change the language from English to French.

Then we would only need to change the string constants and the enumeration literals. For this modification, the use of **IMAGE** and **VALUE** will save us some work.

7.4 SUBTYPES AND SUBRANGES OF ENUMERATIONS

A *subrange* is a limited and contiguous set of values of a previously declared scalar type. The syntax for subtypes and subranges is given in Figure 3–3. The new idea in this chapter is that subrange limitations can be applied to enumeration types. We also discuss how subranges interact with parameters.

Subrange restrictions are possible with enumeration types. The declaration

```
Work_Day: Days range Mon..Fri;
```

declares the variable **Work_Day** to hold a value from a subrange of the type **Days**. The system will automatically check that a variable is only assigned a value within the correct range. If a value that is out of range is detected, a **CONSTRAINT_ERROR** will result.

As in Chapter 3, a *subtype* is a type with a possible constraint. Indeed, we saw that subtypes without any additional constraints are possible and occasionally useful. With a constraint, we are insisting that we be informed if something that we assumed to be true about a value should in fact fail to be true about that value.

The following declarations declare the subtype **Weekday**, two variables (**Work_Day** and **Bad_Day**) of that subtype, and one variable (**Any_Day**) of the original type:

```
subtype Weekday is Days range Mon..Fri;
Work_Day, Bad_Day: Weekday;
Any_Day: Days;
```

Both **Work_Day** and **Bad_Day** have range restrictions.

Recall that subtypes of a common type are compatible. This is also true with enumeration types. Accordingly, the variables **Any_Day** and **Work_Day** are compatible. For example, they can be compared, as in

```
Any_Day = Work_Day
```

or used on opposite sides of an assignment, as in

```
Any_Day := Work_Day;
```

Remember, whenever a value is stored in a variable of a subtype, a check is made to assure that the value satisfies the constraint. Thus, the assignment

```
Work_Day := Any_Day;
```

could cause a **CONSTRAINT_ERROR** if the value stored in **Any_Day** were **Sat** or **Sun**.

Subtypes of a subtype are possible as shown in the declarations:

```
type Days is (Mon, Tue, Wed, Thur, Fri, Sat, Sun);
subtype Weekday is Days range  Mon..Fri;
subtype Week_Start is Weekday range Mon..Tue;
Work_Day, Bad_Day: Weekday;
Very_Bad_Day: Week_Start;
Any_Day: Days;
```

In these declarations, **Week_Start** is a subtype of the subtype **Weekday**. Subtypes inherit type compatibility. Thus, variables of the types **Days**, **Weekday**, and **Week_Start** are all compatible. This means the variables of these types could be used as they are in the following statements:

```
Work_Day := Very_Bad_Day;
Very_Bad_Day := Any_Day;
```

A restriction on the declaration of a subtype is that the additional constraint of the new subtype must be consistent with the constraint of the subtype from which it is formed. This means that the range of the new subtype must fall within the range of the subtype from which it is formed. Thus, in the declarations

```
subtype Weekday is Days range Mon..Fri;
subtype Bad is Weekday range Fri..Sat; --CONSTRAINT_ERROR
```

since the range of **Bad** is not contained within the range of **Weekday** a **CONSTRAINT_ERROR** will occur. Often, this kind of **CONSTRAINT_ERROR** is detected only when the program is run. This sort of error most often occurs when the subrange is declared using variables, as is illustrated in the procedure **Subrange_Demo** in Program 7–3.

```
procedure Subrange_Demo is
  type Days is (Mon, Tue, Wed, Thur, Fri, Sat, Sun);
  subtype Weekday is Days range Mon..Fri;
  First, Last: Days;
  A, B: Weekday;
  procedure Local_Subrange is
    subtype Maybe is Weekday range First..Last;
    subtype Always is Weekday range A..B;
    Z: Always;
  begin ... end Local_Subrange;
begin ... end Subrange_Demo;
```

Program 7–3

The null subrange, no matter how it is expressed, always falls within any other range. For example,

```
subtype No_Days is Weekday range Sun..Wed;
```

is a null subrange and falls within the range of **Weekday** even though this null range is expressed using a value (**Sun**) that is outside the range of **Weekday**.

An important consequence of enumeration types, type compatibility, and constraint checking occurs with procedure parameters. The formal parameter in the procedure declaration

```
procedure Demo(Param: Weekday) is ...
```

is compatible with any actual parameter that is compatible with the type **Weekday**. For example, the call

```
Demo(Very_Bad_Day);
```

is legal because the type of **Very_Bad_Day** is **Week_Start** and this type is compatible with the type **Weekday**. So is the call

```
Demo(Any_Day);
```

Of course, in this latter call, a **CONSTRAINT_ERROR** is possible. In particular, the actual parameter could assume the value **Sat** or **Sun**. But since the formal parameter cannot assume either of these values, a **CONSTRAINT_ERROR** would occur if a call tried to pass in one of these values.

With parameters of mode **in out** or mode **out**, as in

```
procedure In_Out_Demo(In_Out_Param: in out Weekday) is ...
```

the situation is slightly more complex. Within the procedure, the range constraint on the formal parameter is defined by the declaration of the formal parameter. Particularly, the constraint on **In_Out_Param** is always **Mon..Fri**, because that is the constraint of the subtype **Weekday**. Any attempt to assign a value outside of this range results in a **CONSTRAINT_ERROR** no matter what the constraint on the actual parameter. In addition, when a value is passed out, as in

```
In_Out_Demo(Very_Bad_Day);
```

a **CONSTRAINT_ERROR** occurs if the value sent back is outside of the allowable range for the actual parameter. Note that the **CONSTRAINT_ERROR** occurs only after exit from the procedure. During execution of the procedure, **In_Out_Param** may contain any value that is legal for the type **Weekday**, including values in **Wed..Fri**, as long as upon exit from the procedure the value associated with **In_Out_Param** is a legal one for the type of the actual parameter.

In the procedure **Local_Subrange**, the range constraints on both **Maybe** and **Always** are dependent on the values contained in variables. A subtype declared in a subprogram (like other items in a subprogram's declarations) is elaborated each time the subprogram is called. Thus, each time **Local_Subrange** is called, the constraints on the subtypes **Maybe** and **Always** are reevaluated. A **CONSTRAINT_ERROR** could occur in the elaboration of **Maybe**, because **First** and **Last** do not necessarily contain values within **Weekday**. **Always** cannot cause a **CONSTRAINT_ERROR**, because **A** and **B** are of type **Weekday**. This is good programming style. Technically, a **CONSTRAINT_ERROR** could occur during this elaboration if the program were erroneous by having either **A** or **B** be uninitialized. Subtypes declared in the declarative region of a package are elaborated during elaboration of the package.

Now consider what happens when **A>B**. In this case, the declaration of subtype **Always** is still legal. However, the range is empty, just like the null range on a for schema. **Z** is a legal variable, but there are no legal values that can be placed in **Z**. What this means is that the degenerate case for a subtype declaration does not cause any problems due to declarations and will be fine as long as the procedure body correctly handles the degenerate case by not attempting an assignment.

Attributes can be applied to subtypes. Before examining how this is done, we introduce some Ada terminology. Consider the following declarations:

```
type Days is (Mon, Tue, Wed, Thur, Fri, Sat, Sun);
subtype Weekend is Days range Fri..Sun;
subtype Shortend is Weekend range Sat..Sun;
```

In Ada, the original type (**Days**) is called the *base type*. Thus, **Days** is the base type of both **Weekend** and **Shortend**. Observe particularly that, even though **Shortend** is formed from **Weekend**, the base type is always the original type.

The attribute **POS** applies not only to discrete types, but also to subtypes of discrete types, because these subtypes are themselves discrete types. However, you should be alert because the value returned is the position in the enumeration list of the *base type*. For example, the value of **Weekend'POS(Fri)** is 4. This is because **POS** depends on the position of **Fri** in the original enumeration list **Days** and *not* in the subtype **Weekend**. Just remember that **POS**'s of compatible types are identical. The same is true for **VAL**.

In addition, **POS** and **VAL** apply to and return the base type. For example, **Weekend'VAL(2)** is **Tues**. Note that although **Tues** is not in the subtype **Weekend**, a **CONSTRAINT_ERROR** does not occur because the **VAL** attribute requires only that the parameter be consistent with the base type **Days**. It does not require consistency with the subtype **Weekend**.

7.5 SCALAR ATTRIBUTES

Ada has several "classes" of types. One class is the scalar types. The class of *scalar types* includes the integer types, the real types, and the enumeration types. Since these types share some qualities, Ada is able to supply some additional scalar attributes that are designed to allow procedures to be more flexible. It is possible to declare a subtype of a scalar type which includes a range constraint. In doing so, since the bounds of a subtype may be defined by an expression, it is not always trivial to determine the range of a subtype. Ada provides two attributes that return the first and last values in a type or subtype.

The attribute **FIRST** returns the value of the first element in the scalar type or subtype. For the type **Days**, the value of **Days'FIRST** is **Mon**, since **Mon** is the first value in the type. For the subtype **Weekend**, the value of **Weekend'FIRST** is **Fri**, since **Fri** is the first value in the range of the subtype.

Since scalar types include **INTEGER** and **FLOAT**, we can ask for the first value in these types. When we do, we get the most negative integer or floating point number that these types allow.

The attribute **LAST** returns the value of the last element in the scalar type or subtype. For **Days** it returns **Sun**, for **INTEGER** it returns the largest (most positive) integer in the implementation of that type and for **FLOAT** it returns the largest floating point number in the implementation of that type.

For subranges of **INTEGER**, **FLOAT**, and enumeration types, **FIRST** and **LAST** will return the bounds on the range. Thus, given the declarations

```
subtype Angle is FLOAT range -3.14 .. 3.14
```

The value of **Angle'FIRST** is **-3.14**. Remember that **FLOAT** uses approximation, so testing for equality remains a bad idea even when using attributes. However, attributes are very useful for testing inequality and membership.

The function **Future_Day** in Program 7–4 illustrates the power of using attributes within a subprogram. **Future_Day** is assumed to be within the procedure **Pay_Roll** of Program 7–2. The purpose of the function is to figure out which day of the week something will be on. For example, **Future_Day(Mon,2)** should evaluate to **Wed** because Wednesday is two days after Monday. Two subtleties are shown in the function. First, the *if statement* is necessary to handle the case when the number of days into the future causes the computation to wrap around into a new week. Second, the *for schema* limits are computed using the knowledge that the days in a week cycle every seven days. This means that we can "divide out" any multiples of 7. We have chosen to use the **mod** operator to do this because it works on negative as well as positive numbers (i.e., when we ask for days in the past, it returns the correct nonnegative number). Notice that instead of the literal **7**, we expressed the number of days in a week using attributes. Thus, if the number of days in a week changes the function does not need to be rewritten.

7.6 THE CASE STATEMENT

A certain method of decision making is used so often that it rightly has its own construct in Ada. This method is often described by the term "multiple choice." In a multiple-

```
function Future_Day(Base_Day: Days; Days_Ahead: INTEGER) return Days is
  New_Day: Days := Base_Day;
begin
  for Count in INTEGER range 1..Days_Ahead mod
       (Days'POS(Days'LAST) - Days'POS(Days'FIRST) + 1) loop
    if New_Day = Days'LAST then
      New_Day := Days'FIRST;
    else
      New_Day := Days'SUCC(New_Day);
    end if;
  end loop;
  return New_Day;
end Future_Day;
```

Program 7–4

choice exam, you choose *one* option from a list of options. This is the principle of the *case statement*. From the list of choices, choose *one* option. The syntax for the case statement is given in Figure 7–2.

In an if statement, the choice of alternatives is based on a Boolean expression. In a case statement, the choice is based on an expression. Each option in the case statement is a statement list preceded by "**when ... =>**". The position indicated by the dots (. . .), contains an indication of when this particular statement list is chosen.

Suppose the variable **X** is declared to be of type **Days**. Then the following is a legal case statement:

```
case X is
  when Mon =>
    Write("Ditch");
  when Tue..Fri =>
    Write("Work");
    Write(" A Little");
  when Sat | Sun =>
    Write("Rest");
end case;
```

The expression in this case statement is simply the variable **X**. On the basis of this expression, one of the three options listed is performed. The first and third options contain one write statement, and the second option contains two write statements. If **X** contains the value **Mon**, then **Ditch** is printed. If **X** contains the value **Tue**, **Wed**, **Thur**, or **Fri**, then **Work A Little** is printed. If **X** contains the value **Sat**, or **Sun**, then **Rest** is printed. In this example, depending on the value of the expression, one of the three options is chosen. This example also illustrates that as a "choice" you can

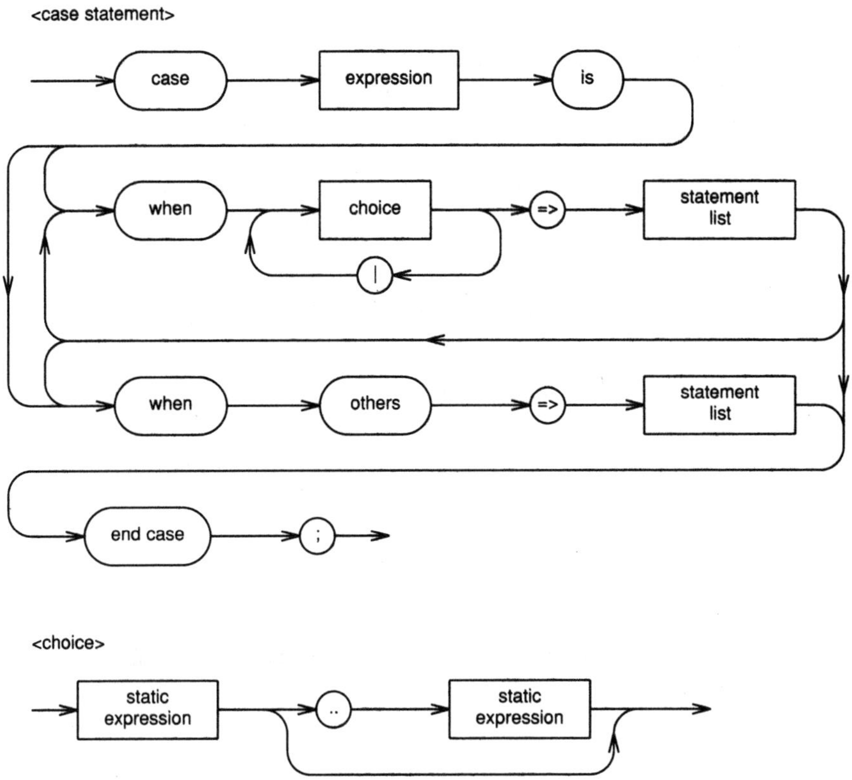

Figure 7–2

have a value (**Mon**), a range (**Tue..Fri**) or a list of values (**Sat|Sun**). In fact even a list of ranges and values such as **Mon..Tue|Thur|Sat..Sun** is allowed.

A number of restrictions must be obeyed when using case statements. First, the type of the expression that is used to select the choice must match the types found in the choices that precede the options. In the preceding example, the expression is of type **Days**, and each of the choices is on the basis of values from the type **Days**. In the preceding example the choice

```
when 3 => ...   -- illegal, needs a value of type Days
```

would be illegal because "**X**" is not an integer expression.

Second, only discrete types can be used. For example, choices cannot be made on the basis of an expression of type **FLOAT**. Third, the choices must be static expressions. Static expressions cannot change during the execution of the program. Thus, "**when Y =>**", where **Y** is a variable, is not allowed. Finally, each possible value of the type must occur in exactly one choice. The following case statement is illegal because **Sun** does not occur in the any of the choices:

```
case X is                                           -- illegal
  when Mon..Fri => Write("Go");
  when Sat      => Write("Stop");
end case;
```

And the following case statement is illegal because **Wed** occurs twice:

```
case X is                                           -- illegal
  when Mon..Fri | Sun => Write("Go");
  when Sat | Wed      => Write("Stop");
end case;
```

In fact, **when Mon..Wed|Wed** is illegal because **Wed** occurs in two choices, even though they are attached to the same statement list.

In some problems, only a few of the values need to be distinguished. For example, when giving a multiple choice exam with five options, **'A'** ... **'E'**, all other letters are errors. In a case like this, we desire to handle the five important letters specially and group the handling of the remaining letters together. Since it would be tedious to list all the remaining letters, Ada provides an easy method to do this called the *others* option. As indicated in the syntax diagram, **others** must appear alone and must occur last. Any values that are not explicitly listed use the **others** option. Thus, in the fragment

```
I: INTEGER range 0..25;
  ...
case I is
  when 0      => Write("Nothing");
  when 1..4   => Write("Small");
  when 5..10  => Write("Medium");
  when others => Write("Large");
end case;
```

the values 1 through 10 are handled explicitly by the first three options and the values 11–25 use the others option.

Since **CHARACTER** is an enumeration type, it may be used in a case statement as in the following example:

```
Ch: CHARACTER;
  ...
case Ch is
  when 'A'..'Z' => Write("Upper case");
  when 'a'..'z' => Write("Lower case");
  when others   => null;
end case;
```

This case statement shows that the statement list can contain the null statement. A null statement is useful when there are cases in which you wish to perform no actions.

Finally, we note that a case statement is allowed to have a single option, as in

```
case Ch is
  when others => Write("Everything");
end case;
```

7.7 TEXT INPUT AND OUTPUT USING TEXT_IO

Input and output in Ada are somewhat complicated. To avoid early discussion of these complexities, we have provided the package **Simple_IO**. In this section, we shall introduce the standard Ada facilities for input and output of text. We consider the simplest forms for input and output of enumeration, integer, floating point, and string values. We will also introduce simple input and output involving disk files. Details and complications will be deferred until Chapter 16. For the type **Normal_Line**, we shall continue to use the facilities supplied by the package **Simple_IO**.

One of the Ada packages that handles input and output is named **TEXT_IO**. Like other packages, it must be named in a context clause before its routines can be accessed. Its principle routines for input are **GET** and **SKIP_LINE**. Its principle routines for output are **PUT** and **NEW_LINE**. The forms of these routines we present at this point are for input and output from the default files, usually the keyboard and the display of the user's terminal.

The procedure **PUT** takes a parameter and outputs the value of that parameter. Since the parameter is of mode **in**, it may be an expression such as

```
TEXT_IO.PUT(CHARACTER'SUCC('A'));
```

which outputs the letter **B**. **PUT** may be used with either **CHARACTER** or **STRING** expressions. An example of how to output a string is

```
TEXT_IO.PUT("How Big? ");
```

Text normally is written on multiple lines. Beginning a new line is the responsibility of the program. To begin a new line, Ada supplies the procedure **NEW_LINE**. For example,

```
TEXT_IO.NEW_LINE;
```

causes the next **PUT** to print its value at the start of a new line. **NEW_LINE** has an **INTEGER** parameter of mode **in** which specifies the number of new lines to be output and whose default value is 1. Values greater than 1 result in blank lines.

The procedure **GET** has a parameter of mode **out**. **GET** places the value read into the variable passed as the actual parameter. In particular, the behavior of **GET** and **PUT** is similar to the behavior of the procedures **Read** and **Write** from the package **Simple_IO**. In the discussion that follows, we shall restrict our use of "**TEXT_IO.GET**" to characters.

The procedure **SKIP_LINE** skips one or more lines of input. If part of a line has been read, **SKIP_LINE** causes the rest of the line to be skipped. This partial line counts as a skipped line. **SKIP_LINE** takes a single **INTEGER** parameter of mode **in** which specifies the number of lines to be skipped and whose default value is 1.

The package **TEXT_IO** itself contains other packages. We will cover three of these packages. These three packages accept types as parameters. In Ada these are called *generic packages* and they will be covered in detail in Chapter 16. At this point, we shall introduce the simplest versions and usages of these packages that allow us to provide input and output. Generic packages must be *instantiated* to be used. Instantiation is accomplished by naming the package, supplying a type and associating the instantiation with an identifier. An instantiation is a declaration and must occur within a declaration section.

The generic package is **ENUMERATION_IO** provides the capability to do input and output on enumeration types. Consider the following declarations:

```
with TEXT_IO;
procedure Day_Handler is
  type Days is (Mon, Tue, Wed, Thur, Fri, Sat, Sun);
  package Day_IO is new TEXT_IO.ENUMERATION_IO(Days);
  X: Days;
begin
  TEXT_IO.PUT("Give me a Day");
  Day_IO.GET(X);
  TEXT_IO.SKIP_LINE;
  Day_IO.PUT(X);
  TEXT_IO.NEW_LINE;
end Day_Handler;
```

Here, a new package called **Day_IO** is formed from the generic package **ENUMERATION_IO** which occurs within the regular package **TEXT_IO**. When **Day_IO** is formed by instantiation, it contains procedures **GET** and **PUT**, which take values of the enumeration type **Days** as parameters. As shown in the example, **Day_IO** enables us to read and write literals corresponding to the type **Days** in the same way we are able to read and write characters.

The generic package **INTEGER_IO** provides the capability to input and output integers. Ada allows many different integer types (see Chapter 13), but for now we consider only the type **INTEGER**. Again, to perform input and output on the type **INTEGER**, we must make an appropriate instantiation, as in

```
package Int_IO is new TEXT_IO.INTEGER_IO(INTEGER);
```

After this instantiation, we may make input and output by calls such as

```
Int_IO.GET(X);
Int_IO.PUT(X);
```

where **X** is a variable of type **INTEGER**. Because **Int_IO.GET** and **Int_IO.PUT** obey the standard rules for types, **X** may be a variable of any subtype that is compatible with **INTEGER**.

The generic package **FLOAT_IO** allows direct input and output of floating point types. A correct instantiation of this package is

```
package Flt_IO is new TEXT_IO.FLOAT_IO(FLOAT);
```

With this instantiation, a correct call for input is

```
Flt_IO.GET(Y);
```

where **Y** is a variable of type **FLOAT**. We can tell you now, that the way the **Simple_IO** package managed to allow you to write integers and floating point numbers was that it used instantiations of **INTEGER_IO** and **FLOAT_IO**. However, **Simple_IO** could not provide enumeration input and output because a separate instantiation is needed for each enumeration type and the enumeration type needs to be declared before an I/O package can be instantiated for it.

We note that on reading input, instantiations of **INTEGER_IO**, **FLOAT_IO**, and **ENUMERATION_IO** ignore leading blanks, including spaces, tab characters, and blank lines.

One word of warning, if the user types something that cannot be interpreted as a value for the type being read, then a **DATA_ERROR** occurs. **Simple_IO** package resolves this problem by asking the user to reenter the value. When using **TEXT_IO**, you, the programmer, must use the structures found in section 8 if you wish to allow the user a chance to reenter the value.

7.7.1 Input and Output Using Files

Thus far, all our input and output have used the default files provided by the system. Although not required by Ada, these files are normally the user's keyboard and display screen. The ability to use disk files is highly desirable, so several techniques for doing this are provided by Ada. One of the simplest of these uses **TEXT_IO**.

The package **TEXT_IO** contains the procedures **CREATE** and **OPEN**. **OPEN** is used with existing files. **CREATE** is used for creating a new file or replacing an old file. For now, both these procedures should be supplied three parameters. The form of their declarations we will use is

```
procedure CREATE(FILE: in out FILE_TYPE; MODE: in FILE_MODE;
                 NAME: in STRING);
procedure OPEN(FILE: in out FILE_TYPE; MODE: in FILE_MODE;
                 NAME: in STRING);
```

There is one additional parameter we have not shown which we allow to assume its default value. The first parameter, **FILE**, is of mode **in out** and contains information about a file. The type of this parameter is **FILE_TYPE**, a type defined in the package **TEXT_IO**. The exact nature of this type is hidden from the programmer by methods defined in Chapter 9. When we wish to do file manipulations, we specify which file we wish to manipulate using a variable of **FILE_TYPE**. A particular variable of **FILE_TYPE** can be associated with a particular file on disk. This association is achieved by calling procedures **OPEN** and **CREATE** and supplying the variable to be associated with the file as the actual parameter for the formal parameter **FILE**. The value of the actual parameter is modified by **CREATE** and **OPEN** to reflect this association. Once the association has been made, we can execute statements that allow us to use **GET** to read information from that disk file or to use **PUT** to write information to that disk file. Essentially, **CREATE** and **OPEN** associate a file with a variable of type **FILE_TYPE**.

The second parameter is the file mode. Its type is an enumeration type declared in **TEXT_IO**. This type has two values:

```
type FILE_MODE is (IN_FILE, OUT_FILE);
```

For now we shall use **CREATE** with a **FILE_MODE** of **OUT_FILE** because we will be putting out information to the newly created file and we will use **OPEN** with a **FILE_MODE** of **IN_FILE** because we shall be getting in information from an existing file. Using **GET** on an **OUT_FILE** or using **PUT** on an **IN_FILE** will cause a **MODE_ERROR**.

The third parameter is the file name. Mostly, we will use a string literal for this parameter. In using **OPEN**, if you try to open a file which does not exist a **NAME_ERROR** occurs. An attempt to create or open a file with a name which is not allowed will also result in a **NAME_ERROR**. The nature of the name depends on the operating system you are using and the file you wish to access.

When you "**OPEN**" a file for input, you would like to know when you have gotten all of the information from that file. There is a function defined within **TEXT_IO** which detects when the entire contents of a file have been read. Its declaration is

```
function END_OF_FILE(FILE: in FILE_TYPE) return BOOLEAN;
```

This function returns the value true if there is no more input left in the file, and false if there is input remaining.

For many files, important divisions of data are signified by starting a new line. It is possible to detect if input from a file has reached the end of a line using the function

```
function END_OF_LINE(FILE: in FILE_TYPE) return BOOLEAN;
```

which returns the value true if the last item read was the last item on the input line.

Another procedure in **TEXT_IO** provides a way to clean up after file operations. The procedure

```
procedure CLOSE(FILE: in FILE_TYPE);
```

closes the file. After a file has been closed it can no longer be written or read until a new **CREATE** or **OPEN** is performed on that file. Every file you create or open should be closed.

Using **GET** and **PUT** with a file is simple. With both of these procedures a file may be indicated. For example, if we have the declarations

```
Letter: CHARACTER;
Our_Data: TEXT_IO.FILE_TYPE;
```

and the statement

```
TEXT_IO.OPEN(Our_Data, TEXT_IO.IN_FILE, "Our_File_Name");
```

has been executed, then we can get a character from the file named "**Our_File_Name**" with the statement

```
TEXT_IO.GET(Our_Data, Letter);
```

Notice that the **OPEN** associated the file name with the variable **Our_Data** and the **GET** used this variable to indicate from which file the character was to be read.

The functions

```
TEXT_IO.STANDARD_INPUT
TEXT_IO.STANDARD_OUTPUT
```

are defined in **TEXT_IO** and return a value of type **FILE_TYPE**. These may be used as the file variable in a **GET** or **PUT** operation. For example:

```
TEXT_IO.GET(TEXT_IO.STANDARD_INPUT, Letter);
```

will get a character from the standard input, usually the keyboard, and

```
TEXT_IO.PUT(TEXT_IO.STANDARD_OUTPUT, Letter);
```

will put a character to the standard output, usually the video display.

The procedure **Add_Numbers** in Program 7–5 illustrates the use of the procedures and functions associated with disk files. Line 4 declares two file variables, associated with the identifiers **Numbers_to_Read** and **Total_of_Numbers**. Lines 9 and 10 write a message to the user; since there is no file specified, this message will go to **STANDARD_OUTPUT**, which is most likely the user's screen. Line 11 opens the file **Numbers_to_Read**. **OPEN** implies that the file already exists, and **IN_FILE** indicates that it is to be used for input. The string **"Numbers"** indicates the name of the file. The interpretation of this name depends on the operating system's naming conventions for files, but the name is the name of some file (probably a disk file) in the file system of the operating system. The name of the file may have to be changed in order to run this program on a particular system.

```
 1:with TEXT_IO;
 2:procedure Add_Numbers is
 3:  use TEXT_IO;
 4:  Numbers_To_Read, Total_Of_Numbers: FILE_TYPE;
 5:  Number: INTEGER;
 6:  Total, Count: INTEGER := 0;
 7:  package Int_IO is new INTEGER_IO(INTEGER);
 8:begin
 9:  PUT("Adding numbers and computing the total");
10:  NEW_LINE;
11:  OPEN(Numbers_To_Read, IN_FILE, "Numbers");
12:  CREATE(Total_Of_Numbers, OUT_FILE, "Total");
13:  while not END_OF_FILE(Numbers_To_Read) loop
14:    Int_IO.GET(Numbers_To_Read, Number);
15:    Total := Total + Number;
16:  end loop;
17:  Int_IO.PUT(Total_Of_Numbers, Total);
18:  PUT("Total completed");
19:  NEW_LINE;
20:  CLOSE(Numbers_to_Read);
21:  CLOSE(Total_Of_Numbers);
22:end Add_Numbers;
```

Program 7–5

Similarly, in line 12, **CREATE** indicates that a new file is being created. This file may be used for output (**OUT_FILE**) and is associated with the name **"Total"** in the operating system's file system. Note that the external (or operating system) names for files ("**Numbers**" and "**Total**") occur only in lines 11 and 12. In all other places, the internal file names (the file objects **Numbers_to_Read** and **Total_of_Numbers**) are used to refer to the files. Lines 11 and 12 associate external file names with internal file names. By changing only lines 11 and 12, we can change the particular files we use.

The while loop in lines 13–16 continues to perform **GET**s until the numbers in the disk file are exhausted. Line 14 uses an instantiation of **INTEGER_IO** to **GET** (read) an integer. If anything other than an **INTEGER** is in the file **Numbers**, a **DATA_ERROR** will occur when we attempt to read that noninteger. In line 17, the **PUT** sends the output to the file associated with the variable **Total_of_Numbers**. Because of the association made in line 12, the number sent by line 17 will appear in the disk file **Total**. Lines 18 and 19 send a message to the user that the total has been completed. As with the message in lines 9 and 10, this probably appears on the user's screen.

Finally, in lines 20 and 21, the files with which we were working are closed. When the procedure is finished running; there will be a new file on disk named **Total**, and it will contain the total of the numbers found in the file **Numbers**.

The procedure **File_Copy** in Program 7–6 also makes use of the capabilities of **TEXT_IO**. The procedure makes a copy of a file a character at a time. While it is

```
with TEXT_IO;
procedure File_Copy is
  use TEXT_IO;
  F_Input, F_Output: FILE_TYPE;
  Ch: CHARACTER;
begin -- File_Copy
  OPEN(F_Input, IN_FILE, "input.txt");
  CREATE(F_Output, OUT_FILE, "output.txt");
  while not END_OF_FILE(F_Input) loop
    while not END_OF_LINE(F_Input) loop
      GET(F_Input, Ch);
      PUT(Ch);  -- echo to standard output
      PUT(F_Output, Ch);
    end loop;
    SKIP_LINE(F_Input);
    NEW_LINE;  -- echo to standard output
    NEW_LINE(F_Output);
  end loop;
  CLOSE(F_Input);
  CLOSE(F_Output);    -- This saves the newly created file
end File_Copy;
```

Program 7–6

making the copy, it echoes the file to the standard output. Characters from a line are read and echoed until **END_OF_LINE** is true. At the end of a line, **SKIP_LINE**, is used to advance to the next line of the input file, and two calls to **NEW_LINE** are used to echo that advance to the screen and the output.

7.8 BLOCK STATEMENTS AND EXCEPTION HANDLERS

A *block statement* is similar to a procedure, except that it is not called; rather, it is executed just like an ordinary statement. The syntax for a block statement is found in Figure 7–3.

As the syntax shows, the block name, the declarative part, and the exception section are optional. If the block has a name, the same name must also appear at the end of the block.

The declaration part of a block statement is like that of any subprogram: variables, subprograms, and even packages may be declared. According to the scope rules, declarations in the declarative part of a block statement are local to the block statement.

Our immediate use for the block statement is to introduce the *exception handler*. Additional details on exception handling are covered in Chapter 10. An exception handler is used to handle "errors" that occur within a block. In Ada, error situations that occur

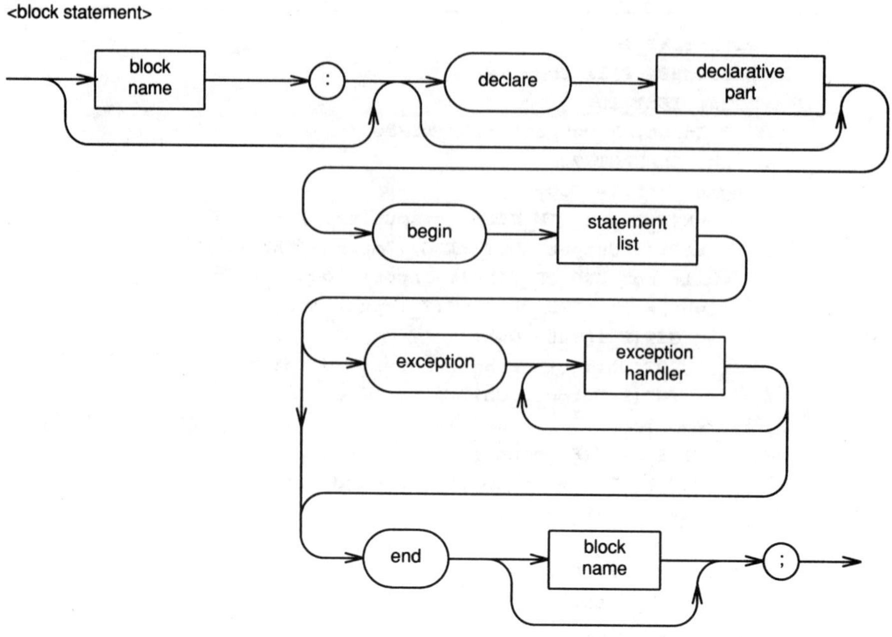

Figure 7–3

during the execution of a program are called *exceptions*. We have seen several exceptions, including **CONSTRAINT_ERROR**, **PROGRAM_ERROR**, and **DATA_ERROR**.

When an exception occurs, normal execution is abandoned and execution transfers to the appropriate exception handler. If there is no appropriate exception handler, execution of the program terminates. This is the behavior we have seen in previous programs which had exceptions. The block statement allows the program to specify an exception handler. If the exception occurs within a block statement, the exception transfers control to the exception handler at the end of the block.

The format of the exception handler, shown in Figure 7–4, resembles that of a case statement, as seen in the following example:

```
begin
  ...
exception
  when CONSTRAINT_ERROR =>
    Simple_IO.WRITE("Out of bounds");
  when DATA_ERROR | PROGRAM_ERROR =>
    Simple_IO.Write("OOPS, assuming 0");
    X := 0;
  when others =>
    Simple_IO.Write("Mysterious Error");
end;
```

<exception handler>

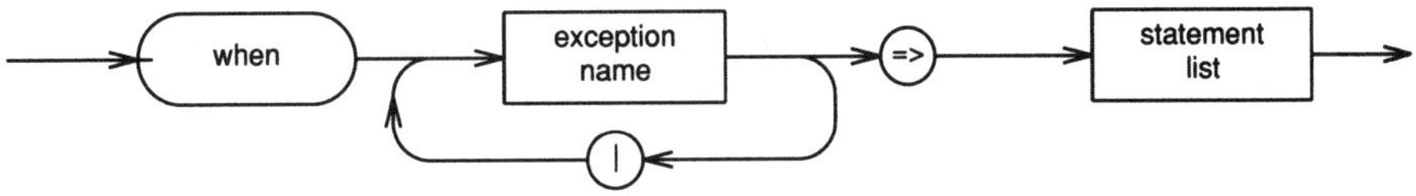

Figure 7–4

One difference from the case statement is in the lack of a selecting expression and another is in that the choices are the names of exceptions. Ranges of choices, such as

```
CONSTRAINT_ERROR..DATA_ERROR    -- illegal
```

are not allowed in an exception handler because the concept of a range has no meaning for exceptions: Exceptions are not a discrete type and they are not ordered. As with a case statement, **others** is optional, but if it occurs, it must be last and stand alone. In the preceding example, if a **CONSTRAINT_ERROR** occurs, "**Out of bounds**" will be written. If a **PROGRAM_ERROR** or **DATA_ERROR** occurs, "**OOPS, assuming 0**" will be written and a corrective action (**X:=0;**) will be taken. If any other exception occurs, "**Mysterious Error**" will be written. Any statements may be used in the statement list of an the exception handler.

Constructs other than block statements may have exception handlers. In general, any **begin** – **end** pair may have exception handlers immediately before the **end**. In particular, this means that exception handlers can occur at the end of any subprogram.

```
function Get_Integer return INTEGER is
  package Int_IO is new TEXT_IO.INTEGER_IO(INTEGER);
begin
  Simple_IO.Write("An integer please");
  loop -- exited by a return
    declare
      I: INTEGER;
    begin
      Int_IO.GET(I);
      return I;
    exception
      when TEXT_IO.DATA_ERROR =>
        Simple_IO.Write("Try again");
        TEXT_IO.SKIP_LINE;
    end;
  end loop;
exception
  when others => Simple_IO.Write("Giving up");
end Get_Integer;
```

Program 7–7

The function **Get_Integer** shown in Program 7–7 illustrates the use of exception handlers. This function reads and returns a legal integer. The loop in lines 5–16 repeatedly performs **GET**s until a legal integer has been obtained. The block in the loop contains an exception handler. If what is read at line 9 is not a legal integer, a **DATA_ERROR** exception will be raised and execution will be transferred to the exception handler starting at line 11. Since **DATA_ERROR** has an exception handler, that handler is executed, and the message "**Try again**" is printed. Execution then leaves the exception handler and resumes at line 16, then loops back to line 5. Notice that the only way out of the loop is the return statement at line 10. This return statement will be reached only if no exception occurred during the **GET**. Thus, we are guaranteed that an integer will be successfully read before the function executes the return. The handler in lines 12–14 contains a call to **SKIP_LINE** to ensure that the input that caused the exception is flushed.

The exception handler beginning at line 17 illustrates that a handler can be associated with the statement list of the procedure. Since there is only an "others" option, this handler will handle all exceptions which cause execution to transfer to line 17 in the same way.

There are many exceptions for input and output. The familiar **DATA_ERROR** occurs when the data was not of the expected type. An **END_ERROR** occurs when an attempt is made to read from a file that has already reached the end of its input. A **NAME_ERROR** occurs when an **OPEN** or **CREATE** uses an invalid file name. Others exceptions are covered in later sections.

A restriction on blocks is that if a loop contains a subprogram or package (or other constructs not yet introduced), we cannot exit that loop from within that subprogram or package. This is shown in the following example:

```
loop
  -- exit of loop allowed
  declare
    procedure No_Exit is
    begin
      -- exit of loop not allowed
    end No_Exit;
  begin
    -- exit of loop allowed
  end;
  -- exit of loop allowed
end loop;
```

This restriction applies even if (indeed, especially if) a loop name is used with the exit.

The procedure **Open_File** in Program 7–8 illustrates the use of exception handlers. This procedure could be named in the context clause of any compilation unit that might need to open a file. The procedure prompts the user for the name of the file and reads the response into a **Normal_Line**. It then converts the **Normal_Line** into a string and attempts to open the file. If it succeeds, the procedure exits; otherwise, control

```
with TEXT_IO, Lines, Simple_IO;
procedure Open_File(F: in out TEXT_IO.FILE_TYPE) is
  File_Name: Lines.Normal_Line;
begin
  Simple_IO.Write("File Name:");
  loop
    begin
      Simple_IO.Read(File_Name);
      TEXT_IO.OPEN(F, TEXT_IO.IN_FILE, Lines.Image(File_Name));
      return;
    exception
      when TEXT_IO.NAME_ERROR =>
        Simple_IO.Write("Bad file name, try again:");
    end;
  end loop;
end Open_File;
```

Program 7–8

transfers to the exception handler, which prints a message, and goes from there back to the start of the loop where it reiterates the request for the name of a file. Notice that only name errors are handled.

7.8.1 Exceptions in Robot

We describe four of the exceptions in the package **Robot**. **Initialize_World_Error** occurs if there is a problem in a call to **Initialize_World**. **Path_Blocked** occurs if the robot attempts to move through an obstacle such as a wall. **Already_Holding_Item** occurs if the robot attempts to pick up an item when it is already holding one. **Need_Item** occurs if the robot attempts to put down an item when it does not have one.

7.9 PROGRAMMING PRACTICES

One of the most important features of enumeration types is that they allow us to use a type that matches the problem. It is best to use an enumeration type instead of encoding information as integers or something else, because this allows the use of meaningful identifiers. In using enumeration types, if a value should be in a restricted range, you should ensure that it is in that range by using a subrange or subtype. Attributes should be used whenever possible with enumeration and other types. Attributes are a way of determining information about a type. It is better to use general forms that are flexible, such as attributes, rather than coding the most specific approach. That way, if the type changes, the attribute reflects the change. Since more than half of the work over the life a program is usually enhancement, flexibility is extremely valuable.

The case statement adds to our repertoire of sequential control structures. The case statement is an alternative decision-making structure. The guideline for choosing a structure is that we should match the program structure to the shape of the problem we wish to solve. If the problem requires a choice among several options that depend on a discrete value, a case statement is appropriate. In general, you should use the most restrictive control structure possible. That makes it easier to understand what the program is doing.

The principle behind the exception handler is that the program should be able to protect itself. This is especially important when the program deals with the outside world, as occurs when inputting values. A program should be structured in such a way that problems caused by unexpected behavior on the part of the outside world are handled gracefully.

7.9.1 Problem Solving

Suppose we are given the following problem:

> A personnel office in a bank keeps running out of office supplies. To deal with this problem, the bank wants us to write a program to help keep track of its inventory of office supplies so that the office staff can make sure to order more before they run out.

As a first step in solving the problem, we interview bank personnel to get more details. We need to know what information they need from the program. For instance, would they be satisfied with a program that just kept track of the number on hand of each item, or do they also need a list of suppliers for each item?

Since we are dealing with inventory, we need to know what types of items are to be kept track of and what information is to be kept on each type of item. Suppose the client indicates that we only need to keep track of how many units of each item are in stock and that we need not worry about the fact that paper is stocked in reams, pencils in dozens, and paper clips by the hundred. We will just report the number of units on hand. The items to be kept track of are pencils, paper, paper clips, file folders, labels, glue, and scissors. The client will not need to add new items later.

Finally, we need to check with the client to determine how the client would like to deal with the program. For instance, we could write a program that would read the inventory information from one file and read its commands from another file which the user would have to prepare in an editor. Suppose the client indicates a preference for having a program interact with staff directly at the keyboard. Also, the client says that we must issue an inventory report at the end of each use of the program.

To write a high-quality program, we should decide on every detail of the interaction of the program with the user before we try to design the internal workings of the program. Specifically, we need to determine what general operations are to be performed by the program (from the user's viewpoint). The program needs to be able to:

- Create a new (empty) inventory when needed.
- Adjust the inventory to a known amount.

- Add to the inventory.
- Subtract from the inventory as items are used.
- Generate the inventory report.

Notice that this list does not mention the file in which the inventory is stored. This is because, unlike the inventory report, the file is not something a user would be concerned about; rather, it is only a part of the implementation.

The documentation of how a program appears to the user is called a *specification* of the program. After careful study, we produce a specification and get the client's approval. The specification looks like this:

1. When the program is first run, it will automatically create an empty (zero) inventory for each item.
2. The program will introduce itself.
3. The program will tell the user the allowed commands and ask the user for a command. The commands are:
   a. Adjust the inventory: **ADJUST_TO**
   b. Add to the inventory: **ADD**
   c. Subtract from the inventory: **SUBTRACT**
   d. Display a description of the commands: **HELP**
   e. Issue a report and leave: **DONE**

   The prompt for a command will look like this:

```
Available commands are:
   ADJUST_TO, ADD, SUBTRACT, HELP, DONE,
Please enter a command: _
```

   The underscore indicates the position at which the user would begin typing.
4. If the user enters the command **ADD**, **ADJUST_TO**, or **SUBTRACT**, the program will list the available items and ask the user to specify one of them. The prompt for an item will look like this:

```
Available items are:
   PENCILS, PAPER, CLIPS, FOLDERS, LABELS, GLUE,
Please enter the name of an item: _
```

5. If the user enters the command **ADD**, **ADJUST_TO**, or **SUBTRACT**, the program will ask the user for the number to **ADD**, **ADJUST_TO**, or **SUBTRACT** and will update the inventory.
6. If the command is not **DONE**, then after the command is completed, the program will go back to step 3. This will permit the user to enter more commands.
7. If an unknown command or item is entered, or if a negative number is entered, then a short message will be printed and the program will continue at step 3.

This specification not only supplies a description of the appearance of the program, but also makes many of the decisions that will be necessary as we proceed to design the internal structure of the program. In fact, if we design the way the program works to match the structure described in the specification, most of the structure of the program has already been designed.

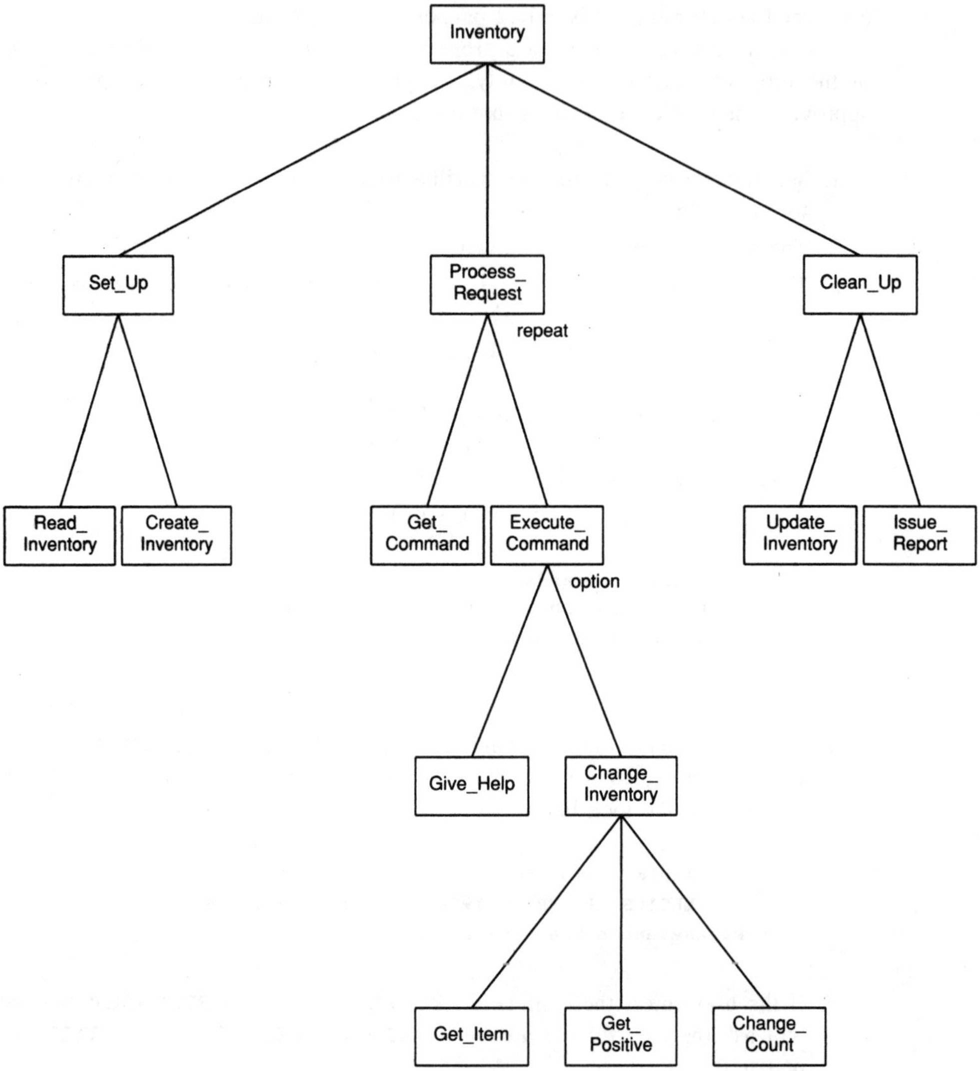

Figure 7–5

We next produce a structure chart for the program (Figure 7–5). Some information has been filled into the chart which is not in the specification, but this is mostly file work that does not concern the user. Notice that the structure chart does not mention anything that is specific to Ada. The chart merely serves to indicate a way to subdivide the problem. See whether you can see the connection between parts of the structure chart and parts of the specification.

The procedure **Inventory** shown in Program 7–9 is our sample solution for this problem. Notice how the structure of the program is developed directly from the structure chart. Since the structure chart is developed directly from the specification, it is relatively easy to determine which parts of the program correspond with which parts of the specification. The prompts are exactly the same as those mentioned in the specification (although enumerations are written using attributes rather than string literals).

As the structure chart is developed, we choose descriptive names for the entries in the chart. We should also document the purpose, parameters, etc., for each entry in the chart, but this documentation is not included here because the program is so long.

Note how all variables and procedures in the program are kept as local as possible. In addition, subranges are used wherever possible, so that certain types of programming errors will not go unnoticed. Finally, the comments in the Ada code were actually written before the procedures were written, so that the development of the code would follow the correct structure.

A program this long and complicated would be very difficult to write correctly if we had not determined its structure in advance, used meaningful names, and carefully broken the program into subprograms. We shall not describe the operation of the program; rather, it will be a good exercise to try to understand the program based on the specification, structure chart, names, and comments.

```
with TEXT_IO, SIMPLE_IO;
procedure Inventory is
  -- Purpose: Program to keep office supplies inventory.
  type Office_Supplies is (Pencils, Paper, Clips,
                           Folders, Labels, Glue, Scissors);
  package Supply_IO is new TEXT_IO.ENUMERATION_IO(Office_Supplies);
  package Integer_IO is new TEXT_IO.INTEGER_IO(INTEGER);
  type Inventory_List is array (Office_Supplies) of INTEGER;
  Supply_Counts: Inventory_List;
  procedure Set_Up_Inventory(Counts: in out Inventory_List) is
  -- Purpose: Read inventory file into Counts.
  -- Description: Open inventory file and read the contents into
  --   the Counts array.
  --   If the file does not exist, set all entries in the array to 0.
  -- Note: The file name may have to be changed to be used on your system.
    Supply_File: TEXT_IO.FILE_TYPE;     -- For reading the Inventory
    Supply: Office_Supplies;            -- Which Item are we reading?
  begin
```

Program 7–9

```
    TEXT_IO.OPEN(Supply_file, TEXT_IO.IN_FILE, "inventory");
    while not TEXT_IO.END_OF_FILE(Supply_File) loop
      Supply_IO.GET(Supply_File, Supply);
      Integer_IO.GET(Supply_File, Counts(Supply));
    end loop;
    TEXT_IO.CLOSE(Supply_File);
  exception
    when TEXT_IO.DATA_ERROR =>
      Simple_IO.Write("Bad data in Inventory file");
      Simple_IO.New_Line;
      Simple_IO.Write("Ignoring all data in Inventory file");
      Simple_IO.New_Line;
      TEXT_IO.CLOSE(Supply_File);
      Counts := (others => 0);
    when TEXT_IO.NAME_ERROR =>
      Simple_IO.Write("No Inventory file");
      Simple_IO.New_Line;
      Simple_IO.Write("Assuming zero inventory");
      Simple_IO.New_Line;
      Counts := (others => 0);
  end Set_Up_Inventory;
  procedure Clean_Up_Inventory(Counts: in Inventory_List) is
  -- Purpose: Report and save inventory.
  -- Note: Inventory will not be reported if the changes cannot be written
  -- to the Inventory file.  This is to ensure that the last reported
  -- inventory corresponds with the contents of the inventory file.
  -- Note: The file name may have to be changed to be used on your system.
    Supply_File: TEXT_IO.FILE_TYPE;     -- For writing the Inventory file.
    procedure Report_Inventory(Counts: in Inventory_List) is
    -- Purpose: Report inventory for each item to user.
    begin
      for Supply in Office_Supplies loop
        Supply_IO.PUT(Supply);
        TEXT_IO.SET_COL(20);
        Integer_IO.PUT(Counts(Supply));
        Simple_IO.New_Line;
      end loop;
    end Report_Inventory;
  begin -- Clean_Up_Inventory
    -- Save inventory
    TEXT_IO.CREATE(Supply_file, TEXT_IO.OUT_FILE, "inventory");
    for Supply in Office_Supplies loop
      Supply_IO.PUT(Supply_File, Supply);
      Integer_IO.PUT(Supply_File, Counts(Supply));
    end loop;
    TEXT_IO.CLOSE(Supply_File);
```

Program 7–9 Continued

```
  -- Report the inventory
  Report_Inventory(Counts);
exception
  when TEXT_IO.NAME_ERROR =>
    Simple_IO.Write("Cannot write Inventory to disk");
    Simple_IO.New_Line;
    Simple_IO.Write("All work in this session lost");
    Simple_IO.New_Line;
end Clean_Up_Inventory;
procedure Process_Request(Counts: in out Inventory_List) is
-- Purpose: Interact with the user to update the inventory in Counts
-- Counts: The inventory to update
-- Description: Prompt the user, read a command.
--  if the command is HELP, print a message.
--  if the command is DONE, return.
--  otherwise, ask for an item name and a count and update Counts
--  repeats until DONE entered.
  type Command_Type is (Adjust_To, Add, Subtract, Help, Done);
  subtype Invent_Command is Command_Type range Adjust_To..Subtract;
  package Command_IO is new TEXT_IO.ENUMERATION_IO(Command_Type);
  Command: Command_Type;              -- Which command?
  Are_We_Done: BOOLEAN := FALSE;      -- To control while loop for exit.
  Procedure Give_Help is
  -- Purpose: Write out a help message
  begin
    Simple_IO.Write("Adjust the inventory to a value: ADJUST_TO");
    Simple_IO.New_Line;
    Simple_IO.Write("Add to the inventory: ADD");
    Simple_IO.New_Line;
    Simple_IO.Write("Subtract from the inventory: SUBTRACT");
    Simple_IO.New_Line;
    Simple_IO.Write("This message: HELP");
    Simple_IO.New_Line;
    Simple_IO.Write("Issue report and leave: DONE");
    Simple_IO.New_Line;
  end Give_Help;
  procedure Change_Inventory(Counts: in out Inventory_List;
                             Action: Invent_Command) is
  -- Purpose: Get the item and count from the user and update the Counts.
  -- Note: The specification says that a count of 0 is not legal for ADD and
  -- SUBTRACT.  Since a count of 0 for these will not change Counts,
  -- we just ignore them.  The behavior which the user sees is the
  -- same as in the specification.
  -- Note: Any exception occurring in this procedure will be handled by
  -- the exception handler in Process_Request, since this procedure
  -- contains no exception handler.
```

Program 7–9 Continued

```
      Item: Office_Supplies;            -- Which supply?
      Count: Natural;                   -- How much?
    begin
      -- Prompt the user for an item
      Simple_IO.Write("Available items are:");
      Simple_IO.New_Line;
      Simple_IO.Write("    ");
      for Item_Prompt in Office_Supplies loop
        Supply_IO.PUT(Item_Prompt);
        Simple_IO.Write(", ");
      end loop;
      Simple_IO.New_Line;
      Simple_IO.Write("Please enter the name of an item: ");
      -- Read the item
      Supply_IO.GET(Item);
      -- Prompt the user for the number to add, subtract, etc.
      Simple_IO.Write("Please enter the value to ");
      Command_IO.PUT(Action);
      Simple_IO.Write(" ");
      Integer_IO.GET(Count);
      -- Make the change
      case Action is
        when Add =>
          Counts(Item) := Counts(Item) + Count;
        when Subtract =>
          Counts(Item) := Counts(Item) - Count;
        when Adjust_To =>
          Counts(Item) := Count;
      end case;
    end Change_Inventory;
  begin -- Process_Request
    while not Are_We_Done loop
      begin
        -- Prompt the user for a command
        Simple_IO.Write("Available commands are:");
        Simple_IO.New_Line;
        Simple_IO.Write("    ");
        for Command_Prompt in Command_Type loop
          Command_IO.PUT(Command_Prompt);
          Simple_IO.Write(", ");
        end loop;
        Simple_IO.New_Line;
        Simple_IO.Write("Please enter a command: ");
        -- Read the command
        Command_IO.GET(Command);
        case Command is
```

Program 7–9 Continued

```
            when Help => Give_Help;
            when Done => Are_We_Done := TRUE;
            when Adjust_To | Add | Subtract =>
              Change_Inventory(Counts, Command);
          end case;
        exception
          when TEXT_IO.DATA_ERROR =>
            Simple_IO.Write("That entry was not acceptable, try again.");
            Simple_IO.New_Line;
          when CONSTRAINT_ERROR =>
            Simple_IO.Write("That would result in a negative inventory");
            Simple_IO.Write(", try again.");
            Simple_IO.New_Line;
        end;
      end loop;
    end Process_Request;
  begin -- Inventory
    Simple_IO.Write("Welcome to the office supply inventory program.");
    Simple_IO.New_Line;
    Simple_IO.New_Line;
    Set_Up_Inventory(Supply_Counts);
    Process_Request(Supply_Counts);
    Clean_Up_Inventory(Supply_Counts);
  end Inventory;
```

Program 7–9 Continued

Inventory uses many of the constructs introduced in this chapter. In some situations, these constructs are used in a more complicated manner than in the examples in the rest of the chapter. Before parting, we discuss the use of these constructs in this program.

Note that subprograms from the **TEXT_IO** package are used extensively in this program. Note also that when we are writing to the display we freely mix the use of **TEXT_IO** and **Simple_IO**. **Simple_IO** is written carefully to permit this.

Exception handlers are used in several places. They permit the program to recover properly if the user enters information that cannot be accepted by the simple interaction procedures in the program. Notice that if an exception is not handled in the procedure in which it arises (e.g., **Change_Inventory**), then it becomes available to be handled in the subprogram (e.g., **Process_Request**) that called the procedure. As good programming practice, we only handle exceptions which we know what to do with, allowing any unexpected problems either to be handled by a calling subprogram or to terminate the program.

Of course, we make use of enumerated types and case statements. Look carefully at the case statement in the **Change_Inventory** procedure. For some commands there is no option listed. This is legal because we are choosing on the basis of the value of the **Action** parameter, which is of a subtype of **Command_Type**. Thus, we only need to list options for values in that subtype.

7.10 ADA SUMMARY

The chief feature of Ada covered in this chapter was the declaration and use of *enumeration types*. We have indicated how attributes and subranges can be used with these (and other) types to produce programs that are more maintainable and more likely to be correct.

The *case statement* completes coverage of the sequential control structures. It is a specialized statement, designed to be used with discrete types when there are multiple choices.

We have introduced the package **TEXT_IO** and, with it, the capability to perform input and output on enumeration types and the standard Ada methods of performing input and output on integers and reals. We have also shown how to perform input and output with files.

In addition, we have covered the fundamentals of *exception handling*, a mechanism for recovering gracefully from errors.

EXERCISES

7.1. The function **Future_Day** in Program 7–4 naively counts off the days. Using the **POS**, **VAL**, and **mod** functions it is possible to reduce this **Future_Day** to a single return statement. Develop the expression for this return statement, and modify **Future_Day** to contain a single return statement using this expression.

7.2. Write a users' manual for the **Inventory** procedure in Program 7–9. The manual should describe how to use the program, but not mention anything about how the program works. Of course, the manual must be written in correct English (including correct grammar and spelling).

7.3. Add a **Report** command to procedure **Inventory**. The procedure should no longer automatically report the inventory when the user enters the **DONE** command. Instead, the **Report** command should write the inventory report to the screen when it is called. In rewriting **Inventory**, be careful, because you will have to change the nesting of procedures. You must maintain good programming style, including using meaningful identifiers and keeping all entities as local as possible. The simpler and easier your solution, the better it is.

7.4. Change the procedure **Inventory** so that if there is no inventory file, the user is asked to enter the initial inventory for each item. You must accept any amount of 0 or more, but negative amounts are not permitted. Maintain good programming style, including using meaningful identifiers and keeping all entities as local as possible.

7.5. Write a program **Days_Between** which calculates the number of days between two dates. Use the following enumeration type:

```
type Months is (January, February, March, April, May, June,
                July, August, September, October, November, December);
```

First your program will open a file called "**daysinmonth**". (You may have to change this name for your system.) This file will contain a month (correctly spelled), followed by an integer indicating the number of days in that month. Each month will occur in the file exactly once, but the months might not be in order. For example, the file could contain

```
February 28
April 30
March 31
  ...
```

Now your program will ask the user for two dates, the "starting date" and the "ending date" (in the same year). It then computes and reports the number of days between the starting date and the ending date. For example, with a starting date of January 12 and an ending date of January 13, the program reports 1 day. Similarly, the number of days between February 23 and April 6 would be 42 — 5 to February 28, 31 more to March 31, and 6 more to April 6. (Assume that we are not in a leap year.)

When the user enters a date, you must detect any illegal input. On entry of each date, the program will first request and read a month. If the month is illegal, it will detect this illegality using an exception handler and repeat the request. (You will need to use **SKIP_LINE** to clear-out the illegal month.) The request will be repeated until a correct month is entered. (The procedure **Get_Integer** in section 7.8 does this.) After the month has been entered, the program will request a date. The date must lie in the legal subrange for the month which was just entered. Again, you must detect any illegal input. Furthermore, you must use an exception handler (and subranges) to perform this detection.

7.6. Write a program that asks for input from the user, carries out the user's instructions, and then asks for the next set of instructions.

The purpose of this exercise is to give you some experience with writing exception handlers. While it is true that you could write this program in such a way as to prevent any exception from being raised (i.e., with **Robot.Look**), that is *not* what we want you to do. Rather, we want to you go ahead and attempt to do what the user specifies, and then to handle any exceptions that may be raised so that you can see the effect of exceptions on the order of execution and how various actions can be taken.

Ask for an input **Normal_Line**, and for each character in that **Normal_Line**, do the following:

```
'L' = turn left
'R' = turn right
'0'-'9' = move the indicated number of spaces
'P' = pick something up in current location
'D' = drop something at current location
<paint chars subset> = set the paint to the indicated "color" and
                       turn painting on
' ' = turn painting off
```

Depending on the exception that gets raised, you are to maintain a count of how many times that exception is raised during the processing of a particular input line. Do *not* handle any exceptions by skipping over the rest of the line and asking for another. When you are through processing the line, inform the user of any mistakes, for example:

```
You bumped into the wall 12 times.
You tried to pick up nonexistent objects 3 times.
```

Finish by asking the user whether to read another input line or quit.

7.7. Modify the **Bank_Account** package and **Teller** procedure built in exercise 5.9. The package specification is

```
package Bank_Account is
  procedure Deposit(Amount_of_Deposit, Account: NATURAL);
  -- Purpose: Record a deposit to the specified account.
  procedure Withdraw(Amount_of_Withdrawal, Account: NATURAL);
  -- Purpose: Record a withdrawal from the specified account.
  function Account_Balance(Account: NATURAL) return NATURAL;
  -- Purpose: Return the balance in the specified account.
  procedure Post_Interest;
  -- Purpose: Post interest to all accounts.
  procedure Initialize_Bank;
  -- Purpose: Starting a new bank, set all account balances to zero.
  procedure Start_Bank;
  -- Purpose: Get the bank ready to open for the day. Read account balances
  -- from the account balance file.
  procedure Close_Bank;
  -- Purpose: Close the bank for the day. Write current account balances
  -- to the account balance file.
end Bank_Account;
```

Add the appropriate capabilities to the **Teller** procedure. The package should keep, in a separate file, a record of each transaction the teller requests.

7.8. Using **TEXT_IO**, write a procedure that copies an input file (**input.txt**) consisting of lines of characters to an output file (**output.txt**), in the process, changing the case of all letters (upper case to lower and lower case to upper). While reading the input file, the procedure should count the following:

(1) Number of lines
(2) Number of characters
(3) Number of upper case letters
(4) Number of lower case letters
(5) Number of digits
(6) Number of arithmetic operators (+, –, *, /)

Once the file has been read in and copied, the procedure should print these items, with suitable identification. For example, one possible output would be:

```
Number of lines = 21
Number of characters = 673
...
```

7.9. Build a procedure that provides an interface for the **Bank_Account** package found in Program 3–14 (or exercises 3.1, 4.5, or 5.9). (This procedure should name the **Bank_Account** package in its context clause.) Banking transactions have the following forms:

Deposit <amount>

Withdraw <amount>

Balance

where <amount> is a nonnegative integer (ignore pennies). The procedure should read and process a series of transactions from the file **"transact.txt"**. An example of the file's format is as follows:

```
DEPOSIT 325
WITHDRAW 50
BALANCE
```

If a transaction fails to conform to this syntax (e.g., "**DEPOSIT**" is spelled "**DEPOSIR**"), the procedure does not process the transaction; instead, it prints an error message, skips the rest of the line, and tries reading a new transaction on the next line. (Hint: use **ENUMERATION_IO**).

7.10. Write a program that reads an Ada source file and prints out counts of the number of times each of the following are found in the source file, excluding from these counts all occurrences that are part of comments, character literals, and string literals:

(1) The number of Ada identifiers

(2) The number of times the compound delimiter "**:=**" occurs

(3) The number of times a semicolon "**;**" occurs, except between parentheses. (Thus, semicolons that terminate statements and most declarations will be included, while those that are within parameter list declarations will not.)

7.11. Write a procedure **Capitalize** that has two input files and one output file. The "dictionary" is an input file consisting of key words. The "source" is an input file whose contents are treated as though they were syntactically correct Ada. The "output" is an output file that is a copy of the source file with the capitalization of all the key words *found* in it changed to match that given in the dictionary. A key word is considered *found* whenever it occurs (with any capitalization) outside of an Ada string literal, outside of an Ada comment and outside a character literal. Thus, if the dictionary file contains only "**Text_IO**", the following line from source file:

```
TEXT_IO.PUT("text_io");   text_io.PUT_LINE;   -- TEXT_IO use
```

would appear in the output file as:

```
Text_IO.PUT("text_io");   Text_IO.PUT_LINE;   -- TEXT_IO use
```

Capitalize starts by reading the dictionary file. Then the program reads the source file, checking each word in it against the dictionary and writing the modified lines to the output file. Remember, the input and output files differ only in that the capitalization of key words that were found in the source file has been changed to match their entries in the dictionary.

8

Structuring Data

8.1 OBJECTIVES

Structuring data is essential to many complex problems. Thus far, we have introduced limited capabilities for structuring data with array types. In this chapter, we supply additional capabilities for the iteration of data, with the introduction of *multidimensional arrays*, and for the handling of data, with an examination of operators that apply to arrays (section 3). We cover the declaration of *record* types, which supply the capability of grouping items of dissimilar types (section 4). For both of these, we introduce attributes that permit the writing of generalized procedures and *aggregates*, which permit values to be assigned to complex data objects. We also show how the programmer can *overload* operators to define functions for complex data types (section 5). Finally, in our discussion of *qualified expressions*, we return to the notion of a type as applied to operators that are overloaded.

CONCEPTS:

- For some problems, matrices are the natural method of expression for both the problem and the answer.
- There are useful operators for arrays beyond those we have already studied.
- For arrays, there is a construct that is similar to a literal. One use of this construct is to define array constants.
- In many problems, it is natural to group related data that are not of identical types.

- Sometimes it is convenient to have a single identifier associated with multiple meanings, especially if those meanings are closely related.
- Operators can be declared by the programmer.

GOALS:

- Use a two-dimensional array to store and retrieve data.
- Build a procedure that sorts complex information.
- Define some overloaded meanings for operators in a package. Use these operators to solve a problem.

8.2 MOTIVATION

In previous chapters, we introduced some elementary capabilities for organizing and expressing data, including iterating data using arrays and associating identifiers with values using enumerations. In many problems the structure of the data is complex. For example, the records a university maintains on its students and staff contain a wide variety of information. Some pieces of information contain further details or information. Modern programming languages allow the programmer to build data structures that reflect the nature of the information required by the problem. In this chapter, we extend our coverage of arrays and introduce the powerful data-structuring capabilities of *records*. Records and the advanced capabilities of arrays allow the programmer to produce programs that both are very understandable and reflect the data organization of the problems the programs solve.

Ada supports these data-structuring capabilities with many of the capabilities it supplied for simple types. This support includes attributes which are helpful in writing code that can be easily understood and modified. The attributes of complex data types are even more useful for achieving this goal. Constants were another construct designed for making programs understandable. The capability to declare constants of complex types leads to the natural introduction of the concept of *aggregates*, which is necessary for this capability. In fact, aggregates have far wider application than just the declaration of constants.

8.3 ADVANCED ARRAYS

A number of capabilities are desirable with respect to arrays. First, there is often a need for a data structure indexed by more than one subscript. Second, some additional attributes would enable us to write more portable programs. Third, some additional operators would be convenient. Fourth, something similar to a literal would be useful in assigning values to arrays. In this section, we consider some capabilities of Ada which solve these problems.

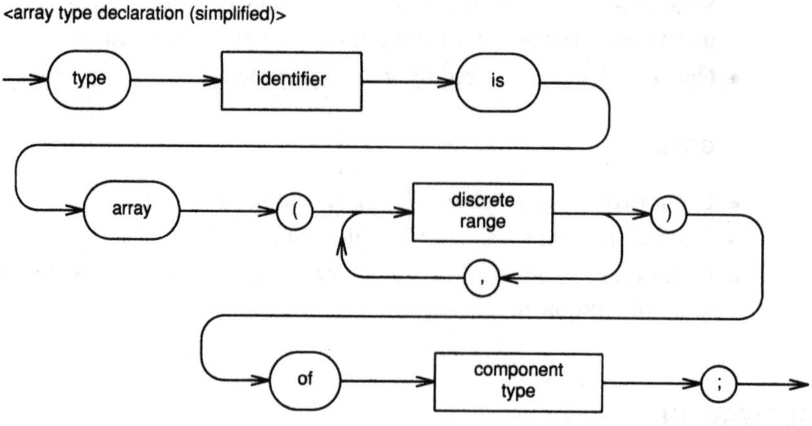

Figure 8–1

8.3.1 Arrays of Arrays

Recall that an array is an indexed collection of components of the same subtype. These components can be of any type. In particular, an array can contain components that are themselves arrays. The syntax for declaring arrays is given in Figure 8–1. This diagram is similar to Figure 5–4, which we used for array type definitions in Chapter 5.

Under the syntax rules, the following declarations are legal:

```
type Bools_4 is array (INTEGER range 4..7) of BOOLEAN;
type Components_22 is array (INTEGER range -6..15) of Bools_4;
B_4: Bools_4;
C_22: Components_22;
```

The array type **Components_22** has 22 components, each of which is of type **Bools_4**. Components of type **Bools_4** are arrays of 4 Boolean values. Thus, the array **C_22**, which is of type **Components_22**, contains 22 arrays, each of which contains 4 Boolean values. That is, **C_22** contains a total of 88 Boolean values.

The organization (22 groups of 4) is very important. Suppose we had 22 vehicles, each containing 4 people (say, 22 cars). That is quite different from having 4 vehicles, each containing 22 people (say, 4 buses). Even though the total number of people is the same, these two configurations would be dealt with quite differently. The same is true with arrays of arrays.

Accessing an element in an array of arrays is reasonably simple. To access an element in a simple array requires an index. To access an element in an array of arrays requires two indices. For **C_22**, the first index indicates one of the 22 arrays that are its components, and the second index indicates one of the 4 Boolean values within that component. Thus,

```
C_22(9)(7) := TRUE;
```

accesses the array whose subscript is 9 and, within that array, accesses the Boolean value whose subscript is 7. The separate sets of parentheses around each index reflect the organization.

As with simple arrays, indices can be expressions of the appropriate type, as illustrated in the assignment

```
C_22(3+4)(2 * 5 - 6) := TRUE;
```

Now that we have given examples we present the terminology. In Chapter 1, we observed that a variable is accessed by using a *name* that refers to it. In Ada, one kind of name is the identifier. In Ada, a name denotes an entity. In Chapter 1, the names were identifiers and the entities were variables. In Chapter 3, we used identifiers to denote two types of objects, variables and constants. We have actually seen other names, including literals, attributes and operators which denote other entities, which we shall discuss further in Chapter 9. In this section, we have seen that objects can have complex types. Accordingly, we can access those objects by a more complex form of name. For example, `C_22(9)` is a name. The entity it denotes is a complex object that happens to be an array object containing 4 Boolean values. In the assignment statement, `C_22(9)(7) := TRUE`, the name `C_22(9)` denotes an object of type `Bools_4`, and the second index, `(7)`, is the subscript of an object of type `Bools_4`, that indicates which of the four components we want.

Since, `C_22(9)` names an object of type `Bools_4`, it is compatible with other array objects of type `Bools_4`. This means that operations like the assignment

```
C_22(9) := B_4;
```

are legal. In this assignment, the right and left sides are compatible with each other because they both denote objects of type `Bools_4`. The semantics of such an assignment are straightforward. There are 4 Boolean values in `B_4`, and there are 4 locations in which to store those values in `C_22(9)`. The 4 values are stored one per location. In particular, the value from `B_4(4)` is stored in `C_22(9)(4)`, the value from `B_4(5)` is stored in `C_22(9)(5)`, and so forth. A good way to think of this is that the right side evaluates to an object with a complex value (i.e., 4 Boolean values), and this complex value is stored in the complex variable named on the left side. This way of thinking about the assignment keeps the 4 values together as a group.

8.3.2 Two-Dimensional Arrays

It is possible to have a two-dimensional array. In mathematics, such an array is called a *matrix*. A typical mathematical matrix has the following form:

$$
\begin{matrix}
A_{11} & A_{12} & A_{13} & A_{14} \\
A_{21} & A_{22} & A_{23} & A_{24} \\
A_{31} & A_{32} & A_{33} & A_{34}
\end{matrix}
$$

In Ada, a two-dimensional array similar to this is expressed by using a comma between discrete ranges (see Figure 8–1). The following declarations are illustrative:

```
type Two_Dim is array (INTEGER range 1..3, INTEGER range 1..4) of INTEGER;
A: Two_Dim;
```

The following declarations create a matrix of Boolean values:

```
type Two_Dim_Bool_Array is array
  (INTEGER range -6..15, INTEGER range 4..7) of BOOLEAN;
B_88: Two_Dim_Bool_Array;
```

The type **Two_Dim_Bool_Array** is a two-dimensional array of Boolean values. The individual components are of the type **BOOLEAN** and are arranged in a two-dimensional pattern. Note that this is *not* an array of arrays, it is a two-dimensional array of Boolean values. The structure is distinct from the type **Components_22** discussed earlier. Indeed, the method of accessing a component of a two-dimensional array is different from that of accessing a component of an arrays of arrays. An example of assigning a value to a component of **B_88** is

```
B_88(9, 7) := TRUE;
```

In referencing a component of a two-dimensional array, the indices are separated by commas. There is no such thing as a component of type **Bools_4** within arrays of type **Two_Dim_Bool_Array**. In the two-dimensional array **B_88**, the components are 88 individual Boolean variables which are accessed using two subscripts.

You should always choose the most natural organization for your arrays. In the case of something like a book, a page is an array of lines and each line is an array of characters. Thus, for this application, an array of arrays should be selected. In the case of representing the world of the robot, there seems to be no difference between rows and columns and no reason why the elements should be grouped by row rather than column or the other way around. For this application, a two-dimensional array is appropriate.

Remember that array components are variables, so they can be used in expressions. If, in addition to the declaration of **B_88** we had the array declarations:

```
type Array_3_by_6 is array (INTEGER range 2..4, INTEGER range 1..6) of INTEGER;
Ints_18: Array_3_by_6;
```

and the assignment

```
Ints_18(3, 2) := 14;
```

then the following are legal:

```
B_88(Ints_18(3, 2) - 1 , 7) := B_88(3, 4);
```

```
C_22(Ints_18(3, 2) - 1)(7) := B_88(3, 4);
```

An element of **Ints_18** is a variable of type **INTEGER** whose value can be used in an integer expression. An integer expression can be used to index the array types **Two_Dim_Bool_Array**, **Bools_4**, and **Components_22**. Because the integer expression

```
Ints_18(3, 2) - 1
```

evaluates to 13, the component of **B_88** that is accessed is **(13,7)** and the component of **C_22** that is accessed is **(13)(7)**.

Notice that even though **B_88** and **C_22** are of different types, the second of these two assignment statements is legal because both **C_22(13)(7)** and **B_88(3,4)** are both of type **BOOLEAN** and therefore compatible. It does not matter that these Boolean values are contained within quite different structures. In this case, the assignment is of a single Boolean value to a single Boolean variable.

Arrays are not limited to two dimensions: More deeply nested declarations and higher dimensions are allowed. Neither is it necessary for all indices to be of an integer type. This is shown in the following declarations:

```
type Three_Dimensions is array (INTEGER range 1..2,
  CHARACTER range 'A'..'Z', INTEGER range 1..3) of CHARACTER;
Three_D_Array, Other_Three_D_Array: Three_Dimensions;
```

These lines declare an array of three dimensions in which the second index has the type **CHARACTER**. We can assign a value to an element of this array as follows:

```
Three_D_Array(1, 'B', 2) := 'C';
```

Since the type **Three_Dimensions** has no intermediate structures, this assignment and reassigning the entire array are the only forms of assignments allowed on **Three_D_Array**.

Since the two arrays are of the same type, the following assignment may be performed:

```
Three_D_Array := Other_Three_D_Array;
```

This results in each value in the array **Other_Three_D_Array** being copied into the corresponding position in the array **Three_D_Array**.

The lines:

```
type Simple_Array is array (INTEGER range 1..3) of CHARACTER;
type Nested_Array is array (CHARACTER range 'A'..'Z') of Simple_Array;
type Double_Nesting is array (INTEGER range 1..2) of Nested_Array;
D_Nested, Other_Nested: Double_Nesting;
```

declare an array with components nested two levels deep. The following statements access various components of this array:

```
D_Nested(1)('B')(2)  := 'C';
D_Nested(2)('X')  := D_Nested(1)('Y');
D_Nested(2)  := D_Nested(1);
Other_Nested  := D_Nested;
```

In the first of these, a component of type **CHARACTER** is assigned a value. In the second, a component of type **Simple_Array** is assigned a value from another component of the same type. In the third, the assignment is performed using components of type **Nested_Array**. The first three of these assignments reflect the fact that components of type **Double_Nesting** contain components. In the fourth statement, an assignment to an entire array is performed.

8.3.3 Comparison of Arrays

A structure of the type **Double_Nesting** has further consequences because the relational operations of equality (=) and inequality (/=) are allowed on objects of the same type. Thus, the comparisons:

```
D_Nested(2)('X')  = D_Nested(1)('Y')
D_Nested(2)  /= D_Nested(1)
```

are legal Boolean relations and could be used in an if statement or while schema.

The requirement for two complex objects to be equal is strict. In the first of the preceding comparisons, the two objects are equal only if they contain the same value in each of their 3 components; that is, only if the following three equalities are true:

```
D_Nested(2)('X')(1)  = D_Nested(1)('Y')(1)
D_Nested(2)('X')(2)  = D_Nested(1)('Y')(2)
D_Nested(2)('X')(3)  = D_Nested(1)('Y')(3)
```

The comparison is always between pairs of components, one from each of the objects. Similarly, the second comparison for inequality returns the value true if *any* of the 78 pairs of characters are not equal.

Of course, entire arrays may be compared, as in

```
Three_D_Array = Other_Three_D_Array
```

This comparison yields the value true only if each component in **Three_D_Array** is equal to the corresponding component in **Other_Three_D_Array**.

One additional type of comparison is allowed in a special case. If the items to be compared are one-dimensional arrays with discrete components, then comparison testing using <, >, <=, or >= is possible. In this case, the comparison is lexicographic, i.e., the first two elements are compared, and only if they are equal are the next elements compared. In the declarations

```
type Days is (Mon, Tue, Wed, Thur, Fri, Sat, Sun);
type Compare_Demo is array(1..3) of Days;
X, Y: Compare_Demo;
```

both **X** and **Y** are one-dimensional arrays whose components are of the discrete type **Days**. Therefore, they can be compared. This means that **X<Y**, **X<=Y**, **X>Y**, and **X>=Y** are legal Boolean expressions. Accordingly, these expressions could be used, say, in an if statement like

```
if X < Y then ...
```

Again, the comparison is lexicographic. Suppose that the values in **X** are **(Mon, Thur, Tue)** and the values in **Y** are **(Mon, Fri, Mon)**. The comparison **X<Y** proceeds as follows. The first element of **X** is compared with the first element of **Y**. Since **Mon** equals **Mon**, the second element of **X** is compared with the second element of **Y**. Since **Thur** is less than **Fri**, **X** is less than **Y**. The value of the third element is not checked. Lexicographically, the third element is not as important as the second in comparisons. The last element will be relevant only if all the preceding elements are equal. As a reminder, the words in an English dictionary appear in lexicographic (also called alphabetic) order.

8.3.4 Logical Operators on Boolean Arrays

Another special case occurs with Boolean operators: Any of the logical operators, including **not**, may be used on one-dimensional arrays of Boolean values. The type **Bools_4** (repeated) in the declaration

```
type Bools_4 is array (INTEGER range 4..7) of BOOLEAN;
B3, B4: Bools_4;
```

is a one-dimensional array of Boolean values. As such, the Boolean operators can be applied to objects of this type. For example, the statement

```
B3 := B3 and B4;
```

is legal. What happens is that the **and** operation is performed for each element in the array. Thus, the assignment has the same effect as the following four statements:

```
B3(4) := B3(4) and B4(4);
B3(5) := B3(5) and B4(5);
B3(6) := B3(6) and B4(6);
B3(7) := B3(7) and B4(7);
```

The only difference between the two forms is that in the single statement all four **ands** on the right-hand side are computed before any assignment occurs, while in the four statements, assignments occur as the values are computed.

Suppose the array **B3** contains the values

```
TRUE, TRUE, FALSE, FALSE
```

and the array **B4** contains the values

```
TRUE, FALSE, TRUE, FALSE
```

Then the previous assignment statement stores the new values

```
TRUE, FALSE, FALSE, FALSE
```

into the variable **B3**.

8.3.5 Array Attributes

We have already seen that attributes are useful for writing flexible procedures. We now introduce extensions to some array attributes we have already seen and some additional array attributes. The attributes **FIRST**, **LAST**, and **RANGE** return information about the index of an array object or array type. In dealing with a multi-dimensional array, there is more than one index, so we need some way to specify which index we are referring to. The syntax for specifying which index is to include a number following the attribute identifier. Thus, **FIRST(1)** returns the **FIRST** value of the first index, and **LAST(3)** returns the **LAST** value of the third index.

In addition to these three attributes, we introduce an additional array attribute. The **LENGTH** attribute specifies the number of values an index has. For example, **LENGTH(2)** returns the number of values the second index can assume. In other words, it returns the size of the array in the second dimension.

Consider the following declaration:

```
type Grade_Array is array(INTEGER range 3..6,
                          CHARACTER range 'A'..'E') of CHARACTER;
```

With this declaration, the value of **Grade_Array'FIRST(1)** is 3, because the smallest (**FIRST**) value of the first (1) index is **3**. Similarly, the value of **Grade_Array'FIRST(2)** is **'A'**. If no index is specified, the attribute returns the value of the first index. Thus, **Grade_Array'RANGE** is the same as **Grade_Array'RANGE(1)** and returns the range **3..6**. Finally, **Grade_Array'LENGTH(2)** returns the value **5**, the number of characters in **'A'..'E'**.

8.3.6 Array Aggregates

An *aggregate* is a method of assigning values to an array. Aggregates are to array objects what character literals are to objects of type **CHARACTER**. An aggregate is a list of values. For example, with the declarations

```
type Agg_Demo is array (INTEGER range 2..11) of INTEGER;
Even: Agg_Demo;
```

the array **Even** can hold 10 integer values. An assignment to **Even** may be performed using an aggregate as follows:

```
Even := (2, 4, 6, 8, 10, 12, 14, 16, 18, 20);
```

Here, the aggregate consists of a list of 10 integer values. This aggregate is compatible with any one-dimensional array type which contains 10 components that are of an integer type. In the assignment, the value **2** is assigned to **Even(2)**, the value **4** to **Even(3)**, and so forth. An aggregate may be used with an array regardless of the type of the components and the type of the indices. Consider the declarations:

```
type Days is (Mon, Tue, Wed, Thur, Fri, Sat, Sun);
type Agg_Day_Demo is array('A'..'E') of Days;
Day_List: Agg_Day_Demo;
```

The array **Day_List** requires 5 values of type **Days**, so a legal assignment using an aggregate is

```
Day_List := (Fri, Wed, Wed, Tue, Sun);
```

All of the preceding aggregates have used positional notation. However, as with parameters, named notation may be used for aggregates. For example,

```
Day_List := ('E' => Fri, 'C' => Wed, 'A' => Wed, 'D' => Tue, 'B' => Sun);
```

supplies values for each of the 5 components of **Day_List**. The syntax of aggregates requires that they be complete and unique; that is, all components must be supplied values, and no component can be designated twice.

If several elements are to be assigned a single value, the vertical bar "|" may be used as in the case statement to separate choices. So the preceding aggregate could be rewritten as

```
Day_List := ('E' => Wed, 'C'|'A' => Mon, 'D' => Thur, 'B' => Mon);
```

Ranges may also be represented either directly as in

```
Day_List := ('A'|'C'..'E' => Fri, 'B' => Sun);
```

or through the use of subtypes, as in

```
subtype Small_Letter is CHARACTER range 'A'..'C';
  ...
Day_List := (Small_Letter => Fri, 'D'|'E' => Sun);
```

As with the case statement, there is an *others* option, that must occur last and that must not be associated with any other choices; that is, it may not be associated with a vertical bar. An example using positional notation is

```
Day_List := (Mon, others => Fri);
```

In this case, the first element of **Day_List** receives the value **Mon**, and all others receive the value **Fri**. The use of **others** with named notation requires qualification and will be discussed in section 6. Unlike parameters, with the exception of the others option, an array aggregate may not mix positional and named association.

The values in an aggregate can be the result of expressions. An example is

```
Day_List := (Mon, others => Day_List('B'));
```

Here, the values in the aggregate are of type **Days** and the expression **Day_List('B')** produces a value of that type. As with other instances of the assignment statement, the expression is evaluated before the assignment occurs. In this case the expression is the aggregate and all expressions included in the aggregate. Thus, the new value of the "others" elements of **Day_List** will depend on the old value of the **'B'**th element of **Day_List**.

When using named association, aggregates can use static expressions as the names. For example, if we had

```
I : constant INTEGER := 6;
```

we could say

```
Y := (I + 1 => 2, ...);
```

The important point is that **I+1** is static, that is, the value of the expression can be determined before program execution begins.

If there is only one choice, nonstatic expressions can be used, as in

```
Ch_1, Ch_2: CHARACTER;
  ...
Day_List := (Ch_1..Ch_2 => Fri);
```

Here, the only choice is **Ch_1..Ch_2**, so this choice can use (**CHARACTER**) expressions, as illustrated by the use of variables. Notice that the equivalent effect could have been obtained by

```
Day_List := (others => Fri);
```

Here the single choice **others** is not static because the size of **Day_List** may not be determinable at compilation time.

A multidimensional array, or an array of arrays, can be initialized by an aggregate of aggregates. Suppose we have the declarations

```
type Agg_Component is array (CHARACTER range 'A'..'C') of Days;
type Agg_Demo is array (INTEGER range 1..2) of Agg_Component;
Data: Agg_Demo;
```

Then a legal aggregate assignment is

```
Data := ((Mon, Tue, Wed), (Thur, Fri, Sat));
```

Data has two components, each containing three variables of type **Days**. Consequently, the aggregate has two components, **(Mon, Tue, Wed)** and **(Thur, Fri, Sat)**, each containing three values of type **Days**. The structure of the aggregate must match the structure of the object for which it is supplying a value.

In the case of this particular assignment, we could have placed the same values into **Data** by the pair of assignments

```
Data(1) := (Mon, Tue, Wed);
Data(2) := (Thur, Fri, Sat);
```

However, remember that with assignment, the right-hand side is evaluated before the assignment is performed. In the assignment

```
Data := (Data(2), Data(1));
```

The aggregate contains two components, **Data(2)** and **Data(1)**, each of which contains three values of the type **Days**. Thus, the assignment is legal. Furthermore, because the right-hand side is evaluated before the assignment is performed, this assignment swaps the values in the two components of **Data**.

The two-dimensional array **Z** declared as

```
type Two_Dim_Agg_Demo is array(INTEGER range 1..3,
                               INTEGER range 3..4) of INTEGER;

Z: Two_Dim_Agg_Demo;
```

can be initialized in the following manner:

```
Z := ((1, 2), (2, 3), (3, 4));
```

Although **Z** is not an array of arrays, for the purposes of an aggregate it is treated as having three components (**1..3**) of two integers (**3..4**) each. Notice that the parentheses in the aggregate reflect this structure.

Aggregates can be used to assign initial values to variables, so we could have written

```
Z: Two_Dim_Agg_Demo := ((1, 2), (2, 3), (3, 4));
```

to declare the variable **Z** and, at elaboration, **Z** would be initialized to the value specified by this aggregate. The others option is available with multi-dimensional arrays, as in

```
Z: Two_Dim_Agg_Demo := ((others => 0), others => (2, 3));
```

The preceding aggregate is equivalent to

```
( (0, 0), (2, 3), (2, 3) )
```

Named notation may also be used:

```
Z: Two_Dim_Agg_Demo := (2 => (3 => 1, 4 => 2), 3 => (2, 3), 1 => (3, 4));
```

Although this declaration uses both named and positional notation, notice that it does not mix the two. The outer aggregate strictly uses named notation. Of the three inner aggregates, one strictly uses named notation and two strictly use positional notation. Of course, this type of mixing is poor style, even though it is legal. All second level aggregates should use the same notation, and the order of entries in a named association should be meaningful.

Constant arrays are allowed. They have the programming advantages of other constant objects. Like other constants, they allow a way of associating an identifier with a value. Aggregates provide a way to specify the value of a constant array:

```
Constant_Array: constant Two_Dim_Agg_Demo := ((1, 2), (2, 3), (3, 4));
```

Of course, in a nested procedure, a constant can be initialized from a variable, parameter, or aggregate. For example, we could form a local constant by

```
procedure Other_Const(Z: Two_Dim_Agg_Demo) is
  C: constant Two_Dim_Agg_Demo := Z;
```

As with other local constants, after it has been elaborated, **C** is constant during execution of the procedure. Of course, its value is recomputed each time the procedure **Other_Const** is elaborated. This means that a constant array cannot be assigned new values, either in part or in whole.

A special rule applies to aggregates containing a single component. Such aggregates must use named association. For example, if an aggregate is used to give a value to the array object in the declaration

```
type Short_Array is array (INTEGER range 6..6) of BOOLEAN;
One_Component: Short_Array;
```

then that aggregate must use named association, as in

```
One_Component := (6 => TRUE);
```

This rule prohibits the only case in which an aggregate might have the same syntax as a parenthesized expression.

8.3.7 Slices

A contiguous portion of a one-dimensional array is called a *slice*. The syntax for a slice is given in Figure 8–2.

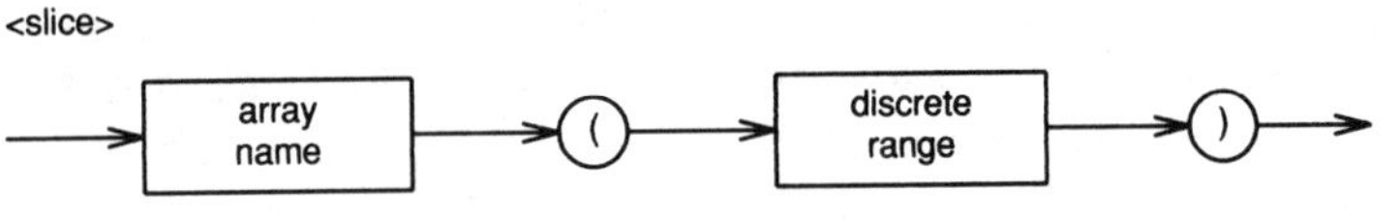

Figure 8–2

Like other variables, slices have types. The type of a slice is the base type of the array from which it is formed. (Until we reach Chapter 12, the type and base type will always be the same for array types.) Thus, two slices are compatible if they are from the same array or arrays of the same base type. A very common operation on slices is assignment. A slice assignment moves a contiguous portion of an array from one location to another.

In the procedure **Slice_It** in Program 8–1, the assignment at line 6 is legal because both slices are from the same array. Since both slices have 5 elements, the assignment proceeds without a constraint error. The values in the array **V2** become

```
(24, 25, 26, 27, 28, 26, 27, 28, 29, 30);
```

Elements 4 through 8 have been copied over into elements 1 through 5. Notice that even though the slices overlapped, the rule that the right-hand side of an assignment is evaluated before any portion of the left-hand side is given a value avoids any confusion.

Because **V1** and **V2** are of the same type, the assignment at line 7 is legal and changes the value of **V1** to

```
(11, 12, 27, 28, 26, 27, 28, 18, 19, 20);
```

```
1:procedure Slice_It(X: INTEGER) is
2:   type Array_Type is array (INTEGER range 1..10) of INTEGER;
3:   V1: Array_Type := (11,12,13,14,15,16,17,18,19,20);
4:   V2: Array_Type := (21,22,23,24,25,26,27,28,29,30);
5:begin
6:   V2(1..5) := V2(4..8);
7:   V1(3..7) := V2(6..10);
8:   V2(2..5) := V2(4..8);     -- constraint error
9:   V1(3..1) := V2(55..54); -- null slice
10:  V1(X..X+2) := V1(X+3..X+5);
11:end Slice_It;
```

Program 8–1

Elements 4 through 8 from **V2** (after having been changed at line 6) are assigned to elements 3 through 7 of **V1**.

The assignment at line 8 is syntactically legal because the types match. However, the slice on the left side of the assignment has 4 elements and the slice on the right side has 5. Ada requires that constraint checking be performed on slices and on slice assignment to ensure that the same number of elements occurs on both sides of the assignment. For this reason, line 8 will result in a **CONSTRAINT_ERROR**.

A null slice occurs when the lower bound of the range exceeds the upper bound. As illustrated in line 9, null slices are legal. An exception to the rule on range checking occurs with null slices: It does not matter if the values are outside the normal range for array indices. Thus, the bounds **55..54** that occur on the right-hand side of line 9 do *not* result in a **CONSTRAINT_ERROR**. Neither does the fact that **3..1** is a wider null range than **55..54**. A null range is a null range, no matter what.

Finally, the assignment in line 10 is legal and indicates that the bounds of a slice can be expressions. In fact, a slice can be made on array aggregates, constant arrays, and array values returned by functions.

8.3.8 Strong Typing

The following variable is of an anonymous type:

```
Anonymous_Array: array (INTEGER range 1..10) of INTEGER;
```

Anonymous types are unusual in the Ada language. A good programming rule is that an anonymous array type should only be used if just one object of the type ever exists. Even then, an array type might be a good idea.

Under the type compatibility rules, objects are not of the same type unless they are of the same nonanonymous type. Thus, in the declaration

```
type Vector is array (INTEGER range 1..10) of INTEGER;
X, Y: Vector;
```

```
type Vector2 is array (INTEGER range 1..10) of INTEGER;
P, Q: Vector2;
A, B: array (INTEGER range 1..10) of INTEGER;
```

the arrays **X** and **Y** are of the same type (**Vector**), and the arrays **P** and **Q** are of the same type (**Vector2**), but of a different type than that of **X** and **Y**. Finally, the array **A** is of a different type than that of all the rest of the arrays, including the array **B**, because both **A** and **B** are of anonymous types. That all these arrays have identical structures is not sufficient to make them compatible.

A convenient way to remember this last rule is to recall that

```
A, B: array (INTEGER range 1..10) of INTEGER;
```

is merely shorthand for

```
A: array (INTEGER range 1..10) of INTEGER;
B: array (INTEGER range 1..10) of INTEGER;
```

This last declaration clearly indicates that **A** and **B** are of different types.

8.3.9 Examples

We conclude this section with some example programs which use arrays. Lines 6–34 of Program 8–2 declare a function **Insertion_Sort** which takes an array parameter and returns an array value. A call to this function occurs in line 36. The function is passed an array value containing the appropriate number (6) of components of the appropriate type (**INTEGER**). This array value is provided using the aggregate **(4,5,6,2,3,1)**. **Insertion_Sort** returns an array that is indexed by characters. Thus, **Insertion_Sort(...)** is the name of an array object (technically, an array value) containing 6 components indexed by the letters **'A'** through **'F'**. Thus the expression in line 36:

```
Insertion_Sort((...))('A')
```

refers to the first of these 6 components; that is, it refers to a single value of type **INTEGER**. This value is converted to a string by the **IMAGE** attribute, and that string is printed by **TEXT_IO**. Because the sort places the smallest value first, what gets printed is the smallest value in the input aggregate, that is, the value **1**.

Within the function **Insertion_Sort**, we see the use of the array attributes **FIRST** in lines 19 and 23, and **LAST** in line 19, to control the loop parameters. Through the use of these attributes, the two loops function correctly regardless of any changes in the size or bounds of the array indices. We also see the use of the discrete attributes **SUCC** in lines 19, 25, and 28, and **PRED** in line 29. Using these attributes is necessary because **+1** and **-1** are not allowed for the type **CHARACTER**. Furthermore, **PRED** and **SUCC** allow the sort to work with arrays with any index type. The local variable **Data**

```
1:with TEXT_IO;
2:procedure Array_Demo is
3:   subtype Index is CHARACTER range 'A'..'F';
4:   subtype Element_Type is INTEGER;
5:   type Array_Type is array (Index) of Element_Type;

6:   function Insertion_Sort(In_List: in Array_Type) return Array_Type is
7:   -- Purpose: return a sorted version of the array using Insertion Sort
8:     -- In_List: the array to be sorted.
9:     Data: Array_Type := In_List;
10:     -- Data: the array in which the sort is performed.
11:     Hold: Element_Type;
12:     -- Hold is where we store the next value to insert.
13:     Put_At: Index;
14:     -- Put_At is where that item will be inserted.
15:   begin
16:     if Data'LENGTH <= 1 then
17:       return Data; -- Array is too small to sort.
18:     end if;
19:     for Look_At in Index'SUCC(Data'FIRST)..Data'LAST loop
20:       -- The next item to insert is at position Look_At.
21:       Hold := Data(Look_At);
22:       -- Find where it goes.
23:       Put_At := Data'FIRST;
24:       while Put_At < Look_At and Data(Put_At) <= Hold loop
25:         Put_At := Index'SUCC(Put_At);
26:       end loop;
27:       -- Open space at Put_At.
28:       Data(Index'SUCC(Put_At)..Look_At)
29:              := Data(Put_At..Index'PRED(Look_At));
30:       -- Put the new item into the list.
31:       Data(Put_At) := Hold;
32:     end loop;
33:     return Data;
34:   end Insertion_Sort;

35:begin
36:   TEXT_IO.PUT(INTEGER'IMAGE(Insertion_Sort((4, 5, 6, 2, 3, 1))('A')));
37:end Array_Demo;
```

Program 8–2

is used because the algorithm sorts by examining and moving elements of the array. This cannot be done with `In_List`, because it is a parameter of mode `in`. Finally, note the use of a slice assignment in lines 28 and 29 to open space for the element to be inserted.

An interesting application of two-dimensional arrays is the game of life. We shall play the game of life in a two-dimensional (10-by-10) array. We shall index the array locations by the integers from 0–9. Each of the 100 array positions represents a location in the world. Each position in the world is either empty or contains a star (asterisk).

The game is played in rounds. Each round, the population of stars in the world is updated. The locations of the stars in the current round determine the locations of the stars in the next round.

Each world position (except those near the edges) is adjacent to 9 world positions (including itself). For example, world position (4,7) is adjacent to world positions: (3,6), (3,7), (3,8), (4,6), (4,7), (4,8), (5,6), (5,7), and (5,8).

The rule to compute the location of the stars in the next round is, If a world position is adjacent to exactly three world positions currently containing stars, then it will contain a star on the next round; otherwise, it will not contain a star on the next round. (Note: Some definitions of the game use "three or four" positions instead of "exactly three".)

The following diagram illustrates the transformation from one round to another in a 5-by-5 world:

```
 Current           Next
 Round             Round
 01234             01234
0.....            0.....
1.....            1..*..
2.***.            2.*.*.
3..*..            3.*.*.
4.....            4.....
```

We shall use the convention that the first index is the row number (down the side) and the second index is the column number (across the top). During the current round, there are stars at four locations: (2,1), (2,2), (2,3), and (3,2). Let us do a few sample computations. In the next round, position (1,2) gets a star because it is adjacent to the three stars at (2,1), (2,2), and (2,3) in the current round. Position (2,2) does not get a star because it is adjacent to four stars ((2,1), (2,2), (2,3), and (3,2)) in the current round.

Note that each of the five positions containing stars in the array on the right corresponds to a position that was adjacent to exactly three positions containing stars in the array on the left. Positions at the boundary of the world must be handled carefully because there are never any stars outside of the world.

We present a partial implementation of the game of life, leaving the remainder as an exercise. The program fragment that follows assumes the declarations

```
subtype World_Range is INTEGER range 0..9;
type World is array (World_Range, World_Range) of BOOLEAN;
Current_Round, Next_Round: World;
```

The Boolean value **TRUE** indicates that a star is present at a given location, and the value **FALSE** indicates that a star is not present at that location. The following program fragment computes the **Next_Round** from the **Current_Round**:

```
 1:  function Has_Star(X, Y: World_Range) return BOOLEAN is
 2:  -- Purpose: Determine whether the position given by X,Y has a star next
 3:  -- round. To determine this, we examine the 9 positions adjacent
 4:  -- to X,Y.
 5:    -- Total_Around: if the total number of stars in the adjacent 9
 6:    --  positions is 3, this position will have a star.
 7:    Total_Around: NATURAL := 0;
 8:  begin
 9:    for I in INTEGER range X-1..X+1 loop
10:      for J in INTEGER range Y-1..Y+1 loop
11:        if I in World_Range and then J in World_Range and then
12:                Current_Round(I, J) then
13:          Total_Around := Total_Around + 1;
14:        end if;
15:      end loop;
16:    end loop;
17:    return Total_Around = 3;
18:  end Has_Star;

19:  for I in World_Range loop
20:    for J in World_Range loop
21:      Next_Round(I, J) := Has_Star(I, J);
22:    end loop;
23:  end loop;
```

The nested loops in lines 19–23 ask for each position in the next round, Will that position have a star? This question is answered by the function **Has_Star**. For the position specified by the parameters, the loop in lines 9–16 checks all nine surrounding positions. For each of these positions, the if statement (lines 11–14) contained in the loop determines whether there is a star there. For each star found, **Total_Around** is incremented. The Boolean expression of the if statement uses a short-circuit form. For a location near the boundary of the world, some of the nine positions might not exist. That is, they might lie beyond the world boundary. Accordingly, for each of these positions, the first two relations check (**in World_Range**) to make sure that the position is within the world boundaries; if it is, it checks for the presence of a star in the current round.

Notice the use of nested for loops with two-dimensional arrays. Notice also the repeated use of the subtype **World_Range**.

8.4 RECORDS

Arrays provide only some of the capabilities for grouping data that we desire. When all the components are of the same type, arrays are appropriate. However, this is not always the case. Consider a library catalog entry. Among other things, it contains a book title, the names of the authors, and a library catalog number. These components are not of the same type, but it is desirable to group them together. Many languages provide the capability to group objects of various types together using a construct commonly referred to as a record.

In Ada, a *record* is a collection of objects that may be of different types. Records are used to store different, but related data items as a unit. For example, the record for a student in a course may contain a name (a **NORMAL_LINE**), status (an enumerated type), and scores (integers).

The syntax for declaring records is given in Figure 8–3. The reserved word **record** indicates the start of a type specification for a record, and the reserved word pair **end record** indicates the end of that type specification. "Subtype indicator" refers to a type or subtype that has already been declared. Anonymous types are never permitted in records. The subtype indicator may include a constraint, such as a range constraint.

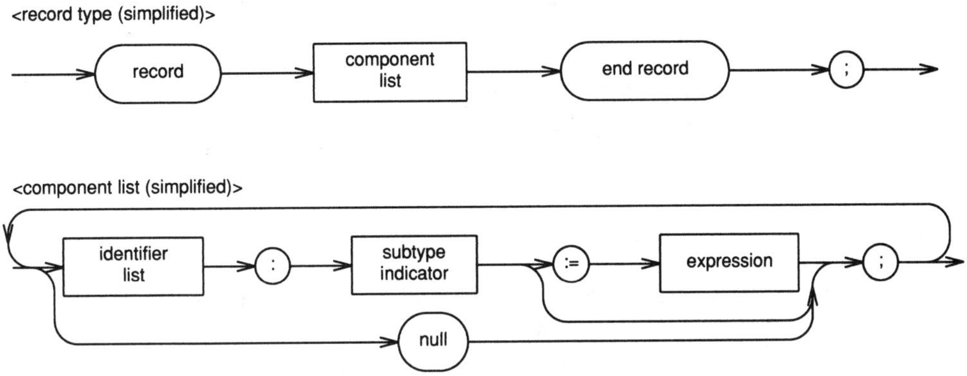

Figure 8–3

The type **Student_Record** in Program 8–3 is an example of a record declaration and its use. In the definition of **Student_Record**, each of the components is of a previously declared type. Any type can be used as a component in a record, including types declared in other packages (the type **Normal_Line** in line 6), enumerations (lines 8–10), and types from **package STANDARD** (lines 7 and 11). Finally, the use of an additional constraint on the type of a record component is illustrated in line 7.

A variable of type **Student_Record** contains 7 components: a variable of type **Normal_Line** associated with the identifier **Name**, a variable of type **INTEGER** associated with the identifier **Final_Score**, a variable of type **Status** associated with the identifier **Result**, two variables of type **Grades** associated with the identifiers **Homework_Grade** and **Course_Grade**, a variable of type **Quarter** associated with the identifier **Taken**, and a variable of type **BOOLEAN** associated with the identifier **Retaking**. Every component in a record is associated with an identifier. As seen in line 9, the familiar shorthand method of declaring multiple variables of the same type is allowed.

A record is a variable even though it has a complex structure. Like an array variable, a record variable can be treated as a single unit. One of the operations that can be applied to a record variable is assignment. In line 14 of our example, a copy

```
1: type Grades is (A, B, C, D, F);
2: type Quarter is (Fall, Winter, Spring, Summer);
3: type Status is (Passed, Failed, Incomplete);
4: type Student_Record is
5:   record
6:     Name: Normal_Line;
7:     Final_Score: INTEGER range 0..100;
8:     Result: Status;
9:     Homework_Grade, Course_Grade: Grades;
10:    Taken: Quarter;
11:    Retaking: BOOLEAN;
12:  end record;
13: A_Student,B_Student:Student_Record;
    ...
14: A_Student := B_Student;
15: if A_Student = B_Student then ...
16: Simple_IO.Write(A_Student.Name);
17: A_Student.Final_Score := B_Student.Final_Score + 6;
```

Program 8–3

of the record **B_Student** is made into the variable **A_Student**. Just as with other assignments, the expression on the right-hand side, which in line 14 is a variable, is evaluated, and that value is stored in the variable named on the left-hand side. For now, there are very few options for an expression that evaluates to a record value, but we shall introduce techniques that can produce more complex expressions in the next section.

The only Boolean operators that are defined for record variables are the comparisons for equality and inequality. Such a comparison is illustrated in line 15.

```
procedure Get_Final_Score(Student: in out Student_Record) is
begin
  Simple_IO.Write("Final score for ");
  Simple_IO.Write(Student.Name);
  Simple_IO.Read(Student.Final_Score);
end Get_Final_Score;
```

Program 8–4

Records may be passed as parameters and returned by functions. Given the declarations for **Student_Record** in Program 8–3, the procedure **Get_Final_Score** in Program 8–4 illustrates passing a record as a parameter. In this case, the parameter has mode **in out** because the procedure uses the **Name** to assist in modifying the **Final_Score**. A call to this procedure would need an actual parameter whose type was **Student_Record** and which was a variable, as in

```
Get_Final_Score(A_Student);
```

Because the record parameter is of mode **in out**, values may be placed into the components of the formal parameter as well as obtained from those components. If the parameter is of mode **out**, values may only be placed into the record or its components, while if it is of mode **in**, values may only be obtained from the record and its components.

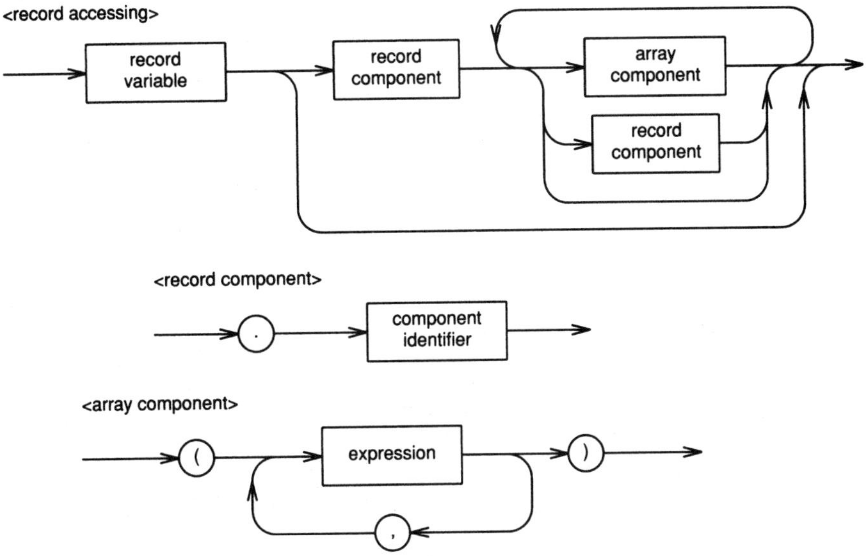

Figure 8–4

The syntax for accessing components in a record is given in Figure 8–4. To access a component in a record, the programmer must indicate the record and then the component within that record. The record variable precedes the component name and is separated from it by a period. Examples of accessing components in a record are found in lines 16 and 17 of Program 8–3. Line 16 prints the name of the student and line 17 accesses the final score of two students. In line 16, "**A_Student.Name**" accesses the **Name** component in the record **A_Student**. This component is a variable of type **Normal_Line**. The identifier **Name** is only valid as the identifier when used as a component of an object of type **Student_Record**. We cannot say

```
Simple_IO.Write(Name);   -- illegal
```

because the the identifier **Name** is visible only as a component of a variable of type **Student_Record**. This visibility rule holds for all identifiers associated with components in a record.

If a component of a record is of a type that allows operations, like the type **INTEGER**, then all appropriate operations may be applied to that component. Since the component **Final_Score** is of type **INTEGER**, any of the integer operators may be applied as is done in line 17 where the final score of one student is computed from the final score of another student using the addition operator. Of course, since there is a range restriction on **Final_Score**, a **CONSTRAINT_ERROR** could occur during execution of the assignment.

```
 1:subtype Class_Range is INTEGER range 1..10;
 2:type Grade_List is array (INTEGER range 1..5) of INTEGER;
 3:type Name is
 4:  record
 5:    Last_Name, First_Name: Normal_Line;
 6:    Middle_Initial: CHARARACTER;
 7:  end record;
 8:type Address is
 9:  record
10:    Street_Address, City: Normal_Line;
11:    Zip_Code: INTEGER;
12:  end record;
13:type Student_Record_2 is
14:  record
15:    Student_Name: Name;
16:    Student_Address: Address;
17:    Grades: Grade_List;
18:  end record;
19:type Class is array (Class_Range) of Student_Record_2;
20:Math_Class: Class
21:A:Address;
     ...
22:Lines.Assign(Math_Class(9).Student_Name.First_Name, "George");
23:Math_Class(9).Student_Address := Math_Class(10).Student_Address;
24:Math_Class(7).Student_Address := A;
```

Program 8–5

A component in a record can be of any type. This is illustrated by the record type **Student_Record_2** in Program 8–5. **Student_Record_2** contains a component **Student_Address** which is a record and another, **Grades**, which is an array. Records and array type declarations may be nested in this manner. In fact, type **Class** is an array of records. All of its components are of the same type (**Student_Record_2**), although this type is a complex record structure.

Lines 22–24 of the program illustrate the use of nested records. In line 22, the access is to the first name of the ninth student. The component **First_Name** is within the record **Student_Name**, so that component name must be preceded by the record name followed by a period. Similarly, **Student_Name** is a component within the ninth component of the array **Math_Class** (this component is of type **Student_Record_2**), so it must be preceded by the name of that ninth component (**Math_Class(9)**) followed by a period.

Line 23 shows that two **Student_Address** components are compatible; they are both of type **Address**. In fact, as shown in line 24, these components are compatible with any value of type **Address**, including the value obtained from the variable **A**. Lines 23 and 24 also show that a complex component is a single variable and may be treated as such, even when it is used in an assignment statement or passed as a parameter.

Records are a powerful tool for structuring data. Like any tool, however, they can be used or abused. The same principle of understandability that we have applied to other programming constructs should also be applied to records. The record structure should reflect the natural organization of the data. For example, **Math_Class** is an array of records, not two arrays, one of names and the other of addresses. Furthermore, related items should be gathered within declared records. For instance, in **Student_Record**, addresses were in one record, names in another. An inappropriate use of records would be to group the first name and state code together, or the last name and street address.

One of the skills of a good programmer is to be able to give an appropriate data structure from a description. For example, suppose a company's employee records consist of a maximum of 450 employees. For each employee, the company maintains a current address, work-related information, tax-related and income-related information, and personal information. The address consists of a valid mailing address. The work-related information consists of a job classification where the possible job classifications are programmer, analyst, accountant, and manager. A start at a correct structure is the following

```
type Address is        record ... end record;
type Work_Type is      record ... end record;
type Money_Type is     record ... end record;
type Person_Type is    record ... end record;
type Employee is
  record
    Current_Address: Address;
    Work_Info: Work_Type;
    Money_Info: Money_Type;
    Personal_Info: Person_Type;
  end record;
subtype Employee_Range is INTEGER range 1..450;
Workers: array (Employee_Range) of Employee;
```

In this structure, the organization of the records reflects the human reader's concept of how the information should be organized. Again, a good organization is one that is understandable to the reader of the program.

8.4.1 Record Aggregates

Aggregates for records are similar to aggregates for arrays. Again, an aggregate must be complete, so it must specify an appropriate value for each of the record's components.

```
 1:type Transaction is (Deposit, Withdraw);
 2:type Bank_Action is
 3:  record
 4:    Amount: FLOAT;
 5:    Type_Of_Transaction: Transaction;
 6:  end record;
 7:Weekly: Bank_Action;
 ...
 8:Weekly := (30.0, Deposit);
 9:Weekly := (Type_Of_Transaction => Withdraw, Amount => 25.0);
10:Weekly := (25.0, others => Deposit);
```

Program 8–6

In the record **Weekly** of type **Bank_Action** in Program 8–6, there are components of two different types. This means that an aggregate for type **Bank_Action** will contain values of two different types. One of these values must be of type **FLOAT**, and the other must be of type **Transaction**. As with arrays, an aggregate may use either named or positional notation. In type **Bank_Action**, the value of type **FLOAT** must precede the value of type **Transaction** in line 8 because **FLOAT** precedes **Transaction** in the declaration. Named association is similar to that used in procedures and arrays. Furthermore, in records, you may mix positional and named association in accordance with the same rules which apply to parameter lists. Also, the *others* option may be used with record aggregates. The others option applies to any components that were not previously specified. All such components must be of the same type, and that type must be compatible with the expression associated with the others option. A use of the others option is illustrated in line 10 of the program.

8.4.2 Default Initial Values

A unique capability of record types is that initial values may be given in the declaration of the type. The syntax for this uses the operator "**:=**" and is shown in Figure 8–3. Because the values are applied only when the record is not otherwise initialized, they are called *default initial values*. Some or all of the components in a record may be given a default value. The syntax is similar to declaring an initial value for a variable. As with variables, although multiple identifiers may be listed for a single type, this is equivalent to declaring them separately. When a variable of the record type is elaborated, the components in that variable are initialized to the default values unless there is an explicit initialization of the variable. This is illustrated in the following example:

```
type Complex is
  record
   Real_Part, Imaginary_Part: FLOAT := 0.0;
   Infinity: BOOLEAN;
  end Record;
```

```
X: Complex;                          -- Gets two (default) zeros
Y: Complex := (3.0, 3.0, FALSE);     -- Gets two threes and a true
```

Upon elaboration, the variable **X** receives the value "**0.0**" for each of its first two components because that is the default specified in the declaration of type **Complex**. The component **Infinity** remains uninitialized because no default value was specified. Since the variable **Y** is explicitly supplied an initial value, it will receive the explicitly defined initial value of two "**3.0**"'s and a **FALSE**. As with other complex variables, the explicit initialization of **Y**, is done using an aggregate. Aggregates must be complete. We cannot say

```
Y: Complex := (Infinity => TRUE);    -- illegal
```

because in this case the aggregate lacks a value for both **Real_Part** and **Imaginary_Part** and is therefore not complete. This completeness requirement means that either the entire record is explicitly initialized or default initialization applies to all components for which defaults are specified.

Constant records are allowed. As with arrays, aggregates provide a way to specify the value of a constant record. Thus we could declare a constant of type **Complex** as

```
I: constant Complex := (0.0, 1.0, FALSE);
```

A constant object must receive explicit initialization, it cannot use the default values. The initial value may be supplied by an aggregate, object, or expression of the same type as the constant object.

In summary, consider the following declarations:

```
Real_Origin: FLOAT;
function Imaginary_Default return FLOAT;
type Complex_2 is
  record
    Real_Part: FLOAT := Real_Origin + 1.0;
    Imaginary_Part: FLOAT := Imaginary_Default;
    Infinity: BOOLEAN;
  end Record;
function Imaginary_Default return FLOAT is ... end;
procedure Nested is
  X_2: Complex_2;
  Y_2: Complex_2;
  Z_2: Complex_2 := (0.0, 0.0);
  C_2: constant Complex_2 := Z_2;
```

The component **Real_Part** is supplied a value by an expression that depends on a variable **Real_Origin**. The component **Imaginary_Part** is supplied a value by an expression that consists of a call to the function **Imaginary_Default**. The defaults are evaluated at the time the record is initialized. Thus, the default values supplied to

X_2 may differ from those supplied to **Y_2**. If an explicit initial value is supplied, the defaults are not evaluated. Thus, in the elaboration of the variable **Z_2**, the function **Imaginary_Default** is not called. Finally, the constant **C_2** is supplied an explicit initial value.

8.5 OVERLOADING OPERATORS

We saw in Chapter 5 that some operators such as "+" had multiple meanings. In Ada terminology, an operator that has multiple meanings is *overloaded*. Because addition ("+") is overloaded: We can use "+" to produce a **FLOAT** by adding two **FLOAT**s or to produce a **INTEGER** by adding two **INTEGER**s. The philosophy of Ada is that programmers should be able to define their own meanings for operators. Thus, in Ada the programmer can overload operators. All that has to be done is to declare a function that supplies a new meaning for the given operator.

```
 1:procedure Add_Vectors is
 2:  type Vector is array (INTEGER range 1..6) of INTEGER;
 3:  X, Y, Z: Vector;
 4:  function "+"(A, B: Vector) return Vector is
 5:    Local:Vector;
 6:  begin
 7:    for I in Vector'RANGE loop
 8:      Local(I) := A(I) + B(I);
 9:    end loop;
10:    return Local;
11:  end "+";
12:begin
13:  X := Y + Z;          -- Infix form
14:  X := "+"(Y, Z);      -- Prefix form
15:end Add_Vectors;
```

Program 8–7

The procedure **Add_Vector** in Program 8–7 contains a programmer-declared overloading of the operator **"+"**. Functions declared using operators always have the operator declaration surrounded by quotation marks, as seen in line 4. Such operators can be used either in prefix form (line 14) or in infix form (line 13).

Within the program **Add_Vectors**, the plus operator is used with two different meanings. A third meaning is, of course, that in which the plus operator applies to the type **FLOAT**. The Ada implementation (technically, the Ada compiler) is required to determine the correct meaning. In line 13, the plus operator is given two vectors. Only one of the three meanings of plus can add two vectors. The compiler can discover which this is by examining the types of the operands. The plus operator in line 8 is given two integers. Again, only one operator is possible.

If we were to declare

```
function "+"(A, B: INTEGER) return INTEGER is ...
```

then there would be two identical declarations for plus. The scope rules would then dictate that the implementation choose the more local declaration. So the user declaration would prevail. In point of fact, the old plus could still be accessed using visibility by selection, as in:

```
STANDARD."+"(2, 3)
```

This function call is forced to refer to one of the plus operators supplied in **package STANDARD**: There is only one such operator that applies to two integers. To declare two plus operators in the same declarative region which are not distinguishable is a syntax error that the compiler is required to detect.

The following operators may be overloaded:

```
and     or      xor
<       <=      >       >=
+       -       &       *       /
mod     rem     **      abs     not
```

An overloading of the operator **rem** might be

```
function "rem"(A, B: Vector) return Vector is ...
```

which would allow it to be used in infix form as

```
X := Y rem Z;
```

and in prefix form as

```
X := "rem"(Y, Z);
```

As is undoubtedly plain by now, a number of operators have been overloaded in the definition of the **Lines** package. These operators include the relational operators, such as "<". For example, to compare two variables, an overloading is

```
function "<"(Left, Right: Normal_Line) return BOOLEAN is ...
```

In addition, several other overloadings were defined because we wanted literals of type **STRING** to behave as though they were of type **Normal_Line**. We shall consider more about the nature of these overloadings in Chapter 12.

There are a number of restrictions regarding the overloading of operators. First, the operators preserve certain properties. The predefined operators **not** and **abs** have one operand and are therefore called *unary* operators. Any function declaration that overloads a unary operator must have one parameter. Any operators with two operand is called a *binary* operator. Any function declaration that overloads a binary operator must have two parameters. The operators + and - may be either binary or unary operators. Function declarations that overload these two operators may have either one or two parameters. All other operators are strictly binary.

A second restriction is that, until we cover limited types in Chapter 10, we will not be able to overload the equality operator. And a third is that, parameters of operators are not allowed to have default values.

Overloaded operators may be used in complex expressions. However, these expressions obey the rules for the predefined operators. For example, if the operators + and * are overloaded the expression

```
X + Y * Z
```

is legal. Furthermore, the precedence rules require that the * operator be evaluated first. The * operator must return a type that is compatible with the + operator. Complex expressions may contain parentheses to force an order of evaluation. Finally, with the predefined meanings of Boolean operators, you cannot mix the operators **and**, **or**, and **xor** in an expression without using parentheses. This rule also applies to expressions containing overloaded definitions of these operators.

8.6 QUALIFIED EXPRESSIONS

Operator overloading provides advantages, but occasionally it introduces difficulties. Sometimes the result type of an expression is not clear. If it is not clear to the compiler, it is an error. If it is not clear to the reader, it is bad programming style. To overcome this difficulty, Ada allows the programmer to state explicitly what type is intended. This is done by using a *qualified expression.* A qualified expression has one of the forms shown in Figure 8–5.

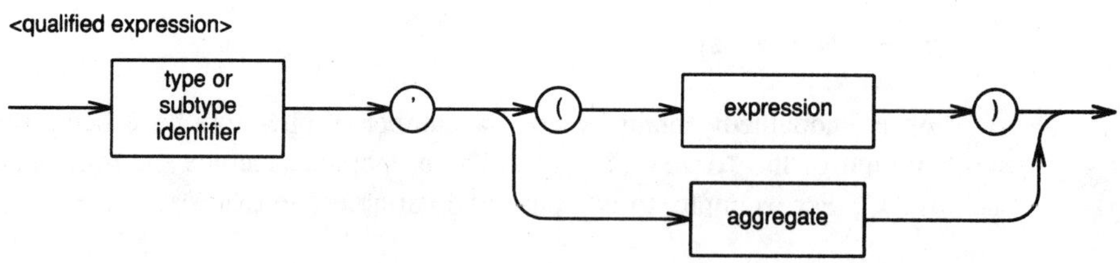

Figure 8–5

For example, consider the following type declarations:

```
type Vector is array (INTEGER range 1..2) of FLOAT;
type Complex is
```

```
    record
      Real, Imaginary: FLOAT;
    end record;
  X: Vector;
  Z: Complex;
```

If there is a "+" operator defined for both the type **Vector** and the type **Complex**, then the following are examples of qualified expressions:

```
Z := Z + Complex'(0.0, 1.0);
X := X + Vector'(0.0, 1.0);
```

In these expressions, the programmer has made it explicit that the type of the aggregate in the first expression is **Complex** and the type of the aggregate in the second expression is **Vector**. Not only can the reader swiftly understand what is being added, but if the programmer has made a syntax error, such as accidently defining **Z** to be of the wrong type, the compiler will be able to detect that error. Of course, having the compiler detect mistakes is far better than trying to find out why a program has failed to run correctly.

Ada requires qualification when combining named notation and the "others" option in an aggregate. For example, the assignment

```
Day_List := ('E' => Fri, others => Wed); --illegal
```

is not allowed, but the assignment

```
Day_List := Agg_Day_Demo'('E' => Fri, others => Wed);
```

is. In this last example, the element associated with the index **'E'** is set to **Fri**; all the other (unlisted) indices denote array positions that receive the value **Wed**.

When a qualified expression is evaluated, a constraint check is performed on the value of the expression or aggregate. If the value does not belong to the subtype, a **CONSTRAINT_ERROR** is raised.

8.7 THE PHONE BOOK PROGRAM

Suppose we wish to maintain a list of names, phone numbers, and addresses. Given any one of these three components, we want to be able to find and report a record that matches that component. The package **Phone_Book** in Program 8–8 supplies some of these capabilities; others are left as exercises.

The package is organized in the most simplistic manner. The fundamental element of the phone book is a **Listing**. The **Listing** contains information about a single phone customer. Each of the components in **Listing** (lines 6–8) is a **Normal_Line** with no further structure. Lines 39–47 show the look-up function for names; those for phone numbers and addresses are left as an exercise, they should be quite similar to

```
with Lines;
package Phone_Book is
  use Lines;
  type Listing is
    record
      Name: Normal_Line;
      Phone_Number: Normal_Line;
      Address: Normal_Line;
    end record;
  function Find_By_Name(Name: Normal_Line) return Listing;
  function Find_By_Address(Address: Normal_Line) return Listing;
  function Find_By_Phone_Number(Phone_Number: Normal_Line) return Listing;
  -- Purpose: Find the first entry in the current book with the
  --  given Name/Address/Number.
  procedure Delete_Listing;
  -- Purpose: Delete a listing to the phone book.
  procedure Add_Listing;
  -- Purpose: Add a listing to the phone book.
  procedure Get_Phone_Book;
  -- Purpose: Read the phone book from a file. The data in the file
  --  replaces any existing entries in the current book.
  procedure Store_Phone_Book;
  -- Purpose: Write the current book to a file.
end Phone_Book;

package body Phone_Book is
  use Lines;
  -- We have a small phone book; it only handles 10 entries
  subtype Phone_Book_Range is POSITIVE range 1..10;
  Book: array(Phone_Book_Range) of Listing;
  Number_Of_Entries: NATURAL range 0..Phone_Book_Range'LAST;
  function No_Such_Listing return Listing is
    Empty: Listing;
  begin
    Assign(Empty.Name, "");
    Assign(Empty.Phone_Number, "");
    Assign(Empty.Address, "");
    return Empty;
  end No_Such_Listing;

  function Find_By_Name(Name: Normal_Line) return Listing is
  begin
    for I in INTEGER range Book'FIRST..Number_Of_Entries loop
      if Equals(Book(I).Name, Name) then
        return Book(I);
      end if;
    end loop;
```

Program 8–8

```
46:    return No_Such_Listing;
47:  end Find_By_Name;
     . . .
48:end Phone_Book;
```

Program 8–8 Continued

the one shown. The look-up function simply examines all records until it finds one that matches. If it does not find a match, it returns a special value called **No_Such_Listing** (line 46). Actually, **No_Such_Listing** is a function call that returns a value of type **Listing** in which all the **Normal_Lines** have length zero. This function is shown in lines 31–38.

The current phone book is maintained in the array **Book** within the package body. In addition, phone books can be stored as disk files. The procedure **Get_Phone_Book** reads such a disk file and makes its contents the current book. The procedure **Store_Phone_Book** stores a copy of the phone book. Both of these should permit the user to specify the file name. In addition, entries can be added to or deleted from the current phone book with the **Add_Listing** and **Delete_Listing** capabilities.

Inside the package, the data is organized as an array of records. Several optimizations could speed the search that is performed. For example, we could sort the data by name or by address.

Several modifications to the phone book package are presented in the exercises at the end of the chapter. They include splitting the name and address into components (as in **Student_Record_2** in Program 8–5), and splitting the phone number into area, prefix, and number.

8.8 PROGRAMMING PRACTICES

Records give us a way to make data objects match the natural structure of a problem. They allow us to explicitly group objects. Appropriate grouping of data into records makes the program more readable and easier to maintain. You should always be able to express the relationship between the elements in a record with a sentence such as "A record contains information about a single student."

Likewise, the organization of arrays should be carefully considered. The choice between an array of arrays and a two-dimensional array should be based on how you would want to describe the information to a person who understands the problem, but not the Ada language.

One of the advantages of subprograms is flexibility. Within subprograms, flexibility should be strengthened by using attributes wherever appropriate. This is especially important with arrays, since they tend to change size as programs are enhanced.

As mentioned before, using an anonymous array type is usually a bad idea. Often, you will want a parameter that is an array of that type or you will want to declare several arrays. Both of these required a named type. Of course, the type name should be meaningful.

In a record type, some components may have defaults supplied, while others do not. If a variable of a record type is not explicitly initialized, then those components with default values are supplied values while the others remain uninitialized. The latter are potentially dangerous, so a good idea is to supply default initialization values for all or none of the components.

Overloading, appropriately used, makes a program easier to understand; carelessly used it can make a program almost impossible to read, even for an experienced programmer.

8.8.1 Problem Solving

Since we now have a considerable ability to structure data, we need a method for documenting that structure while designing our program. The same structure charts we use to design the relationships between subprograms can also be used to design the relationships between parts of a data structure. The method is to look at the problem we are trying to model and determine the structure of the information in the problem. We then attempt to model this structure with a structure chart.

Suppose the problem is to represent information about students in a course. Suppose we need to store names, addresses, and grades for each student. We can think of this information as three collections of data (names, addresses, and grades), or as a collection of students, each with some data. The important point is to choose a view which most closely (or simply) matches the information being described.

Since we have several pieces of information about each student, we could have three arrays indexed by student number, but this would not be the most natural approach. What seems most natural is to have a collection of students, each with a collection of data. The structure chart would look something like Figure 8–6.

As a matter of fact, the figure charts the structure of the type **`Class`** discussed earlier in the chapter. In charting a structure, we use names that explain what is being grouped or repeated. If we do not have a useful name, we can use the name of a type instead. We avoid using the names of objects, because we want to look at the structure of the data, not the holders for the structure; that is, we want to describe the nature of the information, not the identifiers associated with the components and variables.

We use terms like "group" and "repeat" (rather than record and array) as "problem-solving labels" to make it clear that we are designing a structure that is independent of the programming language. Another label, "option" is useful in many situations, but the Ada tools to implement the associated a structure will not be introduced until Chapter 12.

Notice that we are speaking as if the structure chart is produced before the program is written. Although this is not always the case, structure charts are often of great help in representing the ideas behind a data structure before the structure is implemented. Therefore, just as with structure charts for subprograms, it is recommended that a data structure chart be created before writing a program.

The comments to document each subprogram or data object should be developed as that portion of the program is made manifest in the structure chart. Experience shows

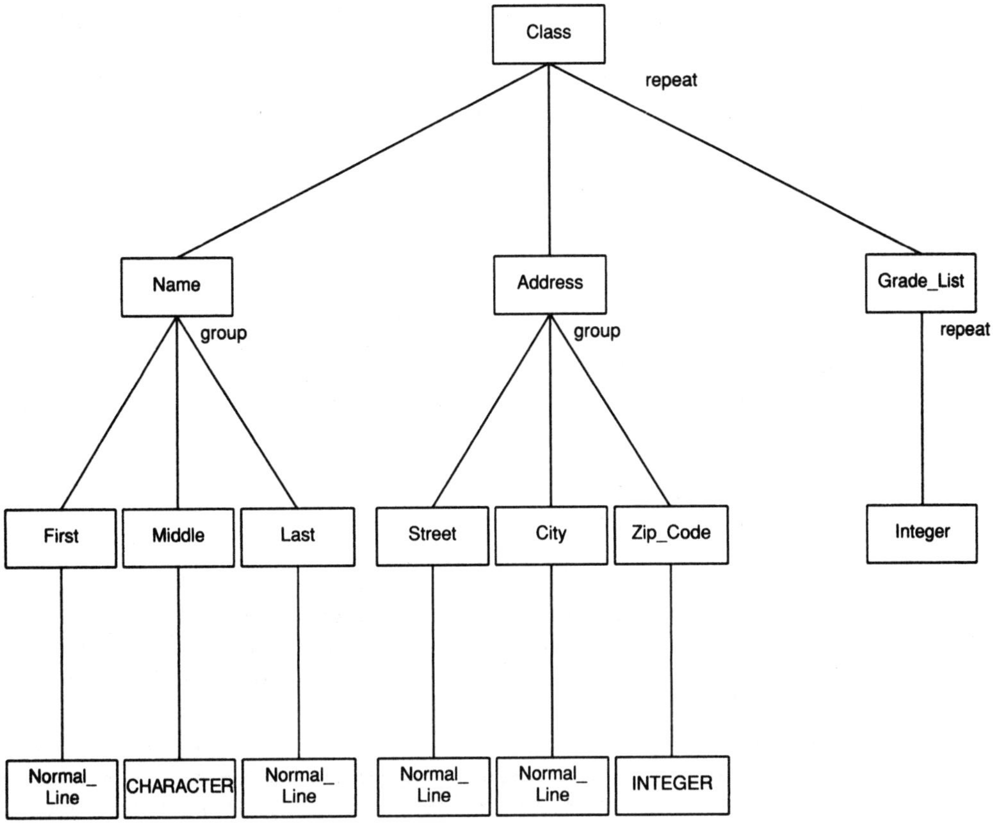

Figure 8–6

that it is much easier to write the Ada code for a program if the structure of the program is properly documented. Documentation is not just torture inflicted by professors; if well done, it can aid in doing the work of programming.

8.9 ADA SUMMARY

In this chapter, we have covered enough data declaration tools to create complex data structures. We have introduced both *multiple-dimensional arrays* and *records* and have seen how to nest array and record declarations to create structures appropriate to the problem being solved. We have examined how *aggregates* provide the effective literals for these structures. We have introduced the concept of *constant objects* that have complex structures. To permit packages to provide operations on complex types, we have shown how to *overload operators*, and to solve possible ambiguities that occasionally arise from overloading, we have introduced *qualified expressions*.

To build flexible procedures, we have covered the *array attributes* **FIRST**, **LAST**, **RANGE**, and **LENGTH**. To assist in array manipulation, we have introduced *slices*. We have seen that logical operations may be applied to one-dimensional Boolean arrays. Finally, we have introduced the anonymous array type.

EXERCISES

8.1. (a) Complete the program for the game of life described in this chapter. Place the life procedures in a package. The package should contain two functions. One of these, **Initialize_World**, allows the user to specify the initial configuration of the world and returns the world which the user specified. The other function, **Compute_Next_Round**, takes **Current_Round** as a parameter and returns the **Next_Round**.

Build a program that names the package. After each round, this program prints the world (use **Simple_IO**) and then allows the user to choose to reinitialize the game, go to the next round of the current game, or quit the program.

(b) Assume that instead of having boundaries the world wraps around. This means that a position on the very left of the world would be adjacent to positions on the very right (and vice versa). For example, the position (0,5) is adjacent to (9,4), (9,5), and (9,6) (plus the other six it is normally adjacent to). Similarly, a position at the very top of the world is adjacent to positions at the very bottom, and vice versa. Modify the function **Has_Star** to reflect this new definition of adjacency.

8.2. Modify the **Bank_Account** package of exercise 7.8 to use an array of records. For each account, in addition to the balance, the package should maintain the name of the customer and tax identification number (both **Normal_Line**). Add subprograms to the package so that if the teller knows either the account number, the customer name, or the tax identification number, the rest of the information about the account can be obtained.

8.3. Build a **Time** package. This package should include two types, **Time_Of_Day** and **Elapsed_Time**. **Time_Of_Day** is expressed in hours, minutes, and AM or PM. The hour is always an integer between 1 and 12, and the minutes are always an integer between 0 and 59. **Elapsed_Time** contains hours and minutes. The only restrictions placed on these integers is that they are not negative (i.e., they are of type **NATURAL**). The package should contain an operator **"+"** which takes a time of day and an elapsed time and produces a new time of day. For instance, if it is currently 11:30 AM and we add an elapsed time of 0 hours and 90 minutes, the new time of day is 1:00 PM. Be sure to handle long periods of time. For instance, if we take any time of day and add exactly 48 hours (2 days), the answer should be the same time of day.

In addition, you should be able to do the other operations indicated in the following (partial) package declaration:

```
package Time is
  type Time_Of_Day  --fill in
  type Elapsed_Time --fill in
  function "+"(Current_Time: Time_Of_Day; Amount_Elapsed: Elapsed_Time)
                return Time_Of_Day;
```

```
  -- Purpose: Computer what time will it be after the amount elapsed.
  function "-"(Current_Time: Time_Of_Day; Amount_Elapsed: Elapsed_Time)
               return Time_Of_Day;
  -- Purpose: Computer what time was it be before the amount elapsed.
  function "-"(Time_Now, Time_Before: Time_Of_Day) return Elapsed_Time;
  -- Purpose: Computer how much has elapsed between two times of the day.
  -- This assumes that both times are during the same day.
  function "+"(Elapsed_1, Elapsed_2: Elapsed_Time) return Elapsed_Time;
  -- Purpose: add two amounts of elapsed time.
  function "-"(Elapsed_1, Elapsed_2: Elapsed_Time) return Elapsed_Time;
  -- Purpose: subtract two amounts of elapsed time.
  procedure Print_Elapsed_Time(Time: Elapsed_Time);
  procedure Print_Time_Of_Day(Time: Time_Of_Day);
end Time;
```

Of course, build a function that tests your package. Make and document a design decision about what to do with negative elapsed times.

8.4. **(a)** Complete the missing procedures in the **Phone_Book** package in Program 8–8.

(b) Modify the package **Phone_Book** so that the record has more structure. Split the name and address into components (as in **Student_Record** in Program 8–3), and split the phone number into area, prefix, and number. Add the appropriate look-up functions.

(c) Modify the package **Phone_Book** so that the find functions return all records that match. These functions should return an array of listings; those components in the array which do not contain valid entries should contain **No_Such_Listing** entries.

(d) Add an enumerated type **Political_Party** where there are only two political parties: **Greens** and **Blues**. Add the appropriate look-up function to return all records on members of the designated political party.

8.5. Modify procedure **Days_Between** from exercise 7.6 to a **Days_Compute** package. The package declaration should be:

```
package Days_Compute is
  type Months is (January, February, March, April, May, June,
                  July, August, September, October, November, December);
  type Date is
    record
      Month: -- You fill in
      Day:   -- You fill in
    end record;
  function "-"(End_Date, Start_Date: Date) return INTEGER;
  -- Purpose: Compute the number of days between Start_Date and End_Date.
  function "+"(Start_Date: Date; Day_Count: INTEGER) return Date;
  function "+"(Day_Count: INTEGER; Start_Date: Date) return Date;
  -- Purpose: Compute the Date which is Day_Count days after the Start_Date.
  function "-"(Start_Date: Date; Day_Count: INTEGER) return Date;
  -- Purpose: Compute the Date which is Day_Count days before the Start_Date.
end Days_Compute;
```

The package should assume that dates are never more than a year apart. However it should perform correctly if dates cross year boundaries, such as in computing 20 days after December 16.

8.6. Design a package **Banner**. This package contains a procedure **Print** which, given a sentence, prints it in large (banner) characters. For example, the word "CAD" could be printed as

```
 CCCC      A     DDDD
C    C    A A    D   D
C        A   A   D   D
C        AAAAA   D   D
C    C   A   A   D   D
 CCCC    A   A   DDDD
```

The pattern for each character is a two-dimensional array. The array for each character needs to be separately designed.

The package also contains a procedure **Select_Font** which initializes the arrays for each character. **Select_Font** asks the user for the name of a file and reads the character patterns from that file. Each character pattern consists of seven lines, each containing five characters. The file contains the characters only for the printable characters (**CHARACTER range ' '..'~'**).

If the font files are not available, design arrays for just the first four capital letters and use them to test the program.

8.7. Build a package that handles rational fractions. The package specification should be:

```
package Fractions is
  type Fraction is
    record
      Numerator: INTEGER;
      Denominator: POSITIVE;
    end record;
  function "+"(L,R: Fraction) return Fraction;
  function "-"(L,R: Fraction) return Fraction;
  function "*"(L,R: Fraction) return Fraction;
  function "/"(L,R: Fraction) return Fraction;
  function "abs"(Val: Fraction) return Fraction;
  function "-"(Val: Fraction) return Fraction;
  function "+"(Val: Fraction) return Fraction;
end Fractions;
```

The package should store fractions exactly; for example, multiplying "3/8" by "3/4" must result in "9/32". Fractions do not need to be reduced.

8.8. Use the following package specification to create a bank package:

```
with Lines;
package Bank is
  use Lines;
```

```
-- Purpose: Provide banking utilities for tellers.
  Max_Bank_Customers: constant NATURAL := 25;

  -- Transactions:
  type Withdraw_Result is (OK, Insufficient_Funds);
  function Withdraw(Account_Number, Amount: POSITIVE) return Withdraw_Result;
  -- Purpose: Withdraw money from an account.
  procedure Deposit(Account_Number, Amount: POSITIVE);
  -- Purpose: Deposit money to an account.
  function Balance(Account_Number: POSITIVE) return INTEGER;
  -- Purpose: Report the balance in an account.

  -- Manager activities:
  procedure Create_Account(Account_Name: Normal_Line;
                           Account_Password: Normal_Line);
  -- Purpose: Creates an account.
  procedure Audit;
  -- Purpose: Dumps all account names, passwords and balances.
  procedure Open_Bank;
  -- Purpose: Opens the bank reading initial information from a file.
  procedure Close_Bank;
  -- Purpose: Closes the bank saving information to a file.

  -- Security:
  -- A customer/manager gets only one transaction per security clearance.
  type Security_Condition is (Approved, Denied);
  type Security_Record is
    record
      Security_Result: Security_Condition;
      Account_Number: POSITIVE;
    end record;
  function Security(Account_Name: Normal_Line;
                    Account_Password: Normal_Line)
                    return Security_Record;
  -- Purpose: Grant or deny a clearance for a customer transaction.
  function Manager_Security(Account_Name: Normal_Line;
                            Account_Password:Normal_Line)
                            return Security_Condition;
  -- Purpose: Grant or deny a clearance for a customer.
end Bank;
```

Each account has a user name, an account number, a password, and a balance. In order to modify the account with a transaction, a password must be correctly sent to the bank through the **Security** function. If the password is the correct one for the account name, the bank returns the value **Approved**, and the account number. Otherwise, it returns **Denied** and the number 0. If a security request is approved, the bank will allow one transaction on that account. In order to perform another transaction, **Security** must be called again. Similarly, if **Manager_Security** is called with a valid password, the value **Approved** is returned and the bank will allow a single management activity. The manager's password is a literal found in the **Manager_Security** function. Information about users is contained in a file named **bank_record**. For each valid account, the file contains four consecutive lines containing the user's name, password, account number, and balance. When the manager opens the bank, this information is read from this file. When the manager closes the bank, an updated version of this information is written to this file.

In addition to the bank, you will need to write a user interface (called a **Teller**) which prompts the user or manager for information, makes requests to the bank, and returns information to the user.

8.9. Change the **Inventory** procedure of Program 7–9 by adding a **NEW_ITEM** command. This command will add a new item to the inventory and ask the user for the current amount of this item on hand. To make this change, you must change the way in which items are dealt with. Instead of representing the list of items as an enumerated type, the names of the items must be stored in an array. Each name is an array of **CHARACTER**s. You should read each name character by character. When the user enters a space, this should indicate the end of the name. The format of the inventory file should be the same (name, space, amount). Item names should be limited to 20 characters each. Allow up to 50 items.

8.10. Write a program which reads a text file and counts the frequency with which letters occur in words of the following seven sizes: 1 to 2 letters; 3 letters; 4 letters; 5 letters; 6 to 8 letters; 9 to 12 letters; and more than 12 letters. Capital and lower case letters should be considered as being the same. Note there are 7 times 26 counts, the count of each letter in each category. The program should print its results.

For the purposes of this exercise, words are consecutive sequences of letters. Your program should directly name **TEXT_IO**.

8.11. The **Word_Count** program has two input files and two output files. The "dictionary" file is an input file that contains one line for each word. This line contains the word (without blanks), followed by one or more blanks, followed by a natural number. Words are always stored in all upper case letters. The number is the number of times the word has been seen before. Words that are not in the dictionary have never been seen before. The lines should be in alphabetic order; if they are not, be sure to issue an appropriate error message.

The "source" file is an input containing words and other objects. A word is any sequence of consecutive letters. Any nonletter separates words.

The "updated dictionary" file is an output file that has the same format as the dictionary file and whose words are in alphabetical order. Each word in the dictionary file also appears in the updated file. The count associated with the word is the original count plus the number of times the word was seen in the source file. A word in the source file should be counted regardless of the capitalization. Thus, "**GlUe**", "**GLUE**", "**gluE**", "**gLUe**", "**Glue**", and 11 other capitalizations count as occurrences of the word "**GLUE**."

The "counts" file is an output file that has the same format as the dictionary file, but the counts represent the number of times the word occurs in the source file (i.e., do not add the original count from the dictionary file).

9

Names, Scope, and Visibility

9.1 OBJECTIVES

This chapter expands upon what we have learned about declaring and accessing entities. Two important capabilities introduced are that of hiding the internal structure of data (section 3) and that of creating an alias for an existing entity (section 4).

We cover several additional details about declarations and elaborations (section 5). In previous chapters we indicated that names denote entities. Here, we summarize the kinds of names there are in Ada and review the details of scope and visibility with respect to the constructs we have previously covered (section 6). To provide a conceptual background, we present a model for expressing scope and visibility (section 7).

Recursion is a problem-solving technique that can be achieved using previously introduced Ada constructs. We discuss recursion and illustrate the concept with some small examples (section 8). Finally, we discuss an algorithm for recursively sorting data (section 9).

CONCEPTS:

- Names denote entities.
- Data and the internal structure of data can be hidden.
- Contour models describe visibility.
- Recursion is a powerful problem-solving methodology.

GOALS:

- Hide the details of a data structure.
- Recursively sort data.

9.2 MOTIVATION

Information hiding is a useful tool for ensuring that values in variables do not become corrupted. Information hiding is accomplished by using the rules for scope and visibility. In this chapter, we present a nearly complete discussion of scope and visibility; the only details left out involve language constructs introduced in later chapters. Several topics related to scope and visibility will be covered, including additional capabilities for information hiding and an additional method, called *renaming*, for making information more easily visible.

The capabilities of packages we have introduced thus far have enabled us to partition the programming task by hiding the implementation of the package from the user of the package. The user can use the routines in the package, but is not permitted knowledge of their internal implementations. These information-hiding capabilities, however, apply only to subprograms; we require similar capabilities for data structures. In this chapter we introduce *private types*, which provide the capability to make a type visible, yet hide its internal organization. This permits the user to declare variables of that type, but prohibits the user from tampering with the contents of those variables.

9.3 PRIVATE TYPES

The **`Lines`** package defines the type **`Normal_Line`** in such a manner that users can declare variables of that type. Variables of type **`Normal_Line`** can be modified by calls to procedures and functions defined in **`Lines`**. However, to ensure the integrity of the value in a variable of type **`Normal_Line`**, the **`Lines`** package does not provide the user with the capability of directly modifying the contents of such a variable. The internal structure of variables of type **`Normal_Line`** is hidden from users of **`Lines`**, thus making it impossible to depend on that structure or to directly modify its components. In Ada, *private types* allow a package to make a type available, yet hide the internal structure of that type. Like other type declarations, a private type declaration is a basic declarative item. However, private types can only be declared in a package declaration.

As shown in Figure 9–1, each package declaration has two parts. The first of these is the *visible part*. The packages we have shown thus far have had only visible parts. The entities declared in the visible part of a package can be referred to by any compilation unit that names the package. The visible part occurs before the reserved word **`private`**. In the package **`Geometry`** shown in Program 9–1, the visible part occurs in lines 2–9. Private types are declared as being private in this part of the package declaration. The full declaration of the private type must occur in the private part of the same package declaration.

<package declaration>

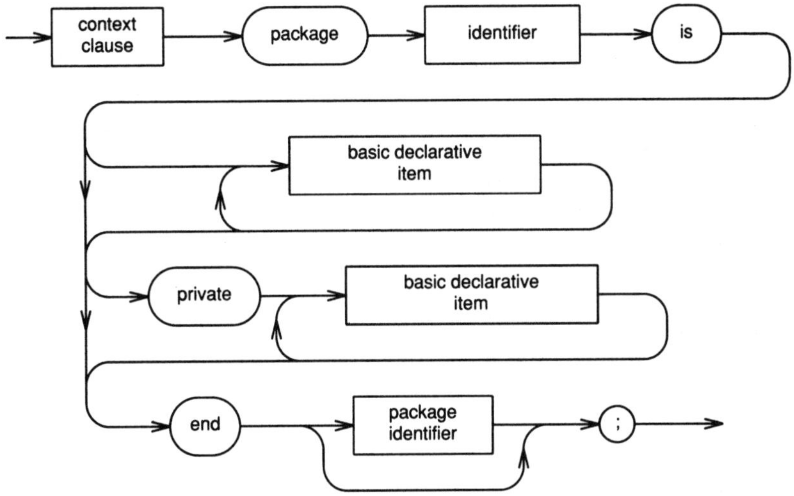

<private type declaration>

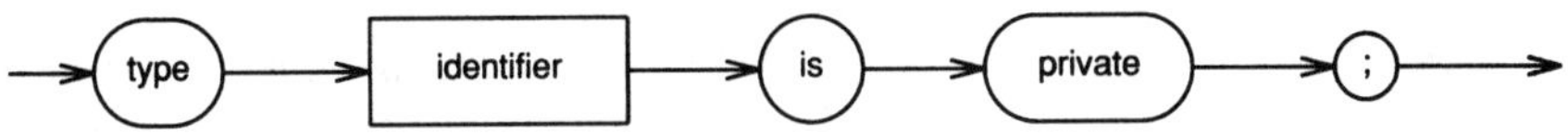

Figure 9–1

For the purpose of illustrating the difference between the two, the package **Geometry** declares both a regular type and a private type. The type **Coordinate** is declared in the visible part of the package (lines 2–5). We can use **Geometry.Coordinate** in any compilation unit which names **Geometry** in its context clause. In addition, **Coordinate** is not private, so if we declare a variable of the type **Coordinate**, as in

```
Where: Geometry.Coordinate
```

then we have direct access to the internal structure of that variable. For example, we could say

```
Where.X := 6;
```

This is because the type **Coordinate** and its components **X** and **Y** are declared in the visible part of the package.

To hide the components of a type, we use the other part of the package declaration, the *private part*. As shown in the syntax, the private part is optional. The private part of a package declaration begins with the reserved word **private** and continues to the end of the declaration.

```
1:package Geometry is
2:  type Coordinate is
3:    record
4:      X, Y: INTEGER;
5:    end record;
6:  Origin: constant Coordinate := (0, 0);  -- visible
7:  type Complex is private;                 -- declare private type
8:  I: constant Complex;                     -- deferred constant
9:  function "+"(Left, Right: Complex) return Complex;
10:private
11:  type Complex is
12:    record
13:      Real, Imaginary: FLOAT;
14:    end record;
15:  I: constant Complex := (0.0, 1.0);
16:end Geometry;
```

Program 9–1

In the package **Geometry**, the private part begins at line 10 and ends at line 16. To declare a private type, we do two things. First, we declare the existence of the private type in the visible part of the package declaration. At line 7 of **Geometry**, the type **Complex** is declared as a private type. The syntax for doing so is given in Figure 9–1. Second, we declare the structure of the type in the private part of the package declaration. For the type **Complex**, this is done in lines 11–14. Components declared in the private part can only be used within the package. The declaration of the structure of the private type occurs in the private part of the package declaration; consequently, that structure is not available outside the package. The reason that the structure of the private type is in the declaration part at all (instead of in the body) is because the compiler needs the private information to compile subprograms that use these private types. In particular, the components **Real** and **Imaginary** of the type **Complex** are declared in the private part of the package **Geometry**. Because of this, naming **Geometry** in the context clause of a compilation unit will not allow that compilation unit to access the internal structure of variables of type **Complex**. The type **Complex** itself is declared in the visible part of the package (line 7), so it can be used outside the package. That is, although we can declare a variable of type **Complex** with the declaration

```
Q: Geometry.Complex;
```

we cannot say **Q.Imaginary**, because **Imaginary** is defined in the private part and is not available outside the package. In fact, if the type **Complex** occurred only in the private part, no one outside the package could use that type. In order to make the type **Complex** available, it also must occur in the visible part of the package (line 7).

Notice how similar this technique is to subprograms; for example, the function **"+"** at line 9 of **Geometry**. In a package declaration, only the information necessary to call the subprogram is made visible. Similarly, only that portion of a private type necessary to the user is declared in the visible part of the package declaration. Thus, line 7 makes the type **Complex** available. In the case of a private type, only the existence of the type and the associated identifier is available outside the package. This provides the user of the package with the ability to declare variables of that type, but prohibits the user from accessing the internal structure of the type. The presence of the reserved word **private** indicates that the definition of the type will be completed in the private part. Again, this is similar to packages in which the subprogram declaration in the package declaration indicates that the implementation (the subprogram body) will be completed in the package body.

Because the user is prohibited from accessing their internal structure, very few operations are predefined for private types. However, a package can define (and possibly make visible) subprograms and operations that use private types. One such operation is the function **"+"** defined in line 9 of the declaration of **Geometry**. Since line 9 is in the visible part of the package, the function **"+"** is available to any compilation unit which names **Geometry** in its context clause. As with other packages, subprograms within the package body but not named in the package declaration cannot be accessed outside the package body. Finally, because **"+"** is declared in the declaration of **Geometry**, its body must occur within the body of that package.

```
package body Geometry is
  function "+"(Left, Right: Complex) return Complex is
  -- Return an aggregate which matches the type complex
  begin
    return (Left.Real + Right.Real, Left.Imaginary + Right.Imaginary);
  end "+";
end Geometry;
```

Program 9–2

Private types hide the internal structure of a data type from the outside world, but within the body of the package, the internal structure is fully visible. Thus, in the body of **Geometry** (Program 9–2), we can use the components **Real** and **Imaginary** in the body of the function **"+"**. Since these components are of type **FLOAT**, we can apply floating point operations (including addition) to the values in these components.

Since the type **Complex** is a record with two **FLOAT** components, aggregates with two **FLOAT** components are compatible with the type. The return statement uses such an aggregate to return a value of type **Complex**. Remember, the structure of **Complex** is visible only within the package body and in the private part after completion of the definition of the type, so only in these positions can an aggregate be used with **Complex**. An aggregate cannot be used where the internal structure of the type is inaccessible.

Because **"+"** is visible, it further overloads the addition operator, so that if we have the declarations:

```
with Geometry;
procedure Complex_Add_Demo is
  use Geometry;
  P, Q, R: Complex
```

we can write the statement

```
P := Q + R;
```

In this case, the **"+"** would refer to the function defined in the package **Geometry**. As illustrated by this example, direct visibility, as well as visibility by selection, are available for private types.

The implementation of the addition operation and the internal structure of the type **Complex** are hidden from the user. We are already familiar with types where the internal structure is hidden. For example, we do not know the internal structure of the type **INTEGER**. However, the **package STANDARD** provides a number of operations on integers which we quite easily use. In a similar manner, the package **Geometry** provides the type **Complex** and operations on that type which are easy to use. The programmer does not need to know, and should not depend on, the nature of the internal structure of **Complex** or the manner in which the supplied operations are implemented.

Some operations on private types are available even if they are not provided in the package declaration. The first is assignment. As shown previously, a value of a private type can be assigned to a variable of a private type. This also implies that private types may be used as parameters. For example,

```
procedure Increment(A: in out Complex; B: Complex) is
-- Purpose: Increment A by the amount B.
begin
  A := A + B;
end;
```

is a procedure that uses two values of type **Complex** as parameters. The parameter **A** is of mode **in out** and receives its value as a result of a computation involving the **"+"** operator defined in **Geometry**. Any mode may be used with parameters of private types, and parameters of mode **in** may have default expressions.

Qualification is another operator that is always available on private types. So we can qualify an expression, as in

```
A := Complex'(A + B);
```

As before, qualification defines the type returned by the expression and can be used to remove ambiguity in the case of overloaded operators.

Finally, equality and inequality are predefined on private types. Thus, **A/=B** and **A=B** are legal Boolean expressions. As with other types, two variables of a private type are equal if all of their components are equal.

Further operations that are automatically available with private types will be covered in Chapters 12 and 13, when the concepts they pertain to are presented.

There may be constants of a private type, for example, as in

```
procedure Increment(A: in out Complex; B: Complex) is
  Z: constant Complex := A + B;
```

As with other constants, the value of a constant of a private type is computed at the time of elaboration. The value will not change during the entire existence of the object. However, in **Increment**, each time the procedure is called, the constant **Z** will be elaborated and its value computed.

Private types also allow "deferred constants." A package may make available some constants which can be used in conjunction with a private type that it has declared. An example is the constant **I** in the package **Geometry**. As line 8 of Program 9–1 shows, no value is supplied for the constant in the visible part of the package. Since the structure of the type **Complex** is not given until the private part of the package, supplying a value for **I** in the visible part would be suppling a value for an object whose structure is not yet defined. Indeed, supplying a structure in the public part would reveal the structure of the type **Complex** in the public part of the package. To avoid doing this, the existence, name, and type of the constant are declared in the public part and supplying a value is deferred until the private part. Deferred constants can only be declared within the same package declaration as the private type. Deferred constants must be completed by supplying a value for them, as is done for the constant **I** in line 15 of **Geometry**. An aggregate may be used at line 15 because at this point the structure of the type is known.

Notice the similarity between deferred constants and subprograms. A subprogram is defined in the visible part of the package, and its implementation is defined in a nonvisible part, i.e., the package body; a deferred constant is defined in the visible part of the package, and its implementation is defined in a nonvisible part, i.e., the private part of the package declaration. In both cases, Ada is consistent in allowing the programmer to achieve modularity by hiding the implementation details from the user.

Suppose we had implemented the types **Complex** and **Coordinate** in Cartesian coordinates and had decided at some point to shift to polar coordinates. Subprograms using **Geometry** could depend on the internal structure of **Coordinate** because that internal structure is available to them. However, changing the implementation of **Coordinate** could require changes in subprograms which use **Coordinate**. By contrast, the implementation of **Complex** is hidden from the user. So even if the internal structure of **Complex** were changed, subprograms using **Complex** would not be required to change as a result of the change of representation.

In closing the section, we point out some details. First, private types can only be declared in package declarations. Second, when a private type is declared, variables of that type cannot be declared in the same package declaration. They can be declared in the package body and, of course, outside the package.

Finally, keep in mind that a well-designed package defines not only the private type, but also an appropriate set of operations that allow meaningful manipulation of that type.

9.4 RENAMING

Renaming introduces additional names for existing entities. Packages, objects, subprograms, enumeration literals, attributes, and some other things yet to be introduced may be renamed. The syntax for renaming several familiar entities is given in Figure 9–2. A renaming is a declaration.

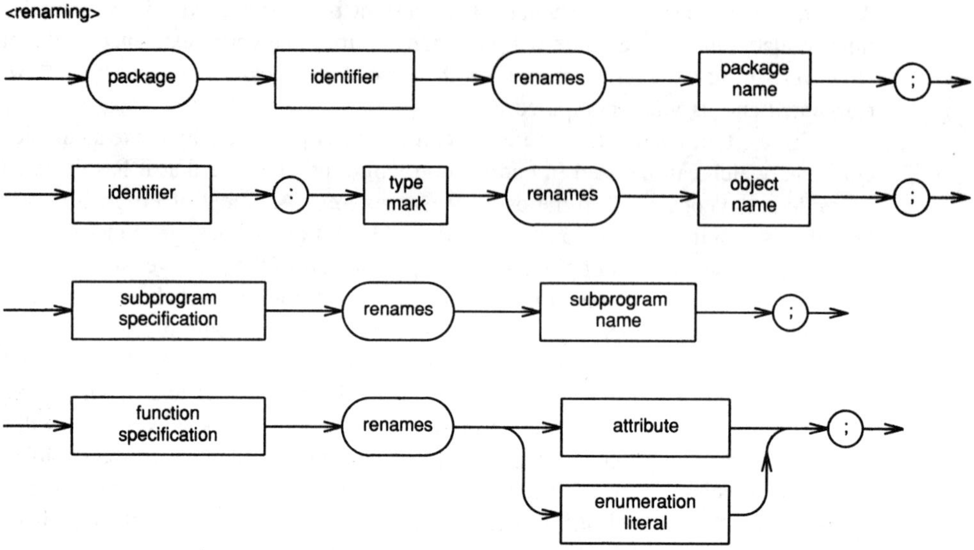

Figure 9–2

A package's actual name should be reasonably descriptive. However, it may be too long for convenient or frequent reference. Renaming allows local definition and use of a shorter name, yet still indicates the package to which an entity belongs. The following code is illustrative:

```
package DBM renames Data_Base_Manager_Utilities;
package ISAM renames Indexed_Sequential_Access_File_Manager;
```

Renaming objects allows the programmer to introduce a shorter local name and also allows a partial evaluation of object. For example, suppose we have the declarations:

```
type Grade is (A, B, C, D, F);
type Grade_List is array (INTEGER range 1..10) of Grade;
type Student_Record is
  record
    Name: Normal_Line;
    Grades: Grade_List;
  end record;
type Student_List is array (INTEGER range 0..15) of Student_Record;
```

```
type Class_Type is
  record
    Class_Name: Normal_Line;
    Class_List: Student_List;
  end record;
ICS_80: Class_Type;
Student_Number, Final: INTEGER;
```

Then we could have the renaming

```
Final_Grade: Grade renames ICS_80.Class_List(Student_Number).Grades(Final);
```

Notice that the exact variable to which the renaming refers depends on the values of the integer variables **Student_Number** and **Final**. As with objects, renamings are declarations that are elaborated. This means that the values of **Student_Number** and **Final** at the time of elaboration of the renaming determine which variable **Final_Grade** renames. If the value of **Student_Number** or **Final** changes after **Final_Grade** has been elaborated, **Final_Grade** will still refer to the same variable that it did at the time of its elaboration.

The syntax for renaming subprograms requires giving an entire specification for the new subprogram name. Doing so allows a renaming to introduce new names not just for the subprogram, but also for the parameters. Suppose we have the declaration

```
procedure Original(Old_Name: INTEGER);
```

Then the renaming

```
procedure New_Improved(New_Name: INTEGER) renames Original;
```

not only changes the name of the procedure, but renames the parameter. We can now write the procedure call

```
New_Improved(New_Name => 5);
```

Of course, this is exactly the same as the call

```
Original(Old_Name => 5);
```

In this example, there is only one procedure whose name is **Original**. The renaming merely supplies an alternative naming scheme by which we can call this procedure. Note that when we call the procedure as **Original** the named formal parameter must be referred to as **Old_Name**, and when we call the procedure as **New_Improved** the named formal parameter must be referred to as **New_Name**. It is illegal to mix the renamed procedure with the nonrenamed formal parameter name and vice versa.

When renaming a subprogram, we are allowed to modify the default values of any parameters of mode **in**. For example, if we have the procedure

```
procedure Default_Values(No_Default: INTEGER;
                         Default_Boolean: BOOLEAN := TRUE;
                         Default_A, Default_B: INTEGER := Initial_Value);
```

the renaming

```
procedure New_Name(Value: INTEGER := 6;
                   No_Default_Boolean: BOOLEAN;
                   New_Default_A: INTEGER := 0;
                   New_Default_B: POSITIVE := 1)
                           renames Default_Values;
```

removes the default value for the second parameter and changes the default values for the other two parameters. Thus, when the identifier **New_Name** is used to call the procedure, say, as in

```
New_Name(No_Default_Boolean => TRUE);
```

a value for the parameter **No_Default_Boolean** must be supplied because it does not have a default value. Furthermore, in this call the parameter **New_Default_A** receives the value 0, the parameter **New_Default_B** receives the value 1, and the parameter **Value** receives the value 6. Notice that, an identifier list can be separated or combined. In this case, we separated the original identifier list

```
Default_A, Default_B
```

into two identifier lists. This allowed us to give separate default values to **New_Default_A** and **New_Default_B**.

In addition, we can change subtypes as long as the renaming declaration is type compatible with the original declaration. For example, any renaming of **Default_Values** must have a first, third, and fourth parameter compatible with **INTEGER** and a second parameter compatible with **BOOLEAN**. This was indeed the case, since **Default_B**, an **INTEGER**, was renamed as **New_Default_B**, a **POSITIVE**, and **INTEGER** and **POSITIVE** are compatible subtypes. In any renaming with a different subtype, the constraints of the original subtype apply. The constraints on renamings are ignored. Thus, when we call **New_Name** the constraint **INTEGER** applies to **New_Default_B** because that is the constraint in the original declaration. The constraint **POSITIVE** of the renaming is ignored. In general, changing the subtype when renaming is poor style. Note that in renaming a function, the return types must be compatible and again, for good style, should be identical. Note also that renaming subprograms does *not* allow changing parameter modes.

Enumeration literals and certain attributes can be renamed as functions. For an enumeration like

```
type Days is (Mon, Tue, Wed, Thur, Fri, Sat, Sun);
```

we could rename the enumeration values as functions, as in

```
function Midweek return Days renames Wed;
```

Midweek thus behaves like a function that always returns **Wed**.

Attributes which Ada defines as functions can also be renamed. For example,

```
function Next_Day(Today: Days) return Days renames Days'SUCC;
```

renames the successor attribute of the type **Days**. Because **Days'SUCC** is applied to an expression of type **Days**, **Next_Day** must have a parameter of type **Days**. A call to **Next_Day** is now the same as a "call" to **Days'SUCC**.

Renaming cannot be applied to types. At first this may seem unfortunate, but renaming types is unnecessary. To achieve the same effect, we can use subtypes. For example,

```
subtype Singularity is Geometry.Coordinate;
```

gives us a new subtype that is completely compatible with an old subtype. With this declaration, we achieve exactly the same effect as if we renamed the subtype **Geometry.Coordinate**.

One important use of renaming is to transfer utilities from one package to another. For example, in the declaration:

```
with Lines, Simple_IO;
package Line_Utilities is
  ...
  procedure Write(Message: Lines.Normal_Line) renames Simple_IO.Write;
end Line_Utilities;
```

the renaming will make available a procedure **Write** to any compilation unit naming **Line_Utilities**. Once you name **Line_Utilities**, the procedure **Line_Utilities.Write** is available. Consequently, you do not need to name **Simple_IO** to obtain this capability. Furthermore, because **Line_Utilities** uses (renames) the procedure from **Simple_IO**, a body for the **Write** procedure does not occur in the body of **Line_Utilities**.

9.5 PACKAGE INITIALIZATION AND DECLARATION

9.5.1 Package Initialization

Many packages must execute a number of instructions before they are ready to do their intended job. For example, with the package **Robot**, if we want a special starting configuration, we need to call **Initialize_World** before beginning to maneuver the robot. Or, the **Bank_Account** package might want to open the files that contain the account records so that the program can determine the balances in the accounts before it allows any calls to procedures that modify those balances. One way to do either of these is to insist that the user of a package call an initialization subprogram before calling any other subprogram. This solution is somewhat inconvenient for the user, because it may involve needing to know details about the package implementation unessential to using the package. It is cumbersome in the package itself because, to achieve this, each subprogram declared the package declaration must contain a test (in the subprogram's body) to ensure that initialization has occurred.

It is most convenient to automatically ensure package initialization is performed before the tools in the package are used. Ada provides a mechanism for doing this using *package initialization code.* Figure 9–3 gives the syntax for the package body. The statement list that occurs at the end of the package body is the package initialization code.

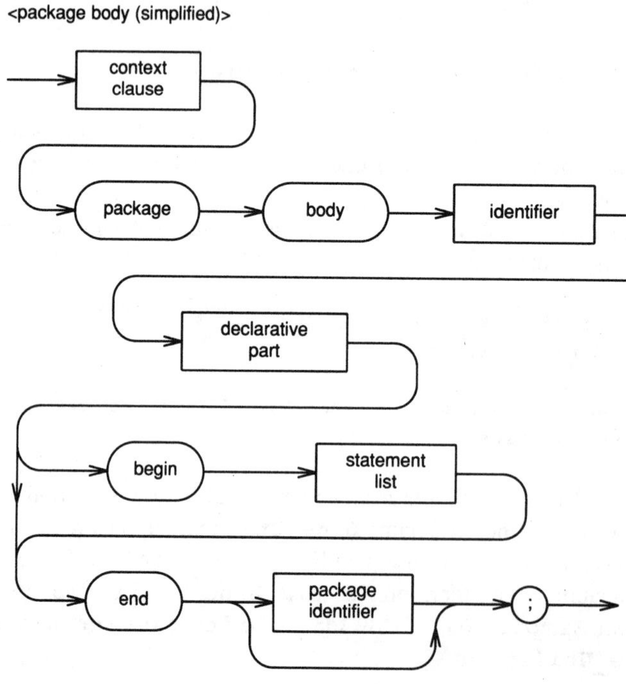

Figure 9–3

Packages must be elaborated. Elaboration of a package consists of three actions: elaboration of the package declaration, elaboration of the declarative part of the package body, and execution of the package's initialization code. Of course, a package is not required to have a body, and a package body is not required to have initialization code.

Packages named in a context clause are elaborated before program execution begins. Packages declared locally are elaborated before the procedure in which they are declared begins execution. Their elaboration occurs in the order of their declaration. Thus, in both cases, the package's initialization code will be executed before calls to the subprograms in the package occur.

As an example, recall the **Phone_Book** package in Program 8–8. This package contained a procedure **Open_Phone_Book** that had to be called before any names, numbers, or addresses could be found. Instead of requiring that the user call this procedure, the procedure could be declared only within the package and called by the package initialization code, as follows:

```
package body Phone_Book is
 -- various declarations
begin
  Open_Phone_Book;
end Phone_Book;
```

9.5.2 Package Declaration

Except for compilation units themselves, declarations occur in *declarative parts*. The declarative part is divided into two portions. In the first of these, only *basic declarative items* may occur; in the second, only *later declarative items* may occur. Any *body*, including a package body or a subprogram body, is always a later declarative item. Any nonbody is always a basic declarative item. Among other things, nonbodies include object declarations and type declarations. Any declaration that can have a related body, such as a package declaration or a subprogram declaration, can be either a basic declarative item or a later declarative item. In addition, use clauses can be either a basic declarative item or a later declarative item. Briefly, the rule is: little things (nonbodies) occur before big things (bodies) and things referring to big things can occur anywhere.

Returning to Figure 9–1, we now point out that the entire declaration part of a package is optional. That is, a package declaration can completely lack a visible part or a private part or both. For example, the package declaration

```
package Nothing_Showing is
end Nothing_Showing;
```

is legal. It offers no utilities or types to the user; however, on elaboration, the initialization code in its body (if it has a body and if that body has initialization code) is run. Also, such a package can actually have other effects (see tasks in Chapter 11). Note that we could have included only a private part in **Nothing_Showing** as follows:

```
package Still_Nothing_Showing is
private
  type Complex is
    record
      Real, Imaginary: FLOAT;
    end record;
end Still_Nothing_Showing;
```

Types declared in the private part are not required to refer to anything that is visible, although that makes them rather useless, in the sense that such declarations could be moved to the package body.

9.6 NAMES, SCOPE, AND VISIBILITY

9.6.1 Names

In Chapter 1, we introduced the idea that identifiers are used to name entities. In Chapter 5, we mentioned that indexing is a way of naming entities that are components of arrays. In this section, we survey the Ada concept of *name*. We shall mention each kind of name that Ada allows, summarize those which we have already considered, and provide references to those yet to be introduced.

The kind of entities that can be named are data objects (which include literals, variables, constants, slices, and parameters), data types and subtypes, packages, attributes, exceptions, subprograms including procedures, functions and operators, blocks and loops, enumeration values, and two items not covered yet, tasks and task entries. The syntax for Ada names is given in Figure 9–4.

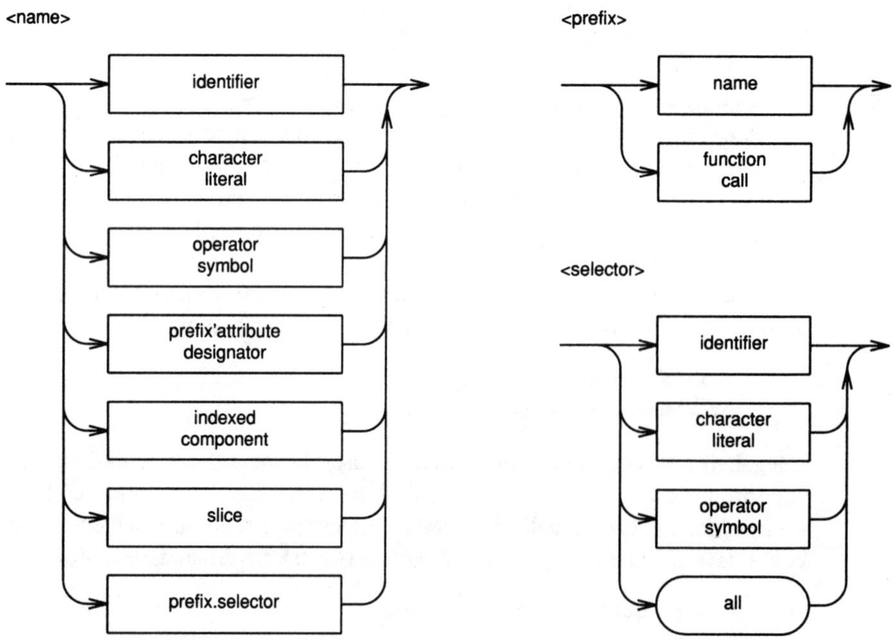

Figure 9–4

A name denotes a declared entity. A name is not the same as an identifier; rather, an identifier is an instance of a name. Identifiers, which are also called simple names, can stand for things such as values (e.g., enumeration literals), variables, and constants. Other items are also names, such as operator symbols (which stand for declared operations), attributes, indexed components (such as **X(2)**), component designators in records, and even slices.

9.6.2 Scope and Visibility

Scope and visibility are defined in terms of declarative regions. The types of declarative regions we have seen are: declarations and corresponding bodies for subprograms and packages, block and loop statements, and record type declarations. The declarative regions we will introduce later are: declarations and corresponding bodies for tasks and generics, entry declarations and corresponding accept statements.

As we have seen, Ada allows declarations to be separated from bodies. In these cases, the declaration comes before or is compiled before the body and defines how the entity appears from the "outside." The declaration "specifies" the essential characteristics of an entity, while the body contains the internal details of an entity.

In a package, the declaration and body must be separate. In a subprogram, declaration and body may be separated, but a separate declaration is optional. If a separate declaration is omitted, the specification part (e.g., **procedure ... is**) of the subprogram body acts as the declaration of the subprogram. In the procedure **Scope_Summary** shown in Program 9–3, the specification of the body of the procedure **B** (line 4) acts as the declaration of **B** because there is no separate declaration.

As mentioned earlier, the scope of an entity is where the name associated with that entity can be used to reference the entity. For example, in **Scope_Summary**, the scope of the parameter **X** declared at line 4 is from the end of its declaration through the end of the procedure **B** (lines 4–17). This includes regions in which visibility is by selection.

The immediate scope of an entity is the region where the entity is declared. For example, the immediate scope of a subprogram declared in a package declaration is the package (including the package body).

The extended scope of an entity is anywhere the entity can be named outside of the declarative region where the entity is declared. For example, the extended scope of a subprogram declared in a package declaration includes any compilation unit that names the package in its context clause.

The procedure **Scope_Summary** illustrates several aspects of scope and visibility. It contains some very bad programming style. In particular, the repeated use of the identifier **X**, while necessary for our illustration, should be avoided in practice.

The integer variable **Y** declared in line 3 has the simplest scope and visibility. This **Y** is visible from the identifier **INTEGER** of line 3 to the reserved word **end** at the beginning of line 30. Its scope is wherever the identifier **Y** is associated with the integer variable and is the same as its visibility.

The scope of the variable **X** declared in line 3 is the same as that of **Y**. However, there is another **X** declared in line 4. Since the scope of the **X** defined in line 4 continues until line 17, the **X** of line 3 is visible by selection in those lines, but not directly visible. As an example, in line 6, visibility by selection (**Scope_Summary.X**) is used to access the variable declared in line 3. Since yet another **X** defined in line 18 has a scope of

```
 1:with A;
 2:procedure Scope_Summary is -- Caution: very bad style
 3:  X, Y, Z: INTEGER;
 4:  procedure B(X: INTEGER) is
 5:    package A is
 6:      X: INTEGER := Scope_Summary.X;
 7:    end A;
 8:    Z: INTEGER;
 9:    procedure C(Z: INTEGER := X) is
10:      X: INTEGER;
11:      use A;
12:    begin
13:      X := B.X + A.X;
14:    end C;
15:  begin
16:    A.X := X + B.A.X + STANDARD.A.X;
17:  end B;
18:  procedure D(X: INTEGER := A.X) is
19:  begin
20:    E: declare
21:      X: INTEGER := D.X;
22:    begin
23:      F: for X in 1..8 loop
24:        E.X := X + F.X;
25:      end loop F;
26:    end E;
27:  end D;
28:begin
29:  B(X => X);
30:end Scope_Summary;
```

Program 9–3

lines 18–27, the **X** of line 3 is only visible by selection in this region also. In line 29 two definitions for **X** are visible within the parameter list. The **X** to the right of "=>" is the variable defined in line 3, while the one to the left is the formal parameter defined in line 4. Both are directly visible in the positions shown.

In addition, the formal parameter defined in line 4 has an immediate scope of lines 4–17. Because of other declarations, such as the **X** in line 10, on most of these lines visibility is by selection (for example, as **B.X** in line 13). However, there are a couple of places in which this parameter is directly visible, including line 9, where it is used in the default expression for the parameter, and line 16, where it is used in an expression. The parameter is also directly visible in line 4. For example, if we had said

```
procedure B(X: INTEGER := X) is     -- illegal
```

the second **X** would refer to the formal parameter. Default initialization of a parameter to its own value is prohibited by Ada; thus, this line of code is illegal. Restating the matter, the parameter **X** becomes visible immediately after the reserved word **INTEGER**; however, it is illegal to use this parameter until after the end of the parameter list. Consequently, the way we have rewritten line 4 is guaranteed to be illegal. On the other hand, it is perfectly legal for a default expression to use a more globally defined **X**, as is done in line 18. In this case, visibility by selection is required to refer to the more global **X**.

Consider carefully the variable **X** declared in the local package **A**. The scope of this variable is from lines 6–17. This **X** is visible by selection throughout this region, as is illustrated by its use (**A.X**) in lines 13 and 16. At line 11, the use clause does not make this **X** directly visible: A use clause never causes direct visibility where there are other choices for the meaning of the identifier. Since there are lots of other choices for the meaning of **X**, visibility by selection (**A.X**) is necessary even with the use clause in line 11. Thus, in line 13, the unselected **X** refers to the variable declared in line 10. In particular, if two packages containing an integer **X** were named in use clauses, neither **X** would be directly visible.

A package that is a compilation unit, that is, is not enclosed in any other unit, is called a *library package*. Visibility of a library package within a compilation unit is achieved by naming the library package in the context clause of the compilation unit. The declaration of the library package is then global to the compilation unit. In Ada terminology, the library package acts as though it were declared immediately within the package **STANDARD**. A package declared inside another compilation unit is called an *internal* or *nonlibrary* package. The scope and visibility of its name are governed by the same rules that apply to objects.

The declaration in lines 5–7 has another effect. A library package **A** is named in the context clause of line 1. The scope of any variables named in the declaration of this package is the entire compilation unit. Since it acts as though it were declared in the package **STANDARD**, the package **A** is visible by selection in the form **STANDARD.A**. The library package is directly visible, except for lines 5–17. Thus, **A.X** at line 18 refers to the **X** declared in the library package named in line 1. In lines 5–17, visibility by selection must be used as in **STANDARD.A.X** in line 16.

As mentioned earlier, names declared in the private part of a package declaration and the package body are not visible outside the package body. Names declared in the visible part of a package declaration are visible wherever a package name is visible. These names are only visible by selection, unless a use clause is present. The use clause provides *direct* visibility, which can be blocked by other declarations. Since there is no use clause applying to the library package **A**, names declared within this package are only visible by selection.

The visibility of library packages is based on compilation units and not on what files those compilation units are in. For example, in a file containing

```
package A is
   ...
end A
```

```
with A;
package B is
   ...
end B;

with B;
procedure C is
   ...
end C;
```

there are three compilation units: the declaration of package **A**, the declaration of package **B**, and the declaration of procedure **C**. Package **B** is visible within **C** because it is named in the context clause of that compilation unit. Package **A** is not visible within **C** because it is not named in the context clause of that compilation unit. That **A** is in the same file as **C** and that **A** is named in the context clause of another compilation unit in the file (i.e., the compilation unit containing the package **B**) is immaterial.

The second section of Program 9–3 illustrates scope with respect to labels. Block statements and loops may have labels. When they do, we can use these labels to provide visibility by selection to loop parameters and entities declared in the block statements. Thus, in line 24, we can refer to the variable **X** of the block statement or the loop parameter **X**. In this line, the only **X** that is directly visible is the loop parameter; so, **X** and **F.X** refer to the same entity. Line 21 reemphasizes the point we made about line 9. The **X** declared in line 21 becomes available after the reserved word **INTEGER**. If we did not use selection (**D.X**) in the default expression, the identifier would refer to the variable that was just declared, and the line would be illegal.

Remember, the use clause is a form of declaration. Normally, it belongs with other declarations in subprograms, package declarations or bodies, or the declarative part of block statements. As a special case, however, it can appear in the "compilation context" (the context clause).

Note that the notion of extended scope applies to subprogram parameters, record components, declarations immediately inside the visible part of package specifications, and several other entities yet to be introduced.

9.7 CONTOUR MODEL OF EXECUTION

A *contour model* of a program is a model of how subprograms (and packages) nest within each other. It is a form of documentation that aids in reading, testing, and correcting a program. There are two types of contour models: static and dynamic.

A *static* contour model shows how subprograms and packages are nested within the text of the program. We draw a box around each such unit. The box visually displays the nesting structure of the program for the reader.

While you can show the same information with indentation, the combination of boxes and indentation makes the program easier to read. In particular, the boxes clearly

```
with A;
procedure Scope_Summary is
  X, Y, Z: INTEGER;
  procedure B(X: INTEGER) is
    package A is
      X: INTEGER;
    end A;
    Z: INTEGER;
    procedure C(Z: INTEGER) is
      use A;
      X: INTEGER;
    begin
      X := B.X + A.X;
    end C;
  begin
    A.X := X;
  end B;
  procedure D(X: INTEGER) is
  begin
    E: declare
      X: INTEGER := D.X;
    begin
      F: for X in 1..8 loop
        E.X := X + F.X;
      end loop F;
    end E;
  end D;
begin
  B(X => X);
end Scope_Summary;
```

show the immediate scope of the items declared immediately within the procedure or package.

A *dynamic* contour model shows how subprograms nest while executing. Each subprogram call spawns a new box. The model is called dynamic because it changes as the program executes. Each diagram represents a snapshot of the program at a particular point in execution.

A dynamic contour model is especially useful if you are having trouble keeping the nesting of procedure calls straight. Concurrency and recursion which we shall discuss subsequently, are programming techniques that are often hard to debug without some form of modeling such as contour models.

9.8 RECURSION

Recursion is a very powerful programming technique. The simplest case of recursion occurs when a subprogram calls itself. Since the specification of a subprogram is completed either by a separate declaration or at the start of the body, the ability to call the subprogram becomes available at the end of the subprogram specification, and the subprogram can be called within its own body.

As a simple example, suppose we wish to substitute all occurrences of a pattern in a string with a replacement pattern. One appropriate problem-solving technique is "Do a piece, then do the rest." Applying this technique, we can substitute for the occurrence of the pattern and then call the same procedure (recursively) to do the rest.

```
 1:procedure Replace(Source: in out Normal_Line;
 2:                  Pattern, Replacement: Normal_Line;
 3:                  Start: POSITIVE := 1) is
 4:-- Purpose: Replace all occurrences of Pattern in Source with Replacement
 5:--  Start: The location in the string at which we wish to start the
 6:--   replacement.
 7:  Position: NATURAL;
 8:begin
 9:  Position := Location(Pattern, Source, Start);
10:  -- Position is 0 if there is no occurrence of the Pattern
11:  if Position /= 0 then
12:    Delete(Source, Position, Length(Pattern));
13:    Replace(Source, Pattern, Replacement, Position);
14:    Insert(Source, Replacement, Position);
15:  end if;
16:end Replace;
```

Program 9–4

The procedure **Replace** in Program 9–4 is a simple recursive procedure which applies this technique. The procedure is supplied a source line **Source**, a pattern **Pattern**, a replacement string **Replacement**, and a starting position **Start** within the source line. The procedure ignores the portion of the source line before the position indicated by the parameter **Start**. In the remainder of the source line, the procedure replaces all occurrences of the pattern with the replacement string. If **Replace** is called with no value for **Start**, the default value causes the replacement of all occurrences of the pattern in the entire source line.

At line 9, the procedure locates the first occurrence of the pattern after the starting position. When there is no occurrence of the pattern, the check at line 11 causes the procedure to return without changing the source line. If there is an occurrence, that occurrence is removed by line 12 and the replacement string is inserted by line 14.

For example, suppose we replace "**ab**" with "**xy**" in '**cabd**" starting with position 1. Line 9 detects the pattern at position 2, and line 12 deletes the pattern, leaving the

the value "**cd**" in the source line. In the recursive call at line 13 the parameter **Source** will contain no occurrences of the pattern, so that call will not modify the parameters. After that call has returned, the replacement "**xy**" is placed in the source line at position 2, so the source line becomes "**cxyd**".

Each recursive call replaces one occurrence of the pattern. After return from the call to **Replace** at line 13, all occurrences after **Position** have been replaced.

Every recursive procedure can be thought of as consisting of five parts:

1. The check to see if we are done
2. Breaking the problem apart
3. Making the recursive call(s)
4. Doing a part of the problem
5. Reassembling the parts to form a solution

These parts always need to be identified. Often, a recursive procedure is designed so that it will not perform step 4 unless no further disassembly of the problem is necessary. Such a procedure will do either steps 2, 3, and 5 or step 4.

9.8.1 Recursively Searching a Maze

As an illustration of recursion, consider Program 9–5. Here, the robot is in a maze and wants to find a goal. The recursive procedure **Search** is designed to have the robot search a maze for a goal. The algorithm is as follows. If the robot has arrived at the goal, the robot is done and the search is stopped. If the robot reaches a dead end, it backs up. If the robot has arrived at a place that has been visited previously, it backs up. Otherwise the robot searchs for the goal starting at the place at which it has just arrived. Essentially, the search is to take one step at a time, backing out of any dead ends or areas already searched. Searching forward involves recursively calling the search procedure; backing out involves exiting recursive calls. One way of using recursion involves restoring the original condition or establishing a predetermined condition. In this program, restoration is done, except when the goal is reached. After reaching the goal, the robot is not moved. Thus, the robot is predetermined to be on top of the goal.

We digress for a moment to discuss the sequence of events that allows a procedure to be called. Technically, a procedure or function can be called anywhere it is visible, i.e., from its declaration to the end of the declarative region. Thus, in **Elaboration_Demo** in Program 9–6, the function **A** is visible following line 2 and can be used in line 10 to initialize another variable, while the function **B** is visible following line 3 and can be used in line 5 to initialize a variable.

Elaboration makes entities available. Elaboration of a variable makes the variable available for use. Elaboration of a subprogram body is necessary before you can call the subprogram. If an entity is not elaborated before it is used, a **PROGRAM_ERROR** occurs. This requirement causes the call to the function **A** in line 15 to produce a **PROGRAM_ERROR**. The elaboration of the body of **A** requires the elaboration of the

```
with Robot;
procedure Searching is
  use Robot;
  Goal: CHARACTER := 'a';
  Wall: constant CHARACTER := '*';
  Marker: CHARACTER := '.';
  function Open_Ahead return BOOLEAN is
  begin
    return Look(Ahead) /= Wall and Look(Ahead) /= Marker;
  end Open_Ahead;
  function Search return BOOLEAN is
  begin
    -- Are we at the goal?
    if Look(Here) = Goal then
      -- We've found it!
      return TRUE;
    end if;
    -- We are not at the goal: continue searching.
    -- Search the path straight ahead.
    if Open_Ahead then
      -- The way is open; take a step forward.
      Move(1);
      -- Recursively search starting here.
      if Search then
        -- We discovered the goal along this path.
        return TRUE;
      end if;
      -- We didn't find the goal from here; back up.
      Move(-1);
    end if;
    -- We didn't find the goal along the path straight ahead;
    --  try a path off to the left.
    -- Search Left.
    Turn(Left);
    if Open_Ahead then
      -- The way is open, take a step forward.
      Move(1);
      -- Recursively search starting here.
      if Search then
        -- We discovered the goal along this path.
        return TRUE;
      end if;
      -- We didn't find the goal from here; back up.
      Move(-1);
    end if;
    -- We didn't find the goal along the path to the left;
```

Program 9–5

```
    --  try a path off to the right.
    -- Back to original direction.
    Turn(Right);
    -- Off to the right.
    Turn(Right);
    -- Search right.
    if Open_Ahead then
      -- The way is open; take a step forward.
      Move(1);
      -- Recursively search starting here.
      if Search then
        -- We discovered the goal along this path.
        return TRUE;
      end if;
      -- We didn't find the goal from here; back up.
      Move(-1);
    end if;
    -- We didn't find the goal off to the right; restore the
    --  original direction.
    Turn(Left);
    return FALSE;
  end Search;
begin
  Initialize_World("maze1");
  Set_Paint(Marker);
  Paint_On;
  Set_Delay(0.2);
  if Search then
    Write("Goal reached.");
  else
    Write("Couldn't find goal.");
  end if;
  Exit_World;
end Searching;
```

Program 9–5 Continued

local variable **X**. The elaboration of **X** requires a call to **B**. This means that **B** must be elaborated before the elaboration of **A** can be completed. But a brief glance shows that the elaboration of **B** requires the elaboration of **A**. So, there is no way to avoid a **PROGRAM_ERROR**.

Within a compilation unit, Ada does *not* try to figure out an elaboration order that works. The actual Ada rule governing elaboration within a compilation unit is simple: Entities are elaborated in the order they are encountered. Thus, even without the mutual dependence we have contrived, when the variable **X** is encountered in line 5, the body of **B** has not been encountered. Consequently, **B** has not been elaborated. This alone will cause a **PROGRAM_ERROR**. Of course, the compiler is permitted to be smart enough to

```
procedure Elaboration_Demo is
  function A return INTEGER;
  function B return INTEGER;
  function A return INTEGER is
    X: INTEGER := B;
  begin
    return X;
  end;
  function B return INTEGER is
    Y: INTEGER := A;
  begin
    return Y;
  end;
begin
  Simple_IO.Write(A);
end Elaboration_Demo;
```

Program 9–6

catch this **PROGRAM_ERROR** at compilation time, but since the compiler is not required to do this, often the error will be reported upon running the program. Another such example is the following:

```
function Recurse return INTEGER is
  X: INTEGER := Recurse;
begin
  return X;
end Recurse;
```

Here, the identifier **Recurse** becomes visible at the end of the function specification. Hence, it can be used in the declaration part of itself. However, when this function is executed, it must elaborate itself before it can elaborate itself. So, a **PROGRAM_ERROR** will always occur when the function is called.

The situation regarding the order of elaboration of library units is somewhat more complex. We will discuss this aspect of elaboration in Chapter 17.

9.9 THE QUICK SORT PROGRAM

Sorting occupies a significant fraction of the total computer time used. Because of this, there has been a lot of interest in developing efficient sorting methods. The goal of the quick sort algorithm is to sort very quickly. The recursive implementation of quick sort is natural. The fundamental observation is that if you sort half as many numbers, you can do it more than twice as fast. The aim, then, is to divide one large sort into two small ones. This shortens the time to perform the sort, but we can get a further improvement if we divide each smaller sort again, so that we have four even smaller sorts. It is this division of divisions which makes the program recursive. In fact, we can continue the process of dividing into smaller sorts until we eventually reach a sort of size 1. When this happens, we do not need to divide any more. Indeed, a list of size 1 is already sorted, so we do not even have to sort.

Suppose we know or can find the *middle* element of the final, sorted list. Using this middle element, we break the list into three parts: those items less than the middle element, the middle element, and those items greater than the middle element. The basic strategy is to perform this split, sort each part, and then recombine the parts. If the elements are part of an array, then the array splits as illustrated in Figure 9–5.

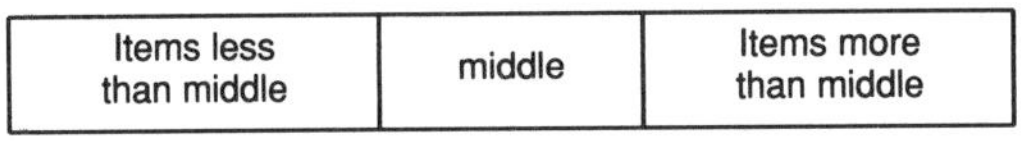

Figure 9–5

If we sort each of the two unsorted parts of the array, then the entire array is sorted. This is because combining arrays is trivial, no action is required.

An important observation is that the sorting time is only slightly affected if we use an element that is close to, but not exactly, the middle element. The upper levels of the structure chart for quick sort are shown in Figure 9–6.

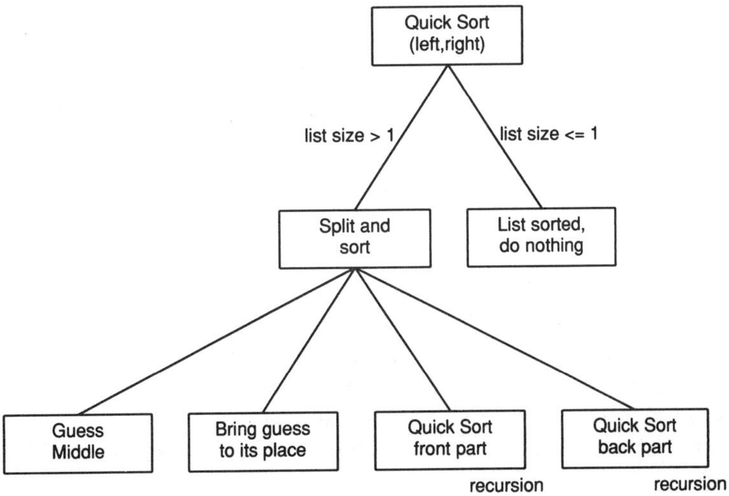

Figure 9–6

Suppose we have an element whose value is reasonably near the middle value. Let us see how we can split the array into three parts. The technique requires that we maintain two indices. Everything to left of the first index (**`Small`**) is less than (or equal to) the middle. Everything to right of the second index (**`Large`**) is greater than (or equal to) the middle. When we check an element, we place it *near* the front or back of the list as appropriate and change the first or second index. At any stage in this process, the array will have the configuration shown in Figure 9–7. In this and the following examples, we use **M** as the value which we guess is close to the middle of the part of the array we are currently considering.

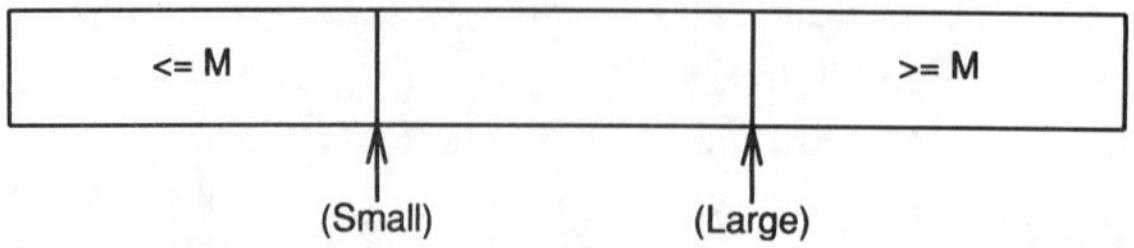

Figure 9–7

We will now illustrate the details of the technique for splitting the list as shown in Figure 9–5. In the following, notice that at each step the array conforms to the configuration of Figure 9–7.

At the start, we have (or bring) **M** to the front of the array. We set **Small** and **Large** to indicate that we have not yet determined the order of any of the values in the array. So our starting configuration is

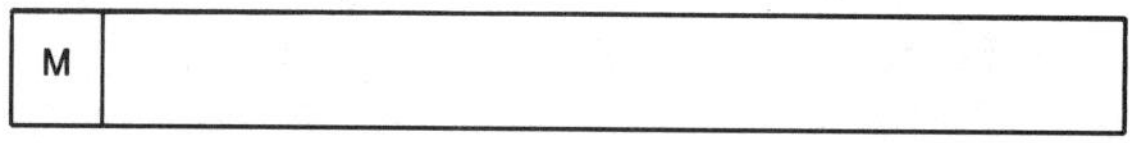

We begin by checking elements at the back of the array to see whether they are greater than or equal to **M**. All such elements which are at least **M** are in the correct position, so as we check each element, we move **Large** so that element is included in those known to be at least **M**. Eventually, we reach an element that is less than **M**, which we designate **S**. Now our configuration is

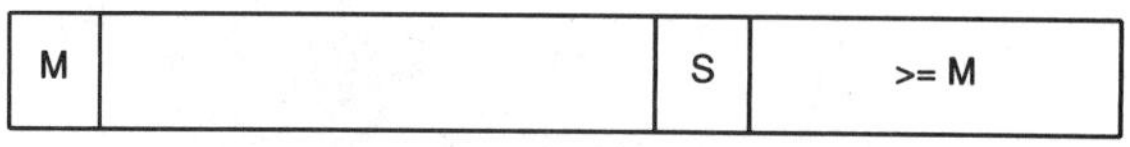

Because **S** is smaller than **M**, it belongs at the front of the array. We place it there by swapping **S** and **M**. Furthermore, we adjust **Large** because the value in the position occupied by **M** is (trivially) at least **M**, and if we ever swap anything else into this position, its value will also be at least **M**. This gets us to the following configuration

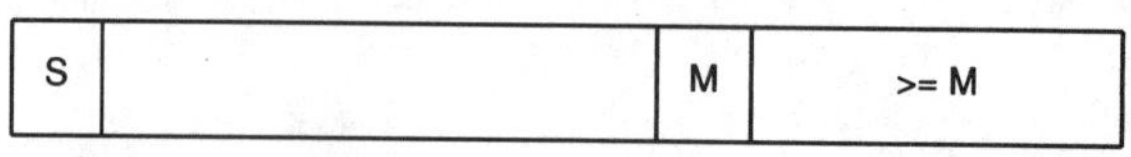

We now begin from the other end of the array. We check elements starting at the front of the array to see whether they are less than or equal to **M**. All such elements are at most **M**, so we move **Small** until we reach a value that is greater than **M**. Let us designate this value as **L**. We now have the following configuration:

S	<= M	L		M	>= M

Because **L** is larger than **M**, it belongs at the back of the array. We place it there by swapping **L** and **M**, giving us the configuration

<= M	M		L	>= M

Notice that we still maintain the constraint of Figure 9–7. The only difference between this last configuration and the starting configuration is that **Small** and **Large** have been adjusted to reflect the fact that we have partially completed dividing the array into two parts. So we repeat the preceding steps. In particular, we again begin by checking elements at the back of the array, starting at **Large**, to see whether they are greater than or equal to **M**.

Each time we repeat this cycle, we get additional portions of the array split into values that are at least **M** and values that are at most **M**. When we have split all the values, we have reached the configuration of Figure 9–5.

The following example shows how the technique works. We start with the array

```
27     99     00     08     13     88     10     64     25     90
Middle Small                                                   Large
```

This means that we have selected the value 27 as being close to the middle and have set **Small** *one place beyond* the index of the first element and **Large** to the index of the last element.

Notice the subtle shift of notation. Elements *in front of* **Small** are less than or equal to **M**, and elements *behind* **Large** are greater than or equal to **M**. In the alternative notation, **Small** would be the index of the last element in the array known to be less than or equal to **M** and **Large** would be the index of the first element in the array known to be greater than or equal to **M**. That is, **Small** would be the index of the component containing 27, and **Large** would be one place beyond the last index. This might not be a problem if the type of the index is **INTEGER**, but we have no guarantee that a legal value exists beyond the last index! Thus, our notation was chosen to avoid constraint errors.

Returning to the algorithm, we begin comparison of values at the end of the array against the middle value. The value 90 is correctly positioned thus: So **Large** is moved:

```
27     99     00     08     13     88     10     64     25     90
Middle Small                                            Large
```

The value 25 is incorrectly positioned, so it is swapped with the middle value (27), and **Large** is adjusted again:

```
25     99     00     08     13     88     10     64     27     90
 Small                                            Large  Middle
```

Now we begin comparing against elements at the front of the array. The value 99 is incorrectly positioned. Hence, it is swapped with 27, and **Small** is adjusted accordingly to yield

```
25      27      00      08      13      88      10      64      99      90
        Middle  Small                                   Large
```

We next return to checking the back of the array; 64 is fine, so we adjust **Large**, but 10 is not, so we swap and adjust **Large**.

```
25      10      00      08      13      88      27      64      99      90
                Small                   Large   Middle
```

Now we return to checking the front of the array. We discover that 00 is fine (adjust **Small**), 08 is fine (adjust **Small**) and 13 is fine (adjust **Small**). These adjustments leave us with:

```
25      10      00      08      13      88      27      64      99      90
                                        Large   Middle
                                        Small
```

We now check 27 against 88 and see that the 88 is incorrectly positioned, so we swap and again adjust **Small** again. This leaves us ready to look at elements at the back end of the array. However, our configuration is

```
25      10      00      08      13      27      88      64      99      90
                                        Large
                                        Middle  Small
```

Small has passed **Large**, indicating that we have achieved the arrangement of Figure 9–5, so we are done. The value 27 is in its correct position, and the array is split into small values and large values.

The algorithm next sorts both halves of the list. For illustration, we shall do just the back part of the list; the front part would be done in the same fashion.

The list we are now interested in is

```
88      64      99      90
```

We select 88 as the value near the middle and set up **Small** and **Large**:

```
88      64      99      90
                        Large
Middle  Small
```

The check proceeds quickly. The entries 90 and 99 are correctly positioned, but 64 is not, so we get

```
64     88     99     90
Large  Middle
              Small
```

With this swap, we discover that the list is split.

Again, at this stage the algorithm needs to sort the two parts of the list. However, the first part consists of the single element 64. A look at Figure 9–6 shows that the algorithm does not need to do anything to sort a list of size one. So the only interesting sort is for the back part of the list. The list of interest is

```
99     90
Middle Large
       Small
```

The value 99 is the middle guess. We begin the comparisons and discover that 90 is out of position, so we swap. This yields

```
90     99
Large  Middle
       Small
```

We are finished splitting the list.

Now we need to sort the front and back parts of the list. The front part is the single value 90, so we do nothing. The back part contains no values, so again, do nothing.

Having done nothing twice, the algorithm has finished sorting the back part of the list. Notice that we could see that the list was sorted a couple of steps before the algorithm was able to decide that it was sorted. Do not be surprised if sometimes the program does nothing except decide that it did not need to sort part of a list.

The principal weakness of the quick sort algorithm is the need to guess a middle element. Statistically, picking a random element usually results in an element that is near the middle value. If the list is random, picking the first element in the portion of the array we are considering is as good as picking a random element. An alternative is to examine several elements and choose the middle of those elements. For example, given a segment of the array to sort (between **Left** and **Right**), pick three elements and choose the middle of those three elements as the guess for the middle. A simple method for doing this is to use the three elements with the indices **Left**, **(Left+Right)/2**, and **Right**. and use the middle of these three values as a guess. The way to use this as the middle element is to swap it with the element at index **Left**.

One last comment is necessary regarding the problem of termination of the algorithm: If you are not careful you could get a **CONSTRAINT_ERROR**, particularly if the index you are using is an enumerated type. Accordingly, in implementing the algorithm, make sure you carefully consider the conditions for terminating the algorithm, especially when the size of the part of the array you wish to divide is small.

9.9.1 Comparing the Speeds of Algorithms

To estimate the speed of the quick sort algorithm, we count the number of comparisons it makes. With good guesses for middle, the number of comparisons used to sort a list of n elements is $n \log n$. With bad guesses for middle, the number of comparisons can be as high as $n(n-1)/2$. The insertion sort we have previously also used as many as $n(n-1)/2$.

To see what this means consider that for a list of size 4 and good guesses for the middle, the quick sort might take $4 \log_2 4$ comparisons (about 8), while the insertion sort would take about 6. Since quick sort is complex, it would probably take longer than the insertion sort. But for a list of size 1000:

$$n \log_2 n \approx 10,000 \qquad \text{(quick sort)}$$

$$n^2 \approx 400,000 \qquad \text{(insertion sort)}$$

This means that even if the quick sort took 3 times as long per comparison, it would still be 15 times faster than the insertion sort. The bigger the list to be sorted, the greater the advantage of the quick sort algorithm.

When analyzing conditions as we did above, the important thing to measure is how fast the time used grows as the size of the problem grows. That is, we are interested in an estimate of the rate of growth. For the purpose of an estimate, "small" factors are ignored. A standard notation for indicating that an estimate is being made is the O-notation. For example, we could estimate that a sort takes $O(n^2)$. When using O-notation, any multiplicative constant is ignored. Thus, $16n^2$ is $O(n^2)$ because the multiplicative constant 16 is ignored. One further point of the O-notation: it indicates an upper bound on how bad time can get. For example, $O(n^2)$ is also $O(n^3)$. Because n^3 is worse than n^2, if the time cannot get any worse than $O(n^2)$, it certainly cannot get worse than $O(n^3)$.

Formally, if a subprogram is $O(f(n))$, then we say that there are constants k and c, such that the subprogram will never take more time than $k \times f(n) + c$. We say that the insertion sort takes $O(n^2)$ time to sort n items. Quick sort also takes $O(n^2)$ time, because if we choose the middle wrong each time, it takes as many comparisons as insertion sort (it is even slower, because k is larger).

We can also use O-notation to analyze the expected time for a subprogram to execute. Thus, we say that the quick sort has an expected time of $O(n \log_2 n)$, while, the expected time for insertion sort is the same as the "worst case" time, that is, $O(n^2)$. Thus, even using the formal notation, we can see that quick sort will *usually* be faster than insertion sort when sorting long lists.

When computer scientists study problems, O-notation is often used to describe the maximum time that a problem takes, using the best algorithm for the problem. Thus, sorting a list of numbers is considered an $O(n \log_2 n)$ problem, because the best available algorithm for the problem takes this amount of time to sort n elements, given the worst possible list of numbers of that length. (This best algorithm is not quick sort.)

Another notation, called Ω-notation, describes the minimum time that a problem could take, using the best algorithm for the problem. Formally, a problem is $\Omega(f(n))$ if we can find constants k and c such that no algorithm can solve the problem in a time less than $k \times f(n) + c$ for the worst-case data. While O-notation expressions are usually derived by analyzing existing algorithms, Ω-notation expressions are usually derived by complicated mathematical proofs.

The problem of sorting a list of n elements using comparisons is $\Omega(n \log_2 n)$. In this situation, we say that the *asymptotic* lower bound (Ω-notation) and upper bound (O-notation) expressions are equal. ("Asymptotic" means for large amounts of data or large n.) When the two expressions are equal, it means that an algorithm is known for sorting which is very close to the theoretically best speed possible.

9.10 PROGRAMMING PRACTICES

The concept of hiding the implementation of a subprogram or a data structure from the programmer is called *information hiding*. The term implies that each subprogram or package hides secrets from other parts of the program. The fewer secrets permitted outside the subprogram or package, the better.

A rule of thumb for deciding how large a subprogram should be is that each subprogram should hide one secret (D.L. Parnas, "On the Criteria To Be Used in Decomposing Systems into Modules", *Communications of the ACM*, 1972). This divides the program up into small pieces that communicate with each other only through known (and well documented) pathways.

Private types can be used to hide secrets about the implementation of a type so that the information involved can only be used inside a given package. Writing a subprogram that uses information about how another subprogram works means that both subprograms need to be changed if the second one is. If good programming practices are not adhered to, these interrelationships can become so complicated that correctly making a change to the program may be as difficult as completely rewriting the program.

Since most useful programs are extended after their development is complete, programs need to be written in a manner that makes them easy to change and extend. Thus, no subprogram should make use of the structure of another, and subprograms should keep data structures secret (or private) whenever possible.

Finally, secrets should be documented. That is, as one designs a subprogram, the description of the subprogram should designate what secrets are hidden in the subprogram. This will make later modification of the subprogram easier.

9.10.1 Problem Solving

Recursion is a powerful tool, but recursion is also a problem solving model. In designing a recursive solution to a problem, you begin with the idea of doing part of the work, but phrase your ideas such that after you have done part of the work the remaining work can be described as one or more smaller versions of the original problem. We can then make recursive calls to solve each of the smaller problems.

For instance, in the **`Searching`** procedure in Program 9–5, the part of the work to be done in each step is to check the current position of the robot. The smaller parts of the problem are searching beginning to the left, right, and front of the current position. We treat these smaller problems exactly as if they were the original problem.

9.10.2 Testing

Special care must be taken in writing and testing subprograms that use recursion. The most common problem is to forget to, or improperly, check for completion. This can lead to a situation in which the subprogram keeps calling itself until it runs out of computer memory. The result is usually a **STORAGE_ERROR**. The best way to eliminate this problem is careful design from the beginning. Identifying, designing, and carefully coding the five parts of the recursive subprogram will help avoid this kind of problem.

As with loops, in testing a recursive procedure, the test data needs to be designed to test all possible combinations. For a procedure like **Searching** it is necessary to move the goal around to test for various conditions such as, (1) the goal is where the robot starts, (2) the goal is one away in each of the three directions, and (3) finding the goal requires backing up. In addition, the procedure should be tested with a missing goal.

When testing recursive subprograms, use of a package such as **Contour** to show you the recursive calls of the procedure can be very helpful in locating errors. Keeping track of how many recursive calls have been made indicates what is happening and makes sure that the correct calls are being made. Any data passed to recursive calls should be printed. Designing such code into a program from the beginning saves time in locating problems.

9.11 ADA SUMMARY

In this chapter, we discussed the Ada concept of *name* and how names can be used to denote entities.

We have also examined the hiding of information using the rules for *scope* and *visibility* and the hiding of the internal structure of information using *private types*. We have introduced the *contour model* as a method of describing either the scope or the visibility of names.

Finally, we have considered *recursive* programs and how recursion can be used to solve problems.

EXERCISES

9.1. Write a package for maintaining the dynamic contour model level, and use it. This package will trace the progress of a program.

```
package Contour is
-- Purpose: Print a dynamic contour model of an executing program.
```

```
--  This package must maintain an internal Contour_Level
--  variable in the body whose initial value is 0.
  procedure Start_Of_Procedure(Procedure_Name: STRING);
  -- Purpose: Increase the contour level.
  -- Increment internal Contour_Level and write a line
  --  containing Procedure_Name prefixed by Contour_Level
  --  copies of the string "| ."
  procedure End_Of_Procedure(Procedure_Name: STRING);
  -- Purpose: Decrease the contour level.
  -- Write a line containing Procedure_Name prefixed by
  --  Contour_Level copies of the string "| _" and then
  --  decrements the internal Contour_Level.
  procedure Contour_Write(Mess:STRING);
  Purpose: Indicate the current contour level.
  -- Write out message preceded by Contour_Level copies of "|  ".
end Contour;
```

9.2. Modify the **Searching** procedure of Program 9–5 so that it remembers how to get from the start to the goal. Do this by adding an array to the program which is used to remember the sequence of moves which got the robot to the goal. As the robot goes forward, record its moves. When the robot is forced to back up, unremember each move that you "undo." When you are done, the array should contain a path in which the robot does not move through the same location more than once. To verify the program, print the path contained in the array when the robot finds the goal. When printing the path, print a series of letters (**R**, **L**, **S**) indicating how a robot at the starting position could follow the path contained in the array. Print **L** if the robot should turn left and then move, **R** if the robot should turn right and then move, and **S** if the robot should move without turning.

9.3. Implement the procedure **Quick_Sort**. Begin with the following declarations:

```
procedure Test_Sort is
  type Sort_Array is array (INTEGER range 1..1000) of INTEGER;
  List: Sort_Array;
  procedure Quick_Sort(Small, Large: INTEGER) is
  begin
    null; -- You fill in here
  end Quick_Sort;
begin
  -- Make test list.
  for I in List'RANGE loop
    List(I) := ((997 * I) mod 1000) + 1;
  end loop;
  -- Call Quick_Sort.
end Test_Sort;
```

Time your program on a list of 1000 elements, and then time insertion sort on the same list.

9.4. Suppose that a maze is square and has n maze locations across each side. (Thus, there are n^2 places in the maze where the robot could step.) Assuming the worst maze possible, how long would it take to search the maze for the goal using the recursive algorithm presented in this chapter? Express your answer in O-notation. Do you think that a faster algorithm could be written? Why or why not?

9.5. In this exercise, you are required to produce a package from a written specification of how that package functions. The implementation is not difficult, but you must make sure that all the details are correctly designed and working.

The **Pager** package, when used by any other program unit, will produce paginated output. The format of the output may be specified by calling subprograms of the **Pager** package.

The output is divided into pages, each page has a heading including the page number, and each line on the page can be numbered. The total number of lines on each page is set by the **Set_Page_Length** procedure, this defaults to 24. The **Page_Length** function returns the value of this setting. The total number of lines includes blank lines that are skipped before the heading, after the heading, and at the end of the page. The number of lines skipped in these three places can be set using the **Set_Lines_Skipped** procedure. The **Lines_Skipped** function can be used to determine how many lines are currently being skipped in each of the three places.

If the number of lines skipped or the total number of lines on a page are not explicitly set, they have the default values: Total number of lines on each page = **Maximum_Page_Length**, (a constant whose value is given in the package specification); lines skipped before heading line = 3; lines skipped after heading line = 2; lines skipped at bottom of page = 4.

The heading that is printed at the top of each page includes a title, as set by the **Set_Page_Heading** procedure, followed by "**Page**" and then the page number. Before the title is explicitly set, it is "**UNTITLED**".

Page numbering starts at 1, unless the **Set_Page_Number** procedure is used. This procedure sets what page number should be used at the start of the next page.

The **Set_Line_Numbering** procedure indicates whether or not the line number should be printed at the start of each line. If it is printed, it is always in the form "xxx: " where each "x" is a digit or a blank. Unless line numbering is explicitly changed by using this procedure, line numbers will appear at the start of each line. On a given page, some line numbers may be printed and others may not, but line numbers are computed whether or not they are being printed out. Line numbering on each page always starts at 1.

The **End_Page** procedure completes the printing of the current page by printing out a suitable number of empty (blank) lines. This procedure is used for printing partial pages, such as at the end of a document or chapter. Whether the blank lines are numbered depends on the last setting of **Set_Line_Numbering**.

The **Write** procedure writes partial lines of output. The **Writeln** procedure writes partial lines of output and then ends the line.

The following is the package declaration (you will need to add comments):

```
with Lines;
package Pager is
  use Lines;
  Maximum_Page_Length: constant INTEGER := 112;
  subtype Line_Count is INTEGER range 1..Maximum_Page_Length;
```

```
  procedure Set_Page_Length(Length: Line_Count);
  function Page_Length return Line_Count;
  type Blank_Regions is (Before_Heading, After_Heading, At_Bottom);
  procedure Set_Lines_Skipped(Where: Blank_Regions;
                              Number_Of_Lines: Line_Count);
  function  Lines_Skipped(Where: Blank_Regions) return Line_Count;
  procedure Set_Page_Heading(Title: Normal_Line);
  procedure Set_Page_Number(Start_Number: POSITIVE);
  procedure Set_Line_Numbering(Print_Numbers: BOOLEAN);
  procedure End_Page;
  procedure Write(S: Normal_Line);
  procedure Writeln(S: Normal_Line);
end Pager;
```

9.6. Write a recursive procedure that generates all permutations of a sequence of characters. Suppose R and S are any sequences of objects and N is the null (empty) sequence. In what follows, it may be helpful to think of the pair of sequences (R, S) as the sequence of objects in R followed by those in S and to think of R as containing the parts of (R, S) that are not yet processed, while S contains what has been processed.

The permutations of a sequence of objects, S, can be computed as the permutations of the objects in the pair of sequences (S, N) by using the following rules:

1. The only permutation of (N, S) is S itself.
2. The permutations of R are those of (R, N).
3. The permutations of (R, S) are the permutations of (R_1, S_1), (R_2, S_2), (R_3, S_3), … (R_n, S_n), where n is the length of R, R_i is R with the i-th character removed, and S_i is S with the i-th character of R put at the beginning of S.

For example, the permutations of "abc" are those of ("abc", ""). The permutations of ("abc", "") are sequences which are permutations of one of the following: ("bc", "a"), ("ac", "b"), ("ab", "c"). The permutations of ("bc", "a") are sequences which are permutations of one of the following: ("c", "ba"), ("b", "ca"). The permutations of ("c", "ba") are sequences which are permutations of one of the following: ("", "cba"). The only permutation of ("", "cba") is "cba". The permutations of ("b", "ca") are sequences which are permutations of one of the following: ("", "bca"). The only permutation of ("", "bca") is "bca". Similarly, the permutations of ("ac", "b") are "cab" and "acb", while those of ("ab", "c") are "bac" and "abc". Thus, we have the six permutations "cba", "bca", "cab", "acb", "bca", and "abc".

In implementing the algorithm, use an array and an integer:

```
type Permutation_Array is array (INTEGER range 1..4) of CHARACTER;
procedure Permute(Current_Array: Permutation_Array; S_Start: INTEGER);
```

The integer **S_Start** will be the index in the array where the sequence S begins. Anything before this index will belong to R. For example, if a call is made to **Permute** with **Current_Array** containing **('a', 'b', 'c', 'd')** and **S_Start** containing **4**, then "d" is the sequence which has already been processed (S) and "abc" is the sequence to be processed (R). This call would generate three recursive calls. For each of these calls **S_Start** would have the value **3**. The three values of **Current_Array** would be: **('c', 'b', 'a', 'd')**, **('a', 'c', 'b', 'd')**, **('a', 'b', 'c', 'd')**.

Observe that the components before **S_Start** can be in any order without changing the correctness of the program, so we have generated the values by swapping components with the third component.

9.7. This exercise extends the **Fractions** package of exercise 8.7. As before, the package maintains rational numbers in a record containing a numerator and denominator. However, there are a number of additional operator overloadings, and **Fraction** is now a private type. The specification of the package should be as follows:

```
package Fractions is
  type Fraction is private;
  function "+"(L, R: Fraction) return Fraction;
  function "-"(L, R: Fraction) return Fraction;
  function "*"(L, R: Fraction) return Fraction;
  function "/"(L, R: Fraction) return Fraction;
  function "abs"(Val: Fraction) return Fraction;
  function "-"(Val: Fraction) return Fraction;
  function "+"(Val: Fraction) return Fraction;
  function "+"(L: Fraction; R: INTEGER) return Fraction;
  function "+"(L: INTEGER; R: Fraction) return Fraction;
  function "-"(L: Fraction; R: INTEGER) return Fraction;
  function "-"(L: INTEGER; R: Fraction) return Fraction;
  function "*"(L: Fraction; R: INTEGER) return Fraction;
  function "*"(L: INTEGER; R: Fraction) return Fraction;
  function "/"(L: Fraction; R: INTEGER) return Fraction;
  function "/"(L: INTEGER; R: Fraction) return Fraction;
  function "/"(L, R: INTEGER) return Fraction;
  function "<"(L, R: Fraction) return BOOLEAN;
  function "<="(L, R: Fraction) return BOOLEAN;
  function ">"(L, R: Fraction) return BOOLEAN;
  function ">="(L, R: Fraction) return BOOLEAN;
  function Equals(L, R: Fraction) return BOOLEAN;
  function Numerator(Val: Fraction) return INTEGER;
  function Denominator(Val: Fraction) return POSITIVE;
private
  type Fraction is
    record
      Numerator: INTEGER;
      Denominator: POSITIVE;
    end record;
end Fractions;
```

10

Handling the Unexpected

10.1 OBJECTIVES

In this chapter, we extend our coverage of the methods Ada provides for handling errors and unusual situations. Combining the *exception handler* control structure introduced in Chapter 7 and several related capabilities enables us to produce subprograms that can either protect themselves against errors or inform the caller of any errors they do not handle (section 3). Using these techniques, we can produce subprograms (and packages) that are more robust.

We cover the details of the type **CHARACTER**, discuss character literals and how they can be used in user declared enumeration types, and introduce the predefined package **ASCII** (section 4). With this knowledge we will be able to do more with user interfaces such as printing prompts and reading user input.

We continue the discussion of techniques for protecting data. In Chapter 9, we gained an appreciation of private types. Private types still have some vulnerabilities, which are curtailed by *limited types* (section 5).

CONCEPTS:

- If something goes wrong, you should either take care of it or report it.
- There is a package specializing in the standard character set.
- A type may be restricted so that values of that type cannot be copied.

GOALS:

- Write a program that uses the full capabilities of exception handlers.

- Write a program that uses the capabilities of the predefined package **ASCII**.
- Build a package that uses limited private types.

10.2 MOTIVATION

Most of the time, operations in Ada proceed in an orderly, expected pattern. Occasionally, an exceptional or unusual event will occur which will not permit execution to continue in the normal pattern. Ada provides the programmer with the exception handler (see Chapter 7) for controlling what happens in this situation. However, sometimes the programmer does not know what should be done in case of an unusual occurrence. For example, suppose a routine that computes a division is asked to divide by zero, or a routine that runs a robot is asked to run the robot through an impassable object. These routines have been asked to do something which is impossible. While they can substitute another action, such as returning 1 or not moving the robot, the caller should be informed that a mistake has occurred. Ada provides this capability by permitting the programmer to *raise* or *propagate* an exception. Ada provides a number of predefined exceptions. Sometimes it is appropriate to raise these, but Ada also permits the programmer to declare exceptions that can be raised when appropriate.

Some character capabilities in Ada are not provided by the regular printable character set. For example, **CHARACTER** had no representation for a carriage return, instead to produce a carriage return, we had to use the **New_Line** procedure. There are other unprintable characters which can occur while using the computer. For instance, when the escape key on the keyboard is pressed, what character is read? And when we wish to output a sound to alert the user, what character do we send? The predefined package **ASCII** assists in handling these characters.

We have emphasized the philosophy of limiting access to information as a means of encouraging correct programs. Ada has many mechanisms for implementing this philosophy, for example, data typing, range restrictions, scope, parameter passing, and private types. But consider the following problem. A package handles the electronic equivalent of a safe deposit box. It issues keys (access authorizations) for individual boxes. However, it does not want those keys to be duplicated. Private types will, of course, prohibit access to the internal structure of a key outside the package; this disallows tampering with the internal structure of a key. However, with private types, assignment is allowed. So anybody who has a key can make and distribute copies of that key to others. What is needed in this situation is a data type whose values cannot be copied. In Ada, these are called *limited* types.

10.3 EXCEPTIONS

To review, we introduced the *exception* as a condition encountered while executing an operation that prevents successful completion of the operation. In Ada, *raising* an exception denotes the act of indicating that the condition has occurred. *Handling* an exception denotes the action taken by the *exception handler*. The occurrence of an exception involves explicit transfer of control to the handlers associated with the frame in which the exception occurred. Since execution remains within the frame, the handlers have access to all objects and subprograms visible in that frame. In addition, the name of the exception causing the transfer of control can be used to select a handler.

We begin with a brief discussion of the concept of exceptions in general. We divide the conditions that cause exceptions to be raised into categories. The first category of exception is that of *domain failures*. A domain failure means that the input to an operation is not valid. For example, subscript out of range, division by zero, and format errors on input constitute domain errors. The second category of exception is that of *range failures*. A range failure says that an operation cannot produce a result even though the input is valid. For example, numeric overflow and output to a closed file constitute range failures. The third category of exception is that of *resource failures*. A resource failure says that a machine limitation has been encountered. Examples of resource failures are insufficient storage, time constraint exceeded, and resource (such as a tape drive) is lacking. The fourth category of exception is that of *logic failures*. In the case of a logic failure what to do next is not defined. For example, no return value specified from a function and no appropriate alternative in a deterministic control structure are cases in which what to do next is unclear. Most exceptions fall into one of these categories, although some fall across the category boundaries.

Exceptions are good for more than error conditions: They can support systematic interactions between different packages. Since packages often represent levels of abstraction, exceptions support abstraction by providing a disciplined way of coordinating actions at different levels in situations where the context in which a condition is detected is not the proper context in which to handle the condition.

To summarize, an *exception handler* is a special construct that is used for processing exceptions. Exception handlers may be inserted after the normal statements, but before the **`end`** of a block statement or the body of a subprogram, package, or task unit (we will examine tasks in later chapters). When talking about exceptions, the set of statements between the **`begin`** and the **`end`** of a subprogram, block, package body, or task body is called an *exception frame*. Figure 10–1 gives the syntax for an exception frame.

An exception frame may include exception handlers. The frame is divided into two parts, the "normal part" and the "exception part." The exception part of an exception frame begins with the reserved word **`exception`**. It is really a collection of exception handlers. As we saw in Chapter 7, the syntax and semantics of an exception handler are very similar to the syntax and semantics of the case statement. Each handler consists of a list of exception names followed by a sequence of statements that will be executed when the exception is raised. As with the case statement, the name **`others`** may be used only by itself and only as the last choice. Unlike the case statement, exceptions are not an enumeration, so ranges cannot be used in defining choices. Also unlike the case statement, the choices do not have to be complete; that is, the list of choices does not have to include every exception.

An exception is said to be *raised* when it occurs. Only one exception at a time can be raised in a frame. When the exception is raised, the computer stops execution of

<exception frame>

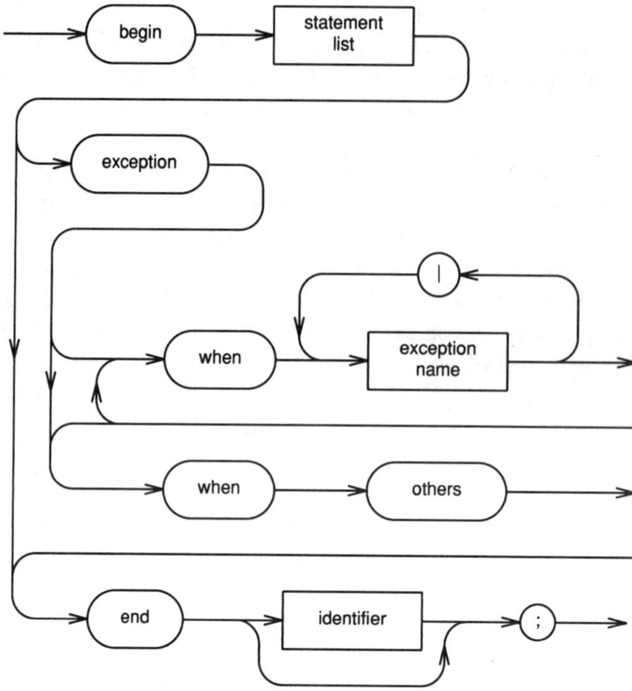

Figure 10–1

the normal sequence of statements in the frame, finds the exception handler in the frame with the correct exception as one of its choices, executes the associated statements, and then exits the frame. After an exception is raised, Ada will not continue execution of the normal sequence of statements; execution will exit the frame.

The following example shows an exception part with two exception handlers.

```
procedure Exception_Example is
begin
   -- sequence of statements
exception
  when NUMERIC_ERROR | CONSTRAINT_ERROR =>
    Simple_IO.Write("Bad value ");
    Simple_IO.Write("in exception example");
  when others =>
    Simple_IO.Write("Unknown exception");
end Exception_Example;
```

If any exception is raised during execution of the *sequence of statements*, execution will immediately transfer to the exception handlers. If the exception was a **NUMERIC_ERROR** or a **CONSTRAINT_ERROR** (two of the predefined exceptions), then the program will print out "Bad value in exception example". Any other exception will cause "Unknown exception" to be printed. When the **Write** is completed, execution will return to the point following the call to procedure **Exception_Example**. Again, execution exits the frame, which in this case means a return from the procedure. Execution cannot be resumed within the sequence of statements in which the exception was raised.

The following five exceptions are predefined in the package **STANDARD**:

```
CONSTRAINT_ERROR
NUMERIC_ERROR
PROGRAM_ERROR
STORAGE_ERROR
TASKING_ERROR
```

These exceptions can be raised by the implementation. For example, if a program attempts to assign a value to a variable, and the value is outside of the range of the variable, then a **CONSTRAINT_ERROR** will be raised by the implementation. The assignment will not be performed; instead, the appropriate exception handler will be found (if it exists) and executed.

Even a **return** statement can raise a **CONSTRAINT_ERROR** if the value being returned is outside the legal range of values for the function to return. The exception will be raised within the function and will prevent completion of the **return** statement. A later example will illustrate this.

The meaning of the exceptions defined in package **STANDARD** is as follows. A **CONSTRAINT_ERROR** occurs when a restriction has been violated. An example is a value that is out of the allowable range for either a subrange or an array index. A **NUMERIC_ERROR** occurs when a predefined arithmetic operation cannot return a valid result. An example is an attempt to divide by zero. A **PROGRAM_ERROR** occurs when a function exits without executing a return, or when there is a call to a procedure that has not yet been elaborated. A **STORAGE_ERROR** occurs when the computer runs out of memory. This often indicates that a recursive subprogram lacks a condition that terminates the recursion. It can also occur if too many variables are declared, particularly if they are extremely large arrays of arrays. A **TASKING_ERROR** occurs with tasks and will be covered in Chapter 19.

The programmer can declare exceptions. Exceptions are declared as though they were identifiers of type **exception**, as shown in Figure 10–2. For example,

```
Robot_Error: exception;
Overflow, Underflow: exception;
```

declares three exceptions. Exception names obey the standard scope and visibility rules. The visibility of the five predefined exceptions is defined by the fact that they are declared in package **STANDARD**. They are always visible, either directly or by selection. Many predefined packages, such as **TEXT_IO**, declare exceptions that become visible when the package is named in the context clause.

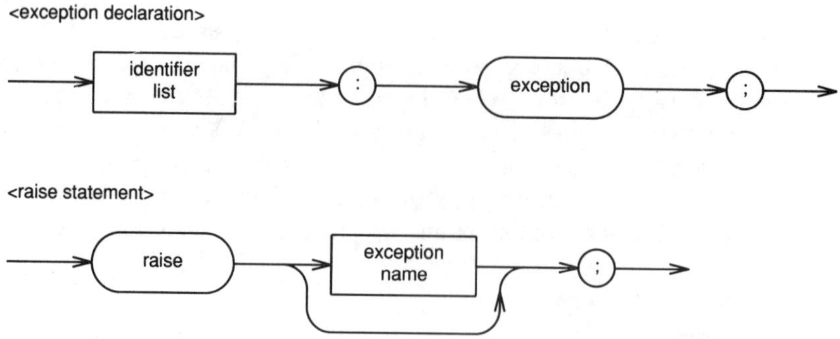

Figure 10–2

An exception may be explicitly raised with the *raise statement*, which has the syntax shown in Figure 10–2. The predefined exceptions may be raised by the implementation or explicitly by the program. Exceptions declared by the program can only be raised by the raise statement. The raise statement allows the programmer to signal an exceptional condition. Again, it is better to raise an exception than to silently do something that might be incorrect.

Consider the function **Get_Positive** in Program 10–1 which reads a positive integer. This function prompts the user for a positive number (line 11) and then gets the number from the user (line 13). If the number is positive, execution continues at line 14 and the number the user entered is returned; otherwise, an exception will be raised. If the user types a legal integer that is not positive, a **CONSTRAINT_ERROR** will be raised at line 13. If the user types something that is not an integer, the exception **DATA_ERROR**, defined in the package **TEXT_IO**, will be raised at line 13. Any exception that arises when the number is being read will be handled within the frame of lines 12–20. If **CONSTRAINT_ERROR** is raised, execution transfers to line 16, and from there to line 17, warning that the function expects a positive number. If **DATA_ERROR** is raised, execution transfers to line 18, and from there to line 19, warning that the function expects an integer.

The exception frame is inside a loop which causes a retry if an exception is raised. Basically, we know that if we have reached line 21, an exception must have been raised, because otherwise we would have exited the procedure by executing line 14. This situation demonstrates that, although you cannot continue executing an exception frame after an exception is raised within that frame, an operation can be retried by placing the entire exception frame in a loop.

When the user has failed five times to enter a legal positive number, the procedure gives up and decides that the situation is hopeless and so raises **Hopeless** at line 24. Although line 24 is not within the exception frame of lines 12–20, it is within the frame of lines 9–31. Consequently, when this exception is raised, control transfers to the handlers beginning at line 27, specifically the handler of lines 28–30. This exception handler prints a message and returns an arbitrary value to permit the calling program to

```
 1:with TEXT_IO;
 2:function Get_Positive return POSITIVE is
 3:  use TEXT_IO;
 4:  package Int_IO is new INTEGER_IO(INTEGER);
 5:  -- Reads a positive number from the user.
 6:  Hopeless: exception;
 7:  Tries_Left: NATURAL := 5;
 8:  Value: POSITIVE;
 9:begin
10:  loop
11:    PUT("Please enter a positive integer: ");
12:    begin
13:      Int_IO.GET(Value);
14:      return Value;
15:    exception
16:      when CONSTRAINT_ERROR =>
17:        PUT("Number not positive");
18:      when others =>
19:        PUT("Not a number");
20:    end;
21:    SKIP_LINE;  -- flush the input
22:    Tries_Left := Tries_Left - 1;
23:    if Tries_Left = 0 then
24:      raise Hopeless;
25:    end if;
26:  end loop;
27:exception
28:  when Hopeless =>
29:    PUT("Out of tries.  Assuming you want 1.");
30:    return 1;
31:end Get_Positive;
```

Program 10–1

continue. The **SKIP_LINE** at line 21 flushes any offending input, but also has the side effect of requiring the user to type a carriage return.

10.3.1 Propagation of Exceptions

Not every exception that might be raised in a frame has to be handled by the frame. Instead, a frame can transfer an exception to another frame; this is called *propagating* the exception. For a subprogram, the same exception will be raised just after the point at which the subprogram was called. For a block statement, the same exception will be raised just after the block statement.

An exception handler can tell Ada to propagate an exception by executing a **raise** statement that does not specify the name of an exception. The only place it is legal to use the **raise** statement without an exception name is inside an exception handler. When used without a name, the raise statement raises the same exception which caused control to be transferred to the exception handler. Also, a program can explicitly raise any exception it wishes within an exception handler. The new exception will be raised at the same place a propagated exception would.

If a frame has no exception handlers, or it has no handler with the reserved word **others**, some or all of the exceptions will not be handled by the frame. Exceptions that are not handled will be propagated. If an exception is propagated out of the program, execution of the program will be abandoned. Most implementations contain a "global exception frame" which displays information for debugging when an exception causes the program to be abandoned.

The function **Get_Positive_2** in the package **Positive_IO** in Program 10–2 contains a modified version of the function **Get_Positive** in Program 10–1. **Get_Positive_2** illustrates some of the points we have just discussed. The purpose of the two functions is the same, although the functions themselves differ. The exception **Hopeless** is declared within the package declaration (line 4). When **Positive_IO** is named in a context clause of a compilation unit, that unit has access to the name of this exception. Of course, unless there is a use clause, it will only be visible by selection, as in

```
when Positive_IO.Hopeless => ...
```

Remember, if the name of an exception is known, the exception can be raised as well as handled. In **Get_Positive_2**, the structure of one handler for the inner frame (lines 16–24) has changed slightly in that **others** of line 18 in **Get_Positive** has been replaced by **DATA_ERROR** (line 22). Recall that **DATA_ERROR** is not one of the five predefined exceptions; rather, it is one of several exceptions defined by the package **TEXT_IO**. If a non-integer is entered, this is the exception that will be raised. If another exception is raised in this frame, such as **PROGRAM_ERROR**, there is no handler, so that exception would be propagated. For example, if **DEVICE_ERROR** was raised by **TEXT_IO**, it would be propagated; that is, **DEVICE_ERROR** would be raised at the point that **Get_Positive_2** was called.

Overuse of the others option can make it more difficult to locate errors. For example, in the function **Get_Positive** in Program 10–1, a **DEVICE_ERROR** exception would mistakenly warn the user that a number was wanted! The poor user, who may have actually entered a number, may be totally misled by such a warning. A safer use of the others option is shown in the outer frame (lines 36–38) of **Get_Positive_2**. In this case, the handler prints a message to indicate to the user that something unexpected has occurred and then executes the raise statement. Handling the exception in this way achieves two goals: First, the user is warned that the error is associated with a call to **Get_Positive_2**; second, the same exception is propagated, so the caller has an opportunity to distinguish between **DEVICE_ERROR** and other exceptions.

Another capability of exception handlers is shown in line 35. When a **PROGRAM_ERROR** is handled, a different exception, **Hopeless**, is raised. This is not spec-

```
with TEXT_IO;
package Positive_IO is
  function Get_Positive_2 return POSITIVE;
  Hopeless: exception;
end Positive_IO;
package body Positive_IO is
  function Get_Positive_2 return POSITIVE is
    use TEXT_IO;
    package Int_IO is new INTEGER_IO(INTEGER);
   -- Reads a positive number from the user.
    Tries_Left: POSITIVE = 5;
    Value: POSITIVE;
  begin
    loop
      PUT("Please enter a positive integer: ");
      begin
        Int_IO.GET(Value);
        return Value;
      exception
        when CONSTRAINT_ERROR =>
          PUT("Number not positive");
        when DATA_ERROR =>
          PUT("Not a number");
      end;
      SKIP_LINE;
      Tries_Left := Tries_Left - 1;
      if Tries_Left <= 0 then
        raise Hopeless;
      end if;
    end loop;
  exception
    when Hopeless =>
      PUT("Out of tries.  Assuming you want 1.");
      return 1;
    when PROGRAM_ERROR => raise Hopeless;
    when others =>
      PUT("Unexpected error in Get_Positive_2.");
      raise;
  end Get_Positive_2;
end Positive_IO;
```

Program 10–2

tacularly useful here, but there are cases in which it is appropriate. For example, in the **Lines** package, any time **CONSTRAINT_ERROR** is raised in one of the subprograms, it would be because of illegal indexing of some form. Here, it makes sense to raise something like **Illegal_Lines_Index** whenever **CONSTRAINT_ERROR** is raised, because **Illegal_Lines_Index** gives a more precise description of the problem.

Finally, consider what would happen if we moved line 4 of Program 10–2 from the package declaration to the package body. Now the exception would not be visible outside the package body. However, if **Hopeless** were raised, say, at line 35, the caller of **Get_Positive_2** would have to handle an exception, but the name of that exception would not be visible. The only way to handle the exception in that case would be with an **others** choice in the exception handler.

Renaming may be used with exceptions. This capability is particularly useful in the case of package declarations. Suppose package **A** names package **B** in its context clause. If package **B** declares some exceptions, package **A** can use renaming to make the names of those exceptions available to programs which name package **A** without requiring those programs to name package **B**.

One package in particular which makes use of this scheme is **TEXT_IO**, in which the following renaming of exceptions is found:

```
STATUS_ERROR: exception renames IO_EXCEPTIONS.STATUS_ERROR;
MODE_ERROR  : exception renames IO_EXCEPTIONS.MODE_ERROR;
NAME_ERROR  : exception renames IO_EXCEPTIONS.NAME_ERROR;
USE_ERROR   : exception renames IO_EXCEPTIONS.USE_ERROR;
DEVICE_ERROR: exception renames IO_EXCEPTIONS.DEVICE_ERROR;
END_ERROR   : exception renames IO_EXCEPTIONS.END_ERROR;
DATA_ERROR  : exception renames IO_EXCEPTIONS.DATA_ERROR;
LAYOUT_ERROR: exception renames IO_EXCEPTIONS.LAYOUT_ERROR;
```

The advantage is that any program that names **TEXT_IO** in its context clause does not also have to name **IO_EXCEPTIONS**. Since the choices in an exception handler must be unique, if a compilation unit names both **TEXT_IO** and **IO_EXCEPTIONS**, it is a syntax error to have

```
when IO_EXCEPTIONS.STATUS_ERROR => ...
when TEXT_IO.STATUS_ERROR => ...
```

in a single exception part because both of these choices refer to the same exception.

We now give a brief explanation of the preceding exceptions. **STATUS_ERROR** is raised when (1) an attempt to is made to read, write or close a file that is not open or (2) an attempt to open a file that is already open. **MODE_ERROR** is raised when an attempt is made to read from an **OUT_FILE**, write to an **IN_FILE**, or ask about **EOF** on an **OUT_FILE**. **NAME_ERROR** is raised when an attempt is made to **OPEN** a nonexistent or to **CREATE** a file with illegal name. **USE_ERROR** is raised when (1) a file or device that can only be read is opened as an **OUT_FILE**, or (2) a file or device that can only be written is opened as an **IN_FILE**. **DEVICE_ERROR** is raised to indicate a system malfunction. **END_ERROR** is raised when an attempt is made to read beyond the end of a file. **DATA_ERROR** is raised when what is read is not of the type expected by the read statement. **LAYOUT_ERROR** is raised when a format control command cannot be performed.

10.3.2 Rules of Exception Propagation

How and where exceptions are propagated occurs in accordance with certain rules. This section describes many of these rules. Other rules will be introduced when we cover the constructs to which they apply.

An exception that is raised immediately within the statement list of a frame can be handled by that frame. This is the case we have seen in all our previous examples. However, exceptions can occur in other places.

An exception can be raised during the elaboration of the declarations within a subprogram or block statement. For instance, a **CONSTRAINT_ERROR** can arise upon assignment of an initial value to a variable. The elaboration of the declarations is immediately abandoned, and it becomes a question of where to propagate the exception. Observe that the declarative part of a subprogram or block is not within the exception frame of the subprogram or block. For example, if an exception was raised during the elaboration of the declarations of **Get_Positive** in Program 10–1, the exception frame within **Get_Positive** would not be given a chance to handle the exception because it was raised before, and not within, the statement list of the frame. Thus, the exception is propagated to the next outer construct. If an exception is raised during the elaboration of the declarations within a subprogram, the exception is raised again at the point that the subprogram was called. If an exception is raised during the elaboration of the declarations within a block statement, the exception is raised again immediately after the block statement.

There are a number of other interesting aspects to exceptions and subprogram calls, most of which are due to compatible subtypes. For example, a parameter or return type could be a subtype with a range constraint.

Consider the procedure **Exception_Demo** in Program 10–3. Depending upon the parameter **X**, various exception combinations occur. If **X** is -1, the value of the parameter **I** (line 4) is not in the subtype **NATURAL**. Since parameters are checked at the point of the call, the exception **CONSTRAINT_ERROR** is raised at line 12. Control then transfers to the handler at line 14.

If **X** is 0, **CONSTRAINT_ERROR** is raised in the elaboration at line 5 because the initial value supplied to **K** is not positive. This error is raised at the point of call, again line 12. Again, control then transfers to the handler at line 14.

If **X** is 1, elaboration is successful. However on execution of line 7, the value of the expression is not in the subtype **NATURAL** and **CONSTRAINT_ERROR** is raised at that line. Control then transfers to the handler at line 9, and execution exits the procedure, setting **Y** to 1.

If **X** is 2, the procedure runs, and **J** is set to 0 at line 7. Upon exit, **CONSTRAINT_ERROR** is raised. It is legal for **J** to assume the value 0, but it is not legal for **Y** to be assigned that value. The exception is raised at the point of call (line 12), and control transfers to line 14.

```
with TEXT_IO;  use TEXT_IO;
procedure Exception_Demo(X: INTEGER) is
  Y: POSITIVE;
  procedure F(I: in NATURAL; J: out NATURAL) is
    K: POSITIVE := I;
  begin
    J := I - 2;
  exception
    when CONSTRAINT_ERROR => J := 1;
  end F;
begin
  F(X, Y);
exception
  when CONSTRAINT_ERROR => PUT("Except_Demo");
end Exception_Demo;
```

Program 10–3

With the robot, exceptions can be avoided most of the time by following the principle of looking first and acting second. However, in a situation where the world has other robots moving around, some exceptions may be unavoidable. Although we do not yet have the capability of having multiple robots, we build the following procedure as an illustration of using exceptions. The attempt is to provide a move command that is secure against the actions of other robots. Other robots could be troublesome by getting in the path of the robot's movement: Even if we do look before each move, another robot might appear between the time we looked and the time we moved.

```
procedure Secure_Move(Distance: NATURAL) is
  Distance_Left: NATURAL := Distance;
begin
  while Distance_Left > 0 loop
    begin
      Move(1);
      Distance_Left := Distance_Left - 1;
    exception
      when Path_Blocked => null;
    end;
  end loop;
end Secure_Move;
```

Program 10–4

The principle of a secure move is embodied in the procedure **Secure_Move** in Program 10–4. We use the type **NATURAL** for the parameter because handling a distance of 0 might avoid multiple checks for this case in routines that use **Secure_Move**. In the procedure, the robot attempts a move. If its path is not blocked, the move occurs and the distance left for the robot to move is decreased by 1. If the decrease in the distance reduces the distance left to 0, iteration is complete and the move is done. If the robot's path is blocked, an exception is raised, the distance is not decreased, and iteration continues. If an exception other than **Path_Blocked** is raised, it is propagated.

The following fragment shows that exception handlers may be nested:

```
begin
  -- statement list of outer exception frame
exception
  when others =>
    begin
      Recovery_Subprogram;
    exception
      when others =>
        TEXT_IO.PUT("Recovery failed");
        raise;
    end;
end;
```

Notice the block statement in the statement list of the exception handler. The block statement includes a procedure call and an exception handler. If an exception is raised in the outer exception frame, control is transferred to its exception handler, which calls **Recovery_Subprogram**. If an exception is raised within **Recovery_Subprogram** which that procedure does not handle, control is transferred to the handler that prints the message that recovery has failed. The point of this example is that exception handlers are able to perform complex tasks, including handling exceptions raised within them. When an unhandled exception occurs in a handler, it propagates out of the "outer" frame as though it were an unhandled exception from that frame.

The propagation of exceptions raised in the elaboration of packages is interesting, but easy to understand. It is important to maintain the distinction between package elaboration and the elaboration of subprograms declared in the package. Elaboration of the declarations within any subprogram occurs each time that subprogram is called. Elaboration of the declarations within a subprogram contained in a package does not occur when the package is elaborated, unless the subprogram is called as part of that elaboration. The rule about propagating exceptions in the elaboration of subprogram declarations to the point of call applies to those subprograms declared in packages.

The propagation of an exception raised in a package declaration or body depends on the location of the package. If an exception is raised in the elaboration of a package declaration or body, the exception is raised again just after that declaration or body. The point of declaration could be the declaration part of a procedure, package declaration, package body, or declare block. The exception will be handled according to which of these the point of declaration is in. In the case of a block statement, the exception is raised immediately following the block statement. If it happens that the procedure is the main program or the package is a library unit, there is no enclosing frame in which to raise the exception and the program is abandoned.

```
function Raise_It return INTEGER is
begin
  if ... then
    raise CONSTRAINT_ERROR;
  else
    return 1;
  end if;
end Raise_It;
```

```
 1:procedure Handle is
 2:  procedure Local is
 3:    package Z is
 4:      X: INTEGER := Raise_It;
 5:    end Z;
 6:      -- Raised again
 7:    package body Z is
 8:      Y: INTEGER := Raise_It
 9:    begin
10:      Y := Raise_It;
11:    exception
12:      when ... => ...
13:    end Z;
14:      -- Raised again
15:  begin
16:    null;
17:  end Local;
18:begin
19:  Local;
20:exception
21:  when others => ...
22:end Handle;
```

Program 10–5

Procedure **Handle** in Program 10–5 illustrates these rules. The only purpose of the function **Raise_It** is to provide a means of raising an exception in the declarations. We have placed the raise statement inside an if statement so that the function will only sometimes raise the exception. When the procedure **Local** is called at line 19, its declarative part is elaborated. This includes the elaboration of the declaration and body of the package **Z**. When the declaration of **Z** is elaborated, the variable **X** is supplied an initial value by a function call (line 4). If the exception **CONSTRAINT_ERROR** is propagated out of that function call, it will be raised at line 4. Because this is during the elaboration of a package declaration, elaboration of that declaration is abandoned and the exception is raised again at line 6. Line 6 is in a procedure declaration. An exception raised during procedure declaration is raised again at the point of call, in this case at line 19. Line 19 is in a sequence of statements, so raising an exception here causes control to transfer to the handler at line 21. Notice that an exception in the elaboration of **Z** has caused a transfer of control to line 21 in the procedure **Handle**.

Suppose that **X** is elaborated without raising an exception and that the first exception raised in the elaboration of **Local** is by the call to **Raise_It** in the elaboration of the variable **Y** in the declarative part of the body of package **Z** (line 8). In this case, the exception is raised again at line 14. Since, this line 14 is in the elaboration of **Local**, the exception is raised again at the point of call (line 19), causing execution to transfer to the handler at line 21.

The initialization code of a package is an exception frame, and it can have an exception handler. The only items propagated to this handler are exceptions raised during execution of the initialization code. An unhandled exception raised during execution of initialization code is an (unhandled) exception that has been raised in elaboration of the package. This means that, like exceptions that are raised during the rest of the elaboration of the package, they propagated to the point of declaration of the package body. Any unhandled exception raised during a call to a subprogram of the package is propagated to the caller. Suppose that, in the procedure **Handle**, no exceptions are raised at either line 4 or line 8. If the call at line 10 raises an exception, control may be transferred to the exception handler at line 12. If the handler at line 12 handles **CONSTRAINT_ERROR**, elaboration has been successful and execution of the body of **Local** can begin. If there had been no exception handlers or if line 12 does not handle **CONSTRAINT_ERROR**, the exception would be raised again at line 14. Once more, this causes the exception to be raised again at line 19 and control to be transferred from there to line 21.

Notice that if the package **Z** were directly within the declarations of main program, or if it were a library unit, execution of the main program would be abandoned.

Now that we have seen the exception handling capabilities of Ada we return to a conceptual discussion of handling exceptions. When an exception occurs, there are four types of action the executing unit can take.

1. The unit can try to execute the code again. This is illustrated by the action of **Get_Positive** in Program 10–1. Since typing mistakes are common, executing the read routine again is likely to fix the problem.
2. The unit can try an alternate path. Although it did not, the procedure **Secure_Move** in Program 10–4, when it detected that the path was blocked, could have attempted to maneuver the robot around the block.
3. The unit can abandon its execution. In the Programming Practices section, we shall see a package containing subprograms which, when asked to do something they are unable to do, raise an exception and propagate it to the caller.
4. The unit can attempt to repair the cause of the error. For example, a program handling student records that gets an exception opening the file containing those records could open a backup version of that file.

Of course, as we have seen with **Get_Positive**, a unit can use a combination of these strategies.

10.4 THE ASCII PACKAGE AND CHARACTER LITERALS

The predefined type **CHARACTER** is an enumerated type containing 128 values, of which, 95 have character literals that represent them. The type **CHARACTER** is defined to be compatible with the ASCII standard. ASCII is an abbreviation for American Standard Code for Information Interchange. For example, ASCII defines upper case A to be associated with the value 65, so **CHARACTER** is defined so that **'A'** has a **POS** of 65.

There is one unusual thing about the type **CHARACTER**: Only the 95 values corresponding to the character literals are directly available. For instance, **CHARACTER'VAL(7)** is a legal value of type **CHARACTER**, but there is neither a character literal nor an identifier that is directly associated with this value. Such an association must be done using the package **ASCII**. This package is predefined in the package **STANDARD**. For example, the package **ASCII** declares the identifier **BEL** to be a constant whose value is equal to **CHARACTER'VAL(7)**. In other words, **ASCII** behaves as though the declaration of **BEL** were as follows:

```
package ASCII is
  ...
  BEL: constant CHARACTER := CHARACTER'VAL(7);
  ...
end ASCII;
```

This declaration allows us to use:

```
ASCII.BEL
```

to refer to the element of the type **CHARACTER** whose **POS** is 7.

We now discuss some of the features in the package **ASCII**. We avoid discussing all the individual characters because for many of them there is no standard manner in which they are used. We also do not indicate the **POS** of these characters, since if you need to use them, you should use the identifiers that the package **ASCII** provides.

We have already mentioned the character **BEL**. When this character is written to a terminal it usually results in a sound similar to a bell or a beep.

There are several characters that are used for formatting. The character **CR** is a carriage return; it usually causes output to move to the start of the line. On some systems it also causes output to move down to a new line. The character **LF** is a line feed and usually moves the output down a line; on some systems straight down, on others to the beginning of the next line. The character **FF** is a form feed. On devices that use paper **FF** often ejects a page. (On a terminal it often will erase the screen.) Thus, the next output begins at the top of the next page. The character **HT** is a horizontal tab. This single character usually causes output to "skip" to the next tab stop, often the next column which is multiple of 8. For example, if you are at column 18, 19, or 20, **HT** would cause the next output to start at column 24. Clearly, the specific formatting performed by each character depends on both the operating system and the device to which the character is written.

There are several characters which might be generated by input from the keyboard. The backspace character, **BS**, is usually generated by the backspace key. Sometimes **BS** is not reported because it is handled by the operating system, causing characters to be erased from the input. The character **ESC** is the escape character, usually generated by the escape key, but often generated by other keys. The character **DEL** is generated by the delete key, sometimes this key is marked as the "rub out" key.

There is a series of names in the package **ASCII** in case the terminal on which you are programming has no key for some characters. For example, **COLON** is the same as the literal `':'`, so that if you do not have a colon on your keyboard, you can still use that character in a program. Another example is **LC_A**, the lower case A, which can also be written `'a'`. Thus, when programming from a terminal without lower case characters you can still write a program which handles the input and output of those characters. For a full description of the package **ASCII**, see Appendix C of the Ada Language Reference Manual.

The package **ASCII** is predefined within package **STANDARD**; thus, you never name **ASCII** in a context clause. As usual, visibility is by selection unless **ASCII** is named in a use clause. Having direct visibility may be useful in procedures that do a lot of character manipulation.

10.5 LIMITED TYPES

In some cases, it is desirable to have a type that does not allow the value of a variable to be duplicated or compared. Ada has *limited types* for which the operations of assignment and the comparisons for equality and inequality are not predefined. Only for limited types may the equality and inequality operations be defined by the program.

<limited private type declaration>

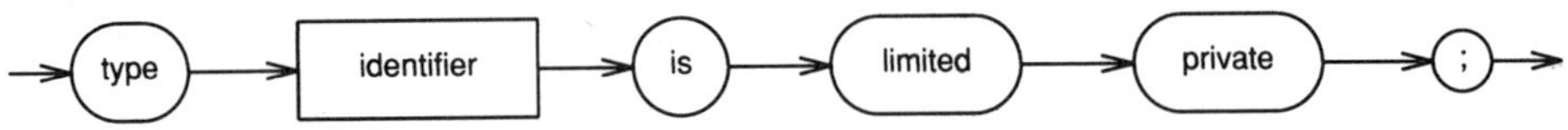

Figure 10–3

There are four kinds of limited types. The first kind is the *limited private type*. The syntax for declaring a limited private type is given by Figure 10–3. These types are both limited and private. Because they are private, they can only be declared in package declarations, and their declaration must be resolved in the private part of the same package declaration. Because they are limited, they cannot be assigned (using `:=`) outside of the package that declares them. Also because they are limited, equality and inequality are not implicitly defined for them. The equality and inequality operators may be overloaded by the package. Finally, because parameters may involve copying values, outside the package in which it is declared a limited type can only be used with mode **in out**.

The second kind of limited type is a composite type (array or record) with a component that is a limited type. Again, because the type is limited, equality and inequality are not implicitly defined, but can be explicitly defined for these types. As with all limited types, assignment is illegal and parameters are restricted to mode **in out**.

The other two kinds of limited types will be discussed in later chapters.

```
 1:package A is
 2:   type X is limited private;
 3:private
 4:   type X is
 5:      record
 6:         Value: CHARACTER;
 7:      end record;
 8:end A;
 9:with A;
10:package Limited_Demo is
11:   type Lim is
12:      record
13:         Index: INTEGER;
14:         Data: A.X;
15:      end record;
16:   function "="(Left, Right: Lim) return BOOLEAN;
17:end Limited_Demo;
18:package body Limited_Demo is
19:   function "="(Left, Right: Lim) return BOOLEAN is
20:   begin
21:      return Left.Index = Right.Index;
22:   end "=";
23:end Limited_Demo;
```

Program 10–6

In the package **Limited_Demo** in Program 10–6, the package declaration (lines 10–17) declares a type **Lim** (lines 11–15) that is limited because one of its components (**Data**, in line 14) is limited. Actually, this component is limited private (line 2). The internal structure of the type **Lim** is available outside the package, so a compilation unit naming **Limited_Demo** in its context clause can access the components **Index** and **Data** in type **Lim**. Because the component **Data** is private, the internal structure of that component is hidden. Because the type **Lim** is limited, the package **Limited_Demo** may overload equality and inequality. (The inequality operator is automatically defined when the equality operator is defined; it is illegal to declare a function with the inequality

(**/=**) operator.) Line 16 declares an overloading of equality. As required, the overloading has two operands of the same limited type and returns a **BOOLEAN**. In lines 19–22 of the package body, the subprogram body for the overloading is declared. Note that the programmer of the package has defined the overloading so that two values of type **Lim** are equal if and only if their **Index** components are equal. If the package **A** had overloaded = for the type **X**, the package **Limited_Demo** could have overloaded = in such a way that it also tested the **Data** components of **Left** and **Right**.

Finally, as a reminder, within the package **A**, variables of type **X** can be assigned and can be used with any parameter mode. That is, limited types are limited only outside the package in which they are declared.

10.6 PROGRAMMING PRACTICES

In developing an interactive system, it is common to find that over half of the program is involved in checking for and correcting unexpected data supplied by the user. It is important to perform enough checks on each value supplied by the user to ensure that it is valid.

A valid data item must be of the correct form and within the appropriate range (for instance, the square of an integer should not be negative). In addition, the data item must be consistent with other data already supplied (for instance, the number of students in a class cannot be more than the number of seats in the room).

As with variables, exceptions should be defined and handled as locally as possible; that is, as close as possible to the point at which the exception is raised. This practice assists readability because the reader can more easily associate the exception with the statements that might raise it. It is important to define an exception and handler for each type of unexpected or improper data item; you should avoid propagating the exception unless you decide that continuing the current subprogram is hopeless.

In most instances, when reading input it is desirable to let the user know what is wrong with the input, and then permit the user to try to reenter the data. In fact, users often appreciate the program providing a more extensive message after a second (or subsequent) try. Finally, it is usually considered a good idea to give up the situation as hopeless (raising another exception to the calling subprogram) after some large number of unsuccessful tries. The function **Get_Positive** in Program 10–1 shows this use of exceptions.

10.6.1 Problem Solving

In previous problem solving sections we have mentioned algorithms as a type of framework for reuse of previous creative problem solving work. That is, by using a standard algorithm you are reusing the work of the computer scientists who developed the algorithm. Examples of algorithms which we have discussed are binary search, insertion sort, and quick sort.

We introduced frameworks with the framework for data processing problems. This is an example of a type of framework which is an abstraction of an approach to an entire range of problems. In this section, we introduce the concept of an *abstract data structure* as a framework for problem solving. Roughly speaking, an abstract data structure is a representation of how values are stored and used. For example, an array is an example of an abstract data structure called a *sequence*. Calling a data structure a sequence only indicates that it is an ordered collection of objects (or values). The abstract data structure corresponding to a record is called a *group*.

The reason these data structures are called *abstract* is because all the information about how the data structure could be implemented is ignored (remember, to abstract means to remove details). We are only interested in the properties and operations of the data structure. Once the details of a particular implementation and application are abstracted away, we can more easily use the data structure as a tool in problem solving.

Another common abstract data structure is a *stack*. A stack is a structure into which values can be placed and removed, but values can only be removed in exactly the opposite order that they were placed on the stack.

One physical equivalent of a stack is a stack of dinner plates. You can put another plate on top of the stack, and you can take a plate off of the top of the stack, but you cannot remove any other plates without causing the whole stack to tumble down. If you think of recording values on the plates, it is easy to see how this is a physical analogue of the abstract data structure we are calling a stack.

Computer scientists have used stacks for many years, so some traditional terms have arisen in regard to them. Putting an item into the stack is called *pushing* the item *onto* (or *on*) the stack. Removing an item from the stack is called *popping* the item *off* the stack.

Suppose we push a 1 onto the stack, then push a 2, and then push a 3. The first time we pop an item off the stack, we will get the value 3. The next pop will yield the value 2, and the third pop will yield the value 1. Thus, the items are returned in the opposite order from the order in which they were pushed.

If we try to pop another item after we have popped all of the items from the stack, this is an error called *stack underflow*. Thus, stack underflow is the error of trying to pop an item when there is no item left to pop.

We do not have to do all of the pushes first and then all of the pops. We can combine them in any suitable order, provided that we only try to pop values after they have been pushed.

Program 10–7 is a partial implementation of a stack. In constructing this package we have used an implementation technique called an *abstract data type*. In Ada, an abstract data type is a package that contains all of the information about a data type and all of the operations (subprograms) for that data type.

Notice that in our implementation of the stack there is an exception called **`Overflow`**. In this implementation of the data structure, it is possible to run out of room on the stack. In fact, in this implementation, each stack is limited to 5 values before **`Overflow`** is raised.

```
package Stack_Package is
  type Stack is limited private;   -- Keeps the implementation abstract.
  subtype Item_Type is INTEGER;
  -- Change the declaration of Item_Type to make a stack package for
  -- another data type.
  Overflow: exception; -- Too many items pushed; no more room.
  Underflow: exception; -- Too many items popped; no more on the stack.
  procedure Push(The_Stack: in out Stack; Value: in Item_Type);
  -- Purpose: Push an item onto the stack.
  -- The_Stack: The stack to push onto.
  -- Value: The value to push onto the stack.
  procedure Pop(The_Stack: in out Stack; Value: out Item_Type);
  -- Purpose: Pop an item from the stack.
  -- The_Stack: The stack to pop from.
  -- Value: The value popped is returned in this parameter.
  function Top(The_Stack: Stack) return Item_Type;
  -- Purpose: Peek at the top item on the stack (the next
  --  which would be popped).
  function Full(The_Stack: Stack) return BOOLEAN;
  -- Purpose: Returns TRUE if and only if a Push would cause Overflow.
  function Empty(The_Stack: Stack) return BOOLEAN;
  -- Purpose: Returns TRUE if and only if a Pop would cause Underflow.
private
  Stack_Size: constant NATURAL := 5;
  -- Pushing more than this number of items will raise Overflow.
  type List is array (NATURAL range 1..Stack_Size) of Item_Type;
  type Stack is record
    Items_On_Stack: NATURAL := 0;  -- Number of items on the stack.
    Item_List: List;
  end record;
end Stack_Package;
package body Stack_Package is
  procedure Push(The_Stack: in out Stack; Value: in Item_Type) is
  -- Purpose: Push an item onto the stack.
  -- The_Stack: The stack to push onto.
  -- Value: The value to push onto the stack.
  begin
    if The_Stack.Items_On_Stack >= Stack_Size then
      raise Overflow;
    else
      The_Stack.Items_On_Stack := The_Stack.Items_On_Stack + 1;
      The_Stack.Item_List(The_Stack.Items_On_Stack) := Value;
    end if;
  end Push;
  procedure Pop(The_Stack: in out Stack; Value: out Item_Type) is
```

Program 10–7

```
    -- Purpose: Pop an item from the stack.
    -- The_Stack: The stack to pop from.
    -- Value: The value popped is returned in this parameter.
    begin
     null; -- You fill this one in
    end Pop;
    function Top(The_Stack: Stack) return Item_Type is
    -- Purpose: Peek at the top item on the stack (the next which would
    --  be popped).
    begin
     null; -- You fill this one in
    end Top;
    function Full(The_Stack: Stack) return BOOLEAN is
    -- Purpose: Returns TRUE if and only if a Push would cause Overflow.
    begin
     null; -- You fill this one in
    end Full;
    function Empty(The_Stack: Stack) return BOOLEAN is
    -- Purpose: Returns TRUE if and only if a Pop would cause Underflow.
    begin
     null; -- You fill this one in
    end Empty;
  end Stack_Package;
```

Program 10–7 Continued

A stack can be used as a repository for values when you are not sure how many values you wish to store. In many of these cases, the programmer does not care about the fact that the stack reverses the order of the information.

Earlier, we mentioned the correspondence between structuring data and structuring the control of program flow. For instance, the correspondence between a loop with a for schema and an array. We also discussed how a structure chart can be produced for data and how this can be used to help design the structure chart for a program. In this section, we see yet another correspondence between data and control: abstract data structures serve roughly the same purposes for data as algorithms serve for control.

A successful program needs both data and control. To successfully design a large program, you should take advantage of both abstract data structures and algorithms. We shall consider several other algorithms and data structures later on in the text.

10.6.2 Testing

Special care must be taken when testing programs that make extensive use of exceptions. In particular, you must be certain that regardless of where in the subprogram an exception is raised, the program will still behave properly.

For example, suppose you are writing a program that reads information from a file, closes the file, opens it again, and writes information back to the same file while processing with both the original information and information derived from the user. If an exception causes the part of the program that closes the file to be skipped, then the file might not be closed. In this situation, if the file is not closed before the program exits, it is possible for all of the information in the file to be lost.

You must test all sections of the program which might raise an exception to ensure that if the exception is raised there, no undesirable results will occur. This sometimes means writing a special version of the program that deliberately raises exceptions which would not normally be raised in certain portions of the program. Remember, defensive programming involves a certain amount of paranoia about what could happen if a later programmer modifies the program.

10.6.3 The Language Reference Manual

The formal definition of the Ada language is given in an official document called *The Programming Language Ada Reference Manual.* This document is issued by the Ada Joint Programming Office of the U.S. government. Informally, the document is called the "Language Reference Manual" or simply the "LRM." The LRM contains many details about the Ada language which are not included in this book.

The LRM was not designed to be a textbook about programming. However, after covering a topic in this book, you should be able to read and understand most of the corresponding material in the LRM. We recommend that as you enter later courses, you use a copy of the LRM. Sometimes, we refer you to the LRM for further details. The capability to use a manual is essential to a computer scientist.

When beginning to use the LRM we recommend you scan the table of contents to note how the manual is divided into 14 major sections, then read the introduction (the first section) which defines many of the terms used in the manual, and then scan the glossary (Appendix D). The glossary contains definitions of Ada terms. After a brief first reading of the glossary, you will want to return to that appendix when you encounter terms in the manual.

In using any manual, you often want to find out something about a particular topic. A good places to start is the index. The LRM has a particularly good index in the back of the manual. Also, at the end of each section is an index of topics related to that section.

10.7 ADA SUMMARY

In this chapter, we have discussed *exceptions* in detail, describing the syntax and semantics of the optional *exception part.* We have discussed how the exception part is related to the *raising* and *propagation* of exceptions. In discussing the declaration of exceptions, we have noted that the rules for their scope and visibility are the same as for a variable. We have covered the package **ASCII** and how it can be used to access the nonprinting characters. Finally, we have introduced both *limited types* and the principles for using them.

EXERCISES

10.1. Complete and test the package **Stack_Package** in Program 10–7.

10.2. Make a stack package for storing values of type **CHARACTER**. Write a program that gets a **Normal_Line** from the user, puts the characters from the **Normal_Line** onto the stack, and then pops the characters off of the stack, printing each character as it is popped. This will reverse the line of characters. Keep popping the stack until the **Underflow** exception is raised (use an exception handler).

10.3. Write a package that reads words from the user, but permits the user to put more than one word on a line. The package must have the following function in it:

```
function Next_Word return Normal_Line;
-- Purpose: returns the next word which has been entered by the user.
```

The package you should create should stack values of type **Normal_Line**. **Next_Word** should pop and return the top item on the stack. If there is no next word, read a line from the user, divide it into words (pushing each onto the stack), and then pop and return the top word. (Notice that this could be recursive.)

Write a test program for your package. The program should exit when the word "end" is returned by **Next_Word**.

10.4. Modify the previous example to keep the words in the correct order. (Hint: Putting the words on the stack reverses the order, so try reversing the order twice.)

10.5. Exercise 8.2 asked you to implement a **Bank_Account** package with multiple depositors by using an array of records hidden within the package. Modify this package so that it uses a limited private type for the depositor's account record. Instead of hiding the records inside the **Bank_Account** package, each depositor can declare their own bank account by declaring a record of type **Account**. Because the type is private, the depositor cannot modify the internals of the account. Because this type is limited, the depositor cannot manufacture money by duplicating the account. Since declaring a record opens an account, the **Bank_Account** package must ensure that objects of type **Account** are initialized before they are used. Use the following declarations as a start for modifying the declarations of the previous **Bank_Account** package:

```
package Bank_Account is
  type Account is limited private
  procedure Deposit( -- you fill in );
  -- Purpose: Record a deposit to the specified account.
  procedure Withdraw( -- you fill in );
  -- Purpose: Record a withdrawal from the specified account.
  function Account_Balance( -- you fill in) return NATURAL;
  -- Purpose: Return the balance in the specified account.
private
  -- you fill in
end Bank_Account;
```

10.6. In the bank account with password security of exercise 8.8, the bank had to maintain information internally so that only one action could be taken per security clearance. Another way to handle security clearance is to modify the declarations of the package so that authorizations are variables of a limited private type. This is shown in the following code:

```
with Lines;
package Bank is
-- Purpose: Provide banking utilities for tellers.
  use Lines;
  Max_Bank_Customers: constant NATURAL := 25;
  -- Transactions:
  type Authorization_Type is limited private;
  type Withdraw_Result is (OK, Insufficient_Funds);
  procedure Withdraw(Authorization: in out Authorization_Type; Amount: POSITIVE;
                     Result: out Withdraw_Result);
  -- Purpose: Withdraw money from an account.
  procedure Deposit(Authorization: in out Authorization_Type; Amount: POSITIVE);
  -- Purpose: Deposit money to an account.
  procedure Balance(Authorization: in out Authorization_Type;
                            Amount: out INTEGER);
  -- Purpose: Report the balance in an account.
  -- Manager activities:
  procedure Create_Account(Authorization: in out Authorization_Type;
                            Account_Name, Account_Password: Normal_Line);
  procedure Audit(Authorization: in out Authorization_Type);
  -- Purpose: Dumps all account names, passwords and balances.
  procedure Open_Bank(Authorization: in out Authorization_Type);
  -- Purpose: Opens the bank reading initial information from a file.
  procedure Close_Bank(Authorization: in out Authorization_Type);
  -- Purpose: Closes the bank writing information to a file.
  -- Security:
  -- A customer/manager gets only one transaction per security clearance.
  procedure Security(Account_Name, Account_Password: Normal_Line;
                      Authorization: in out Authorization_Type);
  -- Purpose: Grant or deny a clearance for a transaction.
private
  type Authorization_Level_Type is (None, Manager, Customer);
  type Authorization_Type is
    record
     Authorization_Level: Authorization_Level_Type := None;
     Account_Number: NATURAL := 0;
    end record;
end Bank;
```

The modified package declaration indicates how to declare an authorization type which replaces the security condition of Chapter 8. Further, each of the subprograms requiring authorization needs an additional parameter, the authorization. We illustrate this by showing how to add authorization to the procedure **Audit**. Because limited private types cannot be duplicated, and the subprograms cancel the authorization when it is used, only one operation can be performed per authorization. Complete the package declaration by adding comments (from Chapter 8), complete the package body, and test the package.

10.7. Modify the **Fractions** package (exercises 8.7 or 9.7) to include the use of exceptions. Any operation that would result in a denominator of zero should raise **NUMERIC_ERROR**.

10.8. Construct a program containing the following declarations and design exception handling for the subprograms:

```
No_Integer, Bad_Value: exception;
function User_Input(Tries: POSITIVE :=1) returns INTEGER;
procedure Get_Positive(I: out POSITIVE);
```

The function **User_Input** uses an instantiation of **TEXT_IO.INTEGER_IO** to attempt to read an integer value. It does not issue any prompt. For **Tries-1** attempts, if the user's input is not in the correct format for an integer, **User_Input** beeps 3 times (by writing the **ASCII.BEL** character 3 times) and gives the user another try. If the input is invalid after **Tries** attempts, **User_Input** propagates the exception raised in **TEXT_IO**.

The procedure **Get_Positive** uses the function **User_Input** to get an integer value from the user, initially giving the user 2 tries to input a valid integer. If **User_Input** raises an exception, **Get_Positive** writes a message asking the user to "Please try harder" and calls **User_Input** again, this time giving the user 3 more tries at a correct entry. If this second invocation of **User_Input** also causes an exception, **Get_Positive** tells the user "Try to be more careful" and again calls **User_Input**, this time allowing only 1 try. If the third use of **User_Input** again raises an exception, **Get_Positive** raises the **No_Integer** exception. If **User_Input** does not raise an exception but the value it returns is negative, **Get_Positive** tells the user "Please don't be negative" and raises the **Bad_Value** exception. Note that **User_Input** prints nothing and does not explicitly raise any exception if the value entered represents an integer greater than or equal to 0. On a **DATA_ERROR**, remember to have **User_Input** flush the input (**SKIP_LINE**) so that the program does not reread the same bad data.

Write a main program that tests the preceding functions. The program should allow the user to continue testing as long as desired, even if some of the tests raise exceptions. The main program should report the nature of any exceptions it handles and should report the value, if any, returned by **Get_Positive**.

10.9. Write a package **Queue_Package** with the following declaration:

```
package Queue_Package is
  type Queue is limited private;    -- Keeps the implementation abstract.
  subtype Item_Type is INTEGER;
  Overflow: exception; -- No room to Store this item.
  Underflow: exception; -- No item to Retrieve.
  procedure Store(The_Queue: in out Queue; Value: in Item_Type);
  -- Purpose: Store an item into the queue
  -- The_Stack: The queue to store in.
  -- Value: The value to store.
  procedure Retrieve(The_Queue: in out Queue; Value: out Item_Type);
  -- Purpose: Get an item from the queue.
  -- The_Queue: The queue to get from.
  -- Value: The value retrieved.
  function Full(The_Queue: Queue) return BOOLEAN;
```

```
  -- Purpose: Returns TRUE if the queue is full.
  function Empty(The_Queue: Queue) return BOOLEAN;
  -- Purpose: Returns TRUE the queue is empty.
  function "="(L, R: Queue) return BOOLEAN;
  -- Purpose: Compare the contents of two queues. They are equal
  --  if they contain the same values.
private
  Queue_Size: constant NATURAL := 5;
  -- Trying to store more than this number of items will raise Overflow.
  type List is array (NATURAL range 1..Queue_Size) of Item_Type;
  type Queue is record
    Items_In_Queue: NATURAL := 0;  -- Number of items in the queue.
    Start_Of_Queue: INTEGER := 1;  -- Index of the start of the queue.
    Items: List;
  end record;
end Queue_Package;
```

A queue is like a line: The first item stored will be the first retrieved. For example, if we stored a 5, and then a 6, and then a 7; we would retrieve a 5, and then a 6, and then a 7. Notice the implementation. Starting with an empty queue: If we store a 8, it is stored in **Items(1)** and set **Items_In_Queue** to 1. If we then store a 9, it is stored in **Items(2)** and set **Items_In_Queue** to 2. If we now retrieve, the 8 is returned, **Start_Of_Queue** set to 2 (**Items(2)** contains the 9, which is the next element that will be retrieved), and **Items_In_Queue** gets set to 1. If we now store 10, 11, 12, and 13 in succession, the 10 goes to location 3, the 11 to location 4, the 12 to location 5, and the 13 to location 1. Notice that storage starts at **Start_Of_Queue** and wraps around to the front of the array if necessary. This avoids moving all the items in the array when **Retrieve** is called. One way to wrap around is to use the **mod** operator.

The equals function should compare the contents of two queues. Suppose **Q1** contains one item, a 5, stored at **Items(4)**, and **Q2** also contains one item, a 5 stored at **Items(2)**. Then **Q1** and **Q2** are equal because they both contain a single item which is a 5, even though they have that 5 in different locations. This means that the **"="** function must contain a loop with the appropriate comparisons.

11

Concurrent Programming

11.1 OBJECTIVES

In this chapter we introduce concurrent programming, how this is achieved in Ada, and how concurrent programs communicate with one another. Additional aspects of concurrent programs are covered in Chapters 18 and 19.

Concurrency is when several things can happen at once. In previous chapters, programs executed only one instruction at a time. In this chapter, we build programs which can be doing several things at a time. We begin with a discussion of the concept of concurrency and the basis of concurrent programming (section 3). We describe the *task*, which is the Ada mechanism for writing concurrent programs (section 4). We show how tasks can coordinate with each other (section 5), and communicate with each other (section 6). We discuss some of the more advanced concepts of coordination and how these concepts can be applied to Ada's features to avoid having one task wait for another task to complete its job (section 7). We consider how a task may be programmed to wait for a fixed amount of time (section 8) and the Ada package which deals with time (section 9). An example of concurrent programming closes the chapter (section 10).

CONCEPTS:

- Work can be done concurrently through the use of tasks.
- Tasks need to cooperate.
- Tasks sometimes are busy and not ready to cooperate.
- Timing is important.

GOALS:

- Write a program that controls several operations simultaneously.

11.2 MOTIVATION

In many computer applications a program needs to do more than one thing at a time. For example, someone using a spread sheet or word-processing program often continues typing even though the program has not finished executing a previous command. In that case, some part of the program must capture the key strokes at the same time as other parts finish executing the previous command. When different parts of a program execute at the same time, we say that they operate *concurrently* with each other. Ada calls the parts of a program that can operate concurrently *tasks*.

Concurrency and tasks open a new area of programming. Doing things concurrently is often a good idea, but some jobs need to be done before others. This requires that tasks cooperate with each other. There are two important forms of cooperation. In the first form, called *synchronization*, the completion of the various portions of a job is coordinated. In the second form, called *communication*, information is exchanged. In Ada, both forms of cooperation are achieved by the *rendezvous*. Because the nature of cooperation depends upon the situation, Ada defines a variety of ways to attempt a rendezvous.

In many problems, timing is important. Particularly, when a program controls objects in the real world, the program should not always run as fast as it can. Such a program needs the capability to wait for something to happen and to know how much time has elapsed. These capabilities are the motivation behind the *delay statement* and the *calendar package*.

11.3 CONCURRENT PROGRAMMING

To visualize concurrent programming, imagine that several independent entities operate at the same time, but in a cooperative fashion, to perform a job. For example, in a restaurant, several people such as cooks, waitresses, and dishwashers must cooperate to accomplish the job of running the restaurant.

In sequential processing, the kind of programming we have discussed up to now, we call a subprogram and wait for it to finish executing before we call another subprogram. This is as if the cook in the restaurant waited for the waitress to finish serving before beginning preparation of the next meal. In concurrent processing, the various entities are not required to wait while another entity is performing its job. In a real restaurant, the cook continues to work in the kitchen while the waitress is serving; when the waitress returns, the next meal is ready to be served.

In Ada, an entity that is capable of executing concurrently with other entities is called a *task*. Tasks may be declared, but, in addition, the main program operates as a task.

The implementation of concurrency can be virtual (simulated) or actual (real). As an analogy, one person can run a restaurant by spending part of their time as cook, part as waitress, and part as dishwasher. Essentially, the one person pretends to be several people or, alternatively, spends time in several different roles. In this case, the concurrency is virtual. In the case where different people perform the separate roles, the concurrency is actual.

In a computing system supporting Ada, concurrent processing may be provided by several processors each handling a task (actual), or by a single processor spending part of its time doing each task (virtual). In the virtual implementation, the single processor behaves as though it were several processors, spending part of its time in each of the different roles. Both implementations should appear the same to the user.

In concurrent processing, several new issues must be addressed. These issues arise when tasks are not independent; that is, when tasks must cooperate to perform a job.

The first issue is called *synchronization*. In some cases, one task must synchronize with another. To go back to the restaurant example, the waitress cannot serve a particular meal until the cook has finished preparing it. That is, the waitress must synchronize her serving with the completion of a particular portion of the cook's task.

The second issue is called *shared resources*. Previously, we indicated that extreme care must be used if several procedures use the same variable. In concurrent processing, additional steps must be taken to ensure that two tasks do not mistakenly use a resource (e.g., a variable) at the same time in a way that could cause an error. In the restaurant example, if the cook is using a pot to prepare soup at the same time the dishwasher is trying to clean that pot, the soup will not be prepared correctly. The cook and the dishwasher must coordinate their efforts in such a way that the pot is being used by only one of them at a time.

Another issue is *information transmission*. In a restaurant, although the cook and the waitress are working on separate tasks simultaneously, it is necessary for the waitress to communicate an order to the cook so that the cook knows what type of meal to prepare. Similarly, in Ada, values must be communicated between tasks. To properly communicate tasks must synchronize in a manner which ensures that a task actually receives the information passed to it. In the restaurant, the cook and waitress use a synchronization mechanism to ensure that when the waitress communicates an order, the cook receives it.

Concurrency, like each new type of programming capability, brings its own problems. Any language that allows concurrent processing must provide mechanisms to address the issues we have just mentioned. Some problems are inherent in concurrent programming, others are inherent in the mechanisms chosen by a particular language. The following are some of the more important problems introduced by concurrency.

A concurrent program can *deadlock*. Because a mechanism must be provided to allow tasks to wait for (synchronize) each other, a program can reach a state in which every task is waiting for some other task. This is like a situation in which the cook is waiting for the waitress to deposit an order, the waitress is waiting for the dishwasher to clear a table, and the dishwasher is waiting for the cook to finish using a pot. Everybody is waiting for someone else to finish some portion of a job. Consequently, nobody is doing anything. If a program deadlocks, the programmer has made a mistake.

A concurrent program can *livelock*. This is similar to deadlock, except that some tasks continue to perform their jobs. Livelock occurs when a task waits forever for something to happen. In the restaurant example, suppose that the cook is waiting for a clean pot from the dishwasher so that soup can be made, but the dishwasher has gone home. The cook continues to prepare food, and the waitress continues to serve food; however, the cook cannot make the soup because of the missing pot. The restaurant still functions, except that customers who ordered soup will wait forever!

When writing a concurrent program, the programmer must remember that several jobs are being performed at the same time. This means that the order in which things happen is not predetermined and is often unpredictable. Will the cook finish preparing the soup before the waitress arrives with the first order? No one knows. If a concurrent program needs to ensure that things happen in a certain order, the programmer must build the appropriate synchronization into the program.

Furthermore, just because concurrent programs do several things at once does not mean that they do their job in a fair manner. Using the restaurant analogy again, there is no guarantee that the cook treats all the waitresses fairly. Orders for the cook's favorite waitress could be prepared first, while orders for other waitresses could wait until the cook has nothing else to do. In a similar manner, fairness is not inherent in Ada. The programmer is responsible for writing the program in such a way that appropriate fairness and priorities for the application are observed.

11.4 SIMPLE TASKS

A task is a part of a program that can operate concurrently with other parts. A task has a task declaration and a task body. A simplified syntax for the task declaration is given in Figure 11–1. In this chapter, we shall illustrate and use only the simpler forms of task declaration. An example of a task declaration is

```
task Divisible_by_Three;
```

A task can be declared in any declarative part. Each task declaration must be accompanied by a task body. Furthermore, the task body must occur in the same declarative region as that of the task declaration. This means that when a task declaration occurs in a package declaration, the task body must occur in the package body.

The syntax for a task body is also given in Figure 11–1. We could write the body of **Divisible_by_Three** as

<task declaration (simplified)>

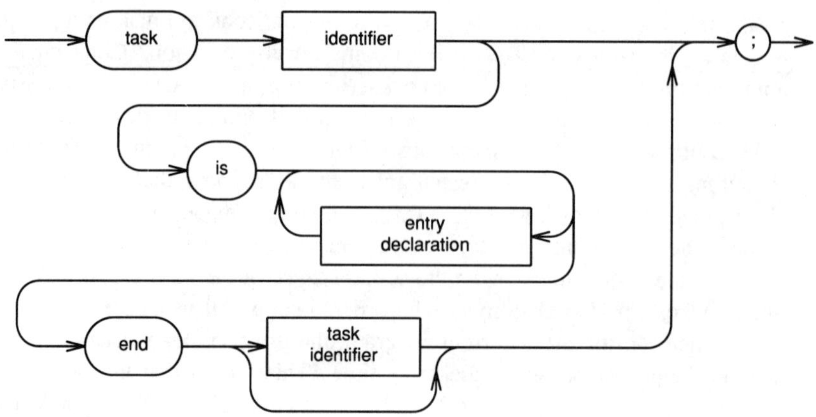

<task body>

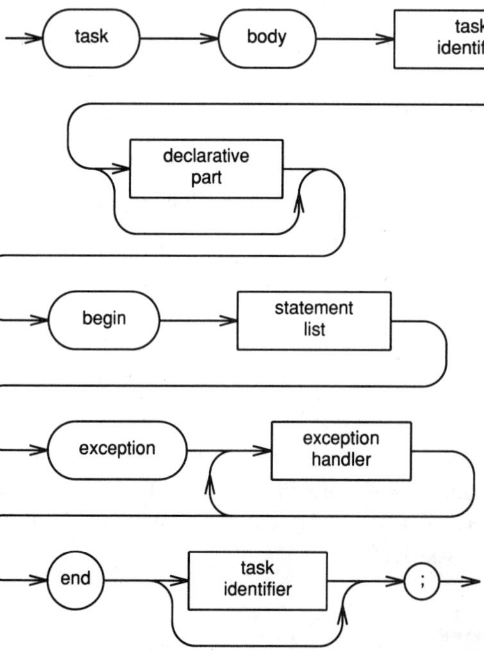

Figure 11–1

```
task body Divisible_by_Three is
  X: INTEGER; Y: BOOLEAN;
begin
  Y := X rem 3 = 0;
end Divisible_by_Three;
```

A task body is very similar to a procedure body. The declarative part of a task body can include declarations of procedures, packages, and even other tasks. In the preceding example, the declarative part of the body of **Divisible_by_Three** includes declarations for the variables **X** and **Y**.

A task has properties of both procedures and objects. Like a procedure, it executes statements; like an object, it remains in existence for as long as all other objects do in the same declarative region. Unlike a procedure, a task exists and is active without being called. It is active concurrently with other tasks.

```
with TEXT_IO;
procedure Divisors is        -- First version
  Number: INTEGER;
  By_Three, By_Four: BOOLEAN;

  procedure Get_Divisors is
    task Divisible_by_Three;
    task Divisible_by_Four;

    task body Divisible_by_Three is
    begin
      By_Three := Number rem 3 = 0;
    end Divisible_by_Three;

    task body Divisible_by_Four is
    begin
      By_Four := Number rem 4 = 0;
    end Divisible_by_Four;

  begin
    null;
  end Get_Divisors;

  package Int_IO is new TEXT_IO.INTEGER_IO(INTEGER);
begin
  Int_IO.GET(Number);
  Get_Divisors;
  TEXT_IO.PUT_LINE("By_Three " & BOOLEAN'IMAGE(By_Three));
  TEXT_IO.PUT_LINE("By_Four " & BOOLEAN'IMAGE(By_Four));
end Divisors;
```

Program 11–1

We illustrate this with the procedure **Divisors** in Program 11–1. This procedure is somewhat contorted and we will rewrite it after we introduce some additional features of tasks. **Divisors** determines whether a number is divisible by three and/or divisible by four. It does this by having two tasks, one which checks whether the number is divisible by three and the other which checks whether the number is divisible by four.

First, we see that tasks may be declared in any declarative region. In **Divisors**, the tasks are declared within the procedure **Get_Divisors**. We have stated that the existence of a task has the same characteristics as the existence of a variable. A variable within **Get_Divisors** does not exist until it is elaborated as a result of the procedure being called. Similarly, our two tasks do not exist before they are elaborated as a result of the call to **Get_Divisors** in line 22. Thus, when we are reading a number at line 21, the tasks do not yet exist.

The process by which a task comes into existence is called *activation*. As we have seen, when a subprogram is called, its declarative part is elaborated. In the case of **Get_Divisors**, this includes the elaboration of the two tasks. Elaboration makes a task available for activation. Activation of a task includes elaboration of its declarative part and starting the execution of its instructions. Thus, on the call to **Get_Divisors**, the task **Divisible_by_Three** is elaborated and then activated, as is the task **Divisible_by_Four**. Activation of these tasks will take place after the elaboration of all declarations in **Get_Divisors**, but before the execution of the first statement in **Get_Divisors**. Specifically, both tasks are activated after the **begin** in line 16 and before the statement in line 17.

After elaboration of the declarations and activation of the tasks of **Get_Divisors**, execution of the statement list of the body of **Get_Divisors** begins. Three things are executing concurrently during the call to **Get_Divisors**: the two tasks and the procedure body. Notice that the tasks always get activated before execution of the statements in the procedure body begins, so the procedure body can rely on their activation having already occurred. Because activation takes place after elaboration of the other declarations the tasks can rely on the elaboration of the variables (and subprograms, etc.) of **Get_Divisors** having already occurred.

We deliberately placed the tasks within **Get_Divisors**. If they had been placed directly within **Divisors**, they would have begun executing before the body of **Divisors** began executing. This means that they would have begun execution before **Number** was read (line 21). Consequently, they might have computed their results on the basis of an uninitialized value in **Number**.

The actual arrangement of the program does not allow these tasks to exist until after **Number** has a value. A number is read, and then **Get_Divisors** is called at line 22. Since this is a procedure call, execution of **Divisors** stops at line 22 until the call to **Get_Divisors** is completed. When **Get_Divisors** is called, the tasks are activated, compute their results and complete. Once the tasks have been activated, execution of the body of **Get_Divisors** begins. Since that body is empty, execution of the body of **Get_Divisors** completes almost immediately. The completion of all its tasks and the completion of its body allows **Get_Divisors** to return. This return allows the execution of **Divisors** to resume following line 22. The answers computed by the tasks are then printed in lines 23 and 24.

A condition for returning from a procedure is that all objects declared in the procedure, including tasks, cease to exist. Since a task cannot cease to exist until it has finished its execution, the return from **Get_Divisors** cannot occur until after its tasks have finished. For example, if we replaced line 14 with

```
loop
  null;
end loop;
```

the task **Divisible_by_Four** would never finish and we would never return from **Get_Divisors**. The moral is to make sure that your tasks finish. There are a number of complex details about how tasks finish and when procedures exit, including issues of what happens when an exception is raised. These are covered in Chapter 19.

11.5 SYNCHRONIZATION

As was plain in the procedure **Divisors**, one way to control task execution is to embed the task within a procedure. However, this form of control is inadequate for many situations, so Ada provides additional mechanisms. The simplest is the *entry call.*

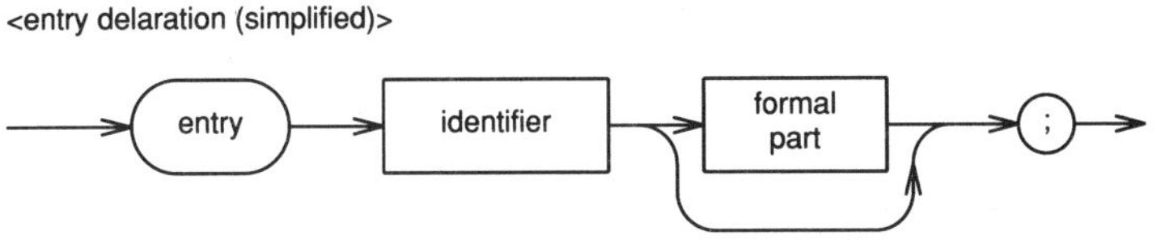

Figure 11–2

Entries must be declared. The declaration of an entry in a task is similar to the declaration of a procedure in a package: It indicates the existence of something that may be called. The syntax for declaring an entry is found in Figure 11–2. The entry call itself is similar to a procedure call. In its simplest form, the caller waits until the call is done. Only after the call is completed does the caller continue execution.

A good way to view an entry call is that the caller requests a service from the task being called. Because the task being called may be doing something else, the caller may have to wait for the task to get around to fulfilling the request. The reverse is also true: The task may be ready to provide a service, but have to wait for someone to call for that service. Thus, an entry provides a way for a caller and a task to synchronize: The caller requests the service and the task provides it; then execution of both continues. Synchronization occurs because the one that arrives first waits for the arrival of the other.

The difference between entries and procedures is that, except when an entry call is made to explicitly force synchronization, tasks run concurrently. When tasks are not involved, procedures never run concurrently.

Entry declarations indicate which types of services are provided by the task. Therefore, entry declarations must be made in the task declaration as shown in Figure 11–1. An entry declaration is a declaration that the task will provide a service or synchronization point.

Within the task body some indication must be provided of when the task is ready to provide the service or synchronization. In Ada, this is done with the *accept statement.* For each entry declaration, there must be at least one accept statement. The accept statement names the entry with which it is associated. We shall discuss accept statements in more detail in section 6, but now we will illustrate their usefulness with an example.

```
 1:with TEXT_IO;
 2:procedure Divisors_2 is      -- Second version
 3:  Number: INTEGER;
 4:  By_Three, By_Four: BOOLEAN;
 5:  task Divisible_by_Three is
 6:    entry Compute;
 7:    entry Done;
 8:  end Divisible_by_Three;
 9:  task Divisible_by_Four is
10:    entry Compute;
11:    entry Done;
12:  end Divisible_by_Four;
13:  task body Divisible_by_Three is
14:  begin
15:    accept Compute;
16:    By_Three := Number rem 3 = 0;
17:    accept Done;
18:  end Divisible_by_Three;
19:  task body Divisible_by_Four is
20:  begin
21:    accept Compute;
22:    By_Four := Number rem 4 = 0;
23:    accept Done;
24:  end Divisible_by_Four;
25:  package Int_IO is new TEXT_IO.INTEGER_IO(INTEGER);
26:begin
27:  Int_IO.GET(Number);
28:  Divisible_by_Three.Compute;
29:  Divisible_by_Four.Compute;
30:  Divisible_by_Three.Done;
31:  Divisible_by_Four.Done;
32:  TEXT_IO.PUT_LINE("By_Three " & BOOLEAN'IMAGE(By_Three));
33:  TEXT_IO.PUT_LINE("By_Four " & BOOLEAN'IMAGE(By_Four));
34:end Divisors_2;
```

Program 11–2

One problem with the procedure **Divisors** in Program 11–1 was that we had to restrain the tasks from computing before a value for **Number** was obtained. **Divisors_2** in Program 11–2 shows how to do this with entry calls and accept statements.

In lines 5–8 and 9–12, we see an expanded version of the task declarations. In line 6, the task **Divide_by_Three** is declared to have an entry named **Compute**. The body of the task must contain at least one accept statement for this entry. Such an accept statement is found in line 15. As a result, the task **Divisible_by_Three** will wait at line 15 until an entry call is made to **Compute**. When that call is made, the task will proceed to line 16 and compute if the number is divisible by three.

A call to this entry is made by **Divisors_2** in line 28. **Divisors_2** will wait at line 28 until the task **Divide_by_Three** arrives at the accept statement. Notice that whichever arrives first, **Divisors_2** at line 28 or **Divide_by_Three** at line 15, waits for the other to arrive.

When both the procedure and the task arrive, they may both proceed. **Divisors_2** proceeds to execute line 29 and **Divisible_by_Three** proceeds to execute line 16. In Ada terminology, a *rendezvous* occurs between **Divisors_2** and **Divisible_by_Three** and then both proceed. This rendezvous forces synchronization between **Divisors_2** and **Divisible_by_Three**.

The main program should not print the result (i.e., execute line 32) until the computation of **Divide_by_Three** is done. This is achieved by providing **Divide_by_Three** with an entry that indicates when it is done. This entry is declared in line 7. The corresponding accept statement is found in line 17. The task **Divisible_by_Three** does not reach line 17 until execution of the assignment statement at line 16 is completed. The call to the entry at line 30 ensures that **Divisible_by_Three** accepts "**Done**" (and hence has completed the assignment statement) before execution continues to lines 32 and the result is printed.

The organization of and calls to **Divide_by_Four** are identical to those of **Divide_by_Three**. The accept at line 21 and the entry call at line 29 ensure that the data is ready before the computation is begun. The accept at line 23 and entry call at line 31 ensure that the computation is completed before the answer is printed.

This style is followed in many concurrent programs. One entry is used to indicate a request for service from a task, and a second entry is used to indicate that the service has been completed. Between entry calls, processing proceeds concurrently.

A task is not a package and cannot be named in a use clause. Thus, as illustrated by lines 28–31, entry calls must use visibility by selection. Consequently, no problems arise in reusing entry names in other tasks because the task to which the entry call is to be made must always be explicitly specified.

Although it does not occur in the preceding examples, entry calls may be made by tasks to other tasks. This means that several entry calls may be waiting for the same entry. If several entry calls are waiting then they get accepted in the order in which the calls were made. We shall return to this point later.

Divisors_2a in Program 11–3 is a slight modification of **Divisors_2**. The differences are that: (1) The lines labeled "a" through "f" have been added between lines 4 and 5 to declare a function **Divisible** and (2) lines 16 and 22 have been modified to call this function. Since both tasks operate concurrently, both can call **Divisible** *at the same time*. Observe that this does *not* cause problems. When a task calls a subprogram, that subprogram is elaborated. Specifically, it is elaborated separately for each call. A similar situation occurs with recursion, where there might be multiple calls pending to the same procedure. Separate elaboration means that each call gets a separate

```
1:with TEXT_IO;
2:procedure Divisors_2a is
3:   Number: INTEGER;
4:   By_Three, By_Four: BOOLEAN;
a:   function Divisible(Number, Divisor) return BOOLEAN is
b:     Answer: BOOLEAN;
c:   begin
d:     Answer := Number rem DIVISOR = 0;
e:     return Answer;
f:   end Divisible;
     ...
13:  task body Divisible_by_Three is
14:  begin
15:    accept Compute;
16:    By_Three := Divisible(Number, 3);
17:    accept Done;
18:  end Divisible_by_Three;
19:  task body Divisible_by_Four is
20:  begin
21:    accept Compute;
22:    By_Four := Divisible(Number, 4);
23:    accept Done;
24:  end Divisible_by_Four;
...
```

Program 11–3

copy of the parameters and of the local variables. Because of this, the separate calls cannot interfere with each other.

This is not so, however, with accesses to global variables. For example, there is only one copy of **By_Four**. If both tasks tried to access this variable, the value that was finally stored there could depend on the order in which the tasks access it. In that case, if the program ran several times, it could produce different answers.

To see what might happen in such a situation, consider the procedure **Conflict** in Program 11–4. Tasks **A** and **B** update the same global variable **X** without any communication or synchronization. Several different results are possible, depending on the order of task execution. It is possible that **A** executes lines 7 and 8 printing a 2, and then **B** executes lines 12 and 13. In this case, executing line 13 prints a 4, because the execution of line 7 by **A** has changed the value in **X** to 2. On the other hand, if **B** executes lines 12 and 13 and then **A** executes lines 7 and 8, what is printed is a 3 followed by a 4. An even more complex execution can occur. Suppose **A** executes line 7 (**X** is now 2), then **B** executes line 12 (**X** is now 4), and then lines 8 and 13 are executed. In this case, two 4's are printed.

In all the previous examples, the final value of **X** was 4. But that is not necessarily always the case. Suppose that **A** begins execution of line 7. It retrieves the value 1 from

```
procedure Conflict is
   X: INTEGER := 1;
   task A;
   task B;
   task body A is
   begin
     X := X + 1;
     Write(X);
   end A;
   task body B is
   begin
     X := X + 2;
     Write(X);
   end B;
     . . .
```

Program 11–4

X and adds 1 to it to get the value 2. **A** is now holding, but has not yet stored, the value 2, consequently **X** is still holding a 1. Now **B** executes. **B** gets 1 (since this value is still in **X**) it adds 2, and it stores the resulting value (3) into **X**. Finally, **B** prints 3. Now **A** resumes its execution. It is holding the value 2, which it stores in **X**, then it prints a 2. Because the tasks have failed to communicate or synchronize, the program has started with the value 1, added a 1, added a 2; and computed the wrong answer.

Suppose instead of **X**, this was your bank account balance and the two tasks were two separate automatic tellers. Plainly, communicating correct values can be very important in tasks.

11.6 INTERPROCESS COMMUNICATION

In **Divisors**, all information communicated between the tasks and the procedure is through the global variables **Number**, **By_Three**, and **By_Four**. To allow the programmer to avoid this undesirable practice, the entry call (see Figure 11–2) is provided with a "formal part." This formal part is precisely the same as the formal part for a subprogram declaration: It defines the formal parameters associated with the entry call.

Accordingly, we might change our entry declarations to those shown in procedure **Divisors_3** in Program 11–5. The declarations in the formal part define the parameters the entry call will pass to the accept statement. These declarations occur in lines 6, 7, 10, and 11 of the procedure. As with other parameter declarations, the formal part must be repeated in the corresponding accept statement. This is done in the accept statements in lines 17, 21, 29, and 33.

The same rules apply as for subprogram parameters: The actual parameter associated with a formal parameter of mode **out** or mode **in out** must be a variable. In

```
with TEXT_IO;
procedure Divisors_3 is     -- Third version
  Global_Number: INTEGER;
  By_Three, By_Four: BOOLEAN;

  task Divisible_by_Three is
    entry Compute(Number: INTEGER);
    entry Done(Divisible: out BOOLEAN);
  end Divisible_by_Three;

  task Divisible_by_Four is
    entry Compute(Number: INTEGER);
    entry Done(Divisible: out BOOLEAN);
  end Divisible_by_Four;

  task body Divisible_by_Three is
    Local_Number: INTEGER;
    Local_Divisor: BOOLEAN;
  begin
    accept Compute(Number: INTEGER) do
      Local_Number := Number;
    end Compute;
    Local_Divisor := Local_Number rem 3 = 0;
    accept Done(Divisible: out BOOLEAN) do
      Divisible := Local_Divisor;
    end Done;
  end Divisible_by_Three;

  task body Divisible_by_Four is
    Local_Number: INTEGER;
    Local_Divisible: BOOLEAN;
  begin
    accept Compute(Number: INTEGER) do
      Local_Number := Number;
    end Compute;
    Local_Divisible := Local_Number rem 4 = 0;
    accept Done(Divisible: out BOOLEAN) do
      Divisible := Local_Divisible;
    end Done;
  end Divisible_by_Four;

  package Int_IO is new TEXT_IO.INTEGER_IO(INTEGER);
begin -- Divisors_3
  Int_IO.GET(Global_Number);
  Divisible_by_Three.Compute(Global_Number);
  Divisible_by_Four.Compute(Number => Global_Number);
  Divisible_by_Three.Done(By_Three);
  Divisible_by_Four.Done(By_Four);
```

Program 11–5

```
44:   TEXT_IO.PUT_LINE("By_Three " & BOOLEAN'IMAGE(By_Three));
45:   TEXT_IO.PUT_LINE("By_Four " & BOOLEAN'IMAGE(By_Four));
46:end Divisors_3;
```

Program 11–5 Continued

lines 40 and 41, any **INTEGER** expressions would be syntactically legal as the actual parameters, but in lines 42 and 43, the actual parameters must be **BOOLEAN** variables.

As with subprogram parameters, the extended scope of the formal parameters is the parameter list of the entry calls, allowing named association to be used in those calls. To illustrate this point, line 40 of the procedure uses positional notation and line 41 uses named association.

Parameter default values are also allowed. The rules and restrictions for mixing named and positional notation, and for omitting parameters with default values, are identical to those applying to subprogram parameters (see Chapter 6).

The immediate scope of a parameter of an entry call is the body of the accept statement. The syntax of the accept statement is given in Figure 11–3. The body of the accept statement is the statement list that occurs between the reserved words **do** and **end**. Notice there is no declarative part in the accept statement, just a body. Of course, a block statement can be placed in the body of the accept if local definitions are necessary.

<accept statement (simplified)>

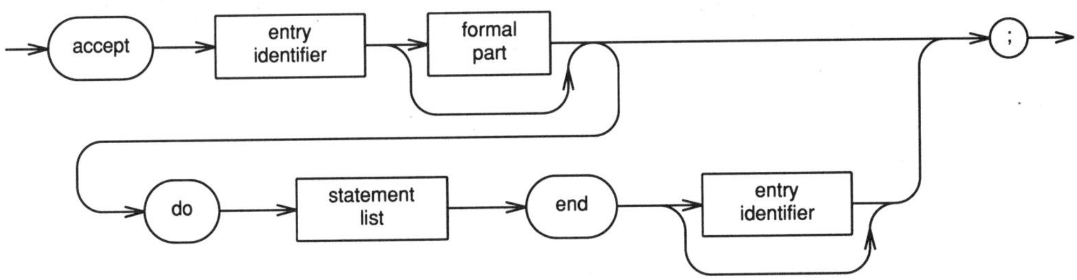

Figure 11–3

Because the immediate scope of a parameter to an accept statement is the statement list of the accept statement, this parameter cannot be used elsewhere in the task. This is why lines 22 and 30 in Program 11–5 save the value of the accept statement parameters.

Observe that the pair consisting of the entry declaration in the task declaration and its accept statement within the task body has visibility of parameters similar to that of the pair consisting of the procedure declaration in the package declaration and the procedure body within the package body. The procedure parameters are visible within the body of the procedure, and the entry call parameters are visible within the body of the accept statement.

The body of the accept statement has one other important effect: It is part of the rendezvous. During a rendezvous, the caller is executing the entry call and the task is executing the accept statement. This means that after the rendezvous begins, the caller waits at the entry call until the statement list in the body of the accept statement has finished executing. Consequently, we do not wish to perform the work of the task within the accept statement, because this would force the caller to wait until the task had completed its work. This influences the organization of **Divisors_3**.

The accept statement in lines 17–19 of **Divisors_3** does the minimum possible work so that it can release the calling procedure from the entry call. This work consists of saving the values of the entry call's parameters. The task then does its principal job of computing divisibility in line 20. Finally, the accept statement in lines 21–23 copies the answers into the appropriate entry call parameter.

One restriction we must note is that the accept statement must be immediately within the appropriate task body. Specifically, although local procedures can be declared within a task, it is syntactically illegal for an accept statement to occur within these local procedures. Accept statements *must* occur in the statement list of the task body, although they may be nested within a block statement.

11.6.1 Renaming Entries

The renaming capabilities introduced in Chapter 9 are available for entry calls. The restriction is that an entry must be renamed as a procedure. The parameter list of the procedure must match the parameter list of the entry it renames. As with other procedures, a renaming may add, remove, or change the default values of the parameters. These points are illustrated in the following example:

```
task Divisible_by_Three is
  entry Compute(Number: INTEGER := 0);
end Divisible_by_Three;
procedure Three_Check(I: INTEGER) renames Divisible_by_Three.Compute;
```

With these declarations, we are allowed to make the call

```
Three_Check(4);
```

in lieu of the call

```
Divisible_by_Three.Compute(4);
```

Note that renaming has removed a default value from the parameter. The entity **Three_Check** behaves like a procedure call. In particular, it cannot be used in place of the entry name in conditional or timed entry calls, defined in the next section. The principle advantage of such a renaming is that visibility by selection is not required for the procedure name.

11.7 CONDITIONAL AND TIMED ENTRY CALLS

The constructs we have presented so far all require entry calls to wait for the task to execute the appropriate accept statement before continuing. If the task never gets to the accept statement, the entry call waits forever. In some cases, you may not be willing to do this, so Ada provides several kinds of entry calls.

There are three mutually exclusive forms of the entry call statement: (1) the *unconditional entry call* which indicates the caller is willing to wait forever, (2) the *conditional entry call* which indicates the caller is not willing to wait at all, and (3) the *timed entry call* which indicates the caller is willing to wait a fixed amount of time.

The entry calls introduced in the previous sections are unconditional entry calls; here, we cover the other two kinds of entry calls. The syntax for these calls is found in Figure 11–4.

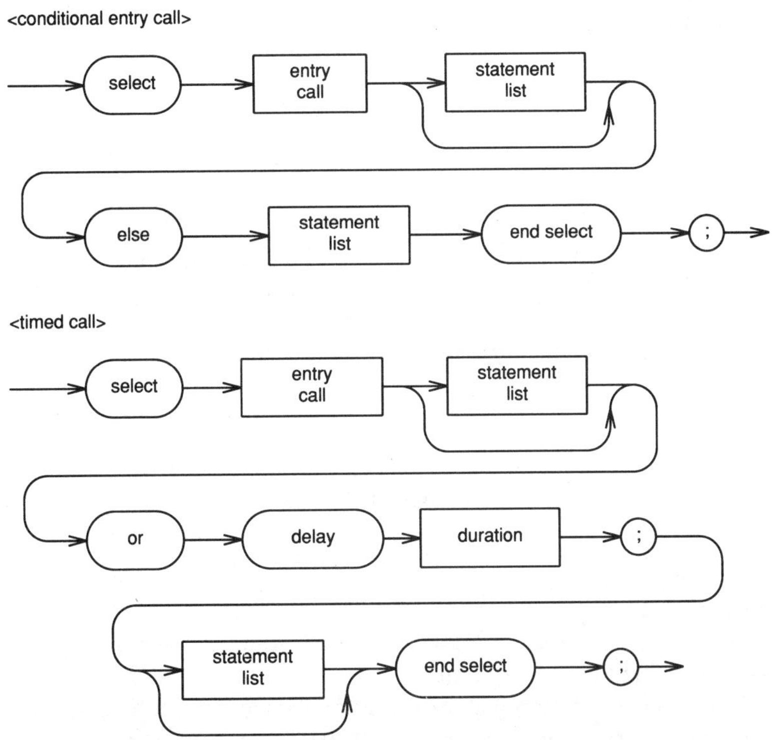

Figure 11–4

The conditional entry call insists that the task containing the entry be ready to immediately accept the entry call, or "else" the caller will take the other action. The conditional entry is a two-way branch whose condition depends on the availability of the task containing the accept statement. Exactly one of the two branches will be taken. If the first branch is taken, the first action will always be the rendezvous associated with the entry immediately following the reserved word **select**. After this rendezvous, the first statement list will be executed if it is present. If the second branch is taken, the statement list following the **else** will be executed. In this case, there is not necessarily an entry call or rendezvous; unless, of course, the statement list following the **else** happens to contain an entry call statement.

The timed entry call insists that the task be ready to accept the entry call within the time limit, "or" the caller will take the other action. The delay statement following the reserved word **or** is part of the timed entry call. Execution waits at the select statement until either an accept has occurred or the time limit specified in the delay statement has expired. If an accept occurs before the time limit expires, a rendezvous occurs during which the corresponding accept is executed. After the rendezvous, the statement list following the entry call (if any) is executed. If the time limit expires before an accept occurs, the entry call is withdrawn and the statement list following the **or** is executed.

To illustrate the details of these rules, let us consider several examples. In the conditional entry call

```
select
  First_Task.Entry1;
else
  null;
end select;
```

the entry call will rendezvous with the task at **Entry1** only if the task is immediately able to accept that entry call. If the rendezvous does not occur, the **null** statement will be executed. Of course, we could replace the **null** with any appropriate statement list, and we could add a statement list following the entry call. This is illustrated in the conditional entry call

```
select
  First_Task.Entry1;
  TEXT_IO.PUT("Task supplied service");
else
  TEXT_IO.PUT("Task not available");
end select;
```

Note that the statement list following the entry call statement is optional, but the statement list following the **else** is required.

In this conditional entry call, the statement lists both contain calls to **TEXT_IO**. There are no restrictions on what can be placed within these statement lists. In particular, nested conditional entry calls are allowed and are often useful.

In the conditional entry call

```
select
  First_Task.Entry1;
else
  Second_Task.Entry2;
end select;
```

the statement list following the **else** consists of a single entry call. The behavior of this conditional entry call is as follows. If **First_Task** is ready to accept **Entry1**, a rendezvous occurs at **Entry1**. Otherwise, the statement list in the else part is executed. This statement list contains the single *unconditional entry call*

```
Second_Task.Entry2;
```

so the caller waits at this unconditional entry call until the task **Second_Task** is ready to perform the accept. Specifically, the conditional entry applies only to the call immediately following the **select**. Whenever execution moves to the else part, any entry call is unconditional, unless there are nested selective entry calls within selective entry calls. An easy way to remember this is to visualize a null statement at the start of the second statement list, as in

```
select
  First_Task.Entry1;
else
  null;
  Second_Task.Entry2;
end select;
```

This indicates more clearly that the call to **Entry2** is not directly associated with the select; it simply is a statement in one of the statement lists. Similarly, entry calls in the statement list following the accept statement are not conditional, as is illustrated by the call to **Entry3** in the following entry call:

```
select
  First_Task.Entry1;
  Second_Task.Entry3;
else
  null;
end select;
```

In this example, the call to **Entry1** is conditional. If it is accepted, then an unconditional call to **Entry3** will be executed.

The following selective entry call illustrates the delayed entry call:

```
select
  First_Task.Entry1;
or
  delay 1.0;
  TEXT_IO.PUT("Your time is up");
end select;
```

If **First_Task** is ready to accept **Entry1** within 1.0 seconds of the caller executing the timed entry call, the rendezvous occurs at **Entry1**. After 1.0 seconds have elapsed without that rendezvous, execution skips to the or part of the selective entry call and the statement list following the delay is executed. In the timed entry call, the delay and duration are part of the **select**. A valid way to visualize the behavior of the delayed call is that execution "waits" at the **select** for either the time limit to expire or the entry call to be accepted. When one of these occurs, execution continues in the appropriate half of the timed entry call.

Again, only the entry call following the **select** is timed. In the timed entry call

```
select
  First_Task.Entry1;
or
  delay 1.0;
  Second_Task.Entry2;
end select;
```

the call to **Entry2** is unconditional. If the or part is executed, the caller will wait indefinitely for **Second_Task** to accept **Entry2**.

11.8 THE DELAY STATEMENT

One major confusion in tasks is not to take note of the distinction between the timed entry call and the delay statement. The two are separate. The delay statement is a request for the execution of a procedure or task to be suspended for the specified amount of time. It is not associated with an entry call. Unfortunately, as Figure 11–5 shows, the two have a similar syntax.

<delay statement>

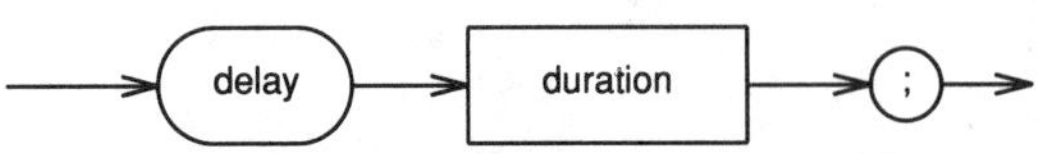

Figure 11–5

In executing a delay statement, Ada requires that execution be suspended for at least the amount of time specified. In a given Ada implementation, the suspension may be for more than the amount of time specified. One situation in which the actual delay may significantly exceed the requested delay is on a very busy multiple-user system. After the delay begins, the system may go off and begin execution of another user's program, not getting back to the system requesting the delay until considerably after the time limit has expired. In fact, there is no guarantee in Ada that

```
delay 2.0;
```

will take any longer than

```
delay 1.0;
```

If, for example, the system is so busy that it does not get back to the program for four seconds, both delays would be for four seconds. Occasionally, the shorter delay may even take more time than the longer delay. Remember, in Ada, the delay specifies a *minimum* amount of time for which execution is suspended.

The following example illustrates an error commonly made by Ada programmers:

```
select
  First_Task.Entry1;
else
  delay 1.0;
end select;
```

This is not a timed entry call, since it does not have the reserved word **or**. Rather, the **else** indicates it is a conditional entry call. If the rendezvous with **Entry1** is not immediately available, execution proceeds *irrevocably* to the else part. Since the else part consists of a delay statement, a delay of at least 1.0 seconds will occur.

Notice that it makes no difference if **Entry1** becomes available during the 1.0 seconds, because execution is no longer waiting at the **select**. Execution has already transferred to the else part and is at the delay statement. For a timed entry call, the reserved word is **or**. In a timed entry call, the reserved word **delay** must follow **or**.

Delays are useful in slowing the execution of a task to match some event in the real world. For example, delays are used in the **Robot** package so that the movement of the robot is slow enough to be seen step by step.

11.9 THE CALENDAR PACKAGE

In Ada, the **CALENDAR** package provides another means of using time. This package defines a private type called **TIME** and uses a real type called **DURATION**.

The type **DURATION** is predefined directly within the package **STANDARD**. In this respect, it has the same status as other predefined numeric types such as **INTEGER** and **FLOAT**. Until we discuss the details of real numbers in Chapter 14, we shall apply only simple arithmetic to values of the type **DURATION**. Real literals are capable of providing values for the type **DURATION**. In fact, the delay statement requires a value of type **DURATION**. We introduce the type here because its principal uses are in conjunction with entry calls, delay statements, and the **CALENDAR** package.

Thus far, the examples we have presented of timed entry and delay statements have used literals, but they could have used variables or constants. For example,

```
Short_Time: DURATION := 2.0;
```

declares a variable of type **DURATION** and sets its value to **2.0**. When used in a timed entry or delay statement, as in

```
delay Short_Time;
```

this is interpreted as a delay of 2.0 seconds.

In package **CALENDAR**, the function

```
function CLOCK return TIME;
```

returns the current time: month, day, year, and time of day. Since the type **TIME** is private, we must use other functions provided by the package to get at these values. There are four such functions and one procedure:

```
function YEAR(DATE: TIME) return YEAR_NUMBER;
```

reports the year as an integer between 1901 and 2099;

```
function MONTH(DATE: TIME) return MONTH_NUMBER;
```

reports the month as an integer between 1 and 12;

```
function DAY(DATE: TIME) return DAY_NUMBER;
```

reports the day of the month as an integer between 1 and 31; and

```
function SECONDS(DATE: TIME) return DAY_DURATION;
```

reports the time of day as a **DURATION** between 0.0 and 86400.0. The time of day is given as the number of seconds since midnight. The procedure

```
procedure SPLIT(DATE: in TIME; YEAR: out YEAR_NUMBER; MONTH: out MONTH_NUMBER;
                DAY: out DAY_NUMBER; SECONDS: out DAY_DURATION);
```

reports all four values in parameters of mode **out**.

An inverse function

```
function TIME_OF(YEAR: YEAR_NUMBER; MONTH: MONTH_NUMBER; DAY: DAY_NUMBER;
                 SECONDS: DAY_DURATION := 0.0) return TIME;
```

permits the formation of a value of type **TIME** from values of the components.

In addition, the package defines several arithmetic operators. The three functions

```
function "+"(LEFT: TIME; RIGHT: DURATION) return TIME;
function "+"(LEFT: DURATION; RIGHT: TIME) return TIME;
function "-"(LEFT: TIME; RIGHT: DURATION) return TIME;
```

take a time of day and an amount of time and compute a new time of day. For example, if **CALENDAR** is named in a use clause, you can compute what time it would be in 120.0 seconds with the expression

```
CLOCK + 120.0
```

One other function,

```
function "-"(LEFT: TIME; RIGHT: TIME) return DURATION;
```

computes the amount of time between two clock readings. Using this function, the following program will report the number of seconds it took to execute:

```
 1:with TEXT_IO, CALENDAR;
 2:procedure Time_It is
 3:  use CALENDAR;
 4:  Start_Time, Finish_Time: TIME;
 5:  package Duration_IO is new TEXT_IO.FIXED_IO(DURATION);
 6:begin
 7:  Start_Time := CLOCK;
 8:  null;
 9:  Finish_Time := CLOCK;
10:  Duration_IO.PUT(Finish_Time - Start_Time);
11:end Time_It;
```

The subtraction operator in line 10 operates on the starting and finishing times to compute the duration of the program. The output call on that line works because of the generic instantiation (line 5), but we shall not describe the details of this until Chapter 14. For now, we note that this notion is similar to output for enumerated types as described in Chapter 7.

11.10 THE ROBOTS PACKAGE

A more advanced version of robots is designed to be used with concurrent programming. This version allows the user to control multiple robots. In fact, the **Robot** package itself performs its operations by calling subprograms in the multiple robot package, while restricting the number of robots to one. Because of this, most of the functions in the advanced package are similar to functions you are already familiar with.

The advanced package is called **Robots**, and it has an important new type called **Robot**. If a program used two robots, we could begin the program as follows:

```
with Robots;
procedure Twins is
  A, B: Robots.Robot;
```

The type **Robot** is a limited private type, so robots cannot be duplicated using assignment statements. The type is implemented as a record with default initialization. In the package, this initialization uses a function call in the following manner:

```
private
  function Init_Robot return CHARACTER;
  type Robot is
    record
      Name: CHARACTER := Init_Robot;
    end record;
end Robots;
```

Since **Robot** is a limited private type, explicit initialization is impossible outside the package. Thus, at the time a variable of type **Robot** is elaborated, it is initialized by a call to the function. The function allocates a different name to each robot, giving the first robot declared the name **'A'**, the second robot declared the name **'B'** and so on. There is a limit of 26 robots, and each is assigned a distinct capital letter.

All the familiar functions and procedures of the original **Robot** package are available, with the difference that now a robot must be specified. For example, to move a robot in procedure **Twins** 10 spaces you must specify either:

```
Robots.Move(A, 10);
```

or

```
Robots.Move(B, 10);
```

In either case, the robot associated with the variable is moved.

Most of the declarations in **Robots** are the same as in **Robot**. In fact, **Robot** mostly renames declarations from **Robots**. The following declarations are changed only in that they take the name of a robot:

```
procedure Move(TheRobot: in Robot; Distance: in INTEGER);
procedure Turn(TheRobot: in Robot; Amount: in Turns);
procedure Paint_On(TheRobot: in Robot);
procedure Paint_Off(TheRobot: in Robot);
procedure Set_Paint(TheRobot: in Robot; New_Paint: in Paint_Char);
function Look(TheRobot: in Robot; Where: in Look_Dir) return CHARACTER;
procedure Pick_Up(TheRobot: in Robot);
procedure Put_Down(TheRobot: in Robot);
```

The following new declarations allow the robots to interact:

```
procedure Give_Item(TheRobot :in Robot);
Too_Many_Robots, No_Receiving_Robot: exception;
```

A robot is allowed to hand an item directly to another robot, under either of two conditions: (1) the robots are immediately adjacent and the robot giving the item is facing the robot receiving the item, or (2) the robots are immediately adjacent to opposite sides of a window and the robot giving the item is facing the window. The window, designated by the character `'='`, is a new feature introduced into the robot world. Like the wall, it prohibits movement. Unlike the wall, items may be handed between robots on opposite sides of the window. An exception, **`No_Receiving_Robot`**, is raised if there is no receiving robot available to receive the item being handed off.

Although fundamentally the same as in the package **`Robot`**, the exception **`Initialize_World_Error`** can also occur in **`Robots`** if the number of variables of type **`Robot`** does not match the number of robots in the file that initializes the world. The world does default to empty and any robots declared do have default positions but, in practice, we will always specify a file that initializes the world.

Procedure **`Stop_Sign`** in Program 11–6 uses multiple robots to illustrate some of the items discussed in this chapter. The goal of this procedure is to simulate a simplified flow of traffic at an intersection with a stop sign. Two robots are each controlled by a separate task. One operates on the north-south "street," the other on the east-west. To prevent collisions, a third task, called **`Controller`**, allows one robot at a time through the intersection. Each of the robot-controlling tasks makes an entry call to **`Controller.Enter`** whenever its robot wishes to cross the intersection. The task then waits for permission to be granted before moving through the intersection. Since the controller permits only one robot at a time to enter the intersection, collisions will be avoided. When a robot has passed through the intersection, it makes an entry call to **`Clear`** to indicate to the controller that the intersection is empty again.

The program makes use of the first-come, first-serve property of the entry call **`Enter`**. Ada stipulates that the calls to an entry will be serviced in the order they arrive. Robots wishing to cross the intersection line up by making a call to **`Enter`**, and these entry calls are accepted in the order they were made. As a consequence, the robot that has been waiting the longest is the next one permitted through the intersection.

Note the use of the entry call **`Start`** to guarantee that the robot world has been initialized before the robots start moving. Note also that, to keep the example simple, we did not include a way for the program to terminate.

11.11 PROGRAMMING PRACTICES

One of the problems of concurrent programming is that concurrency allows things to happen in several different orders. A difficult task for the programmer is determining when order matters and when it does not. Generally, order matters when tasks share a resource such as a global variable or the locations in the robots' world.

It behooves us here to be reminded about the difference between the program and reality. In a correctly written program such as **`Stop_Sign`**, the state of reality (which in this case is the position of the robots in the robot world) matches the state of the program. However, programs are not required to match reality. For example, suppose

```
with Robots;
procedure Stop_Sign is
  task Controller is
    entry Enter;
    entry Clear;
  end Controller;
  task N_S_Robot is
    entry Start;
  end N_S_Robot;
  task E_W_Robot is
    entry Start;
  end E_W_Robot;
  task body Controller is
  begin
    loop
      accept Enter; -- Permit one "vehicle" to cross
      accept Clear; -- Vehicle is out of intersection
    end loop;
  end Controller;
  task body N_S_Robot is
    NS_Robot:Robots.Robot;
  begin
    accept Start;
    Robots.Turn(NS_Robot, Robots.Left);         -- Initial orientation
    loop
      Controller.Enter;           -- Permission to enter intersection
      Robots.Move(NS_Robot, 2);        -- Move through intersection
      Controller.Clear;           -- We have cleared the intersection
      Robots.Turn(NS_Robot, Robots.Left); -- Turn around, and do it
                                          -- again
      Robots.Turn(NS_Robot, Robots.Left);
    end loop;
  end N_S_Robot;
  task body E_W_Robot is
    EW_Robot: Robots.Robot;
  begin
    accept Start;
    loop
      Controller.Enter;           -- Permission to enter intersection
      Robots.Move(EW_Robot, 2);        -- Move through intersection
      Controller.Clear;           -- We have cleared the intersection
      Robots.Turn(EW_Robot, Robots.Left); -- Turn around, and do it again
      Robots.Turn(EW_Robot, Robots.Left);
    end loop;
  end E_W_Robot;
begin
```

Program 11–6

```
    Robots.Initialize_World("traffic_world");
    N_S_Robot.Start;
    E_W_Robot.Start;
  end Stop_Sign;
```

Program 11–6 Continued

we omitted the call to the entry **Clear** from the body of **E_W_Robot**. Then when this robot moved out of the intersection, the intersection would become clear, but since no one would have told the controller, the controller would not give permission for another robot to enter the intersection. As with sequential programs, ensuring that the program addresses the problem being solved is the responsibility of the programmer.

11.11.1 Problem Solving

An example of the use of timed entry calls is the procedure **Get_Delivery_Item** shown in Program 11–7. This procedure is a fragment of a program that includes definitions of other procedures and tasks. We assume that **A_Server** and **B_Server** are tasks with entries **Get_A** and **Get_B**, respectively. The purpose of the procedure is to have the robot pick up an item from one of two windows and deliver it to a predefined place. The robot is to get an item as soon as possible, but we do not know which window will have an item available first. The procedure causes the robot to move repeatedly between the windows until an item becomes available.

The robot begins by waiting at the first window for one second. If an item arrives, the robot delivers the item and leaves the procedure. If no item arrives, the robot moves to the second window. At the second window, the robot again waits for one second. If, as before, an item arrives, the robot delivers the item and leaves the procedure. If no item arrives, the robot moves back to the first window.

Waiting at the first window is accomplished by the timed entry call found in lines 5–18. If an item arrives during the second the robot waits, execution of lines 6–8 occurs. If no item arrives, execution shifts to line 10. This line cause the robot to move to the second window. The wait at the second window is accomplished by the timed entry call found in lines 11–17. Notice that this timed entry call is nested inside the timed entry call for the first window. If an item arrives during the second the robot waits, execution of lines 12–14 occurs. If no item arrives, execution shifts to line 16, completing the execution of the nested entry calls. Because these entry calls are contained in the loop of lines 3–19, execution loops back to line 4, causing the robot to return to the first window and to execute the timed entry in lines 5–18. The robot will leave this procedure only when it has delivered an item.

11.11.2 Testing

In concurrent programs, it is difficult to test all paths because the paths depend on the order in which the tasks execute, and you have little control over this order of execution.

```
procedure Get_Delivery_Item(Delivery_Robot: Robot) is
begin
  loop
    Move_To_First_Window(Delivery_Robot);
    select
      A_Server.Get_A;
      Move_To_Delivery_Place(Delivery_Robot);
      return;
    or delay 1.0;
      Move_To_Second_Window(Delivery_Robot);
      select
        B_Server.Get_B;
        Move_To_Delivery_Place(Delivery_Robot);
        return;
      or delay 1.0;
        null;
      end select;
    end select;
  end loop;
end Get_Delivery_Item;
```

Program 11–7

Nevertheless, you should design tests that exercise the synchronization between the tasks as much as possible. These tests should be run several times, with different delays if possible. For example, in **Stop_Sign**, we could test the program with differing delays placed inside the loops in the task bodies.

11.12 ADA SUMMARY

In this chapter, we have introduced several Ada constructs which permit concurrent programming. The fundamental component of concurrent programming is the *task*. Tasks run concurrently, although within each task execution is sequential. In order to permit tasks to cooperate, Ada provides *entry calls* and *accept statements*. An *entry* is a point of synchronization between two tasks. One of the tasks makes the entry call, while the other accepts the entry. The task which declares an entry is the only one that can accept that entry.

Entry calls have several options which determine how long the caller is willing to wait for the called task to accept. In the *unconditional entry call* the caller is willing to wait forever, in the *timed entry call* the caller is willing to wait a specified amount of time, and in the *conditional entry call* the caller is not willing to wait at all.

Concurrency is often used for programs that involve events in the real world. To assist in interfacing with the world, Ada provides some timing capabilities. One of these, the *delay statement*, allows a program to adjust its speed. Another, the **CALENDAR** package, allows a program to compute the time or how much time has passed between two given times.

EXERCISES

11.1. Implement a **Timer** package that could be invoked by a program to inform the user how long execution some portion of that program took. The specification of **Timer** is as follows:

```
package Timer is
  procedure Start_Timer;
  procedure Stop_Timer;
  procedure Report_Timer;
  Timer_Not_Stopped, Timer_Not_Started: exception;
end Timer;
```

A sequence of calls to **Start_Timer**, then **Stop_Timer** and then **Report_Timer** will cause the time between the calls to **Start_Timer** and **Stop_Timer** to be written to the screen in hours, minutes, and seconds. When asked to start the timer or report the time, you will need to check that the timer has already been stopped. When asked to stop the timer, check that it was started. Use an old program of yours to try this package out by placing the call to **Start_Timer** at the beginning of the main program and the calls to **Stop_Timer** and **Report_Timer** at the end of the main program. **Timer** should make use of the **CALENDAR** package.

11.2. In this exercise, you are going to simulate a post office. You will have three customer robots which wait in line for a post office window to become available. Each customer robot waits its turn in line, moving forward as robots ahead of it move toward the window. When the customer robot is at the window of it will let the clerk know who it is. If there is any mail for the customer, the clerk will give the customer the mail. If the customer gets mail, it goes home, drops the mail off, and returns to the end of the line for more mail. If there is no mail, the customer goes home and goes to sleep, that is, the controlling task should complete execution of its statement list.

The clerk waits at the window until a customer requests mail. If the clerk finds mail, it gives it to the customer. The clerk always informs the customer if there is or isn't mail. All the mail is stored in stacks within the post office. The stack of **a** items is mail for **A** and so on.

Of course, there may be collisions between robots, and you must be prepared to handle them.

The clerk will have to maintain a list of which customers have no more mail. The clerk can go home when all the mail has been delivered. As with the customer robot, this means the task for the clerk robot should complete execution.

Hints: Be careful about getting things set up before starting the post office. Plan the traffic flow of the customer robots so they don't have head on collisions.

The following diagram illustrates the initial configuration of the post office world:

```
* * * * * * * * * * * * * * * * * * * * * *
...
*                     *                    *
*                     *    a               *
*        C>B>A>       = D> b               *
*                     *    c               *
*                     *                    *
...
* * * * * * * * * * * * * * * * * * * * * *
```

11.3. In this exercise, you are to have three robots participating in a relay race. The first robot starts out with a pile of objects, which is a stack of any number of "**a**"s. It starts taking each object, one at a time, to the window for the second robot. The second robot, meanwhile, has been waiting for the first one to appear at the window. When the first robot appears at the window, it gives the object it is carrying to the second robot. The second robot then ferries the object over to the window where the third robot is waiting. The third robot then places the object received from the second robot by the far wall. When the first robot finds that there are no more objects left in the stack, it informs the second robot, which in turn informs the third robot.

The initial robot world is shown in the following diagram; the first robot, **A**, is sitting on top of the objects it has to give to the second robot (**B**).

```
* * * * * * * * * * * * * * * * * * * * * *
...
*          *          *                    *
*          *          *                    *
*A>        =B>        =C>                  *
*          *          *                    *
*          *          *                    *
...
* * * * * * * * * * * * * * * * * * * * * *
```

11.4. Build a multiple-task program that satisfies the following specification:

1. All printing will be done through the special printing task, **Print_A_Line**. This task will receive a string (via an entry call) and print that string to the screen.
2. There will be a task **Slow_Primes** that will compute all the primes between 1 and 100. Every time it finds a prime, it will call (entry call) **Print_A_Line** to print that prime before proceeding to compute the next prime. It will **delay** (at least) 1.0 seconds between each prime it prints.
3. There will be a task **Fast_Primes** that will compute all the primes between 1 and 100. Every time it finds a prime, it will call **Print_A_Line** to print that prime before proceeding to compute the next prime. It will **delay** (at least) 0.5 seconds between each prime it prints.
4. There will be a main procedure that is not required to do anything except declare the preceding tasks. The main procedure should have the following format:

```
with Lines, Simple_IO;
procedure Prime_Printer is
  use Lines;

  task Print_A_Line is
    entry Print_A_String(Message: Normal_Line);
  end Print_A_Line;

  task Slow_Primes is
    -- you fill in
  end Slow_Primes;

  task Fast_Primes is
    -- you fill in
  end Fast_Primes;

begin
  -- you fill in
end Prime_Printer;
```

12

Parameterizable Data Structures

12.1 OBJECTIVES

In Ada, it is possible to parameterize data structures. Although the arrays we have seen up to now have had fixed bounds, we emphasized the use of attributes to build programs in such a manner that they did not depend on the exact bounds of the array. In fact, it is not necessary for the bounds on an array type to be fixed. This is an instance of an unconstrained type. Both record and array types can be unconstrained. In this chapter, we consider *unconstrained array types* and their usage (section 3). An example of an unconstrained array type is the type **STRING**, defined in the package **STANDARD**. We have previously covered string literals, we now cover string types and variables (section 4). In many applications of unconstrained array types, it is natural to concatenate two array values to form a third. Accordingly, we introduce the Ada *catenation* operator, with particular attention to how it is applied to strings (section 5). Then, to complete the discussion of unconstrained types, we cover the constraining of records, using what Ada calls *discriminants* (sections 6 and 7). We extend our coverage of the topic of overloading by covering the overloading of subprograms (section 8). Finally, we introduce the remainder of the **Lines** package and how it is implemented using the constructs presented in this chapter (section 9).

CONCEPTS:

- Data structures are more flexible when they are parameterized.
- There are constrained and unconstrained types of data.
- Properties of objects are not always identical to those of types.
- The same identifier may be used for several related subprograms.

GOALS:

- Build a procedure that handles unconstrained array parameters.
- Build a program that uses discriminated records.

12.2 MOTIVATION

The usefulness of procedures is greatly improved by parameters. Similarly, data declarations are more useful when they are parameterized. Like procedures, not every data declaration needs a parameter, but often it is highly desirable. Parameterized data structures combined with the use of attributes allows us to build procedures of greater flexibility. Hence, we can concentrate on correctly building a few excellently designed procedures which solve a cluster of related problems, rather than building a cluster of related procedures, each of which solves a specific instance of a more general problem.

The rule for choosing a data structure is that the structure chosen should reflect the natural organization of the data in the problem. A good program cannot be built around a bad choice for a data structure. Consequently, structuring data deserves time and thought.

12.3 UNCONSTRAINED ARRAYS

Related arrays are not always of the same size. For example, on a calendar, a month consists of an array of days, indexed between 1 and the last day of the month. Some months have 30 days, some have 31, and one has 28 or 29. However, all months are related, so it would be redundant to declare a separate array type for each month. For this and many other purposes the most reasonable solution is to use arrays that are of the same type, but of different sizes. For this purpose, Ada supplies *unconstrained array types*. These types allow the declaration of compatible arrays of various sizes.

The syntax for declaring an unconstrained array type is given in Figure 12–1. It is similar to the syntax for declaring constrained array types in that the type of the component is fixed and the type of the range is fixed. However, the bounds of the range are not given. Instead, the range is given by what is called a box, that is, "**<>**". Sample declarations of two unconstrained array types are included in the following:

```
type Days is (Mon, Tue, Wed, Thur, Fri, Sat, Sun);
type Vector is array (INTEGER range <>) of FLOAT;
type Project is array (Days range <>) of INTEGER;
```

The types **Vector** and **Project** are both unconstrained array types. The index of **Vector** is of type **INTEGER**, and the index of type **Project** is of type **Days**. Neither of these declarations specify the bounds on the indices.

<unconstrained array type>

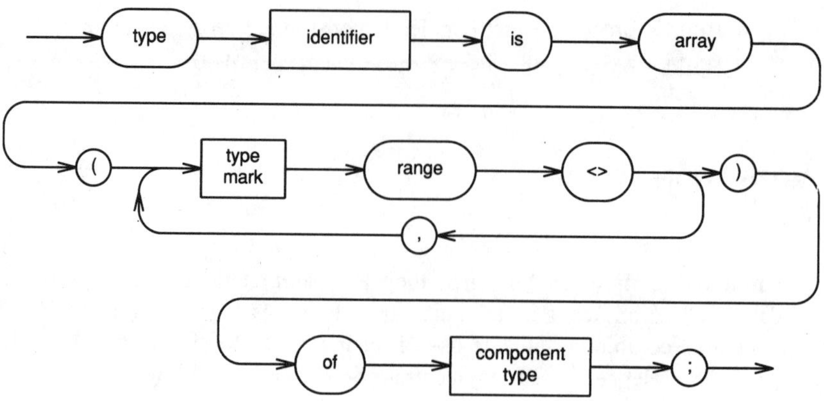

Figure 12–1

<subtype>

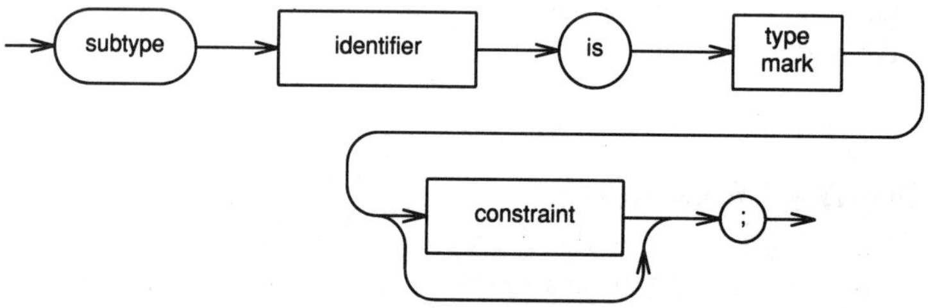

Figure 12–2

Previously, we formed a subtype by applying a range constraint to a previously declared type. This principle applies to more than range constraints: We can apply constraints to unconstrained array types to form *constrained array subtypes*. The syntax of a subtype is given in Figure 12–2. For example, using this syntax, we can declare the following constrained array subtypes from the previously declared unconstrained array types:

```
subtype Five_Vector is Vector(1..5);
subtype Short_Project is Project(Mon..Tue);
```

Here, a range constraint of **(1..5)** is applied to the type **Vector** to form the subtype **Five_Vector**. This means that arrays of this subtype will contain 5 variables of type **FLOAT**. Similarly, arrays of the subtype **Short_Project** will contain 2 variables of type **INTEGER**. Array objects may be defined from either constrained or unconstrained types. When defining an array object from an unconstrained array type, constraints must be explicitly supplied. This is illustrated in the following declarations:

```
V: Vector(1..5);
W: Five_Vector;
X: Vector(-3..6);
Y: Short_Project;
Z: Vector(1..6);
```

In these declarations, **V**, **X**, and **Z** are array variables defined from the unconstrained array type **Vector**, while **W** and **Y** are array variables defined from constrained subtypes formed from unconstrained types. With these declarations, **X** contains 10 variables of type **FLOAT**, both **V** and **W** contain 5 variables of type **FLOAT**, **Y** contains 2 variables of type **INTEGER**, and **Z** contain 6 variables of type **FLOAT**. As with other range constraints, the bounds of an array subtype or object may be given by an expression of the index type. In the declaration

```
What_Bounds: Vector(Y(Mon)..Y(Tue));
```

the array bounds are given by integer expressions that depend on the values stored in a previously declared array. The array bounds are computed when the subtype or object is elaborated.

Notice that all the preceding array objects are constrained. Array types may be unconstrained, but array objects, both array variables and array constants, are *always* constrained.

As expected, type checking applies to constrained and unconstrained types. The situation is similar to the one we are familiar with concerning range constraints. As discussed in Chapter 7, Ada uses the term *base type* to describe the compatibility of subtypes. Objects with range constraints and subtypes with range constraints are compatible if they have the same base type. A subtype has the same base type as the type from which it is formed. In general, two types are compatible if they have the same base type. Note that an unconstrained type can be a base type. For example, the type **Project** declared earlier is a base type. In fact, **Project** is its own base type and it is the base type of **Short_Project**, because **Short_Project** is a subtype of **Project**. Of course, according to the rules presented in Chapter 7, **Project** would also be the base type of any subtype formed from **Short_Project**, although in this case it is only possible to form trivial subtypes such as

```
subtype New_Short_Project is Short_Project.
```

because there are no additional constraints which we can apply. Nevertheless, the base type of **New_Short_Project** is **Project**, so **New_Short_Project** is compatible with both **Short_Project** and **Project**.

Subtypes are compatible if they have the same base type, even if that base type is an unconstrained type. In the previous declarations, the array variables **V**, **W**, **X**, and **Z** all have the base type **Vector**, and so all are compatible. For example, this means that the following assignments are syntactically legal:

```
V := W;
Z := X;
```

As with other subtypes, the constraint determines the nature of the array. Hence, you cannot always store the values from one array into another by simple assignment. To illustrate, the assignment

```
V := W;    -- No problems
```

is syntactically legal and executes without error. But even though the assignment

```
Z := X;    -- CONSTRAINT_ERROR
```

is syntactically legal, it will cause a **CONSTRAINT_ERROR** because **Z** is constrained to have 6 components while **X** is constrained to have 10 components.

In an assignment, if two compatible arrays have the same number of components, but different bounds no exception occurs. Thus,

```
Z := X(-3..2);    -- No problems
```

will not cause an exception.

To summarize, unconstrained types provide type compatibility and, at the same time, retain the safety features that ensure that there will be a correspondence between the compatible subtypes. Further, using slice assignment, we can handle those situations in which the number of components differs.

12.3.1 Aggregates and Unconstrained Array Types

Aggregates may be used with arrays formed from unconstrained types. Since, with respect to arrays, aggregates supply values only to array objects and array objects are always constrained, no new rules are necessary. Of course, the number of values and type of the values in the aggregate must match the object. For example, we could supply a value to the array **X** in the earlier sample declaration by the assignment

```
X := (1.1, 1.2, 1.3, 1.4, 1.5, 1.6, 1.7, 1.8, 1.9, 1.10);
```

The array **X** contains 10 components of type **FLOAT**. As is required, the aggregate is compatible because it has 10 components each of which is compatible with the type **FLOAT**.

We can also use aggregates to supply initial values to array variables, as in

```
New_Short: Project(Mon..Wed) := (1,6,5)
```

or to declare constant array objects, as in

```
A: constant Short_Project := (0, 1);
B: constant Project(Mon..Tue) := (0, 0);
```

When we declare a constant from a constrained subtype (e.g., the constant **A**), the aggregate must match the subtype. When we declare a constant directly from a unconstrained type (e.g., the constant **B**), we must also supply the explicit constraints.

The **others** option is allowed with these aggregates. For example, we could supply a value to **X** by the assignment

```
X := (1.0, 2.0, others => 0.0);
```

As with other aggregates and expressions in general, qualification is possible. In the case of an aggregate, qualification is sometimes necessary to determine the number of components. If the aggregate does not contain the **others** option, the number of components is explicit in the aggregate; if an aggregate contains the **others** option, it should be qualified by a constrained subtype. For example,

```
Vector'(1.0, 2.0, 4.0)
```

is qualified by an unconstrained array type, but the aggregate makes it explicit that there are three components, while

```
Five_Vector'(1 => 1.0, others => 0.0)
```

is known to have 5 components because **Five_Vector** is constrained and has 5 components. On the other hand, with the qualified expression

```
Vector'(1.0, others => 0.0) --illegal
```

there is no method of determining the number of components. Consequently, this expression is not legal. In essence, this is an attempt to create an unconstrained object (in this case an aggregate).

As a final remark on compatibility, note that the assignment

```
V: Vector(1..5);
  ...
V := Five_Vector'(1 => 1.0, others => 0.0);
```

is legal and does not raise a **CONSTRAINT_ERROR**. The assignment is legal because **V** is of a subtype compatible **Five_Vector**. A constraint error is avoided because the number of components in the subtype **Five_Vector** is the same as the number of components in **V**. In fact, a constraint error would not occur even if the range of **V** was **2..6**, as long as **V** and **Five_Vector** had the same number of components. Array assignment requires that the number of components be the same, not that the bounds be identical.

12.3.2 Parameters of Unconstrained Array Types

Parameters represent a unique opportunity to exploit unconstrained types. If we declared

```
Q: Vector(1..6);
function Total(B: Five_Vector) return FLOAT;
```

and we called this function with any parameter that had a different constraint, such as

```
Simple_IO.Write(Total(Q));
```

the type of the actual and formal parameters would match, but a constraint error would be raised. The reason is because **Five_Vector** is a constrained type with a range of **1..5**. What we desire is the capability to write a subprogram that is able to handle any vector compatible with the type **Vector**. Recognizing this need, Ada allows formal parameters to be of an unconstrained type, as in the following two subprogram declarations:

```
function Total(A: Vector) return FLOAT;
procedure Check_Schedule(B: Project);
```

Since array objects must be constrained, the actual parameter will have to be constrained. Thus, for any given call to the procedure, the parameter will be constrained. However, the constraints may differ from call to call. Using a formal parameter of an unconstrained type announces that constraints on the actual parameter do not matter, so there will never be a constraint error due to mismatched index bounds in passing the parameter into the procedure.

```
function Total(A: Vector) return FLOAT is
  Sum:FLOAT := 0.0;
begin
  for I in A'RANGE loop
    Sum := Sum + A(I);
  end loop;
  return Sum;
end Total;
```

Program 12–1

When we use an unconstrained formal parameter, the attributes supply vital information about the constraints of the actual parameter. In the body of the function **Total** in Program 12–1 we have used the attribute **RANGE** for the bounds on the loop. The value of **RANGE** is the same as the value of **RANGE** for the actual parameter passed into **Total**. No matter what actual parameter is passed, the function correctly returns the sum of the components of the vector. For example, if we made the call

```
Total(Q);
```

where the range of **Q** was **1..6** then **A'RANGE** would be **1..6**.

To illustrate these points more fully, consider the construction of a function that adds two real vectors. In the function **Addition** in Program 12–2, the first element of the "left" vector **L** should be added to the first element of the "right" vector **R**, the second element of **L** should be added to the second element of **R**, and so forth. The result of the addition is a vector with the same number of components as the input vectors.

```
 1:function Addition(L, R: Vector) return Vector is
 2:  Answer: Vector(1..L'LENGTH);
 3:begin
 4:  if L'LENGTH /= R'LENGTH then
 5:    Simple_IO.Write("Length Mismatch Error");
 6:    raise CONSTRAINT_ERROR;
 7:  else
 8:    for I in Answer'RANGE loop
 9:      Answer(I) := L(I - Answer'FIRST + L'FIRST) +
10:                   R(I - Answer'FIRST + R'FIRST);
11:    end loop;
12:    return Answer;
13:  end if;
14:end Addition;
```

Program 12–2

In the declaration of **Addition**, not only are the formal parameters unconstrained types, but so is the return value. The actual value returned will be an array object and will be constrained, but there is no restriction on what its constraints will be. Specifically, **Addition** does not have to return a vector with the same number of components as the parameters have. Neither does the vector returned have to have "1" as its first index. These aspects of the return value are merely results of how the function was written; it could have been written differently.

As constructed, in order for the **Addition** to be execute correctly, the input vectors must be of the same length. This is not an Ada restriction, but a result of how we wish to define vector addition. To enforce this concept of vector addition, the check at line 4 ensures that the vectors have the same length. Since we do not know what constraints the vectors will have, line 4 uses attributes to determine this. If the vectors are not of the same length, an error message is printed and an exception is raised. If they are of the same length, the addition is performed.

As we build the answer to be returned, we need to store it. How big of a vector do we need? This depends on the length of the input vectors. Consequently, the solution is to make the constraint on the local variable dependent on the length of one of the parameters. This is done in the declaration of **Answer** in line 2.

It is also necessary to "align" the vectors. At lines 8–11, we know that all three vectors are of the same length, but we have no guarantee that their ranges are identical. Thus, the loop parameter **I** will go through the range of one of the vectors (**Answer**), and the program will carefully compute the appropriate matching elements in the other vectors (**L** and **R**). From a brief consideration of the expression

```
I - Answer'FIRST + L'FIRST
```

it should be obvious that when **I** starts at **Answer'FIRST**, the expression evaluates to **L'FIRST**. The fact that both **Answer** and **L** are accessing their first element means that they are appropriately aligned for the first addition. By a similar argument, both **Answer** and **R** are appropriately aligned for the first addition. Thus, since the vectors are appropriately aligned for the first addition, and all three indices step with **I**, all the additions will be appropriately aligned.

The vector returned will always be the same length as the input vectors, no matter what **L'FIRST** and **R'FIRST** are. Since **Answer** always has a range of **1..L'LENGTH**, the vector returned will have a **FIRST** of 1. A comment explicitly stating this should be added to the function.

Remember, array objects passed into or out of subprograms have bounds that must not be violated.

Using the declarations of **Vector** and **Addition**, plus the declarations

```
E, F, G: Vector(1..5);
Q: Vector(2..6);
H: Vector(1..11);
```

we can use the function in the following manner:

```
E := Addition(F, G);
E := Addition(F, H(3..7));
```

The vectors produced are stored in **E**, which has the same number of components as that returned by the function. In fact, we could modify four components of **H** if we used the slice assignment

```
H(8..11) := Addition(F, Q)(2..5);
```

Finally, we could use aggregates for parameters, as in

```
E(2..5) := Addition(Q(2..5), (2.2, 2.3, 2.4, 2.5));
```

We have emphasized that parameters that are passed and values that are returned have bounds. This required the use of attributes or slices. On the other hand, assignment removes bounds. For example, the assignment

```
Q := G;
```

is legal because both variables are of the same type. Although they do not have the same bounds (**Q** is **2..6** and **G** is **1..5**), there is no constraint error because they have the same number of components.

An alternative way of defining addition of two vectors would be to use an operator. The declaration of addition could be modified as follows:

```
1:function "+"(L, R: Vector) return Vector is
   --lines 2-13 don't change
14:end "+";
```

With this definition, we could add two vectors using infix notation, as in

```
E := F + G;
```

In either case, the function operates on vectors of various sizes.

```
procedure Insertion_Sort(List: in out Vector) is
  -- Sort the array using Insertion Sort
  Hold: FLOAT; Put_At: INTEGER;
begin
  for Look_At in INTEGER range List'FIRST + 1..List'LAST loop
    -- The next item to insert is at position Look_At
    Hold := List(Look_At);
    -- Find where it goes
    Put_At := List'FIRST;
    while List(Put_At) < Hold loop
      Put_At := Put_At + 1;
    end loop;
    -- Open space at Put_At
    List(Put_At + 1..Look_At) := List(Put_At..Look_At - 1);
    -- Put the new item into the list
    List(Put_At) := Hold;
  end loop;
end Insertion_Sort;
```

Program 12–3

We illustrate the power of unconstrained array types with the procedure **Insertion_Sort** in Program 12–3. **Insertion_Sort** was first presented in Chapter 5 and extended in Chapter 8 to use attributes. In this new version, **Insertion_Sort** receives the array it is to sort as a parameter of mode **in out**. Note that the parameter is declared to be of an unconstrained type. This type is compatible with any parameter whose base type is the unconstrained array type **Vector**. Thus, with the declarations

```
X: Vector(-3..6);
Z: Vector(1..5);
```

both of the calls

```
Insertion_Sort(Z);
Insertion_Sort(X);
```

are legal, even though **Z** and **X** are of different sizes.

The actual parameter to this procedure must be an array object. (In fact, because the formal parameter has mode **in out**, it must be an array variable.) Since array objects are always constrained, the actual parameter will always be constrained. When we execute **Insertion_Sort**, the attributes associated with the formal parameter **List** will be determined by the attributes of the object passed as the actual parameter. When we pass **Z** as the actual parameter, **List'FIRST** evaluates to 1, and when we pass **X** as the actual parameter, **List'FIRST** evaluates to −3.

Whenever **Insertion_Sort** is called, **List** will be constrained because the actual parameter will be constrained. But since the constraints can differ from call to call, the procedure can sort an array of any length. The only differences between this procedure and the one in Chapter 5 are that the list to be sorted is a parameter (line 1), the type of **Hold** is **FLOAT** (line 3), and the loop to open space has been replaced by a slice assignment (line 14). The additional power is obtained because the parameter **List** is now an unconstrained type.

Unconstrained formal parameters of mode **out** can also be handled by these methods. While it is illegal to obtain the value of an **out** parameter, it is perfectly legal to inquire about its **FIRST**, **LAST**, and **RANGE**. Because an array parameter of mode **out** must be associated with a variable, and a variable must have a constraint, these attributes have values. The attributes do not supply any information that reveals the value within the parameter; they simply convey the "shape" of that parameter.

12.3.3 Array Comparisons

In Chapter 8, we saw how one-dimensional arrays of a scalar type were compared. The introduction of unconstrained array types means that it is syntactically legal to compare two arrays of different sizes. Consider the following declarations:

```
type Days is (Mon, Tue, Wed, Thur, Fri, Sat, Sun);
type Project is array (Days range <>) of INTEGER;
A: Project(Mon..Wed)  := (3, 2, 1);
B: Project(Fri..Sun)  := (3, 2, 2);
C: Project(Tue..Fri)  := (3, 2, 1, 1);
```

Since the three arrays are one-dimensional arrays with scalar components, any two of them can be legally compared. For example, the Boolean expression

```
A < B  -- TRUE
```

evaluates to true. The first two components (**3** vs. **3**) are compared. Because they are equal, the second two components (**2** vs. **2**) are compared. Because these are also equal, the third two components (**1** vs. **2**) are compared. This last comparison establishes that **A** is less than **B**. The comparison

```
A < C   -- TRUE
```

also evaluates to true. As before, because the first, second, and third components of these arrays are equal, the comparison proceeds to the fourth component. **A** has no fourth component and **C** does. This establishes that **A** is less than **C**.

Finally, the comparison

```
C < B   -- TRUE
```

evaluates to true. Because the first and second components of the two arrays are equal, the comparison proceeds to the third component. Since the third component of **C** (**1**) is less than the third component of **B** (**2**), **C** is less than **B**. Notice that the fact that **C** is longer than **B** does not matter, since they differed at the third component.

12.3.4 Multiple Dimensions and Complex Components

Ada allows multidimensional unconstrained array types (see Figure 12–1). The declaration

```
type Schedule is (CHARACTER range <>, Days range <>) of INTEGER;
```

declares such a type. Note that the syntax forces all or none of the dimensions to be unconstrained. In declaring an array object of a multidimensional unconstrained array type, constraints must be supplied for all dimensions, as in

```
Map: Schedule('A'..'E', Mon..Wed);
```

Unconstrained array types can contain complex components. In the declarations

```
type Priority is array (INTEGER range 1..5) of INTEGER;
type Days is (Mon, Tue, Wed, Thur, Fri, Sat, Sun);
type To_Do is array (Days range <>) of Priority;
```

the components of unconstrained array type **To_Do** are a constrained array type. However, an array component is not allowed to be an unconstrained array type. So the declaration

```
type Vector is array (INTEGER range <>) of FLOAT;
type Vector_List is array (CHARACTER) of Vector; -- illegal
```

is not legal. However, this declaration can be made legal by constraining the component type, as in

```
type Legal_List is array (CHARACTER) of Vector(1..5);
```

12.4 THE TYPE STRING

The unconstrained array type **STRING** is predefined in Ada as

```
subtype POSITIVE is INTEGER range 1..INTEGER'LAST;
type STRING is array (POSITIVE range <>) OF CHARACTER;
```

Using this type, we can declare string variables as follows:

```
Short_String: STRING(1..3);
Long_String: STRING(55..370);
```

Here, **Short_String** contains 3 **CHARACTER**s and **Long_String** contains 316 **CHARACTER**s.

String literals are defined in Ada as a sequence of characters between quotation marks (see Chapter 1) and can be used in the same manner as an aggregate. For example, to provide 3 character values to the components of **Short_String**, we can write

```
Short_String := "Bye";
```

In conformity with the rules for aggregates, the number of characters must *exactly* match the size of the string object.

We could also express this same assignment as

```
Short_String := ('B', 'y', 'e');
```

Here, we can clearly see that **Short_String** is being assigned a value from an aggregate whose components are characters. In the case of the type **STRING**, aggregates are so common in programs that Ada supplies the string literal as a shorthand form of the aggregate.

```
procedure Set_String(Target: out STRING; Contents: in STRING) is
begin
  Target(Target'FIRST..Target'FIRST + Contents'LENGTH - 1) := Contents;
  Target(Target'FIRST + Contents'LENGTH..Target'LAST) := (others => ' ');
end Set_String;
```

Program 12–4

As with other unconstrained array types, the type **STRING** may be used as a formal parameter or as the return type of a function. The procedure **Set_String** in Program 12–4 illustrates the use of a parameter of type **STRING**. The purpose of this procedure is to initialize a string so that the front of the string has the specified contents and the remainder of the string contains blanks. The procedure uses the attributes of a parameter of mode **out**. It contains two statements, the first of which puts the contents at the front of the string and the second of which puts blanks in the remainder of the string.

In the previous section, we discussed the comparison of unconstrained one-dimensional array types with scalar components. The type **STRING** is an unconstrained one-dimensional array of characters and, consequently, these comparison rules apply. As previously discussed, the comparison is lexicographic. Because comparison of strings is so common, we review a few examples. The comparison,

```
"ABCDE" <= "ABXA"
```

evaluates to true because the strings are equal in the first two positions and in the third position **C** is less than **X**. The comparison,

```
"ABCDE" > "ABCD"
```

evaluates to true because the strings are equal in the first four positions and the right-hand string is of length 4. The comparison,

```
"ZZZZZ" < "aaaa"
```

evaluates to true because in the predefined type **CHARACTER**, the character **Z** is less than the character **a**.

Note that under Ada's rules, string comparisons yield the same order as found in the dictionary (except that upper versus lower case matters).

12.5 THE CATENATION OPERATOR

We have waited until now to introduce the catenation operator because much of the usefulness of catenation occurs when it is used with unconstrained array types, slice assignments, and aggregates. The catenation operator is represented by the ampersand. As an example of its use, we can concatenate three strings with the expression

```
"First" & " and " & "Third"
```

Like the other operators, both infix and prefix forms are allowed for catenation, and the prefix form uses quotation marks. We can rewrite the preceding expression in prefix form as

```
"&"("First" , "&"(" and " , "Third"))
```

Catenation is defined for one-dimensional array types. For example, the declarations

```
type Vector is array (INTEGER range <>) of FLOAT;
E: Vector(2..6);
F: Vector(2..3);
G: Vector(1..8);
R: FLOAT;
```

allow the assignment

```
E := F & G(5..7);
```

The first rule of catenation is that the type of the result of the operation is the same as the type of its operands. The second rule is that the starting index of the result is taken from the starting index of the left hand operand, providing it has a determinable starting index. The third rule is that the length of the result is the sum of the lengths of the operands. Thus, in the preceding assignment, the type of the result is **Vector** because that is the type of the operands, the starting index of the result is **2** because that is the starting index of **F**, and the length or the result is 5 because the length of **F** is 2 and the length of **G(5..7)** is 3.

Aggregates can also be operands of catenation. This was the case with the strings we catenated in the first two examples. The result of both of these two string catenations is

```
"First and Third"
```

the length which is the sum of the lengths of the three strings catenated. Remember, the number of components on both sides of an assignment must be the same. The above result has length 15, assigning it to a string variable that does not contain exactly 15 components will raise **CONSTRAINT_ERROR**. Of course, slice assignment could be used to place the 15 characters into a portion of a larger string.

In addition, a component can be catenated with an array, or two components can be catenated. For example, the catenations

```
F & R
'A' & "BCD"
3.0 & 2.4
```

are allowed. The first returns the type of **F**, the second returns type **STRING**, and the third returns any array type whose components are **FLOAT** in the same manner as the equivalent aggregate

```
(3.0, 2.4)
```

would match any array type whose components are **FLOAT**.

As with other operators, the ampersand can be overloaded by the programmer. Like other dyadic operators (i.e., operators having two operands), such overloadings must specify exactly two parameters.

12.6 DISCRIMINANTS

Like unconstrained arrays, discriminated records are a means of building a parameterized data structure. Discriminants enable the creation of selectable data types. One instance where we might want to use a discriminant is in a personnel record that needs to have different components for married and single persons.

The use of a discriminant is highly restricted. In the first place, a discriminant may only be used with record types, or with private types that refer to record types. Furthermore, a discriminant may only be used to (1) supply an initial value for a component, (2) supply an index constraint, (3) supply a discriminant to an unconstrained component, or (4) select a variant part.

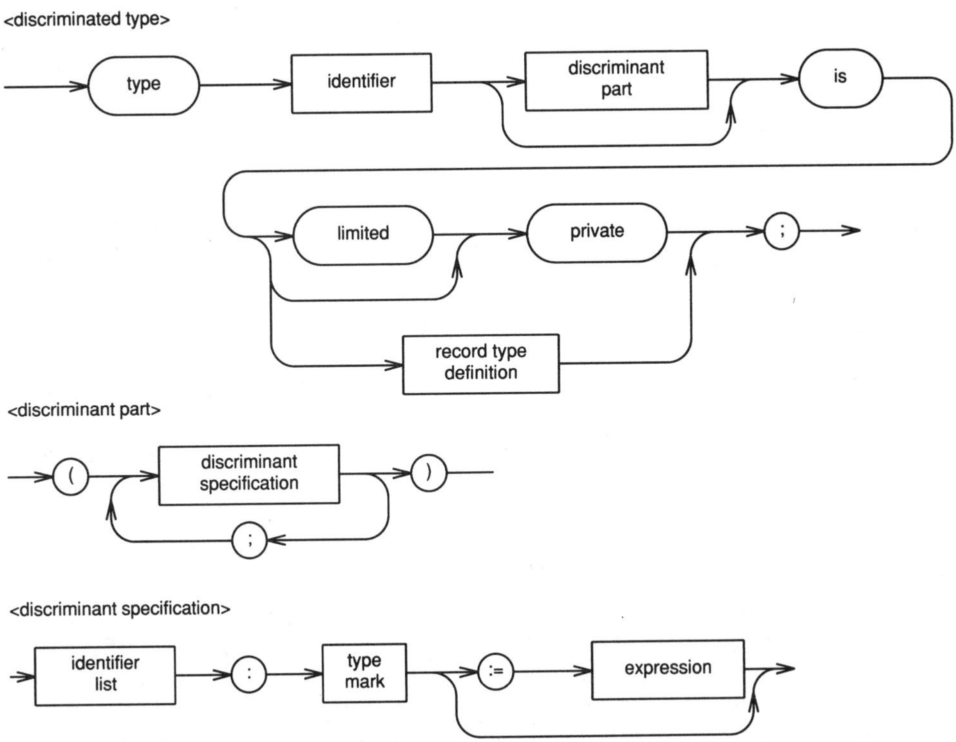

Figure 12–3

The syntax for declaring discriminated types is shown in Figure 12–3. The figure shows that any record type definition can have a discriminant part. This means a private type can have a discriminant, provided that the private type is a record type.

The figure also shows the syntax for the discriminant part. This syntax is similar to the syntax for a parameter list (Figure 6–3). A discriminant provides parameters for a record declaration. Note that multiple discriminants of multiple types are allowed.

In the rest of this section, we will step through a number of discriminant definitions of increasing complexity. As we discuss these definitions, we will cover the rules and subtleties of using discriminants.

```
 1:procedure Initial_Value is
 2:  type Down_Counter(Minutes: POSITIVE) is
 3:    record
 4:      Seconds_Left: NATURAL := 60 * Minutes;
 5:    end record;
 6:  X: Down_Counter(3);
 7:  Y: Down_Counter(2);
 8:begin
 9:  while X.Seconds_Left > 0 loop
10:    X.Seconds_Left := X.Seconds_Left - 1;
11:  end loop;
12:  Y.Seconds_Left := 13;
13:  X.Seconds_Left := Y.Minutes * 60;
14:end Initial_Value;
```

Program 12–5

In the procedure **Initial_Value** shown in Program 12–5, the type **Down_Counter** is a discriminated record. The identifier associated with the discriminant is **Minutes** and the type of the discriminant is **POSITIVE**. In this record declaration, the discriminant is used to supply an initial value to a component in the record. The elaboration of an object of the type **Down_Counter** causes the **Seconds_Left** component to be initialized to 60 times the value passed as the discriminant. Thus, the elaboration of **X** causes the **Seconds_Left** component of that record to be initialized to the value 180. Note that the value of the **Seconds_Left** component can subsequently be changed as in lines 10, 12, and 13.

Records of type **Down_Counter** actually have two components. This is because the discriminant (**Minutes**) is itself a component. Like parameters of mode **in**, discriminant components cannot be changed. Thus, the value of **Y.Minutes** will be 2 for the entire existence of the object. Also like an **in** parameter, the value of the discriminant component can be used, as in line 13. Of the four uses of discriminants in declaring a record, the only one in which the discriminant can appear as part of an expression is when it is used to initialize the value of a component. In all other cases it is not allowed to be part of a larger expression.

The second use of a discriminant is to supply an index constraint to one or more components of a record. Thus, discriminants yield structures of selectable sizes. The procedure **Array_Discriminant** in Program 12–6 illustrates this. The type **Grade_List** contains an array of selectable size. Specifically, a component in **Grade_List** is of an unconstrained array type (**Vary**). The discriminant (**Class_Size**) is used to provide an index constraint. The effect of the declarations is that **Math** and

```
1:procedure Array_Discriminant is
2:  type Vary is array (INTEGER range <>) of INTEGER;
3:  type Grade_List(Class_Size: INTEGER) is
4:    record
5:      List: Vary(1..Class_Size);
6:    end record;
7:  Math: Grade_List(5);
8:  Chem: Grade_List(5);
9:  Biol: Grade_List(10);
10:begin
11:  Math.List(5) := 96;
12:  Math.List(3) := Chem.Class_Size;
13:  Chem := Math;
14:end Array_Discriminant;
```

Program 12–6

Chem contain 6 **INTEGER** components and **Biol** contains 11 **INTEGER** components. For **Math** and **Chem**, this is 5 integers in **List** and 1 integer discriminant component in **Class_Size**; for **Biol**, this is 10 integers in **List** and 1 in **Class_Size**.

Again, the discriminant component is a constant: it can be used but not modified. Thus, for **Math** and **Chem** it will always remain 5, and for **Biol** it will always remain 10. Since **List** is a component in a record variable, **List** itself is a variable. This means that the elements in the array **List** can be assigned values. This is illustrated in lines 11 and 12. In fact, the entire list could be assigned, as in

```
Math.List := Chem.List;
```

Both sides of this assignment are of type **Vary** and have five components.

Variables of type **Grade_List** are type compatible. This is illustrated in line 13, where the entire contents of the object **Chem** are replaced with a copy of the contents of **Math**. Notice that the discriminants **Math** and **Chem** are the same. This is not the case with the assignment

```
Math := Biol;        -- CONSTRAINT_ERROR
```

The discriminants are different and the arrays are of two different sizes. This assignment causes a constraint error. The constraint error is caused because of the difference in the discriminants. This is illustrated by attempting to do the assignment

```
X := Y;              -- CONSTRAINT_ERROR
```

with the variables of type **Down_Counter** from Program 12–5. Even though these discriminated records do not contain arrays; a constraint error occurs because their discriminants differ. It is the discriminant that provides a constraint on the object, and it is the discriminants which must match to avoid a constraint error.

A difference between discriminants may be detected, and the error declared, at either compilation time or run time. The run-time detection often occurs when the objects are used in the fashion

```
Math: Grade_List(A);
Chem: Grade_List(B);
```

where **A** and **B** are variables declared at some outer level or are dependent on parameters to the procedure. Until the procedure declarations are elaborated at execution time, we do not know whether **Math** and **Chem** have different sizes.

When used to supply an index constraint, a discriminant may not be part of a larger expression. The declaration

```
List: Vary(1..Class_Size + 1); -- illegal version of line 5
```

would violate this rule.

A record with a discriminant can have a component that is itself a discriminated record. The third use of a discriminant is to supply a discriminant to a record component. Such a use is illustrated in the procedure **Complex_Discriminants** in Program 12–7. Within the type **Scan_Lines** of this procedure, the components **First_Line**, **Second_Line**, and **Third_Line** are of the type **Line**, which is a discriminated record. As before, when used to supply a constraint for an unconstrained component, a discriminant may not be part of a larger expression.

The procedure **Complex_Discriminants** illustrates four aspects of discriminants:

1. A discriminant can supply a discriminant to an unconstrained component. For example, in line 10, the value of the discriminant to the type **Line** depends on the discriminant **Another_Width**.
2. A record may contain more than one unconstrained component. For example, records of type **Scan_Lines** contain three unconstrained components.
3. A discriminant can be used more than once. For example, the discriminant **Width** is used in lines 8 and 9.
4. A discriminated record may have any number of discriminants. For example, **Scan_Lines** has two discriminants.

12.6.1 Default Discriminant Values

We note from the syntax diagram in Figure 12–3, that an expression may be attached to a discriminant. Like parameters, discriminants may have a default value. If no explicit value is supplied, the discriminant assumes the default value. In **Complex_Discriminants**, the discriminant **Maximum** in line 2 has a default value of 40. If no value is supplied for this discriminant, it will assume the value 40. In the case of multiple discriminants, all or none of the discriminants must have defaults, and all or none of the discriminants must be supplied explicit values.

```
 1:procedure Complex_Discriminants is
 2:  type Line(Maximum: POSITIVE := 40) is
 3:    record
 4:      Data: STRING(1..Maximum);
 5:    end record;
 6:  type Scan_Lines(Width, Another_Width: POSITIVE ) is
 7:    record
 8:      First_Line: Line(Width);
 9:      Second_Line: Line(Width);
10:      Third_Line: Line(Another_Width);
11:    end record;
12:  A_Line: Scan_Lines(10, 2);
13:  Default_Line: Line;
14:  type Nested_Default(Long: POSITIVE := 20) is
15:    record
16:      The_Line: Line(Long);
17:    end record;
18:  NDLine: Nested_Default;
19:begin
20:  A_Line.First_Line.Data(2) := 'X';
21:end Complex_Discriminants;
```

Program 12–7

The declaration in line 12 of **Complex_Discriminants** supplies discriminants. This is required because the discriminants of **Scan_Lines** do not have default values. By contrast, the declaration of **Default_Line** at line 13 does not supply the discriminant. Rather, the default value is assumed, i.e., **Maximum** will be 40 and **Data** will be **(1..40)**.

The declaration of **NDLine** at line 18 shows what happens with nested discriminated records and defaults. This declaration does not supply a constraint. This means that **Long** assumes a default value of 20. The record declaration indicates that the component **The_Line** (at line 16) will have the discriminant value equal to that of **Long**. Even though **Long** was set by default, it was set, and it has the value 20. Thus, we elaborate **Line** with a discriminant of 20.

As illustrated in line 20, access to nested discriminated records proceeds exactly as does access to nested records without discriminants.

Using a discriminant with a default, as done in lines 2–5, can cause a numeric error or storage error to occur in some implementations. This usually happens if the implementation tries to allocate the maximum amount of storage necessary for the largest possible version of the discriminant. Suppose the discriminant determines the size of an array and that it can assume any integer value. The number of elements could be up to the size of the largest allowable integer. The machine, however, may not be able to store such an array, causing the program to run out of storage. A numeric error is possible because, as the machine computes the amount of storage necessary, it adds the potential size of the array (the largest possible integer) to the size of any other components, and the resulting number is greater than the largest integer it can handle. In those implementations that adopt a "wait and see" method of allocating storage, these errors do not usually occur, because when the array is actually given a size, it is usually much smaller than the maximum size. If such a problem occurs, it can be avoided by using a subtype with a more restrictive constraint for the discriminant. For example, by changing the type of **Maximum** in line 2 from **POSITIVE** to some other subtype that has a smaller range.

Like parameters and record aggregates, discriminants may be referred to by name. Positional and named notation may be mixed, but all positional notation must come first. Thus, we could have declared **A_Line** in Program 12–7 as

```
A_Line: Scan_Line(Another_Width => 2, Width => 10);
```

A discriminant does not have to be used at all. In that case, the component is still present and can be read, but it cannot be changed. Consider the code

```
type Student_Record(Student_Number: POSITIVE) is
  record
    Grade: INTEGER;
  end record;
Steve: Student_Record(86);
```

In the declaration of **Student_Record**, the discriminant component **Student_Number** is not used. In elaborations of objects of type **Student_Record**, a value is supplied for **Student_Number** when the object is elaborated. That value is permanently attached to the record. A discriminant used this way supplies a constant component within a record.

A record with a discriminant may be assigned a value by means of an aggregate. This is illustrated in the procedure **Disc_And_Aggreg** in Program 12–8. As discussed in a previous example, because the discriminants of **Chem** and **Math** are identical, the assignment of line 10 does not raise a constraint error. A similar rule applies to aggregates: An aggregate must have a structure corresponding to the object to which it supplies values. The type **Grade_List** has two components, **Class_Size** and **List**. Thus, an aggregate that is compatible with **Grade_List** must have two components. The first must be compatible with **Class_Size** and the second must be compatible with **List**. Since, in line 11, **Class_Size** for **Chem** is a discriminant whose value is 3, the aggregate must contain a 3 as the value of its first component. Also, since the component **List** in the variable **Chem** contains three integers, the second component of the aggregate must contain three integers. That is, the second component must be an aggregate itself, since **List** is an array. In line 7, an initial value is given to the variable **Math** at elaboration. Both of the 3's on this line are required. The first supplies the discriminant for **Math**, while the second is so the discriminant in the aggregate will be compatible with the discriminant in **Math**. Briefly, the discriminants cannot be changed, they must be repeated.

```
 1:procedure Disc_And_Aggreg is
 2:   type Vary is array (INTEGER range <>) of INTEGER;
 3:   type Grade_List(Class_Size: INTEGER) is
 4:     record
 5:       List: Vary(1..Class_Size);
 6:     end record;
 7:   Math: Grade_List(3) := (3, (45, 37, 99));
 8:   Chem: Grade_List(3);
 9:begin
10:   Chem := Math;
11:   Chem := (3, (22, 27, 34));
12:end Disc_And_Aggreg;
```

Program 12–8

Note that the variable **Math** could have been declared as a *constant* record, in which case none of its components could be changed.

Default record initialization can be applied to records with discriminants. For example, we could modify line 5 of **Disc_And_Aggreg** to read

```
List: Vary(1..Class_Size) := (27, 84, 35);   -- Dangerous
```

This default value would apply to any declaration of type **Grade_List** which did not have an explicit initial value indicated. For example, upon declaration of **Chem**, this default value would be supplied. An obvious problem with this type of default is that it has exactly 3 values. Thus, declarations not having a **Class_Size** of 3, such as

```
Biology: Grade_List(4);
```

would result in a **CONSTRAINT_ERROR**. We repeat, the elaboration of a declaration *can* cause an exception, such as **CONSTRAINT_ERROR**, to be raised. In the case of the preceding component declaration, a more reasonable default initialization is

```
List: Vary(1..Class_Size) := (others => 0);
```

which always produces an aggregate with the appropriate number of components, thus avoiding a constraint error. In using named association in aggregates, remember the requirement that the choices must be static unless there is only one choice. In the immediately preceding initialization of **List**, the choice is not static because the size of the array, and hence the size of the aggregate, depends on a discriminant. Because **others** is the only choice in this initialization, it is legal. However,

```
List: Vary(1..Class_Size) := (1, others => 0);     -- illegal
```

is illegal because there are two choices, and one of them, the **others** choice, is not static.

12.7 VARIANT RECORDS

The fourth use of a discriminant is to select a *variant part*. Figure 12–4 gives the full syntax for a record type declaration. A variant part may be the last component in the record. The syntax of a variant part resembles the case statement. The variant part is optional: It may follow other (nonvariant) components, but it may also be the only thing in a record. In all cases, there must be at least one component or the reserved word **null** within the record declaration. Any number of components may occur before the variant part.

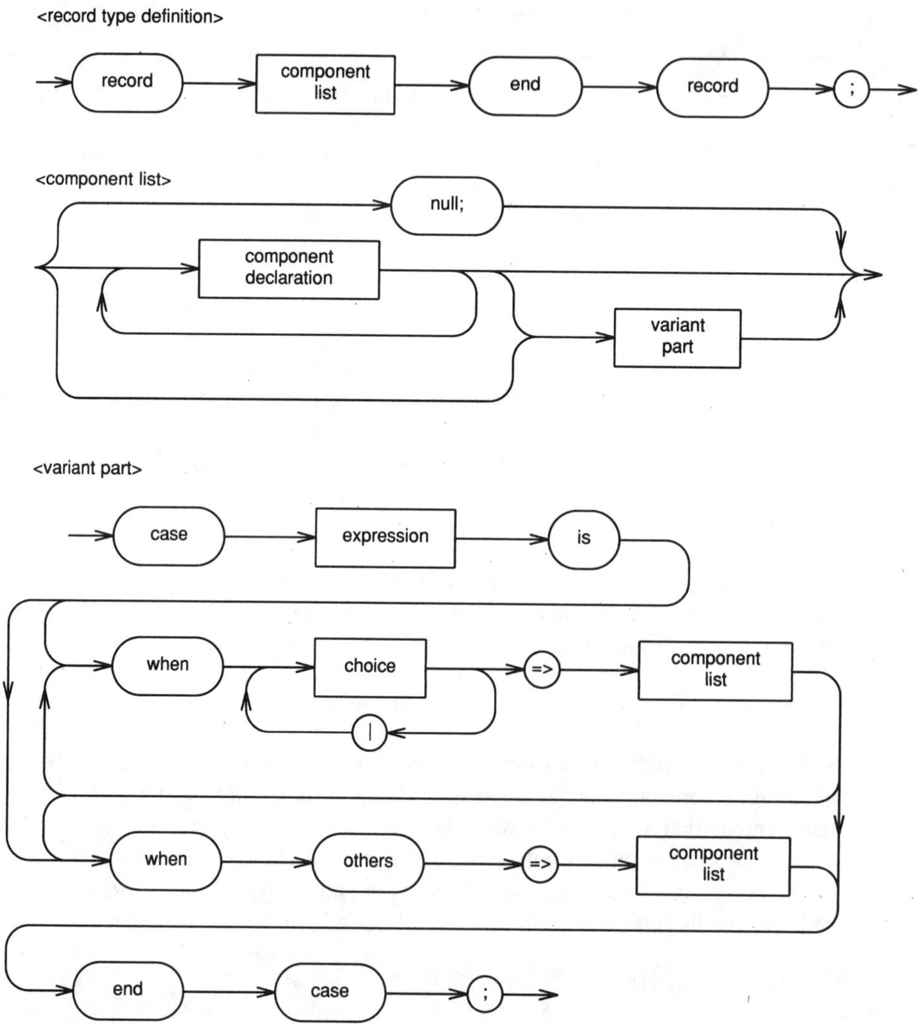

Figure 12–4

Selecting a variant part with a discriminant allows the selection of a record structure. Specifically, one variant of the record structure is selected upon elaboration of an object.

```
 1:type Shape is (Rectangle, Circle, Triangle);
 2:type Color is (Red, Yellow, Green, Black, White);
 3:type Figure(Kind: Shape) is
 4:  record
 5:    Figure_Body: Color := Black;
 6:    Border: Color := White;
 7:    case Kind is
 8:      when Rectangle => Width, Height: NATURAL;
 9:      when Circle => Radius: NATURAL;
10:      when Triangle => Side_1, Side_2: NATURAL;
11:        Interior_Angle: NATURAL range 0..180;
12:    end case;
13:  end record;
14:Box: Figure(Rectangle);
```

Program 12–9

In the type **Figure** in Program 12–9, there are two regular component declarations, **Figure_Body** and **Border**. All objects of type **Figure** will have these two components. Lines 7–12 are the variant part of **Figure**. The variant part will be one of three possible structures. If the value of the discriminant **Kind** is **Rectangle**, as is the case with the variable **Box**, then there are two components in the variant part: **Width** and **Height**. If the value of the discriminant is **Circle**, then there is one component, **Radius**, and if the value of the discriminant is **Triangle**, there are three components. An object of type **Figure** will have exactly one of the variant parts. For example, such an object will never have both **Width** and **Radius** components, because these components are parts of different variants.

A variant part resembles a case statement, each of whose choices is a list of component declarations. The final component declaration of a variant part may also be a variant part. Thus, variant parts may be nested within variant parts. This is illustrated in the following declaration:

```
type Model is (Regular, Deluxe);
type Size is (Little, Medium, Large);
type Color is (Red, Blue, Green);
type Bread_Box(How_Big: Size; Which: Model) is
  record
    case How_Big is
      when Little =>
        null;
      when Medium =>
        Its_Color: Color;
        case Which is
```

```
              when Regular => null;
              when Deluxe  => Side: Color;
            end case;
          when Large =>
            Top: Color;
            Bottom: Color;
        end case;
      end record;
    B: Bread_Box(Medium, Regular);
    C: Bread_Box(Large, Deluxe);
    D: Bread_Box(Medium, Deluxe);
```

The type **Bread_Box** has two discriminants, **How_Big** and **Which**. If the first discriminant has the value **Medium**, the second discriminant **Which** is used to select either "**null;**" or "**Side:Color;**" to be included in the object. Of the three objects declared, only **D** has a **Side** component.

Several discriminant values can refer to the same variant part, as in

```
when Medium | Large => ...
```

Also, ranges may be used, as in

```
when Mon..Wed | Sun => ...
```

and an **others** option may be used as the last selection. As with a case statement, each choice must occur exactly once.

As regards type compatibility, variants follow the same rules as do all discriminated records. Thus, if the variables **A** and **B** are of the same type, as in the declarations

```
A: Bread_Box(Medium);
B: Bread_Box(Little);
```

then the assignment

```
A := B;
```

is legal, but raises a constraint error because the discriminants are different. Again, the discriminants must match, and not just the record structures. Even if the declaration of **Bread_Box** contained

```
when Medium | Little =>
```

so that both **A** and **B** contained exactly the same components, a constraint error would still be raised because, again, the values of the discriminants of **A** and **B** would differ.

Subtypes of discriminated record types may be declared. As is true of all subtypes, subtypes with the same base type are compatible.

```
subtype Medium_Bread_Box is Bread_Box(Medium, Regular);
subtype Little_Bread_Box is Bread_Box(Little, Regular);
A: Medium_Bread_Box;
B: Bread_Box(Medium, Regular);
begin
  A := B;
end;
```

As shown above, subtypes may be declared which are always **Medium** or **Little Bread_Box**es. **A** and **B** are compatible because the base type of both is **Bread_Box**, and in fact, their discriminants are the same, so no constraint error occurs.

As with other discriminated records, aggregates may be used to assign to and/or initialize variants. Aggregates use either named or positional notation, as in the following:

```
  A: Bread_Box(Medium, Regular);
  B: Bread_Box(How_Big => Large, Which => Regular);
begin
  A := (Medium, Regular, Green);
  B := (Which => Regular, Top => Blue, Bottom => Red, How_Big => Large);
end;
```

The standard rules for discriminated records apply, so all components must be specified and all discriminants must be repeated.

Discriminants used as variants may have defaults. Again, as with other discriminants, all or none of the discriminants must have defaults, and all or none of the discriminants must be supplied explicit values. (Notice that this differs from procedure parameters.) Thus, in the declarations

```
type Size is (Little, Medium, Large);
type Color is (Red, Blue, Green);
type Bread_Box(How_Big: Size := Medium) is
  record
    case How_Big is
      when Little => null;
      when Medium => Its_Color: Color;
      when Large => Top: Color; Bottom: Color;
    end case;
  end record;
A: Bread_Box;
B: Bread_Box(Little);
```

until otherwise informed, **A** is a **Medium** sized **Bread_Box**. On the other hand because the explicit value **Little** is supplied, **B** is always a **Little Bread_Box**.

If a discriminated variable was declared using default values, the discriminant values may be changed during execution. Changing the default value changes the nature of the record during execution. In the previous declaration for **A**, the default value of the discriminant was used. Because of this, the discriminant may be changed during execution. Thus,

```
A := (Little);
```

changes the size of **A** from **Medium** to **Little**. Even after this reassignment, **A** may be further changed, as in

```
A := (Large, Blue, Red);
```

Now **A** is a **Large Bread_Box**. In fact, a variable or expression can be used on the right-hand side of the assignment operation. The assignment

```
A := B;
```

will always change **A** to be a **Little Bread_Box**.

When an unconstrained object formed from a default has its discriminant overridden, the entire record must be reassigned. So

```
A.How_Big := Large;      -- illegal
```

is illegal. An aggregate or object must be used to reassign the entire record.

Finally, the combination

```
A := (Little);
A.Its_Color := Blue;     -- CONSTRAINT_ERROR
```

always causes a **CONSTRAINT_ERROR** because at execution **A** becomes **Little** and does not possess the component **Its_Color**.

Let us summarize the rules for variants. First, the discriminant of an object may not be changed if the object is declared with its discriminant constrained. Second, all objects must have values for all their discriminants. Third, whenever no default is given in the type definition, the discriminant value must be explicitly supplied for each object of that type when the object is declared. Fourth, when a default discriminant is used, it can be changed, but the whole record must be reassigned.

As mentioned, private types that are record types may have discriminants. In fact, a private type that has discriminants may have unconstrained components and variants. Also, the discriminants of a private type may have default values. A sample private type declaration with discriminants is the following:

```
type Line(Maximum: POSITIVE := 40) is private;
  ...
private
  type Line(Maximum: POSITIVE := 40) is
    record
      Length: NATURAL := 0;
```

```
      Data: STRING(1..Maximum);
    end record;
```

The discriminants must be given in the visible part of the declaration and must be repeated in the private part. Since they are given in the visible part, the user knows the names and the types of the discriminants. So the variable declarations

```
V1: Line(20);
V2: Line(Maximum => 20);
```

are legal anywhere the type **Line** is visible, and the component reference

```
V2.Maximum
```

is legal anywhere the variable **V2** is visible. Finally, because **Line** has a default value for the discriminant, in the declaration

```
V3: Line;
```

Maximum assumes the default value of 40.

The attribute **CONSTRAINED** is available for objects and private types that have discriminants. On an object, this attribute may be used as shown in the following procedure:

```
procedure Check_Constraint(A_Line: in out Line) is
begin
  if not A_Line'CONSTRAINED then
    A_Line := V2;
  end if;
end Check_Constraint;
```

If this procedure is called as

```
Check_Constraint(V3);
```

then the attribute **A_Line'CONSTRAINED** will return **FALSE**. While **V3** has "constraints," it got them from the default values for the discriminant. Since such constraints can be changed, **V3** is considered unconstrained. On the other hand, in the call

```
Check_Constraint(V2);
```

the attribute **A_Line'CONSTRAINED** will return **TRUE** because the constraints (i.e., the discriminant) on **V2** cannot be changed.

On a private type, **CONSTRAINED** indicates if the type is a subtype in which the discriminants have been constrained. Given the definition following of the unconstrained private type, **Un_Line**:

```
type Un_Line(Maximum: POSITIVE) is private;
 ...
private
  type Un_Line(Maximum: POSITIVE) is
    record
      Length: NATURAL := 0;
      Data: STRING(1..Maximum);
    end record;
```

the value of **Un_Line'CONSTRAINED** would be **FALSE** because the discriminant **Maximum** is not constrained to a specific value. However, subtypes may be formed from private types. The following private subtype

```
subtype Old_Line is Un_Line;
```

is unconstrained, while the private subtype

```
subtype Little_Line is Un_Line(10);
```

is constrained. Specifically, in the type **Little_Line** the value of **Maximum** is constrained to be 10.

Remember that although a type may be unconstrained, objects have constraints. With objects of type **Un_Line** a **CONSTRAINT_ERROR** may be raised; for example, in an assignment statement involving objects with differing constraints. With the exception of total reassignment of an object formed using a default (such as was done earlier with **V3** in **V3:=V1;**), the constraint of an object cannot be changed after elaboration.

12.7.1 Renaming Components

Record components may, in general, be renamed. However, certain restrictions apply to discriminated records. Consider again the following definitions:

```
type Size is (Little, Medium, Large);
type Color is (Red, Blue, Green);
type Bread_Box(How_Big: Size := Medium) is
  record
    case How_Big is
      when Little => null;
      when Medium => Its_Color: Color;
      when Large => Top: Color; Bottom: Color;
    end case;
  end record;
A: Bread_Box;
B: Bread_Box(Large);
```

Renaming can be used only when the component is sure to exist. Thus, we can rename components in **B**, such as

```
Paint_Needed: Color renames B.Top;
```

The record **B** is constrained: If at the time of the renaming it has a component **Top**, it will always have a component **Top**. On the other hand, we cannot rename components in the record **A**, such as in

```
May_Have_It: Color renames A.Its_Color;  -- illegal
```

The record **A** is unconstrained. So, even though it might have an **Its_Color** component at the time of renaming, a complete reassignment such as

```
A := B;
```

would cause that component to cease to exist. The rational behind making such a renaming illegal is that it could rename an entity which could become nonexistent.

12.8 OVERLOADING SUBPROGRAMS

Visibility involves one definition hiding another. We have seen that in the case of operators that a new definition for an operator as in:

```
function "+"(L: Days; R: INTEGER) return Days;
```

did not hide the original **"+"** operator. Instead it *overloaded* the operator. This meant that it supplied another definition and that both definitions were directly visible simultaneously. Overloading may also be applied to subprograms. This allows the declaration of multiple meanings for a single identifier.

Overloading of subprograms can only occur with subprograms that are distinguishable. If the subprograms are in different declaration parts, visibility by selection may be used to distinguish them. With such programs, we may or may not have overloading. Ada allows subprograms with the same identifier to be declared in the *same* declaration part. In this case, visibility by selection cannot be used to distinguish the subprograms. One way to ensure that such subprograms are distinguishable is for their parameters to be of different types.

One instance of subprogram overloading we have already seen occurs in the package **Simple_IO**. Recall that we used the procedure **Write** with integers, characters, and strings. How did we avoid the requirement that **Write** accept a parameter of a given type? In fact, we did not avoid it; we simply used overloading. Consider the following package declaration:

```
package Simple_IO is
  procedure Write(Value: CHARACTER);
  procedure Write(Value: INTEGER);
  procedure Write(Value: STRING);
end Simple_IO;
```

In this declaration, three different procedures are declared. The identifier for each of these procedures is the same, but the procedures are different. The identifier "**Write**" is *overloaded* with three different meanings.

The requirement is that these three procedures be distinguishable. As a matter of fact, they can be distinguished from the context of their call. In the call

```
Write('A');
```

the parameter is of type **CHARACTER**. Since only one of the three procedures can take a parameter of type **CHARACTER**, we know exactly which procedure the call refers to. If there is ever more than one procedure to which a call could refer, it is a syntax error that will be detected by the compiler.

The two concepts of overloading and hiding can be somewhat confusing. Overloading is when an identifier or operator has multiple meanings that are simultaneously directly visible. Hiding is where a identifier or operator masks another definition of the same identifier or operator.

In the declarations

```
procedure A is
  procedure B is
    procedure A is
      -- The global A is visible only by selection
      begin null; end;
  ...
```

the global **A** is hidden from the point of declaration of the local **A** until the end of the declarative region of **B**. Qualified visibility may be applied to the global **A** so that it may be used in this region, but it is not directly visible. There is no overloading in this example.

By contrast, in the declarations

```
procedure A is
  procedure B(C: CHARACTER) is ...
  procedure B(I: INTEGER) is ...
    -- B is overloaded
  ...
```

both declarations of **B** are directly visible simultaneously, so the identifier is overloaded. In a call to **B**, the implementation distinguishes which **B** is intended by the type of the actual parameter. Selection does not help with **B** although we could assure which **B** is chosen by qualifying the actual parameter, as in the call

```
B(INTEGER'(I));
```

By forcing the parameter to be interpreted as type **INTEGER**, the implementation is forced to infer that the second declaration of **B** was intended in the call. Other instances in which qualification is useful or required will arise as we introduce additional Ada constructs.

To summarize, overloading occurs when a name allows multiple meanings. Qualification is a method of specifying to what type an expression (or name) belongs. Qualification can assist in disambiguating names that are overloaded. Selection can serve the same purpose by distinguishing the entity to which a name belongs. For example, selection disambiguates between procedures declared in different packages.

In some cases, the context is sufficient to distinguish between meanings for a name. For example, multiple declarations for the same procedure name in a single package are distinguished by the types of the parameters used in the call.

12.9 THE LINES PACKAGE (3): UNCONSTRAINED TYPES AND OVERLOADING

The **Lines** package uses a discriminated record, an unconstrained array, and overloading. The type **Normal_Line** which we have previously used is actually a subtype of an unconstrained type **Super_Line**. So that users of **Lines** will not depend on the organization of **Super_Line**, **Super_Line** is a private type. The declarations of these types is as follows:

```
package Lines is
  subtype Line_Size is NATURAL;
  Normal_Size: constant Line_Size := 96;
  type Super_Line(Size: Line_Size) is private;
  subtype Normal_Line is Super_Line(Normal_Size);
  -- Other declarations
private
  type Super_Line(Size: Line_Size) is
    record
      Length: Line_Size := 0;
      Data: STRING(1..Size);
    end record;
end Lines;
```

The discriminant **Size** is the maximum number of characters that can be stored in the line. In the case of **Normal_Line**, this is 96 characters. From the type **Super_Line**, you may declare subtypes with different maximum lengths. For example,

```
subtype Short_Line is Super_Line(5);
```

declares a line that can store at most five characters.

Within the type **Super_Line**, the discriminant is used to constrain an unconstrained array component **Data** which is of type **STRING**. Notice also that within the record, the actual number of characters stored in the line is kept in the component **Length**.

The procedures and functions in the **Lines** package use the type **Super_Line**. For example, a comparison operator is declared by

```
function "<="(Left, Right: Super_Line) return BOOLEAN;
```

Within the body of the **Lines** package, this comparison is done with the slice comparison capabilities defined for arrays of scalar types. The body of the function is as follows:

```
function "<="(Left, Right: Super_Line) return BOOLEAN is
begin
  return Left.Data(1..Left.Length) <= Right.Data(1..Right.Length);
end "<=";
```

The index of the first character of the **STRING** component in the type **Super_Line** is always **1**. The component **Length** defines how many of the characters in that component contain meaningful values. The portions of the two **STRING** components that contain meaningful values are compared to obtain the value to be returned.

The procedures and functions of the **Lines** package allow the substitution of string literals for **in** parameters of type **Super_Line**. This is achieved by overloading the procedure and function names. The previous comparison operator is overloaded with the following two additional meanings:

```
function "<="(Left: Super_Line; Right: STRING) return BOOLEAN;
function "<="(Left: STRING; Right: Super_Line) return BOOLEAN;
```

The bodies of these overloadings are as straightforward as the previous body. For example, the body of the second overloadings is

```
function "<="(Left: STRING; Right: Super_Line) return BOOLEAN is
begin
  return Left <= Right.Data(1..Right.Length);
end "<=";
```

In this overloading the entire string is compared against the meaningful portion of the **Super_Line**.

Lines overloads many subprogram names. The following are two examples:

```
-- Comparison routines for Super_Lines and STRINGS. Comparison is
--   lexicographical.
function Equals(Left,              Right: Super_Line) return BOOLEAN;
function Equals(Left: Super_Line; Right: STRING)      return BOOLEAN;
function Equals(Left: STRING;      Right: Super_Line) return BOOLEAN;
-- Purpose: insert characters into a line.
--   Destination: characters will be inserted into this line.
--   Insertion: the thing to be inserted.
--   Location: where in Destination the insertion is to occur.
```

```
procedure Insert(Destination: in out Super_Line; Insertion: Super_Line;
                 Location: Line_Size);
procedure Insert(Destination: in out Super_Line; Insertion: STRING;
                 Location: Line_Size);
procedure Insert(Destination: in out Super_Line; Insertion: CHARACTER;
                 Location: Line_Size);
```

As mentioned before, the principle behind these overloadings is to cause string literals to have the appearance of literals of the type **Super_Line**. The overloadings allow the programmer to forget which parameters are of type **Super_Line** and which are of type **STRING** in these comparison operators. In fact, in the case of insertion, characters, strings, and lines can be interchanged. This abstraction makes the utilities in the **Lines** package easier to use.

12.10 PROGRAMMING PRACTICES

The capability of parameterizing data structures permits Ada procedures to be written which work with multiple variations of a basic data declaration. Using attributes and discriminants, subprograms can be constructed which appropriately handle these variations. For ease of understanding, it is important that there be a reason for the variation of the data structure. For example, declaring a single type that is an unconstrained array of integers and using that type for several purposes which are unrelated is poor practice. It is better to have each fundamental data type associated with a separate declaration and to limit grouping using constraints and discriminants to those data types which are logically associated with each other in the solution of the problem.

Reducing the information that someone needs to keep track of in order to understand a program is called *abstraction.* When we make a concept more abstract, we remove the details and retain only the "high-level," essential information about that concept. In effect, we present only a summary of the concept.

A (well-documented) package declaration is an abstraction of the package. Likewise, a well-designed parameterized data type can serve as such a summary. It summarizes a collection of types into one. In the next chapter, we shall see more applications of abstraction to data types.

12.10.1 Returning Unconstrained Types

We return to the **Lines** package and examine the procedure **Assign** because it illustrates a solution to a common problem encountered in the use of discriminated types. The declaration of **Assign** is:

```
procedure Assign(Destination: out Super_Line; Source: Super_Line) is
begin
  Destination.Data(1..Source.Length) := Source.Data(1..Source.Length);
  Destination.Length := Source.Length;
```

```
exception
  when CONSTRAINT_ERROR =>
    raise Illegal_Lines_Index;
end Assign;
```

Why should **Assign** be a procedure? Why not just use assignment (:=)? The reason is because an assignment such as

```
A := B;
```

will raise a constraint error, unless **A** and **B** have the same constraint. But this is counter to the purpose of having variable-length lines. The procedure, on the other hand, does not have such a restriction. The first line of the procedure moves the meaningful part of the **Source** into the **Destination**. Provided there is enough room to fit this meaningful part, no error will occur. Only if there is not enough room will this assignment cause **CONSTRAINT_ERROR** to be raised. The handler converts that constraint error into an **Illegal_Lines_Index** exception. Notice the order of the two assignments in the procedure. The second assignment will not raise an exception. Thus, if an exception occurs, it will be because the first assignment could not be performed. This means that when an exception is raised, neither the **Data** nor the **Length** components of **Destination** will be changed. If we had reversed the order of the assignments, the **Length** component would have been changed even when an exception occurred. This would leave the **Destination** containing a meaningless value. A good programming practice is to ensure that whenever a procedure exits with an exception, its parameters of modes **out** and **in out** have not been changed.

12.10.2 Problem Solving

Let us again consider stacks and queues. Although these two abstract data structures have different properties (e.g., queues are first-in, first-out structures, whereas stacks are last-in, first-out structures), they do have features in common. Both store and retrieve data, and both can become full or empty. Once the user has selected which of these two structures to use, the operations that can be applied to the structures are very similar. Discriminants permit the natural development of a **Storage_Handler** package that combines the two abstract structures.

Before reading the following discussion you may want to review the Problem Solving section of Chapter 10 (10.6.1) where we discussed the **Stack_Package** and exercise 10.9, which deals with the **Queue_Package**. In the exercises of this chapter, you are asked to complete **Storage_Handler**.

The **Storage_Handler** package implements the following operations:

Store: Given a structure and an item, stores that item according to the protocol of the structure.

Retrieve: Given a structure, removes the appropriate item (again, determined by the type of the structure), and returns that item.

Full: Returns **TRUE** if the given structure is full.

Empty: Returns **TRUE** if the given structure is empty.

"=": Returns **TRUE** if the two structures are of the same type and the contents of the two structures are the same.

Storage_Handler implements the structure as a discriminated record and uses these four operations to deal appropriately with the structure. In this manner, once the user has decided on a queue or a stack and chosen the structure by choosing the appropriate discriminant, the user can forget about the structure and rely on the package to take care of the details. **Storage_Handler** implements both the stack and the queue in such a way that **Store** and **Retrieve** do not move elements around, instead the package keeps track of the first element and/or number of elements stored. The declaration of the package **Storage_Handler** and a partial implementation of the package body are shown in Program 12–10.

In **Storage_Handler**, the limited private type **Storage_Structure** has two discriminants. One indicates the nature of the structure (either a **Stack** or a **Queue**), the other indicates the maximum number of items that can be stored in the structure. The implementation described in the exercises of Chapter 10 requires a slightly different record for a queue than for a stack. This difference is embodied in the variant part of the **Storage_Structure** record.

The structure of the procedure **Store** illustrates how a subprogram could handle records with different discriminants. **Store** first does those operations shared by all records, and then on the basis of the discriminant, it performs the operations unique to each value of the discriminant.

The advantage of the **Storage_Handler** package is that it abstracts the concept of storing items even further than the packages which handled only stacks or queues. The decision whether an object of type **Storage_Structure** is a stack or a queue is made when the object is elaborated. Furthermore, because the value of a discriminant is an expression that is evaluated at elaboration, it is possible to choose the type of structure needed during execution of the program.

12.11 ADA SUMMARY

This chapter has dealt primarily with parameterizing data structures. *Unconstrained array types* provided arrays of selectable size which are of the same base type and hence, type compatible. This allows us to abstract the array structure by ignoring the size of the array. With the use of parameters which are unconstrained array types and attributes we are able to build subprograms that perform correctly for any array size.

Records could be parameterized using *discriminants*. This kind of parameterization yields us the same benefits as do unconstrained array types. In addition, discriminants can be used with *variant parts* to vary the structure of the record, providing another level of flexibility. Because constraint checks are performed, the use of discriminants and variants assists in detecting programming mistakes.

```
package Storage_Handler is
  type Structure_Type is (Stack, Queue);
  type Storage_Structure(Size: NATURAL; Structure: Structure_Type)
                                                   is limited private;
  subtype Item_Type is INTEGER;
  -- Change the declaration of Item_Type to make a storage handler for
  -- another data type.
  Overflow: exception;  -- Too many items stored; no more room.
  Underflow: exception; -- Too many items retrieved; no more to retrieve.
  procedure Store(Storage: in out Storage_Structure; Item: Item_Type);
  -- Purpose: Store an item into a structure.
  -- Storage: The structure to store into.
  -- Value: The value to store into the structure.
  procedure Retrieve(Storage: in out Storage_Structure; Item: out Item_Type);
  -- Purpose: Retrieve an item from a structure. The item is removed
  -- from the structure.
  -- Storage: The structure to retrieve the item from.
  -- Value: The value to store into the structure.
  function Full(Storage: Storage_Structure) return BOOLEAN;
  -- Purpose: Returns TRUE if and only if a Store would cause Overflow.
  function Empty(Storage: Storage_Structure) return BOOLEAN;
  -- Purpose: Returns TRUE if and only if a Retrieve would cause
  -- Underflow.
  function "="(Left, Right: Storage_Structure) return BOOLEAN;
  -- Purpose: Returns TRUE if the structures are the same type and are
  -- storing identical values in the identical order.
private
  type List is array (NATURAL range <>) of Item_Type;
  type Storage_Structure(Size: NATURAL; Structure: Structure_Type) is
    record
      Data: List(1..Size);
      Number_Of_Items: NATURAL := 0;  -- Number of items in the structure
      case Structure is
        -- Left as an exercise.
      end case;
    end record;
end Storage_Handler;
package body Storage_Handler is
  procedure Store(Storage: in out Storage_Structure; Item: Item_Type);
  -- Check if there is room to store the Item. Raise Overflow if there
  -- is no room.
  -- Check the type of structure. Perform the appropriate storage for
  -- that type of structure.
  begin
    if Storage.Number_Of_Items >= Storage.Size then
      raise Overflow;
```

Program 12–10

```
      elsif Storage.Structure = Stack then
        -- Push the Item onto the top of stack.
        Storage.Number_Of_Items := Storage.Number_Of_Items + 1;
        Storage.List(Storage.Number_Of_Items) := Item;
      else
        -- Put the Item on end of the queue.
        -- Left as an exercise.
      end if;
    end Store;
    -- The other subprograms are left as an exercise.
  end Storage_Handler;
```

Program 12–10 Continued

Many times we wish to perform similar operations on different types. Using the same identifier for each of these operations decreases the complexity of the program for the programmer. Ada permits us to do this by *overloading* subprogram identifiers.

EXERCISES

12.1. Modify **Insertion_Sort** in Program 12–3 so that its parameter is an unconstrained array type indexed by the type **CHARACTER**. Remember, the arithmetic operators are not available for characters. (Hint: See the version of **Insertion_Sort** given in Program 8–2 or your solution to exercise 5.7.)

12.2. Write a procedure **Reverse_String** that has a single parameter of mode **in out**. When passed a **STRING** variable, the procedure reverses the order of the letters in the string. The procedure should work on any string regardless of the range of its index.

12.3. Build a queue package. A queue is like a line of people waiting for service. New arrivals are placed at the back of the line. The next person receiving service is the one at the front of the line. A queue allows three operations: **Add** places an element at the back of the queue, **Remove** removes the element at the front of the queue, **Count** indicates how many items are waiting in the queue. The queues will contain characters. The description of exercise 10.9 may be helpful. Use the following declarations:

```
Package Queue_Handler is
  type Queue (Size: POSITIVE) is limited private;
  Procedure Add(Which_Queue: in out Queue; Element: CHARACTER);
  --Purpose: Adds an element to a queue.
  procedure Remove(Which_Queue: in out Queue; Element: out CHARACTER);
  -- Purpose: Removes an element from a queue. Returns that element in
  -- Element.
  function Count(Which_Queue: Queue) return NATURAL;
  -- Purpose: Returns how many items are in the queue.
  procedure Print_Queue(Which_Queue: Queue);
```

```
  --Purpose: Prints the current contents of the queue, for debugging.
  Queue_Empty, Queue_Full: exception;
private
  --Yours to fill in.
end Queue_Handler;
```

The type **Queue** should be a discriminated record with discriminant **Size**. **Queue** should be declared so that objects of type **Queue** are initialized to the empty queue; that is, the initial number of elements in the queue is zero.

12.4. Implement a package that supplies some **Lines** kind of capabilities for the type **STRING**. Remember that with **STRING**, each object will be of a fixed size. Build a package that contains a set of **Insert** functions. These functions return a **STRING**. Implement the capabilities to insert one string into another, to insert a character into a string, and to insert a **Normal_Line** into a string. Do this by overloading the identifier **Insert**.

12.5. Complete the implementation of the **Storage_Handler** package in Program 12–10.

12.6. In most banks, you have a variety of options available to you. Which options are available depend on the amount of minimum balance you agree to keep in the account.

Modify the **Bank_Account** package (Program 3–14; exercises 3.1, 4.5, 5.9, 7.8, 8.2, 10.5, or 10.6) to allow three possible minimum balances: \$100, \$1000, and \$10000. Following is a description of the various benefits at each level:

\$100: The interest rate of $5\frac{1}{2}$ %.

\$1000: You have an ATM card (and therefore a PIN number) and an interest rate of $6\frac{1}{2}$ %.

\$10000: You have an ATM card, overdraft protection, and an interest rate of $8\frac{1}{2}$ %.

You will need to add **ATM_Deposit** and **ATM_Withdraw** routines which demand the PIN number before proceeding with the request. In addition, a **Create_Account** procedure that interactively makes a new account and fills it in with appropriate values will be necessary. The old procedures, **Deposit**, **Withdraw**, **Interest**, and **Account_Balance** will be retained, although they must be modified to handle the new account type.

Overdraft protection means that the balance is permitted to fall below the minimum (but not below zero) to cover a withdrawal, provided that the next action is to deposit some money to bring the balance back up. No interest is paid on an account whose balance is below the minimum.

The specification for this version of **Bank_Account** is as follows:

```
package Bank_Account is
  type Account_Description is (Good_Service, Better_Service, Best_Service);
  type Account_Type(Description: Account_Description) is limited private;
  procedure Create_Account(New_Account: out Account_Type);
  procedure Withdraw(Account: in out Account_Type; Amount: POSITIVE);
  procedure Deposit(Account: in out Account_Type; Amount: POSITIVE);
  procedure ATM_Withdraw(Account: in out Account_Type; Amount: POSITIVE);
  procedure ATM_Deposit(Account: in out Account_Type; Amount: POSITIVE);
  procedure Interest(Account: in out Account_Type);
  procedure Account_Balance(Account: Account_Type);
private
```

```
  type Account_Type(Description: Account_Description) is
    record
      -- this is for you to fill in
    end record;
end Bank_Account;
```

12.7. A "pool" is a group of items from which selections may be made. Once an item has been selected, it may not be selected again. Implement a **Pool_Utilities** package that allows pools of integers of varying sizes. Use the following specification:

```
package Pool_Utilities is
  type Pool_Type(Size: INTEGER) is private;
  procedure Choose(Pool: in out Pool_Type; Choice: INTEGER);
  -- Purpose: Chooses an element from the Pool.
private
  type Pool_Values is array(INTEGER range <>) of INTEGER;
  type Pool_Type(Size: INTEGER) is
    record
      Values: Pool_Values(1..Size);
      Number_Left: INTEGER := Size;
      Initialized: BOOLEAN := FALSE;
    end record;
end Pool_Utilities;
```

One way to implement a pool is as follows. Suppose we have a pool **I** of size 5 containing the integers 1, 2, 3, 4, and 5. We randomly select an element from the pool by selecting a random integer between 1 and 5. Suppose our random integer is 3, then the number we select from the pool is 3 because **I.Values(3)** is 3. Now there are only 4 values left in the pool, so we set **Number_Left** to 4. Also, we move the contents of **Values(5)** into the location **Values(3)**. The **Values** array now contains **(1,2,5,4,5)**. On our next **Choose**, we pick a random number between 1 and 4. Suppose that number is again 3, then the number we now select from the pool is 5 because **Values(3)** is 5. This time we will move the contents of **Values(4)** into **Values(3)** and the array will contain **1,2,4,4,5** of which the first 3 values are eligible to be picked. We may summarize the algorithm as follows: Select a random number between 1 and the number left in the pool. Use that random number as an index into the array to select a value. Adjust the array so the unselected values are at the front. Decrement the number left. Note that if the pool has not been initialized, **Choose** must initialize the pool by setting up the array to contain the numbers **1..Size**.

13

Abstract Data Types

13.1 OBJECTIVES

The Ada language is structured so that types and type checking can be used by the compiler to detect many common errors. One capability which we have not yet covered is the ability to make a copy of a type — that is, to create a new type that has the capabilities of an old type. In this chapter we will show how Ada provides this capability with *derived types* (section 3) and with the ability to derive new integer types (section 4). Both of these capabilities are directed at the programming practice of *data abstraction* (section 7).

We have encouraged the use of enumerations as a programming tool. When there are a substantial number of enumerations within a program, repetition of enumeration literals often occurs. The overloading of enumeration literals (section 6) allows an enumeration literal to occur in more than one enumeration type. In the same section we discuss character literals as enumeration literals.

CONCEPTS:

- The same fundamental type may be safely used for two different types that should not be mixed.
- Hiding and differentiating data avoid errors.
- Character literals are like other enumeration literals.
- Object-oriented programming is a powerful programming methodology.

GOALS:

- Write a program that uses derived types.
- Write a program that defines an enumeration that includes character literals.

13.2 MOTIVATION

Often you must deal with different physical units. For example, angles are measured in degrees or radians and volumes are measured in gallons or liters. When a program must deal with different types of units it should protect itself against accidentally mixing those units. Suppose we have 3 gallons and add 2 liters for an incorrect answer of 5. Gallons and liters do not add directly because, even though they both are measures of volume, they represent different amounts of volume. If these measures must be mixed, you want some assurance that one has been converted to another before they were added. *Derived types* are the appropriate Ada tool for protecting the program in these situations.

In a similar vein, Ada allows many different integer types. Separating these types makes writing reliable programs easier for the same reasons as for derived types.

Ada recognizes that in programs that make appropriate use of its package structure, identifiers may sometimes be repeated. Rather than constantly worrying about those identifiers interfering with each other, Ada establishes a set of rules to prevent the ambiguous use of an identifier. As we have discussed before, *overloading* is the term used when an operator or identifier has multiple meanings. In this chapter we extend our coverage of overloading to the overloading of enumeration literals.

We have mentioned that the type **CHARACTER** is an enumerated type. In fact, character literals are enumeration literals. Many things, for example course grades, involve letters (i.e., character literals). In many of these cases, the inclusion of all the character literals or the ordering of the characters, as done in the type **CHARACTER**, is inappropriate. In these cases, defining an enumeration type with character literals permits a natural representation of the data in a program. Ada permits the use of character literals in the declaration of enumeration types.

13.3 DERIVED TYPES

A derived type is a new type which takes its properties from an existing type. Derived types allow the programmer to create related, but distinct, types. In many problems, the programmer needs to use closely related types for several different jobs. For example, in a large scheduling program, a simple error might be to add the time to type in a program to the time to compile the program, forgetting that the first is given in units of minutes and the second is given in units of seconds. Both values are integers; they are closely related because the same operations apply to them and they both measure time. However, it is a mistake to directly add them. One unit of measure should be converted to match the other before addition is conceptually correct. If they were distinct types the compiler

<derived type>

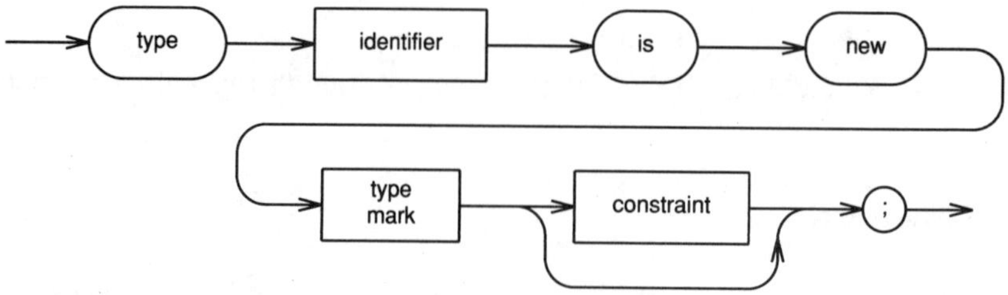

Figure 13–1

would detect any failure to convert, thus helping avoid errors. In such situations derived types are very useful.

The syntax for a derived type is given in Figure 13–1. As mentioned in Chapter 5, the reserved word **type** indicates that a new, distinct type, rather than a subtype, is being declared. The reserved word **new** indicates that the type is a derived type. Note that in previous declarations of array and record types, the reserved word **new** was not present, indicating that these types were *not* derived from existing types. The type mark is the name of the existing type on which the new type is based.

Recall that a subtype is compatible with its base type. A derived type differs from a subtype in that each derived type is a new and distinct type. A derived type is a new base type; it is *not* compatible with the type from which it is derived. Furthermore, types which are derived from the same type are not compatible. This means that values from two different types cannot be operated upon together by the same operator even if one type is derived from the other. The *parent type* of a derived type is the type from which the derived type was derived. Derived types *inherit* the operations and a copy of the available values of their parent type.

```
procedure Derived_Type_Demo is
   type Orange_Count is new INTEGER;
   type Apple_Count is new INTEGER;
   Oranges_In_Box, Oranges_On_Shelf: Orange_Count;
   Apples_In_Box: Apple_Count;
   Dropped_Fruit, Total_Fruit: INTEGER;
begin
   Oranges_On_Shelf := Apples_In_Box;        -- illegal
   Oranges_In_Box := Dropped_Fruit;          -- illegal
   Oranges_On_Shelf := 100 - Oranges_In_Box;
end Derived_Type_Demo;
```

Program 13–1

The procedure **Derived_Type_Demo** in Program 13–1 illustrates the various incompatibilities. To avoid mixing up the counting of apples and oranges, two distinct derived types are created. Line 8 has a syntax error because the assignment operator requires the type of the right-hand side be compatible with the type of the left-hand side, and distinct derived types are not compatible. Line 9 illustrates that the derived type **Orange_Count** is not compatible with the **INTEGER** type from which it was derived.

Line 10 shows a legal use of derived types. Both variables are of the same type, **Orange_Count**. The subtraction operator is defined on values of type **Orange_Count** because a derived type inherits the properties of its parent. The parent of **Orange_Count** is **INTEGER**, for which a subtraction operator is defined. The literal 100 is legal because a derived type receives a copy of the values of the parent type. So both **Orange_Count** and **Apple_Count** are allowed to use all the values available for the type **INTEGER** and all the operations that are predefined for the type **INTEGER**. However, being distinct types, using one type where the other should have been used will be detected by the compiler as a syntax error.

Derived types allow the specification of a range constraint, as in

```
type Small_Count is new INTEGER range -100..100;
```

Keep in mind the important distinction that a derived type (with or without a range constraint) is not compatible with the type from which it was derived, whereas a subtype (with or without a range constraint) is compatible. The type **Small_Count** is very different from

```
subtype Little_Count is INTEGER range -100..100;
```

Little_Count is compatible with **INTEGER**; **Small_Count** is not.

Derived types of discriminated types and of unconstrained types are allowed. For example, in

```
type Days is (Mon, Tue, Wed, Thur, Fri, Sat, Sun);
type Project is array (Days range <>) of INTEGER:
type New_Project is new Project;
```

the type **Project** is an unconstrained array from which the type **New_Project** is derived. As with other derived types, **Project** and **New_Project** are not compatible. Both **Project** and **New_Project** are unconstrained types.

Derived types may (or may not) have discriminants or constraints supplied. We have illustrated the case of not supplying them with the definition of **New_Project**. By contrast, in the declaration:

```
type Weekend_Project is new Project(Sat..Sun);
```

a constraint is supplied. The type **Weekend_Project** is a constrained type. Of course, it is not compatible with either **New_Project** or **Project**. However, this is because it is derived, not because of the constraint.

Constraints are inherited. Thus, if we declare

```
type Short_Project is new Weekend_Project;
```

The type **Short_Project** is a constrained array type with a range of **Sat..Sun**. Remember, that in contrast to types, objects must have constraints. Thus, in declaring an object of type **New_Project**, as in

```
Paint_House: New_Project(Sat..Sun);
```

a constraint must be supplied. Again, the variable **Paint_House** is not compatible with variables of type **Weekend_Project**, despite the fact that the constraints are the same. Constraints can result in **CONSTRAINT_ERROR**, but they do not affect type compatibility.

If a discriminant is not supplied, the defaults on discriminants are inherited. Thus, in the declarations

```
type Employee_Record(Hourly: BOOLEAN := TRUE) is
  record
    case Hourly is
      when TRUE  => Hourly_Rate: INTEGER;
      when FALSE => Monthly_Rate: INTEGER;
    end case;
  end record;
type Public_Employee is new Employee_Record;
type Executive_Employee is new Employee_Record(FALSE);
```

the default value of the discriminant component is inherited by the derived type **Public_Employee**. If we declare an object without supplying the default, as in

```
George: Public_Employee;
```

that record uses the default value of the discriminant, in this case the value **TRUE**. Remember this is a default value; record objects of type **Public_Employee** can be explicitly declared with a discriminant of either value, **TRUE** or **FALSE**. On the other hand, if the derived type supplies a value for the discriminant, as is the case for the type **Executive_Employee**, all records of that type are constrained to have that discriminant.

Initial values on record types are inherited. So in the declarations

```
type Bank_Balance is
  record
    Amount: INTEGER := 0;
    User_Id: INTEGER;
  end record;
type New_Account is new Bank_Balance;
```

record variables of the type **New_Account** have a default initialization of **0** for the **Amount** component.

13.3.1 Type Conversions

Sometimes it is necessary to convert from one type to another. For example, in **Derived_Type_Demo** in Program 13–1, we might want to compute **Total_Fruit** by adding the numbers of **Apples_In_Box** and **Oranges_In_Box**. If it is necessary to convert from one derived type to another, explicit type conversion must be used. The syntax for explicit type conversion is given in Figure 13–2.

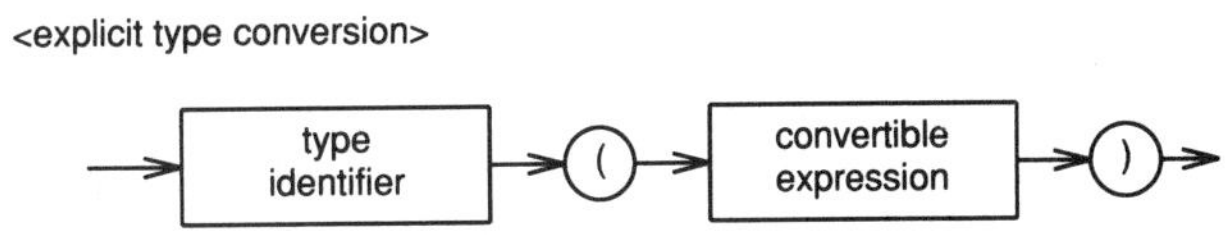

Figure 13–2

A type conversion takes a value of one type and converts it into the equivalent value in another type. If the expression is converted to a type with a constraint, that constraint is checked. The following are examples of explicit type conversions that could occur within **Derived_Type_Demo**:

```
Total_Fruit := INTEGER(Apples_In_Box) + INTEGER(Oranges_In_Box);
Apples_In_Box := Apple_Count(Oranges_In_Box + 1);
```

Type conversions are possible between types derived from the same ancestor, even if the derivation is several steps long. No matter how long the derivation, the conversions themselves are direct.

All the type conversions in the procedure **Convert_Types** shown in Program 13–2 are legal. For example, at line 12, **INTEGER** is an ancestor of both **Apple_Count** (the type of **Crabs**), **Small_Count** (the type of **Little_Oranges**), and **Green_Count** (the type of **Unripe**). Thus, these types are convertible to each other. In line 15, we consider **INTEGER** to be an ancestor of itself, so that **Dropped_Fruit** (type **INTEGER**) and **Unripe** (type **Green_Count**) are convertible. In fact, since **INTEGER** is an ancestor of every type declared in this procedure, all the types declared here are convertible to each other. Finally, note that the conversion to **Small_Count** in line 14 may cause a constraint error if the value of **Dropped_Fruit** is outside the allowable range for **Small_Count**. This error would be raised at the point of the conversion.

An explicit type conversion may be used in an actual parameter list. For example, if the procedure **Count_Fruit** is declared as

```
procedure Count_Fruit(X: in out Apple_Count) ...
```

it could be called as

```
Count_Fruit(Apple_Count(Little_Oranges));
```

```
procedure Convert_Types is
   type Orange_Count is new INTEGER;
   type Small_Count is new Orange_Count range -100..100;
   type Green_Count is new Small_Count;
   type Apple_Count is new INTEGER;
   Oranges_In_Box: Orange_Count;
   Little_Oranges: Small_Count;
   Unripe: Green_Count;
   Crabs: Apple_Count;
   Dropped_Fruit: INTEGER;
begin
   Unripe := Green_Count(Crabs) + Green_Count(Little_Oranges);
   Oranges_In_Box := 100 - Orange_Count(Unripe);
   Little_Oranges := Small_Count(Dropped_Fruit);
   Dropped_Fruit := INTEGER(Unripe);
end Convert_Types;
```

Program 13–2

Conversion occurs before and/or after the procedure is called. Parameters of mode **in** are converted and then passed. Parameters of mode **out** are passed (out) and then unconverted. Parameters of mode **in out** are converted and then passed in, passed out and then unconverted. With the preceding declaration, a constraint error occurs if **Count_Fruit** attempts to exit with a value outside the range of **Small_Count** in the formal parameter **X**. Because the conversion is part of the actual parameter list, exceptions raised during conversion are raised at the point of call.

The standard rules of parameter association and the "all or nothing" rule on defaults apply to derived types with discriminants. Procedure **Derived** in Program 13–3 illustrates the interaction of derived types and discriminants. In this procedure, two types, **True_Case** in line 9 and **False_Case** in line 11, are derived from the discriminated type **Discriminated** declared in lines 2–8. According to the rules of Ada, conversion between these two types is possible. Thus, the conversion in line 14 is syntactically legal. However, a **CONSTRAINT_ERROR** is raised because a value with a discriminant of **FALSE** cannot be changed into a value with a discriminant of **TRUE**.

13.3.2 Derivable Subprograms

As mentioned before, subprograms may be derivable. Since operators are a specific kind of subprogram, this discussion also applies to them. By derivable Ada means that a subprogram is inherited by a derived type. There are two ways for a subprogram to be derivable. Subprograms of a parent type are derivable by derived types if:

1. The parent type and the subprogram are declared in the visible part of the same package, or
2. The parent type is a derived type which has inherited the subprogram under rule 1.

```
procedure Derived is
  type Discriminated(B: BOOLEAN) is
    record
      case B is
        when TRUE => Y: INTEGER;
        when FALSE => Z: CHARACTER;
      end case;
    end record
  type True_Case is new Discriminated(TRUE);
  True_Var: True_Case;
  type False_Case is new Discriminated(FALSE);
  False_Var: False_Case;
begin
  True_Var := True_Case(False_Var);     -- CONSTRAINT_ERROR
end Derived;
```

Program 13–3

The derived subprogram behaves as though it were declared at the point of the derived type declaration.

In Program 13–4, the type **Money** and the subprogram **Interest** are declared within the visible part of the package **Banker**. Therefore, by rule 1, **Interest** is derivable. When the derived type **Dollars** is declared in line 14, it inherits the subprogram **Interest**. This inherited version behaves as though it were declared at line 14 — that is, as though it were declared at the same point as the type **Dollars**. Thus, in line 20, the subprogram **Interest** refers to this derived subprogram.

The derived type **Checking** is declared from the derived type **Dollars**. Consequently, by rule 2, it inherits all subprograms inherited by **Dollars**. Thus, the subprogram **Interest** is inherited by **Checking** under rule 2. This derived version of **Interest** behaves as though it were declared at line 16. The call in line 21 refers to this derived subprogram **Interest**.

In the case of a derived subprogram, the effect is equivalent to converting the inputs, calling the function, then unconverting the outputs. For example, the call at line 20 is equivalent to converting the parameters from type **Dollars** to from type **Money**, then calling the function. On return it is equivalent to returning, and then converting the return value from type **Money** to type **Dollars**. At these implicit conversions, constraints are checked and **CONSTRAINT_ERROR** can be raised.

Not all subprograms are derivable. If, later in the declaration of **Derived_Subrograms**, there appeared the package

```
package Not_Derivable is
  function Weight(Amount: Money; Unit_Weight: INTEGER) return INTEGER;
end Not_Derivable;
```

the subprogram **Weight** would not be inherited by types derived from the type **Money**.

```
procedure Derived_Subprograms is
  package Banker is
    type Money is new INTEGER;
    function Interest(Amount: Money; Rate: INTEGER) return Money;
  end Banker;
  package body Banker is
    function Interest(Amount: Money; Rate: INTEGER) return Money is
    begin
      return Amount * Money(Rate);
    end Interest;
  end Banker;
  procedure Compute_Interest is
    use Banker;
    type Dollars is new Money;         -- inherits Interest from Money
    Adjustment, Savings: Dollars;
    type Checking is new Dollars;      -- inherits Interest from Dollars
    Account_1, Account_2: Checking;
    Interest_Rate: INTEGER;
  begin
    Adjustment := Interest(Savings, Interest_Rate);
    Account_1 := Interest(Account_2, Interest_Rate);
  end Compute_Interest;
  ...
```

Program 13–4

This is because the declaration of **Weight** is not in the *same* package declaration as the type **Money**. Similarly, the type **Money** does not inherit subprograms (or operators) defined for the type **INTEGER**, except for those declared in package **STANDARD**, which is where the type **INTEGER** is defined.

In the case of rule 1, the subprogram becomes derivable after the visible part of the package. Thus, in the declarations

```
package Not_Derivable_2 is
  type X is
    record
      Y: INTEGER;
    end record;
  type Z is new X;
  ...
```

the derived type **Z** does *not* derive any subprograms declared in **Not_Derivable_2**. If type **Z** were declared outside the visible part of the package declaration, it would derive those subprograms.

Derived types are allowed within package declarations; this is the way they create derivable subprograms. But there is a restriction: A derived type or private type may not be used to create another derived type within the visible part of the declaration part in which it is defined. For example, in the declarations

```
package Not_Good is
  type X is new INTEGER;
  type Z is new X;          -- illegal
  type P is private;
  type Q is new P;          -- illegal
private
  type P is ...
end Not_Good;
```

X is a legal derived type, but type **Z** cannot be derived from **X** in the same visible part. Furthermore, since the private type **P** is declared in this package, the type **Q** cannot be derived from **P** in this visible part. In other packages, types can be derived from **X** and **P**. In fact, types can even be derived from **X** and **P** within the body of package **Not_Good**.

13.4 INTEGER TYPES

We have seen one of Ada's integer types and one of its real types. Ada allows other numeric types. Numeric types are similar to derived types. For integers, Ada defines a type called *universal integer*. Integer literals are defined to be of this type. Arithmetic operations apply to literals and produce results of type universal integer. There are even universal constants, such as

```
Little_Prime: constant := 3;
Minus_Number: constant := Little_Prime - 4;
```

Notice that neither of these constants indicates a type, and both values are expressions of type universal integer. In Ada terminology, these are *named numbers*. Named numbers are allowed and named integers are of type universal integer, but there are never variables or parameters of type universal integer.

Instead, for parameters and variables, we must use an integer type which inherits operations and literals from the type universal integer. The type **INTEGER** is such a type. Other such types are possible. A new integer type can be declared as follows:

```
type My_Int is range 1..18;
```

The range cannot exceed the implementation bounds on predefined types. The type **INTEGER** is always predefined. The types **LONG_INTEGER** and **SHORT_INTEGER** may also be predefined. The exact nature of the latter two types is not specified by Ada, in fact, it is legal for an implementation not to supply one or either of them.

But when they are supplied, the range of **LONG_INTEGER** is at least that of **INTEGER**. That is **LONG_INTEGER** can store values as big as, and possibly bigger than, **INTEGER**. Analogously, the range of **SHORT_INTEGER** is at most that of **INTEGER**. Conceptually, **LONG_INTEGER** supplies a possibly bigger number than **INTEGER**, but possibly takes more space to store and more time when used in computations, while **SHORT_INTEGER** possibly takes less space and time.

Conceptually, we can think of the arithmetic operations as defined for universal integer and that the arithmetic operators are derivable for all other integer types.

Since all integer types are considered to be derived from a common type, explicit conversion is allowed between integer types. An example of this is in the following code:

```
procedure Convert_Integers is
  type My_Int is range 1..18;
  X: INTEGER;
  Y: LONG_INTEGER;
  Z: My_Int;
begin
  X := INTEGER(Y);
  Y := LONG_INTEGER(X);
  X := INTEGER(Z);
  ...
```

The predefined types and the user-defined types are not compatible, but they are explicitly convertible. Of course, in converting to a type with a more restricted range, as when **Y** is converted to **INTEGER**, a **CONSTRAINT_ERROR** could occur.

The loop parameter of the for schema has a unique interaction with universal integers. Like other parameters and variables, the loop parameter is not permitted to be of the type universal integer. If both bounds on a for schema are integer literals or named numbers, the loop parameter implicitly assumes the type **INTEGER**. Thus, in both for schemata contained in the declarations

```
X:constant := -1;
...
for I in 1..10 ...
for I in X..10 ...
```

the loop parameter **I** has type **INTEGER**. On the other hand, the for schema

```
for I in -1..10  -- illegal
```

is illegal because "**-1**" is neither a literal or a named number; it is an expression. To make this schema legal one would have to say

```
for I in INTEGER range -1..10
```

Again, explicitly stating the type of a range even when it is not required is a good programming practice.

13.4.1 Predefined Integer Operators

We now complete our coverage of two of the predefined integer operators **rem** and **mod**. As mentioned in Chapter 4, with positive operands, these functions produce identical results. With negative operands, they differ. The **rem** operator follows the mathematical conventions for computing remainders. In the expression

```
A rem B
```

the remainder will have same sign as **A**. The magnitude of the remainder does not depend upon the sign of the operands. Specifically, the formula

```
abs(A rem B) = abs(A) rem abs(B)
```

always holds. By hand, it is often best to compute the remainder using positive numbers and then examine **A** to determine the sign of the result.

The **mod** operator follows the mathematical conventions for computing the modulus. The best way to think of **mod** is that the answers cycle. For example, for **mod 3** the answers will cycle in the sequence

```
0 1 2 0 1 2 ...
```

That is, whenever **I mod 3** is **1** then **(I+1) mod 3** will be **2** and **(I+2) mod 3** will be **0**.

In the expression

```
A mod B
```

the expression is always between **0** and one short of **B**. For example, if **B** is **-3** the cycle will be

```
0 -2 -1 0 -2 -1  ...
```

To get the cycle correct, one only has to get started correctly. This is easy because the small numbers of the correct sign are their own mods. For example, with our example of **B** being **-3**, **-2 mod B** will be **-2**. Notice what this does to the positive numbers when we line up **-2 mod B** and **-1 mod B** in the following table.

```
number:    -2 -1 0  1  2  ...
mod B:     -2 -1 0 -2 -1  ...
```

We see that **2 mod B** is **-1**!

An alternative way to remember this is that the cycle always increases. For **B** of **3** the cycle goes **0**, **1**, **2**, and then cycles. For **B** of **-3** the cycle goes **-2**, **-1**, **0**, and then cycles. In both cases, numbers divisible by **B** have a **mod** of **0**.

Using these simple tricks, it is easy to compute **rem** and **mod** whenever it is necessary to do so to check the correctness of a program.

13.5 TYPE CONVERSION

We have seen type conversion between derived types and integer types. In Chapter 14 we will see that conversion applies between all numeric types. One additional case of type conversion is allowed with arrays. Two array types may be converted if they have the same dimension, the type of their components is the same and their indices are convertible. For example, consider the following declarations:

```
type My_Int is range 1..18;
type A is array (INTEGER range 1..10) of INTEGER;
type B is array (My_Int range 1..10) of INTEGER;
type C is array (My_Int range 1..10) of My_Int;
subtype Small_Count is INTEGER range 1..10;
type D is array (My_Int range 1..10) of Small_Count;
A1: A; B1: B; C1: C; D1: D;
```

Type conversion is allowed between types **A** and **B**: Both are one dimensional, both have components of type **INTEGER**, and the index of type **INTEGER** is convertible to an index of type **My_Int**. Thus, the assignment

```
A1 := A(B1);
```

is legal. The type **C** is not convertible to either **A** or **B** because the components of **C** are not the same type as the components of **A** or **B**. The type **D** is technically convertible to **A** and **B** because the components of **D** are the same type as the components of **A** and **B**. However, in an assignment such as

```
D1 := D(A1);   -- CONSTRAINT_ERROR
```

a constraint error will occur because the constraints on **Small_Count** are not the same as the constraints on **INTEGER**. The constraints on the components must be the same for the conversion to occur.

Derived types, numeric types, and convertible arrays are the only three cases where explicit conversion is allowed. Thus, with the declarations

```
type A is
  record
    X: INTEGER;
  end record;
```

```
type B is
  record
    X: INTEGER;
  end record;
A1: A;
B1: B;
```

the conversion

```
A1 := A(B1);    -- illegal
```

is illegal because it is not one of the three legal cases.

13.6 OVERLOADING ENUMERATION LITERALS

An identifier or operator is overloaded whenever it has more than one possible meaning. We saw in Chapter 10 that subprogram identifiers can be overloaded. Overloading of operators and subprogram identifiers allows the creation of families of subprograms. If unrelated subprograms utilize the same identifier, or if unrelated operations use the same operator, readability is decreased. So in good programming practice, subprograms with similar names should perform similar actions.

Enumeration literals can also be overloaded. Sometimes such an overloading improves the readability of a program. The rules for overloading allow an identifier to be used in several enumeration lists. Thus, the declarations

```
type Traffic_Signal is (Green, Yellow, Red);
type Wire_Color is (Red, Black, White);
```

are legal, even when they occur in the same declaration part. In these declarations, the identifier **Red** is overloaded. Within the declarative region, **Red** can refer either to a value of type **Traffic_Signal** or to a value of type **Wire_Color**. A program containing overloaded enumeration identifiers is legal, provided that for each occurrence of an overloaded identifier, there is exactly one legal interpretation. This is the same rule as for overloaded subprogram identifiers. Thus the code

```
X: Traffic_Signal;
  ...
X := Red;
```

would be legal because the overloaded identifier **Red** must be interpreted as of type **Traffic_Signal** for the statement to be legal. This use of **Red** could not be interpreted as a value of type **Wire_Color**, because this would cause a syntax error due to conflict between the type of **Red** and the type of **X**.

Sometimes the context is insufficient to restrict the number of legal interpretations to one. To allow the programmer to force an interpretation, Ada provides *qualified reference*. Qualified reference declares the type of the qualified expression, thus forcing a particular interpretation. For example,

```
Wire_Color'(Red)
```

forces the expression "**Red**" to be interpreted as of type **Wire_Color**. Qualification can be applied to any expression.

The use of qualification to disambiguate overloaded identifiers is illustrated by the following procedure:

```
procedure A is
  type Water_State is (Solid, Liquid, Gas);
  type Assests is (Liquid, Fixed);
  procedure Usable(Water_Condition: Water_State);
  procedure Usable(Investment_Condition: Assets);
  ...
begin
  Usable(Liquid);                          -- illegal
  Usable(Water_Condition => Liquid);
  Usable(Assets'(Liquid));
end A;
```

The first call to **Usable** is illegal because it is impossible to distinguish which procedure is supposed to be called. One interpretation would be for **Liquid** to be of **Water_State** and the procedure to be

```
procedure Usable(Water_Condition: Water_State);
```

A second interpretation would be for **Liquid** to be of **Assets** and the procedure to be

```
procedure Usable(Investment_Condition: Assets);
```

Since both interpretations are possible, the call is ambiguous and, consequently, illegal.

The second call to **Usable** is distinguishable and legal because only one of the procedures has a formal parameter named **Water_Condition**. The third call is distinguishable and legal because only one of the procedures has a formal parameter of type **Assets**. In this last call, a qualified expression is used to force the actual parameter to be interpreted as being of type **Assets**.

13.6.1 Character Literals

Character literals actually are much more similar to identifiers than we have previously shown. Thus far, we have used character literals only in conjunction with the type

CHARACTER. This type is predefined in package **STANDARD** in the same way as the type **BOOLEAN** is predefined there. The type **CHARACTER** contains the character literal values in the same way as the type **BOOLEAN** contains the values **FALSE** and **TRUE**. Because **FALSE** and **TRUE** are not reserved words, we can create new meanings for these identifiers. For example, we could create a new enumeration type by the declaration

```
type Fuzzy_Logic is (False, Maybe, True);
```

The type **CHARACTER** is an enumeration which contains the character literals. In the same way that we can declare new enumeration types using the identifiers **True** and **False**, we can also declare new enumeration types using the character literals. For example, we could declare

```
type Grades is ('A', 'B', 'C', 'D', 'F', No_Report);
```

This new enumerated type has six values: five character literals and an identifier. Together, the character literals and the identifier constitute the enumeration literals of the type **Grades**. A few examples point up the difference between **Grades** and **CHARACTER**. The value of **Grades'POS('A')** is 0 because **A** is the first value in the enumeration list of the type **Grades**. By contrast, the value of **CHARACTER'POS('A')** is 65 because in the enumeration list of the type **CHARACTER**, there are 65 values in front of **'A'**. The value of **Grades'SUCC('D')** is **'F'**, because **F** follows **'D'** in the enumeration of **Grades**. By contrast, the value of **CHARACTER'SUCC('D')** is **'E'**, because **E** follows **'D'** in the enumeration of **CHARACTER**.

To repeat our point, character literals can be overloaded in enumeration lists and can be mixed with identifiers in the same enumeration list. The order of the enumeration defines the ordering of all identifiers and character literals in a particular enumeration.

The package **Roman_Numerals** in Program 13–5 uses an enumeration type containing character literals. In the enumeration type **Roman_Literal** the lowest four Roman numeral values (**'I'**, **'V'**, **'X'**, **'L'**) and a place holder (**' '**) are defined. The procedure **Roman_Read** is designed to read in a string and convert it into a Roman numeral. Note that character literals include the apostrophes. This distinguishes them from identifiers. For example, if we directly said

```
Count: Roman_Literal := 'V';
  ...
Roman_IO.PUT(Count);
```

the three characters **'V'** would have been printed. Similarly, if we directly read a Roman literal we would need to type quotes around each of the characters. In the case of **CHARACTER**, **TEXT_IO** removes the characters on printing and adds the characters on reading. With respect to reading, we accomplish this with the procedure **Roman_Read**. This procedure reads a string in line 13. The **Get_Line** procedure in line 13 places the characters read into **Number** and reports how many characters were read in **Size**. The

```
1:package Roman_Numerals is
2:   type Roman_Literal is (' ', 'I', 'V', 'X', 'L');
3:   type Roman_Numeral is array (NATURAL range <>) of Roman_Literal;
4:   procedure Roman_Read(N: out Roman_Numeral);
5:end Roman_Numerals;

6:with TEXT_IO;
7:package body Roman_Numerals is
8:   package Roman_IO is new TEXT_IO.ENUMERATION_IO(Roman_Literal);
9:   procedure Roman_Read(N: out Roman_Numeral) is
10:     Number: STRING(1..80);
11:     Size: NATURAL;
12:  begin
13:     TEXT_IO.GET_LINE(Number, Size);
14:     for I in NATURAL range 1..Size loop
15:       N(I) := Roman_Literal'VALUE(''' & Number(I) & ''');
16:     end loop;
17:     for I in NATURAL range Size + 1..N'LAST loop
18:       N(I) := ' ';
19:     end loop;
20:  end Roman_Read;
21:end Roman_Numerals;
```

Program 13–5

loop in lines 14–16 converts this string into a Roman numeral. Line 15 uses the **VALUE** attribute, but notice that it adds apostrophes to the letter before applying the attribute.

13.7 PROGRAMMING PRACTICES

13.7.1 Abstraction

Throughout this text, we have emphasized how packages provide a method of encapsulation. Package declarations define services and definitions that are available to the user of the package. Subprograms are the services, and types and variables are the definitions. Package bodies define the implementations of the services. Since only the declarations are visible, the implementation is hidden from the user.

Packages provide an *abstraction* of the implementation of subprograms. That is, they hide the internal structure of the services while still providing the user with those services. They contain the subprogram bodies, hidden variables, and hidden types which are used to provide those services.

Because the user has no access to package bodies, the user cannot make assumptions about how the package is implemented. This prevents situations which are common in other languages, where the programmers using a component make assumptions which become incorrect when the implementation of the components is changed. Such changes often occur on fixing an error or on moving to a different operating system.

A type provides a method of encapsulation for data. Private types allow the internal structure of the data to be hidden, while still enabling the user to declare objects and subprograms using the type. Declaring a private type within a package allows the programmer of the package to provide a set of values and a set of operations, while hiding from the user the internal structure of the data and the internal implementation of the operations which act on the data. In this way, private types provide data structure abstraction. Thus, data declarations as well as subprogram bodies can be changed at will (as long as they implement the intent of the declaration).

The design of Ada supports a philosophy that different degrees of restriction are appropriate in different cases. The least degree of restriction is a subtype that provides an additional constraint. Most often this is a range constraint. The subtype provides the least protection and the greatest degree of compatibility with other variables. It should be used when the subtypes with the constraint are continually used in conjunction with subtypes that lack the constraint. The derived type provides a greater degree of protection and a lesser degree of compatibility. It should be used when the types interact occasionally. The points of interaction are obvious because explicit type conversion is required. Derived types should also be used when a new type is supposed to inherit the values and operations of an existing type. A separate type provides the greatest degree of protection and the least degree of compatibility. Separate types should be used when types do not interact and inheritance is not needed.

As has been stressed so often in this text the philosophy supported by the constructs of the Ada language is that it is better to get compiler errors and constraint errors than to compute incorrect answers with no warning.

13.7.2 Object-Oriented Programming

A concept that is related to information hiding, abstraction, and abstract data types is *object-oriented programming*.

Object-oriented programming is a program design technique in which the program designer concentrates on objects (e.g., variables, constants, and values) rather than on the manipulation of values. Most of us who speak English as our native language tend to concentrate on operations, rather than concentrating on the objects and examining how the operations relate to them. The English language encourages this type of thought pattern.

But suppose we turned our thinking around. Suppose that we thought of the bank account as the major item, with the operations (open, deposit, withdraw, close) as "belonging to" the account. We would then think in terms of packages that each corresponded to a single type (and all objects of that type). We would group ideas by data type, rather than by actions to be performed.

Of course, we have been doing this all along in this book. We have been emphasizing the importance of making the structure of objects match the natural structure of the information being stored. We have also often arranged packages around a type or a collection of types. In many situations, it is more natural to model the objects and then the corresponding operations.

One important concept in object-oriented programming is *inheritance*. If a type of object is created as a restricted or otherwise modified version of another type, the operations from the original type should be inheritable by the modified type.

Moreover, when a type (e.g., a record) is defined as a collection of smaller types, we think of the smaller types as keeping their identity and operations. Sometimes the bigger type inherits (at least in the abstract) some of the operations of the smaller types.

Information hiding and data abstraction are also design techniques. These techniques are ways of preventing reliance on trivial (implementation) details, rather than concentrating on the higher level, published information about an operation or data structure. That is, by keeping most information secret, it is possible to prevent abuse of that information.

Abstract data types and packages are tools that can be used to assist in data abstraction, information hiding, and object-oriented programming. All three of these are techniques for designing quality software. In addition, abstract data types and packages are implementation techniques that assist in conveying the intent of the design into the implementation. Representing the agendas of the design in the actual, implemented program is important because it keeps those agendas alive while the program is being modified after development is completed.

Object-oriented programming, information hiding, and data abstraction are terms that have become widely used in computer science. Since the techniques they refer to are often used together, their meanings are often confused. By keeping in mind that there are three separate techniques, and that you can choose one on which to concentrate while designing a program or a piece of a program, you will have a set of tools that can be applied as the need arises.

In a practical sense, confusion between these techniques is not very important. But we summarize them here, so that they can be distinguished at a glance. Object-oriented programming is the technique of concentrating on the objects, rather than the operations. Information hiding is the technique of keeping secrets within subprograms in order to reduce the dependence of one portion of the program on another. Finally, data abstraction is the technique of hiding (or delaying the presentation of) information about a data type to reduce the portions of the program that depend on the specifics of how the type is represented.

13.7.3 Design Techniques

Design of a program should begin with an understanding of the problem to be solved. Some problems involve mostly numerical manipulation, but many involve the maintenance of complex data. For these, plan your data structures first. Consider what sort of data you will need to keep and how you need to organize that data. Next, consider data validity. Design with enumeration types, derived types, and subranges so that the appropriate checks are automatically performed.

Next, structure the program. Consider the operations you will need on the data. Group the appropriate data and operations together. Plan on hiding or protecting as much of the data as possible. These groupings will form your packages.

For very large programs, the process of designing and grouping will need to be repeated at several levels of detail.

13.7.4 Problem Solving

We close this section with the description of a sample program which uses derived types. Many companies use computers to compute their payroll and to maintain records on their employees. The procedure **Payroll** in Program 13–6 is a simplified example of a payroll program that uses derived types. Our first step in creating this program is to structure the data. There are two basic categories of employee data to be stored: data about the employee having to do with the company and data about the employee not related to company business. To reflect this dichotomy the employee's record will be divided into two parts. The personal (non-company) part will contain the minimum data about the employee necessary for company business, the employee's name, and how to contact the employee (phone number and address). We do not want to mix names, phone numbers, and address, but inside the program we may need to manipulate them by insertion or deletion. We choose to do this by deriving these types from the subtype **Normal_Line** in the **Lines** package. This causes these types to inherit the **Insert**, **Delete**, and other subprograms from that package. **Lines** is named in a use clause to make these subprograms directly visible within the procedure.

The employment-related information includes an employee identification number (in case two employees have the same name), a rate at which the employee accrues vacation, a record of the current amount of vacation the employee has accrued, a rate at which the employee is paid, the total salary paid so far this year, and the total amount of tax withheld so far this year. For many of these items, we use types derived from **INTEGER**. Explicit conversion is always available for integer types, so declaring separate integer types (as opposed to derived types) would not give us additional protection.

Notice that we chose very natural categories for these integer types which are reflected in their identifiers. Since all are derivations from the type **INTEGER**, the type conversion in **Compute_Pay** (lines 43–44) is legal. Within the **Employment_Record**, we have chosen to apply explicit range constraints to several components. These range constraints help ensure compliance with company rules. We could also have declared separate types for these ranges, particularly if these restrictions were used outside of the record.

The instantiation in **Get_Employee_Number** (line 61) names the derived type **Employee_Number_Range**, allowing us to **Get** (line 63) a value of that derived type.

13.7.5 Testing: Audit Trails

An *audit trail* is a file into which all input to a program is copied so that when an error occurs, the situation causing the error can be reconstructed. Originally, audit trails were

```
with Text_IO;
with Lines;
procedure Payroll is
-- Purpose: A payroll manager for a company.
  use Lines;
  type Employee_Name is new Lines.Normal_Line;
  type Employee_Address is new Lines.Normal_Line;
  type Employee_Phone is new Lines.Normal_Line;
  type Personal_Record is
    record
      Name: Employee_Name;
      Address: Employee_Address;
      Phone_Number: Employee_Phone;
    end record;

  type Dollars_Per_Hour is new NATURAL;
  type Hours_Per_Month is new NATURAL;
  type Hours is new NATURAL;
  type Dollars is new INTEGER;
  type Employment_Record is
    record
      Vacation_Rate: Hours_Per_Month;
      Vacation_Accrued: Hours;
      Regular_Hours, Overtime_Hours: Hours range 0..40;
      Salary: Dollars_Per_Hour range 4..50;
      Income, Total_Income: Dollars;
      Taxes: Dollars;
    end record;
  type Employee_Record is
    record
      Valid_Record: BOOLEAN := FALSE;
      Personal: Personal_Record;
      Employment: Employment_Record;
    end record;

  type Employee_Number_Range is new POSITIVE range 1..50;
  Employee_Number: Employee_Number_Range;
  -- The employee identification number is same as the position in the array.
  Employees: array (Employee_Number_Range) of Employee_Record;

  procedure Compute_Pay(Who: in out Employment_Record) is
  -- Purpose: Compute the pay for the employee. The record contains
  --   the salary information; use it to update the Income field
  --   of the record.
  begin
    Who.Income := Dollars(Who.Regular_Hours + Who.Overtime_Hours)
                   * Dollars(Who.Salary);
```

Program 13–6

```
    Who.Total_Income := Who.Total_Income + Who.Income;
  end Compute_Pay;

  procedure Get_Hours(Who: in out Employee_Record) is
  -- Purpose: Get the number of hours worked this week by the employee.
  --   Record the number of hours worked in the employee record.
  --   Data is from the keyboard.
  begin
    null;
  end Get_Hours;

  procedure New_Employee(Who: out Employee_Record) is
  -- Purpose: Get information about a new employee. Build an employee
  -- record for this new person. Data is from the keyboard.
  begin
    null;
  end New_Employee;

  procedure Get_Employee_Number(Number: out Employee_Number_Range) is
    package Emp_IO is new TEXT_IO.INTEGER_IO(Employee_Number_Range);
  begin
    Emp_IO.Get(Employee_Number);
  end Get_Employee_Number;

begin  -- Payroll
  loop
    Get_Employee_Number(Employee_Number);
    if not Employees(Employee_Number).Employment.Valid_Record then
      New_Employee(Employees(Employee_Number));
    end if;
    Get_Hours(Employees(Employee_Number));
    Compute_Pay(Employees(Employee_Number).Employment);
    Assign(Employees(2).Personal.Name, "joe");
  end loop;
end Payroll;
```

Program 13–6 Continued

the paperwork saved so that an auditor could check to ensure that a company was keeping its books accurately. Later, the term was applied to a computer file that kept the same information; the auditor could check the data calculated against the information entered.

A common use of an audit trail is as a source of information for rebuilding a data base that has been corrupted by either a program error or a system "crash". In this case, the data base is periodically copied to preserve an error-free copy of the data base as of some particular date and time. The copy is called a *checkpoint*. In case of disaster, the last checkpoint file can be loaded and the program can execute the commands that have been saved in the audit trail to rebuild the data base to the state that existed just before the crash.

If the problem is a bug in the program, rather than a system crash, the checkpoint and audit trail allow the data base to be reconstructed up to the point just before the error occurred. This copy of the data base can then be used as a new checkpoint, and processing can continue. Of course, the inputs that triggered the bug cannot be included in the reconstruction, as this would just trigger the bug again. In fact, this technique is often used to determine that the problem is a bug in the program, rather than a hardware error. By copying the partially restored data base and executing the program on the last few inputs in the audit trail, with testing statements in place, the programmer can determine exactly what went wrong. Once the problem is located, the program can be fixed.

In many programs, there are no checkpoint files and there is no data base to restore. An audit trail file is also useful in this type of program to provide the programmer with a tool with which to determine exactly what went wrong with the program in case of an error. This technique is often called *instrumenting* the program. In this case, the audit trail is often saved only for one execution of the program and is replaced the next time the program is executed.

The audit trail is much better than the user's explanation because the user may not remember exactly what was entered. In fact, the user will often remember only what the user intended to enter, while the bug may have been triggered by a typing error. It is then possible that entering the information with just a one character difference would fail to trigger the bug again.

As with other testing assistance, the amount of time required for instrumenting a program can be quite large. Usually, the audit trail must be written to a file, and output to files is quite slow on most computer systems. Instrumentation is often removed before releasing the program, in order to improve the execution speed of the program. Unfortunately, instrumentation is most useful when the program is being used by real users, that is, after the program is released.

13.8 ADA SUMMARY

This chapter provides coverage of *derived types*. It gives a full explanation of how to declare them, how to use them, and why to use them. It illustrates how the values of the old type are inherited by the new type. It also provides details about when subprograms and operators are *derivable*.

The related topic of integer types was also covered. Although derived types of the type **INTEGER** are allowed, integer types may also be directly declared by specifying the range of allowable numbers. Although integer types are distinct, integer literals are compatible with any type and *explicit conversion* between types is allowed.

This chapter continues the coverage of overloading in Ada. It introduces the concept of the *overloading of enumeration literals*. A literal may belong to multiple types and may be used throughout a program, as long as the compiler can always unambiguously use the context of the literal to determine to which type it belongs. We have illustrated qualified reference as a means of disambiguating any literal. We have shown that *character literals* are enumeration literals.

Finally, we have discussed the concept of *abstraction* and how this concept can be used in designing programs.

EXERCISES

13.1. Convert the procedure **Payroll** in Program 13–6 to a package and the type **Dollars** into a type **Money**. In a main program, declare the derived types **Dollars** and **Lire**. Modify **Payroll** so that employee records can be maintained in either denomination, using a record with a variant part.

13.2. Change **Compute_Pay** to time-and-a-half for overtime up to 20 hours and double-time for overtime hours over 20.

13.3. Write a **Computations** package that provides a set of functions to calculate various areas based on some unit of measure. The package declaration is as follows:

```
package Computations is
  type Unit is new FLOAT;
  function Area_Of_Rectangle(Height, Width: Unit) return Unit;
  function Area_Of_Circle(Radius: Unit) return Unit;
  function Area_Of_Triangle(Base, Height: Unit) return Unit;
end Computations;
```

Now, write a program that declares two specific units of measure: centimeters and inches. You will need to make conversion functions that convert inches to centimeters and vice versa. In addition, you should maintain a current total of the areas you compute. Present the user with the following selection of actions:

1. Choose one of the computations to perform. You will have to request further information, based on which computation is chosen. When such a computation is done, it needs to be done twice, once for each measure.

2. Display the current total of all the areas computed so far in both square inches and square centimeters.

3. Reset the current total to zero.

4. Quit the program.

13.4. Implement a variation of the **Phone_Book** package in Program 8–8. To prevent possible mixups between names and addresses and phone numbers, you will need to derive new **Normal_Line** types. An example would be a new **Name_Type** for the components in the name record.

13.5. Modify the **Roman_Numerals** package in Program 13–5. 1) Define the operation addition on the type **Roman_Numeral**. 2) Define conversions between **INTEGER** and **Roman_Numeral**.

13.6. Hexadecimal numbers are numbers represented in base 16. Hexadecimal digits are 0, 1, 2, 3, 4, 5, 6, 7, 8, 9, A, B, C, D, E, F. Thus, hexadecimal A is the equivalent of decimal 10, hexadecimal F is decimal 15, hexadecimal 10 is decimal 16, and hexadecimal 1A is decimal 26.

You are to write a hexadecimal package that declares a type for a hexadecimal number and that declares and implements the following functions:

```
type Hex_Chars is ('0', '1', '2', '3', '4', '5', '6', '7', '8', '9',
                   'A', 'B', 'C', 'D', 'E', 'F');
type Hexadecimal is array (INTEGER range <>) of Hex_Chars;
function Hex_To_Decimal(Number: Hexadecimal) return INTEGER;
-- Purpose: Convert a given hexadecimal number to its decimal equivalent.
function Decimal_To_Hex(Number: INTEGER) return Hexadecimal;
-- Purpose: Convert a given decimal number to its hexadecimal equivalent.
function "+"(Left, Right: Hexadecimal) return Hexadecimal;
-- Purpose: Return the result of adding two hexadecimal numbers together.
function Image(Number: Hexadecimal) return STRING;
-- Purpose: Return the string representation of the given hexadecimal number.
function Value(Number: STRING) return Hexadecimal;
-- Purpose: Return the hexadecimal number of the given string representation.
```

In a separate file, implement a testing routine for this package.

13.7. Implement a **Truncate** function, along with a main program to test the function. The function should take a parameter of type **FLOAT** and return a value of type **INTEGER**. The value returned should be the integer portion of the parameter. Remember, conversion rounds instead of truncating.

14

Numeric Types

14.1 OBJECTIVES

This chapter discusses the nature of real numbers in Ada (section 3). The first of two categories of real types is the floating point types (section 4). Floating point numbers are used in many scientific applications. We discuss these types in detail and mention a few of the concerns in programs that use floating point types. The second category is the fixed point types (section 5). Fixed point types are used in many business calculations. We show how to use these types to achieve representations of numbers that are appropriate to the dollars and cents of business applications. Finally, we extend our coverage of numeric literals by introduced based literals (section 6) that allow us to express previous numeric literals in bases other than base 10.

CONCEPTS:

- Numbers have varying degrees of precision.
- A knowledge of precision, accuracy, and their consequences is necessary for those who write numeric programs.

GOALS:

- Write a program that uses floating point numbers.
- Write a program that uses fixed point numbers.

14.2 MOTIVATION

There are two fundamental numeric types: integer and real. In Chapter 13, we saw that there may be several predefined integer types and the user may declare additional integer types. In Chapter 6, we have seen one real type, the type **FLOAT**. In this chapter, we cover the full range and power of the real types that are available in Ada.

The real types in Ada can support both scientific and business calculations. The domain that defines how best to perform the computations in these areas is called numerical analysis. Numerical analysis is beyond the scope of our presentation. However, we shall discuss some of the problems that arise with real types. We shall also discuss the tools Ada provides so that you as a programmer will have sufficient familiarity with them to apply Ada to the concepts learned in a numerical analysis course.

14.3 REAL NUMBERS

As we discussed in Chapter 6, unlike in mathematics, the storage of real numbers on a computer is of limited precision and computations with real numbers are of limited accuracy. In writing programs using real numbers, it is often necessary to know the precision of the numbers you are using and the accuracy of the computations performed. We will find within the real types the capabilities to declare types with a given precision and to ascertain the precision of a given real object. For most computers, the accuracy of the individual arithmetic operations is at least equal to the precision with which they may be stored.

Ada has two classes of real types: floating point types and fixed point types. The predefined type **FLOAT** is a floating point type. Floating point types provide a given number of digits of precision. The concept of precision is traditionally used by people in areas such as science, where measurements have inherent inaccuracies.

Fixed point types provide a fixed number of digits after the decimal point. This is the form usually used in business calculations. For instance, money, when expressed in dollars, always has two places after the decimal point.

14.4 FLOATING POINT TYPES

The basis of floating point numbers is scientific notation. Scientific notation is a method of writing fractions and large numbers that has traditionally been used by scientists and engineers. Scientific notation reflects the fact that most numbers in scientific computations are approximations.

Scientific notation uses a *mantissa* and an *exponent*. For example, the number 6.02×10^{23}, has a mantissa of 6.02 and an exponent of 23. The mantissa defines the number and its precision, while the exponent defines the location of the decimal point. Positive exponents mean that the decimal point belongs to the right of where it is shown. Negative exponents mean that it belongs to the left. A zero or no exponent means that it belongs where it is shown. In our example, the exponent of 23 means that the decimal point belongs 23 places to the right of where it is shown. The number represented is thus 602,000,000,000,000,000,000,000. The first reason a scientist would use scientific notation rather than the latter form is the ease with which zeros can accidentally be added or dropped in the latter form. The second reason is that, due to the approximate nature of the number, we do not know these digits are zeros. So writing them really misrepresents what we know.

In scientific notation, a number can be written any number of ways. The number 3.14159 is the same as the number 314.159×10^{-2}. Expressed the second way, the number says the decimal point belongs two places to the left. Expressed the first way, the number says the decimal point belongs where it is. Yet another way of writing the same number is 0.314159×10^{1}.

In scientific notation, it is customary to write a number with one nonzero digit in front of the decimal point. Thus, the notation 3.14159 is "standard," although the other forms are permitted. Other examples of numbers in standard scientific notation are 6.023×10^{23}, 2.71828, and 6.63×10^{-34}. Standard scientific notation consists of a mantissa of at least 1.0, but less than 10.0, and an exponent part indicating where the decimal point belongs.

We measure precision as the number of digits given in the mantissa. It does not depend on the exponent. Precision is often measured as the number of significant digits. This representation of precision is called *relative* precision. In standard form the relative precision is one plus the number of digits after the decimal point. Thus, 6.023 has four significant digits of precision and 3.14159 has six significant digits of precision.

The scientific concept is that we can only measure with limited accuracy. Writing down more digits than the accuracy of measurement is a fanciful guess as to what those additional digits should be. Within a computer the number of digits is an issue for another reason. The precision of a computer's floating point number is related to the amount of room allocated to store that number. Thus, for a given variable, we might allocate only enough storage space to store three digits for the mantissa. Likewise, the amount of storage space for the exponent limits the size of the exponent that can be stored. These limitations imposed by storage create some problems when using floating point numbers in programs.

In Ada, the definition of *canonical form* for real numbers differs slightly from standard scientific notation. In Ada's canonical form, the mantissa always has a zero before the decimal point and the first digit after the decimal point is nonzero. Canonical forms for our preceding examples are 0.6023×10^{24}, 0.271828×10^{1}, and 0.663×10^{-33}.

By *digits* of precision, Ada means the number of digits after the decimal point in canonical form, which for the preceding numbers is 4, 6, and 3, respectively. Thus, the number of digits of precision in Ada is the same as the number of digits of precision in scientific notation.

The syntax for real literals, which include floating point literals, is given in Figure 14–1.

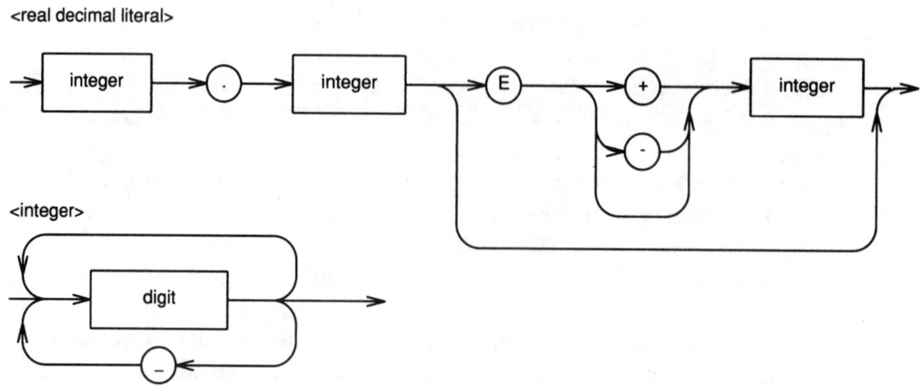

Figure 14–1

As examples of literals in this format, we give two representations of each of the preceding floating point numbers:

```
0.6023E24        27.1828          0.663E-33
60.23E22         2.718_28E+1      6.63E-3_4
```

Although, underscores are allowed in the integer representing the exponent, in general, exponents are too small to warrant the use of underscores. The last number listed represents a poor use of the underscore.

The declaration of a floating point type always uses the reserved word **digits**. The syntax for defining a floating point type is shown in Figure 14–2.

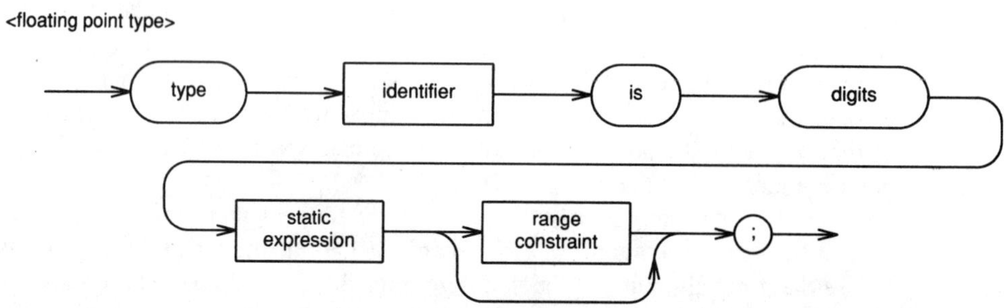

Figure 14–2

In every Ada implementation, there is always one predefined floating point type **FLOAT**. On a typical machine **FLOAT** might be expected to have about six digits of precision. In addition, the floating point types **LONG_FLOAT** and **SHORT_FLOAT** may be predefined. The syntax allows the programmer to define floating point types. Some examples of floating point declarations are:

```
type A is digits 10;
type B is digits 6;
type C is digits 6 range 0.0 .. 1.0;
type D is digits 8 range 0.0 .. 1.0E10;
type E is digits 4 range -100.0 .. 100.0;
```

When declaring a floating point type, the number of digits *must* be specified. A range constraint may also be specified. As with other range constraints, the implementation is responsible for ensuring that the range constraint is enforced on objects of that type. If no range is provided, the system supplies a default range.

Subtypes of floating point types may be constructed. Some example declarations are:

```
subtype F is FLOAT digits 5;
subtype H is A digits 5;
subtype I is C range 0.0 .. 1.0;
subtype J is C digits 4;
subtype K is D range 0.0 .. 0.5;
```

Floating point subtypes may specify a number of digits and they may specify a range. The flowing rules apply:

1. The number of digits requested must not exceed that of the type from which the subtype is formed.
2. The range requested must not exceed that of the type from which the subtype is formed.

Violation of either of these rules constitutes a **CONSTRAINT_ERROR**. If the number of digits or range is omitted, it is the same as that of the type from which it is formed.

The difference between floating point types and floating point subtypes is similar to the difference between derived types and subtypes. Floating point types are not type compatible with each other and must be explicitly converted. Floating point subtypes are type compatible; however, as with other subtypes, constraint errors may occur.

As a word of warning, some of the preceding declarations may result in errors because a given implementation cannot support either the requested number of digits or the requested range. This is because **digits** defines the *minimum* number of digits of precision which the implementation must supply and range defines the range the implementation must supply. If the implementation is unable to supply the required number of digits or the required range, an error must be reported at compilation time. This is in keeping with the Ada philosophy that it is better to declare a mistake than to quietly do something that may be wrong.

The existence of numeric types which are not compatible is an important safety feature of Ada. However, since there are a variety of numeric types, there may be a need to convert from one to another. Type conversions are always available between numeric types. The following are some examples:

```
AX: FLOAT;
BX: B;
CX: C;
DX: D;
EX: E;
I: INTEGER;
 ...
AX := FLOAT(CX);
CX := C(BX);
EX := E(CX);
BX := B(I);
I  := INTEGER(EX);
```

In this fragment, all the type conversions shown are legal. Of course, conversions to integer types round the floating point number to the nearest integer. Conversions between floating point types also round: In converting to a floating point type that has less accuracy, whatever rounding is necessary will be performed.

Rounding numbers in a computer is a little different from the rounding you are used to, because computers work in binary. In binary, we use powers of 2, such as halves, fourths, and eighths instead of tenth and hundredths which are powers of 10. Often, computers are in the situation of rounding up or down on the basis of "a half." Various computers have chosen to round up or down by different methods. Ada's definition of rounding seeks to cover most of these methods. Simply stated, in Ada, if a value falls between two mantissas that are representable by the computer, it may be rounded to either one. As a decimal example, 1/3 could be rounded to 0.333 or 0.334, depending on the computer you are using.

In a computer, as with decimal notation, some numbers can be accurately represented using a fixed number of binary digits, while other numbers (like 1/3) repeat. Since floating point numbers have a fixed number of digits, numbers requiring more digits are approximated by a number with our "fixed" number of digits. That is, those numbers which are completely accurate are used as approximations for those which are not.

A *model number* is a number that is exactly representable by the computer. Ada uses model numbers to define the precision of its real types. The model numbers of a floating point type depend on the number of **digits** in that type. We shall denote the number of digits in a type by D.

Computers operate in binary (base 2), while digits are in decimal (base 10), so it happens that there are very short decimal numbers that cannot be exactly represented by the computer. For example, 1.3 requires two decimal digits, however, no matter how much storage you allocate, you cannot exactly represent this number in binary using "standard" notation. Since you cannot exactly represent numbers of D digits of accuracy you must settle for some approximation. The fundamental goal is that no two numbers with D or fewer digits map to the same model number. Thus, the model numbers are the approximations used for D-digit numbers. As defined in Ada, the model numbers are no more accurate than necessary to achieve these goals while allowing for certain differences in rounding.

The rule for Ada is that the model numbers are represented in base 2. That means that places represent powers of 2, such as 1, 2, 4, and 8, instead of representing powers of 10, such as 1, 10, 100, and 1000. In addition, places after the binary point represent powers of 1/2, such as 1/2, 1/4, 1/8, 1/16, 1/32. So model numbers are defined by the number of bits that are needed to achieve the goals. The number of bits B can be defined in terms of the number of digits D by the formula

$$B = \lceil D \times \log(10)/\log(2) \rceil + 1$$

where the notation $\lceil\ \rceil$ means "round up to the next integer."

Model numbers for a type are those with B bits of mantissa after the binary point in binary canonical form.

The preceding formula requires that B be the smallest integer such that

$$2^{-B} \leq \frac{1}{2} \times 10^{-D}$$

The two preceding formulae are equivalent. However, from the second formula, we can more easily see that the distance between model numbers is at most half the distance between D-digit numbers. This means that for each D-digit number there is some model number closer to it than to any other D-digit number. Using the second formulae we can compute the following sample values for B:

For $D = 1$, $\frac{1}{2} \times 10^{-1} = 1/20$. So, the smallest B such that $2^{-B} \leq 1/20$ is 5 ($2^{-5} = 1/32$). Thus, digits of 1 requires 5 bits to store the mantissa.

For $D = 2$, $\frac{1}{2} \times 10^{-2} = 1/200$. So, the smallest B such that $2^{-B} \leq 1/200$ is 8. Thus, digits of 2 requires 8 bits of mantissa.

For $D = 6$, $\frac{1}{2} \times 10^{-6} = 1/2,000,000$. So, the smallest B such that $2^{-B} \leq 1/2,000,000$ is 21. Thus, digits of 6 requires 21 bits of mantissa.

Let's consider in detail the case when digits is 1. As we observed above, in this case B is 5. Canonical binary form always has a 0 in front of the binary point and a 1 after it. For example, canonical binary form for $1\frac{1}{16}$ is 0.10001×2^1. Note: it has 5 bits after the binary point. The model numbers just above 1.0 are 1 , $1\frac{1}{16}$, $1\frac{2}{16}$, $1\frac{3}{16}$, ..., 2. The canonical form for 31/32 is 0.11111×2^0. The model numbers just below 1.0 are: 17/32, 18/32, ..., 31/32, 1. Notice that at 1, the distance between model numbers shifts from 32nds to 16ths. Another such shift happens at 2, a third shift happens at 4, and, indeed, a shift happens at every power of 2. Shifts also happen at every power of 1/2.

Now consider 0.7 and 0.8, which are canonical decimal numbers with one digit of accuracy. Suppose we attempt to represent them using only 4 bits instead of 5 required by the formula. Then the model numbers in this range would be 11/16, 12/16, and 13/16. These translate into decimal as 0.6875, 0.75, and 0.8125. The value 0.7 must be converted (i.e., rounded) to some model number. The value 0.7 lies between 11/16 and 12/16. By the Ada rounding rules, 0.7 might be converted to 0.75. Similarly, the value 0.8 lies between 12/16 and 13/16. By the Ada rounding rules, the value 0.8 might also be converted to 0.75. In order to force 0.7 and 0.8 to be converted to different model numbers we need a minimum of 5 bits. With the appropriate 5 bits, 0.7 lies between 22/32 and 23/32 and 0.8 lies between 25/32 and 26/32. They cannot be converted to the same model number.

Ada limits the range of the model numbers. The rule in Ada is that a model number with B bits in the mantissa is only guaranteed to support an exponent in the range $-4 \times B \cdots +4 \times B$. Remember, this exponent expresses the power of 2 by which the mantissa is multiplied to obtain the actual number. Since $D = 1$ gives $B = 5$, the model numbers of types with one digit have exponents in the range ± 20. That is they are no larger than $2^{\pm 20}$. This means that model numbers for types with one digit of accuracy go up to about $10^{\pm 6}$. Computations outside this range may result in a constraint error or may be inaccurate. According to this formula, the more digits of accuracy, the bigger the guaranteed exponents. For example, with two digits of accuracy ($D = 2$), we have $B = 8$, so our numbers may range up to $2^{\pm 32}$.

An implementation must be able to represent the model numbers for a type, or that type is not legal for that particular implementation. The compiler must detect this illegality. Note that a type may be illegal on one computer, but legal on another that is capable of supplying a greater precision. By declaring a number of digits, you indicate that you are unwilling to have the program run with less than the number of digits declared.

Another type of numbers are the *safe numbers*. The safe numbers are a super set of the model numbers. Safe implies accuracy will be preserved. The difference between safe numbers and model numbers is that safe numbers allow (possibly) bigger exponents. For example, numbers with digits equal to 1 may be allowed to safely have exponents in excess $10^{\pm 6}$. How big the safe numbers can be depends on the implementation and is usually $2^{\pm 127}$, or about $10^{\pm 39}$. The concept is that the implementation guarantees that these additional numbers exist and that they can be used safely and accurately in computations.

14.4.1 Floating Point Attributes

To assist the numerical programmer, Ada supplies several floating point attributes and some additional information.

For each Ada implementation, there is a constant that depends on the implementation called **SYSTEM.MAX_DIGITS**. Actually this constant is a predefined named number **MAX_DIGITS** which is declared in the package **SYSTEM**. The package **SYSTEM** also contains a number of other definitions that depend on the particular implementation. Every Ada implementation includes the package **SYSTEM**. Like other packages, **SYSTEM** must be named in the context clause of the compilation unit which wishes to use its definitions. **MAX_DIGITS** defines the maximum number of digits in the largest floating point type. If you define a floating point type which asks for more precision than this you will get a syntax error because your requested precision will "exceed that of parent type".

The following attributes can be applied to any floating point type. The attribute **DIGITS** returns the number of digits of precision. The attribute **MANTISSA** returns the number of bits used in the model numbers. The attribute **EPSILON** returns the distance between 1.0 and next model number, i.e., the guaranteed relative accuracy. The attribute **LARGE** returns the largest positive model number. The attribute **SMALL** returns the smallest positive model number. The attribute **EMAX** returns the largest exponent allowed on a model number. The attribute **SAFE_SMALL** returns the smallest positive safe number. The attribute **SAFE_LARGE** returns the largest positive safe number; range specifications should not exceed this number. Finally, the attribute **SAFE_EMAX** returns the largest exponent allowed on a safe number.

14.4.2 Arithmetic Operations on Floating Point Numbers

The same operators apply to both floating point and fixed point numbers. When applied to two real numbers of the same type, the operators +, -, *, and / produce a real result of that type. For example, with the declarations

```
type A is digits 10;
X, Y, Z: A;
```

the statement

```
Z := X + Y;
```

computes a result of type **A** from the two operands of type **A** and stores that result in **Z**.

The operator **abs**, when applied to a real type, produces a result of the same real type. Thus, the expression

```
abs X
```

produces a result of type **A**. Similarly, the exponentiation operator allows a value of any real type to be raised to any integer power, and produces a result of the same type. Thus, the expression

```
X ** 3
```

produces a result of type **A**.

The accuracy of any real operation is defined in terms of model numbers. Consider any single real operation. Its inputs are any two model numbers. The exact mathematical result will either be a model number or will be between two model numbers. If the mathematical result is a model number, the operation must yield that model number. If the mathematical result is between two model numbers, the actual result must be at or between those model numbers.

14.4.3 Limitations of Floating Point Numbers

Despite all the capabilities and assistance that Ada provides, the programmer must still handle the various unique problems present in floating point computations. The appropriate place for a detailed discussion of these problems is in a course on numerical analysis. In this chapter we present an overview, so that the student is acquainted with the existence and nature of the various problems.

The first problem we will discuss is *overflow*. Overflow also occurs with integers. Overflow means that the magnitude of a number is too large to represent. For a given floating point type, there is an upper limit on the size of exponent the computer can store. If this limit is exceeded, the number cannot be represented within that type, and overflow will occur.

A second problem of floating point numbers is *underflow*. Underflow occurs when the magnitude of a number is too small to represent. For a given floating point type, there is a lower limit on the value of exponent the computer can store. Small numbers have negative exponents, and the more negative the exponent, the smaller the number. If this limit is exceeded, in the negative direction, the number cannot be represented within the type, and underflow can occur. With underflow the number is so small that it is very close to zero. In some cases we can approximate the number by zero, but it may also be a mistake to do this. This depends on the nature of the computation.

The third problem of floating point numbers is *precision*. Since any floating point type has a fixed number of decimal digits, a number may not be exactly representable. The limitation on the number of places causes approximations to occur. For example, even 1/3 can not be represented exactly.

The limitation on precision causes approximations. Approximations yield small errors in the values stored. If computations are performed in the wrong order or formulae are computed by the wrong method, these errors can accumulate to become very serious.

For example, suppose we wish to add eleven numbers using three-digit precision. (Note: Since the computer adds in binary, the results may not be exactly as illustrated in what follows, but the principle is the same.) Ten of these numbers are 0.001 and the other is 1.0. One method for adding the numbers is:

```
0.001 + 0.001 + 0.001 + 0.001 + 0.001 +
0.001 + 0.001 + 0.001 + 0.001 + 0.001 + 1.00
```

By this notation, we indicate that the addition is from left to right. When adding the left most two numbers ($0.001 + 0.001$), we get an answer of 0.002, which only requires one digit of precision to store. When adding the next 0.001 to this, the total of 0.003 is still storable within our precision. When we add the last of the 0.001s we get a total of 0.01, which we now add to 1.00. This last addition results in the value 1.01, which is representable in 3 digits of precision.

Now, let us see what happens when we add the numbers in the opposite order:

```
1.00  + 0.001 + 0.001 + 0.001 + 0.001 +
0.001 + 0.001 + 0.001 + 0.001 + 0.001 + 0.001
```

The first addition ($1.000 + 0.001$) results in an answer of 1.001. To store this number requires four digits of precision. We are forced to round in order to store. When we round we get 1.000. The same thing happens when we add the next number. So when we reach the end of the additions, the total is still 1.00. The difference between this and the correct total is due to the accumulation of successive rounding errors. In just ten additions we have lost one place of accuracy.

The moral of this rounding example is to avoid adding small numbers to large ones. When accumulating totals, start with the smallest number. More fundamentally you need to pay attention to your computations and how rounding error affects them.

Precision affects computation in other ways also. It is particularly dangerous when it occurs in conjunction with testing. Consider the following program where **A** is a floating point number with three decimal places of accuracy.

```
A := 1.0;
if A = 3.0 * (A / 3.0) then ...
```

The computation within the expression of the if statement proceeds as follows. First we compute **A/3.0** and obtain a value of one-third. Because we must represent this with three decimal places of precision our actual answer is **0.333**. Now multiply this answer by 3, **3.0*0.333** gives an answer of **0.999**. So the right-hand side of the expression evaluates to 0.999. When we compare this against 1.0, we discover that 0.999 is not equal to 1.0. So, even though we know mathematically that the two sides should be equal, the limitation on precision forced us to round, resulting in numbers which were not equal. The moral here is that since floating point numbers are of limited precision, *never depend on floating point numbers being exactly equal.*

Another problem with numbers is that certain orders of evaluating a formula can result in an overflow while others do not. For example, suppose the largest number representable in an implementation is 10^{30}. Consider the evaluation of the expression:

$$10^{25} \times 10^{25}/10^{25}$$

If you multiply first, there is an unrepresentable intermediate result of 10^{50}. If you divide first, the computation works. The moral is that you must *watch the order of your computation.*

When programming using floating point remember these rules. Computations are not completely accurate. Ada measures precision in the number of decimal places. Two numbers which are the result of approximate calculations will almost never be exactly equal even if they (theoretically) should.

In order to overcome the various problems illustrated above, those programming sophisticated numerical computations need to know how accurately numbers are stored, what size numbers (exponents) can be stored, and how much accuracy is lost in numeric computations. Ada defines answers to these questions and/or provides attributes which help to answer these questions.

14.5 FIXED POINT TYPES

The declaration of a fixed point type always uses the reserved word **delta**. The syntax for declaring a fixed point type is given in Figure 14–3. In fixed point types, the numbers are at fixed intervals. For example, fixed point is usually used for money. With United States currency, accuracy in prices is always in hundredths of a dollar (cents), no matter how large the amount.

<fixed point type>

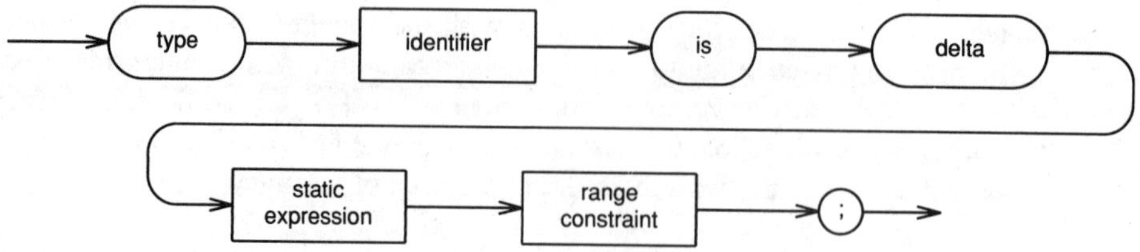

Figure 14–3

For fixed point types the predefined types are anonymous; that is, there is no predefined type which can be used. Rather, specific declaration of fixed point types is required.

A sample declaration of fixed point types is:

```
type A is delta 0.2 range -1.0 .. 3.0 ;
type B is delta 0.01 range 0.0 .. 30.0 ;
```

A fixed point type must have a delta specified. Furthermore, a fixed point type must have a range constraint or be derived from a fixed point type with a range constraint. As before, the implementation must be able to supply the accuracy and the range, or the compiler must report an error.

Subtypes of fixed point types can be declared. Some sample subtype declarations are:

```
subtype C is B delta 0.1;
subtype D is B range 0.0 .. 1.0;
```

The rules for fixed point subtypes are the same as for floating point types: the range of a subtype can be no larger than range of the type from which it is formed, and the accuracy can be no greater than the accuracy of the type from which it is formed. The latter rule means that the delta of a subtype must be at least as large as the delta of the type from which it is formed. As with floating point types, if the range of a fixed point subtype is omitted, it is the same as that of the type from which it is formed. Similarly, if the delta of a subtype is omitted, it is the same as that of the type from which it is formed.

Be careful about the bounds on a fixed point type. For example, in the type

```
type End_Drop is delta 0.3 range 0.0 .. 1.0;
```

the upper bound (`1.0`) is not a multiple of the **`delta`** (`0.3`). The largest multiple of `0.3` within this range is `0.9`. In this type, model numbers are multiples of `0.25`. The largest model number less than `0.9` is `0.75`. As a consequence, **`End_Drop'LAST`** is `0.75`. Technically, this is the largest model number within the type.

As with floating point types, Ada uses model numbers to define the precision of fixed point types. The difference is that a fixed point number is stored as a mantissa only. The value of the number stored is the mantissa multiplied by a value called **SMALL**. This means a fixed point value is represented as an integer. This integer is the mantissa. To obtain the value of a fixed point number from the integer representation, the integer is multiplied by a scale factor. This scale factor is the value **SMALL**. The default value for **SMALL** is the next power of 2 smaller than or equal to the delta. The model numbers are then multiples of this value. When the default value for **SMALL** is used, the model numbers are only as close together as is necessary to assure that two mantissas differing by at least delta can be stored as different model numbers. For example, for fixed point type **A** declared above, the model numbers are

$$-1,\ -\frac{7}{8},\ -\frac{6}{8},\ \ldots,\ 2\frac{6}{8},\ 2\frac{7}{8},\ 3$$

The fixed increment size of 1/8 is less than the delta of 0.2. An increment size of 1/4 could not be used because that size is bigger than 0.2. The compiler can optionally use more than the minimum number of bits.

When a fixed point value is to be stored, it is rounded to an adjacent model number. This model number is a multiple of **SMALL**. It is this multiple which is stored. For example, if the model number is n times **SMALL**, the integer n will be stored and will represent the model number.

As with floating point types, there are a number of attributes which the programmer can inquire about so that appropriate numerical computations may be performed. The attribute **DELTA** returns the requested value of delta. The attribute **MANTISSA** returns the allocated number of bits. The attribute **SMALL** returns the smallest positive model number. The attribute **LARGE** returns the largest model number.

With fixed point, as well as with other types, certain requirements can be specified by the programmer. The programmer can specify the number of bits used in storing a fixed point number of a given type. This is done by a representation clause that follows the type declaration. In the declarations

```
type A is delta 0.2 range -1.0 .. 3.0 ;
for A'SIZE use 6;
```

the representation clause is second of the two lines. This directive for **SIZE** causes exactly 6 bits to be used when objects of type **A** are stored. When specifying **SIZE** for a particular type, you must indicate enough bits to provide for **delta** and the range of that type. In particular

$$2^{\mathtt{SIZE}} \geq \frac{\mathtt{LAST} - \mathtt{FIRST}}{\mathtt{delta}}$$

For type **A** this formulae indicates that $2^{\mathtt{SIZE}}$ must be at least $(3.0 - (-1.0))/0.2 = 20$. Thus, if you specify **SIZE** for type **A** you must specify at least 5 because 2^5 is larger than 20, while 2^4 is not.

A far more common practice is to specify **SMALL** and hence fix the model numbers. An illustration of how this can be accomplished is

```
type A is delta 0.3 range -0.6 .. 0.6
for A'SMALL use 0.015;
type D is delta 0.2 range 10.00 .. 30.00 ;
for D'SMALL use 0.01;
```

This directive forces a distance between model numbers. The preceding directive forces the model numbers of the type **D** to be 0.01 apart. This means that the model numbers for **D** are 10.00, 10.01, 10.02, ... 29.99, 30.00. Obviously, if we were dealing with money, this would far better than accepting the default value for **SMALL** of 1/128. The rule that must be followed in specifying **SMALL** is that **SMALL** may not exceed **delta**.

As with integer literals, real literals are of type *universal real*. A copy of the real literals is inherited by each fixed and floating point type. Further, constants of the type universal real can be declared, as in

```
Pi: constant := 3.14159;
```

Such constants can be formed from universal expressions, as in

```
Two_Pi: constant := 2.0 * Pi;
```

In fact, universal expressions can use integer literals with the multiplication and division operators in the following three forms:

```
Two_Pi_2: constant := 2 * Pi;
Two_Pi_3: constant := Pi * 2;
Half_Pi : constant := Pi / 2;
```

These three mixtures of univeral real and universal integer literals produce universal reals.

Fixed point types have additional overloadings for the multiplication and division operations. With any fixed point type, you can multiply (on either side) by an expression of type **INTEGER** or divide by an expression of type **INTEGER**. Thus the following are legal for **I** of type **INTEGER** and **D** a fixed point type, such as the one previous declared.

```
D * I          I * D          D / I
```

Finally, multiplying any two fixed point types is legal and the result can be explicitly converted to any fixed point type. Thus, for the types **A** and **D** of the preceding fixed point type declarations, the expression

```
A * D
```

results in a value of type universal fixed.

14.6 BASED LITERALS

All of the integer and real literals we have seen thus far have been decimal or base 10 numbers. Ada allows literals to be written in bases other than 10. These are called *based literals*. The syntax for a based literal is given in Figure 14–4.

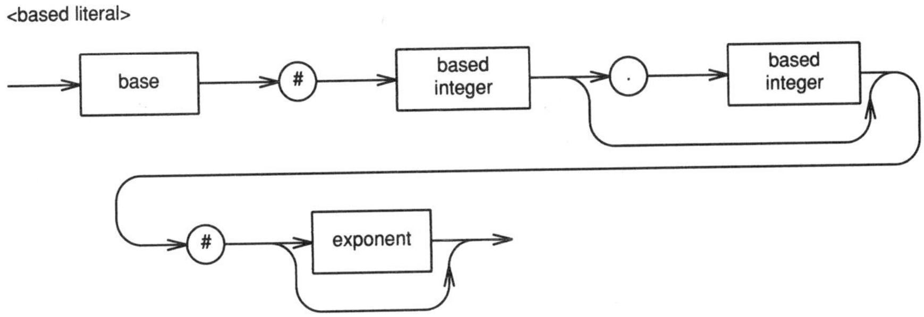

Figure 14–4

A based literal is divided into three parts separated by two pound signs (**#**). The first part indicates the base of the literal, the second part indicates the mantissa of the literal, and the third part indicates any exponent. The following are examples of based integer literals:

```
2#111_111#        16#FF#E2        8#7034#E9
16#e8#            2#1101#E11      3#20122#e14
```

The following are examples of based real literals:

```
2#10.0101#        16#f.b3#E2          8#134.74#E+7
16#2F.E3#         2#1110.111#E-11     3#122.11#e-5
```

The only bases Ada allows are those from 2 through 16. In specifying a based literal, the base and the exponent are given as a decimal integer literals. The exponent indicates multiplication by a power of the base. For example,

```
2#1001#E16
```

indicates that **1001** must be multiplied by 2^{16}, that is, the base **2** raised to the exponent **16**.

The mantissa of the based literal is found in the second part. The value of the mantissa is expressed as a number in the base; it is the only part of the literal expressed in the base. In the case of a based real it contains an embedded decimal point, in the case of a based integer it does not. It may contain *extended digits*. This means that for bases greater than 10, the letters **A** through **F** stand for the numbers 10 through 15, respectively. Of course, an extended digit of the based integer is not allowed to equal or exceed the base. For example, in a base 8 integer, you may not use the digits **8** and **9** or the extended digits **A** through **F**; or in base 12 integer, you may use all the digits and the extended digits **A** and **B**, but not **C** through **F**.

Finally, note that, in a based literal, (1) upper and lower case letters are equivalent, and (2) underscores may be used in any of the parts, provided they obey the standard rules requiring them to be embedded and noncontiguous.

14.7 PROGRAMMING PRACTICES

If you are going to be writing a lot of numerical programs, we recommend an advanced course in numerical analysis so that you are fully aware of the dangers and pitfalls of floating point numbers. For someone who is not a numerical analyst there are a few rules that usually avoid trouble. First, remember reals are only approximate, so do not count on anything exactly equaling anything else. Second, accumulating small numbers to get large numbers, or subtracting large numbers to get small numbers, will lose accuracy rapidly. Third, watch the order of your calculations to avoid underflow and overflow. Leaving division until last provides the most precision, provided that overflow does not occur.

Fixed point types have similar problems to floating point types unless the fixed point type exactly represents what you want, such as dollars and cents. Even then, rounding errors can occur when you multiply by fractional constants.

A good rule is to decide upon a strategy for handling rounding inaccuracies before beginning to write a procedure. If you cannot figure out how to handle these, you should discuss your problem with an expert.

14.7.1 Computing the Sine Function

Many times, numerical routines depend on the number of digits or bits of precision available to perform the computations. The following algorithm for computing the sine function is such a routine. For a full discussion of the issues raised in this section and a description of algorithms for other functions, see *Software Manual for the Elementary Functions* by William J. Cody and William Waite (Prentice-Hall 1980).

Sine is a cyclic function, that is, it repeats on a regular basis. Because of this, mathematically we know that $\sin(X) = \sin(2\pi N + X)$ for integer values of N. In fact, $\sin(X) = \sin(\pi N + X)$ if N is even, and $\sin(X) = -\sin(\pi N + X)$ if N is odd. The approach used to compute the sine function is to divide out all multiples of N, compute the sine of a number between 0 and π and adjust the sign of the answer if N is odd.

The first consideration is for large values of X. If X is sufficiently large, the imprecision of the value stored in X becomes close to π. For example, suppose we have (exactly) 4 decimal digits of precision and we take the sine of 2.0E4. With 4 decimal digits, the nearest representable numbers to 2.0E4 are 19990 and 20010. This means that 2.0E4 is used to represent values in the range 19995–20005, a difference of 10. Depending on which of these values 2.0E4 represents, the sine of the number being represented could be any value between -1 and 1. So, returning a value for $sin(2.0E4)$ represents a guess based on what number 2.0E4 represents. Hence, if X is too large, any computation of the value of sine is meaningless. For this reason, if X exceeds $\pi 2^{b/2}$, where b is the number of bits in the mantissa of X, the sine function should raise an exception (**NUMERIC_ERROR** would be appropriate).

Now that we know that sin(X) is meaningful, we wish to remove multiples of π from X. First, we compute the number of multiples of π in X using the formula

$$N = X \times \frac{1}{\pi}$$

using the value 0.31830_98861_83790_67154 for $1/\pi$. Precomputing $1/\pi$ avoids an extra division.

For increased accuracy, multiples of π are removed in two steps. First, we remove exactly representable multiples with the formula $F = X - 3.140625N$. The advantage of using 3.140625 is that it can be exactly representable with very few bits. We can easily see this by noting that we can exactly represent 3.140625 by the based literal **8#3.11#**. Now, the rest of the multiples may be removed by $F = F + 8.9089\_10206\_76153\_73566\_17E-6N$. Actually, the first subtraction removes too much, and the second formula corrects this by adding in the difference. The two constants add to π.

Now, F is a number between 0 and π, and we shall approximate the value of sin(F) using a polynomial. Because of the nature of the sine function, only even powers of F occur in this polynomial. So, instead of using F directly, this polynomial will use g which is defined to be $g = F^2$.

The best polynomial to use depends on b, the number of bits in the mantissa. If $b \leq 24$, the appropriate polynomial is:

$$(((r_4 g + r_3)g + r_2)g + r_1)g$$

and the appropriate values of the constants are as follows

$$\begin{aligned} r_1 &= -0.16666\_65668E+0 \\ r_2 &= 0.83330\_25139E-2 \\ r_3 &= -0.19807\_41872E-3 \\ r_4 &= 0.26019\_03036E-5 \end{aligned}$$

If $24 < b \leq 32$, the polynomial is

$$((((r_5 g + r_4)g + r_3)g + r_2)g + r_1)g$$

and the appropriate values of the constants are as follows

$$r_1 = -0.16666\_66660\_883E+0$$

$$r_2 = 0.83333\_30720\_556E-2$$

$$r_3 = -0.19840\_83282\_313E-3$$

$$r_4 = 0.27523\_97106\_775E-5$$

$$r_5 = -0.23868\_34640\_601E-7$$

Notice that the polynomials compute and add the smaller numbers before computing and adding the larger numbers.

Now that we have the value of $\sin(X)$, we need to compute its sign. If X was positive and N was even, or if X was negative and N was odd, the sine is positive. In all other cases, we must multiply by -1.

Several additional improvements of the algorithm have been omitted from the above discussion to simplify it. Both the algorithm presented and the improvements perform calculations in a carefully designed order. The purpose of this order is that the maximum value of the error in the computation is restricted as much as possible.

When testing the sine algorithm we should select a series of points between 0 and 2π. A reasonable choice would be 0.5, 1.0, 1.5, ..., 5.5, 6.0. These points should be tested and the results compared against a table. We should make a few special tests near 0, π, and 2π to see if we get reasonable values when the sine of the number is near zero. Finally, we should test the reductions by computing the sine of a few large values such as $\pm(100\pi)$ and $\pm(101\pi + 1.0)$. Note that these tests are designed merely to detect gross mistakes in the implementation of the algorithm; they will not tell you, for example, if the above coefficients are actually the best coefficients to use.

14.7.2 Testing: Assertions

We have discussed testing programs by writing information to the screen while the program is executing. Unfortunately, this technique can write enormous amounts of information and drastically slow down the program. Another approach, programming with *assertions*, is to display a message only when things go wrong.

When using assertions, you determine a way to check the correctness of each subprogram as it executes. For instance, you check that the parameters into the subprogram have meaningful values. You would check that the values computed are correct before returning or writing them. Finally, you would check the values that are being computed in a loop at the top of the loop.

Some of this checking is performed automatically for you in Ada whenever you use subtypes to limit the values of your variables and parameters. However, this technique only checks each value against a static range. For example, in a square root function, the requirement that the parameter be greater than or equal to zero can be enforced with a subtype. To completely check a value, you may need a substantial Boolean expression.

For instance, to check that the value to be returned by a square root function is correct, you need to subtract the square of the proposed square root from the original value and check that the difference is small. This requirement cannot be enforced automatically through the use of subtypes, and the calculation of how small the difference should be is complicated. Furthermore, in a square root routine implemented with a loop you should also check that each time through the loop the value calculated gets closer to the square root. Finally, you should place a limit on the number of times the loop is executed and issue a message if this number of iterations is exceeded.

There are several ways to find which kinds of checks are appropriate. First, as in the square root case, it is often possible to calculate whether the answer is correct. Second, it is often possible to ensure that the answer is at least the correct order of magnitude. Third, you can calculate the values using two different algorithms and compare the results (e.g., checking a quick sort procedure by comparing the results with those obtained by an insertion sort). Finally, you can check that the calculation is leading in the correct direction and that loops terminate.

The following procedure could be useful in enforcing assertions:

```
Assert(Condition: in BOOLEAN;  Warning: in STRING);
-- Purpose:      Warns the user if the assertion is violated.
--  Condition:   The assertion which must be true.
--  Warning:     The message to print if the assertion is false.
-- Note: Sends ASCII.BELL to the terminal before printing the message.
--          Requires that the user "Press Return" before permitting
--          execution to continue.
```

Opinions differ as to whether code that checks assertions should be removed from a program before the program is released for use. Some feel that assertions require a considerable amount of computer time to execute and display messages that are only of interest to a programmer. On the other hand, if an assertion is false, continuing normal execution could lead to a serious error.

One way to settle this problem is to indicate which statements are temporary assertions by placing an appropriate comment (e.g., **-- AT**) at the end of each line involved in the calculation. Then, before the program is released, each line marked as temporary should be commented out (i.e., place -- in the left margin), and the program should be retested to ensure that no essential parts of the program are commented out. Finally, the assertions should never be removed from the program source, they should remain in the source so that they can be used in testing future versions of the program.

14.8 ADA SUMMARY

In this chapter we have covered the details of the *real types*. We have introduced the *fixed point* and *floating point* types. We have covered the various attributes available for real types. We have discussed some of the issues and pitfalls associated with real numbers including the problems of *overflow*, *underflow*, *rounding error*, and the *accuracy* of operations. We have discussed the concept of *model numbers* upon which Ada builds its definitions of the precision of real variables and the accuracy of real computations.

We introduced several *representation clauses*, which control how real numbers are represented when stored. We illustrated how the precision and accuracy of a program using numeric types could be changed by using representation clauses. Finally, we introduced based literals as way of writing numeric literals.

EXERCISES

14.1. Modify the **Bank_Account** package (Program 3–14, exercises 3.1, 4.5, 5.9, 7.8, 8.2, 10.5, 10.6, or 12.6) so that it uses fixed point arithmetic with dollars as whole numbers and pennies as hundredths.

14.2. One method of obtaining the square root of a positive number is to divide and average. To find the square root of a positive number X using this method, we may use the following algorithm:

1. Guess a number Y. For an initial guess, use $X/2.0$.

2. Compute X/Y. If Y is the square root of X, then X/Y will equal Y. If Y is smaller than the square root of X, then X/Y will be larger than Y, and if Y is larger than the square root of X, then X/Y will be smaller than Y. Thus, the average of Y and X/Y will be closer to the square root of X than Y is.

3. If X/Y and Y are close, stop. Otherwise, compute their average and use this as the new guess.

Implement this algorithm as a program. In step 3, whether or not two numbers are close should depend on the attribute **EPSILON**. Exactly how this should depend on **EPSILON** is tricky, so think about it carefully.

Your program should read a number, print the square root and print the square root times itself (which should be close to the original number).

14.3. Implement a **Sin** routine on the basis of the dicussion in section 7 as a function contained in a package called **Numeric_Routines**. Assume that the function is passed and returns a floating point subtype that is compatible with **FLOAT**. Be sure to use floating point attributes where appropriate.

14.4. This is an exercise to increase your grasp of the technical details of model numbers. Write a program that takes the following input from the user:

1. An integer **D** between **1** and **FLOAT'DIGITS**

2. A positive **FLOAT** value, **Value**, with at most **D** significant digits

The program should print the **FLOAT** values corresponding to the model number closest to **Value** from below and the model number closest to **Value** from above. When using the formula for the number of bits in the model number, use the value 3.321929 to approximate the value of $\log(10)/\log(2)$. When printing a floating point value, print it both in decimal form and as a base 2 numeric literal. For example, **2#0.101100#E10** is a base 2 numeric literal.

As an example, suppose the program is given **D=1** and **Value=2000**. This means that **B** is 5 and that all numbers can be written in the form

$$\frac{x}{32} \times 2^N$$

where **X** is a value between 16 and 31. To find the model numbers surrounding **Value**, we must find **N** such that

$$\frac{1}{2} \le \frac{\textbf{Value}}{2^N} < 1$$

For **2000**, **N=11** and **X=31**. So the values printed should be:

```
Lower     1984.000    2#0.11111#E11
Upper     2048.000    2#0.10000#E12
```

The program should allow testing of multiple values.

14.5. Write a program that computes compound interest. The program lets the user input an account balance, an annual interest rate, the number of interest periods per year, and a number of years. The program should output what the account balance would be at the end of the number of years the user has specified. This balance should include the compound interest.

Compound interest should be calculated as follows. Each interest period the balance in an account is replaced by

```
Balance := Balance * (1.0 + Interest_Rate_During_Period);
```

During the next interest period the new value of **Balance** is used when this computation is repeated. The interest rate during a period can be computed as

```
Interest_Rate_During_Period := Annual_Interest_Rate / Periods_Per_Year;
```

For example, if the annual interest rate was 12% and the number of periods per year was 12, then the interest rate per period would be 1% (i.e., about 1% per month).

All values in the program should be maintained as fixed point values. The number of periods per year and the number of years which the user inputs should be required to be integers (but may subsequently be converted to fixed point).

All interest computations should be repeated twice, first using two fixed point *decimal digits* of accuracy (i.e., dollars and cents) and then using four fixed point decimal digits of accuracy. The program should report the results of both computations.

Notice what happens when greater accuracy is used. Examine especially the case where there are a lot of periods per year.

15

Access Types

15.1 OBJECTIVES

To solve some programming problems, you need to create variables on demand, during execution of a program. This chapter deals with mechanisms for dynamically creating variables. The most important mechanism is the *access type*. This chapter covers this class of types in detail (section 3). We cover several additional programming techniques made possible by the ability to create dynamic variables (sections 4–6).

CONCEPTS:

- Variables can be created when executing a statement.
- Data structures can be constructed that can be changed by the program.
- Recursive data structures can be built that contain arbitrarily large numbers of variables.

GOALS:

- Implement a dynamic and recursive data structure using access types.

15.2 MOTIVATION

Thus far, all the variables we have used were declared and each variable was associated with an identifier. With this kind of variable, you have to know at compile time how many variables of each type you need because you have to declare them. These are *static* variables. Indeed, all objects introduced thus far have been static objects. This is true even though the number or type of components of these variables may be determined at execution time. In many situations, the flexibility provided by adjusting the number or type of the components is not adequate. Except for unconstrained variants, the size of these structures can only be set at elaboration. With unconstrained variants the size can only be set by completely reassigning the structure.

Suppose you have a group of student records filling all your available variables and you wish to add one more student record to your data. It is impossible to use constrained objects to do this because to change their size, you must exit and then reenter their declarative region. Since an object ceases to exist when you exit its declarative region, the existing data about students does not survive this technique of creating more space. Similarly, it is impossible to use unconstrained variants because to change the size of an unconstrained variant you must reassign the entire record. Again, the data does not survive the reassignment.

What we need to do in this situation is to create additional variables during execution. This is the concept behind *dynamic variables.* Ada provides a mechanism that allows variables to be created by the program while it is running. Because the number of these variables is not known when you compile, clearly these variables cannot be associated with identifiers in the normal way. Some way of naming (referring to) these variables must be supplied.

15.3 ACCESS TYPES

Ada provides dynamic variables and access to them through the mechanism of *access types.* The syntax for an access type is given in Figure 15–1.

<access type declaration>

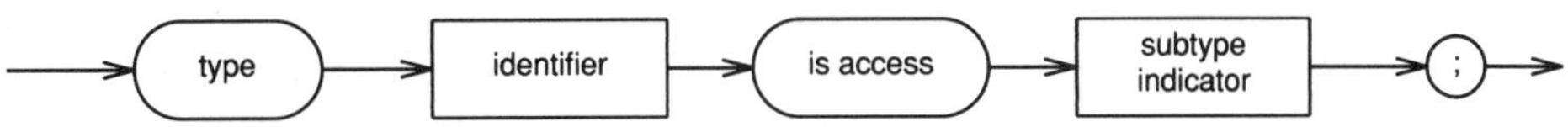

Figure 15–1

In the following declarations, **X** and **Z** are access types, while **C** and **D** are variables of access type:

```
type X is access INTEGER;
type Z is access BOOLEAN;
C: X;
D: Z;
```

A variable of access type is most often referred to as an *access variable.* An access variable is one kind of *access object.* An *access constant* is another kind of access object. Sometimes access objects are called pointers or addresses.

As with most objects, an access type must be explicitly declared before declaring an object of that access type; that is, anonymous access types are illegal. Thus, the declaration

```
A: access ...    -- illegal
```

is syntactically illegal.

An access object is similar to your address. Your address is not you, but it tells me how to find you. To find you, I only need to follow the directions on the address. Your address provides me with the means of accessing you. Your address does not provide me with you. You and your address are different types of objects. You are quite easily distinguishable from your address. Furthermore, if I need you, it is not enough just to look at your address; I must use your address to find you.

Similarly, an access object is a different type of object from the dynamic variable to which it provides access. Both are objects. The access object contains the information on how to access a dynamic variable, just as your address contains the information on how to access you. If I need the dynamic variable, it is not enough to just use the access object; I must use the access object to access the dynamic variable. Many mistakes in using access objects result from the programmer confusing the dynamic variable containing the data with the access object providing access to the variable containing the data. When using access types, it is always good practice to comment and to recheck your code to make sure you have kept the distinction between dynamic variables and access objects. Remember, *to find the contents (person), you only need to know how to access them (address).*

In the previous declarations, **D** is a variable of access type that provides access to a dynamic **BOOLEAN** variable. In Ada you can access the variable to which **D** provides access using the name **D.all**. **D.all** is a **BOOLEAN** variable. Particularly, **D.all** is the **BOOLEAN** variable to which **D** provides access. Similarly, **C.all** is the **INTEGER** variable to which **C** provides access.

Ada's strict restriction on types means that the access variable **C** in the example can only provide access to an **INTEGER** variable; **C** can never provide access to a **BOOLEAN** value.

Access variables involve at least two types: the access type and the type of the variable being accessed. In Ada terminology, the type of the variable being accessed is called the *designated type*. In the previous example, **C** is a variable of access type and its designated type is **INTEGER**. **D** is also a variable of access type, but its designated type is **BOOLEAN**. Furthermore, because objects other than variables can be accessed, Ada uses the term *designated object* for the object being accessed. With the exception of task types (see Chapter 19), access types always refer to variable objects. This is because an access type names a designated type and there is no such thing as a constant type.

Again, an access variable is *not* a dynamic variable; it merely allows access to a dynamic variable. Recall that the goal of access types is to create dynamic variables during execution. To achieve this we must have a means of creating dynamic variables. In Ada, dynamic variables are created using the **new** operator. The syntax for the **new** operator is given in Figure 15–2.

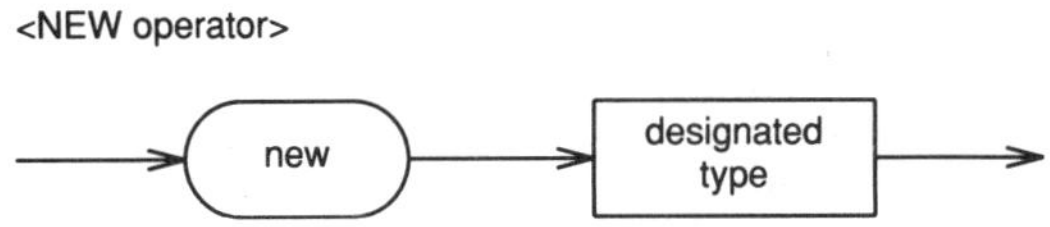

Figure 15–2

The **new** operator creates an object (variable) of the designated type and the capability to access that newly created dynamic variable. In Ada terms, **new** creates an object of the designated type and returns the access value of that object. Thus, "**new BOOLEAN**" creates a dynamic variable of type **BOOLEAN** and returns the access value of that object. Since **new** returns a value, it is like a function, or, more accurately, it is like an operator such as the addition or "**+**" operator. Thus, as in the case of functions and operators, something must be done with the access value returned by **new**. The options are similar to those that exist for values of other types that are returned by operators. In some sense, the simplest option is to store the value. With the previous declarations, this could be done by the statement

```
D := new BOOLEAN;
```

This statement creates a **BOOLEAN** variable, returns an access value to this created variable, and stores that access value in the variable **D**. The variable which has been created can be accessed as **D.all**. Note that until the **new** operation was performed, there was no Boolean variable for **D** to access.

In Ada terminology, **new** is called the *allocator*. It allocates or creates a dynamic variable. The type of the variable created is given by the *designated type*. The allocator **new** creates (allocates) an object of the designated type (or subtype) and yields (returns) an access value to that object.

An access variable contains an access value. This access value may be changed, tested, or used to access a dynamic variable. The preceding assignment modified the access value stored in **D**. Appending **.all** to an access value references the dynamic variable. Access variables without suffixes refer to the access value.

Many times an access value supplies access to a dynamic variable. But there are situations in which it does not, such as before a dynamic variable has been created. In these cases some way is needed to indicate that there is no variable to access. Ada fulfills this need through the special access value **null**. If an access variable contains the value **null**, the access variable does not supply access to anything. Access variables default to **null** on elaboration. Thus, an access variable always has a valid value. Either they contain the access value of a dynamic variable or they contain the value **null**.

The use of access values, allocators and access variables is illustrated in the procedure **Access_Demo** in Program 15–1. In line 2 an access type is declared, and in line 3 three variables of this access type are declared. The designated type of these variables is **BOOLEAN**. In lines 5 and 7, the allocator is used to create dynamic **BOOLEAN** variables. The statements in these lines store the access values for these dynamic variables in the access variables **B1** and **B2**, respectively. At line 6, the first dynamic variable created

```
 1:procedure Access_Demo is
 2:   type Bool_Access is access BOOLEAN;
 3:   B1, B2, B3: Bool_Access;
 4:begin
 5:   B1 := new BOOLEAN;
 6:   B1.all := FALSE;
 7:   B2 := new BOOLEAN;
 8:   B2.all := B1.all;
 9:   B1 := null;
10:   B1.all := FALSE;          -- CONSTRAINT_ERROR
11:   B3.all := FALSE;          -- CONSTRAINT_ERROR
12:   B3 := B2;
13:   B3.all := TRUE;
14:   if B1 = null then B1 := new BOOLEAN; end if;
15:end Access_Demo;
```

Program 15–1

receives a value. In line 8, both dynamic variables are accessed. On the right-hand side, the expression **B1.all** refers to the Boolean variable accessed by **B1**. Technically, **B1.all** is a Boolean expression consisting of a single Boolean variable and no operators. This Boolean expression returns the value **FALSE** because this is the value which was stored in line 6. This value **FALSE** is stored into the second dynamic variable **B2.all** (line 8). Both **B1.all** and **B2.all** are designated objects.

Line 9 illustrates a use of the value **null**. This line declares that **B1** no longer has access to a dynamic variable. At line 10 no dynamic variable is accessed by **B1**, so there is no place to store **FALSE**. Consequently, the assignment in line 10 is illegal. Attempting an assignment when there is no dynamic variable results in a **CONSTRAINT_ERROR**. Conceptually, there is a condition or constraint on the use of the **null** access value. You may not use the value **null** when attempting to access a dynamic variable because it is reserved for the case where such a dynamic variable does not exist. Similarly, line 11 is illegal because **B3** received the value **null** at elaboration and that value was never replaced.

Line 12 is legal, although somewhat difficult to understand at first glance. In this line both **B2** and **B3** have the type **Bool_Access**, so the assignment is legal. What **B2** contains is access to the **BOOLEAN** variable created at line 7. The assignment makes a copy of that access and stores it in **B3**. After this assignment, both **B3** and **B2** provide access to the same variable. Thus, after the assignment at line 13 is performed and the value of this variable changes, both **B3.all** and **B2.all** will evaluate to **TRUE**.

An interesting way of thinking about what is going on in lines 12 and 13 is with phone numbers. A phone number provides access to a person. If I have your phone number, I can use it to access you. If I give someone else a copy of your phone number, that person can also use it to access you. If you move out and a new person moves in, when I or someone else calls the phone number, we will reach that new person.

Comparisons can be made between access variables. As with other variables, these comparisons are legal only if the access variables are of the same type. With access variables, only tests for equality and inequality are allowed.

Equality testing, as in **B1=B2**, asks whether both access variables access the same variable. For example, after line 12 of Program 15–1, **B2=B3** returns **TRUE** because both **B2** and **B3** access the same variable. Of course, the inequality **B1/=B2** can also be tested. This comparison returns **TRUE** except when **B1** and **B2** access the same variable.

Comparisons against **null** are allowed. In the comparison **B1/=null**, the value **TRUE** is returned whenever **B1** accesses an object. The comparison **B1=null** returns **TRUE** when **B1** is not currently accessing an object. Note that **B1=B2** returns **TRUE** if both are **null**. Line 14 of the program illustrates an instance of a comparison. This comparison is used to cause the creation of a variable if **B1** does not already access one.

In dealing with access types, it is convenient to draw pictures. In these pictures, boxes indicate variables. These variables may be of access type or of other types. With access variables, we indicate the value by an arrow that points to the dynamic variable to which the access variable provides access. With variables of other types we indicate the value of the variable by writing that value inside the box. When we change an ordinary variable, we change the contents of a box. When we change an access variable, we change where the arrow points. The reserved value **null** is represented by an arrow that points to a small circle.

```
 1:procedure Box_Demo
 2:   type Int_Access is access INTEGER;
 3:   A: INTEGER;
 4:   B, C, D: Int_Access;
 5:begin
 6:   A := 14;
 7:   B := new INTEGER;
 8:   B.all := 7;
 9:   C := B;
10:   C.all := A;
11:end Box_Demo;
```

Program 15–2

The procedure **Box_Demo** in Program 15–2 shows how this works. Just after executing line 9, the procedure generates the box diagram shown in Figure 15–3. The box labeled **A** represents the integer variable associated with the identifier **A**. Since **A** was assigned the value 14 in line 6, the box contains a 14. The box labeled **D** represents an access variable. The fact that **D** contains the value **null** is clearly indicated by the arrow going nowhere. The reason **D** contains **null** is that it received that value at elaboration and the value was not changed during execution of the program. The box labeled **B** also represents a variable which is of an access type. Originally, it contained an arrow similar to the one still in box **D**. However, during the execution of line 7, a dynamic variable (a new box) was created and the access value of this new variable was stored in **B**. So the box labeled **B** now contains an arrow pointing to the box (variable) created by the allocator. Since **B.all** was assigned the value 7 (in line 8), this box contains a 7. Note that after it is created in line 7 and before it is given a value in line 8, the dynamic variable is uninitialized and behaves as does any other uninitialized variable.

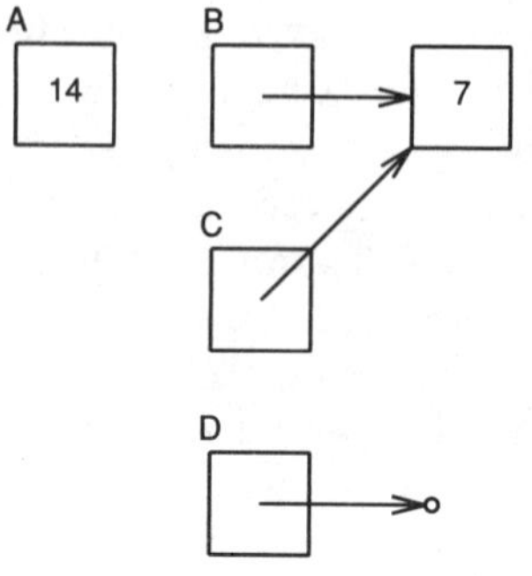

Figure 15–3

The assignment in line 9 causes a copy of the value stored in **B** to be stored into **C**. Now **C** provides access to the same variable as **B**. In Figure 15–3, this is indicated by the existence of arrows from **B** and **C** pointing to the same dynamic variable.

Observe closely what happens when we execute line 10. The variable **A** contains the value 14, so **C.all** receives the value 14. Because **C** supplies access to the box containing the value 7, the 7 is replaced by a 14. Notice that **B** provides access to the same dynamic variable as **C**. Consequently, the value of **B.all** will also change to 14, even though **B** was not even mentioned in line 10.

15.3.1 Access Types, Records, and Arrays

The principle of an access type is that any type may be the designated type. In particular, records and arrays may be designated types. The procedure **Component_Access** in Program 15–3 illustrates how to declare, create, and access dynamic array variables, dynamic record variables, and their components. The box diagram corresponding to this procedure is shown in Figure 15–4.

Accessing components of a dynamic variable is very simple. A suffix on an access type indicates that the appropriate portion of the dynamic variable should be accessed. If the dynamic variable is a record, the suffix can be the name of the component or **.all**. If the designated type of the dynamic variable is an array type, the suffix can be an index or **.all**. Of course, use of a component name is syntactically legal only if the designated type is a record type with an appropriate component, while use of an array index is syntactically legal only if the designated type an array type with an appropriate index type. If you attempt to access a nonexistent component it is a syntax error. If you attempt to access a nonexistent index it is a **CONSTRAINT_ERROR**. Type checking applies fully to dynamic variables.

```
with Lines;
 1:procedure Component_Access is
 2:   type Grade_List is array (1..4) of INTEGER;
 3:   type Student_Record is
 4:     record
 5:       Name: Lines.Normal_Line;
 6:       Grades: Grade_List;
 7:     end record;
 8:   type Grade_Access is access Grade_List;
 9:   type Stu_Access is access Student_Record;
10:   Some_Grades: Grade_Access;
11:   Student: Stu_Access;
12:begin
13:   Some_Grades := new Grade_List;
14:   Some_Grades.all(4) := 98;
15:   Some_Grades(4) := 98;
16:   Student := new Student_Record;
17:   Lines.Assign(Student.all.Name, "Smith");
18:   Lines.Assign(Student.Name, "Smith");
19:   Student.Grades(1) := 43;
20:end Component_Access;
```

Program 15–3

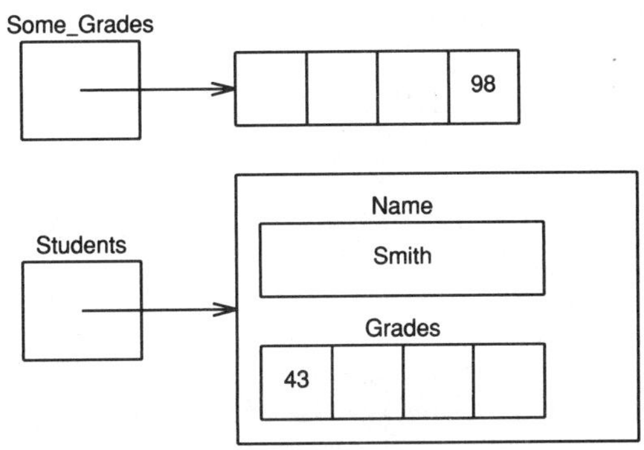

Figure 15–4

The notation **.all** is a special suffix notation that refers to the whole dynamic variable. Thus, the reference to **Some_Grades.all** in line 14 of Program 15–3 refers to the entire array, while the reference to **Student.all** in line 17 refers to the entire record. The **.all** may stand alone, as was shown in Programs 15–1 and 15–2, or it can be combined with components or indices, as shown in Program 15–3.

In Program 15–3 we have an access type **Grade_Access** whose designated type is an array type **Grade_List**, and an access type **Stu_Access** whose designated type is a record type **Student_Record**. In line 13, we create an array and store its access value in the access variable **Some_Grades**. Line 14 gives a value to an element in this array. Here, we use **Some_Grades.all**, which accesses the whole array. This whole array has 4 components, of which we specify one, **(4)**, to be accessed. A second way to do this is shown in line 15. Here, the index is used directly. Lines 14 and 15 are equivalent.

The dynamic variable **Some_Grades** is an array. Had we wanted, we could have assigned values to the components of this array using slice assignment because it is legal on one-dimensional arrays, or using aggregates because they are also legal on arrays. Although it is a dynamic variable, this array behaves like all other arrays.

In line 16, we create a record of type **Student_Record**. This record contains two components. Lines 17 and 18 are equivalent ways of performing an assignment to one of those components. Again, either a direct suffix is equivalent to a suffix indicating the whole record, followed by a suffix indicating a component within the record. In both lines, a component of a dynamic variable is used as the parameter to a procedure. This parameter happened to be of mode **out**, allowing a new value to be assigned to the component.

The record has two components. We have filled in the **Name** component and one of the grades in the **Grades** component. Line 19 illustrates access to a nested component. This line accesses the first component of the **Grades** component of the dynamic record. As we can see in Figure 15–4, the procedure has created two dynamic variables, and given a value to one component in the dynamic array variable, a value to the first component in the dynamic record variable, and a value to the second component in the dynamic record variable.

```
procedure Records_With_Access_Types is
  type Grade_List is array (1..4) of INTEGER range 0..100;
  type Grade_Access is access Grade_List;
  type School_Record is
    record
      Name: STRING(1..5);
      Math: Grade_Access;
      Chem: Grade_Access;
    end record;
  type School_Access is access School_Record;
  A_School: School_Access;
begin
  A_School := new School_Record;
  A_School.Name := "Local";
  A_School.Math := new Grade_List;
  A_School.Math := (86, 78, 67, 77);
end Records_With_Access_Types;
```

Program 15–4

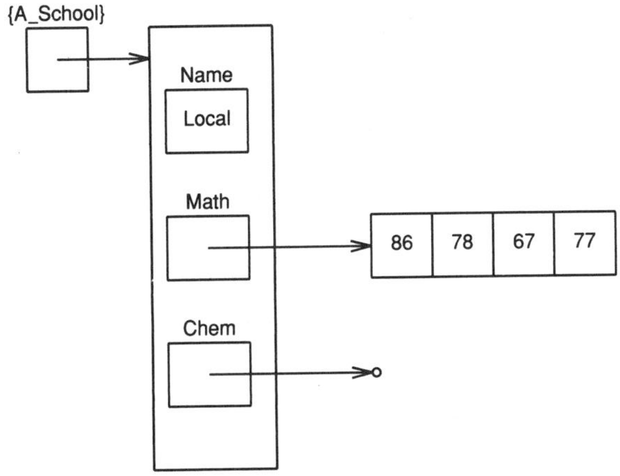

Figure 15–5

One of the most powerful aspects of access types is that an access type can access an object that itself contains access types. In fact, it is legal to access a value which is an access type. This is illustrated by the procedure **`Records_With_Access_Types`** in Program 15–4. The variable **`A_School`** is an access type which accesses an object of type **`School_Record`**. **`School_Record`** contains 3 components. Two of these components are access variables.

In line 13, a dynamic record variable of type **`School_Record`** is created. One component is given a value in line 14. The other two components are of type **`Grade_Access`**.

Recall that whenever a variable of an access type is created, it has a default initialization value of **`null`**. This applies whether the creation is by elaboration or by use of the allocator. Thus, when the dynamic variable is created in line 13, both its **`Math`** and **`Chem`** components receive the value **`null`**. In line 15, a dynamic array variable is created. Access to this variable is stored in the **`Math`** component of the dynamic record created in line 13. Line 16 assigns an aggregate to give this variable of type **`Grade_List`** a value. The final configuration of the variables in this program is shown in Figure 15–5.

Suppose we wanted to get the value of the third grade in the math class. Several appropriate means of accessing that grade are as follows

```
A_School.Math(3)
A_School.Math.all(3)
A_School.all.Math(3)
A_School.all.Math.all(3)
```

All of the above are equivalent. In Ada terminology, they all name the same variable. All of them provide access to the variable containing the value 67. In each of these there is either a component or **`.all`** after **`A_School`**, so all refer to the dynamic record accessed by **`A_School`**. In each of these there is either an index or **`.all`** after **`Math`**, so all refer to a component in the dynamic array accessed by the **Math** component the dynamic record.

Although all the above names are legal, we suggest the style of using **.all** only when referring to an entire dynamic object. In other cases, leave **.all** out whenever possible. The reason for this is that we wish to focus on the fact that we are accessing a component in a record, and not on whether that component is in a static or dynamic record.

As with all records, there is no limitation on the number of levels of nesting. Complex structures with many levels of nesting are often built for situations involving complex data. Any of these levels of nesting may contain access types.

15.3.2 Incomplete Types

We now wish to show how to use dynamic variables to create arbitrary numbers of variables during procedure execution. First however, we must discuss *incomplete types.* An incomplete type declaration gives the identifier and any discriminants of the type, but it does not give the definition of the type. Two example of incomplete types are the following:

```
type Not_Yet;
type Discriminated_Not_Yet(Is_It_Blue: BOOLEAN);
```

Like procedure declarations, incomplete types are easily recognizable by having the terminating semicolon instead of the reserved word **is**. Also like procedure declarations, incomplete types must eventually be completed. For a subprogram, the full type declaration that completes the incomplete type must be in declarations of the subprogram. If the incomplete type was defined in the visible part of a package declaration, the completion must be in the visible part of the package declaration. If the incomplete type was defined in a private part of a package the completion may be in the private part or in the package body. In completing a type, the discriminants must be repeated. The following could complete the preceding incomplete types:

```
type Not_Yet is new INTEGER;
type Discriminated_Not_Yet(Is_It_Blue: BOOLEAN) is
  record
    Size: INTEGER;
    case Is_It_Blue is
      when TRUE =>  Dark: BOOLEAN;
      when FALSE => Height: INTEGER;
    end case;
  end record;
```

Technically, the discriminant need not be repeated exactly, however, the repetition must "conform" to the incomplete type declaration. Good style requires exact repetition.

Until an incomplete type has been completed, it may only be used as the designated type of an access type. After completion, the previously incomplete type is like any other type and may be used as such.

Using incomplete types, we can build *linked lists.* Linked lists are an extension of the concept of dynamic records containing access values. They provide a method for building structures whose size can be changed while the program is executing.

```
 1:procedure Linked_List is
 2:  type Linked_Int;
 3:  type Next_Int is access Linked_Int;
 4:  type Linked_Int is
 5:    record
 6:      Data: INTEGER;
 7:      Link: Next_Int;
 8:    end record;
 9:  A, B, C: Next_Int;
10:begin
11:  C := new Linked_Int;
12:  C.Data := 14;
13:  B := new Linked_Int;
14:  B.Data := 34;
15:  B.Link := C;
16:  A := new Linked_Int;
17:  A.Data := 73;
18:  A.Link := B;
19:end Linked_List;
```

Program 15–5

The fundamental concepts of linked lists are illustrated in the procedure **Linked_List** in Program 15–5. In the declarations, the first occurrence of **Linked_Int** in line 2 is an incomplete type definition. It declares that the type will be defined later in the declaration section. The definition of **Next_Int** in line 3 is an access type whose designated type is a type whose definition is incomplete. Since the definition of **Linked_Int** has a component that refers to **Next_Int**, which itself accesses **Linked_Int**, the definition of **Linked_Int** is recursive.

Since the definition of **Linked_Int** in line 2 is incomplete it can only be used as a designated type (as is done in line 3) until after the completion of its definition (line 8). On the other hand, **Next_Int** as defined in line 3 is a complete type definition. This is easily determined by the presence of the reserved word **is** in that line.

Examining the program in detail we see that there are three access variables declared in line 9 whose designated type is **Linked_Int**. The final result of the program is illustrated in Figure 15–6. In line 11, a dynamic variable is created and access to it is stored in **C**. In line 12, the **Data** component of the dynamic variable to which **C** provides access is given the value 14. At this point, **C** has an arrow to the dynamic variable whose

Data component contains 14. The **Link** component of this dynamic variable is **null**. In line 13, another dynamic variable is created and access to it is stored in **B**. In line 14 the value 34 is stored in the **Data** component of this dynamic variable and, in line 15 the **Link** component this dynamic variable gets a copy of the value stored in **C**. Two arrows now point to the record containing 14. In line 16, the third dynamic variable is created and access to it is stored in **A**. Its components are given the values 73 and a copy of **B**. The configuration shown in 15–6 is now complete.

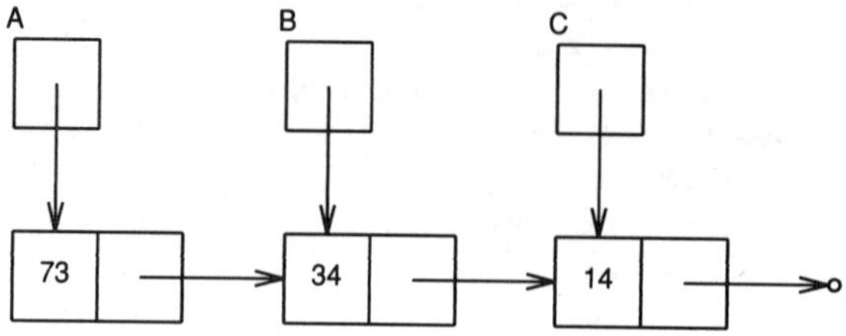

Figure 15–6

All records in the linked list can be found by starting at **A** and traversing the list. The principle for traversing a linked list is simple. Each member of the list contains the access value of the next member. Wherever we are in the list, we can use the access value of that record to get to the next item in the list. The procedure **Find** described later in this chapter shows how to do this.

15.3.3 Initializing Access Objects

Ada allows the components of a dynamic variable to be initialized upon allocation. This is similar to supplying initial values at elaboration. In the case of the type **Linked_Int** in Program 15–5, the dynamic variable is a record so we must use an aggregate. The following three lines are equivalent to the body of the procedure **Linked_List**:

```
C := new Linked_Int'(14, null);
B := new Linked_Int'(34, C);
A := new Linked_Int'(73, B);
```

These lines give exactly the same final configuration as before. The allocator **new** is now followed by a qualified expression. In this case, the expression is evaluated, a dynamic variable is created whose subtype is the same as that of the qualified expression, this dynamic variable is initialized to the value of the qualified expression, and its access value of the dynamic variable is returned.

Specifically, the evaluation of the qualified expression, the creation of the dynamic variable, and the initialization of the dynamic variable to the value of the qualified expression occur *before* the access value becomes available. Because of this, only one static variable (**A**) is really needed to create the list. Thus, we can create the list by rewriting the preceding instructions as

```
A := new Linked_Int'(14, null);
A := new Linked_Int'(34, A);
A := new Linked_Int'(73, A);
```

Because parameters are evaluated before assignment is done, the evaluation of the aggregate uses the *old* value of **A**. Each statement uses the aggregate to initialize the record and, then, when the access value becomes available, stores this *new* value in **A**. This sequence of statements accomplishes the same task as before, except that the variables **B** and **C**, which were used to save the intermediate access values, are no longer needed and can be eliminated. The final configuration is shown in Figure 15–7.

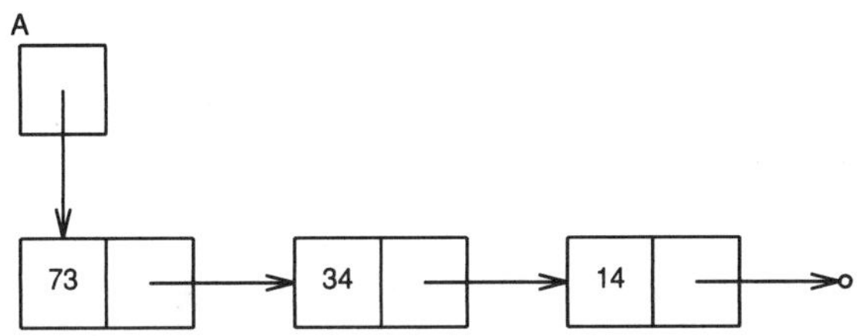

Figure 15–7

Like other variables, access variables may be given values at declaration. Thus, in **Linked_List**, we could have declared the access variables as follows:

```
C: Next_Int := new Linked_Int'(14, null);
B: Next_Int := new Linked_Int'(34, C);
A: Next_Int := new Linked_Int'(73, B);
```

The result of these declarations is that the linked list of Figure 15–6 is built before execution of the body of **Linked_List** begins.

An object of access type may be a constant. Given the declarations of **Linked_List**, we could define the following access constants:

```
D: constant Next_Int := new Linked_Int'(7, null);
E: constant Next_Int := new Linked_Int;
```

A constant access object cannot be changed. Like other constants, an access constant must be given a value at elaboration; that is, the dynamic variable to which it supplies access must be determined by the declaration of the access constant. As shown in the preceding example, both **D** and **E** are explicitly supplied values. In addition, the dynamic variable that **D** accesses is supplied with an initial value. **D** will always provide access to the same dynamic variable, the one created during its elaboration. **D** can never be changed to access another dynamic variable. That is, the assignment **D:=A** is illegal. However, what **D** accesses is *not* a constant, it is a dynamic variable. Thus,

```
D.all  := A.all;
E.all  := D.all;
D.Data := 6;
```

are all perfectly legal. In these, neither **D** nor **E** change, they remain constant. However, the values stored in the dynamic variables they access are changed. In addition to directly using the allocator, you can use any other expression that returns an access value of the correct designated type to initialize a constant access object. For example,

```
F: constant Next_Int := E;
```

is legal because the expression "**E**" yields an access value of the correct type. Of course, a constant access object may be initialized to the value **null**, in which case it will never access a dynamic object.

15.3.4 Access Types and Unconstrained Types

In our previous discussion of unconstrained types we noted that although types and formal parameters may be unconstrained, all objects must have constraints. An access type may have a designated type which is unconstrained. But the rule on objects having constraints still applies to dynamic variables. In fact it applies to all types of designated objects. Thus, if the designated type is an unconstrained type, then a constraint must be supplied when creating the dynamic variable.

The procedure **Access_Discriminant** in Program 15–6 illustrates the interaction of discriminants and constraints with access types. The syntax for access types given in 15–1 allows a subtype indicator. However, for access types, the allowable constraints on the designated type are limited to index constraints on unconstrained array types and discriminant constraints on discriminated records. The type **Vary** declared in line 2 is an unconstrained array type and the type **Grade_List** declared in lines 3–6 is a discriminated record. Both may be used as designated types.

Again, while unconstrained types are allowed, a dynamic variable, like all other objects, must have constraints. Thus, when we use the allocator **new** to create a designated object, any necessary constraints must be supplied. In **Access_Discriminant**, when allocating a dynamic variable of type **Grade_List**, a discriminant must be supplied as is illustrated in lines 9, 15, and 20. In line 15, an explicit discriminant supplies the constraint and causes a record containing a list of size 4 to be created. In line 20, a qualified expression supplies the type, the constraint, and a value. This causes a dynamic record constraining a list of size 3 to be created and initialized. A qualified expression or discriminant could also be used at the point of declaration, as is illustrated by the use of a qualified expression in line 9.

```
 1:procedure Access_Discriminant is
 2:   type Vary is array (INTEGER range <>) of INTEGER;
 3:   type Grade_List(Class_Size: INTEGER) is
 4:     record
 5:       List: Vary(1..Class_Size);
 6:     end record;
 7:   type Grade_Access is access Grade_List;
 8:   Math, Chem: Grade_Access;
 9:   Empty: constant Grade_Access := new Grade_List'(2, (0, 0));
10:   type Constrained is access Vary(1..6);
11:   Z: Constrained := new Vary(1..6);
12:   type Incompatible is access Grade_List(4);
13:   subtype Compatible is Grade_Access(4);
14:begin
15:   Math := new Grade_List(4);
16:   Math.all := (4, (84, 33, 67, 72));
17:   Math.List(2) := 96;
18:   Chem := Math;
19:   Math.List(1) := Chem.Class_Size;
20:   Math := new Grade_List'(3, (40, 47, 36));
21:   Z.all := (1, 2, 3, 4, 5, 6);
22:end Access_Discriminant;
```

Program 15–6

The same rules for supplying constraints hold for dynamic array variables, as illustrated in line 11. Again, while the array type may be unconstrained, the array object is constrained.

As with other variables, existing dynamic variables with discriminants may be supplied values using aggregates. This is illustrated in line 16. Again, as with other discriminated records, the discriminants must be repeated in the aggregate and must agree with the discriminants of the dynamic variable. Discriminants cannot be changed by an aggregate, except when they have values as a result of default initialization. This is the same rule that applies to static discriminated variables. Of course, individual elements may be modified as illustrated in line 17. As always, the discriminant is a component in the dynamic record as illustrated in line 19.

Dynamic array variables may also be given values by aggregates, but, as with array variables, constraints are not supplied. This is illustrated in line 21. A dynamic array variable is an array variable and the array operations and rules apply.

As with other situations involving discriminated records, **CONSTRAINT_ERROR**s can occur. For example, given the allocations

```
Math := new Grade_List(3);
Chem := new Grade_List(2);
```

the assignment

```
Chem.all := Math.all;
```

will result in a **CONSTRAINT_ERROR** because of the attempt to store the 3 values in **Math.all** into **Chem.all**. Actually, as with other discriminated records, the constraint error does not depend on the difference in size, but occurs because there is an attempt to modify the discriminant.

On the other hand, the assignment in line 18 is always fine. This is because **Chem:=Math;** does not attempt to change a discriminant. Rather, it changes the value of **Chem** — that is, it changes which dynamic record **Chem** accesses. The designated type of **Chem** is an unconstrained type. Therefore, the access variable **Chem** can access a dynamic variable with any discriminant that is legal for its designated type. After this assignment, both **Math** and **Chem** access the same dynamic variable with 3 integers. In short, assigning new access values never requires that the discriminants of the designated types match. However, assigning new values to designated objects does.

The subtleties of type compatibility are illustrated in lines 7 and 12. In Ada, strong typing means that the type declared in line 12 is incompatible with the type declared in line 7. This is indicated by the use of the reserved word **type** in these declarations, which is perfectly consistent with our previous discussions of types and subtypes. Thus, access variables of type **Grade_Access** and type **Incompatible** are incompatible. Note that even though these types are incompatible, the designated objects of both types are of type **Grade_List** and remain compatible. This is similar to records, in that incompatible record types can contain compatible components. For example, with an access variable declared as

```
Inc: Incompatible := new Grade_List'(4, (23, 34, 56, 28));
```

the assignment

```
Math := Inc; -- illegal
```

is a syntax error, while the assignment

```
Math.all := Inc.all;
```

is legal, although it could result in a **CONSTRAINT_ERROR**.

On the other hand, subtypes of access types can be declared as shown in line 13. These subtypes can contain constraints. These constraints apply to the designated type. For example, **Compatible** can only provide access to a dynamic variable in which **Class_Size** is 4. To summarize: access types are not compatible even if their designated types are, but access subtypes are compatible even though a **CONSTRAINT_ERROR** may result. Note that the compatibility of access subtypes allows us to build a single subprogram that allows access variables of any compatible access subtype to be passed as parameters.

As with discriminated records, the constraint may be supplied by a default. For example, suppose we change the declaration of **Grade_List** to

```
3: type Grade_List(Class_Size: INTEGER := 20) is
```

With this declaration, if we do not give an explicit constraint at the time of allocation then the default value is used in the creation of the dynamic variable. For example, in the statements

```
Math := new Grade_List;
Chem := new Grade_List(5);
```

Math has 20 grades because the default value is assumed, while **Chem** has 5 because a value is explicitly supplied. Had we used

```
Inc := new Grade_List;
```

we would get a **CONSTRAINT_ERROR** because the allocator produces a record with a default constraint of 20, even though **Inc** can only access records with a constraint of 4. To summarize, there are three ways to supply the constraint when allocating a dynamic record: explicitly, in parentheses following the designated type; by a qualified expression; and by default.

Dynamic discriminated and variant variables behave in the same way as static discriminated and variant variables. In the rules, substitute "allocation time" for "elaboration time." This means that dynamic variables that use defaults may have their discriminants changed by complete assignment.

You can have dynamic variables that have variants, as illustrated in the procedure **Variant** in Program 15–7. At the time of creation, a discriminant is supplied and the dynamic variable assumes the characteristics of one of the variants. The type **Box** declared on lines 4–15 is a variant record. When we create a **Box**, we give it a size. The variable **A** declared on line 17 can provide access to a **Box** of any size. Since variants are compatible, access variables are compatible with any and all variants. This means that the assignment

```
A := B;
```

is always syntactically legal. In fact, it merely causes **A** to access the same dynamic variable as **B**. Since no **Box** data is being changed by this assignment, it never gets a **CONSTRAINT_ERROR**. On the other hand, caution is required with the assignment

```
A.all := B.all;
```

Here, a copy is made of the values from the dynamic variable to which **B** provides access, and these values are assigned into the dynamic variable to which **A** provides access. If the constraint on **A.all** does not match the constraint on **B.all**, then a **CONSTRAINT_ERROR** occurs.

```
procedure Variant is
  type Size is (Little, Medium, Large);
  type Color is (Red, Blue, Green);
  type Box(How_Big: Size) is
    record
      case How_Big is
        when Little =>
          null;
        when Medium =>
          Its_Color: Color;
        when Large =>
          Top: Color;
          Bottom: Color;
      end case;
    end record;
  type Box_Access is access Box;
  A, B: Box_Access;
begin
  A := new Box(Medium);
  A.Its_Color := Green;
  B := new Box(Large);
  B.Top := Blue;
  A := new Box'(A.How_Big, Green);
  B := new Box'(Large, Blue, Red);
end Variant;
```

Program 15–7

15.3.5 Functions Returning Access Types

An access value can be returned by a function as illustrated by the function **`Get_Next`** in the procedure **`Access_Functions`** in Program 15–8. The function's return type is the access type **`Next_Int`**. The value returned by the function provides access to a dynamic variable. This variable is

```
Get_Next(A).all
```

Providing the function does not return **`null`**, you can use the value returned by the function to access a variable. The suffix **`.all`** accomplishes this and provides access to the entire variable. Similarly, the suffix **`.Data`** in lines 16 and 17 provides access to a component of the record whose access value is returned by the function.

The declaration in line 9, along with the statement in line 15, builds a linked list of two items, the first of which contains a 34 in its **`Data`** component and the second of which contains a 14. In line 16, **`Get_Next`** returns the access value of the dynamic record containing the 14. Thus, this line will print a 14.

```
 1:procedure Access_Functions is
 2:  type Linked_Int;
 3:  type Next_Int is access Linked_Int;
 4:  type Linked_Int is
 5:    record
 6:      Data: INTEGER;
 7:      Link: Next_Int;
 8:    end record;
 9:  A: Next_Int := new Linked_Int'(14, null);
10:  function Get_Next(A: Next_Int) return Next_Int is
11:  begin
12:    return A.Link;
13:  end Get_Next;
14:begin
15:  A := new Linked_Int'(34, A);
16:  Simple_IO.Write(Get_Next(A).Data);
17:  Get_Next(A).Data := 12;
18:end Access_Functions;
```

Program 15–8

Line 17 is somewhat tricky. Notice that a function occurs on the left-hand side of the assignment. We have seen cases before in which a function occurs on the left-hand side of the assignment. For example, if **R** is an array and **F** is a function then

```
R(F(3)) := 2;
```

is legal provided we have the appropriate types. In this example the function was used to determine which component, that is which variable, receives the value 2. The same is true with line 17. The function **Get_Next** is used to determine which dynamic variable gets the value 12 placed in its **Data** component. Again, **Get_Next** returns the access value of the record containing a 14, so the assignment replaces the 14 with the value 12. The function is not being reassigned; its result is being evaluated. That evaluation yields a dynamic variable which can have the value 14 assigned to one of its components. Observe that it is still true that you cannot change the function result for example,

```
Get_Next(A) := A; -- illegal
```

is illegal. But you can change the dynamic variable to which the function's result provides access as is done in line 17.

Obviously, the access value returned by **Get_Next** in line 17 is always computed before the assignment occurs. Thus, the question, "When does Ada determine which access value is returned?" only becomes important if the expressions within the statement do something that potentially changes the value returned by **Get_Next**. When the access value is determined is not defined by the language; consequently, any procedure containing assignments that attempt these sorts of changes is not guaranteed to work the same on all Ada implementations. Obviously, this kind of programming practice should be avoided. It is fine to use functions that return access types, but it can be very dangerous if they have side effects that change access values.

15.3.6 Access Types and Private Types

The interaction of access types with private types is simple. Access types may have private or limited private types as their designated types. Furthermore, a private type declaration can serve the same function as an incomplete type declaration. Consider the following fragment from a package declaration:

```
  type Linked_Int is private;
  type Next_Int is access Linked_Int;
private
  type Linked_Int is
    record
      Data: INTEGER;
      Link: Next_Int;
    end record;
```

The type **Linked_Int** becomes available at the point at which it is declared to be a private type. Thus, an access type to **Linked_Int** can be declared anytime thereafter. In the private part, the structure of **Linked_Int** reveals a definition that is appropriate for a linked list. The fact that **Linked_Int** is private means that the structure of the designated objects is hidden from the user of the package. Specifically, if **X** and **Y** are variables of type **Next_Int**, use of:

```
X.Data
```

is not allowed outside the package, although of course it is allowed inside the package body. But

```
X.all := Y.all;
```

is an allowable expression, because this assignment does not involve knowing the structure of the designated objects. Thus, we can apply **.all** to any access type, regardless of the designated type. In addition, tests such as

```
X = null
```

are allowed. This is because in the public part **Next_Int** is declared to be an access type, and all access types can be compared against **null**.

With limited private types, assignment is disallowed (see Chapter 10). Suppose that we changed the definition of **Linked_Int** to be:

```
type Linked_Int is limited private;
```

then for variables **X** and **Y** of type **Next_Int**, assignment statements such as

```
X.all := Y.all;
```

would not be allowed. Because the designated type is a limited type, the restrictions on limited types apply to the dynamic variables. However, as with private types, there are no additional restrictions on access types or access variables whose designated types are limited private. Thus, even with a limited private designated type, the assignment of access values, as in

```
X := Y;
```

and the comparison against **null** are allowed. It is the designated type, not the access type, which is restricted.

15.3.7 Compiler Issues

For clarification, we provide a note about one other possibility. Suppose we have a private (or limited private) type that is an access type, as in

```
  type An_Access is private;
private
  type An_Access is access ...
```

In this situation, the user of the package cannot use the fact (i.e., effectively "does not know") that the private type is an access type. That is, if the private type is an access type, the standard rules for private types still apply.

The existence of the private part of a package declaration is strictly for the benefit of the compiler. In Ada, all the information the compiler needs to make use of the things that are visible in the package must be contained in the package declaration. This means that compilation of a unit that names a package depends only on the package declaration. A unit that names a package can declare variables from private types that are available in the named package. The compiler will need to allocate storage for these variables and will need to be able to perform this allocation on the basis of information contained in the declaration of the named package. Specifically, the allocation of storage requires the information in the private part of the package declaration. Any information that is not so required may be deferred to the package body.

As an example, consider the declaration

```
package Deferred is
  type An_Access is private;
private
  type Something;
  type An_Access is access Something;
end Deferred;
package body Deferred is
  type Something is ...
end Deferred;
```

Compilation units naming **Deferred** can declare objects of type **An_Access**. The compiler needs to determine from the private part how much space to provide for such objects. The declaration that **An_Access** is an access type provides sufficient information to determine this amount of space. The type **Something** is not available outside the body of **Deferred**. So outside the package, it is not possible to allocate an object of type **Something**. Consequently, the compiler does not need to know about this type to compile units naming **Deferred**. In this case, the resolution of the incomplete type can be deferred to the inside of the package body, as is shown in the following example

```
package Deferred is
  type Regular_Private is private;
private
  type Something;
  type Known_Size is access Something;
  type Regular_Private is Known_Size;
end Deferred;
package body Deferred is
  type Something is ...
end Deferred;
```

Here, the type **Regular_Private** is an access type; consequently, its size is known. It is not possible to declare a variable of type **Something** outside the package. This permits deferring the definition of **Something** to inside the package body.

15.3.8 Running Out of Storage

Creating dynamic variables causes space to be allocated for those dynamic variables during execution. Under some circumstances, the implementation could run out of space to allocate. Then it becomes impossible to create new dynamic variables. An attempt to create a dynamic variable when there is no space available results in a **STORAGE_ERROR** exception. This exception is predefined in package **STANDARD**. Most often, **STORAGE_ERROR** occurs because of another error, such as a **new** contained in an inadvertent infinite loop or infinite recursion, but occasionally they occur because your program has attempted to allocate very large amounts of storage.

15.4 PROGRAMMING PRACTICES

Access types must be used very carefully. It is very easy to develop structures in which the interlocking accesses come to resemble a dish of spaghetti. Such structures are highly prone to errors. Fortunately, they can usually be avoided by careful design of the data structures and careful attention to implementation. Two of the most commonly used structures are linked lists and trees. We have previously mentioned linked lists in this chapter. In this section, we discuss and implement the simplest type of linked lists package. Following that, we will discuss another strategy for organizing linked lists. Trees will be discussed in the Programming Practices section of the next chapter.

15.4.1 The Linked List Package

We develop a package for the manipulation of linked lists. We describe the subprograms available in this package and give the Ada implementation for them. This package will hide the structure of the linked list. All access to and modification of the list will be through the subprograms provided by the package.

```
 1:package Linked_List is
 2:  type List is private;
 3:  subtype Key_Type is STRING;
 4:  subtype Data_Type is INTEGER;
 5:  function Get_Data(The_List: List; Key: Key_Type) return Data_Type;
 6:  procedure Insert(The_List: in out List; Key: Key_Type; Data: Data_Type);
 7:  procedure Delete(The_List: in out List; Key: Key_Type);
 8:  function Get_Front_Key(The_List: List) return Key_Type;
 9:  function Key_In_List(The_List: List; Key: Key_Type) return BOOLEAN;
10:  List_Error: exception;
11:private
12:  type List_Element(Data_Size: POSITIVE);
13:  type List is access List_Element;
14:end Linked_List;

15:package body Linked_List is
16:  type List_Element(Data_Size: POSITIVE) is
17:    record
18:      Key:Key_Type(1..Data_Size);
19:      Data:Data_Type;
20:      Next:List;
21:    end record;
      ...
```

Program 15–9

The declaration of the **Linked_List** package shown in Program 15–9 includes the type declarations for a linked list and the subprogram declarations that operate on linked lists. The structure of the linked list is hidden by using a private type (line 2). Conceptually, each element of the linked list has a **Key** and a **Data** component (plus a link). The types of these components are declared in lines 3 and 4. Although these declarations simply set **Key_Type** to be the same as **STRING** and **Data_Type** to be the same as **INTEGER**, they provide flexibility because we can change the type of **Key** or **Data** by changing a single line. In the private part, we see that the type **List** (line 13) is an access type for a dynamic object of the type **List_Element**. Since no subprogram outside the package can create an object of type **List_Element**, we defer completion of its declaration to the package body (lines 16–21). Conceptually, the

Key is the identification by means of which an element of the linked list is found, and the **Data** is the information associated with that **Key**. In most of the pictorial examples that follow, we shall simplify the diagrams by omitting the **Data** component.

First, we briefly summarize the subprograms of the **Linked_List** package, and then we cover these subprograms individually. Five subprograms are provided to the user of the package. Three of these are related to locating information in the list. Since locating information involves a **Key**, two of these three help determine which keys are in the list. The other two subprograms allow records to be inserted or deleted from a list. Any time a subprogram cannot successfully complete an operation or return a valid value, it will raise the exception **List_Error**.

```
 1:function Get_Data(Which_List: List; Key: Key_Type) return Data_Type is
 2:  Current_Record: List := Which_List;
 3:begin
 4:  while Current_Record /= null loop
 5:    if Current_Record.Key = Key then
 6:      return Current_Record.Data;
 7:    end if;
 8:    Current_Record := Current_Record.Next;
 9:  end loop;
10:  raise List_Error;
11:end Get_Data;
```

Program 15–10

The first subprogram we discuss is the one which locates data in the list. The function **Get_Data** shown in Program 15–10, is given a key to look for and a linked list in which to look. Its task is to search the linked list and to return the data in the record associated with that key. If the key is not found in the linked list, **Get_Data** raises **List_Error**. **Current_Record** indicates the record being examined. Its declaration at line 2 initializes it so that it will examine the first record (if any) of the linked list. Line 8 advances the search to the next record in the list. The conditions on the loop (line 4) indicate that the loop terminates if we have exhausted the list (**null**). If we have found the record (line 5), we return the value of its **Data** component (line 6). If we exhaust the list without locating the key, execution proceeds to the raise statement at line 10.

The effect of line 8 is illustrated in the before and after comparison of Figure 15–8. If **Current_Record** contained the access value of the record containing the key **"73"**, **Current_Record.Next** contains the access value of the next element of the linked list. That is, **Current_Record.Next** provides access to the record containing the key **"34"**. This access value is returned by the expression on the right-hand side of the assignment in line 8. Then this value is stored into **Current_Record**. After executing line 8, **Current_Record** contains the access value of the record containing the 34.

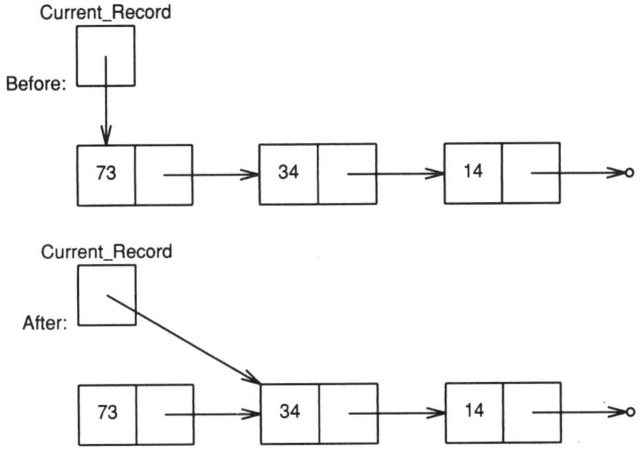

Figure 15–8

```
1:procedure Insert(Which_List: in out List; Key: Key_Type; Data: Data_Type) is
2:  New_Element: List := new List_Element'(Key'LENGTH, Key, Data, Which_List);
3:begin
4:  Which_List := New_Element;
5:end Insert;
```

Program 15–11

The next subprogram we describe is the procedure **Insert** shown in Program 15–11. This procedure inserts a new record into a list. The record is inserted as the first element in the list. **New_Element** is an access variable containing the access value of the new record to be inserted. This access value is assigned at elaboration (line 2). The qualified expression on this line creates a dynamic variable with the correct discriminant; that is, the component **Key** will be exactly the right size to hold the key. Line 2 also places the key, the data, and the correct value for the **Next** component into that dynamic variable. Note that the **Next** component contains the access value for the current first element in the list. As soon as the new element is inserted, the current first element will become the second element in the list. If the list was empty, the value **null** is in **Which_List**, and this is the value assigned to the **Next** component. At line 4, the list is set to access the new first element.

For a further example, we present another version of insert with an additional parameter which specifies a location at which the new element is to be inserted. Although conceptually slightly more tricky, it is remarkably simple. The procedure **Internal_Insert** shown in Program 15–12, is given an additional parameter **Behind_What**. **Behind_What** indicates the location at which the new element is to be inserted. Most of the procedure (lines 6–7 and 11–14) is identical to **Get_Data** and serves the purpose of finding the element with the key indicated by **Behind_What**.

```
1:procedure Internal_Insert(Which_List: in out List; Behind_What: Key_Type;
2:                          Key: Key_Type; Data: Data_Type) is
3:  New_Element: List := new List_Element'(Key'LENGTH, Key, Data, null);
4:  Current_Record: List := Which_List;
5:begin
6:  while Current_Record /= null loop
7:    if Current_Record.Key = Behind_What then
8:      New_Element.Next := Current_Record.Next;
9:      Current_Record.Next := New_Element;
10:     return;
11:   end if;
12:   Current_Record := Current_Record.Next;
13: end loop;
14: raise List_Error;
15:end Internal_Insert;
```

Program 15–12

When this key is found, execution of lines 8–10 occurs. When executing line 8, **Current_Record** contains the access value of a record containing the key **Behind_What**. The new record is to be inserted into the list just behind this record. Figure 15–9 shows how this insertion is accomplished.

The new dynamic variable accessed by **New_Element** was created in line 3. Its **Key** and **Data** components of this dynamic variable are initialized at the time it is allocated. When line 8 begins execution, the data is in the configuration shown in the "Before" section of Figure 15–9. Note that at this point, the **Next** component of the newly created record retains its default initialization value of **null**.

When line 8 is executed, the link of the new element is set so that the new element will provide access to the rest of the list. Note that, at this point the rest of the list is accessed by **Current_Record.Next**. This achieves the configuration labeled "Middle" in the figure.

When line 9 is executed, the value of **Current_Record.Next** is changed so that it provides access to the new record. This achieves the configuration labeled "After" in the figure. At this point, the insertion of the new data into the list has been accomplished.

The order of the two statements in lines 8 and 9 of **Internal_Insert** is critical. The assignment statement in line 8 must be before the assignment statement in line 9 because the value of **Current_Element.Next** must be used before it is changed. If the statements are reversed, the back end of the list "falls off"; that is, no one saved the value of **Current_Element.Next** so we no longer have an access value which leads to whatever element was accessed by that value. That element and all elements behind it would no longer be accessible. This sort of error is quite common in the manipulation of access values.

In building **Internal_Insert**, we should ask about the boundary conditions. First, what happens if **Current_Record** is the end of the list? In this case, **Cur-**

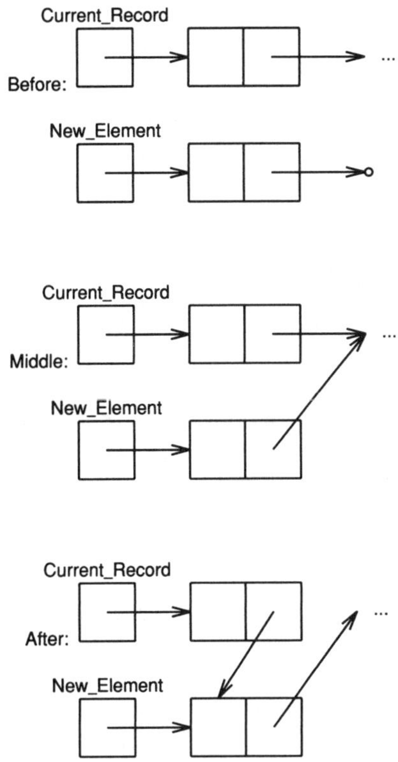

Figure 15–9

rent_Record.Next contains the value **null**. So in Figure 15–9, at "Middle," the access value stored in **New_Element.Next** becomes **null**. The steps performed by **Internal_Insert** still result in a correct list. Notice that if the list contains no elements (**Which_List = null**), the loop is not entered and **List_Error** is raised. In the case of an empty list, it is impossible to find **Behind_What**, so there is no possibility of an internal insertion.

Second, what happens if **Behind_What** refers to the first element of the list. In this case, when lines 8–10 are executed, **Current_Record** refers to the static variable that provides access to the list and not the **Next** component of a dynamic variable within the list. Observe that neither **Internal_Insert** nor Figure 15–9 make any assumption about whether **Current_Record** is a static variable or a **Next** component in a dynamic variable. If **Current_Record** is a static variable, then after the execution of **Internal_Insert**, the new element is the first element of the linked list.

The procedure **Delete** shown in Program 15–13 looks for a record containing the indicated key and removes that record from the list. If the record is not found, **Delete** raises **List_Error**. First the procedure checks to make sure it has a list (line 4). If it does, it checks the special case in which the record to be deleted is the first record

```
 1:procedure Delete(Which_List: in out List; Key: Key_Type) is
 2:  Current_Record: List := Which_List;
 3:begin
 4:  if Which_List = null then
 5:    raise List_Error;
 6:  elsif Which_List.Key = Key then
 7:    Which_List := Which_List.Next;
 8:  else
 9:    while Current_Record.Next /= null loop
10:      if Current_Record.Next.Key = Key then
11:        Current_Record.Next := Current_Record.Next.Next;
12:        return;
13:      end if;
14:      Current_Record := Current_Record.Next;
15:    end loop;
16:    raise List_Error;
17:  end if;
18:end Delete;
```

Program 15–13

in the list. If the record to be deleted is not the first record in the list, the loop in lines 9–15 goes down the list looking for the indicated key, using the if test in line 10. If it finds the key, line 11 removes the record from the list and line 12 exits the procedure. If it does not find the key, line 14 steps one link further down the list. If the key is not found in the list, execution will reach the raise statement at line 16.

Notice that the procedure looks ahead. In technical terms, **Current_Record** is a *trailing access value*. That is, it is always one list element before the one we are considering. That is why we so often see **Current_Record.Next** in this procedure. The reason for this is so that removal of an element can be accomplished.

As shown in Figure 15–10, we must change the **Next** component of the element before the one with the correct value of **What**. If we are deleting the 34, then it is the **Next** component of the record containing the 73 which must be changed. **Current_Record** must retain the access value of the record containing the 73 while we examine the next record to discover the 34. In line 11, **Current_Record.Next.Next** is the access value of the record containing 14. (This value is stored in the record containing the 34). A copy of this value is made into the record containing the 73 (**Current_Record.Next**). The record containing the 34 still exists, but it is no longer in the linked list.

The functions **Get_Front_Key** and **Key_In_List** shown in Program 15–14 are designed to see what is in the list. **Get_Front_Key** returns the key of the first record in the list. **Key_In_List** returns **TRUE** if it finds the key in the list. This function uses the by-now familiar loop to traverse the list, looking for a record with the correct key.

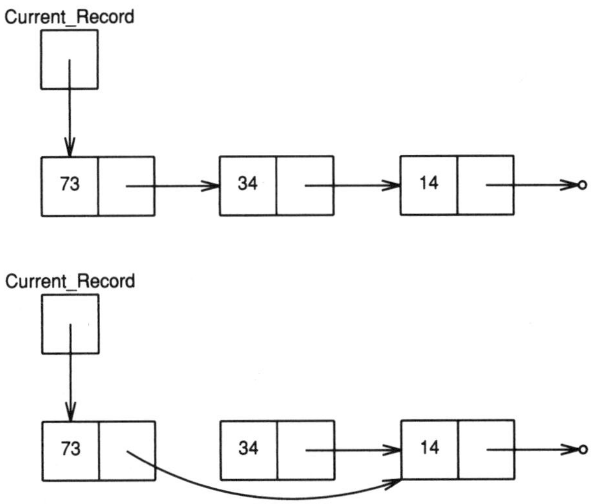

Figure 15–10

```
function Get_Front_Key(Which_List: List) return Key_Type is
begin
  if Which_List = null then
    raise List_Error;
  end if;
  return Which_List.Key;
end Get_Front_Key;

function Key_In_List(Which_List: List; Key: Key_Type) return BOOLEAN is
  Current_Record: List := Which_List;
begin
  while Current_Record /= null loop
    if Current_Record.Key = Key then
      return TRUE;
    end if;
    Current_Record := Current_Record.Next;
  end loop;
  return FALSE;
end Key_In_List;
```

Program 15–14

15.4.2 The Doubly Linked List Package

With singly linked lists, it is very difficult to move backward through the list. To avoid this problem, doubly linked lists are often used. In a doubly linked list, each node contains access values for the nodes before and after it.

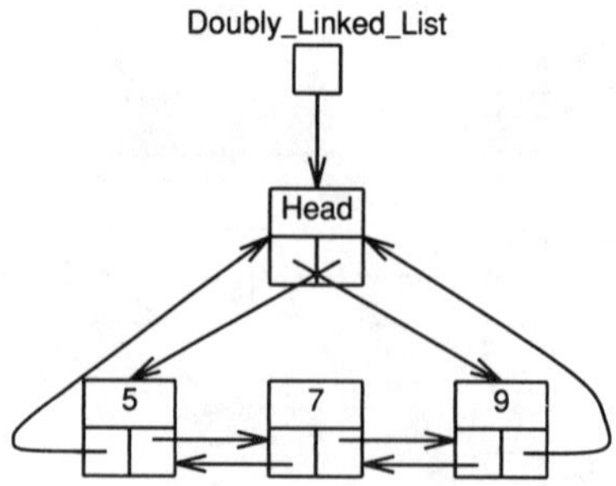

Figure 15–11

A sample doubly linked list is illustrated in Figure 15–11. When we insert a node into a doubly linked list, we need to adjust four access values. For example, if we wished to add a node between the nodes containing the data values 7 and 9 in the figure, we would have to change the right access value in the node with 7 and the left access value in the node with 9 and set the two appropriate values in the new node.

The delete procedure for doubly linked lists is much simpler than that for linked lists. In the package **Linked_List** in Program 15–9, we could not simply supply the access value of the node to be deleted, because we needed to find the node just before it in the linked list. This required going to the start of the list and traversing the list to the node just before the node to be deleted. Because the doubly linked list provides access to nodes in both directions, it is easy to find the nodes before and after a node. To delete the node whose access value is given in an access variable **X**, we can adjust the access value of the node in front of that accessed by **X** with the statement

```
X.Left_Access.Right_Access := X.Right_Access;
```

Because this does not change the node to which **X** provides access, the statement

```
X.Right_Access.Left_Access := X.Left_Access;
```

will correctly adjust the node following the one we wish to delete. Although the node **X.all** still contains access to nodes in the list, **X.all** has been removed from the list by these commands.

One trick with a doubly linked list is to use a special head node to eliminate the special cases which would otherwise apply to empty lists. The head node is never deleted or searched for. It is easy to detect because the static variable (**A_List**) contains its access value. Figure 15–12 illustrates an empty doubly linked list. The list is empty if

```
A_List.Right_Access = A_List
```

Of course, we could have equivalently compared against **Left_Access** and gotten the same result.

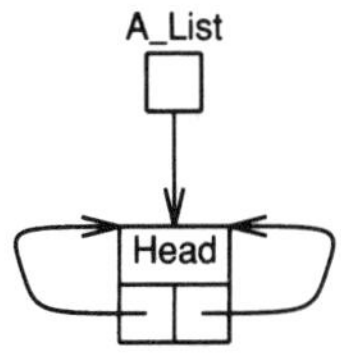

Figure 15–12

One of the advantages of doubly linked lists is that there is no difference between the front and the back of the list. Insertions or deletions work the same way at both ends. This makes the doubly linked list a natural structure to use for implementing queues.

15.4.3 Testing and Debugging

Most problems with linked structures occur because the program built is different from the structure the programmer intended it to build. Often this is because a mistake in the program leads to a piece of the structure getting lost. Even if this loss occurs in testing, it may not be discovered unless a search is made of the key of one of the nodes that was lost. Even more subtle problems are possible, and care must be taken to detect them.

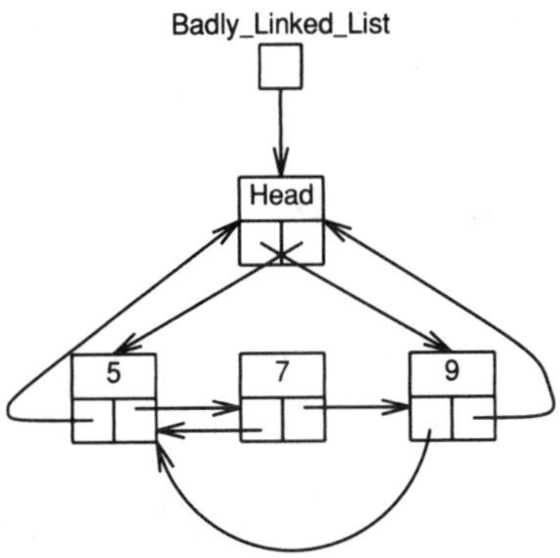

Figure 15–13

As an example of a problem involving a linked structure, suppose a doubly linked list package builds the list shown in Figure 15–13. One of the links is clearly wrong. However, traversing the list forward or backward does not reveal the problem, unless we notice that the nodes reported in the list are different. Certain orders of insertions, deletions, and queries may fail to detect this sort of problem. In general, in order to detect and locate problems, it is advisable to examine the entire structure after each step in the test. Unfortunately, the package itself makes testing hard because it hides the structure. To make testing easier, the package could supply a subprogram that printed the contents of the lists. In a doubly linked package, such a subprogram could print the list twice, once going from front to back (using the **Right**) links and again going from back to front (using the **Left**) links. When supplying such a subprogram, be careful that it does not accidentally modify the structure it is printing.

15.5 ADA SUMMARY

The single theme of this chapter was *access types*. We examined the concept of dynamic variables and data structures which can be built during program execution. We examined how to declare access types and use them to implement dynamic data structures. We illustrated one kind of adjustable structure, the *linked list*. Because they are often used with access types, we introduced *incomplete type declarations*. To point out some ways in which access types could be used, we discussed the interaction of access types with other aspects of the Ada language, including discriminated types and private types.

EXERCISES

15.1. In a bank, the number of depositors is continually changing. Change the implementation of the **Bank_Account** package (Program 3–14, exercises 3.1, 4.5, 5.9, 7.8, 8.2, 10.5, 10.6, 12.6, or 14.1) so that it uses a linked list of customers. To keep our examples simple, the **Data** component in our linked list examples consisted of a simple integer. You will need to modify the declarations and procedures of the linked list package to handle a more complex **Data** component, that is, a bank account.

15.2. Build a **Doubly_Linked_List** package. The visible part of this package should be identical to the **Linked_List** package in Program 15–9. The private part and the body will need to be somewhat different, but the similarity will surprise you. One tricky but valuable part is to set up the record initialization so that every time a doubly linked list is declared, it gets initialized to the empty list, that is, initialized to look like Figure 15–12.

15.3. Implement the **Storage_Handler** package (Program 12–10 or exercise 12.5) as a linked list rather than as an array. Be sure to remove the discriminant indicating the maximum size of the stack/queue, and take out the **Queue_Full** exception since it is no longer applicable.

15.4. In this exercise, you will be building a dictionary utility. For this exercise, you should not use the **Lines** package or **Simple_IO** packages.

First, write a dictionary package with the following specification:

```
package Dictionary is
  function Definition(Word: STRING) return STRING;
  -- Purpose: Get a definition from the dictionary.
  procedure Store(Word, Definition: STRING);
  -- Purpose: Add a definition to the dictionary.
  Word_Not_Found, Word_Already_Present: exception;
end Dictionary;
```

Store stores the word as given, along with the definition. The exception **Word_Already_Present** is raised if the word is found to be in the dictionary already.

`Definition` does a *case-insensitive* search for the given word; that is, "BEGIN" is the same word as "begin". This function returns the definition of the word. If the word is not found, the exception **`Word_Not_Found`** should be raised.

The package should store the words and their definitions into a linked list. We suggest two of several ways in which you might represent a node of this linked list:

```
type Node(Word_Length, Definition_Length: NATURAL);
  type Node_Ptr is access Node;
  type Node(Word_Length, Definition_Length: NATURAL) is
    record
      Word: STRING(1..Word_Length);
      Definition: STRING(1..Definition_Length);
      Next_Word: Node_Ptr;
    end record;
```

or

```
type String_Ptr is access STRING;
  type Node;
  type Node_Ptr is access Node;
  type Node is
    record
      Word, Definition: String_Ptr;
      Next_Word: Node_Ptr;
    end record;
```

Each method has its advantages. These declarations are inside the package body. The package declaration should remain the same no matter what representation you choose.

Implement a main program that will read a file of words and definitions and enter them into the dictionary. Then the main program should interactively allow the user to look up words and add words to the dictionary.

16

Generics: Abstraction and Reuse

16.1 OBJECTIVES

In this chapter, we cover *generic units*, an Ada construct for writing reusable components. We will describe in detail how to declare and use a generic unit (section 3). This description will include the various methods of parameterizing these units which enable their reuse in different situations. We will look in detail at an example, a generic sort procedure (section 4). We will also cover in detail the **TEXT_IO** package, showing how to use the generic units it supplies for controlling input and output (section 5). As a larger example, a generic binary tree package is designed and implemented (section 6).

CONCEPTS:

- In many cases, the exact type of an object is not required for a subprogram to be written correctly.
- It is better to spend more time getting a single elegant parameterized solution than multiple related solutions.

GOALS:

- Write and use a generic unit.
- Write a program that makes use of advanced input and output capabilities.

16.2 MOTIVATION

Abstraction is the process of stepping back from a specific problem and handling a more general problem. If we can solve the general problem, we can apply that solution to the specific problem, as well as many other problems. Programming languages support various forms of abstraction.

The first form of abstraction we introduced in Ada was the procedure. The procedure solved a general problem. The parameters allowed us to apply that solution to a specific problem. A parameterized procedure solved a family of programming problems; that is, the parameters permitted selection or variation of actions in a program.

Two other forms of abstraction in Ada were the discriminated record and the unconstrained array. The record or array solved a general problem. The discriminant or constraint allowed us to apply that solution to a specific problem. A parameterized type solved a family of data problems. Discriminants and constraints permitted selection or variation of components and sizes of data.

The benefits of these types of abstraction are conciseness, because you only need to express something once, and accuracy, because you only need to get something right once. Thus you can concentrate on doing the job right once rather than repeating it with minor variations. An abstract solution gives you flexibility. Since you have solved the fundamental problem, it is easier to use that solution in another situation, changing the parameters, discriminants, or constraints.

Packages were an abstraction of a different nature. They permitted construction of sets of tools that could be applied to various problems. Again, the time taken to build a good set of tools was repaid by the ease with which those tools allowed us to solve more complex problems. This form of abstraction says you need not know how a problem is solved, only that it is solved correctly.

Scope was an abstraction of the storage of values that complements the idea of packages. Scope permitted identifiers to be limited to local access, thus protecting a solution against unauthorized and mistaken interference. Again, this form of abstraction meant that no one could depend on the details of how a problem was solved. Thus, you were forced to ignore the method by which a tool used various data in its solution.

Types were a form of abstraction. Types had operations and values. Type values removed us from the constraints of the numeric representations that underlie all computer data. With operations, types restricted the uses of variables and literals in such a way as to encourage the programmer not to deal with the internal workings of a type or the internal structure of tools (operations) provided for that type.

The benefits of the last two forms of abstraction are maintainability and understandability. These forms make programs more maintainable because you can fix one thing without the risk of upsetting something else. These forms make programs more understandable because it is easier to see what is being done and how it is being done when you do not have to be concerned about implementation details.

Overloading encouraged abstraction because it permitted you to build a family of subprograms associated with the same identifier, all of which had similar functionality.

The capability we now introduce is the Ada *generic*. Generic subprograms permit the building of a single metasubprogram that can be used to create other subprograms. The advantage of generic units is that you can build a general-purpose subprogram. Building and reusing a general-purpose subprogram rather than building many subprograms which are quite similar saves time. The time saved can be spent on getting a correct and elegant general-purpose subprogram. Generic packages offer similar benefits.

16.3 GENERIC UNITS

Generic units permit the selection of types, subprograms, and objects. Procedures take actual parameters that supply values to formal parameters; generic units take actual parameters that supply types, subprograms or objects to formal parameters. The syntax for declaring a generic unit is given in Figure 16–1.

<generic declaration>

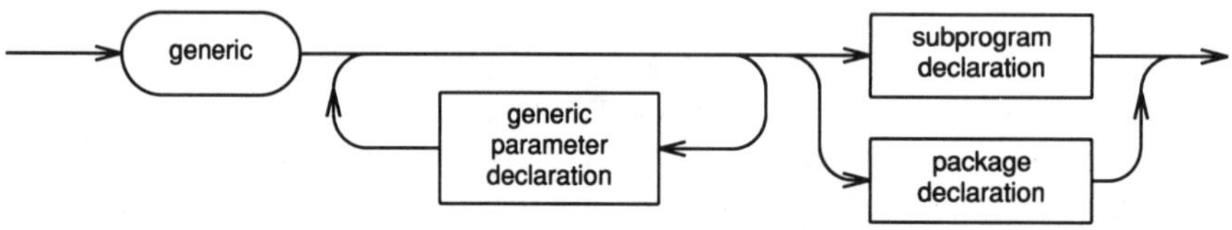

Figure 16–1

A generic unit is a *template* for a set of related program units. A generic unit is either a generic subprogram or a generic package. A generic subprogram is a template for a set of subprograms, while a generic package is a template for a set of packages. We can think of a procedure as performing variations on actions in accordance with its parameters. A generic unit can have *generic formal parameters* that indicate how members of the set differ.

The procedure **Generic_Demo** in Program 16–1 contains the generic procedure **Exchange**. This generic procedure contains a generic formal parameter **Elem**, which is declared in line 4. A generic declaration always begins with the reserved word **generic** (line 3) and ends at the end of the subprogram or package declaration (line 5). Consequently you can only declare one subprogram or package per occurrence of the reserved word **generic**. However, by repeating the reserved word **generic**, you can make as many generic declarations as desired. In fact you can nest generic or nongeneric declarations within a generic declaration. For example, a generic package may declare many subprograms and generic subprograms in its visible part.

Unlike other procedures, the body of a generic procedure is required to be separate from the declaration. The declaration of the body of the generic procedure **Exchange** is found in lines 6–10 of **Generic_Demo**. The only "unusual" thing about the body of a generic unit is that it can use the generic parameters. The body of **Exchange** looks like any normal procedure, except for the use of the identifier **Elem**. Even then, **Elem** is used exactly as though it were a type.

```
 1:procedure Generic_Demo is
 2:  X, Y: INTEGER;
 3:  generic
 4:    type Elem is private;
 5:  procedure Exchange(U, V: in out Elem); -- End generic declaration
 6:  procedure Exchange(U, V: in out Elem) is
 7:    T: Elem := U;
 8:  begin
 9:    U := V; V := T;
10:  end Exchange;
11:  procedure Swap is new Exchange(Elem => INTEGER);
12:begin -- Generic_Demo
13:  Swap(X, Y);
14:end Generic_Demo;
```

Program 16–1

A subprogram or package that is *instantiated* (i.e., obtained, created, built) from a generic unit is called an *instance* or instantiation of that generic unit. The reserved word **new** is used for generic instantiation. For each instantiation of a generic unit, *generic actual parameters* corresponding to the generic formal parameters must be supplied. Generic formal parameters may have default values. Once a subprogram or package has been instantiated from a generic unit, it is just like any other subprogram or package.

The only thing a generic declaration is good for is instantiation. For example, a generic procedure cannot be executed or called; it can only be used to instantiate procedures.

An instantiation of the generic procedure **Exchange** in line 11 of Program 16–1 creates the procedure **Swap**. **Swap** is an instance of **Exchange** in which the generic parameter **Elem** is associated with the actual parameter **INTEGER**. Consequently, **Swap** has formal parameters **U** and **V** that are of type **INTEGER**. **Swap** is a normal procedure and may be used as such, as shown in line 13. When called, **Swap** will swap the values found in the two **INTEGER** variables that are supplied as its actual parameters. Thus, the call in line 13 will swap the value in **X** with the value in **Y**.

In a sense, instantiation is to a generic unit what a call is to a procedure. That is, a generic unit exists only for the purpose of being instantiated, while a procedure exists only for the purpose of being called.

As with packages and subprograms, a generic unit may be a separate compilation unit. In fact, when a generic declaration is a compilation unit, the corresponding generic body will be separate compilation unit from the generic declaration. For example, we could separate **Generic_Demo** as follows. First we would compile the declaration of the generic unit:

```
generic
  type Elem is private;
procedure Exchange(U, V: in out Elem);
```

This declares the presence of the generic procedure **Exchange**. Then we compile the body of the generic procedure:

```
procedure Exchange(U, V: in out Elem) is
  T: Elem := U;
begin
  U := V; V := T;
end Exchange;
```

We have now specified how the procedure works. The Ada implementation is responsible for associating the body with the declaration. Like other body-declaration pairs, the body and the specification must match. Notice that the reserved word **generic** is not repeated in the generic body. The fact that the declaration is labeled generic causes the body to be a generic body.

A subprogram can be a library unit. This includes subprograms that are formed by instantiating generics. Thus, we can make **Swap** a library unit by instantiating it in a separate compilation unit:

```
with Exchange;
procedure Swap is new Exchange(Elem => INTEGER);
```

Because **Exchange** is now a library unit, it must be named in the context clause in order to be available. The two lines shown constitute the entire compilation unit. There is no body for **Swap**; rather, its body is defined by the body of **Exchange**. **Swap** is an instantiation of **Exchange**.

Now we can compile the procedure **Generic_Demo**:

```
with Swap;
procedure Generic_Demo is
  X, Y: INTEGER;
begin
  Swap(X, Y);
end Generic_Demo;
```

Because it is a library unit **Swap** must be named in the context clause. Of course, if we had named **Exchange** in the context clause, other procedures could have been instantiated inside **Generic_Demo**.

16.3.1 Generic Formal Parameters: Formal Types

There are three kinds of generic formal parameters: generic formal types, generic formal subprograms, and generic formal objects. We will cover each of these in separate sections. Generic formal parameters are what allow an instantiation to select its types, subprograms, and objects.

<generic parameter declaration -- formal type>

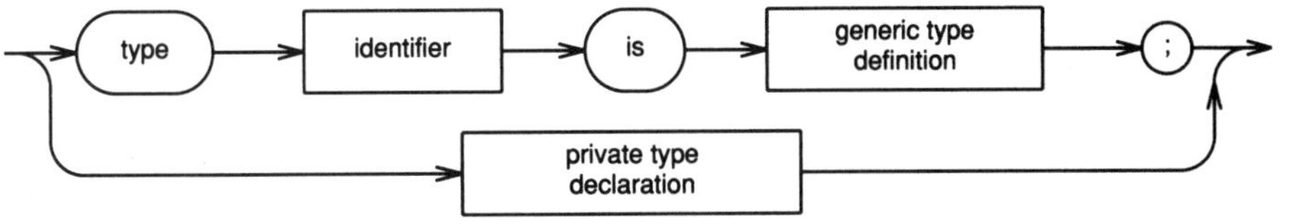

Figure 16–2

The first kind of generic formal parameter we cover is the generic formal type. The syntax for generic formal types is given in Figure 16–2. The available types are discrete, integer, float, fixed, array, access, private, and limited private.

We begin by examining the generic private type declaration using the procedure **Generic_Demo** in Program 16–1. The syntax for a generic private type is given in Figure 16–3. The type **Elem** is a generic private type. Instantiation of **Exchange** creates a procedure that exchanges a specified type. Because **Elem** is supplied the type **INTEGER** in the instantiation of **Swap**, the procedure **Swap** exchanges two integers. Had we supplied the type **BOOLEAN** we would have instantiated a procedure that swapped two Booleans.

The generic actual parameter must be a type mark, that is, a name that corresponds to a type or subtype. As with formal parameters of subprograms, you may not add a constraint to a subtype within the parameter list of the instantiation. For example,

```
procedure Exchange is new Swap(INTEGER range 1..5);    -- illegal
```

is not legal because the parameter is not simply a type mark.

<private type declaration>

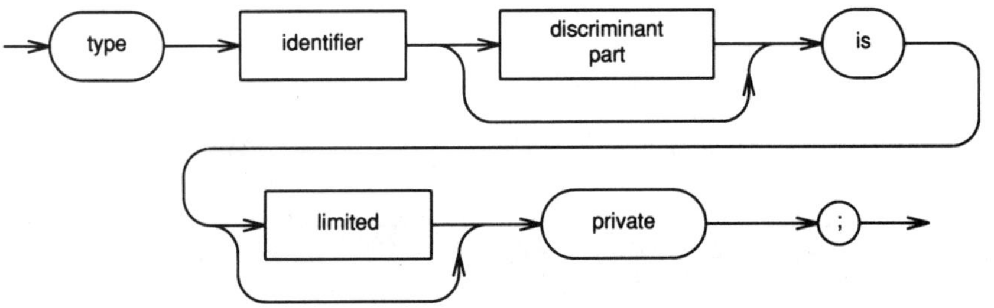

Figure 16–3

With generic formal types, the compiler performs type checking to ensure that the actual and formal parameters match. In generic private types, **private** may match any actual type or subtype except a limited type. Thus, the association of **Elem** with **INTEGER** by the instantiation in line 11 is legal. It would also be legal for an instantiation to associate **Elem** with any array type, record type, or access type, as long as that type was not a limited type. Similarly, **limited private** may match any type or subtype.

The use of the reserved word **private** indicates that the type is private from the viewpoint of the generic. Because of the matching rules, the generic has no idea what type is being passed, except that the type is *not* limited. Thus, the generic may only assume that assignment and equality are available. The type **Elem** is private and only assignment was used inside **Exchange** (lines 7 and 11). A statement using an operator, such as

```
U := V + T;    -- illegal
```

is illegal inside **Exchange**. Even though the instantiation of **Swap** associated **Elem** with **INTEGER**, an instantiation could associate **Elem** with a record type, for which an addition operation is not defined. Thus, the matching rules say, only operators guaranteed to be defined on any type associated with **Elem** are predefined within the generic. Again, for a private type, these are assignment and equality.

The reserved word pair **limited private** indicates that the actual parameter may be of any type, including a limited type. Because the type may be anything, the generic cannot make any assumptions, even that assignment and equality are available. Again, the type is limited private from viewpoint of the generic. This means that, within the generic no operations are guaranteed to be predefined on the type. However, the generic can be explicitly told that certain operations exist using the mechanism of generic formal subprograms to be described shortly.

As indicated in Figure 16–3, generic private types and types passed as generic actual parameters can contain discriminants. When discriminants occur, the match is legal if the generic formal type does not have discriminants, or if the generic formal type has discriminants and the generic actual parameter has matching discriminants. The following program fragment illustrates these points:

```
type No_Constraint(Char: CHARACTER) is
  record
    Letter: CHARACTER := Char;
  end record;
subtype Has_Constraint is No_Constraint('C');
generic
  type Formal_With_Discrim(Ch: CHARACTER) is private;
  type Formal is private;
package Generic_Privates is
  procedure Analyze(First: Formal_With_Discrim; Second: Formal);
end Generic_Privates;
package body Generic_Privates is
  Local: Formal_With_Discrim('C');
  ...
end Generic_Privates;
package Good_1 is new Generic_Privates(No_Constraint, Has_Constraint);
package Good_2 is new Generic_Privates(No_Constraint, No_Constraint);
```

```
17:package Bad is new Generic_Privates(Has_Constraint, No_Constraint);
   --illegal
```

In these declarations **Formal** and **Formal_With_Discrim** are generic private types. This means that within **Generic_Privates**, the operations allowed on objects of these types are those allowed on private types; that is, assignment, equality, explicit conversion (to a derived type) and membership testing. For example, these are the only operations which could be applied to the variable **Local**.

Although, **Formal_With_Discrim** is a generic private type, it is also declared that it is a discriminated type and the discriminant is of the type **CHARACTER**. Because we know the type of the discriminant we can apply the operators available for that type to the discriminant. For example, within the body of **Analyze** we could use an expression of type **CHARACTER**, such as:

```
CHARACTER'SUCC(Local.Ch)
```

When we instantiate the package **Generic_Privates**, the discriminants must match. In line 7, the generic formal parameter **Formal_With_Discrim** has a discriminant of type **CHARACTER**. So any actual parameter associated with this formal parameter must contain a discriminant of type **CHARACTER**. In the instantiations in lines 15 and 16, the actual parameter (**No_Constraint**, declared in line 1) has a discriminant of type **CHARACTER**, so the matches are legal. The declaration in line 7 implies three things about the actual parameter associated with **Formal_With_Discrim**: that it is not a limited private type, that it has a discriminant of type **CHARACTER** and that it is an unconstrained type. In line 17, the actual parameter, **Has_Constraint**, has a discriminant of type **CHARACTER**, but it is a constrained type and therefore cannot match **Formal_With_Discrim**.

Certain attributes may be applied to generic private types. Some of these have to do with representation information (Chapter 17). For now we introduce the attribute **CONSTRAINED**. The declaration of **Formal** in line 8 indicates only that the actual parameter is not of a limited private type. This declaration neither requires nor disallows a match against a type which has discriminants. Within **Generic_Privates**, the type **Formal** cannot access any discriminant, because the actual type may not have one. In the instantiations in lines 15 and 16, the actual parameter does have a discriminant. In line 15 the actual type is constrained, in line 16, it is unconstrained. If it is necessary to know within **Generic_Privates** whether or not the actual type is unconstrained, the attribute **Formal'CONSTRAINED** may be used. For the instantiation in line 15, this attribute will yield **FALSE**; for the instantiation in line 16, it will yield **TRUE**. Of course, other associations are possible for **Formal**. For example, if associated with the type **FLOAT**, it would be constrained; if associated with the type **STRING**, it would be unconstrained.

If you want to perform operations on a generic formal type, one solution is to restrict which types can be passed. This is done by using generic type definitions. The syntax for generic type definitions is given in Figure 16–4. With these definitions, the type of the actual parameter is restricted. Certain operators will always be available for

<generic type definition>

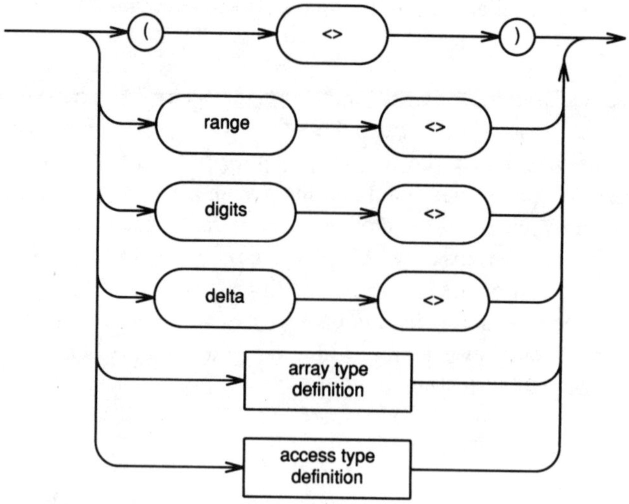

Figure 16–4

these restricted types and these operators can be used within the generic. The compiler is responsible for ensuring that instantiations conform to the required type restrictions. Failure to conform is a syntax error.

The first form of generic type definition indicates that the actual parameter will be a discrete type. Thus, in the declaration

```
 1:generic
 2:  type Discrete_Type is (<>);
 3:procedure Discretes;
 4:procedure Discretes is
 5:  A, B: Discrete_Type;
 6:  type X is array (Discrete_Type) of INTEGER;
 7:begin
    ...
 8:  if A > B then
 9:    B := Discrete_Type'SUCC(A);
10:  end if;
11:  TEXT_IO.PUT(Discrete_Type'IMAGE(B));
12:  for Y in Discrete_Type loop ...
13:end Discretes;
```

Discrete_Type will only match a discrete type. We do not know any details of that discrete type, but within the generic unit we may use the type as a discrete type. For example, discrete types may be compared (line 8), any discrete attribute can be applied (lines 9 and 11), discrete types may be used as array indices (line 6) and discrete types may be used in the for schema (line 12). Any instantiation of **Discretes** must associate **Discrete_Type** with a discrete type as is done in the following examples

```
procedure Day_Instance is new Discretes(BOOLEAN);
procedure Integer_Instance is new Discretes(INTEGER);
```

The next three generic type definitions correspond to numeric types. These are illustrated in the following generic procedure declaration:

```
 1:generic
 2:  type Integer_Type is range <>;
 3:  type Floating_Point_Type is digits <>;
 4:  type Fixed_Point_Type is delta <>;
 5:procedure Numeric_Generics;
 6:procedure Numeric_Generics is
 7:  I: Integer_Type;
 8:  X: Floating_Point_Type;
 9:  R: Fixed_Point_Type;
10:begin
11:  I := I + Integer_Type(X);
12:  if Floating_Point_Type'DIGITS > 5 then
13:    R := 0.0;
14:  end if;
15:end Numeric_Generics;
```

The notation **range <>** indicates that the generic actual parameter must be an integer subtype. Within the generic package, we can use any operators and attributes applicable to integer types. As examples, addition and explicit conversion from other numeric types are illustrated in line 11.

The notation **digits <>** indicates that the generic actual parameter must be a floating point subtype. Thus, we may apply any operations or attributes that are legal for floating point types. As an example, line 12 uses the attribute **DIGITS**. In particular, a generic package could contain statements which make the computation of a function depend on the accuracy of the type supplied as the generic actual parameter. Because conversion exists between any two numeric types, the conversion of a floating point type to an integer type in line 11 is legal.

The notation **delta <>** indicates that the generic actual parameter must be a fixed point subtype. So, the generic may apply any operations or attributes that are legal for fixed point types. For example, real literals can be used with generic fixed point types, as illustrated by the assignment statement of line 13.

An instantiation that uses the generic procedure **Numeric_Generics** is the following:

```
with Numerics_Generic;
procedure Generic_Type_Demo is
  subtype Small is INTEGER range 0..4;
  type A_Float is digits 3;
```

```
type A_Fixed is delta 0.1 range 0.0..1.0;
procedure Make_Generic is new Numeric_Generics(Small, A_Float, A_Fixed);
...
```

In the instantiated procedure **Make_Generic**, the addition of variables of the generic formal type **Integer_Type** (line 11 in the body in **Numeric_Generics**) is, in fact, the addition of variables of the subtype **Small**. Further, the **DIGITS** attribute applied to the formal type **Floating_Point_Type** (line 12 in **Numeric_Generics**), is, in fact, the attribute **DIGITS** applied to the type **A_Float**. For example, in this instantiation, **Floating_Point_Type'DIGITS** is 3 and **Integer_Type'FIRST** is 0.

There are two additional allowable generic type definitions. These types are the only ones that allow the direct association of actual structures with generic structures. These are generic array types and generic access types.

The syntax for this *generic array type* definition is the same as that for any array type. The actual parameter must be an array type. This actual parameter must have the same dimension, the same index type(s), and the same component type as the generic formal parameter. Furthermore, if the generic formal array type is constrained, the actual parameter must also be constrained; if the formal array type is unconstrained, the actual parameter must be unconstrained. Consider the following declarations:

```
1:generic
2:   type Cons_Formal_Type is array (INTEGER range 0..4) of BOOLEAN;
3:   type Uncons_Formal_Type is array (CHARACTER range <>) of FLOAT;
4:package Arrays is
5:   Array_1:Cons_Formal_Type;
6:   Array_2:Uncons_Formal_Type('A'..'E');
7:end Arrays;

8:with Arrays;
9:package Generic_Array_Parameters is
10:  type Cons_Type is array (INTEGER range 0..4) of BOOLEAN;
11:  type Uncons_Type is array (CHARACTER range <>) of FLOAT;
12:  package Good_Package is new Arrays(Cons_Type, Uncons_Type);
13:end Generic_Array_Parameters;
```

In the generic package **Arrays**, **Cons_Formal_Type** is a constrained generic array type and **Uncons_Formal_Type** is an unconstrained generic array type. The instantiation of **Good_Package** (line 12) is legal because the parameters match: Both the formal parameter **Cons_Formal_Type** and the actual parameter **Cons_Type** are arrays of dimension 1, have indices of type **INTEGER** and components of type **BOOLEAN**. Further, both types are constrained. Both the formal parameter **Uncons_Formal_Type** and the actual parameter **Uncons_Type** are arrays of dimension 1, have indices of type **CHARACTER** and components of type **FLOAT**, and both are unconstrained. Remember, that an object always has constraints, so when an object of the generic formal type **Uncons_Formal_Type** is declared in line 6, constraints must be supplied.

The last restricted generic type definition is the *generic access type*. For generic access types (or subtypes) the designated type of the formal parameter must match the designated type of the actual parameter, and the designated types of the formal and actual parameters must either both be constrained or both be unconstrained. Consider the following declarations:

```
 1:procedure Generic_Access_Parameters is
 2:  type Uncons_Type is array (CHARACTER range <>) of FLOAT;
 3:  generic
 4:    type Cons_Formal_Type is access INTEGER;
 5:    type Formal_Access_Uncons is access Uncons_Type;
 6:  package Accesses is
     ...
 7:  end Accesses;
 8:  type Access_Integer is access INTEGER;
 9:  type Access_Uncons is access Uncons_Type;
10:  subtype Cons_Subtype is Uncons_Type('A'..'E');
11:  type Access_Cons_Subtype is access Cons_Subtype;
12:  package Good_Access_Package is new Accesses(Access_Integer, Access_Uncons);
     ...
```

In the procedure **Generic_Access_Parameters**, the generic package **Accesses** has two formal access type parameters. The access type in line 4 has a designated type of **INTEGER** which is a constrained type. The access type in line 5 has a designated type which is an unconstrained array type. In the instantiation of **Good_Access_Package**, it is required that the designated objects match. The designated objects of the formal parameter **Cons_Formal_Type** and the actual parameter **Access_Integer** are both of type **INTEGER**, so they match. The designated objects of the formal parameter **Formal_Access_Uncons** and the actual parameter **Access_Uncons** are both of type **Uncons_Type** so they match. Furthermore, both designated types are constrained. Notice that, it would be illegal to use **Access_Cons_Subtype** in place of **Access_Uncons** at line 12: Although **Access_Cons_Subtype** is compatible with **Formal_Access_Uncons**; the actual parameter is a constrained type and the formal parameter is an unconstrained type, so the match would be illegal. During execution, additional checks are performed. For example, if we changed the declaration in line 4 from **INTEGER** to **NATURAL**, then when the package was instantiated, **CONSTRAINT_ERROR** would be raised. At instantiation, constraints of the formal and actual parameters are checked to ensure that they are the same.

In the preceding discussion, what we have done with generic units is very limited. What provides the flexibility of generic units is the rules for the visibility of generic parameters. The scope of a generic parameter is (1) from its point of definition to the end of the generic declaration and (2) the body corresponding to that generic unit. In particular, a generic parameter may be used in the definition of later generic parameters. This is shown in the following example:

```
generic
  type T is private;
  type A is access T;
package Visibility is ...

with Visibility;
procedure Show_Visibility is
  type Access_Integer is access INTEGER;
  package Good_Package is new Visibility(INTEGER, Access_Integer);
  package Bad_Package is new Visibility(BOOLEAN, Access_Integer); --illegal
  package Bad_Package2 is new Visibility(NATURAL, Access_Integer);
  ...
```

Here, the generic formal type **T** is used in the definition of the generic formal type **A**. Ada requires that both the formal parameter **A** and the actual parameter have the same designated type. But the generic package defines the designated type of **A** to be the type of the formal parameter **T**. If we correctly instantiate the package (as is done with **Good_Package**), the designated type of type **A** will be the type **T**. In the case of **Good_Package**, the actual parameter for **T** is the type **INTEGER**, so the designated type of **A** must be compatible with **INTEGER**. The actual parameter for the type **A** is the type **Access_Integer**. Because the designated type of **Access_Integer** is **INTEGER**, it matches **A**. In the case of **Bad_Package**, the supplying of **BOOLEAN** for **T** requires that the designated type of **A** be **BOOLEAN**. **Access_Integer** does not satisfy this requirement. The instantiation of **Bad_Package2** shows another kind of error. In this case, the match is compatible, but at instantiation, **CONSTRAINT_ERROR** will be raised. This is because supplying **NATURAL** for **T** requires that the designated type of **A** be a subtype of **INTEGER** whose constraints are the same as the subtype **NATURAL**. However, **A** is associated with the actual parameter **Access_Integer** whose designated type (**INTEGER**) has constraints different from those of **NATURAL**.

Program 16–2 illustrates how generic type definitions and the visibility rule for generic formal parameters can be applied in the construction of a generic function. The generic function **Get_Max** has three generic formal parameters. The first two formal parameters, **Index** and **Item**, are used in the definition of the third, (**Row**). The objective of **Get_Max** is to return the maximum or largest number in a vector. The function restricts the types of its generic actual parameters. In line 2, the declaration of the generic formal type **Index** indicates that it can only match a discrete type. This restriction is required because **Index** is used as the index of an array (line 4), and only discrete types can be used as array indices. In line 3, the declaration of the generic formal type **Item** indicates that it can only match a floating point type. This restriction is somewhat arbitrary, since neither arithmetic operations nor floating point attributes are used in the function body. Nevertheless, the function restricts itself to searching for a maximum in an array of floating point numbers.

The procedure **Generic_Demo** names the generic function **Get_Max**. In the instantiation of this generic function as the function **Get_Real_Max** (line 21), we have been careful to correctly match the parameters. By the rules for generic parameters, **Vec** must match **Row**. Because the instantiation at line 21 associates **Short** with **Index** and

```
1:generic
2:  type Index is (<>);
3:  type Item is digits <>;
4:  type Row is array (Index) of Item;
5:function Get_Max(Vector: Row) return Item;
6:function Get_Max(Vector: Row) return Item is
7:  Max_So_Far: Item := Vector(Vector'FIRST);
8:begin
9:  for I in Vector'RANGE loop
10:   if Max_So_Far < Vector(I) then
11:     Max_So_Far := Vector(I);
12:   end if;
13:  end loop;
14:  return Max_So_Far;
15:end Get_Max;

16:with Get_Max;
17:procedure Generic_Demo is
18:  subtype Short is INTEGER range 1..5;
19:  type Our_Real is digits 6;
20:  type Vec is array(Short) of Our_Real;
21:  function Get_Real_Max is new Get_Max(Short, Our_Real, Vec);
22:  A_Vec: Vec := (3.0, 2.4, 1.3, 2.6, 4.2);
23:  The_Max: Our_Real
24:begin
25:  The_Max := Get_Real_Max(A_Vec);
26:end Generic_Demo;
```

Program 16–2

`Our_Real` with **`Item`**, the type associated with **`Row`** must be an array indexed by the type **`Short`** whose components are of type **`Our_Real`**. The type **`Vec`** satisfies these requirements.

The instantiation **`Get_Real_Max`** is called at line 25. When it is passed the vector **`A_Vec`**, the instantiation of lines 6–15 will be executed. In the instantiation of these lines associated with **`Get_Real_Max`** the type **`Item`** (line 7) is the type **`Our_Real`** and the type **`Row`** (line 6) is the type **`Vec`**. Since the index type of **`Vector`** is **`Short`**, the type of the loop parameter **`I`** (line 9) is **`Short`**. Notice the comparison (**<**) in line 10. This relational operator is overloaded. Since in this instantiation both **`Max_So_Far`** and **`Vector(I)`** are of type **`Our_Real`**, the only overloading allowed is the one that compares two values of the type **`Our_Real`**. This overloading exists, because the comparison operators are predefined for all numeric types, in particular, they are predefined for the numeric (floating point) type **`Our_Real`**. The function call at line 25 will return the value **`4.2`**.

16.3.2 Generic Formal Parameters: Formal Subprograms

The second kind of generic parameter is the generic formal subprogram. The syntax for generic formal subprograms is given in Figure 16–5. The reserved word **with** serves to distinguish a subprogram that is a formal parameter from the generic subprogram that is being declared. The two options involving the reserved word **is** have to do with the default subprogram to be used if no actual parameter is supplied and will be covered later. To illustrate the use of a generic formal subprogram, we present the following alternative declaration of the function **Get_Max**.

<generic parameter -- formal subprogram>

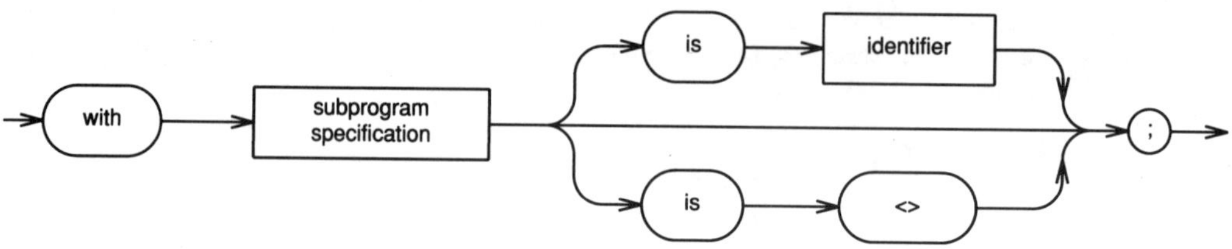

Figure 16–5

```
 1:generic
 2:   type Index is (<>);
 3:   type Item is private;
 4:   type Row is array (Index) of Item;
 5:   with function "<"(Left, Right: Item) return BOOLEAN;
 6:function Get_Max_2(Vector: Row) return Item;
 7:function Get_Max_2(Vector: Row) return Item is
 8:   Max_So_Far: Item := Vector(Vector'FIRST);
 9:begin
10:   for I in Vector'RANGE loop
11:     if Max_So_Far < Vector(I) then
12:       Max_So_Far := Vector(I);
13:     end if;
14:   end loop;
15:   return Max_So_Far;
16:end Get_Max_2;
```

The only differences between the declarations of **Get_Max_2** and **Get_Max** of Program 16–2 are the addition of the generic formal subprogram parameter in line 5 and the change in the declaration of **Item** from a floating point type to a generic private type in line 3. The generic formal subprogram parameter indicates that every instantiation of **Get_Max_2** will include an actual parameter that is the name of a function that compares two values of type **Item** and returns a **BOOLEAN**. In the body of **Get_Max_2**, the relational operator at line 11 will refer to the function that was passed as the actual parameter. In fact, because the type **Item** is a generic private type, there is no predefined operation "<", so the generic formal subprogram is the only legal option for this relational operation. Consider the following procedure:

```
 1:with Get_Max_2;
 2:procedure Record_Max is
 3:  subtype Short is INTEGER range 1..3;
 4:  type Data_Record is
 5:    record
 6:      Student_Number: INTEGER;
 7:      Grade: CHARACTER;
 8:    end record;
 9:  type Class is array(Short) of Data_Record;
10:  Class_List: Class := ((1, 'B'), (2, 'C'), (3, 'A'));
11:  The_Max: Data_Record;
12:  function Compare(Record_1, Record_2: Data_Record) return BOOLEAN is
13:  begin
14:    return Record_1.Grade < Record_2.Grade;
15:  end Compare;
16:  function Get_Highest is new Get_Max_2(Short, Data_Record, Class, Compare);
17:begin
18:  The_Max := Get_Highest(Class_List);
19:end Record_Max;
```

In the instantiation **Get_Highest** in line 16, the type associated with the formal private **Item** is the record type **Data_Record**. In this instantiation the operator **<** at line 11 of **Get_Max_2** is associated with the function **Compare** at lines 12–15 of **Record_Max**. Because of this, when **Get_Highest** compares two records, it does so by comparing their **Grade** components. Notice that in **Compare**, the grade **'C'** is higher than the grade **'A'** because **'C'** comes after **'A'** in the type **CHARACTER**. For the purpose of **Get_Highest**, we could reverse this so that **'A'** is the highest grade by changing the operator **<** in **Compare** (line 14) to **>**. One advantage of the generic in this situation is that whatever comparison function is most appropriate may be supplied as the actual parameter to the instantiation. The call to the function at line 18 of **Record_Max** will return the value **(2,'C')**.

16.3.3 Generic Formal Parameters: Formal Objects

The third kind of generic formal parameter we discuss is the generic formal object. The syntax for generic formal objects is given in Figure 16–6. A generic formal object has one of two modes. Mode **in** is the default mode. A generic formal object of mode **in** is a constant whose value is used in the instantiation. A generic formal object of mode **in out** is a formal variable denoting the variable supplied as the actual parameter. Mode **in** is the default, mode **in out** must be explicitly declared. Obviously, the actual parameter must be a variable.

The package **Integer_Stack** in Program 16–3 is a generic package with generic formal objects. In this package, **Max_Size** and **Secure** are of mode **in** and **Cur-**

<generic parameter declaration -- formal object>

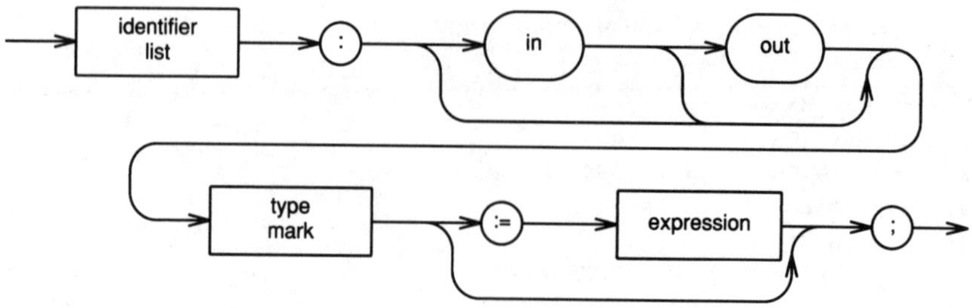

Figure 16–6

```
1:generic
2:   Max_Size: POSITIVE;
3:   Current_Size: in out POSITIVE;
4:   Secure: in BOOLEAN := FALSE;
5:package Integer_Stack is
6:   procedure Push(X: in INTEGER);
7:   procedure Pop(X: out INTEGER);
8:   Stack_Full: exception;
9:end Integer_Stack;
10:package body Integer_Stack is
11:   The_Stack: array (1..Max_Size) of INTEGER;
12:   procedure Push(X: in INTEGER) is
13:   begin
14:     if Current_Size >= Max_Size then
15:       raise Stack_Full;
16:     end if;
17:     Current_Size := Current_Size + 1;
18:     The_Stack(Current_Size) := X;
19:   end Push;
      ...
20:end Integer_Stack;
```

Program 16–3

rent_Size is of mode **in out**. Within **Integer_Stack**, **Max_Size** is a constant, but the value of **Current_Size** may be changed. The formal object **Max_Size** is used in line 11 to determine the size of an array and again in line 14 to determine whether the stack is full. The formal object **Current_Size** indicates how many elements are currently in the stack. The value of **Current_Size** is incremented in line 17.

We may instantiate the **Integer_Stack** package as follows:

```
with Integer_Stack;
procedure Use_Stack(Z: INTEGER) is
```

```
  X, Y: INTEGER := 0;
  package Stack1 is new Integer_Stack(10, X, TRUE);
  package Stack2 is new
    Integer_Stack(Max_Size => Z + 4, Current_Size => Y, Secure => TRUE);
  package Stack3 is new Integer_Stack(10, X);
  ...
end Use_Stack;
```

With the mode **in** parameters, we may supply any expressions, including constants, variables, and complex expressions, as actual parameters. In the instantiation **Stack1**, **Max_Size** receives its value from a variable (**Y**). In the instantiation **Stack2**, it receives it from an expression (**Z+4**). In both instantiations, **Secure** receives its value from an enumeration literal (**TRUE**). The value of the expression is computed at the time of instantiation and this value is then used in the process of instantiation. As part of good programming practice, you should verify that variables used as actual parameters of an instantiation (such as **Y**) have been initialized at the point of *instantiation.*

The generic formal parameter **Current_Size** is of mode **in out**. Hence, it must be associated with a variable. In **Stack1**, it is associated with the variable **X**, in **Stack2** it is associated with the variable **Y**. Consequently, a **Push** within the instance **Stack1**, as in the statement

```
Stack1.Push(5);
```

modifies the value of **X**, while a **Push** within the instance **Stack2** modifies the value of **Y**.

As illustrated in the instantiation of **Stack2**, named association may be used with generic parameters. The same rules apply as with named and positional notation in procedure calls.

Type checking applies to formal objects. In the previous example, **X** and **Y** are of type **INTEGER**, while **Current_Size** is the integer subtype **POSITIVE**. For generic formal objects compatible subtypes are legal, and constraint checks are performed. Because **Max_Size** is of mode **in** its constraint will be checked at instantiation. For a parameter of mode **in out**, the constraints of the actual parameter are applied. In our example, this means that the constraint **POSITIVE** on **Current_Size** is ignored. Instead the constraint of the actual parameter prevails. Thus, for **Stack1**, the constraint **INTEGER** of the parameter **X** is applied as the constraint on the type **Current_Size**. Because they are ignored, a good programming practice is to use base types for generic parameters of mode **in out**. Thus, good practice says that the type of **Current_Size** should be **INTEGER**.

The value of generic formal objects is determined at instantiation. Instantiation occurs upon elaboration of the declarations. Specifically, the packages **Stack1** and **Stack2** are reinstantiated every time the procedure **Use_Stack** is called. Because the parameter **Z** can assume different values between calls, the size of the array (**The_Stack**) in **Stack2** can be different each time **Use_Stack** is called. In fact, the parameter **Current_Size** could also vary. For example, suppose we had

```
package Stack1 is new Integer_Stack(Y, Z.Int, TRUE);
```

where **Z** is an access variable whose designated type has a component **Int** of type **INTEGER**. Thus, depending on the value of **Z**, **Current_Size** could access a different variable on each instantiation of **Use_Stack**, but once instantiated, **Current_Size** will continue to refer to the same variable even if **Z** is changed to access a different integer. A similar effect can be achieved if **X** is an **in out** parameter of **Use_Stack** instead of a local variable.

A generic formal object may have a default value. The syntax for the default value is the familiar "**:= expression**" used in most other forms of default. In **Integer_Stack**, the parameter **Secure** has a default value of **FALSE**. Thus, if an instantiation of **Integer_Stack** omits a value for this parameter, as is done in the instantiation of **Stack3**, **Secure** assumes the value **FALSE**. The type of the default expression must match the type of the parameter to which it applies.

16.3.4 Generics and Contexts

The *instantiation context* is the context in which the generic is instantiated. The *declaration context* is the context in which the generic is declared. In the declarations

```
1:package Declaration_Context is
2:   Initial_Value: constant INTEGER := 6;
3:   procedure G;
4:   generic
5:     Defaults: INTEGER := Initial_Value;
6:     with procedure E is <>;
7:     with procedure F is G;
8:   procedure Q;
9:end Declaration_Context;

10:with Declaration_Context;
11:package Instantiation_Context is
12:   use Declaration_Context;
13:   procedure E;
14:   procedure New_Q_1 is new Q;
15:   Initial_Value: constant INTEGER := 5;
16:   procedure New_Q_2 is new Q (Initial_Value);
17:end Instantiation_Context;
```

Declaration_Context is the declaration context of the generic procedure **Q**, while **Instantiation_Context** is the instantiation context of **Q**. Actual parameters are evaluated in the instantiation context. For example, the actual parameter **Initial_Value** in the instantiation of **New_Q_2** (line 16) is evaluated in the instantiation context so it refers the integer constant **Initial_Value** declared at line 15 in the package **Instantiation_Context**. Default values for generic formal objects (such as **Defaults** at line 5) and entities within the generic body are evaluated in the declaration context. Thus, the default initial value (**Initial_Value**) of **Defaults** refers to the constant declared at line 2 in the package **Declaration_Context**. We should note that the body of the generic procedure **Q** will be defined within the body of the package **Declaration_Context**.

For generic formal subprograms, there are two forms of default values. The form that uses the box (<>) indicates that the default refers to the instantiation context. The form that uses the identifier indicates that the default refers to the declaration context.

For procedure **E** (line 6), if no actual parameter is explicitly given, whatever **E** is visible in the instantiation context (i.e., the **E** declared in line 13) will be used. Most often, this form of default is used with formal subprograms of the type

```
with function "+"(X, Y: T) return T is <>;
```

in which case whichever addition operator **"+"**, that is available for the type **T** in the instantiation context is used as the default. If no such operator is visible, it is a syntax error.

For procedure **F** (line 7), if no actual parameter is explicitly given, whatever **G** is visible in the declaration context (i.e., the **G** declared in line 3) will be used.

To summarize, for a generic instantiation, the actual parameters are resolved in the instantiation context. For a generic declaration, the subprogram default <> is resolved in the instantiation context, while all other items in the declaration are resolved in the declaration context.

16.4 THE GENERIC SORT PROCEDURE

In this section, we develop a generic package for sorting the contents of an array. As a basis we shall use the insertion sort developed in Chapter 5. It is interesting to compare the generic sort with the sort in Chapter 5 to notice how little extra effort is required to generalize the sort procedure. The declaration of the generic sort package can be as follows:

```
1:generic
2:   type Index_Type is (<>);
3:   type Element_Type is private;
4:   type Array_Type is array (Index_Type) of Element_Type;
5:   with function "<="(L, R: Element_Type) return BOOLEAN;
6:procedure Generic_Insertion_Sort(Data: in out Array_Type);
```

The declaration in line 2 requires that the actual parameter to **Index_Type** be a discrete type. Since **Index_Type** is used as an array index in line 4, this restriction is required. The element type is **private**, which allows us to sort any type that is not a limited type. Since sorting moves elements around in the array, if we declared **Element** to be **limited private** so that we could also sort limited types, we would need an additional generic formal procedure that moves elements. Because **Element_Type** is merely private, assignment is available. However, **Element_Type** is not restricted to being a type for which there is a predefined comparison routine. Therefore, it is necessary to have a generic formal subprogram parameter that compares objects of **Element_Type** (line 5). Given a correct comparison routine, arrays of any component type will be correctly sorted by our generic procedure.

Notice that **Array_Type** is constrained. Specifically, it has one element for each value in the full range of **Index_Type**. When we create an instance from **Generic_Insertion_Sort**, a constrained array type will have to be associated with the generic formal parameter **Array_Type**. Alternatively, we could have written line 4 as

```
4:  type Array_Type is array (Index_Type range <>) of Element_Type;
```

in which case the associated generic formal parameter would have to be an unconstrained array type.

The body of **Generic_Insertion_Sort** will be compiled separately and is as follows:

```
 1:-- Sort an array using Insertion Sort.
 2:procedure Generic_Insertion_Sort(Data: in out Array_Type)  is
 3:  -- Data: the array to be sorted.
 4:  Hold: Element_Type;
 5:  -- Hold is where we store the next value to insert.
 6:  Put_At: Index_Type;
 7:  -- Put_At is where that item will be inserted.
 8:begin
 9:  if Data'LENGTH <= 1 then
10:    return; -- Array is too small to sort.
11:  end if;
12:  for Look_At in Index_Type'SUCC(Data'FIRST)..Data'Last loop
13:    -- The next item to insert is at position Look_At.
14:    Hold := Data(Look_At);
15:    -- Find where it goes.
16:    Put_At := Data'FIRST;
17:    while Put_At < Look_At and Data(Put_At) <= Hold loop
18:      Put_At := Index_Type'SUCC(Put_At);
19:    end loop;
20:    -- Open space at Put_At.
21:    Data(Index_Type'SUCC(Put_At)..Look_At)
22:          := Data(Put_At..Index_Type'PRED(Look_At));
23:    -- Put the new item into the list.
24:    Data(Put_At) := Hold;
25:  end loop;
26:end Generic_Insertion_Sort;
```

Within the body we have used attributes because we do not wish to assume how big the array is or what values are used as indices. In line 9, the **LENGTH** of the array is checked. For arrays of 0 or 1 elements, a sort is unnecessary. In fact, lines 12–25 can handle arrays of this size, but there can be a problem with the **Index_Type**. That is, using the **SUCC** attribute can result in a **CONSTRAINT_ERROR** if there are 0 or 1 values in this type.

At lines 18 and 19, you might have expected to see "**+1**" instead of **SUCC**, but remember that addition works only for numbers, while **Index_Type** may be any discrete type. If you attempt to use addition with **Index_Type** it is a syntax error that will be detected by the compiler.

In line 17, **<=** is applied to two values of type **Element_Type** and refers to the generic formal subprogram parameter. In this line, the **<** operator is legal because comparison is predefined for all discrete types.

Again, notice that there is very little difference between the generic version of insertion sort and previous versions. It took very little additional effort to generalize the procedure to handle sorts of many different types.

We can instantiate **Generic_Insertion_Sort** as follows:

```
with Generic_Insertion_Sort, TEXT_IO;
procedure Sort_It is
  subtype Array_Range is CHARACTER range 'A'..'F';
  type Table is array (Array_Range) of INTEGER;
  List: Table := (3, 4, 1, 6, 5, 2);
  procedure Insertion_Sort is
     new Generic_Insertion_Sort(Array_Range, INTEGER, Table, Standard."<=");
begin
  Insertion_Sort(List);
  for I in List'RANGE loop
    TEXT_IO.PUT_LINE(INTEGER'IMAGE(List(I)));
  end loop;
end Sort_It;
```

In **Sort_It**, the elements of the arrays are integers, so the standard comparison for integers can be passed as the comparison routine. Had they been records, we would have had to pass the name of a function which compared records. Of particular importance is the declaration of the subtype **Array_Range** and its use in the type **Table**. The generic formal parameter declarations in **Generic_Insertion_Sort**, together with the combination of **Array_Range** and **INTEGER** as the first two actual parameters, require that the actual type **Table** be an array indexed by **Array_Range** with components of type **INTEGER** in order to match the formal type **Array_Type**. **Sort_It** sorts and prints an array of integers indexed by characters.

16.5 INPUT AND OUTPUT

The packages that perform input and output are the most complex of the predefined packages in Ada. All of Chapter 14 of the language reference manual is dedicated to the detailed explanation of these packages. We introduced the **TEXT_IO** package in

Chapter 7. In this section, we seek to cover the most critical aspects of **TEXT_IO**, pointing out how the package makes use of Ada language constructs. We also introduce several of the other I/O packages. For details on the numerous commands available in these packages, you should refer to the Ada language reference manual.

16.5.1 The Package TEXT_IO

We introduced a number of capabilities supplied by **TEXT_IO** without explaining how they were allowed by Ada, saying only that they were generics. Having discussed generics and unconstrained arrays, we now examine the **TEXT_IO** package more fully.

The most often used routines in package **TEXT_IO** are those which allow input and output with the types **CHARACTER** and **STRING**. We have discussed input and output with the type **CHARACTER**. The type **STRING** is an unconstrained array of **CHARACTER**s. The input and output subprograms introduce for **STRING** are **GET**, **PUT**, **GET_LINE**, and **PUT_LINE**. **GET** and **PUT** are, of course, overloaded.

The **PUT** procedures have a parameter of mode **in**. With an object of type **STRING** as a parameter, **PUT** prints the value of the string object. All objects must have constraints, consequently the number of characters in a string is known by the procedure, and all these characters are printed. **PUT_LINE** is the same as **PUT** followed by a **NEW_LINE**.

The procedure **GET** has a parameter of mode **out**. It takes input and places it into that parameter. For strings, the number of characters read is exactly equal to the length of the string. For the purpose of reading, a carriage return does not constitute a character. Thus, a string may span several lines. Subsequent reads begin with the next unused character and not at the beginning of a line.

The procedure **GET_LINE** is declared as

```
procedure GET_LINE(ITEM: out STRING; LAST: out NATURAL);
```

As with **GET**, **GET_LINE** takes input and places it into a string. However, **GET_LINE** stops on one of two conditions: The first (like **GET**) is when there are enough characters to fill the string, the second is when an end of line (i.e., carriage return) is encountered. In either case, the integer parameter (**LAST**) is set to the number of characters placed into the string. If **GET_LINE** terminates by encountering an end of line, the contents of any unfilled characters in the string are undefined. Specifically, an implementation may or may not change their value, so you cannot count on them remaining unchanged or being set to blanks.

A word of warning: When **GET_LINE** stops because of encountering a carriage return, a **SKIP_LINE** causes the end of line to be skipped and the next input to begin at the start of the next line. When **GET_LINE** stops because there are enough characters to fill the string the rest of the characters on the line are available for subsequent reads. If the number of characters before the end of line exactly matches the number in the string, the end of line remains and is not skipped!

TEXT_IO contains several generic packages. We now know that many different integer types can be declared. This means it is impossible to supply a single set of I/O routines. Instead, **TEXT_IO** declares a generic package, **INTEGER_IO** that accepts as a parameter a generic formal type that is an integer type. Thus the declaration:

```
package Int_IO is new TEXT_IO.INTEGER_IO(INTEGER);
```

instantiates a set of I/O routines for the type **INTEGER**. This instantiation makes available the procedures **GET** and **PUT** for the particular type named in the parameter. These procedures, as well as all other procedures from **TEXT_IO** which we shall discuss in this section, are overloaded so that a file may be specified.

With floating point and fixed point types we have a similar situation. Input and output routines are obtained by instantiations of **FLOAT_IO** and **FIXED_IO**, respectively.

With all the numeric types, the input and output routines have additional parameters. These parameters specify the format to be used when writing the numbers. For example, the number of places before and after the decimal point may be specified. We refer you to the Language Reference Manual for the exact details.

The existence of many different enumerations also requires the use of a generic package. This package is **ENUMERATION_IO** It takes as its parameter the enumeration type for which you wish to perform input and output. Inputs and outputs will match the enumeration literals. As with other identifiers, identifiers corresponding to enumeration literals that are read using an instantiation of **ENUMERATON_IO** may contain any mixture of upper and lower case characters. The **GET** procedure skips leading blank space, reads an identifier, and matches that identifier to an enumeration value. If an enumeration value cannot be obtained, the exception **DATA_ERROR** is raised and no characters are read.

Output of enumeration types will be in a single case. The particular case used can be controlled either by setting a variable within the package (**DEFAULT_SETTING**) to **UPPER_CASE** or **LOWER_CASE** or by passing one of those two values to the **PUT** procedure. In addition to a parameter for the enumeration value to be printed, the **PUT** procedure has a **WIDTH** and a **SET** parameter. **WIDTH** is similar to that for integers and reals; **SET** allows the programmer to specify **UPPER_CASE** or **LOWER_CASE**.

16.5.2 Sequential I/O and Direct I/O

In this section, we introduce two generic packages that allow you to perform I/O on nontextual items. For example, suppose we have an array of records and we wish to store the contents of these records in a file. We can do this by an instantiation of either **SEQUENTIAL_IO** or **DIRECT_IO**. The parameter in the instantiation is the type of the elements to be written. For example, if we declared a record type named **Student_Record** we could instantiate perform I/O on that type with the declaration

```
package Student_IO is new SEQUENTIAL_IO(Student_Record)
```

With **SEQUENTIAL_IO** there are only two modes: **IN_FILE** and **OUT_FILE**. There are two procedures for doing input and output which are declared as follows:

```
procedure READ(FILE: in FILE_TYPE; ITEM: out ELEMENT_TYPE);
procedure WRITE(FILE: in FILE_TYPE; ITEM: in ELEMENT_TYPE);
```

As the name implies, **SEQUENTIAL_IO** accesses a file sequentially. For example, on an **IN_FILE** the first **READ** returns the first element in the file, the second **READ** returns the second element, and so forth. **READ** may be applied only to an **IN_FILE**, **WRITE** may be applied only to an **OUT_FILE**. As with all files, an **END_OF_FILE** function is available. In the case of previously instantiated **Student_IO** package, each read reads an entire **Student_Record** and each write writes an entire **Student_Record**.

The generic package **DIRECT_IO** has all these capabilities and some additional ones. First, an additional file mode **INOUT_FILE** is allowed. This mode allows both reads and writes on the same file. Furthermore, the read and write procedures have a parameter which indicates the element to be read or written. The read procedure is declared as follows:

```
procedure READ(FILE: in FILE_TYPE; ITEM: out ELEMENT_TYPE; TO: POSITIVE_COUNT);
```

The parameter **TO** is an index that specifies the element to read. An **END_ERROR** is raised if **TO** exceeds the number of elements in the file. The type **POSITIVE_COUNT** is a subtype of an integer type **COUNT** declared in **DIRECT_IO**. **COUNT**, is *not* a subtype of **INTEGER**. With the declarations

```
package Update_IO is new DIRECT_IO(Student_Record)
F: Update_IO.FILE_TYPE;
Current_Student: Student_Record;
```

the call

```
Update_IO.READ(F, Current_Student, 4);
```

reads the fourth student record in the file.

The **WRITE** procedure is similar to the **READ** procedure, however **END_ERROR** will never occur. Instead, the size of the file will be increased to include the indicated element. So that you can determine the number of elements in a file, the function **SIZE** takes a single parameter of type **FILE_TYPE** and returns the index of the last record in the file. This index is a value of type **COUNT**. The package **DIRECT_IO** is ideal for updating a data file.

16.6 PROGRAMMING PRACTICES

Throughout this book we emphasize the need for writing flexible subprograms. With generic units we have introduced a powerful Ada tool for doing this. Using generics accomplishes two things. First, it provides a unit which may be reused in many situations. Second, it forces the programmer to think about an abstraction of the problem.

For example, instead of being concerned about the details of the record structure, the generic sort only needed to know that it had a function that compared two records and determined their correct order. The details of the comparison did not matter, as long as the comparison was appropriate for the problem. In fact, different problems can be solved by substituting different comparison routines; the generic sort does not depend on which is used.

Generics are particularly useful for generalizing data structures. For example, in one of the exercises you are asked to implement a generic storage handler. Why build a separate storage or queue handler package for each type when you could build one that is generic and then whenever you needed one for a particular type, instantiate it. To illustrate how this might be done, the problem solving section steps through the implementation of a package for a storage structure known as a binary tree.

16.6.1 Problem Solving

Like a linked list, a binary tree is a dynamic structure that uses access types. However, whereas a linked lists had one link at each node, a binary tree has two. In a binary tree, these links are used to build a data structure that expands as you go down the links. Binary trees are a recursive structure and hence are often used in conjunction with recursive programs. For binary trees, the term *root* refers to the node that locates the entire structure, as shown in Figure 16–7. The term *leaf* refers to any node whose links do not provide access to other nodes. In Figure 16–7, the nodes containing 7, 11, 14, and 17 are leaves.

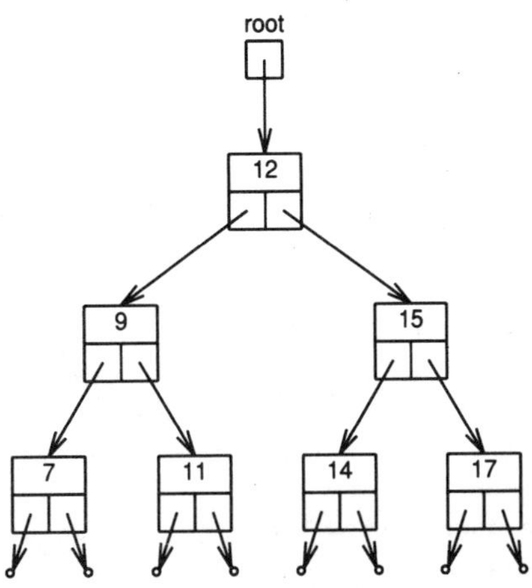

Figure 16–7

In representing the two access values in the node of a binary tree, we draw arrows out from each node. For example, from the node containing 12, arrows go to the nodes containing 9 and 15. The arrow going to 9 is drawn to the left of the arrow going to 15. Computer scientists use the terms "left" and "right" in talking about binary trees.

Notice that, as a result of the recursive structure of a binary tree, the node containing the value 9 and the nodes below it form a tree. This is called the *left subtree* of the node containing 12. Similarly, the node containing 15 and the nodes below it are the *right subtree* of the node containing 12.

Because of the structure of binary trees, insertion and deletion of nodes is easiest at the leaves of the structure. When modifying the interior of the structure, care must be taken to not lose pieces of the tree when nodes are manipulated.

Binary trees are often used in searching. One way this is done is to have each node in a binary tree contain a value called a key and to have the nodes in the tree organized with respect to the keys. In the tree of Figure 16–7 the keys have such an organization. For example, the key 12 occurs in the root. All nodes in the left subtree of the root contain keys less than 12, (these nodes have keys 7, 9, and 11) and all nodes in the right subtree of the root contain keys greater than 12 (these nodes have keys 14, 15, and 17). This organization is the same for each node in the tree. For example, for the node with key 15, the node in its left subtree has a smaller key (14) and the node in its right subtree has a larger key (17).

A search of the binary tree proceeds as follows. We look at the key of the node we are currently considering. If we have found what we are looking for, we are done. If we have reached a leaf and not found what we are looking for, we are done and we know that the node we wanted does not exist in the tree. Otherwise, if our key is greater than what we are looking for, we search the right subtree; if it is less, we search the left subtree. The declaration of the generic binary tree package is as follows:

```
generic
  type Key_Type is private;
  type Data_Type is private;
  with function "<"(Left, Right: Key_Type) return BOOLEAN;
  with function Equals(Left, Right: Key_Type) return BOOLEAN;
  with procedure Print_Data(Value_To_Print: Data_Type);
package Binary_Trees is
  type Tree is private;
  function Get_Data(Which_Tree: Tree; Key: Key_Type) return Data_Type;
  procedure Insert(Which_Tree: in out Tree; Key: Key_Type; Data: Data_Type);
  procedure Print_Tree(Which_Tree: in Tree);
  Key_Not_Found, Key_Found: exception;
private
  type Tree_Node;
  type Tree is access Tree_Node;
end Binary_Trees;
```

You will notice this declaration is quite similar to the declaration of the linked lists package in Program 15–9. The data type and key type are now generic parameters. Observe how these declarations hide the binary tree nature of the structure. In fact, even in the private part, the only thing shown is that the type **Tree** provides access to a **Tree_Node**. Notice that a tree is defined by its root, and that the root of a tree is a variable which provides access to a node in the tree.

The package declaration represents several implementation choices. We decided to pass a comparison function. This allows the keys to be records or other structures for which comparison is not necessarily defined. The alternative was to restrict **Key_Type** to a discrete type so that comparison was guaranteed to be predefined. We decided to pass a function that defines when two keys are equal. This allows keys to be things like **Normal_Line**, in which equality is based on part of the record's value. We could have chosen to call this function **"="**, but that would require making **Key_Type** limited private, which would force us to pass an assignment function to be able to insert a node. Since we also need to copy the data when we insert a node and when we retrieve the data associated with a key, we chose not to make **Data_Type** a limited type. The decision to make **Key_Type** and **Data_Type** generic private types has another consequence: Neither **Key_Type** nor **Data_Type** will match an unconstrained array type. For example, we cannot instantiate a binary tree with **STRING** as the key or data type.

For debugging purposes, we have included a procedure **Print_Tree** which prints the current contents of the tree. As we shall see in the package body, this procedure prints the **Data** component of each node.

Now let us consider the parts of the package body. The first is the declaration of the type **Tree_Node**:

```
type Tree_Node is
  record
    Key: Key_Type;
    Data: Data_Type;
    Left, Right: Tree;
  end record;
```

The **Key**, **Left**, and **Right** components correspond exactly to the nodes in Figure 16–7. We did not include the **Data** component in that figure. Although data is stored in each node of the tree, data plays no part in determining the tree's structure and does not effect how we search for or insert nodes. The function **Get_Data** is declared as follows:

```
function Get_Data(Which_Tree: Tree; Key: Key_Type) return Data_Type is
begin
  if Which_Tree = null then
    raise Key_Not_Found; -- Key was not found, can't return Data
  elsif Equals(Which_Tree.Key, Key) then
    return Which_Tree.Data;
  elsif Key < Which_Tree.Key then
    return Get_Data(Which_Tree.Left, Key);
  else
    return Get_Data(Which_Tree.Right, Key);
  end if;
end Get_Data;
```

The purpose of **Get_Data** is to return the data associated with a key. If there is no node with the key, **Key_Not_Found** is raised. A recursive function is natural because a tree is a recursive structure.

At each call to **Get_Data** there are 4 possibilities. If the subtree we are searching has no nodes (**Which_Tree = null**), the key is not in the tree. This may be because the tree was originally empty or because we have recursively gotten to the bottom of the tree without finding the key. The next check is to see whether the node being examined contains the key. If it does, the data value of the node is returned; if it does not, yet another check determines whether the left or right subtree should be searched.

Consider two examples using the tree shown in Figure 16–7. Suppose we ask for the data associated with the key 11. **Get_Data** starts at the root. The root is not null, so we do not raise an exception. The key 12 is not equal to 11, so we do not return. The key 12 is greater than 11, so we search the left subtree. Notice that when we are done searching the subtree, **Get_Data** will return the value returned to it by the recursive call. That is, once a node with the correct key has been found, each of the recursive calls in turn returns that value.

When we search the left subtree, we check the key 9. Since 9 is less than 11, we search the right subtree. This brings us to the node containing the key 11, so we return the **Data** component of that node.

Now suppose we search instead for the key 13. At the root, 12 is less than 13, so we search the right subtree. The recursive call examines the node with key 15, so we search the left subtree of the node containing 15. The next recursive call examines the node with key 14, so we search the left of the node containing 14. The left subtree of 14 is empty. So this recursive call finds that **Which_Tree** equals **null**. This call raises **Key_Not_Found**. This exception is then propagated by each of the recursive calls to **Get_Data** so that it will eventually be propagated to the original caller of **Get_Data**.

The procedure **Insert** is declared as follows:

```
procedure Insert(Which_Tree: in out Tree; Key: Key_Type; Data: Data_Type) is
begin
  if Which_Tree = null then
    Which_Tree := new Tree_Node'(Key, Data, null, null);
  elsif Equals(Key, Which_Tree.Key) then
    raise Key_Found;
  elsif Key < Which_Tree.Key then
    Insert(Which_Tree.Left, Key, Data);
  else
    Insert(Which_Tree.Right, Key, Data);
  end if;
end Insert;
```

Insert is similar to **Get_Data** and is also recursive. The procedure recursively searches the tree to determine where to insert the new node. If the key is found to be in the tree already, **Key_Found** is raised.

Notice that the decision whether to insert to the left or the right of a given node is identical to the comparison used when **Get_Data** searches for the node. The difference is that when **Insert** reaches the value **null** it has reached the bottom of the tree, and this is exactly where the new node should be inserted. The new node is created and initialized using the allocator. It is then attached to the tree by storing its access value in the variable (associated with the **in out** parameter) that formerly contained **null**.

For example, suppose we insert a node with key 13 into the tree of Figure 16–7. At 12 we go right, at 15 we go left, and at 14 we go left. When the recursive call is made from the node containing 14, the access variable that is passed contains the value **null**. This recursive call creates a node and stores the access value of this new node in the parameter **Which_Tree**. Because, at this point, **Which_Tree** refers to the **Left** component of the node containing 14, the new node is inserted into the tree to the left of 14. Finally, this recursive call returns, this return subsequently causes the other recursive calls to return. The tree after this insertion is shown in Figure 16–8.

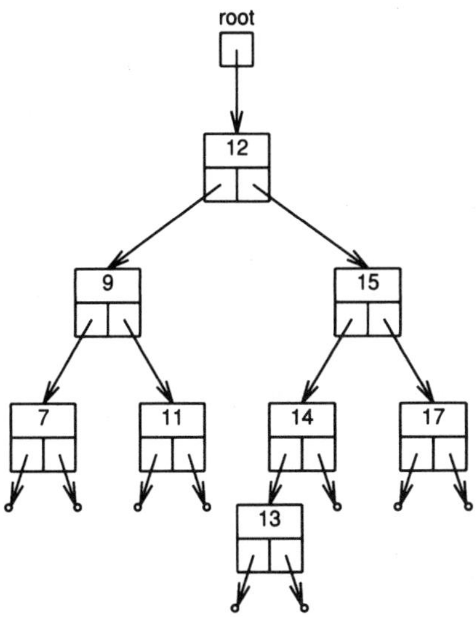

Figure 16–8

The final procedure in the body of the generic package **Binary_Trees** is **Print_Tree**:

```
procedure Print_Tree(Which_Tree: in Tree) is
begin
  if Which_Tree /= null then
    Print_Tree(Which_Tree.Left);
    Print_Data(Which_Tree.Data);
    Print_Tree(Which_Tree.Right);
  end if;
end Print_Tree;
```

The purpose of **Print_Tree** is to permit the user to examine the **Data** components of the tree. The nodes are printed using the generic formal procedure **Print_Data**. Since the generic package does not know what the data looks like, the print procedure must be supplied at the point of instantiation. Examining the body of the procedure we see that, first **Print_Tree** uses a recursive call to print the contents of all the nodes to the left of the current node, then it prints the contents of the current node, and finally it uses a recursive call to print the contents of all the nodes to the right of the current node.

Regardless of the structure of the tree, **Print_Tree** will print the nodes in order from the smallest key to the largest key. The reason for this can be described by considering what happens to a specific node which we shall call the current node. The first recursive call prints all nodes in the left subtree (**Which_Tree.Left**) of the current node, the keys for these nodes are less than the key of the node current node. Next we print the current node. Finally, the second recursive call prints all nodes in the right subtree (**Which_Tree.Right**), the keys for these nodes are greater than the key of the current node. Thus, for the current node, nodes printed before it have keys less than it, while nodes printed after it, have keys greater than it. Since each node, at some point, is a current node; all nodes are printed according to the order of their keys.

16.6.2 Testing

In testing, we have suggested that you use data which tests all paths through each subprogram. Generics add the capability to have different types. In testing generic declarations we should test instantiations with the different combinations of the generic parameters. With the binary tree package, we should test an instantiation of the simplest case, where the data and key are integers. In addition, we should also test instantiations where the data type is a record, the key type is a record and where both are records. Further tests should include instantiations in which the data and keys are access types or contain access types. A valuable test would be with the type **Normal_Line**. Note that the formal parameters **Key** and **Data** cannot be matched with unconstrained array types. This means that **Key** and **Data** cannot be associated with the type **STRING**.

In designing the generic binary tree package we planned ahead for testing by providing the procedure **Print_Tree**. However, **Print_Tree** would be even more useful if it somehow indicated the structure of the tree. This is an exercise.

16.7 ADA SUMMARY

We have covered the Ada concept of a *generic unit*. We have shown how to declare and instantiate generic units. We have examined *generic formal parameters*, including generic formal *objects*, generic formal *types*, and generic formal *subprograms*. We have illustrated the use of generics by constructing a sort procedure and a binary tree package, both of which can be used with many different types.

The predefined package **TEXT_IO** contains a number of generic units which we have discussed. In addition, we have discussed the advanced file-handling capabilities which are embodied in **SEQUENTIAL_IO** and **DIRECT_IO**.

EXERCISES

16.1. One unsatisfying thing about an instantiation like **Insertion_Sort** is that its formal parameter (**Data**) is constrained. Thus, **Insertion_Sort** can only sort arrays of a fixed size. This is a result of the generic formal type **Array_Type** being a constrained type.

Modify **Generic_Insertion_Sort** so that the **Array_Type** is unconstrained, and modify **Sort_It** so that when instantiated, it can sort arrays of any size. That is, make the modifications so that the array index of the actual parameter to **Sort_It** may be any subrange of the type **CHARACTER**.

According to the rules for generic parameters, unconstrained formal parameters must be matched by unconstrained actual parameters, so the modification of **Sort_It** is forced (if you want it to compile).

(Hint: the modification to the generic sort requires a small change to one line; the modification to **Sort_It** requires changes in three lines.)

16.2. Build a generic quick sort package. Instantiate the package to sort records.

16.3. Build a procedure that sorts strings alphabetically regardless of capitalization. That is, a word like "**BooK**" will be sorted to the same place as the word "**bOOk**". Since **STRING** is an unconstrained array type you cannot have an array of **STRING**; instead use an array with components that access **STRING**. Build your procedure by instantiating a sort routine with a generic formal comparison function associated with an actual function that compares strings without respect to the case of the letters. You can instantiate **Generic_Insertion_Sort** without modification or you can modify **Generic_Insertion_Sort** to an unconstrained array (i.e., when instantiated it can sort an array with any number of elements) as described in exercise 16.1.

16.4. In a binary tree, each node has one key and two subtrees. We could construct trees with more than two subtrees per node. These are sometimes called k-ary trees, where k is the number of subtrees per node. Such trees contain $k - 1$ keys (and data components) per node. If the key we want is between the ith and $i + 1$st keys in a node, we search the $i + 1$st subtree.

Modify the **Binary_Trees** package so that it instantiates a k-ary tree, where k is a generic formal object. Instead of **Left** and **Right**, the record for a node should contain an array of length k. Also, instead of a single key, there should be an array of length $k - 1$. Note that you will need to modify the search and insert procedures of **Binary_Tree** to use loops.

16.5. Implement the **Storage_Handler** package (Program 12–10, exercises 12.5, 15.3) so that it is a generic package. Use a generic parameter for the type of the data being stored. Note: this exercise should be almost trivial to implement.

16.6. Modify **Print_Tree** of the **Binary_Tree** package (section 16.6.1) to indicate the level in the tree of each node printed. Consider the root as level 1. The level of any other node is one higher than the level of its parent.

16.7. Add a **Print_Level** procedure to **Binary_Tree**. **Print_Level** should print all nodes in a specified level.

16.8. Add a **Delete** procedure to the binary tree package. Deleting a leaf is no problem. The big problem is to figure out how to hook the two subtrees back together after an interior node is deleted.

16.9. Change the implementation of the **Dictionary** package in exercise 15.4 so that it uses a binary search tree instead of a linked list to store the words. The dictionary is a single binary tree.

16.10. Design, implement, and test a **Dictionary_Handler** package. **Dictionary_Handler** is an extension of the **Dictionary** package which allows its users to define variables of type **Dictionary**. Each such variable when it is elaborated is initialized to an empty tree. Each node contains two string components: **Key** and **Data**. The nodes in each tree are arranged in alphabetic order with respect to the **Key** values. The declaration of **Dictionary_Handler** is

```
package Dictionary_Handler is
-- Purpose: Maintain a dictionary.
  type Dictionary is private;
  function Definition(Which_Dictionary: Dictionary; Word: STRING) return STRING;
  -- Purpose: Look up a word in the dictionary and return its definition.
  --  Word_Not_Found will be raised if the word is not in the dictionary.
  procedure Store(Which_Dictionary: in out Dictionary;
                  Word, Definition: STRING);
  -- Purpose: Define a word not in the dictionary. World_Already_Present
  -- will be raised if the word is in the dictionary.
  Word_Not_Found, Word_Already_Present: exception;
private
  -- You must add type declarations.
end Dictionary_Handler;
```

16.11. The **Print_Tree** procedure of the **Binary_Trees** package prints the left subtree, prints the data from the current node, and then prints the right subtree. This is known as an *inorder* traversal because the current node is printed in between the printing of the subtrees. Two other types of traversal are *preorder*, in which the current node is printed before printing the subtrees, and *postorder*, in which the current node is printed after printing the subtrees.

Add a procedure to the **Binary_Trees** package that prints the tree in preorder and another procedure that prints it in postorder.

16.12. Many things, such as days of the week cycle. For example, Wednesday is 9 days after Monday. You should build a generic package called **Cycle** which provides cyclic arithmetic for discrete types. Use the following package declaration:

```
generic
  type Discrete is (<>);  -- any discrete type
package Cycle is
-- This package allows the computation of discrete values that are any
-- specified number of values before or after another value. The
-- discrete values are considered to cycle as do the days of the week.
  function "+"(Left: Discrete; Right: INTEGER) return Discrete;
```

```
  -- Purpose: return the Discrete that is Right values after
  --   the value Left.
  function "-"(Left: Discrete; Right: INTEGER) return Discrete;
  -- Purpose: return the Discrete that is Right values before
  --   the value Left.
end Cycle;
```

The functions **+** and **-** should be implemented without recursion or iteration (i.e., you should use attributes and integers). You may ignore the possibility of numeric overflow that might happen when a discrete type has too many elements or when very large integer values are used.

Now write a test program that tests this generic unit by testing its instantiations for at least the following types:

```
type Month is (Jan, Feb, Mar, Apr, May, Jun, Jul, Aug, Sep, Oct, Nov, Dec);
type Week is (Sun, Mon, Tue, Wed, Thur, Fri, Sat);
subtype Hour is NATURAL range 1..12;
```

(*Warning:* The cycle subtype **Hour** may uncover a number of errors in your implementation because **Hour'FIRST** is not 0.)

16.13. Implement a genealogical tree in which the record for each person consists of a name, place and date of birth, and parents. The parental information should use access values for other persons listed in the tree.

The program should allow a person interested in his genealogy to add information found over the course of time to the tree, such as some great grandparent or the birthplace or birthdate of some ancestor. Adding information will have to be done interactively, of course, to determine which side of the family to follow at each stage.

You will need to implement a **Print_Family** routine which, given a person and number of generations, prints his or her genealogy back through that number of generations by printing the names of the ancestors. If the routine finds that the name of a specific ancestor is unknown (i.e., the name component is a zero length **Normal_Line**), it should print "unknown ancestor." An example of a printout 2 generations back is

```
Lisa Smith
       Horace Smith
         Harold Smith
         Melissa Montgomery
       Linda Jones
         Larry Jones
         Mary Craig
```

where Horace Smith and Linda Jones are the parents of Lisa Smith, and Harold Smith and Melissa Montgomery are the parents of Horace. The parents of Larry Jones would appear indented two more spaces underneath his name.

To simplify the family tree, it will only be concerned with direct ancestors; that is, no siblings will be included.

The main program that makes use of this package should allow user-directed specification of where to add an ancestor, or of which ancestor to change or update information on.

The package specification is as follows:

```
with Lines;
package Genealogy_Tree is
  use Lines;
  type Person is private;
  No_Such_Person: constant Person;
  function Create_Person(Name, Birthdate, Birthplace: Normal_Line)
                         return Person;
  -- Purpose:  Creates a person record.
  --  Name: Name of person.
  --  Birthdate: Date person was born.
  --  Birthplace: City or town plus country the person was born in.
  -- Description:
  --  Returns a person based on the given information.
  --  Any of the information may be "unknown," i.e., a Normal_Line
  --  consisting of all spaces or null.
  function Return_Mother(Child: Person) return Person;
  function Return_Father(Child: Person) return Person;
  -- Purpose: Returns the requested parent.
  --  Child: The child of the requested parent.
  -- Description:
  --  Return the indicated parent of the child.  If the parent
  --  does not exist, then No_Such_Person is returned instead.
  function Name_Of(Individual: Person) return Normal_Line;
  function Birthdate_Of(Individual: Person) return Normal_Line;
  function Birthplace_Of(Individual: Person) return Normal_Line;
  -- Purpose: Returns the requested information on an individual.
  --  Individual: The person with the requested information.
  -- Description:
  --  Return specific information on an individual.
  procedure Add_Mother(Child: in out Person; Mother: Person);
  procedure Add_Father(Child: in out Person; Father: Person);
  -- Purpose: Add the parent to the child's information.
  --  Child: The person who is getting the parent.
  --  Parent: The parent to be added to the Child's parents.
  -- Affects: Child, who gains a parent.
  -- Description:
  --  Add the appropriate parent to the specified Child.
  --  WARNING: if the Child already has that parent, the old
  --  information will no longer be available from that Child
  procedure Update_Name(Who: in out Person; New_Name: Normal_Line);
  -- Purpose: Modify the name of a person
  --  Who: The person whose name is to be changed
  --  New_Name: The new modified name for that person.
  -- Affects: Who, which gets a new value for Name.
  procedure Update_Birthdate(Who: in out Person; New_Birthdate: Normal_Line);
  -- Purpose: Modify the birthdate of a person
```

```
  --  Who: The person whose birthdate is to be changed
  --  New_Birthdate: The new modified name for that person.
  -- Affects: Who, which gets a new value for birthdate.
  procedure Update_Birthplace(Who: in out Person; New_Birthplace: Normal_Line);
  -- Purpose: Modify the birthplace of a person
  --  Who: The person whose birthplace is to be changed
  --  New_Birthplace: The new modified name for that person.
  -- Affects: Who, which gets a new value for birthplace.
  procedure Print_Family_Tree(Child: Person; Number_Of_Generations: POSITIVE);
  -- Purpose: Print out the family tree.
  --  Child: The "root" of the family tree to print out.
  --  Number_Of_Generations: How far back to print the family tree.
  -- Affects: None.
  -- Description:
  --  Print the family tree back to the specified number of generations.
  --  1 = just prints the name of the child and his parents out,
  --  2 also prints out the four grandparents.
  --  If the name of some ancestor is all spaces or null, only
  --  writes "unknown ancestor" in lieu of the name.
private
  -- you fill in
end Genealogy_Tree;
```

17

Program Development Tools and System Interfacing Capabilities

17.1 OBJECTIVES

This chapter emphasizes those tools that Ada provides for the construction of large programs and the capabilities that allow Ada to interface with the hardware and the operating system. We discuss the Ada library and compilation structure. We discuss what units can be named in context clauses and the bodies of those units (section 3). We discuss how to separately compile the body of a procedure or package whose declaration is not a library unit (section 4). Then we examine the order of compilation required by Ada (section 5) and a method for determining a valid order of compilation called *topological sort* (section 6). This chapter also discusses how *pragmas* can be used to direct the Ada compiler and to override some of Ada's features. Finally, a number of options, including representations clauses, designed to allow Ada to interface to hardware or an operating system are presented (sections 7 and 8).

CONCEPTS:

- The Ada compilation rules provide the capabilities needed in building a larger program.
- A compilation order for library units can be determined by topological sort.
- Pragmas can be used to direct the compiler and to interface with other languages.
- Representation clauses can be used to control how data is represented and how much storage it takes to store data.
- Representation clauses can be used to interface with the computer's hardware.

GOALS:

- Implement a topological sort.
- Design and implement a program that makes use of Ada's separate compilation capabilities.

17.2 MOTIVATION

We have introduced all the capabilities in the Ada language that are designed to support the principles of modularization. However, what we have introduced is inadequate in the sense that some additional details are necessary to support projects that involve large programs and many people. In this chapter, we consider these details, and discuss how these capabilities provide for construction of a program from parts.

In a large program or team effort, it is desirable to separate the program into modules, each in its own file. This allows several people to work simultaneously on different modules. To make the use of separate modules practical, Ada provides the capability of separate compilation. With this capability, an individual on a team may modify and recompile a specific portion of the program without recompiling other portions. Of course, the effectiveness of this technique depends heavily on how well the overall modularization of the program has been designed.

This chapter also discusses some features of Ada that are necessary for writing operating systems and other hardware-dependent software. Most of these are only mentioned in passing, as they are not required for most programs, and they can be quite dangerous.

17.3 LIBRARY UNITS AND SECONDARY UNITS

In Ada the term *compilation unit* refers to an entity that may be separately compiled. Multiple compilation units may be in the same file. However, we recommend that each compilation unit be in a separate file. Putting more than one compilation unit in a file makes it hard to compile the compilation units separately, thus somewhat defeating the purpose of having such units. Ada has two types of compilation units: *library units* and *secondary units*. The syntax for a compilation unit is shown in Figure 17–1.

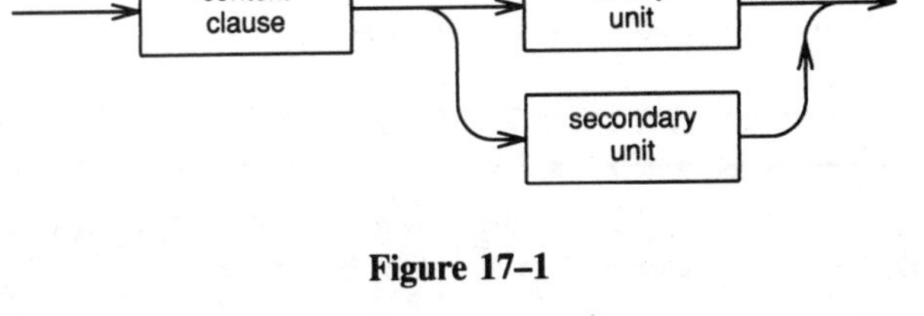

Figure 17–1

Library units are those compilation units which define capabilities that can be accessed by other compilation units. That is, library units declare entities that can be used by other units. In previous chapters we have used library units regularly.

When the following are compilation units, they are also library units:

1. The declaration part of a package
2. The declaration of a subprogram
3. The declaration of a generic
4. The instantiation of a generic
5. A subprogram body when there is no separately compiled declaration of the procedure.

An example of the first kind of library unit is

```
package X is
  ...
end X;
```

Through this declaration, the package and its capabilities become potentially available. To make this availability an actual fact, the package must be named in the context clause of another compilation unit.

An example of the second kind of library unit is:

```
procedure Z(X, Y: INTEGER);
```

As with the package, the subprogram and its capabilities become potentially available. The subprogram can now be named in the context clause of another compilation unit. Although we have shown a subprogram that is a procedure, subprograms that are functions can also be compilation units. When the compilation unit is a procedure that has no parameters, the Ada implementation must allow it to be used as the main program. An implementation may also allow other kinds of subprograms (such as functions or procedures with parameters) to form main programs, but is not required to do so.

An example of the third kind of library unit is

```
generic
  type Index_Type is private;
  type Element_Type is private;
  type Data_Array is array (Index_Type range <>) of Element_Type;
  with "<"(Left, Right: Element_Type) return BOOLEAN;
procedure Sort(Data: in out Data_Array);
```

When this library unit is compiled, the generic declaration becomes available. A context clause can name **Sort** to gain access to that library unit's capabilities. Of course, the only capability provided by a generic library unit is the ability to produce an instantiation. Note that generic packages can also be library units.

An example of the fourth kind of library unit is

```
with Decls_Package, Sort;
procedure Sort_Students(Data: Student_Records) is
        new Sort(INTEGER, Decls_Package.Student,
                  Decls_Package.Student_Records, Decls_Package."<");
```

This entire compilation unit consists of a generic instantiation. Assuming that **Student**, **Student_Records**, and **"<"** are appropriately defined by **Decls_Package**, this compilation unit forms a library unit that is a procedure capable of sorting student records.

Provided the procedure **Q** is not declared by one of the previously mentioned kinds of library units, an example of the fifth kind of library unit is

```
procedure Q(X, Y: BOOLEAN) is
begin
   ...
end Q;
```

This declaration makes **Q** potentially available.

Secondary units define the bodies of library units. Secondary units cannot be named in a context clause (although their corresponding declarations might be named). Secondary units include package bodies, generic bodies for both generic packages and generic subprograms, and subprogram bodies. In addition, secondary units include entities called subunits, which we shall define later in the chapter.

Notice that a subprogram body is a secondary unit if its declaration is separately compiled and is a library unit if its declaration is not separately compiled. This makes little difference to a person writing a module that uses the subprogram, but it can have a considerable impact on how much of the program must be recompiled if the subprogram is altered. For example, if for the procedure **Q**, whose body was a library unit in the previous declaration, we also had the declaration

```
procedure Q(X, Y: BOOLEAN);
```

then the preceding declaration of the body of **Q** would constitute a secondary unit instead of a library unit. If the body of **Q** is a secondary unit, a change to that body would not require recompilation of units that named **Q**; if the body of **Q** is a library unit, a change to it would require recompilation of units that named **Q**. We recommend that all subprograms that are intended as library units have a declaration, and that the declaration be in a separate file from the body of the subprogram.

17.3.1 The Main Program

In many programming languages, the syntax of a program indicates that a particular portion of the program is the main program and the rest of the program is included within this main program. In Ada, the main program is that portion of the program which initiates execution. The main program may not necessarily contain the first instructions executed, because the initialization code of library packages is always executed before the main program begins execution and tasks may execute instructions before the execution of the first instruction in the main program. However, in Ada, the *subprogram* in which execution begins is the main program. There is no syntactic difference between the main program and any other subprogram. It is not until the program is linked together that there is any indication of which subprogram initiates execution.

As previously mentioned, Ada requires that all implementations allow any parameterless procedure to become a main program. In addition, an implementation can allow subprograms with parameters and functions to become main programs. However, something has to be done about the parameters of the subprogram and the return values of the function. When you call such a subprogram within another subprogram, Ada defines what happens to these. Ada does not say what happens if the subprogram is a main program. In this case what happens is defined by each particular implementation. The specific practice of an implementation is required to be reported in Appendix F.

Appendix F is the extension of the Ada language reference manual that deals with implementation-dependent details. This appendix must be included in the documentation for the implementation. In order to make a program portable, the use of subprograms with parameters as the main program should be avoided.

17.4 BODY STUBS AND SUBUNITS

A *body stub* indicates that the body is compiled someplace else. By allowing a body to be compiled separately, Ada permits the programmer to recompile the body without recompiling the entire compilation unit that "includes" the body. The reserved word indicating that a body is in a separate compilation is **`separate`**. Only bodies can be separate, declarations never can. The syntax for a body stub is given in Figure 17–2. A body stub may only occur directly within a compilation unit. It may never occur in a subprogram body, package body or task body that is nested within a compilation unit.

<body stub>

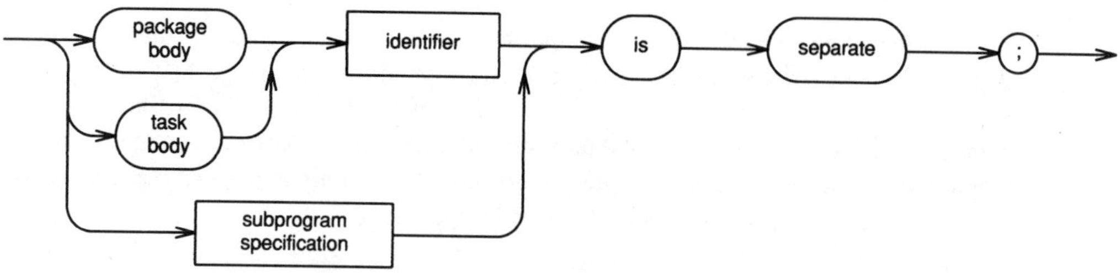

Figure 17–2

The following declaration is an example of a compilation that indicates that two bodies are separately compiled:

```
1:with Simple_IO;
2:package body Separate_Demo is
3:   procedure Y(I: INTEGER) is separate;
4:   package Z is -- Never separate
      ...
5:   end Z;
6:   package body Z is separate;
7:end Separate_Demo:
```

This declaration indicates that the body of the procedure **Y** and the body of the package **Z** will be found in separate compilations. Note that the declaration of the package **Z** at line 4 cannot be separate.

Since a body stub stands for a body, it can only be used where such a body could occur. For example, a body stub can never occur in a package declaration.

A *subunit* is compiled separately and contains the body for a body stub. The unit in which the subunit is declared to be separate is called the *parent unit* of that subunit. The separate compilation names the parent unit. Subunits are easily recognizable by the presence of the reserved word **separate** with an indication within parentheses to which unit the body stub belongs. The syntax for a subunit declaration is given in Figure 17–3.

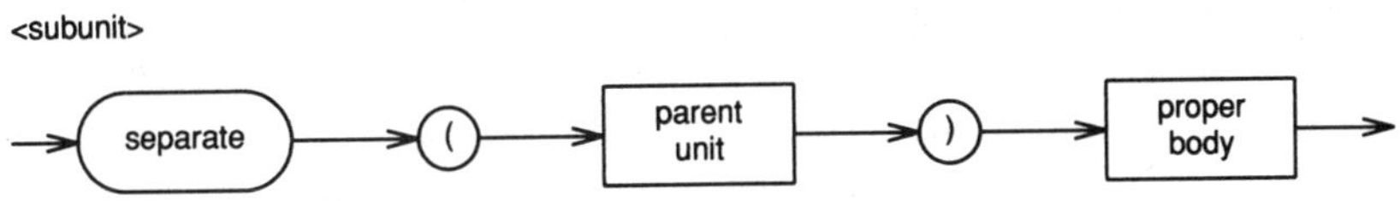

Figure 17–3

The following compilation is the stub for the procedure **Y**:

```
1:separate(Separate_Demo)
2:procedure Y(I: INTEGER) is
3:begin
   ...
4:end Y;
```

Note how the secondary unit indicates that the compilation unit **Separate_Demo** is the parent unit which contains the body stub corresponding to the secondary unit. Notice particularly that there is no semicolon at the end of line 1.

The body of procedure **Y** compiles exactly as if it were compiled at line 3 in the body of **Separate_Demo**. The rules for the body of **Y** are the same as if it were at line 3 in the body of **Separate_Demo**, including the rules for conformance of parameters, visibility and scope.

The following compilation unit is the secondary unit that corresponds to the body stub for the package **Z**:

```
1:with Lines;
2:separate(Separate_Demo)
3:package body Z is
4:  A_Line: Lines.Normal_Line;
5:  procedure Sub_Sub is separate;
6:begin
7:  Simple_IO.Read(A_Line);
8:  Y(3);
9:end Z;
```

The body of **Z** emphasizes the context of a body stub. Because **Z** behaves as if it were compiled at line 6 in the body of **Separate_Demo**, the context of the parent unit is available. Since the parent unit names the package **Simple_IO**, that package is available within **Z**, as is illustrated in line 7. Furthermore, if a use clause made **Simple_IO** directly visible in **Separate_Demo**, it would also be directly visible in **Z**. Since **Y** is declared at line 3 of **Separate_Demo** and the body stub of **Z** is at line 6 of **Separate_Demo**, the declaration of **Y** is available in the body of **Z** as is illustrated in line 8.

Because a subunit is a compilation unit, it may have a context clause. The context clause for the subunit containing the body of **Z** names the package **Lines** (line 1). As illustrated in line 4, that package becomes available within the compilation. The context clause of a subunit applies *only* to that subunit. So naming **Lines** for the body of **Z** does not make **Lines** available outside the body of **Z**. Specifically, this naming does *not* make **Lines** available in the portion of **Separate_Demo** that follows the body stub for **Z**. Note that the only statements in the body of **Z** is the initialization code in lines 7 and 8.

As illustrated in line 5 of the body of **Z**, a subunit may contain a body stub. The only thing that is subtle is the naming of the parent unit. If the parent unit is a subunit, visibility by selection must be used. Thus, the subunit corresponding to the body of procedure **Sub_Sub** would have to be declared as

```
separate(Separate_Demo.Z)
procedure Sub_Sub is
...
end Sub_Sub;
```

This indicates that the procedure is a subunit of the compilation unit named **Z**, which in turn is a subunit of the compilation unit **Separate_Demo**. There is no limit on the number of levels of nesting of such subunits.

17.5 COMPILATION ORDER

Ada restricts the order in which compilation units may be compiled. These restrictions ensure that if a unit uses declarations from another unit, the declarations from that other unit are compiled first. The rules governing the order in which compilation units are compiled are:

1. Each compilation unit must be compiled after all library units listed in its context clause.
2. Any library unit body must be compiled after its corresponding library unit.
3. Any subunit must be compiled after its parent unit.

When one compilation unit is recompiled (even when it does not change) other units may need to be recompiled. All recompilation must obey the preceding compilation order rules. Specifically, if a unit is recompiled, all other units which were required to be compiled after it, must be recompiled. For example, with the declarations

```
with A;
package body B is
  procedure X is separate;
end B;
```

if **B** is recompiled, then the body of **X** must be recompiled. If **A** is recompiled, then **B** must be recompiled and, after that, **X** must be recompiled.

Changing a library unit, such as a package declaration, can require that most of a program to be recompiled. Since many Ada programs contain tens or even hundreds of thousands of lines of code, recompiling most of the program can require a significant amount of time and effort. Therefore, interfaces and specifications should be carefully designed early in the development process to avoid the necessity of recompiling (and possibly changing) large amounts of code.

On the other hand, changing secondary units requires little recompilation. If a subprogram body is changed, only the file containing the body needs to be recompiled.

On many systems, the library units and secondary units used by a program must be explicitly combined by a program called a linker. The linker combines the portions of the program together into one file and changes the compiled code to permit one portion of the program to make use of other portions of the program. Changes in part of the program do not affect execution of the program until the program is relinked and execution is begun. On other systems, linking is done automatically when the program is loaded into memory to be executed.

17.6 TOPOLOGICAL SORTING

Sorting is the ordering of data according to certain rules. When we sort numbers, we usually compare the numeric value of the numbers and order them from smallest to largest (or largest to smallest). When we sort alphabetic data, we often sort the entries into dictionary order, being particularly careful that the sort does not differentiate between upper and lower case letters. Other orderings are also possible. Often, sorting is implemented as a generic package, with the function which compares two items and indicates which is larger being one of the parameters of the package.

This type of sorting is useful if there is a general rule for determining which item is larger. When there is a general rule for comparing two items, mathematicians say that there is a *total ordering* of the items. Another form of ordering is *partial ordering*. A partial ordering is a function which takes two items (A and B) as its domain and returns a value indicating that one of the following three holds:

1. A is known to be less than B.
2. B is known to be less than A.
3. Nothing is known about the direct relationship between A and B.

Even if we know quite a lot about elements in a collection, the existence of pairs of items which cannot be compared makes an ordering partial rather than total.

As an example of a partial ordering, consider the order in which a meal is prepared. Certain actions must be taken before other actions; that is, they are "less than" others. For example, soup must be removed from the refrigerator before it can be cooked. But some pairs of actions may be taken in either order; that is, neither of the actions is less than another action. For example, the table may be set either before or after the soup is removed from the refrigerator.

The relative order in which two compilation units must be recompiled is a partial ordering. In some cases, one unit must be compiled before another, while in other cases, it does not matter which unit is compiled first. So if we know how to sort according to a partial ordering, we can determine a legal order in which the packages in a large program can be compiled.

A normal sorting algorithm would not work well if it were given a partial ordering function as its ordering function. For example, with the quick sort algorithm, if we do not know how to compare an item with the middle item, then there is no way to determine in which of the two partitions the item should be placed.

Sorting algorithms that can handle partial orderings are called *topological sorting* algorithms. The input to these algorithms is a list of relations between pairs of items. For example,

```
(A < B), (C < D), (C < E), (B < E)
```

is such a list. The output is a list of items in an order that obeys the restrictions of the input. Notice that in this example we do not know the relationships between **A** and **C** or **B** and **D**. On the other hand, some orderings must occur even though the ordering is not included in the list. For example, the combination of **A < B** and **B < E** means that **E** must follow **A** even though there is no explicit relationship listed for **E** and **A**.

There are many orderings for the preceding list which are legal, some examples are:

```
A B C D E
A B C E D
C D A B E
A C D B E
```

The topological sort algorithm handles the list of relations one at a time. We will sort so that the smallest item is first. With each relation the algorithm performs the following steps:

1. Make sure both items named by the relation are in the list of items we know about. If they are not, add them to the list.
2. Create a pointer from the smaller item to the larger item.
3. Each item keeps count of the number of relations in which it is the larger item, so increment the count for the larger item.

When all the relations have been processed the algorithm proceeds to a second phase. Notice that for any item whose count is zero, there is no item which is smaller than it, so it can be the first item in the sorted list. Observe also that, an item can be placed in the sorted list whenever all the items which are smaller than it have been placed in the sorted list. The second phase of the algorithm repeats the following steps until all the items have been placed in the sorted list:

4. Pick any item whose count is zero. A zero count will mean either that no items were smaller than it or that all smaller items have already been placed in the sorted list.
5. The chosen item has pointers (built in the first phase) to each other item which was known to be larger than it.
   For each such pointer, decrement the count associated with the item pointed to.
6. Place the chosen item into the sorted list and remove it from the list of items to be sorted.

We shall illustrate the topological sort algorithm using the list of relations previously given. When we examine the first relation (**A<B**), we enter the items **A** and **B** into the list of known items, setting their count to 0 (step 1). Then, because **B** is the larger of the two items, we create a pointer from **A** to **B** (step 2) and increment the count of **B** to 1 (step 3). The data structure now looks like this:

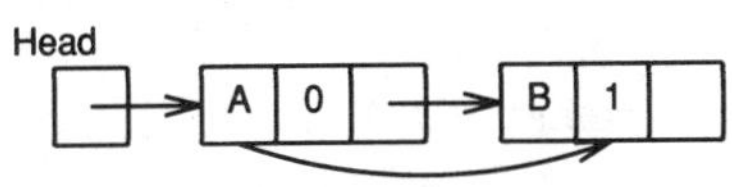

The next relation we examine is **(C<D)**. We create the items **C** and **D**, enter them into the list, set their counts to 0, add a pointer from **C** to **D**, and increment the count of **D** to 1. The data structure now looks like this:

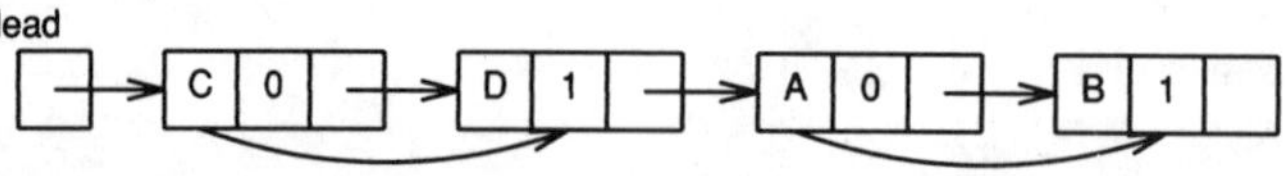

Next, when we examine the relation **(C<E)** we discover that **C** is already in the list so we only need to add **E**. We add a pointer from **C** to **E** and the increment count of **E** to 1. The data structure now looks like this:

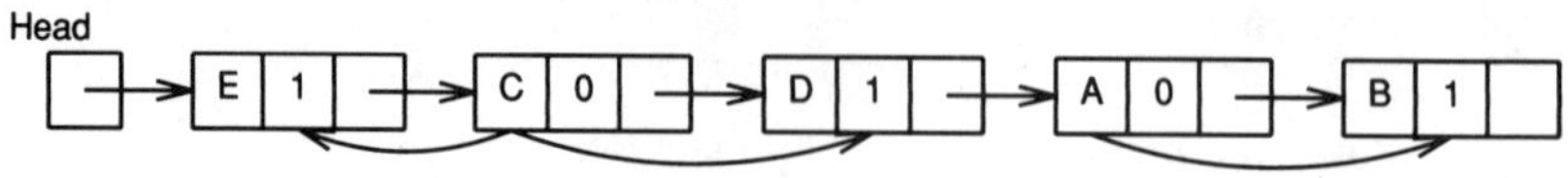

Finally, we examine the relation **(B<E)**. Both of these items have already been seen so nothing is added to the list. However, we add a pointer from **B** to **E** and increment the count of **E** to 2. At the end of the first phase the data structure looks like this:

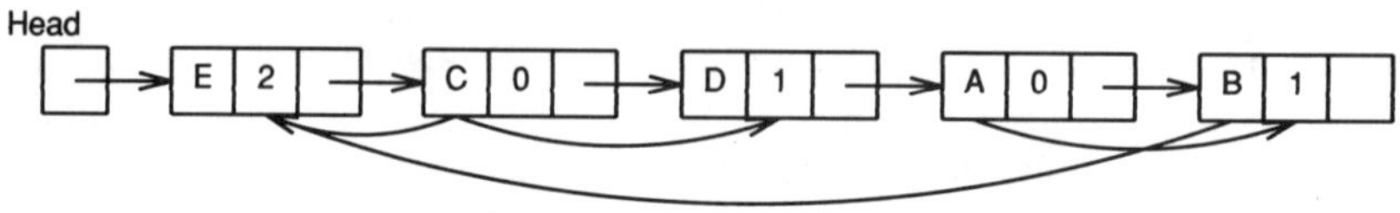

At the start of the second phase of the algorithm, the counts of both **A** and **C** are 0. We can pick either to be the first element in the sorted list. Suppose we pick **C** (step 4). Because **C** has pointers to **D** and **E**, the counts of both of these are decremented (step 5). **C** is then placed in the sorted list and removed from the list of items to be sorted. The data structure now looks like this:

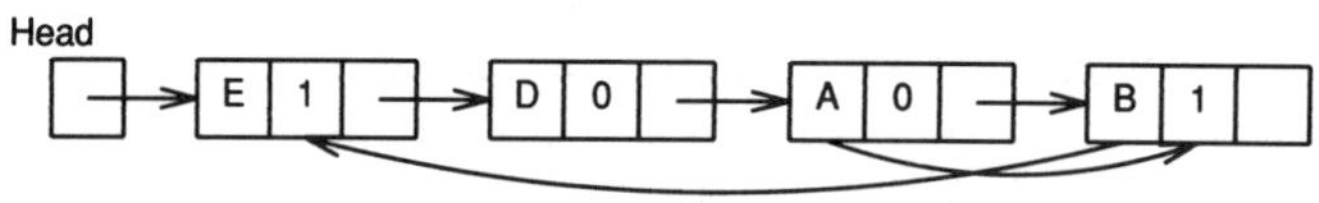

At this point, the counts of both **A** and **D** are 0. So, we may pick either to be next in the sorted list. Suppose we pick **D** (step 4). Then since **D** has no pointers, no counts are decremented (step 5). **D** is then placed in the sorted list and removed from the list of items to be sorted. The data structure now looks like this:

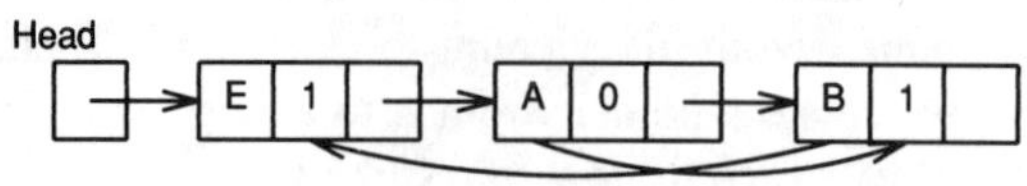

At this point, only **A** has a count of zero so we must pick **A**. **A** has a pointer to **B**, so we decremented the count of **B**. **A** is then placed in the sorted list and removed from the list of items to be sorted. The data structure now looks like this:

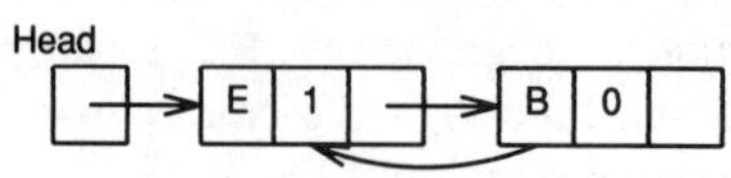

At this point, only **B** has a count of zero, so we must pick **B**. **B** has a pointer to **E** so we decrement the count of **E**. **B** is then placed in the sorted list and removed from the list of items to be sorted. The data structure now looks like this:

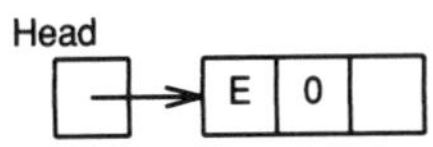

At this stage, only **E** is left in the list, and it has a count of zero. After it is picked and removed, the list to be sorted is empty and we are done.

The above data structure is a linked list. Elements of this linked list contain four components, the item name, the count of the items this item is smaller than, a link to the next element of the list and a list of items that this item is smaller than. Because we do not know how many items will be in the list maintained in this last component, this last component, which we diagrammed as a set of arrows coming out of the item name, must be implemented as a linked list of access values. So the entire structure is a linked list of elements in which the elements contain a component that is linked list.

In addition to the principal data structure just described, implementations of the algorithm sometimes use auxiliary data structures. For instance, instead of searching the above structure to find an item by name or an item whose count is 0, we could use data structures which are indices. To find items by name, we might maintain a binary tree using the item names as the keys. To find items whose count is 0 we might maintain a linked list of those items. Finally, we might want to have a data structure, such as a linked list, that stores the sorted list. (The principal data structure works fine if you just want to print the items in sorted order, but did not provide for their storage.)

In the *Art of Programming*, Volume 1 (Reading, Addison-Wesley, 1973), Donald Knuth goes into detail about this algorithm and analyzes its execution time. Knuth assumes that the items are integers and that every integer from 1 to N is used, where N is the number of items to be sorted (This eliminates the need for an index.) Knuth finds that the worst case execution time of the algorithm is $O(N+M)$, where M is the number of pairs in the input. $O(x)$ denotes a function whose value is at most $k*x+c$, where k and c are constants that depend on the function (they do not change with changes in x).

When we discussed normal sorting previously we said that in the worst case, the fastest sorting algorithms using comparisons require time $O(N\log_2 N)$ to sort N items. From the values of $O(x)$, it would appear that topological sorting is even faster. Actually, topological sorting is not faster if we deal with the general case in which the item names are not restricted. In order to process a pair from the input, we need to search the index to find where each item in the pair is in the linked list. Even if the index is in a known order (e.g., dictionary sorted), the worst case time to find an entry in the list with a binary search is $O(\log_2 N)$ (remember, N is the length of the list). Since we need to do this M times, the total time to search the index is $O(M\log_2 N)$. Finally, since in normal situations each item will appear in at least one pair, N is less than M, so the total topological sorting time is at least $O(M + M\log_2 N)$, which is more time than some sorting algorithms for total orderings.

17.7 PRAGMAS

A *pragma* is a way of conveying information to the compiler. Some pragmas provide ways to control the specifics of a compilation for efficiency. Others eliminate the safeguards built into Ada to prevent errors. The latter should generally be avoided. The syntax for a pragma is shown in Figure 17–4.

<pragma>

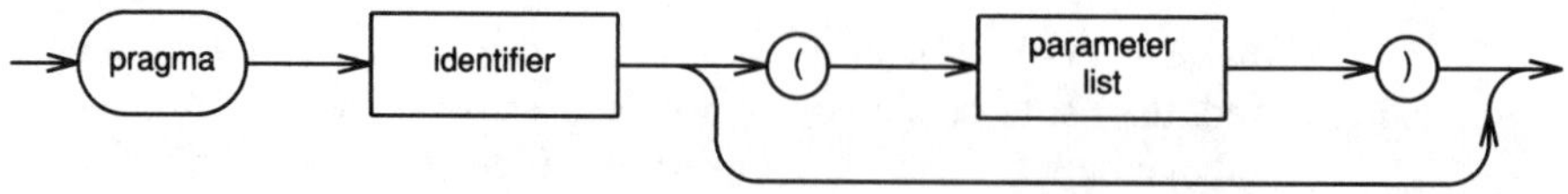

Figure 17–4

Pragmas may appear after the semicolon of declarations, statements, clauses, compilation units, and exception category variants. Essentially, this includes context clauses, declarations and statement lists. Except for their own syntax, pragmas have no effect on the syntax of a program.

A standard list of pragmas defined by the Ada language is included in the Ada Language Reference Manual (Annex B). In addition, an implementation may define other pragmas. If an implementation defined pragma is not recognized, the pragma is ignored and does not make the program illegal. The same is true if a language defined pragma is used with parameters which are not recognized. It is generally considered that the compiler should issue warning messages when pragmas are ignored, but this is not required and many compilers do not generate such warnings. The specific details of which pragmas are supported on a particular compiler are reported in Appendix F of the reference manual for that compiler.

In the following subsections we mention each of the Ada standard pragmas. We discuss the details of the more commonly used pragmas.

17.7.1 Controlling Elaboration Order

The problem of elaboration order arises with respect to compilation units that are bodies of library units. Consider the following fragment from several compilation units. Here lines with four dashes represent the divisions between compilation units.

```
package Me_First is
  function Count return INTEGER;
end Me_First;
----
with Me_First;
-- pragma ELABORATE(Me_First);    -- the pragma could go here
package Need_Count is
  X: constant INTEGER := Me_First.Count;
  -- other stuff;
```

```
end Need_Count;
----
package body Need_Count is
----
package body Me_First is
```

Because of the with clause, the compiler must elaborate the declaration of **Me_First** before elaborating the declaration of **Need_Count**. Also the compiler must elaborate the declaration of **Need_Count** before the corresponding body and the declaration of **Me_First** before its body. But between the declaration of **Need_Count** and the body of **Me_First**, which should be elaborated first? Suppose the compiler chose to elaborate the declaration of **Need_Count** before the body of **Me_First**. During this elaboration it becomes necessary to give a value to **X**. This requires a call to **Me_First.Count**. Since the body of **Me_First** has not been elaborated, the attempted call to **Count** raises **PROGRAM_ERROR**. For this reason, the body of **Me_First** must be elaborated before the declaration of **Need_Count**.

A similar problem occurs if the initialization code in the body of **Need_Count** calls **Count**. In this case, the body of **Me_First** would have to be elaborated before the body of **Need_Count**.

There are circumstances in which a compiler cannot figure out the correct order of elaboration to avoid a **PROGRAM_ERROR**. There are also circumstances in which a compiler could figure it out, but Ada does not require it do so. In all these circumstances the pragma **ELABORATE** can be used to direct the compiler to use a certain order of elaboration. The preceding example indicates where we could place this pragma to direct that the body of **Me_First** be elaborated before the declaration of **Need_Count**. The format for the **ELABORATE** pragma is

ELABORATE (*Library_Unit_Names*) ;

The pragma means that the bodies of the designated library units must be elaborated before elaborating this unit. Of course, if you force the elaboration of units in an incorrect order **PROGRAM_ERROR** will be raised. To emphasize, although **ELABORATE** names library units, it is the elaboration of the corresponding secondary units which the pragma is requiring.

17.7.2 Calling Subprograms Written in Other Languages

Sometimes utilities, libraries, and operating system routines will have been written in languages other than Ada. The pragma **INTERFACE** provides a means to call these routines from Ada programs. The format of the pragma is

INTERFACE (*Language*, *Subprogram_Names*) ;

The pragma specifies that the bodies of the subprograms named are implemented in another language. These subprograms have been previously declared as Ada subprograms. The specifics of how to prepare a subprogram in another language so that it is acceptable to Ada can be quite complicated and will vary from implementation to implementation.

Pragma **INTERFACE** need not be provided by an implementation, and even when it is provided, interfaces may be defined for some languages and not for others.

Suppose we have a program provided by the operating system called **Status** which takes an integer indicating a printer and returns an integer indicating the status of that printer. Our declarations could be as follows

```
package Printer_Information is
  procedure Get_Status(Which_Printer: INTEGER; Status_Report: out INTEGER);
end Printer_Information;
package body Printer_Information is
  procedure Status(Printer, Printer_Status: in out INTEGER);
  pragma INTERFACE(FORTRAN, Status);
  procedure Get_Status(Which_Printer: INTEGER; Status_Report: out INTEGER) is
    The_Printer: INTEGER := Which_Printer;
    The_Status: INTEGER;
  begin
    Status(The_Printer, The_Status);
    Status_Report := The_Status;
  end Get_Status;
end Printer_Information;
```

The actual procedure being interfaced to is the one named **Status**. This procedure is really implemented in a language called **FORTRAN**. Notice that we have isolated the interface: Instead of directly calling **Status**, Ada users call **Get_Status**, which then provides parameters of the appropriate modes **in** and **out**. By contrast, the actual procedure **Status** uses parameters of mode **in out**. It does this because we have "inside information" about our Ada and FORTRAN compilers, as well as the "real" **Status** procedure which says that this the way we must pass the parameters. This kind of information will vary with compilers and computers, that is why we isolated this call so that only **Get_Status** can use it. In this manner, if we switch compilers or machines, only **Get_Status** will have to be modified. We could actually have made **Get_Status** even more convenient by providing an enumeration list of printers and appropriately converting between this enumeration type and the integers that **Status** would expect.

17.7.3 Other Pragmas

The following other pragmas are defined by the Ada language:

LIST(*option*); — This pragma is used to produce a compiled listing of a program. The allowed options are **ON** and **OFF**. **ON** says to list the lines of the program that follow while compiling them. This is quite useful for debugging, as error messages will appear together with the lines to which they refer. Additional information for debugging is sometimes also provided.

PAGE; — This pragma also has to do with creating listings when compiling. It directs the compiler to start a new page on the listing.

OPTIMIZE (*option*) ; — The allowed options are **TIME** and **SPACE**. High-quality compilers will attempt to improve the code generated in order to improve the speed of execution (**TIME**) or reduce the memory required for the program (**SPACE**). This pragma tells the compiler what to do if a choice needs to be made between a faster program and a larger program.

INLINE (*Subprogram_Names*) ; — This pragma recommends that inline code be generated instead of branch-return code. Inline code executes faster, but requires a copy of the code for a subprogram for each of call made to that subprogram. Thus, declaring a subprogram to be inline can require a significantly larger amount of memory if the subprogram is called at more than one place in the program. The implementation may choose when to apply and when to ignore the **INLINE** pragma.

CONTROLLED (*Access_type*) ; — The specified access type is not subject to automatic storage reclamation. There is no requirement in Ada that storage be reclaimed. However, some implementations reclaim storage used by dynamic variables. Such reclamation may take considerable time and cause the program to become unacceptably slow. The **CONTROLLED** pragma ensures that reclamation will not be attempted on the specified access types.

PACK (*Record_Or_Array_Type*) ; — This pragma requests the use of minimum space in representing the indicated type, often with a great penalty in execution time. For instance, on many computers, an array of Boolean is normally stored with one element per computer word. If the computer word is 16 bits, this means that 15/16 of the memory used to store the array is wasted. Using **PACK** can avoid wasting this memory, but on some machines each access to a **PACK**ed element can require as much as 10 times as long as access to the same array element if the array is not packed. An implementation is permitted to ignore this pragma.

PRIORITY (*Static_expression*) ; — This pragma specifies the priority of a task or the main program. The expression must be in the range of the **INTEGER** subtype **SYSTEM.PRIORITY**. A task is not allowed to be executing when a task of higher priority could sensibly be executing instead. *Sensible* takes into account several considerations. For example, the higher priority task might require special capabilities or too much memory to be executed by the same processor and in the same memory as is being used by the lower priority task. In this case it would not be sensible to attempt to run it.

SHARED (*Simple_Variable_Name*) ; — The named variable must be a scalar or an access type. Both the pragma and the variable declaration must be in the same declaration part. The pragma makes reading and writing of the named variable become an indivisible operation. That is, if multiple tasks are operating and the named variable is accessed by several of them, no read or write can be interrupted by a read or write from another task.

MEMORY_SIZE (*Numeric_Literal*) ; — The named number **SYSTEM.MEMORY_SIZE** is the number of storage units normally available. This pragma redefines this number of storage units for this particular compilation. This pragma, like the next two pragmas, must occur before the first compilation unit of the compilation. All three of these pragmas implicitly "recompile" the package **SYSTEM**, forcing the recompilation of units naming that package.

STORAGE_UNIT (*Numeric_Literal*) ; — The named number **SYSTEM.STORAGE_UNIT** is the number of bits per storage unit. This pragma redefines this number of bits for this particular compilation.

SYSTEM_NAME (*Enumeration_Literal*) ; — **SYSTEM.NAME** is an enumeration type defined by the implementation that contains the allowable system names. These enumeration literals name the machine configurations handled by the implementation. The named constant **SYSTEM.SYSTEM_NAME** is one of these and is the default target configuration of the compiler. The pragma specifies the name of an allowable target configuration.

SUPPRESS (*Check*) ; — Most of the Ada execution-time checks can be suppressed. The next subsection gives more details on this particular pragma.

17.7.4 Suppression of Predefined Exceptions

Ada checks for many unusual situations as the program executes. If one of these situations arises, a predefined exception will be raised. There may be a need to suppress these checks. For this reason Ada provides the **SUPPRESS** pragma. Suppression of these checks is dangerous; therefore, we leave a detailed description of suppression to the Chapter 11 of the Language Reference Manual. The following is a simplified description of this pragma.

```
pragma SUPPRESS(Check, ON => name);
```

The pragma gives permission to the implementation to omit the specified check. This means that an implementation can always omit check, ignore the directive and never omit the check, or partially ignore the directive and omit the check some of the time. In particular, if a certain check is automatically performed by the hardware of the implementation, it may be impossible to avoid performing that check, or it may be avoidable only for certain instructions.

The pragma must be immediately within a declarative part of a package specification. The *name* must be the identifier of an object, subtype, or subprogram in the declarative part of the package specification. The *check* that will be suppressed is one of the following:

ACCESS_CHECK — This suppresses the check that raises a constraint error when the program attempts to use an access object containing the value **null** to access a dynamic variable.

DISCRIMINANT_CHECK — This suppresses the check that raises a constraint error when discriminants do not match.

INDEX_CHECK — This suppresses the check that raises a constraint error when an index is outside the legal bounds of an array.

LENGTH_CHECK — When applying Boolean operators to one dimensional arrays of Booleans, Ada requires the arrays have equal length. This suppresses the check on the length of the arrays.

RANGE_CHECK — This suppresses the check that raises a constraint error when the subrange restriction on an object or type is violated.

DIVISION_CHECK — This suppresses the check that raises numeric error when a division by zero is attempted.

OVERFLOW_CHECK — This suppresses the check to ensure that the result of a computation is not a number too large or too small for the precision of the numbers involved.

ELABORATION_CHECK — This suppresses the check to ensure that the body of a procedure has been elaborated before it is called or the body of a package has been elaborated before its contents are accessed.

STORAGE_CHECK — This suppresses the check that determines whether the program has run out of memory.

17.8 HARDWARE DEPENDENCIES AND INTERFACES

Some Ada programs must interact directly with hardware. The portions of a program which access the hardware should always be kept separate from the rest of the program, kept as small as possible and should be very well commented. It is a common practice to combine these portions into packages which are designed to hide the specifics of the hardware with which the program is interacting.

At the outset of the Ada project, the goal was to provide a programming language that would support software development for "embedded military systems." This software, such as aircraft or missile navigation and guidance systems, runs on computers that are built into equipment, rather than computers that exist as individual pieces of equipment. Many of these systems are small and require control of the equipment by the computer. In those portions of a program which must interact in a hardware-dependent manner the programmer may need to force certain interpretations. For example, the programmer may need a certain pattern of bits to represent a value or may need some entity to be associated with a certain address. To achieve this Ada provides powerful tools for interfacing with hardware.

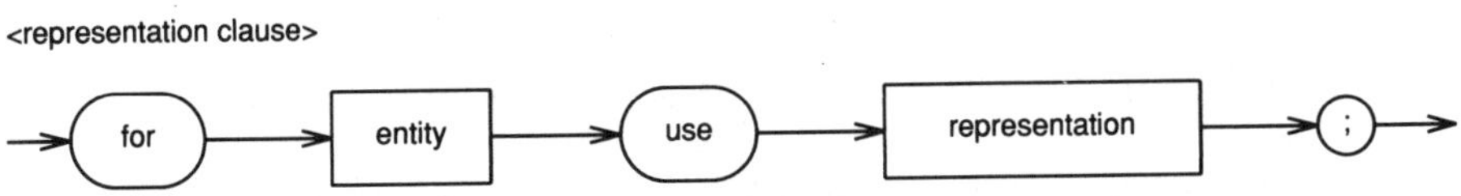

Figure 17–5

17.8.1 Representation Clauses

The pragma **PACK** discussed in section 7 is the only predefined pragma that is considered a representation clause. Other implementation-defined pragmas may effect representation. Like other implementation dependencies these will be described in Appendix F of the reference manual for the given implementation. Most other representation clauses have the format shown in Figure 17–5.

One group of representation clauses is the *length clauses*. They are called this because they effect the amount of storage used by a type. The entity named is an attribute of the type. One of these representation clauses is is associated with the fixed point attribute **SMALL** and effects the model numbers of the fixed point type. Because the choice of model numbers can change the amount of size needed to store a value of that type, it is considered a length clause. We have already discussed this representation clause in Chapter 14.

Another attribute that may be named is **SIZE**. In a length clause this attribute is used to place an upper bound on the number of bits used to store values of the specified type. For example,

```
for Days'SIZE use 3;
```

specifies that objects of type **Days** use at most 3 bits of storage. We have already used this attribute with real numbers. The same rule that applied to the use of this clause with real numbers applies to other types: The number of bits must be sufficient to store the values of the type.

A third attribute, **STORAGE_SIZE**, is used in two different kinds of length clauses. When used with an access type, it indicates the number of storage units for a designated object accessed by that type. When used with a task type (see Chapter 19), it specifies the number of storage units reserved for the activation of a task of that type.

A second group of representation clauses is the *enumeration representation clauses*. Using this class of clause, it is possible to specify the values associated with the literals of an enumerated data type. The specified values are used to represent the enumeration values. In this form of the use clause, the entity is the name of the type and the expression is an aggregate indicating the representation values associated with the enumeration values. An example is

```
type Register is (FP, AP, PC);
for Register use (12, 14, 15);
```

The aggregate contains universal integers that define the representation values for the type. Note that each value in the type must be provided a representation. The attributes **SUCC**, **PRED**, and **POS** are not affected by the representation clause.

A third group of representation clauses is the *record representation clauses*. These allow the programmer to specify how a record is stored. For example, the declarations

```
type Instruction is
  record
    Operation_Code: INTEGER range 0..15;
    First_Address_Mode: INTEGER range 0..7;
    First_Register: INTEGER range 0..7;
```

```
    Second_Address_Mode: INTEGER range 0..7;
    Second_Register: INTEGER range 0..7;
  end record;
for Instruction use
  record at mod 2;
    Operation_Code      at 0*WORD range 0..3;
    First_Address_Mode  at 0*WORD range 4..6;
    First_Register      at 0*WORD range 7..9;
    Second_Address_Mode at 0*WORD range 10..12;
    Second_Register     at 0*WORD range 13..15;
  end record;
```

specify the locations of the various components within records of type **Instruction**. This specification places the **Operation_Code** component in the first 4 bits, the **First_Address_Mode** component in the next 3 bits, and so forth. If the record needed more than one word of storage then, "**1*WORD**" would precede those components stored in the second word, "**2*WORD**" would precede those components stored in the third word, and so on. This of course assumes that **WORD** is associated with an appropriate value for the difference in addresses between words in the target machine. This entire arrangement is quite dependent upon the particular hardware on which the implementation is run.

The final group of representation clauses is the *address clauses*. These are used to associate a specific address with an entity. Address clauses can be applied to objects, executable units (subprograms, packages, tasks), and task entries. When applied to an object, the address clause indicates the address at which that object is to be stored. When applied to an executable unit, the address clause indicates the address at which the executable code for that unit will be placed. In each of these uses, the programmer is associating an object or section of code with a particular portion of the computer's hardware. This most often occurs when that object or code is associated with control of certain computer hardware.

When applied to a task entry, the address clause associates an *interrupt* with that entry. An interrupt is a hardware-generated signal which indicates an unusual condition. Common useful interrupts include those which indicate that data is available from a specific hardware device. The association of a task entry with a hardware interrupt causes a call to the task entry whenever that particular interrupt occurs. This permits the software to respond to the situation that caused the interrupt. In the following task declaration

```
task Input_Handler is
  entry Character_Has_Arrived;
  for Character_Has_Arrived use 8#177544# ;
end Input_Handler;
```

an interrupt associated with the specified address (**8#177544#**) becomes a call for the entry **Character_Has_Arrived**. The address expression must conform to the type

SYSTEM.ADDRESS. For the purposes of this example we have assumed that this is an integer type, but this will vary with the implementation.

Sometimes interfacing with hardware requires direct generation of *machine code*. Procedures can be written in which the body of the procedure is written in either machine code or assembly language for the computer on which the program is intended to execute. This permits access to portions of the machine that are not accessible in Ada. It also permits procedures to be written which execute extremely quickly. These procedures are dangerous, as the normal checks performed by Ada to help prevent errors are not made in these procedures. The use clause

```
use MACHINE_CODE;
```

invokes a predefined package that allows direct generation of machine code. This package is implementation dependent, and an Ada implementation is not required to supply it.

17.9 PROGRAMMING PRACTICES

Ada offers many features to ease team efforts in software development. These are among the most important features in the language. In order to best use these features, we suggest the following rules of thumb:

1. Keep declarations in separate files, and separate declarations from bodies.
2. Get declarations right first. You can fix or build a single procedure without recompiling everything else, but if a declaration changes, this can be a mess.
3. Design a program from the top down (from the entire program with no details down to the details).
4. Build the program from the bottom up, and test each part of the program as it is built. If the little things do not work, the bigger things cannot work.
5. Stub bodies until they can be implemented. That is, write bodies that will compile correctly, but do not actually perform their functions. Often, stubs print messages to enable the programmer to follow the execution of the (partial) program. For example, if you have implemented one of the subprograms in a package and wish to test it, stub the other bodies so the package will compile and you can perform the test.
6. Use structure charts or diagrams to plan your program. They can be a significant aid in making decisions about the design of the program and the program's data types.

17.9.1 Problem Solving

To illustrate some of the capabilities of separate compilation we shall sketch the structure of a program that maintains accounts for a bank. This program slightly extends the capabilities of the previous bank programs (Program 3–14, exercises 3.1, 4.5, 5.9, 7.8,

8.2, 10.5, 10.6, 12.6, 14.1, and 15.1). The bank will have a single teller; however, our design will anticipate the multiple-teller bank developed in Chapter 19.

Briefly, the bank needs to be able to maintain information about each customer account and to send a monthly bank statement to each customer. All account information will be maintained in a permanent file. For each account, the bank will allow the following transactions: deposit, withdraw, open, and close. The bank will close each night and shut down the bank program. When the bank opens, it will restart the program.

We shall separate the functions of the teller from the other functions of the bank. The teller will identify a customer, perform a sequence of operations for that customer, then go to the next customer (or close the bank). Deposits are simple: The bank accepts the amount and updates the account. Closing an account is also simple: The bank marks the account closed and returns all the money in that account. For a withdrawal, the customer requests a certain amount. The bank will not perform this withdrawal unless the account has sufficient funds. Information must be transmitted both ways, the teller tells the bank how much the customer wants, and the bank returns either that amount or an indication that the account has insufficient funds. Opening an account requires getting information about the customer. The teller must get that customer information and pass it to the bank, which returns an account.

According to these specifications, the procedure that interfaces with the teller could appear as follows

```
with Bank;
procedure Teller is
  type Choices is (Deposit, Withdraw, Close_Account, Close_Bank, Done);
  Choice: Choices;
  type Customer_Type is (Old_Customer, New_Customer);
  Customer_Choice: Customer_Type;
  Amount: Bank.Money;
  Current_Customer: Bank.Account;
  procedure Display_Customer_Options is separate;
  procedure Get_Customer_Type(User_Choice: out Customer_Type) is separate;
  procedure Read_Choice(User_Choice: out Choices) is separate;
  procedure Get_Customer(A_Customer: out Bank.Account) is separate;
  procedure Get_New_Customer(A_Customer: out Bank.Account) is separate;
  procedure Display_Options is separate;
  procedure Get_Amount(How_Much: out Bank.Money) is separate;
  procedure Give_Amount(How_Much: in Bank.Money) is separate;
begin
  loop
    Display_Customer_Options;
    Get_Customer_Type(Customer_Choice);
    case Customer_Choice is
      when Old_Customer =>
        Get_Customer(Current_Customer);
      when New_Customer =>
        Get_New_Customer(Current_Customer);
```

```
      end case;
      loop
        Display_Options;
        Read_Choice(Choice);
        case Choice is
          when Deposit =>
            Get_Amount(Amount);
            Bank.Deposit(Current_Customer, Amount);
          when Withdraw =>
            Bank.Withdraw(Current_Customer, Amount);
            Give_Amount(Amount);
          when Close_Account =>
            Bank.Close_Account(Current_Customer, Amount);
            Give_Amount(Amount);
            exit;  -- This customer is done.
          when Close_Bank =>
            Bank.Close_Bank;
            return;              -- Exit the program.
          when Done => exit;     -- This customer is done.
        end case;
      end loop;
    end loop;
  end Teller;
```

We leave the **Display_Customer_Options**, **Display_Options**, and **Read_Choice** procedures as an exercise. The **Get_Customer** procedure can work one of two ways. If the teller is an automated teller machine (ATM), the ATM gets the customer's account number (in a real ATM this is done by reading the magnetic information on the bank card) and the customer's personal identification number, and then verifies these with the bank. A human teller gets either the customer's name or account number and verifies the customer's identity by using a picture or signature. For this discussion we will assume a human teller because ATMs do not open accounts. If the customer has an existing account, **Get_Customer** locates the account. If the customer is opening a new account, **Get_New_Customer** gets the information and opens the account. Either way, when **Display_Options** is called, **Current_Customer** refers to a valid account. By declaring the procedures as subunits, we can defer their implementation.

We will concentrate on the bank package. First, consider the data structures. We need the following information for each account:

1. A unique account number.
2. The names of the persons authorized to perform transactions on this account. We shall allow up to four names on each account.
3. The type of account. The allowable types are savings, checking, and commercial.
4. The address to which the bank statements will be sent. The address will include a street address, city, state, and zip code. In addition, a commercial account address may contain the company or organization name.

5. The account balance.
6. The date on which the bank should send out the bank statement. To send all statements on the same day would clog the mail system, so accounts have statements sent on different days of the month, but always on the same date each month. When the bank is opened, it should send statements for each account for the current day and for each day since the bank last opened. (The bank stays closed on weekends and holidays.)
7. The lowest balance since the last statement. When a statement is sent, the bank calculates the account's monthly interest. This interest is based on the lowest balance since the last statement was sent.
8. A personal identification number, that is, a password.

The complete data structure is needed only within the package so we can place the following declaration in the package body:

```
type Bank_Account is
  record
    Account_Number: Account;
    Names: Name_List;
    Account_Type: Account_Types;
    Statement_Address: Address_Record;
    Statement_Date: CALENDAR.DAY_NUMBER;
    Account_Balance: Money;
    Lowest_Balance: Money;
    Personal_Identification_Number: NATURAL;
  end record;
```

Because they are used by the teller, **Account** and **Money** must occur in the package declaration. We use the declarations:

```
type Money is delta 0.01 range 0.0 .. 10.0E8;
for Money'SMALL use 0.01;
subtype Account is POSITIVE;
```

Most of the procedures made visible by **Bank** are similar. For example, the procedure **Deposit**. will read the user's account, modify the account balance and write the modified account back to the file. An implementation of **Deposit** is:

```
procedure Deposit(Customer: Account; Amount: Money) is
  -- Purpose: Make a deposit to a customer's account.
  Customer_Info: Account;
begin
  Bank_IO.Read_Account(Customer, Customer_Info);
  Customer_Info.Account_Balance := Customer_Info.Account_Balance + Amount;
  Bank_IO.Write_Account(Customer, Customer_Info);
end Deposit;
```

This procedure reads the account information, updates the balance, and writes the modified account information. Notice that we have placed the input and output routines in another package.

The interface between **Get_New_Customer** and the bank is more complicated. Here, the teller needs to get the list of names, the account type, and the address from the customer and pass this information to the bank. The teller also needs to get the account number from the bank and give it to the customer. The bank package should declare the procedure for opening an account as follows:

```
procedure Open(Names: in Name_List;
               Account_Type: Account_Types;
               Statement_Address: Address_Record;
               Account_Number: out Account);
```

This implies that the types named in this parameter list are declared in the package declaration.

Sending out statements when the bank opens requires that a procedure **Send_Statements** be called in the package initialization code. **Send_Statements** will go through the current accounts, sending statements and paying interest (by making deposits) to the appropriate accounts. An account is appropriate if its statement date is after the last time statements were issued and on or before the current date. This implies that the date must be saved (in a file) each time statements are issued. It also requires **Bank_IO** to supply a method for systematically reading all the accounts one at a time.

The last major piece is the **Bank_IO** package. Because accounts are accessed in whatever order the customers arrive, this package should use **DIRECT_IO**. The permanent file contains records of type **Account**. Since we hide this declaration in the body of **Bank**, we shall also place **Bank_IO** within that body. There will be two ways to access a bank account: sequentially (to send statements) and by account number. The only potential difficulty with sequential reads is recognizing and skipping records for closed accounts. When accessing an account by account number, we do not want to read the entire file, searching for the account with that number. Instead, we would maintain a data structure in which the account number would be the key and the record number would be the data. This can be done by instantiating the binary search tree package of Chapter 16. We still have to read the permanent file through once to insert the account numbers and record numbers into the tree, but after that we can look up the account number in the tree to find the record number. Opening an account should also cause an addition to the tree. Closing an account could delete from the tree, or it could mark the account record in the permanent file as closed.

This completes our sketch of the parts of the bank. Each part we have described is reasonably small and easy to implement. A good strategy is to implement and test the bank from the bottom up. First implement the **Bank_IO** and test it. Then implement and test the procedures in **Bank**, and then test the whole **Bank** package. Finally, test **Teller**. For testing, a procedure should be added to **Bank_IO** that dumps all the bank accounts. This procedure should be used to watch what happens to the bank accounts after each operation.

17.9.2 Testing: Designing for Testing

Just as it is possible to design a program so that it may be easily and reliably extended, it is possible to design a program so that it may be easily and reliably tested. A plan for testing should be included from the beginning when designing the program.

For example, in a program that uses windows for interaction with the user, it is helpful if one line of the screen is kept available for testing. This is often the next to the bottom line on the screen, and is often used to display the bottom of the box separating the windows when testing is not being performed. If a line is always available for use in testing, then testing messages can always be displayed there and a smaller number of testing subprograms can be used for displaying the testing information.

As another example, it is easier to test a program if all input from the user is initially handled by one routine. This routine can then be used in keeping an audit trail, a list of the keystrokes entered by the user. It can also be used when it is necessary to execute a series of commands from a file, rather than directly interacting with the user (e.g., playing back the audit trail).

In general, the programming practices recommended in this book serve to simplify testing by dividing the program into small, easily tested pieces. Also, following these practices would lead to similar operations being handled by the same subprogram or at least by subprograms housed in the same package. Finally these programming practices keep you aware that things can go wrong and indicate ways to check whether things are still correct.

The following are a few more rules of thumb that are helpful in designing for testing:

- Concentrate output through a small number of routines. This will permit you to test the output routines separately from the rest of program and thus simplify the decision as to whether the problem is in the calculation or in displaying the result.
- Permit the output to be sent to a file instead of the screen. This permits comparison of the results calculated by a new version of the program with the results from a previous version.
- Reuse algorithms and data structures which are already tested.
- When designing an interaction, make sure that you have specified exactly what will happen to any particular keystroke at any particular time. Consider using a formal model such as a finite-state machine.
- When designing any subprogram, program defensively. That is, check the input values for validity before using them.

17.10 ADA SUMMARY

In this chapter we have completed our coverage of *compilation units*. Compilation units were designed so that large Ada programs could be compiled in separate pieces in an orderly and safe fashion. We have seen the division of compilation units into *library units*, which can be named in a context clause, and *secondary units*, which cannot. Secondary units were divided into two types: *library unit bodies* and *subunits*. Library unit bodies supply bodies for their corresponding library units, while subunits supply bodies for corresponding body stubs of other compilation units. Related to the concept of compilation order, we presented the concept of a *topological sort*.

The second thrust of this chapter was interfacing with and controlling the environment in which the Ada implementation is running. We discussed the various Ada *pragmas* and how they could direct the compiler. We discussed methods to write programs that needed to interface with other languages or the system hardware. In both cases we emphasized that extreme care should be taken when dealing with code containing pragmas or hardware-dependent sections, because many of Ada's normal safety features become suppressed.

EXERCISES

17.1. Implement topological sorting as described in the chapter. After you have read in the data, write out the list in sorted order.

17.2. In the following situation, indicate the partial ordering pairs which represent the required compilation order, and then indicate a legal compilation order.
package `A` indicates **`with`** `B, C, D`
package `B` indicates **`with`** `C`
package `D` indicates **`with`** `C`

17.3. Implement and test the **`Bank`** package and the **`Teller`** procedure. You may let the account number be the same as the record number of the account in the file, thereby eliminating the need for a data structure to storing this information.

17.4. A school asks you to design and implement a program which enrolls students in classes. You are given the following brief description.

Each class has a time, a location, a class number, a maximum number of students allowed in the class. Each student has a name.

A student will use this program to enroll in classes.

An administrator will use this program to add classes, delete classes, change the time, location or maximum size of a class, and admit students (so they can enroll).

Develop a full description of the program, design the structure of the solution, and then construct an implementation.

18

Concurrent Control Structures, I

18.1 OBJECTIVES

In Chapter 11 we introduced concurrent programming. In this chapter we introduce additional structures for controlling concurrent programs. The timed entry call and conditional entry call discussed earlier allowed the caller some control over entry calls. Here, we focus on those structures that allow a task receiving the entry call the flexibility to wait for one of several occurrences, including the arrival of an entry call. We introduce an attribute for determining the number of calls pending on an entry (section 3), examine the construct that permits a task to wait for one of a number of events (section 4), and discuss the concept of a family of entries (section 5). Then, to put these concepts and constructs into perspective, we summarize entry calls and accept statements (section 6). Finally, we provide a detailed discussion of some programs that use these features (section 7).

CONCEPTS:

- A task can control which entry calls it accepts.
- There are provisions for the orderly completion of concurrent programs.

GOALS:

- Build a moderately complex concurrent program.

18.2 MOTIVATION

We have seen that it is useful to provide some options when making an entry call. Similarly, a task may need to have options when accepting an entry call. For example, a task which provides two services may not want to refuse one of the services just because it is waiting to provide the other service. In the restaurant example in Chapter 11, the cook may be willing to receive an order or, if no orders are pending, begin preparing some soup. In other words, the cook is willing to accept an order, but does not want to be stuck waiting for orders if there are none.

In Ada, the combination of entry calls and accept statements allows the caller and the called task to rendezvous. Either the caller or the called task may have to wait for the other. During this wait, either can give up the request for a rendezvous. For the caller, options are provided by the timed entry call and the conditional entry call. For the accepter, options are provided by the *selective wait*. However, once the rendezvous starts, both are committed to it. In this chapter, we introduce those structures that provide options for the called task.

18.3 THE ENTRY ATTRIBUTE COUNT

The only attribute which applies to entries is **COUNT**. For example, the task **Storage** (see Program 18–1) has two entries, **Store** and **Recall**. Within this task, we can ask for **Store'COUNT** or **Recall'COUNT**. The attribute yields the number of calls pending on an entry. For example, if there were 4 outstanding calls to **Store**, then **Store'COUNT** would yield the value 4. **COUNT** returns a universal integer (see Chapter 13), so this value is compatible with any integer type.

Like accept statements, **COUNT** can be used directly within the body of the appropriate task, but it cannot be used within any subprogram, generic unit, or locally declared task. In addition, **COUNT** can be used directly within the declarative region of the task body, for example, to supply an initial value to variable.

Caution must be observed in interpreting the meaning of **COUNT**. Entry calls occur concurrently; thus, the value returned by **COUNT** may change immediately after its evaluation. For example, if entry calls are arriving rapidly, values for **COUNT** often will not include the latest calls. In that case, by the time any use is made of the value yielded by **COUNT**, the number of pending entry calls may have increased.

In fact, **COUNT** can also lead to overestimates of the number of entries waiting. Suppose, for example, **COUNT** happens to be evaluated when a conditional or timed entry call has occurred. Then the value of **COUNT** could include such calls, but these entry calls might immediately disappear. Thus,

```
if Store'COUNT >= 1 then
  accept Store(Value: INTEGER);
end if;
```

may get stuck because, at the time **COUNT** is evaluated, a timed entry call is pending so the Boolean expression yields **TRUE**, but by the time the accept statement is executed, the entry may have timed out and disappeared. If this happened, we would find ourselves at the accept waiting for the *next* call to **Store** because no calls were pending. Of course, if those calling the entry are correctly and carefully programmed (that is, they did not make timed or conditional entry calls to those entries which checked **COUNT**), the latter problem could be avoided. In any case, **COUNT** is useful for providing an estimate of the number of backlogged entry calls.

18.4 SELECTIVE WAIT

The purpose of the *selective wait statement* is to provide "accept" options to the called task. The semantics of the selective wait is similar to that of the case statement in that it allows a task to choose one of a number of options.

Like accept statements, selective wait statements may only occur immediately within a task body. They cannot occur outside a task body, or in the declarative region of the task body (i.e., in a nested subprogram or task). Selective wait statements can occur within block statements and within exception handlers, provided that these statement or handlers are within the task body (and not the declarative region of that body). Placing accepts and selective wait statements inside block statements allows a task to handle exceptions without being forced to complete. The syntax for the selective wait is given in Figure 18–1.

There are two restrictions: first, there must be at least one accept alternative. and second, the delay alternative, terminate alternative, and else part are mutually exclusive; that is, at most one of these may occur as part of a selective wait.

Confusion sometimes results because the reserved word **select** is used for timed entry calls and conditional entry calls in addition to the selective wait. Beware, these statements are quite different. The entry call statement is a request for a rendezvous with a task; the accept statement and the selective wait are the mechanisms by which a task grants a rendezvous. Anybody can make an entry call, but only the task body can contain an accept or selective wait.

The simplest form of the selective wait occurs when a task is willing to service any of a number of entry calls. This is illustrated in the task **Storage** in Program 18–1. **Storage** provides for storage and recall of an integer value. When the task is activated, the elaboration of the variable **Current_Value** causes an initial value of zero to be stored. When the task body begins executing, it enters the loop at line 8 and executes the selective wait statement of lines 9–18.

This selective wait indicates that the task is willing to either store a new value or recall an old value. If an entry call is made to **Store**, execution moves from the select statement to the accept statement at line 10, and a rendezvous occurs. The movement from the select into the rendezvous is *atomic*. That is, even if the entry call is a conditional or delayed entry call, there is no opportunity for the entry call to "back out" once a selection has been made.

If an entry call is made to **Recall**, execution moves from the select statement to the accept statement at line 14, and a rendezvous occurs. If entry calls are made to both statements, execution may move to either line 10 or line 14. Ada allows either selection to be made, but in either case a rendezvous occurs.

A task at a selective wait is simultaneously waiting on all alternatives. It will select one of the alternatives or the else part. When it selects an accept alternative it

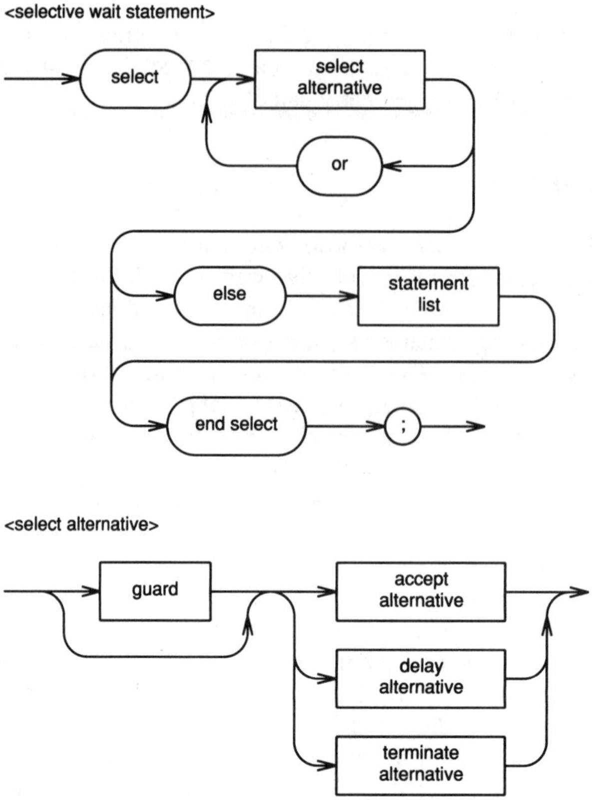

Figure 18–1

moves immediately into a rendezvous. Once it has moved into such a rendezvous it is no longer waiting at the select. For example, when two conditional entry calls arrive simultaneously and the task is waiting at the select, one of those calls will be selected and the other call will execute its else part.

We have indicated that if calls are waiting on several entries of the select, one of the appropriate accept alternatives is selected. Which alternative is selected depends on the implementation. If the programmer wishes to guarantee priorities, such as handling stores before recalls, additional steps must be taken. The only restriction Ada places on the implementation is that calls to the same entry must form a queue; that is, they will be accepted in the order the calls were made. Calls to different entries may be accepted in any order, regardless of the order in which the calls were made.

Both lines 10–12 and lines 14–17 of Program 18–1 are accept alternatives. The syntax for an accept alternative is given in Figure 18–2. An accept alternative always begins with an accept statement. Every selective wait contains at least one accept alternative. Line 17 illustrates that a statement list may be included in an accept alternative following the accept statement.

```
task Storage is  -- Version 1
  entry Store(Value: INTEGER);
  entry Recall(Value: out INTEGER);
end Storage;
task body Storage is
  Current_Value: INTEGER := 0;
begin
  loop
    select
      accept Store(Value: INTEGER) do
        Current_Value := Value;
      end Store;
    or
      accept Recall(Value: out Item) do
        Value := Current_Value;
      end Recall;
      TEXT_IO.PUT("Data recalled");
    end select;
  end loop;
end Storage;
```

Program 18–1

<accept alternative>

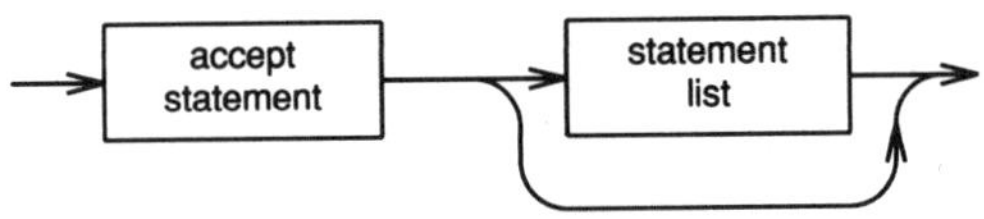

Figure 18–2

18.4.1 Guards

In the syntax diagram of Figure 18–1, we see that an optional *guard* can be applied to the alternatives of the selective wait. The syntax for a guard is given in Figure 18–3.

<guard>

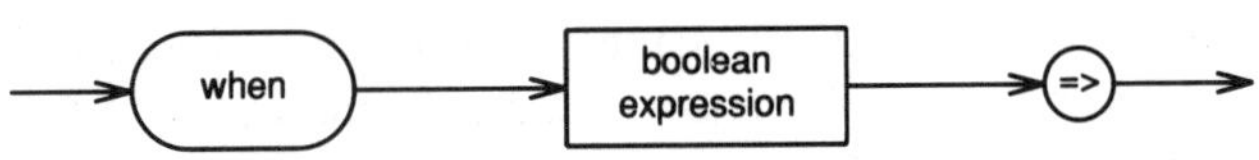

Figure 18–3

Each guard contains a Boolean expression. An alternative is said to be *open* if the guard associated with that alternative evaluates to **TRUE**, and is said to be *closed* if the guard evaluates to **FALSE**. When execution of a selective wait commences, the guards are evaluated. If the guard of an alternative evaluates to **FALSE**, that alternative cannot be used. Execution of the selective wait occurs as though that alternative did not exist. Alternatives without guards are always open. Thus, we can consider an alternative without a guard as having an implicit guard that always evaluates to **TRUE**.

```
 1:task Storage_2 is    -- Version 2
 2:  entry Store(Value: INTEGER);
 3:  entry Recall(Value: out INTEGER);
 4:end Storage_2;
 5:task body Storage_2 is
 6:  Current_Value: INTEGER;
 7:  Value_Stored: BOOLEAN := FALSE;
 8:begin
 9:  loop
10:    select
11:      when Recall'COUNT = 0 =>
12:      accept Store(Value: INTEGER) do
13:        Current_Value := Value;
14:      end Store;
15:      Value_Stored := TRUE;
16:    or
17:      when Value_Stored =>
18:      accept Recall(Value: out Item) do
19:        Value := Current_Value;
20:      end Recall;
21:    end select;
22:  end loop;
23:end Storage_2;
```

Program 18–2

The task **Storage_2** of Program 18–2 is a version of **Storage** with guards placed on both alternatives. The guards try to service requests to **Recall** before requests to **Store** and try to avoid allowing **Recall** when no value has been stored. The task contains inadequacies that illustrate some of the points discussed in the previous paragraph.

The guards are found in lines 11 and 17. When execution reaches the selective wait statement at line 10, all guards are evaluated. If **Recall'COUNT** is not 0 (line 11), the accept to **Store** is closed, and only entry calls to **Recall** will be accepted. If **Value_Stored** is **FALSE** (line 17), the entry call to **Recall** is closed, and only calls to **Store** will be accepted.

The guards are evaluated only once. If **Recall'COUNT** initially evaluates to 0, the Boolean expression at line 11 yields **TRUE**, and the accept is open. Even if entry calls to **Recall** are made, the Boolean expression is not reevaluated, so the accept alternative remains open. Thus, if entry calls to **Store** and **Recall** arrive just after the guards are evaluated, the call to **Store** could be accepted. For the alternative of lines 12–15 to close, the select statement would have to finish by accepting an entry call. Then, when the loop forces reexecution of the selective wait statement, the guards will be reevaluated. Similarly, the guard at line 17 is evaluated when execution reaches 10. If **Value_Stored** is **FALSE** when execution reaches line 10, the alternative of lines 17–21 will be closed. In that case, only the alternative of lines 11–15 would be available. Since this alternative assigns **TRUE** to **Value_Stored**, the next time line 10 is reached, the alternative of lines 17–21 will be open.

Since guards are evaluated only once during the execution of a selective wait, if all alternatives are closed, no alternative can be selected and a select could never be made. In this case, the task would be stuck permanently at the selective wait. Instead of permitting the task to remain silently stuck, Ada specifies that the exception **PROGRAM_ERROR** will be raised.

In the task **Storage_2**, if both **Recall'COUNT** is not 0 and **Value_Stored** is **FALSE**, both alternatives will be closed and **PROGRAM_ERROR** will be raised. Execution of that task will then be transferred to the exception handler for the block containing the selective wait statement. In particular, **PROGRAM_ERROR** will be raised if a **Recall** occurred before the first **Store**. The error could be fixed by replacing the Boolean condition in line 11 by

```
not Value_Stored or Recall'COUNT = 0
```

so that the alternative will always be open until the first call to **Store** has been accepted.

<terminate alternative>

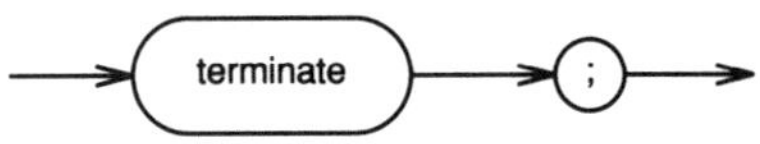

Figure 18–4

18.4.2 Terminate Alternative

Both versions of **Storage** have only accept alternatives, easily recognizable by the occurrence of the accept statement just after the guard. The terminate alternative is equally easy to recognize: it contains the reserved word **terminate** just after the guard. The syntax for the terminate alternative is given in Figure 18–4. For example, we could modify **Storage_2** as follows:

```
task body Storage_2 is -- Version with terminate alternative.
  Current_Value: INTEGER;
  Value_Stored: BOOLEAN := FALSE;
begin
  loop
    select
      when not Value_Stored or Recall'COUNT = 0 =>
```

```
 8:        accept Store(Value: INTEGER) do
 9:          Current_Value := Value;
10:        end Store;
11:        Value_Stored := TRUE;
12:      or
13:        when Current_Value /= -99  =>
14:        terminate;
15:      or
16:        when Value_Stored =>
17:        accept Recall(Value: out Item) do
18:          Value := Current_Value;
19:        end Recall;
20:      end select;
21:    end loop;
22:end Storage_2;
```

In this modification, we have placed a terminate alternative as the next to last alternative (lines 13–14). The terminate alternative is not required to be the last alternative: It may be used as any of the alternatives. However, only one terminate alternative is allowed per selective wait. As with other alternatives, the guard (line 13) is optional. Notice that the terminate alternative never includes any statements.

We now introduce two Ada terms: *completion* and *termination.* Completion can apply to a task, subprogram or block. A task, subprogram, or block is completed if the execution of its statement list has been completed—that is, if its main body has completed execution. Termination applies to tasks. A task becomes terminated when it is completed and all dependent tasks are terminated.

Tasks can also become terminated through the terminate alternative. The terminate alternative allows the task to terminate its execution if its services "cannot be required". The terminate alternative is only available to a task if the guard indicates that the alternative is open. The Ada rule for determining if a task can terminate is simple. A task's services "cannot be required" if every subprogram which could contain an entry call has completed and every task which could contain an entry call has completed or is executing a selective wait with an open terminate alternative. Obviously, completed tasks or subprograms cannot make an entry call. The requirement that all uncompleted tasks are at a selective wait means that none of them are currently making an entry call. In Ada, terminate alternatives, delay alternatives, and else parts are mutually exclusive. This means that if all uncompleted tasks are at a selective wait with a terminate alternative, those selective waits have no delay alternatives and no else parts. The only way a task could leave such a selective wait (other than by terminating) is if it receives an entry call. But because every task is completed or waiting, no task can make an entry call. Consequently, it is not possible for any task to perform an action, except termination. If some of the entries are associated with interrupts through address clauses, the implementation may place additional restrictions on what is required for selection of the terminate alternative.

<delay alternative>

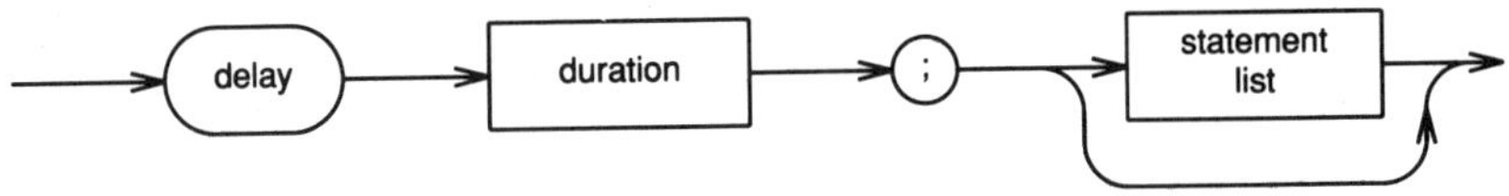

Figure 18–5

18.4.3 Delay Alternative

The *delay alternative* of the selective wait is distinct from the timed entry call as well as the delay statement. The syntax for the delay alternative is given in Figure 18–5. There may be more than one delay alternative per selective wait. However, as mentioned before, a selective wait with a delay cannot contain either a terminate alternative or an else part. Again, we could modify **Storage_2** to add a delay alternative as follows:

```
1:task body Storage_2 is -- Version with delay alternatives.
2:   Current_Value: INTEGER;
3:   Value_Stored: BOOLEAN := FALSE;
4:begin
5:   loop
6:     select
7:       when not Value_Stored or Recall'COUNT = 0 =>
8:       accept Store(Value: INTEGER) do
9:         Current_Value := Value;
10:      end Store;
11:      Value_Stored := TRUE;
12:    or
13:      when not Value_Stored =>
14:      delay 5.0;
15:      TEXT_IO.PUT("Failed to store a value");
16:    or
17:      when Value_Stored =>
18:      accept Recall(Value: out Item) do
19:        Value := Current_Value;
20:      end Recall;
21:    or
22:      delay 10.0;
23:      TEXT_IO.PUT("Entry call overdue");
24:    end select;
25:  end loop;
26:end Storage_2;
```

In this version of the task, the selective wait statement contains two delay alternatives, the first at lines 13–15 and the second at lines 22–23. Notice that a selective wait can have more than one delay alternative, but if it has any delay alternatives, it cannot have a terminate alternative or an else part. Usually, if there is more than one delay alternative, their guards will differ, but this is not required. Neither is it required that their delays be different. Thus, it is possible that several delays will expire simultaneously.

Semantically, an open delay alternative is selected if its time limit expires before there is an entry call to an open accept alternative. When multiple delay alternatives are open, the one with the shortest delay will be selected if its time limit expires before there is an entry call to an open accept alternative. When several delay alternatives share the shortest delay, one of them is arbitrarily selected.

In the preceding modification of **Storage_2**, if there is an entry call for one or more open accept alternatives when the selective wait is executed, an accept alternative would be accepted and a rendezvous would occur. If there were no entry calls waiting at open accept alternatives and one arrived within five seconds, the appropriate open accept alternative would be selected and a rendezvous would occur. If no entry call arrived at an open accept alternative for five seconds, and the delay alternative at lines 13–15 was open, that delay alternative would be selected. This would cause the message "**Failed to store a value**" to be printed. If the alternative at lines 13–15 was closed and no entry call arrived at an open accept alternative for 10 seconds, the delay alternative at lines 22–23 would be selected and the message "**Entry call overdue**" would be printed.

The delay alternative provides the accepting task with a capability similar to that which is supplied to the entry caller by the timed entry call. If nothing happens within the specified time period, the task ceases to wait for an entry call and goes on to do other things.

18.4.4 Else Part

The *else part* is for the impatient task. If present, the else part must occur last. The syntax (Figure 18–1) does not allow a guard on the else part. If none of the open accept alternatives can be selected immediately, the else part is selected. An else part can begin with a delay statement or an accept statement, but keep in mind that such a delay or accept statement is *not* a delay or accept alternative. Such a statement would simply be unconditionally executed if the else part were selected.

If an else part is present, it is permissible for all alternatives to be closed. In this case, the else part is the only thing available to be selected. Again, if an else part is present there cannot be delay or terminate alternatives. We could modify **Storage_2** to add an else part as follows:

```
task body Storage_2 is -- Version with an else part.
  Current_Value: INTEGER;
  Value_Stored: BOOLEAN := FALSE;
begin
  loop
    select
      when not Value_Stored or Recall'COUNT = 0 =>
      accept Store(Value: INTEGER) do
        Current_Value := Value;
```

```
10:       end Store;
11:       Value_Stored := TRUE;
12:       TEXT_IO.PUT("Failed to store a value");
13:     or
14:       when Value_Stored =>
15:       accept Recall(Value: out Item) do
16:         Value := Current_Value;
17:       end Recall;
18:     else
19:       TEXT_IO.PUT("Nobody calling");
20:     end select;
21:   end loop;
22:end Storage_2;
```

The else part is located in lines 18–19. With this modification, if there is an entry call waiting at one or more open accept alternatives, an accept alternative is chosen and a rendezvous occurs. If there are no such entry calls waiting, the else part is selected and the message "**Nobody calling**" is printed.

The else part provides the accepting task with a capability similar to that supplied to the entry caller by the conditional entry call. If no entry call is waiting, the task immediately goes on to do other things. As a word of warning, if the caller uses conditional entry calls and the task uses a selective wait with an else part, no task is willing to wait for any other task, so it may difficult for a rendezvous actually to occur.

18.4.5 Examples

We close our discussion of the selective wait with a number of short examples. In these examples we will assume that **E1**, **E2**, and **E3** are entries and **G1**, **G2**, and **G3** are Boolean variables.

Our first example shows a selective wait with an else part:

```
 1:select
 2:  when G1 =>
 3:  accept E1;
 4:  TEXT_IO.PUT("E1");
 5:or
 6:  when G2 =>
 7:  accept E2;
 8:  TEXT_IO.PUT("E2");
 9:else
10:  TEXT_IO.PUT("Else");
11:end select;
```

The else part occupies lines 9 and 10. The else part is selected if there is no pending entry call to an open accept statement. For example, if **G2** is true and **G1** is false, an entry call to **E2** will be accepted if such an entry call is available; otherwise, the else part will be selected. If both **G1** and **G2** are false, the else part will be selected.

The following example illustrates the difference between alternatives and statements:

```
1:select
2:  accept E1;    -- Accept alternative
3:  TEXT_IO.PUT("E1");
4:or
5:  accept E1;    -- Accept alternative
6:  TEXT_IO.PUT("E2");
7:  delay 10.0;  -- Delay statement
8:  TEXT_IO.PUT("delayed 10.0 seconds");
9:or
10:  delay 5.0;   -- Delay alternative
11:  TEXT_IO.PUT("5.0 seconds without a call");
12:  accept E3;   -- Accept statement
13:  TEXT_IO.PUT("E3");
14:end select;
```

Lines 2–3 and 5–8 are accept alternatives. Lines 10–13 are a delay alternative. Line 12 is an accept statement that occurs within a delay alternative. Line 7 is a delay statement that occurs within an accept alternative. In the accept and delay alternatives, the reserved words **accept** and **delay** immediately follow the reserved words **select** and **or**. In timed entry calls, **delay** immediately follows **or**. All other occurrences of **accept** and **delay** refer to (unconditional) statements. When execution reaches line 7, there is an unconditional delay for 10 seconds. When execution reaches line 12, execution waits unconditionally for an entry call to **E3**. On the other hand, when execution reaches line 1 (the selective wait), one of the three alternatives will be chosen. Which one is chosen depends on the time of arrival of the entry calls.

This example also shows that a select alternative may contain multiple accept statements for an entry. In this case, accept alternatives for **E1** occur at lines 2–3 and 5–8. These alternatives may be open simultaneously, as they are in this case since there are no guards. One of these open alternatives is arbitrarily selected when an **E1** entry call is accepted.

The following example contains two delay alternatives:

```
select
  accept E1:
  TEXT_IO.PUT("E1");
or
  when G2 =>
  delay 10.0; -- Delay alternative
  TEXT_IO.PUT("10.0 seconds without a call");
or
  when G3 =>
  delay 5.0;  -- Delay alternative
  TEXT_IO.PUT("5.0 seconds without a call");
end select;
```

In this selective wait statement, preference is given to accepting calls to the entry **E1**. If **G2** is true, the task is patient and waits 10 seconds for a call before printing a message and exiting the selective wait. If **G3** is true, the task is impatient and waits only 5 seconds for a call before printing a message and exiting the selective wait. If both **G2** and **G3** are false, only the accept alternative at line 2 is open, so the task is very patient and will wait forever for an **E1** entry call. Remember, the guards will not be reevaluated, so the delay alternatives cannot become open unless an **E1** call occurs and the selective wait is in a loop which causes it to be executed again. If both **G2** and **G3** are true, the shortest delay will be selected, which, in this case, is the delay alternative of lines 9–11. If there are several shortest delays of equal duration, one is arbitrarily selected.

Negative delays and zero delays are allowed. These are available for immediate selection. However, entry calls for open accept alternatives are selected before any delay alternatives with negative or zero delays.

18.5 ENTRIES AND ENTRY FAMILIES

In addition to single entries, it is possible to declare *entry families*. The syntax diagram in Figure 18–6 indicates an optional discrete range. The presence of the discrete range declares an entry family. If the discrete range is omitted a single entry is declared. For example,

```
entry Bus(INTEGER range 1..10)(Full: BOOLEAN);
```

declares a family of 10 entries indexed by the integers 1 through 10. Each of these entries has a Boolean parameter. The following:

```
subtype Clerk_Names CHARACTER range 'A'..'E'; -- not in task
...
entry Clerks(Clerk_Names);
```

declares a family of five entries indexed by the characters **'A'** through **'E'**. Note that the declaration of the subtype **Clerk_Names** cannot occur within the task declaration. As with other subranges, the bounds may be given by any expression of the appropriate type. This means that the number of entries in the family may not be known until the task declaration is elaborated during program execution.

An entry can have a discrete range (making it an entry family), a parameter list, both, or neither. In an entry declaration, the discrete range and the parameter list are discernible from the syntax of the items between the parentheses. In particular, the parameter list will always contain a colon (:), while the discrete range will never contain one.

A call to a member of an entry family specifies which entry is intended as in:

```
Task_Name.Bus(3)(TRUE);
Other_Task.Clerks('A');
```

<entry declaration>

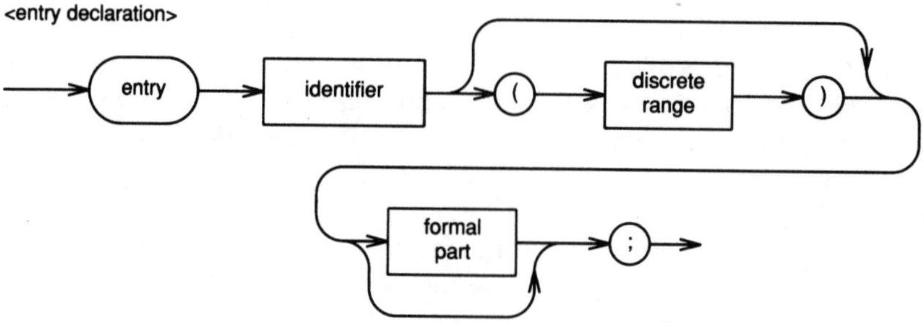

Figure 18–6

The index for the call can be any expression of the appropriate type. For example, the loop

```
for I in INTEGER range 1..10 loop
  Task_Name.Bus(I)(FALSE);
end loop;
```

calls each of the 10 entries in the family and passes the value **FALSE** on each call.

Observe that the task (**Task_Name**) will have to execute 10 accepts, one for each member of the entry family, before execution of this loop could complete.

Within the task body, an accept statement may name a member of an entry family using an expression. For example,

```
task body Task_Name is
  Bus_Full: array (INTEGER range 1..10) of BOOLEAN;
begin
  for I in INTEGER range 1..3 loop
    accept Bus(I)(Full: BOOLEAN) do
      Bus_Full(I) := Full;
    end Bus;
  end loop;
end Task_Name;
```

contains a valid accept statement. Which member of the entry family it accepts depends on which iteration of the loop is being executed. When execution of this accept statement begins, the entry index is computed to determine which entry in the family is being accepted. The accept refers to that entry and no other. Thus, the first iteration of this loop waits for an entry call to **Bus(1)**. Until such an entry call occurs, the first iteration cannot complete. Only after accepting a call for **Bus(1)** will the loop perform the second iteration, and an accept for **Bus(2)** will occur. This loop handles 10 entry calls, in order of ascending entry index, before the loop completes execution.

The selective wait statement can be used to wait for several entries in an entry family. For example,

```
select
  accept Clerks('A');
or
  accept Clerks('B');
or
  accept Clerks('C');
end select;
```

will wait until an entry call to one of the first three entries in the **Clerk** family can be accepted. This is effective when you know the range of the entry indices. Another alternative is to use a loop to scan the entries:

```
for I in Clerk_Names loop
  select
    accept Clerks(I);
  else
    null;
  end select;
end loop;
```

This loop scans the members of the entry family in order. For each entry in the family, if there is a call waiting, it is accepted and a rendezvous occurs. However, if there is no call pending when an entry is checked, the else part of the selective wait is executed. This loop accepts one call to each member of the family which has calls pending. Notice that this loop never waits for an entry. If there are no calls pending for any entries, the loop will iterate 5 times, doing nothing on each iteration, and then execution will proceed to the statement following the loop. The disadvantage of this kind of loop is that it does a lot of looping when no entry calls are waiting.

18.6 SELECTIVE WAIT STATEMENT: SUMMARY

Earlier, we said that the capability of selecting an option that the selective wait statement provides is similar to the capability provided by a case statement. However, as is plain from the discussion, execution of the selective wait is far more complex. Many more things have to be considered than during execution of a case statement. Nevertheless, considered a step at a time, the execution of a selective wait is easy to follow. This section summarizes what happens when a selective wait statement is executed.

Upon execution of a selective wait the following happen in the order given. First, all guards are evaluated. The order in which the guards are evaluated is not defined by Ada, so programs should not depend on a particular order. Closed alternatives are eliminated from any further consideration.

Next, for each open alternative, any entry index (for accept alternatives using entry families) or delay expression (for delay alternatives) is evaluated. Again, the order in which evaluation of indices and expressions occurs is not defined by Ada, so programs should not depend on a particular order.

At this point, it is known which entries can be accepted by open alternatives and which is the shortest delay alternative. If there is an entry call waiting for any open accept alternative, one such alternative is selected and executed. If there are no entry calls waiting and there is an else alternative, it is selected and executed. If there are no calls waiting and there is no else alternative, the task waits for the first entry call to an open accept alternative. The shortest open delay alternative is selected only after the delay has elapsed and no accept alternative has been selected.

18.7 PROGRAMMING PRACTICES

Several common techniques and concepts are useful in building concurrent programs. In this section, we describe these techniques and then examine two programs that use tasks.

An important concept is the *critical region*. A critical region is a section of code that should be executed by only one task at a time. Accordingly, critical regions are useful in handling resources (including data and files) that should only be accessed by a single task at a time. For example, suppose we have several tasks which access a file containing student data. If two tasks attempted to modify the same data at the same time, incorrect data values could be stored.

Use of a critical region occurs in the package **Robots**. The package is designed to allow a different task to control each robot. Each of these tasks will be calling procedures in the package (**Move**, **Turn**, etc.) that cause the screen (and the robots' world) to be updated. If two procedure calls caused updates at the same time, an incorrect screen display or an illegal action could occur. (By an illegal action, we mean that the program might manage to do something like move two robots into the same location.) These are prevented from occurring by the use of critical regions within the package. These critical regions ensure that only one move or turn at a time causes an update. To establish these critical regions the package body uses a task called **Control** defined as follows:

```
task Control is -- Prevent two tasks from changing the world at one time.
  entry Start;  -- Call this at the beginning of your procedure.
  entry Stop;   -- Call this at the end of your procedure and in
end Control;    --  your exception handler.

task body Control is
begin
  loop
    select
      accept Start;
    or
      terminate;
    end select;
    accept Stop;
  end loop;
end Control;
```

The procedures in the package use **Control** to keep the manipulation of the robots' world well defined. For example, the procedure **Move** has the form

```
procedure Move is
 -- declarations
begin
  -- noncritical region
  Control.Start;
  -- critical region
  Control.Stop;
  -- noncritical region
end Move;
```

as do other procedures in the package. Suppose now that two tasks attempt a move simultaneously. This results in two separate calls to **Move** at the same time. Both calls elaborate the declarations, execute the noncritical region at the start of the **Move** procedure, and call the entry **Start**. The task **Control** accepts one of these entry calls, and the procedure whose entry call was accepted commences execution of its critical region, updating the screen and the world. The other procedure waits at its entry call. The task **Control** will not accept another call to **Start** until it has been informed that the critical region has been completed by an entry call to **Stop**. Thus, calls to **Control** are used to allow at most one procedure at a time to execute its critical region. To make the critical regions work correctly, all procedures must make the appropriate calls to **Start** and **Stop**. If any procedure does not make such a call, we could end up with two procedures executing their critical regions at the same time. In the case of the **Robots** package, only the procedures in the package body update the robots' world, so they are the ones that have to make these calls correctly.

Notice the comment on the **Stop** entry of **Control**. Calls to **Move** can raise exceptions. It is important that a call to **Stop** be made even if an exception is raised. For example, suppose that in the critical region of a call to **Move**, the procedure determines that a robot has bumped an object. The procedure will raise an exception to indicate this to the caller of **Move**. The caller can handle that exception and would expect robots to keep running. If **Move** does not call **Stop**, no other call to **Start** will ever be accepted, and the the robots' world will be frozen. Notice also in **Control** that **Start** occurs within a selective wait statement with a terminate alternative. This allows the **Control** task to terminate when the main program and all its tasks are done. In turn, termination of **Control** will allow the main program to exit.

To summarize, the fundamental requirement for controlling access to a critical region is to ensure that one task at a time enters such a region. In Ada, this can be achieved by calls to a controlling task. **Control** implements what computer scientists often call a *semaphore*.

Another important technique is the *monitor*. A monitor is a collection of capabilities which allow access to a resource. In the case of Ada, a monitor is usually a task that controls a resource. In the monitor technique, only the monitor directly updates the resource. Other tasks cause updates to the resource by making entry calls to the monitor.

For example, if we had used the monitor technique with **Robots**, we would have made **Robots** a task and converted **Turn**, **Move**, and all other procedures that cause the world to be changed into entry calls. A monitor could also be used in maintaining a data file. Only the monitor would read and write the data in the file. Other tasks would make entry calls indicating what information they wanted the monitor to read or what updates they wanted the monitor to make.

The **Post_Box** task shown in Program 18–3 is a monitor which allows access to the storage resources of the post office.

While some techniques assist in designing concurrent processes, there are few simple approaches to avoiding errors due to problems in synchronizing processes. The use of monitors and the identification of critical regions are important steps in this direction. Unfortunately, while some tools have been developed, there is not yet an equivalent to the structure chart for adequately representing the communication (entry) relationships among tasks in a complex program.

18.7.1 The Post Office

The **Post_Office** package in Program 18–3 illustrates the use of entry families. Conceptually, a post office is somewhere messages can be deposited and picked up. In our post office, each piece of mail will be addressed to a post office box. Post office customers will send mail to any box they desire, but will pick up mail only from their own box. Normally, when the post office issues a box, it has a lock for which the customer is issued the combination, but we shall avoid that complication and assume that our customers are strictly honest. We shall also include a way to close the post office.

The **Post_Office** package illustrates a number of the concepts introduced in this chapter. Since tasks are not compilation units, it is necessary to place tasks inside a compilation unit. Hence, the **Post_Box** task is placed inside a package. The task declaration in the package declaration makes the task and its entries visible to any compilation unit naming the package **Post_Office**. The corresponding task body is declared in the package body of **Post_Office**.

The goal of **Post_Box** is to provide a postal system in which two other tasks can receive messages. One of these tasks receives its mail in box 1, the other in box 2. There is room for a single character in each of the two post boxes. A box is either empty or full. If it is empty, a message can be placed into the box (filling it). If it is full, a message can be removed from the box (emptying it). Initially, the boxes are empty. When box 1 is empty, the guard at line 25 closes the accept alternative of lines 26–29. Thus, we disallow **Pick_Up**, because there is no message in the box. The guard at line 31 does the same for the other box. Similarly, when the box is full, the guards at lines 13 and 19 disallow **Drop_Off**.

There is one other alternative, found in lines 37–44. This delay alternative allows **Post_Box** to terminate. It is open only if all the boxes are empty. Furthermore, there must be no postal activity (i.e., **Drop_Off**s) for 5 seconds. When this delay alternative is selected, lines 39–44 are executed. These lines contain a selective wait statement. If a **Stop** entry call is pending, the execution of the exit statement at line 41 will move execution to line 47, causing the completion of the task. Since there is an else part for this selective wait, if no **Stop** is pending, the **null** of line 43 is executed. Execution of line 43 completes the execution of both the selective wait of lines 39–44 and the selective

```
package Post_Office is
  subtype Item is CHARACTER;
  subtype Box_Numbers is INTEGER range 1..2;
  task Post_Box is
    entry Stop;
    entry Drop_Off(Box_Numbers)(Message: in Item);
    entry Pick_Up(Box_Numbers)(Message: out Item);
  end Post_Box;
end Post_Office;
```

```
package body Post_Office is
  task body Post_Box is
    type Box_Status is (Empty, Full);
    type Box_Type is
      record
        Value: Item;
        Status: Box_Status := Empty;
      end record;
    Boxes: array(Box_Numbers) of Box_Type;
  begin
    loop  -- Post Office is open
      select
        when Boxes(1).Status = Empty =>
        accept Drop_Off(1)(Message: in Item) do
          Boxes(1).Value := Message;
        end Drop_Off;
        Boxes(1).Status := Full;
      or
        when Boxes(2).Status = Empty =>
        accept Drop_Off(2)(Message: in Item) do
          Boxes(2).Value := Message;
        end Drop_Off;
        Boxes(2).Status := Full;
      or
        when Boxes(1).Status = Full =>
        accept Pick_Up(1)(Message: out Item) do
          Message := Boxes(1).Value;
        end Pick_Up;
        Boxes(1).Status := Empty;
      or
        when Boxes(2).Status = Full =>
        accept Pick_Up(2)(Message: out Item) do
          Message := Boxes(2).Value;
        end Pick_Up;
        Boxes(2).Status := Empty;
      or
        when Boxes(1).Status = Empty and Boxes(2).Status = Empty =>
```

Program 18–3

```
38:          delay 5.0;
39:          select
40:            accept Stop;
41:            exit;
42:          else
43:            null;
44:          end select;
45:        end select;
46:      end loop;
47:   end Post_Box;
48:end Post_Office;
```

Program 18–3 Continued

wait of lines 12–45. Thus, the else part allows execution of the selective wait statements to finish. Note that the selective wait statements are in a loop (lines 11–46). If line 43 is executed, this loop will cause execution to return to the selective wait beginning at line 12. Thus, the condition required for shutting down the post boxes is that there be no messages in the boxes, no activity for 5 seconds, and an entry call to **Stop**.

```
generic
   type Item is private;
package Post_Office is
   subtype Box_Numbers is INTEGER range 1..2;
   task Post_Box is
     entry Stop;
     entry Drop_Off(Box_Numbers)(Message: in Item);
     entry Pick_Up(Box_Numbers)(Message: out Item);
   end Post_Box;
end Post_Office;
```

Program 18–4

A more flexible declaration is that of the generic package **Post_Office** shown in Program 18–4. In this declaration, the type of the message is a generic formal private type. Using this generic, the program can instantiate a post box which can send and receive messages of any type other than a limited type. This declaration does *not* create a **Post_Office** task. In order to create such a task, it is necessary to instantiate a post office. For example, the declaration

```
package Sentence_Post_Office is new Post_Office(Normal_Line);
```

creates a task with two post boxes, each of which is capable of storing a **Normal_Line**.

18.7.2 The Traffic Light Controller

The traffic light controller package illustrates the development of a concurrent program from a specification. The goal is to develop a program that controls a traffic light. Inputs to the program will indicate the presence of cars and pedestrians. What we will actually develop is a package containing some tasks.

The traffic light system at an intersection contains 4 lights, one for north-south vehicles, one for east-west vehicles, one for north-south pedestrians, and one for east-west pedestrians, A vehicle light is either red, yellow, or green. A pedestrian light is either red, blinking, or green. We shall represent the condition of the traffic light by printing a line indicating the new color of the lights.

The controller has 6 inputs, one that detects the arrival of north-south vehicles, one that detects the departure of north-south vehicles, one that detects the arrival of east-west vehicles, one that detects the departure of east-west vehicles, one that detects when a pedestrian pushes the north-south button, and one that detects when a pedestrian pushes the east-west button.

The pedestrian lights behave as follows. A light should go green if and only if a pedestrian has pushed the appropriate button. When the light goes green, it remains green for 2 seconds, then blinking for 3 seconds, and then turns red. A pedestrian light is green only if the vehicle light in the same direction is also green.

The vehicle lights behave as follows. If a light turns green, it remains green until at least 7 seconds have passed and there is traffic waiting in the other direction. The pedestrian light must be red for at least 2 seconds before the vehicle light turns yellow. The vehicle light must be yellow for 2 seconds before turning red. The vehicle light must be red 2 seconds before the light in the other direction turns green.

Whenever there is a pedestrian or vehicle waiting, the traffic light controller must eventually go green in the direction the pedestrian or vehicle wants to go. The controller is incorrect if any vehicle or pedestrian can be kept waiting forever through the behavior of other vehicles or pedestrians.

The above specification contains a number of ambiguities. There are several correct implementations with quite different behavior. We develop one of these here.

The declaration of our traffic light controller package is as follows:

```
package Traffic_Light_Controller is
  -- Purpose: Control a traffic light. Each procedure represents
  --  an input from the traffic sensors.
  procedure North_South_Vehicle_Sensor_On;
  procedure North_South_Vehicle_Sensor_Off;
  procedure East_West_Vehicle_Sensor_On;
  procedure East_West_Vehicle_Sensor_Off;
  procedure Push_North_South_Button;
  procedure Push_East_West_Button;
end Traffic_Light_Controller;
```

In the package we will allow these procedures to be called simultaneously.

Each vehicle sensor uses two procedure calls. For example, the north-south sensor calls the procedure **North_South_Vehicle_Sensor_On** whenever it begins to sense a vehicle and calls **North_South_Vehicle_Sensor_Off** whenever it ceases to sense a vehicle. Whenever vehicles are present in a given direction, the last procedure call for that direction will be to "**Sensor_On**". Whenever no vehicles are present in a given direction, the last procedure call for that direction will be to "**Sensor_Off**". This reflects the fact that once the car has arrived at the intersection, it may remain present, or it may disappear from the intersection (either by going because the light became green or by making a right turn on red).

Each time a pedestrian button is pushed, it causes a call to the either the procedure **Push_North_South_Button** or the procedure **Push_East_West_Button** (depending on which button was pushed).

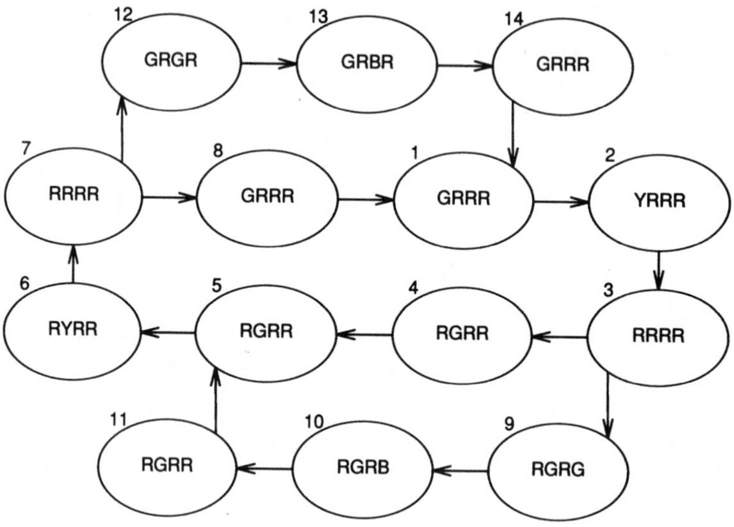

Figure 18–7

We begin our analysis of the problem by using what is called a *state diagram*. The state diagram we have designed for this problem is found in Figure 18–7. In designing a state diagram do not expect the first design to be exact. The one shown in the figure is the result of building preliminary diagrams and correcting them. To make it easy to discuss the diagram, each of the states is numbered. Each of the states contains four letters that represent the status of the four traffic lights. For example, state 10 contains **RGRB**, meaning that the north-south vehicle light is red, the east-west vehicle light is green, the north-south pedestrian light is red, and the east-west pedestrian light is blinking. From this state, the arrow indicates that we will go to state 11, which contains **RGRR**. The change from state 10 to state 11 corresponds to the east-west pedestrian light becoming red. Some states have two arrows out of them, and which one is taken depends on the traffic conditions.

In state 1, the north-south vehicle light is green and the other lights are red. We can allow the traffic light to remain in state 1 until an east-west vehicle or a pedestrian arrives. When one of these happens, we need to change the light. Notice that to know when to change the light, we have to know the status of the traffic. If the traffic requires it, the light goes yellow (state 2) for 2 seconds and then goes red (state 3). After remaining red for 2 seconds, there are two options. If an east-west pedestrian is present, we go to state 9; otherwise we go to state 4. If we go to state 4, we wait 7 seconds and then go to state 5. Notice that the lights are **RGRR** in states 4, 5 and 11. The difference is in state 4 we are waiting 7 seconds, while in state 11 we are waiting 2 seconds. Since, once we have chosen state 4 or state 9, there are no choices in the state diagram we can implement these states as a series of delays and commands to change the lights. State 5 is similar to state 1. We remain in state 5 until the traffic requires that we leave it.

Now we can see that there are two principal tasks in controlling the traffic light. One is to control the sequence of light changes and the other is to keep track of the status of the traffic. Our traffic controller package will contain two tasks, **`Sequencer`** and **`Status`**.

The **`Sequencer`** task is shown in Program 18–5. We have kept this implementation simple to keep the program short. A number of extensions and improvements to this program are suggested as exercises.

Line 31 represents state 1. We are willing to wait in state 1 until the status of the traffic requires us to change the lights. Thus, the natural implementation of state 1 is an entry call to the **`Status`** task. **`Status`** will accept this call only if the traffic status indicates that the lights should change. When **`Status`** accepts this entry call it returns a Boolean value indicating whether a pedestrian is waiting in the east-west direction. Line 32 turns the light yellow for 2 seconds, implementing state 2. Line 33 turns the light red for 2 seconds, implementing state 3. When we leave state 3, the if statement at line 34 decides whether we go to state 4 or state 9. This decision is based on the value returned at line 31. If a pedestrian pushed the east-west button during states 2 or 3, the east-west pedestrian light will go green during the light cycle after the current one.

The sequence of states 9, 10, and 11 is implemented by lines 35–37, and state 4 is implemented by line 39. At the end of the if statement, we find ourselves in state 5 (line 41).

```
1:  task Sequencer;
2:  -- Purpose: Commands the lights to cycle. Bases its commands
3:  --   on calls to the Status task.

4:  task body Sequencer is
5:    Need_Green_Ped_Light: BOOLEAN;
6:    -- The four lights
7:    North_South_Vehicle_Light: Vehicle_Light_Colors := Green;
8:    North_South_Pedestrian_Light: Pedestrian_Light_Colors := Red;
```

Program 18–5

```
   East_West_Vehicle_Light: Vehicle_Light_Colors := Red;
   East_West_Pedestrian_Light: Pedestrian_Light_Colors := Red;

   procedure Set_Lights(
         N_S_Vehicle_Light, E_W_Vehicle_Light: in Vehicle_Light_Colors;
         N_S_Ped_Light, E_W_Ped_Light: in Pedestrian_Light_Colors;
         Hold_Time: DURATION) is
   -- Purpose: "Saves" the new light status and implements the delay.
   --  Print the new values of the lights.
   begin
     North_South_Vehicle_Light := N_S_Vehicle_Light;
     North_South_Pedestrian_Light := N_S_Ped_Light;
     East_West_Vehicle_Light := E_W_Vehicle_Light;
     East_West_Pedestrian_Light := E_W_Ped_Light;
     TEXT_IO.PUT_LINE(
       Vehicle_Light_Colors'IMAGE(North_South_Vehicle_Light) & " " &
       Pedestrian_Light_Colors'IMAGE(North_South_Pedestrian_Light) & " " &
       Vehicle_Light_Colors'IMAGE(East_West_Vehicle_Light) & " " &
       Pedestrian_Light_Colors'IMAGE(East_West_Pedestrian_Light));
     delay Hold_Time;
   end Set_Lights;

begin -- Sequencer
   loop
     Status.Go_Green_E_W(Need_Green_Ped_Light);          -- State  1
     Set_Lights(Yellow, Red, Red, Red, 2.0);              -- State  2
     Set_Lights(Red, Red, Red, Red, 2.0);                 -- State  3
     if Need_Green_Ped_Light then
       Set_Lights(Red, Green, Red, Green, 2.0);           -- State  9
       Set_Lights(Red, Green, Red, Blinking, 3.0);        -- State 10
       Set_Lights(Red, Green, Red, Red, 2.0);             -- State 11
     else
       Set_Lights(Red, Green, Red, Red, 7.0);             -- State  4
     end if;
     Status.Go_Green_N_S(Need_Green_Ped_Light);          -- State  5
     Set_Lights(Red, Yellow, Red, Red, 2.0);              -- State  6
     Set_Lights(Red, Red, Red, Red, 2.0);                 -- State  7
     if Need_Green_Ped_Light then
       Set_Lights(Green, Red, Green, Red, 2.0);           -- State 12
       Set_Lights(Green, Red, Blinking, Red, 3.0);        -- State 13
       Set_Lights(Green, Red, Red, Red, 2.0);             -- State 14
     else
       Set_Lights(Green, Red, Red, Red, 7.0);             -- State  8
     end if;
   end loop;
end Sequencer;
```

Program 18–5 Continued

Except for swapping east-west with north-south, lines 41–50 are the same as lines 31–40.

The variables declared on lines 7–10 store the status of the traffic lights. Technically this is not necessary, because the state indicates the color of the lights, but in a real traffic light representation clauses (see Chapter 17) could be used to make the variables correspond to physical devices that controlled the lights.

Program 18–6 contains the remainder of the traffic light controller package. The procedures of lines 54–77 correspond to the procedures declared in the package interface. Each of these procedures contains an entry call to **Status**. We could have placed the task declaration (lines 5–12) inside the package declaration so that the entry calls were visible outside the package, but that would also have made the **Go_Green** entries visible outside the package.

Status has 4 entries corresponding to inputs to the traffic sensor, two for vehicles and two for pedestrian buttons. Whenever the status of the north-south vehicle sensor changes, the entry **N_S_Vehicle** will be called with a Boolean value that indicates whether the new sensor status is "on" or "off". Whenever the north-south pedestrian button is pushed, **N_S_Ped_Button** is called. The east-west sensors operate the same way.

The body of the task is a selective wait statement (lines 21–47) nested inside a loop (lines 20–48). Because we expect the traffic light to run forever, we make no provision for termination of the task. The selective wait is always willing to accept entries corresponding to the sensors. For example, if the north-south pedestrian button is pushed, the call to **N_S_Ped_Button** will be accepted (line 30), and the Boolean variable **N_S_Ped_Waiting** will be set to **TRUE** (line 31). If the north-south vehicle sensor changes, the call to **N_S_Vehicle** will be accepted (line 22) and the value of **N_S_Veh_Waiting** will be set according to whether the sensor went to "present" or "not present."

The other two entries are the ones used by the **Sequencer** task. Suppose **Sequencer** has made a call to **Go_Green_E_W** (i.e., the sequencer is in state 1). **Sequencer** will unconditionally wait until that call is accepted. The accept statement for that call (lines 42–47) contains a guard that allows the call to be accepted only if the status of the traffic requires a change. That is, the call will be accepted only when there is a pedestrian waiting or a vehicle waiting in the east-west direction. Also remember that the call can be accepted only if **Sequencer** has made the call; that is, only if **Sequencer** is waiting in state 1. When such a call is accepted, **Status** determines whether the pedestrian light should go green (line 44) and passes this information back to **Sequencer**. Since (if necessary) the pedestrian light will be going green in the appropriate direction, **Status** assumes that the pedestrian will cross the street and modifies the pedestrian waiting status (line 46). If the pedestrian misses the chance to cross, he will have to press the button again.

In designing the traffic controller, tasks were necessary because events occurred simultaneously. In the solution set out here, one task (**Sequencer**) uses the services of another task (**Status**). The entry calls are made in one direction. That is, calls were made by the task being served to the server. A number of other implementations are

```
with TEXT_IO;
package body Traffic_Light_Controller is
  type Vehicle_Light_Colors is (Red, Yellow, Green);
  type Pedestrian_Light_Colors is (Red, Blinking, Green);
  task Status is
    entry N_S_Vehicle(Present: in BOOLEAN);
    entry E_W_Vehicle(Present: in BOOLEAN);
    entry N_S_Ped_Button;
    entry E_W_Ped_Button;
    entry Go_Green_N_S(Pedestrian: out BOOLEAN);
    entry Go_Green_E_W(Pedestrian: out BOOLEAN);
  end Status;
  task body Status is
    -- Whenever the button is pushed we assume a pedestrian will wait.
    -- When a vehicle is present, we assume it is waiting only if
    --  the light is red.
    N_S_Veh_Waiting, E_W_Veh_Waiting,
    N_S_Ped_Waiting, E_W_Ped_Waiting: BOOLEAN := FALSE;
  begin
    loop
      select
        accept N_S_Vehicle(Present: in BOOLEAN) do
          N_S_Veh_Waiting := Present;
        end N_S_Vehicle;
      or
        accept E_W_Vehicle(Present: in BOOLEAN) do
          E_W_Veh_Waiting := Present;
        end E_W_Vehicle;
      or
        accept N_S_Ped_Button;
        N_S_Ped_Waiting := TRUE;
      or
        accept E_W_Ped_Button;
        E_W_Ped_Waiting := TRUE;
      or
        when N_S_Ped_Waiting or E_W_Ped_Waiting or N_S_Veh_Waiting =>
        accept Go_Green_N_S(Pedestrian: out BOOLEAN) do
          Pedestrian := N_S_Ped_Waiting;
        end Go_Green_N_S;
        N_S_Ped_Waiting := FALSE;
      or
        when N_S_Ped_Waiting or E_W_Ped_Waiting or E_W_Veh_Waiting =>
        accept Go_Green_E_W(Pedestrian: out BOOLEAN) do
          Pedestrian := E_W_Ped_Waiting;
```

Program 18–6

```
        end Go_Green_E_W;
        E_W_Ped_Waiting := FALSE;
      end select;
    end loop;
  end Status;

  -- Calls to these procedures by tasks (sensors) outside the
  --   package indicate any change in status of the sensors.
  --   This change is recorded by making the appropriate entry calls
  --   to the Status task.
  procedure North_South_Vehicle_Sensor_On is
  begin
    Status.N_S_Vehicle(Present => TRUE);
  end North_South_Vehicle_Sensor_On;

  procedure North_South_Vehicle_Sensor_Off is
  begin
    Status.N_S_Vehicle(Present => FALSE);
  end North_South_Vehicle_Sensor_Off;

  procedure East_West_Vehicle_Sensor_On is
  begin
    Status.E_W_Vehicle(Present => TRUE);
  end East_West_Vehicle_Sensor_On;

  procedure East_West_Vehicle_Sensor_Off is
  begin
    Status.E_W_Vehicle(Present => FALSE);
  end East_West_Vehicle_Sensor_Off;

  procedure Push_North_South_Button is
  begin
    Status.N_S_Ped_Button;
  end Push_North_South_Button;

  procedure Push_East_West_Button is
  begin
    Status.E_W_Ped_Button;
  end Push_East_West_Button;

  -- Sequencer goes here
end Traffic_Light_Controller;
```

Program 18–6 Continued

possible in which **Status** calls **Sequencer** and **Sequencer** calls **Status**. In these designs it is easy to have each task making an entry call to the other and neither able to accept a call, or both executing an accept when neither is making a call. In designing the interaction of tasks, it is best to keep the flow of service (entry calls) in one direction and keep the interaction between tasks simple.

18.7.3 Testing: Symbolic Debuggers

Throughout this text we have emphasized the importance of including debugging statements in subprograms when they are written. This makes it easier to test the programs and to have more confidence that they work correctly. However, the approach is difficult to apply in many circumstances. For example, programs that use the entire screen for interactive windows leave no place for interactive debugging information to be placed. Also, some errors can "disappear" when debugging statements are added to a program. That is, you may not be able to get the error to reoccur with these statements in the program. *Symbolic debuggers* are designed to handle these and other situations.

In general, a debugger permits the programmer to watch the execution of a program, stop the program whenever it reaches particular places called *breakpoints*, examine the values in variables, and modify the values in variables. Debuggers can usually display a part of the program so that the programmer can accurately set breakpoints. Many can even execute the program one statement at a time so that it is easy to see exactly what is happening.

Unfortunately, most debuggers display program statements in assembly language (the low-level language of the computer). This means that to use these debuggers effectively, the programmer must be fluent in the particular assembly language as well as Ada (or whichever high-level language is being used). A symbolic debugger allows the programmer to interact with the program using Ada constructs and Ada identifiers.

Debugging in assembly language has its advantages. In particular, it permits the programmer to examine exactly what is happening on the computer, even if the problem is a bug in the compiler, and not a bug in the program being debugged. The most powerful debuggers permit the programmer to switch back and forth between debugging in assembly language and debugging in the high level language. In general, it is usually harder to debug a program with a symbolic debugger than by using debugging statements designed into the program.

18.8 ADA SUMMARY

In this chapter we have covered the options associated with accepting entry calls. We have introduced the **COUNT** attribute, which can be used to estimate the number of calls pending on an entry. We have shown how the *selective wait* can provide the capability to wait for one of several events. Associated with the selective wait were the select alternatives. The *accept alternative* lets us choose among entry calls. The *delay alternative* lets us take an alternative after a specified amount of time passed with no entry calls accepted. The *else part* of the selective wait is for the task which does not wish to wait for an entry call. The *terminate alternative* allows tasks to quit when there is no more business to perform.

Also associated with the selective wait is the *guard*, which provides a means of controlling which alternatives can be taken. With its alternatives and guards, the selective wait allows you to control the conditions under which a task waits for a rendezvous to occur.

Another topic of this chapter was *entry families*. Similar to array accessing, you may compute the index of the particular entry call you wish to make or, if you are the task, the particular entry you wish to accept.

EXERCISES

18.1. Modify the generic `Post_Office` package in Program 18–4 to allow the instantiation of a post office with any number of boxes. Modify the body of `Post_Office` (Program 18–3) so that it works no matter how many boxes exist. The selective wait statement will have to be replaced with something that allows all calls to the entry families `Pick_Up` and `Drop_Off` to be examined, no matter how many entries there are in the family. Close (`Stop`) the post office only if all boxes are empty and no activity has occurred for 5 seconds.

18.2. Extend the previous exercise by modifying the generic `Post_Office` package declaration to allow a box to store multiple messages in a queue. Continue to disallow `Pick_Up` when a box is empty. Disallow a `Drop_Off` when there is no more room to store a message. The queue size, number of boxes, and message type should be generic parameters. (Consider using the queue capability of the generic storage handler package you built in Chapter 16.)

18.3. Extend the post office world of exercise 11.2. There will be 3 customer robots (**A**, **B**, **C**) and 2 clerk robots (**D**, **E**) at two different windows. The customer robots will be both picking up mail from the post office as well as dropping mail off at the post office. The clerks will need to be able to accept a robot's request to drop off mail and/or pick it up.

Each customer robot has under it a pile of mail to take to the post office. All of the mail in the pile is meant for another robot; i.e., robot **A** has mail for **B** and **C**, robot **B** has mail for **A** and **C**, and robot **C** has mail for **A** and **B**. Each robot takes a piece of mail from the top of its pile, and takes it to the post office, where it hands the mail to the first clerk available. Then, the robot checks to see whether there is any mail waiting for it. If there is, the robot takes the mail from the post office and takes it home, building a second pile of its own mail. When the original pile is depleted, the robot then continues to go the post office to see whether there is any mail for it to pick up. When waiting at the front of the line for a clerk, the customer repeatedly checks to see if first one then the other clerk is ready to serve a customer. The customer moves to the window of the first clerk it finds is available.

The clerks wait at their respective windows ready to accept customers. If they accept a customer with mail, they take any mail the customer wants to give, and deposit it in the correct stack. The clerk then checks the appropriate stack to locate mail for the customer, and returns to the window to give the customer any such mail.

When a customer robot's pile of mail is empty and the robot is told at the post office there is no mail to be picked up, it goes back home, waits for 20 seconds, then comes back to the post office. If there still is no mail for the robot, it goes back home and quits for good. If there is mail, the robot picks it up, takes it home, and goes back to checking for more mail at the post office.

When all three of the customer robots quit, the two clerk robots should then quit. (Hint: the clerks can use the terminate alternative.)

18.4. In our design of the traffic light controller of Programs 18–5 and 18–6, a pedestrian who pushes the button after the light turns yellow will have to wait until the next cycle for a green walk light. This occurs because there are no entry calls to **Status** between lines 31 and 34 or between lines 41 and 44. Modify the traffic light controller so that as long as the pedestrian pushes the button before the vehicle light goes green, the pedestrian light goes green (at the same time as the vehicle light). (Hint: This modification is easier if you declare two new entry calls to **Status**.)

18.5. In the traffic light controller, when the light is green for the north-south direction and a pedestrian pushes the north-south button, the east-west light goes green before cycling back to allow the pedestrian to cross. Modify the controller so that the east-west light does not have to go green before the north-south pedestrian is allowed to cross. This involves modifying the state diagram by adding an arrow from state 5 to state 9 and from state 1 to state 12. To decide which arrow to follow out of states 1 and 5, add a parameter to the **Go_Green** entry calls.

18.6. Add a left-turn arrow to the traffic light controller. Specify how the arrow is to work, rebuild the state diagram, and implement the modified package.

19

Concurrent Control Structures, II

19.1 OBJECTIVES

The more complex aspects of tasks are covered in this chapter. In these we see more clearly the dual nature of the task as part object and part program. We examine task types (section 3), from which task objects may be declared. We provided detailed coverage of the termination of tasks by introducing the Ada concept of task masters (section 4). We cover how a task may be aborted by another task (section 5) and the details of how exceptions interact with tasks (section 6). We conclude the chapter with a discussion of how tasks terminate (section 7) and the attributes that are available for tasks (section 8).

CONCEPTS:

- Task types provide a simple mechanism for creating multiple identical tasks.
- Tasks may be created during execution.
- A task may be terminated by another task.

GOALS:

- Build a complex concurrent program.

19.2 MOTIVATION

In many applications we desire a number of tasks, all of which are similar. For example, we may need to declare a user interface task for each terminal on a computing system. In these cases, we do not wish to write many identical tasks. Ada provides a solution in the *task type*. Like other types, a task type does not create a task object, but it allows for the declaration of many "identical" task objects. A task type also provides the mechanism for dynamically creating new tasks during program execution.

In order for a program to finish, its tasks must *terminate*. The details of what terminates when, and when a return from a subprogram can occur, are important in concurrent programming. Ada defines the conditions under which termination and return from a subprogram can occur. In addition, sometimes it is necessary to force a task to terminate. Ada also supplies this capability.

Because tasks run independently and concurrently, error handling is complicated in a program with tasks. This makes it necessary for Ada to provide special rules about tasks and exceptions. In addition, tasks have certain attributes which can be used to detect and avoid some types of problems.

19.3 TASK TYPES

As mentioned earlier, a task is a cross between a subprogram and an object. One aspect in which a task is like an object is in the ability to declare *task types*. The only syntactic difference in declaring a task type versus a task is the presence of the reserved word **type**, as shown in Figure 19–1. For example,

```
task type Robot_Controller is
  entry Start;
  entry Assign_Robot(Which_Robot: CHARACTER);
end Robot_Controller;
```

declares a task type in which there are two entries.

Remember, a type declaration is different from an object declaration. When a type is declared, no object is created. Thus, the declaration of a task type does not create a task. One use of types, including task types, is to create objects. A task is created by declaring an object of the task type. Thus, the declaration

```
A_Robot, B_Robot: Robot_Controller;
```

creates two tasks named **A_Robot** and **B_Robot**. Each of these tasks has the entries declared by the task type. An entry call to the first of these tasks would be

```
A_Robot.Start;
```

Specifically, there is *no* task named **Robot_Controller**, so there is no entry:

<task declaration>

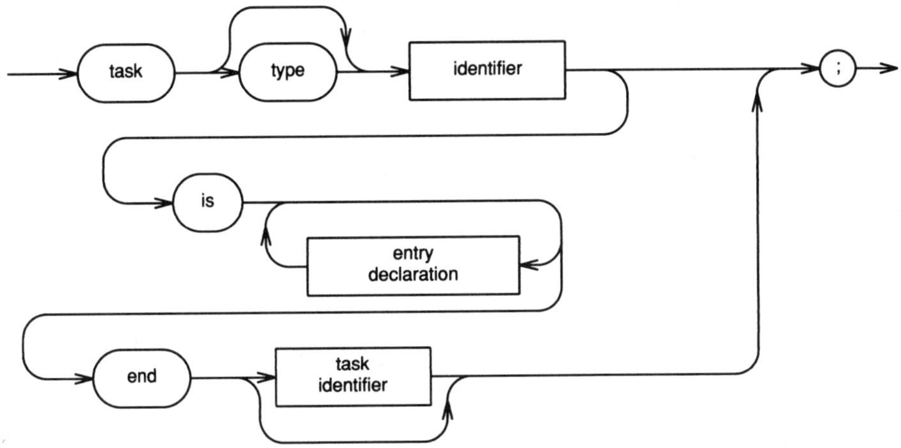

Figure 19–1

```
Robot_Controller.Start; -- illegal
```

because **Robot_Controller** is a type, not an object.

Task types may be used to declare either task objects or other types. In the following example a task type is used to declare a type which is an array of task objects:

```
type Controller_Array_Type is array ('A'..'E') of Robot_Controller;
Controller_Array: Controller_Array_Type;
```

These declarations create 5 tasks of type **Robot_Controller**. These tasks are named **Controller_Array('A')** through **Controller_Array('E')**. Just a reminder, the declaration of the type **Controller_Array_Type** does not create any tasks, but the declaration of the object **Controller_Array** does. Typical entry calls are contained in the loop

```
for Which_Robot in CHARACTER range 'A'..'E' loop
  Controller_Array(Which_Robot).Assign_Robot(Which_Robot);
end loop;
```

The first time through the loop, an unconditional entry call is made to the **Assign_Robot** entry of the **Controller_Array('A')** task. Execution of the loop does not continue until that entry call has been accepted and the resulting rendezvous completed. Then execution of the loop continues, causing a call to the **Assign_Robot** entry of the **'B'** task. Again, the call is unconditional, and execution of the loop waits until the accept and rendezvous complete. The loop continues until an entry call to each of the 5 tasks has been made.

A task type can also be a component in a record type declaration. The following is an example of such a declaration:

```
type Search is
  record
    Top_Of_Maze, Bottom_Of_Maze: Robot_Controller;
  end record;
```

Each time a record of type **Search** is declared, two tasks of type **Robot_Controller** are activated.

A task type is a *limited type*. As with other limited types, assignment is not allowed, there is no predefined comparison for equality and inequality, and generic formal parameters of mode **in** are not allowed. Normally, procedures with parameters of mode **out** may only be declared in the package declaring the limited type. However, with task types, mode **out** parameters may *never* be used. These restrictions reflect the more general principle that a task may not be duplicated and it is not a "value" that may be copied.

This general principle defines the semantics that applies to parameters of a task type. Subprograms may have task type parameters of mode **in** and mode **in out**. For example, we may declare

```
procedure Start_Robot(Which_Robot: Robot_Controller) is
begin
  Which_Robot.Start;
end Start_Robot;
```

In the case of task types, the effect of mode **in** is the same as mode **in out**. The formal parameter refers to the task supplied as the actual parameter. So if we make the call

```
Start_Robot(Controller_Array('C'));
```

the entry call within the procedure becomes a call to the **Start** entry in the task **Controller_Array('C')**. In the case of task types, we do not get a copy of the task, rather, the formal parameter *always* refers to the task that is the actual parameter.

The behavior of generic formal parameters of a task type obeys the same general principle. Only mode **in out** is allowed for a generic formal parameter of a task type. The generic formal parameter will refer to the task object that is supplied as the generic actual parameter at the time of instantiation. Again, in this case a new task is not created; the formal parameter refers to the task supplied as the actual parameter.

For example, consider the following declaration:

```
procedure Generic_Task_Parameter is
  task type Task_Type is
    entry Start;
  end Task_Type;
```

```
 5:  A_Task: Task_Type;
 6:  generic
 7:    Which_Task: in out Task_Type;
 8:  package Start_Task is
 9:    procedure Start_It;
10:  end Start_Task;
11:  task body Task_Type is
12:  begin
13:    accept Start;
14:  end Task_Type;
15:  package body Start_Task is
16:    procedure Start_It is
17:    begin
18:      Which_Task.Start;
19:    end Start_It;
20:  end Start_Task;
21:  package Start_A is new Start_Task(A_Task);
22:begin
23:  Start_A.Start_It;
24:end Generic_Task_Parameter;
```

Line 7 declares a generic formal parameter of a task type. The generic package contains a procedure that makes an entry call to the generic formal task type (line 18). The instantiation at line 21 creates a package in which this entry call will refer to the task declared at line 5. The call to the procedure **Start_It** at line 23 results in the call at line 18 becoming a call to **A_Task.Start**. The principle is simple: Formal parameters whose type is a task type always refer to the tasks which are used as actual parameters. Copies of a task are never made.

Task types may also be used in declaring access types, as in

```
type Robot_Access is access Robot_Controller;
New_Task_Access: Robot_Access;
```

These declarations create an access type and a variable of that access type. Because they do not create an object, these declarations do not create a task. To create a task from these declarations, we must create an object using the allocator **new**. The statement

```
New_Task_Access := new Robot_Controller;
```

creates a task and stores access capability to that task in an access variable. An entry call to that task would have the form

```
New_Task_Access.Start
```

In a manner similar to referencing components of other access types, reference to an entry is obtained by prefixing the entry name with an access value. Further, although we cannot use assignment with limited types, we can perform assignment on access types whose designate types are limited. In other words, the access value for a task could be stored in several separate access variables. There will be just one task, but many ways to access it.

Proceeding one step further, the declarations

```
type Task_List;
type Link is access Task_List;
type Task_List is
  record
    This_Task: Robot_Access;
    Next_Task: Link;
  end record;
```

would allow creation of a linked list of tasks. Indeed, linked lists or trees of tasks can be useful. One observation should be made. In dealing with dynamic objects, a sequence of statements such as

```
New_Task_Access := new Robot_Controller;
New_Task_Access := new Robot_Controller;
```

would lose the ability to access a dynamic object. In particular, access capability to the first of the two tasks created by this pair of statements is not retained by the program. The task object does not cease to exist, but it cannot be accessed. In particular, the task itself continues to run, however, there is no way to make an entry call to it.

In Ada terminology, the elaboration of an object of a task type will cause the elaboration and activation of a task of that type. If a task object is created by a declaration, the task declaration is elaborated immediately, and the task is activated after elaboration of the declarative part in which the task object was declared. This rule is similar to the more familiar rule for task elaboration used in previous chapters. Indeed, Ada defines the declaration of a task (as opposed to a task type) to be equivalent to the declaration of an anonymous task type followed by the declaration of an object of that type.

For task objects created by the allocator **new**, activation occurs at the point of execution of the allocator. Elaboration of the task specification still occurs at the point of declaration. This elaboration defines the entry calls (and representation clauses) for the task type. Elaboration of the task body also occurs at its point of declaration. In all cases, elaboration of the task body makes the task available for execution and has no other effects. This means that the declaration part of a task body will be elaborated upon activation of the task, and not upon elaboration of the task body. This means that exceptions raised in elaborating the declaration part of a task body will be raised upon activation. Similarly, initial values for variables within the declaration part of the task will be computed at activation.

The foregoing rule has consequences with respect to exception handling. Recall that a task declared in a procedure is activated just after the **begin** of the procedure body. If, during the elaboration of the declarations in the body of such a task, an exception is raised, it will be reraised just after the **begin** of the procedure body. Similarly, a task created from a task type by the allocator **new** is activated at the point of allocation, so an exception raised in the elaboration of such a task will be reraised at the point of allocation. For example, if a task is declared in a procedure and an exception is raised during the elaboration of the declarations in the task body, the exception will be raised just after the **begin** of the procedure body.

The foregoing rule has other effects. Consider the following procedure:

```
 1:procedure Task_Elaboration is
 2:   task type Task_Type;
 3:   A_Task: Task_Type;
 4:   type Access_Task_Type is access Task_Type;
 5:   Dynamic_Task: Access_Task_Type;
 6:   X: INTEGER := 5;
 7:   task body Task_Type is
 8:     Z: POSITIVE := X;
 9:   begin
10:     TEXT_IO.PUT(INTEGER'IMAGE(Z));
11:   end Task_Type;
12:begin
13:   X := 6;
14:   Dynamic_Task := new Task_Type;
15:end Task_Elaboration;
```

The task **A_Task** is declared in line 3. Obviously, the corresponding task type body in lines 7–11 is not elaborated at the point where the task is declared. Rather, its elaboration (lines 7–11) follows that of the variable **X**. However, the elaboration of the body of a task type only makes the task body available; it does not include elaboration of the declarations within the body. Because **A_Task** is in the declarative part of **Task_Elaboration**, it is activated immediately following the **begin** at line 12. At this point the declarations within the task body are elaborated and the value of **Z** is set to 5. When this task executes the statement at line 10, it will print a 5. At line 14, a dynamic task object is allocated. This allocation includes the activation of the task and, consequently, the elaboration of the declarations within the task body. Since, at line 14, the value of **X** is 6, **Z** is set to 6, and this is the value that will be printed when this task executes line 10. Because tasks run independently and concurrently, we cannot say that 5 will be printed by **A_Task** before 6 is printed by the dynamically created task. In fact, the values could be printed in either order. But the initial value of **Z** will always depend on the value of **X** at the time the task is activated.

An important case occurs when the value of **X** is negative. This would cause a **CONSTRAINT_ERROR** to be raised upon the elaboration of **Z**. In the case of **A_Task**, the exception is raised in the main procedure just after the **begin** of line 12. In the case of the task created by the allocator, the exception is raised during execution of the allocator at line 14. Most importantly, it never occurs at line 8. This is a point to be aware of when debugging a program.

19.4 TASK MASTERS

Many aspects of tasks may be explained in terms of task masters. In Ada, the term "depend" is the other side of the term "master." A task depends on its master or masters. Only tasks have masters, and each task must have at least one master. A master can be another task, a currently executing block statement, a subprogram, or a library package. Every task directly depends on one master. This *direct master* is defined by how and where the task was created. There are two cases: the second case consists of those tasks activated by using the allocator **new**, the first case consists of all other tasks.

In the first case the direct master is the task, block, subprogram, or library package whose execution activates the task. As a consequence of this rule, if the task is activated by an object declaration, the subprogram, block, task, or library package directly containing that declaration is the task's direct master. In the following example

```
procedure Direct is
  task A;
  task body A is
   ...
  end A;
begin
  ...
end Direct;
```

the task object **A** is declared directly within the subprogram **Direct**. Because a call to **Direct** activates **A**, **Direct** is the direct master of **A**. In the following example

```
package Library is ... end Library;
package body Library is
  task B;
  task body B is
   ...
  end B;
end Library;
```

the task **B** is declared directly within the library package **Library**, so **Library** is the direct master of **B**. This would still be true if the declaration of **B** occurred in the visible part of **Library**. In the following example:

```
task body Master is
  task Dependent;
  task body Dependent is;
   ...
  end Dependent;
begin
  ...
end Master;
```

the task **Master** is the direct master of the task **Dependent** because **Dependent** is declared within the body of **Master**. The activation of **Master** causes the activation of **Dependent**. Note that a task declaration cannot be a compilation unit, so the declaration of **Master** must be within a package, subprogram or block.

The next concept is that of an *indirect master*. When a task depends on a master which is a block or subprogram that is being executed by another master, the task depends on that other master. In the following example:

```
procedure Indirect is
begin
  Direct;
end Indirect;
```

the procedure **Indirect** calls the procedure **Direct** defined previously. **Indirect** is an indirect master of the task **A** that was declared within **Direct**. In the following example we define a subprogram that includes the task **Master**:

```
procedure Both is
  task Master;
  task body Master is
    task Dependent;
    ...
  end Master;
end Both;
```

The procedure **Both** is the indirect master of **Dependent**, as well as the direct master of **Master**.

As a final example, we present a block included within a procedure:

```
procedure Run_Right is
begin
  loop
    declare
      task Local ...
    begin
      ...
      return;
    exception
      when others => null;
    end;
  end loop;
Run_Right;
```

The direct master of the task **Local** is the block statement. The procedure **Run_Right** is an indirect master of **Local**. Any procedure calling **Run_Right** will also become an indirect master of **Local**.

In the second case the task is created by the allocator **new**. Such a task can be accessed using some access type. The direct master of the task is the task, block, subprogram or library package in which that access type is declared. The indirect masters of the task are the same as in the previous case.

Suppose the following library package has been declared:

```
package Task_Library is
  task type A;
end Task_Library;
```

Then the declaration

```
with Task_Library;
procedure Type_Carrier is
  type Task_Access is access Task_Library.A;
  procedure Not_Me is;
    X: Task_Access;
  begin
    X := new Task_Library.A;
  end Not_Me;
begin
  ...
end Type_Carrier;
```

the procedure **Type_Carrier** becomes the direct master of all tasks of type **Task_Access**. Even though a call to **Not_Me** dynamically creates a task, **Not_Me** is not a master of that task. When execution returns from **Not_Me**, the task continues to exist. Of course, because **X** is local to **Not_Me**, the program loses the access value of the task. However, that could be prevented by storing the access value in a global variable. Because **Task_Access** is declared immediately inside **Type_Carrier**, the access value for the task could be stored as long as execution has not exited the procedure **Type_Carrier**.

For an example using a block or a task as a master, we simply replace "**procedure Type_Carrier is**" with "**declare**" or "**task body Z is**" as shown in the program fragments:

```
declare
  type Task_Access is access Task_Library.A;
  ...
end;
```

```
task body Z is
  type Task_Access is access Task_Library.A;
  ...
end Z;
```

In the first fragment, the block is the master of tasks associated with the access type. In the second, the task **Z** is the master of tasks associated with the access type.

The one remaining case is that of masters that are library packages. Suppose we change the declaration of **Task_Library** to be:

```
package Task_Library is
  task type A;
  type Task_Access is access A;
end Task_Library;
```

Here, the package provides the definition of the access type, so it becomes the master of dynamically created tasks which use that access type. The following program creates a task whose master is the library package:

```
with Task_Library;
procedure Make_Task is
  A_Task: Task_Library.Task_Access;
begin
  A_Task := new Task_Library.A;
end Make_Task;
```

The main program, **Make_Task**, is neither a direct master nor an indirect master.

To summarize, who is the master of a task created with the allocator depends on where the access type is declared; for other tasks who is the master depends on where the task object is declared.

19.5 THE ABORT STATEMENT

Sometimes it is necessary to force a task to terminate. Although it is preferable to use terminate alternatives, the *abort statement* can be used to force the completion of tasks so that a subprogram may execute a return. For example, an abort may occur in the exception handler of a subprogram. Because execution cannot return from a subprogram until all dependent tasks have terminated, the program awaits this termination before the exception can propagate to the point at which the subprogram was called. The occurrence of the exception, however, may indicate that it is useless or counterproductive to wait for the dependent tasks to terminate normally. In this case, it is appropriate to use the abort statement. An abort statement may specify any task whose name is visible. The syntax for the abort statement is given in Figure 19–2.

Conceptually, the named tasks are aborted. Technically, the named tasks become abnormal unless they are already terminated. Abnormal tasks waiting at accept statements, executing selective waits, waiting at entry calls, or not activated become complete. An aborted task waiting at an entry call is removed from the entry queue. If a task which made an entry call has already entered a rendezvous before it becomes abnormal, it does not complete until the rendezvous is completed. An entry call to an abnormal task raises

<abort statement>

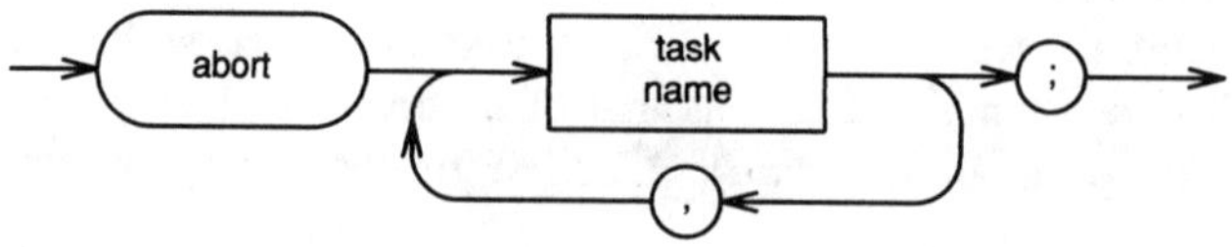

Figure 19–2

TASKING_ERROR. This occurs regardless of whether or not a rendezvous has begun. For example, if task **A** has called task **B** and is involved in a rendezvous when **B** becomes abnormal, **TASKING_ERROR** is raised in **A** at the point of the call. In addition, any further entry calls to **B** raise **TASKING_ERROR** at the point of the call.

Even though a task has been aborted, an Ada implementation can allow it to continue to run until it reaches a delay, accept, selective wait, or entry call. In particular, there is no requirement that a task ever complete if it is stuck in an infinite loop or waiting for input.

19.6 TASKS AND EXCEPTIONS

Errors due to the interaction of tasks usually result in the exception **TASKING_ERROR**. Among such errors are making an entry call to a task that has completed. In addition, a number of new issues are raised by the occurrence of exceptions in concurrent programs.

In some cases, the occurrence of an exception is independent of concurrency. For example, consider the following task:

```
 1:task body Has_Handler is
 2:begin
 3:  loop
 4:    begin
 5:      ... -- exception here
 6:    exception
 7:      when others => null;
 8:    end;
 9:  end loop;
10:end Has_Handler;
```

If an exception is raised in the body of the block statement—that is, at line 5—it would be handled by the exception handler at the end of the block (lines 6 and 7). Because the exception is handled and not reraised, execution would loop back to line 3. In all of this the task would continue to run and other tasks would not even know that an exception had occurred. Any exception that occurs in the execution of the "sequential" statements within a task and is handled within the task is handled in the manner that is normal for exceptions occurring in sequential statements. For this purpose, we do not consider statements related directly to tasking (entry calls, accept statements, and selective wait statements) to be "sequential" statements.

The remainder of this section is concerned with how exceptions relate to the special properties of tasks. Consider what happens when an exception is handled by the exception handler for the task body. Since execution cannot return to a point within the task, execution of the body becomes completed. For example, in the following:

```
1:task body Has_Handler is
2:begin
3:  -- raised here
4:exception
5:   when others => -- handled here
6:end Has_Handler;
```

an exception raised at line 3 and handled at line 5 means that the execution of the task body completes. There is nothing wrong with this, provided that nobody needs the services of the task.

Next consider what happens when an exception is not handled within the task. The task:

```
1:task body No_Handler is
2:begin
3:  -- raised here
4:end No_Handler;
```

has no exception handler. As with the previous task, the task becomes completed. Furthermore, the exception is not propagated. Initially you may find the lack of propagation surprising; however, since a task is not "called" like a procedure, it is unclear as to what point in the program the exception should be propagated. You might consider propagating the exception to the task's master, but where in the master would the exception be raised?

A slight variation on this situation is when the task gets an exception during activation, as is shown in the following example:

```
1:task body Bad_Activation is
2:  -- raised here
3:begin
4:   ...
5:end Bad_Activation;
```

The task itself has no opportunity to handle exceptions occurring during its activation. Again, the task becomes completed. In addition, the exception **TASKING_ERROR** is raised at the point at which activation of the task would have occurred. In particular, if the task is activated because it was declared as an object in a declaration part, the exception is raised at the start of execution of the body associated with that declaration part. For example, in the activation of the task **Bad_Activation** in the following procedure:

```
procedure Declaration_Part is
  task Bad_Activation;
  task body Bad_Activation is
    -- raised here
  begin
    ...
  end Bad_Activation;
begin    -- Body of Declaration_Part
         -- TASK_ERROR here
  null; -- First statement in body
  ...
exception
  -- TASK_ERROR could be handled here.
end Declaration_Part;
```

the exception may be handled by the exception handler for the body of the subprogram **Declaration_Part**. If it is not, the exception may be propagated to the point at which the subprogram was called. If **Declaration_Part** were a task, the exception would not be propagated out of that task. Notice that in either case, the body associated with the declaration that causes the error to be raised is not executed.

Exceptions can also occur at an entry call. One way this can happen is when an entry call is made to a completed task or a task completes while the call is in the entry queue. In this case, **TASKING_ERROR** is raised at the point of the entry call. Note that the exception is raised even if you make a timed or conditional entry call. This exception is how Ada informs the caller that the call cannot possibly result in a rendezvous. If the caller plans to continue even though a task has completed, the entry call may be embedded in an exception frame.

Another way an exception can occur at an entry call is if an exception occurs during a rendezvous. If the exception is handled within the accept statement, nothing extraordinary happens. Note that the accept statement itself does not have an exception handler (or declarative part), so to handle the exception, there must be a block statement nested within the accept statement or in a procedure that is called within the statement list of the accept statement. An exception handled within such a block statement or procedure is not propagated outside, nor is it reported to the task which made the entry call. When the exception is not handled within the accept statement, the exception is raised both in the accept statement and at the entry call. That is, both parties to the rendezvous are informed of the unhandled exception.

The final way an exception can occur at an entry call is if a task abnormally completes during rendezvous. If the task accepting the entry call completes abnormally, that entry call abnormally completes and **TASKING_ERROR** is raised at the point the entry call was made. If the task making the entry call completes abnormally, the rendezvous completes in the normal fashion. That is, the task accepting the entry call proceeds normally. The only way a task ever abnormally completes during a rendezvous is due to an **abort** statement.

There is an asymmetry about the raising and handling of exceptions: The accepting task is protected from the calling task, but the converse is not true. An entry call cannot raise or cause an exception in an accepting task. Even if the caller is a task that completes or aborts, the caller at most completes the rendezvous and disappears. Thus, tasks requesting service cannot damage the server. On the other hand, an entry calling task is highly vulnerable to the accepting task. If the server disappears or has an error while providing service, an exception is raised at the point of the entry call. Consider the following analogy, if a grocery store closes, the customers must be informed, but if a customer disappears, the grocery store can operate without being informed.

19.7 TASK TERMINATION

To review the Ada terminology, a task, subprogram, or block has *completed* when the sequence of statements directly within it has finished executing; a task has *terminated* if it has completed and all tasks which depend on it have terminated. Execution can leave (return from) a subprogram or block only if that subprogram or block has completed and all tasks which depend on that subprogram or block have terminated.

Completion does not apply to packages. The sequence of statements directly within a package is the package initialization code. Completion of this code completes the initialization of the package. A package supplies subprograms and data structures. The subprograms within a package "complete" before the return, but the concept of completion does not apply to the package itself.

We will now describe the rules for termination, exit and return using the concept of masters. Termination of a task implies that the task and all dependent tasks cease execution. Consider the following declarations:

```
task X;
task body X is
  task Y;
  task body Y is
  begin
    loop null; end loop;
  end;
begin
 null;
end X;
```

Because the body of **X** is null, **X** completes very quickly. However, because **X** is the master of the task **Y**, **X** cannot terminate until **Y** terminates. Since **Y** contains an infinite loop, **X** cannot terminate. **X** has ceased to execute, but it cannot cease to exist because it is master of a task object **Y** which has not ceased to exist. This is an example of the general rule that, until a task has terminated, masters of that task cannot terminate, exit, or return. Put another way, a master cannot terminate, exit or return until all its dependent tasks have terminated.

Another way for tasks to terminate is through the terminate alternative of the selective wait. This is the only way a task which has not completed can terminate.

The rules are as follows. A task can terminate if its direct master has completed or the task is executing a selective wait with an open terminate alternative, and all tasks dependent on its direct master have completed or are executing selective waits with open terminate alternatives. The principle in this type of termination is that a group of tasks should terminate together. Consider a master and the group of tasks which depend on that master. If the master has completed and all the tasks that depend on that master are either terminated or at a select with an open terminate alternative, then the tasks terminate and the master exits (if it is a subprogram or package) or terminates (if it is a task).

Because the master is complete, it cannot make an entry call. Also, because all tasks which are dependent on the master are at selective waits, they are not in the process of making entry calls. In fact, all tasks and the master are willing to terminate at this point in time. Furthermore, since terminate alternatives, delay alternatives and else parts cannot occur in a single selective wait, none of these tasks has any possibility of making a selection unless an entry call is made. Since all tasks which could make such entry calls are at these selective waits, no entry call could possibly be made.

If this sort of situation is reached without terminate alternatives a tasking error could occur because there are no runnable tasks. With terminate alternatives, all the tasks may terminate, provided they do so all at the same time.

The procedure **`Termination`** in Program 19–1 illustrates some of the preceding points. Suppose we make the call

```
Termination("AB");
```

Then the loop of lines 31–37 is iterated twice. The first time, a call is made to **`A.Call`**. This call is accepted by the task **`A`** by the accept statement of line 11. Task **`A`** then executes the selective wait of lines 12–16. In the second iteration, a call is made to **`B.Call`**. This call is accepted by the task **`B`** by the accept statement of line 22. Task **`B`** then executes the selective wait of lines 23–27. When **`Termination`** finishes the second iteration, it exits the loop and becomes completed. At this point, both tasks **`A`** and **`B`** are at selective wait statements with terminate alternatives. The only other entity in which entry calls to **`A`** or **`B`** are syntactically legal is the procedure **`Termination`**. But this procedure has completed, so it is not capable of making an entry call. Consequently, all entities which could make legal entry calls to **`A`** or **`B`** are either at selective waits with terminate alternatives or have completed. So under the rules for termination, **`A`** and **`B`** become terminated. This means that all tasks for which **`Termination`** is the master have terminated. Hence, since the procedure has completed, a return from the procedure call occurs.

Now suppose instead that we made the call

```
Termination("A");
```

Then the loop of lines 31–37 is iterated once. After accepting the call to **`A.Call`**, the task **`A`** executes the selective wait statement of lines 12–16. The procedure **`Termination`** then becomes completed. The task **`B`** is executing the unconditional accept at line 22. Termination cannot occur because the task **`B`** is not at a selective wait statement with

```
procedure Termination(S: STRING) is
  task A is
    entry Call;
  end A;
  task B is
    entry Call;
  end B;

  task body A is
  begin
    loop
      accept Call;
      select
        accept Call;
      or
        terminate;
      end select;
    end loop;
  end A;

  task body B is
  begin
    loop
      accept Call;
      select
        accept Call;
      or
        terminate;
      end select;
    end loop;
  end B;

begin
  for I in S'RANGE loop
    if S(I) = 'A' then
      A.Call;
    else
      B.Call;
    end if;
  end loop;
end Termination;
```

Program 19–1

a terminate alternative. However, all entities which could make calls to **A** or **B** are completed or waiting, so the tasks and the procedure are waiting for events that cannot occur. Hence, because **A** and **B** cannot terminate, a return from the procedure cannot occur.

As a final example, suppose we make the call

```
Termination("ABABAB");
```

Then the loop of lines 31–37 is iterated six times. After the first two iterations, tasks **A** and **B** are both at selective waits with terminate alternatives. However, the procedure **Termination** has not completed, so they are not allowed to terminate. At the third iteration of the loop, the entry call to **A.Call** causes the selective wait to choose the accept alternative of line 13. At the fourth iteration of the loop, the entry call to **B.Call** causes the selective wait to choose the accept alternative of line 24. **A** and **B** are now waiting at the unconditional accept statements of lines 11 and 22, respectively. After the fifth and sixth iterations, **A** and **B** are again at the selective waits. After the sixth iteration, the procedure **Termination** completes so that at this point the terminate alternatives will be selected, the tasks will terminate, and a return from the procedure will occur.

Finally, Ada does not specify how termination occurs for tasks whose masters are library packages. We know only that the library package (and hence any included tasks) must remain for duration of the execution of the main program and that the main program "does not await termination of tasks which depend on library packages."

19.8 TASK ATTRIBUTES

There are three attributes associated with tasks. Two of these pertain to the tasks themselves, the third **COUNT** pertains to entries and was discussed in Chapter 18. Both the other task attributes return Boolean values. The first attribute is **CALLABLE**. For example, **Box'CALLABLE** evaluates to **FALSE** if calls to entries in **Box** are impossible. This is the case if the task is no longer capable of executing instructions, as for example, when an exception has occurred within the task body.

The second attribute is **TERMINATED**. This attribute returns **TRUE** if the task has terminated and **FALSE** otherwise.

Note that a task can never be both **CALLABLE** and **TERMINATED**. However, an abnormal or completed task could be neither **CALLABLE** nor **TERMINATED**.

19.9 PROGRAMMING PRACTICES

One of the most difficult aspects of tasks is the handling of exceptions. The lack of an appropriate place to propagate an exception that occurs directly within the body of a task means that tasks can easily complete due to an exception. Since such completion is not reported by any Ada mechanism, the error may not manifest itself until sometime later when an entry call is made to the task. In fact, the error may not be reported to the user until the main program makes an entry call to a task which has already completed due to an exception. This task may be several tasking errors away from the task which originally had the exception. We suggest that each task body conclude with an exception handler which at least reports (**TEXT_IO.PUT**) that the task has completed due to an exception.

19.9.1 Problem Solving

Task types are useful when many tasks perform the same operations. For example, every teller in a bank performs the same operations. To illustrate task types, we discuss how to use the **Bank** package of Chapter 17 to implement a bank with multiple tellers. In this discussion we assume that a bank package with a single teller and a single teller program have been implemented and tested.

The chief problem is to avoid two tellers simultaneously modifying the same account. We prevent this by the simple method of allowing only one account modification at a time. What we build is a package **Big_Bank** containing a task **Bank_Task**. To modify an account, the teller will make an entry call to the task. When the task accepts an entry call, it will make an appropriate call to **Bank**. **Big_Bank** is built as follows:

```
with Bank;
package Big_Bank is
  type Account renames Bank.Account;
  ... other renames declarations
  task Bank_Task is
    entry Deposit(Current_Customer: Account; How_Much: Money);
    ... other entry declarations
  end Bank_Task;
end Big_Bank;
```

By renaming, **Big_Bank** makes available exactly the same types as does **Bank**. Also, for each procedure in the declaration of **Bank**, **Big_Bank** makes available a corresponding entry call. Recall that **Bank** declared the procedure **Deposit** as

```
procedure Deposit(Current_Customer: Account; How_Much: Money);
```

Notice how closely the entry in **Bank_Task** corresponds to this declaration.

Now consider the package body. Since the purpose of the package is to serve as an interface between the tellers and the **Bank** package, the body simply translates entry calls to procedure calls:

```
package body Big_Bank is
  task body Bank_Task is
    Bank.Send_Statements;
    loop
      select
        accept Deposit(Current_Customer: Account; How_Much: Money) do
          Bank.Deposit(Current_Customer, How_Much);
        end Deposit;
      or
```

```
        ... other accept statements
      end Bank_Task;
    end Big_Bank;
```

Bank_Task is a monitor. The task handles one teller request at a time. For each entry call it makes a procedure call. This prevents simultaneous modifications to bank accounts. Direct calls to the procedures have been replaced with entry calls which, in turn, call the original procedure.

The tellers are implemented as follows:

```
with Big_Bank;
procedure Our_Bank is
  task type Teller;
  Bank_Staff: array(1..20) of Teller;

  task body Teller is
    ... declarations are the same as the procedure Teller
  begin
  At_Work:
    loop
      Display_Customer_Options;
      Read_Choice(Choice);
      case Choice is
        when 'A' =>
          Get_Customer(Current_Customer);
        when 'B' =>
          Get_New_Customer(Current_Customer);
      end case;
      begin
        loop
          Display_Options;
          Read_Choice(Choice);
          case Choice is
            when 'A' =>
              Get_Amount(Amount);
              Big_Bank.Bank_Task.Deposit(Current_Customer, Amount);
            when 'B' =>
              Big_Bank.Bank_Task.Withdraw(Current_Customer, Amount);
              Give_Amount(Amount);
            when 'C' =>
              Big_Bank.Bank_Task.Close_Account(Current_Customer, Amount);
              Give_Amount(Amount);
              exit;              -- This customer is done.
            when 'D' =>
              Big_Bank.Bank_Task.Close_Teller;
              exit At_Work;      -- The teller goes home.
            when 'E' => exit;    -- This customer is done.
          end case;
```

```
            end loop;
          exception
            when Big_Bank.Account_Closed => null;
          end;
        end loop At_Work;
      end Teller;
    end Our_Bank;
```

The teller task type differs from the teller procedure in that procedure calls are replaced by entry calls, there is a modification to exit the task instead of return from a procedure, and an exception handler has been added. In addition to what is shown here, the calls to procedures in **Bank** from **Get_Customer** and **Get_New_Customer** must be converted to entry calls.

As presented, the conversion to multiple tellers is quite simple. The monitor converts simultaneous requests into a sequence of requests about various customers. This decision avoids most of the problems associated with simultaneous requests. One problem that persists occurs because we assume that whenever the program is at **Display_Options** there is a valid customer. With simultaneous requests, this assumption would be violated if the customer's account was closed by another teller. This problem may be solved by raising an exception whenever an operation occurs on a closed account. Because the place where it will be discovered that an operation is requested on a closed account is the package **Bank**, the exception should be declared in that package. The package **Big_Bank** should make this exception available by renaming it.

This last problem points out the difficulty of testing a program with multiple tasks. It is often impossible to test all possible orders of requests, but certain orders will uncover special difficulties, so an effort must be made to test as many orders of entry calls as possible.

19.10 ADA SUMMARY

This chapter has covered several constructs for concurrent programming. The *task type* makes possible the dynamic creation of tasks. This provides a means for adjusting the number of tasks during execution. However, the task type complicates the rules for completion and termination. To express these rules, Ada introduces the concept of *task masters*. The *abort statement* may be used to force a task to abandon execution. With respect to tasks, Ada defines specific rules for the raising and propagation of *exceptions*. Task attributes can be used to inquire about the status of a task. Although task types lack parameters, they may be embedded in other constructs. For example, by embedding a task or task type in a generic package you can select the types allowed in the parameter list of the entry calls or the size of certain data structures within the task. However, this selection is available when defining a task or task type, but not at the time a task is dynamically created.

EXERCISES

19.1. Modify the robot version of the post office (exercise 18.3) to use task types. You will have to design a way to communicate to each task where "home" (location of the original piles of mail) is and which robot (**A**, **B**, or **C**) it controls. Clerk task types will have to know which window they operate (D window, or E window).

19.2. Design a program that performs matrix multiplication using multiple tasks. For the array declarations

```
subtype I1 is INTEGER range 1..M;
subtype I2 is INTEGER range 1..N;
subtype I3 is INTEGER range 1..T;
type Left_Operand is array(I1, I3) of INTEGER;
type Right_Operand is array(I3, I2) of INTEGER;
type Answer_Type is array(I1, I2) of INTEGER;
Left: Left_Operand;
Right: Right_Operand;
Answer: Answer_Type;
```

one way to do this is to have each task take a row of **Left** and multiply it by **Right** to produce a row of **Answer**. This means using **M** tasks.

19.3. In exercises 18.1 and 18.2, there was a single post office. In real postal systems, there are many post offices. Modify the post office so that it handles messages that are addressed to a post office box at a given post office. Assume there is one post office per zip code (i.e., each post office is identified by a **POSITIVE** number). Change the post box task to be a task type. Add an entry **Start(Zip_Code: INTEGER)** that allows you to tell the post box task which zip code it represents. An array of post office box tasks will represent the postal system.

Appendix A

Syntax Diagrams

Because the diagrams within the text are scattered and often simplified, we provide this appendix as a summary of the major syntactic components of Ada. This appendix is meant as a quick reference for the programmer and is not intended to be a complete syntax for the language. The diagrams are organized into sections as follows:

1. Compilation units
2. Formal parameters
3. Task and entry declarations
4. Declarative items
5. Statements
6. Exception part

Within the declarative items section, a few major items are listed first, and the remainder of the diagrams follow in alphabetical order. The statements section is entirely in alphabetical order.

A.1 COMPILATION UNITS

<compilation unit>

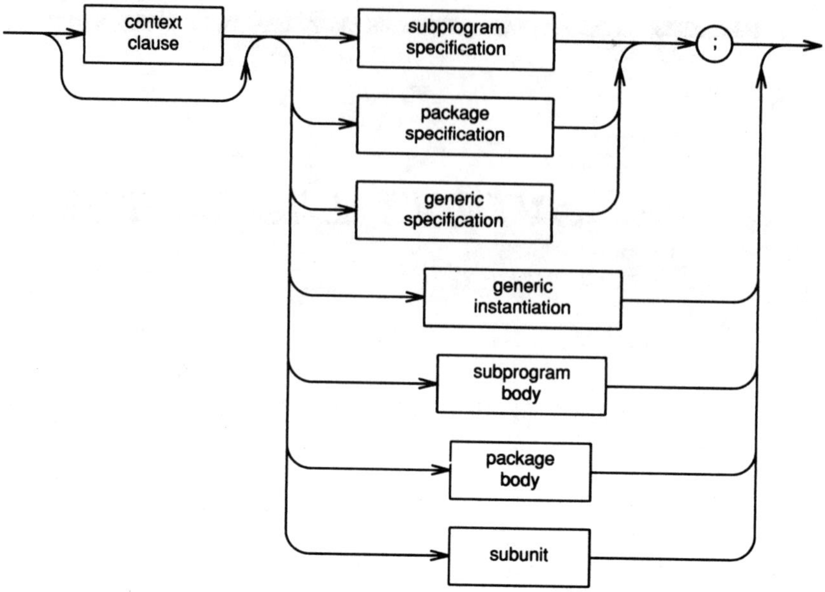

<context clause>

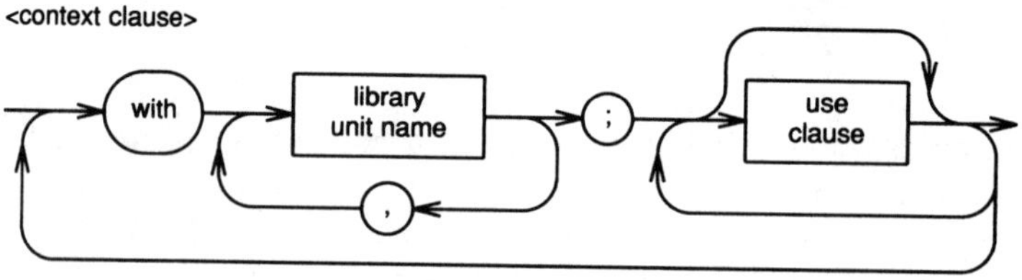

<package specification>

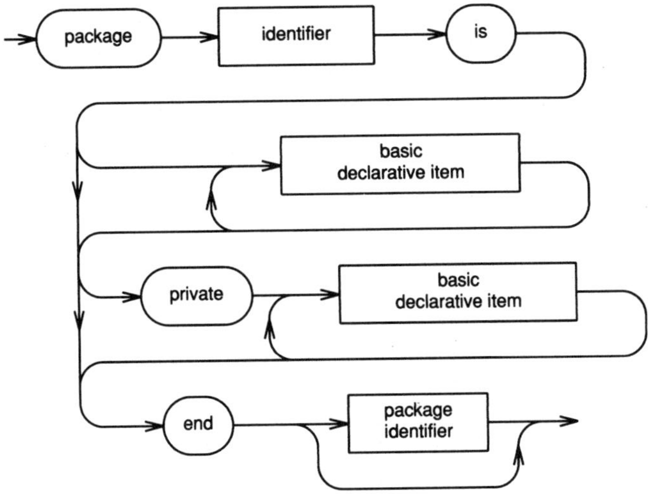

<subprogram specification>

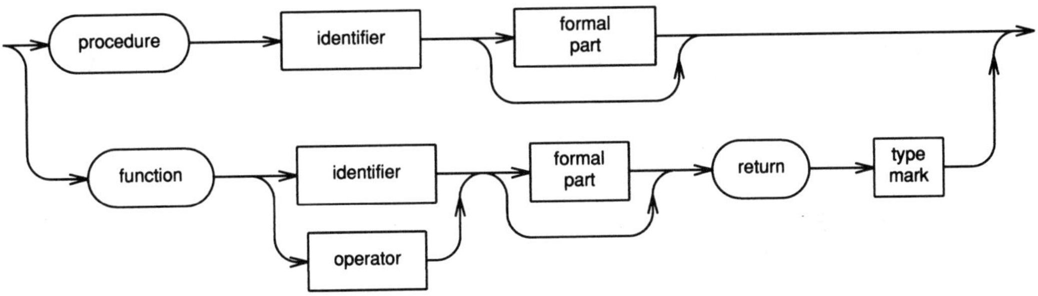

<package body>

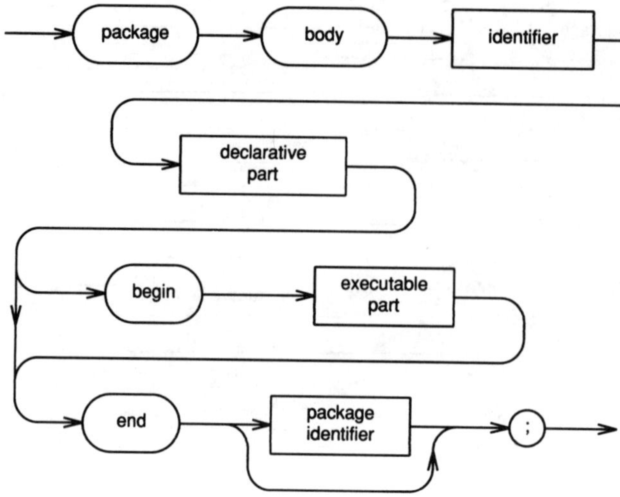

<subprogram body>

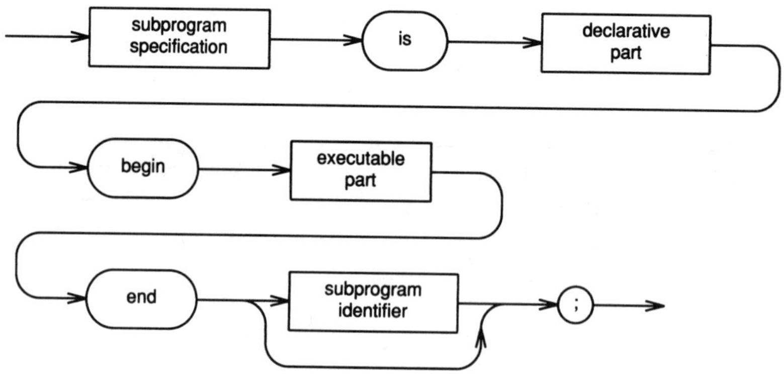

<subunit>

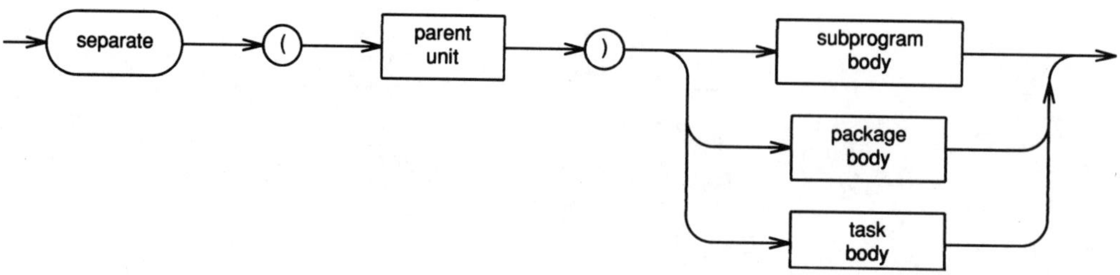

<generic specification>

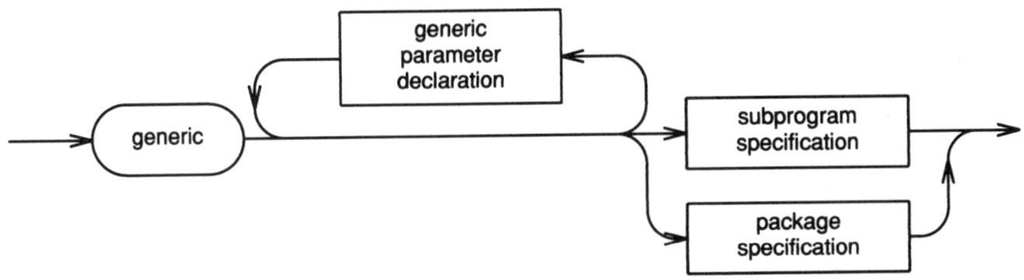

<generic instantiation>

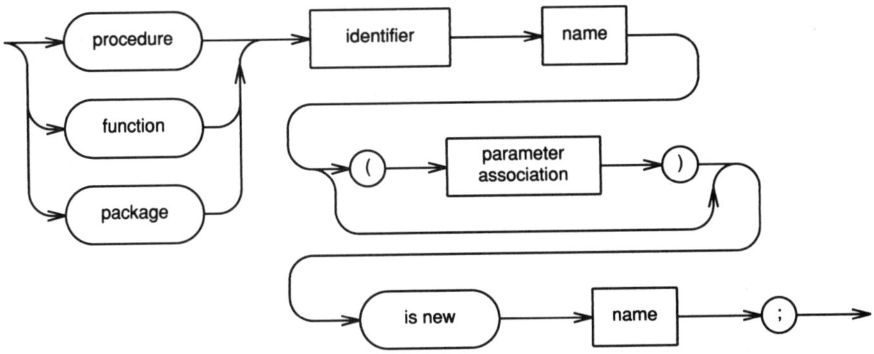

<executable part>

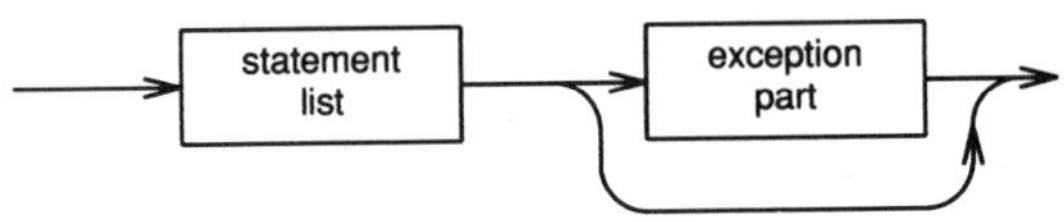

A.2 FORMAL PARAMETER DECLARATIONS

<formal part>

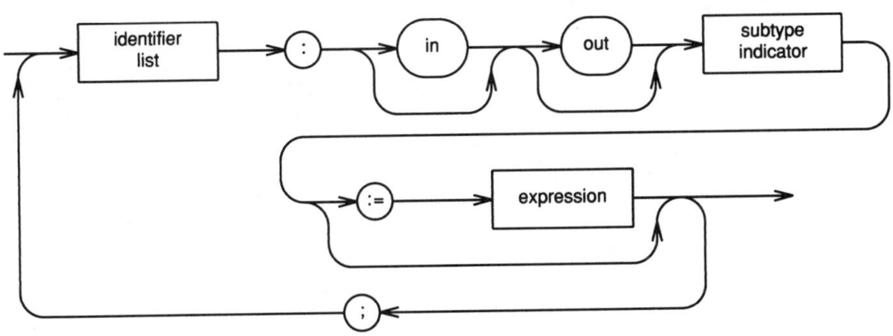

<generic parameter declaration>

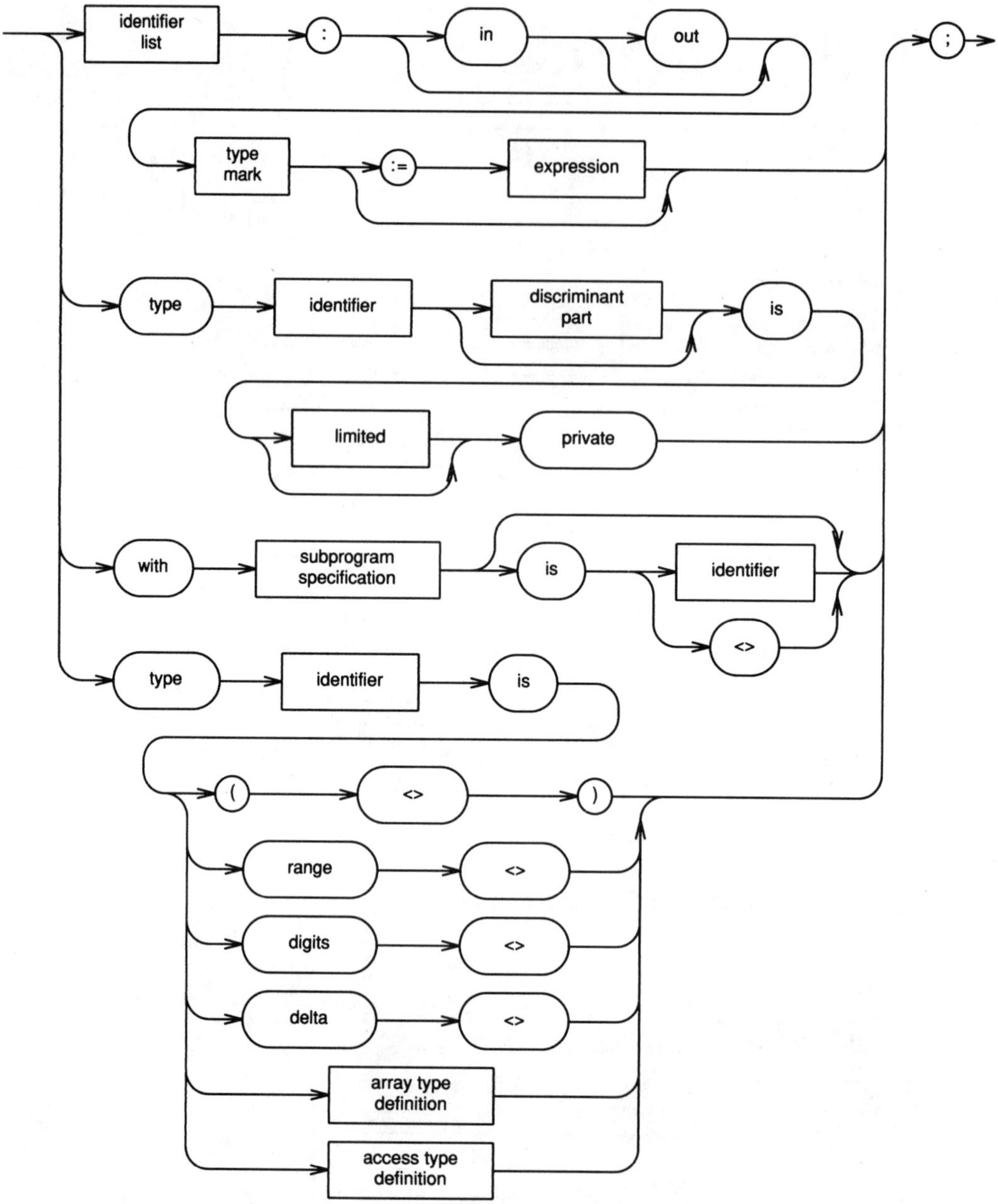

A.3 TASK AND ENTRY DECLARATIONS

<task declaration>

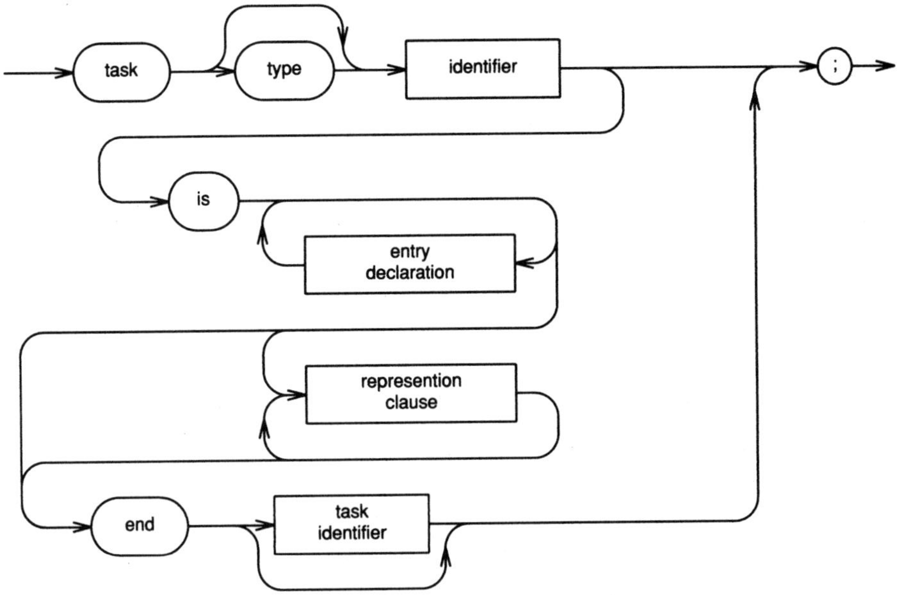

<task body>

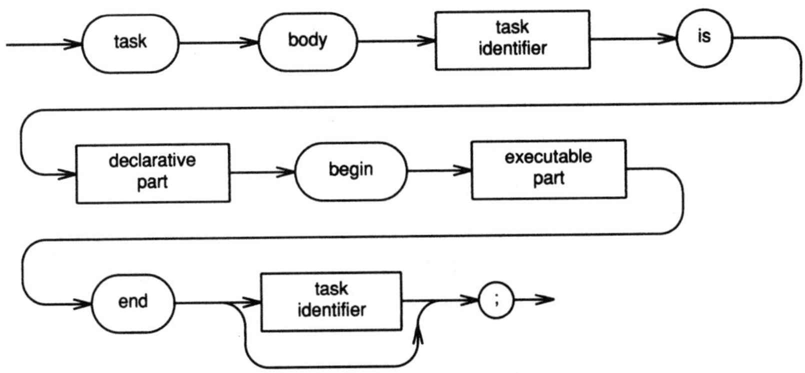

<entry declaration>

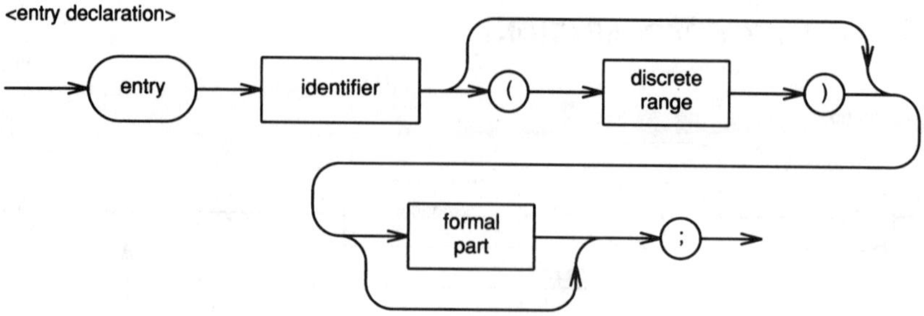

A.4 DECLARATIVE ITEMS

<declarative part>

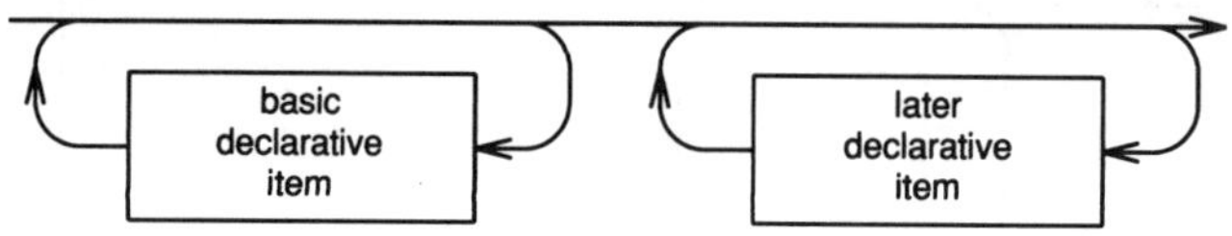

<basic declarative item>

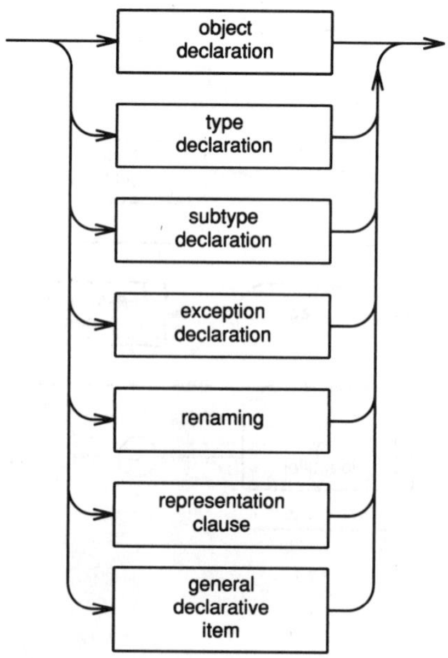

<later declarative item>

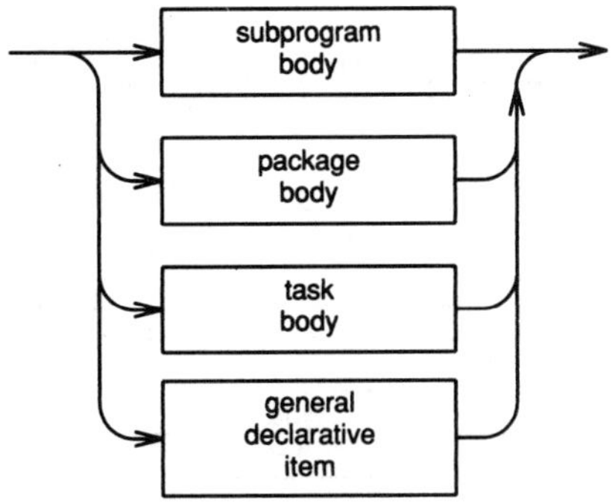

<general declarative item>

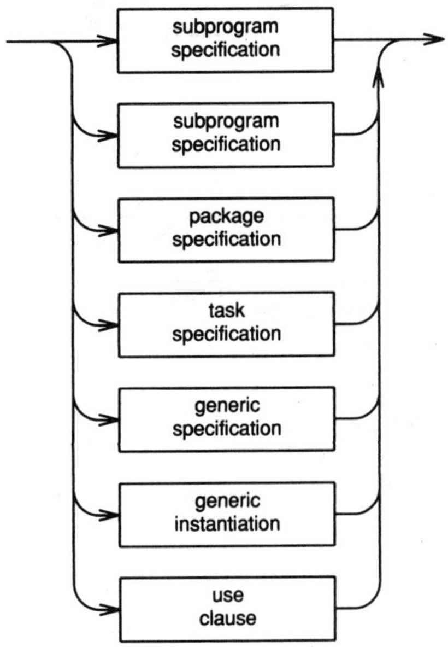

<access type definition>

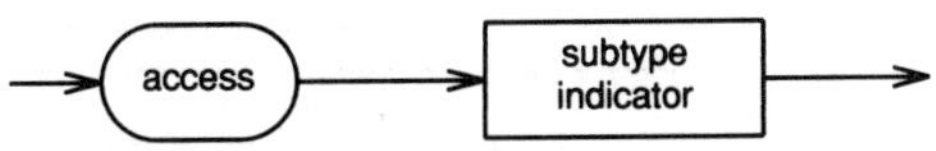

<array type definition>

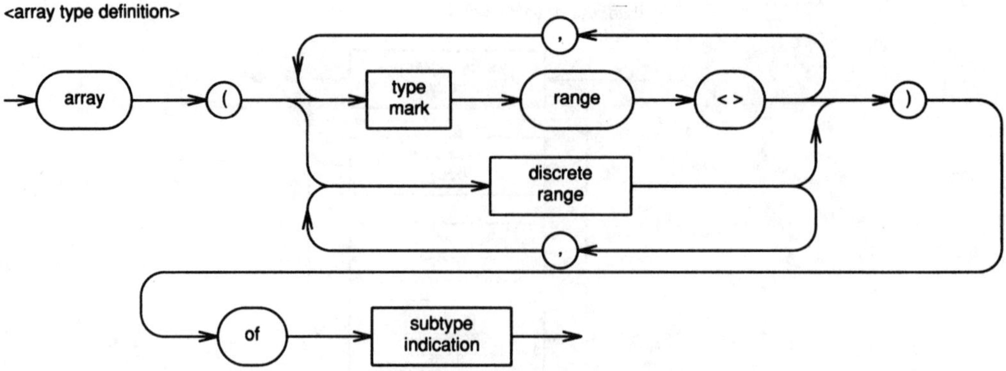

<discrete range>

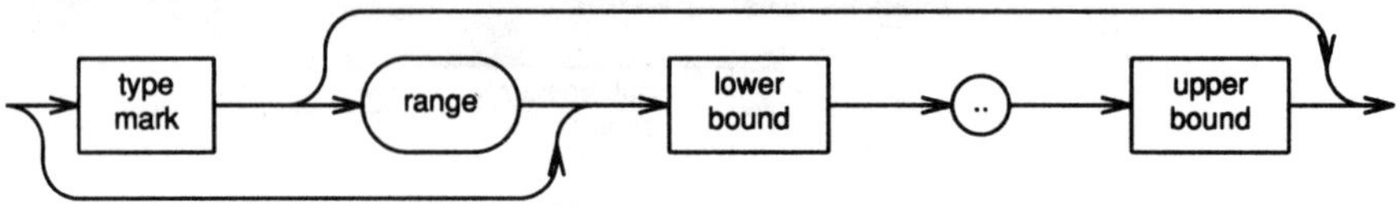

<discriminant part>

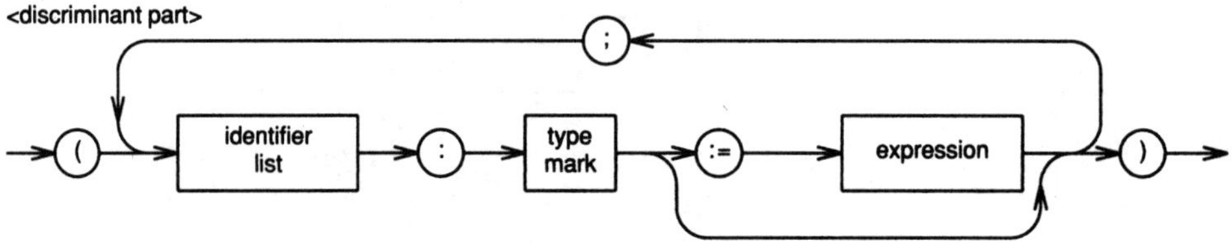

<exception declaration>

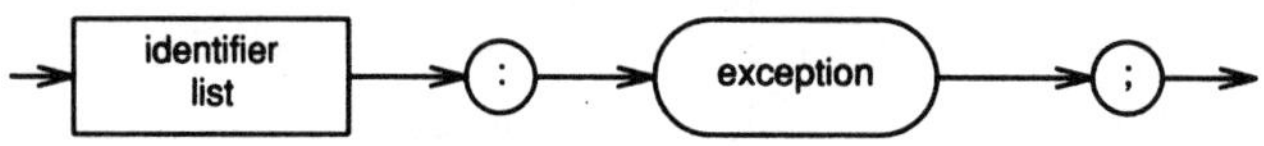

<object declaration>

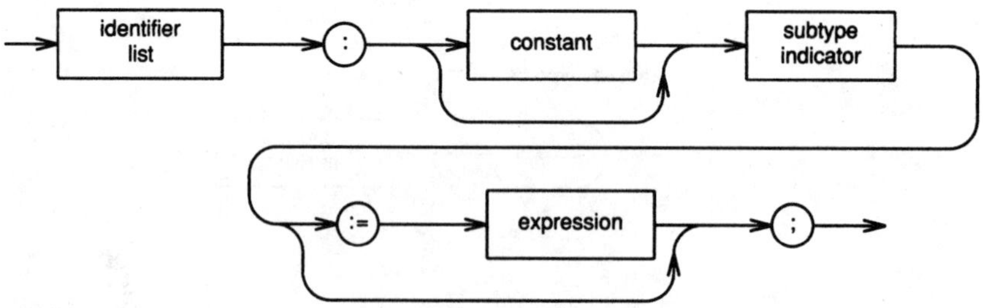

<record type definition>

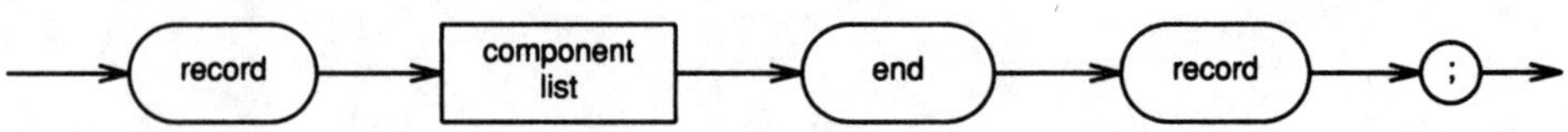

<component list>

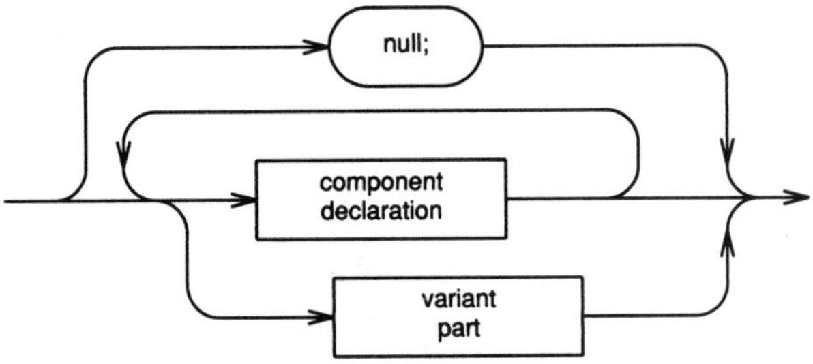

<variant part>

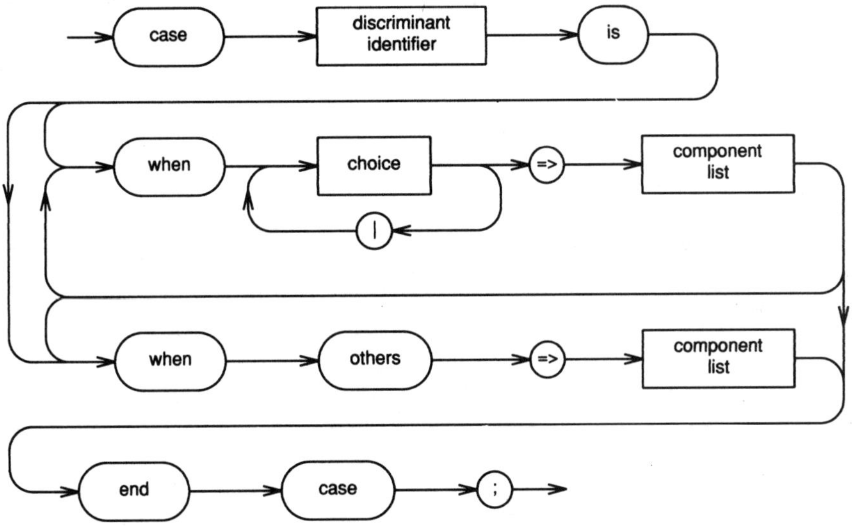

<component declaration>

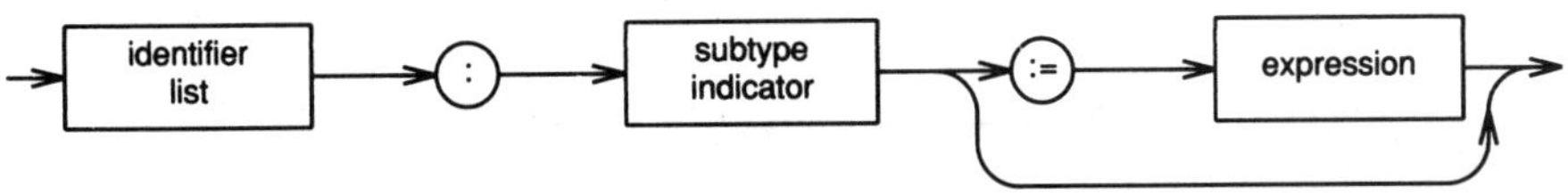

<renames declaration>

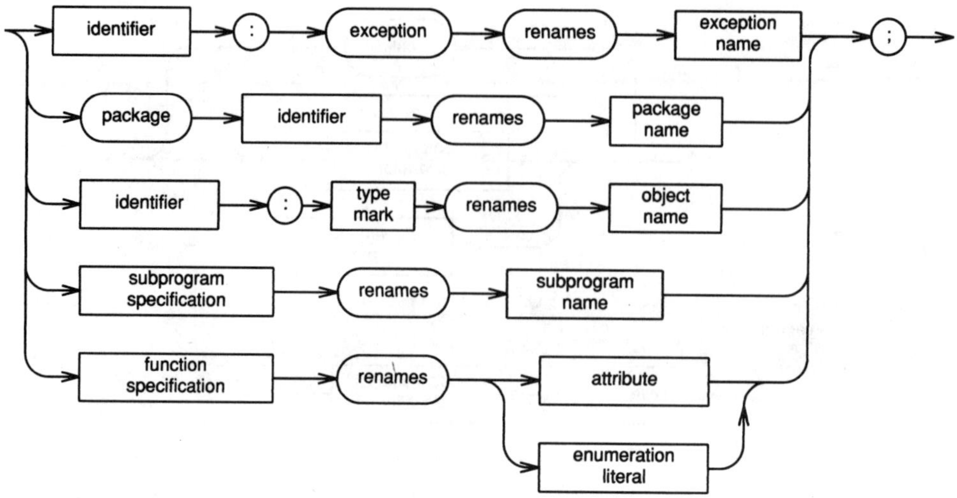

<subtype declaration>

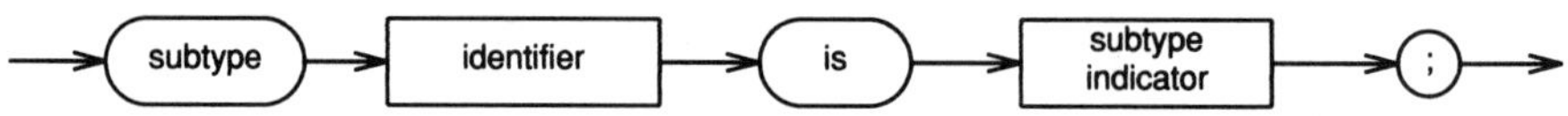

<subtype indicator>

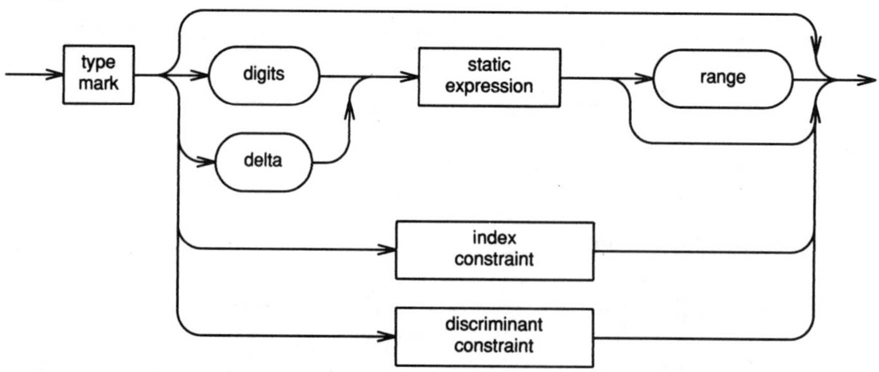

<type declaration>

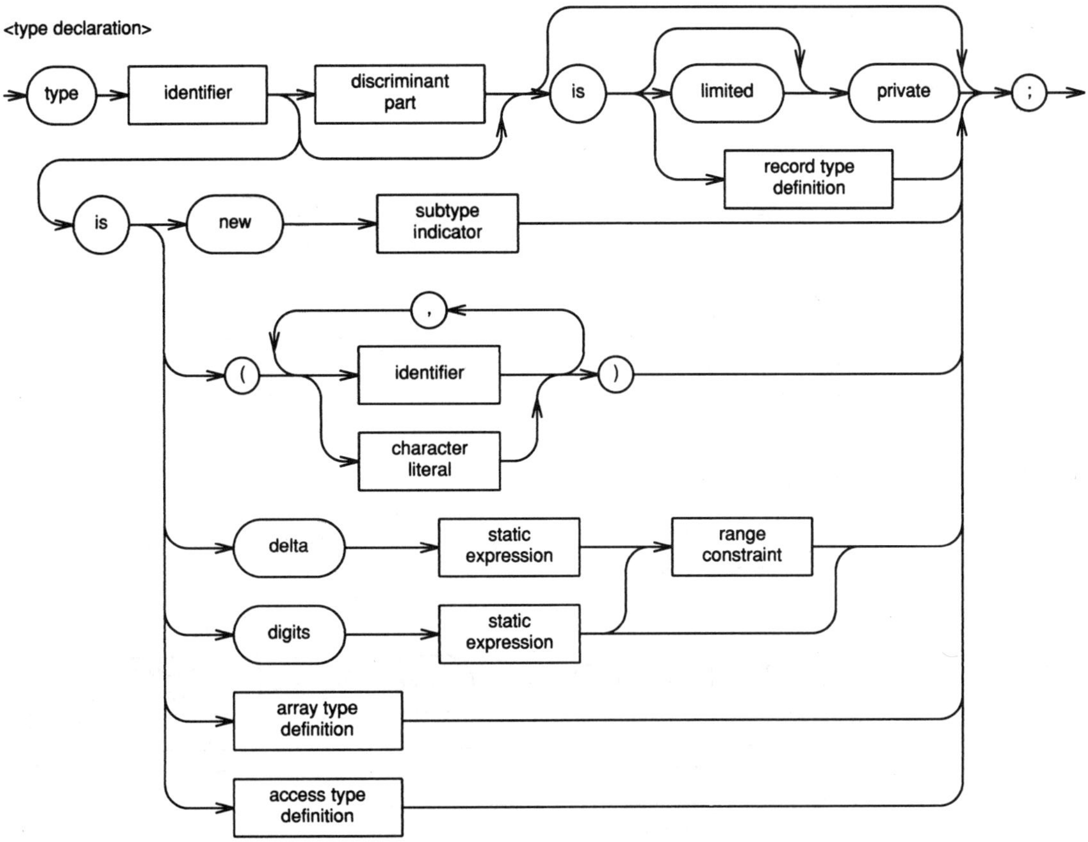

<use clause>

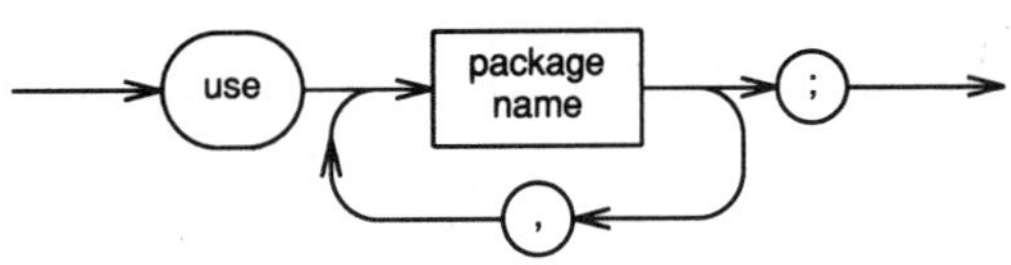

A.5 STATEMENTS

<abort statement>

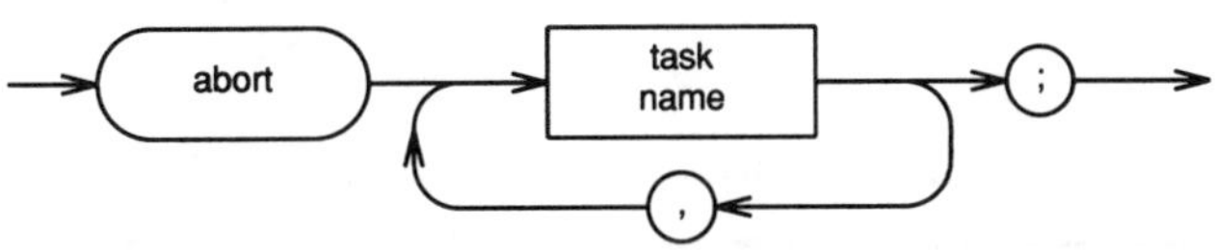

<accept statement>

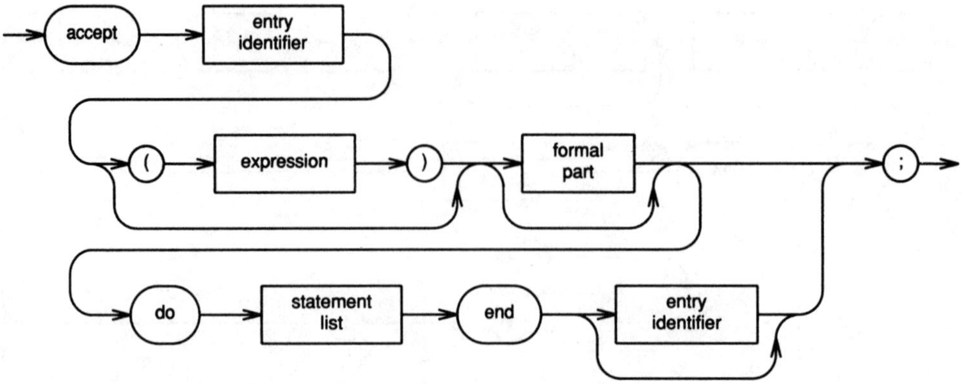

<assignment statement>

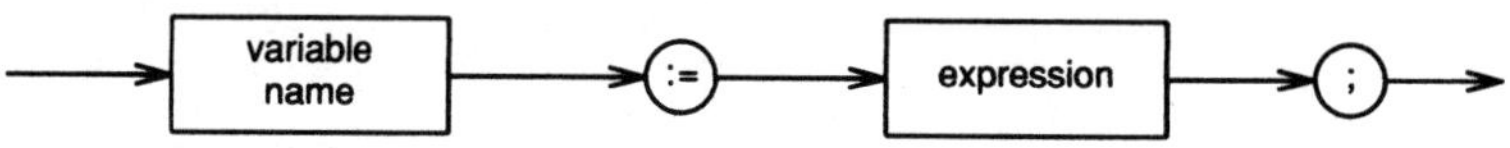

<block statement>

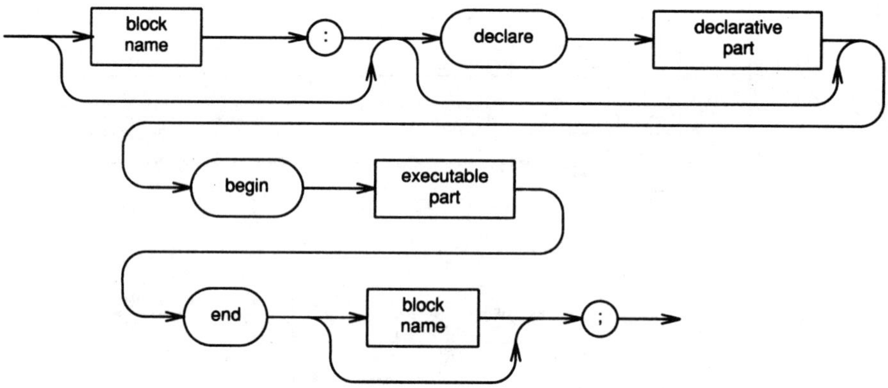

<case statement>

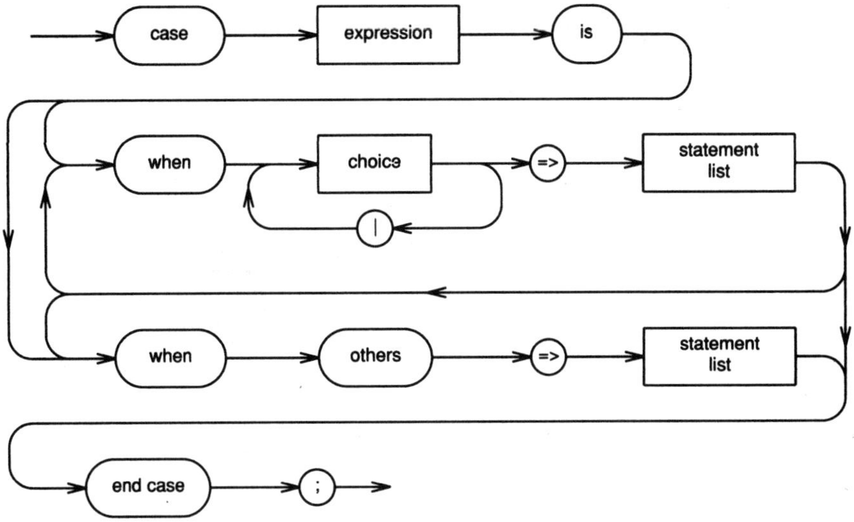

<choice>

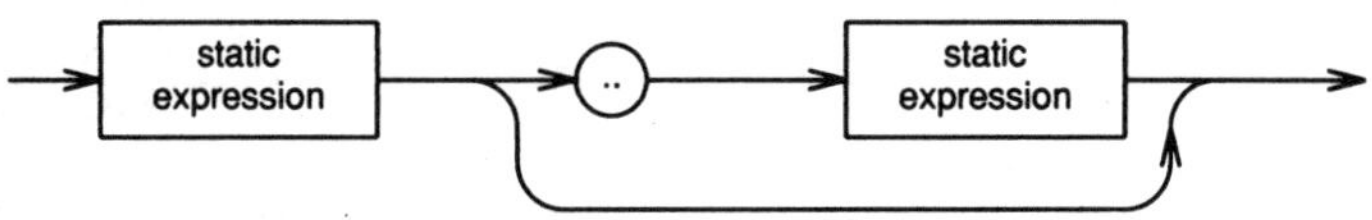

<procedure call>

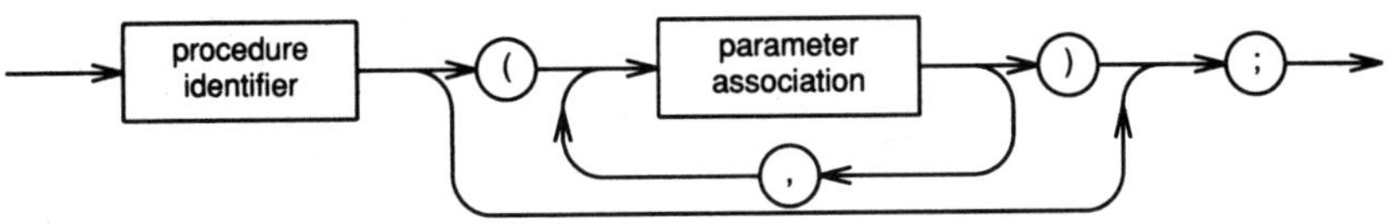

<delay statement>

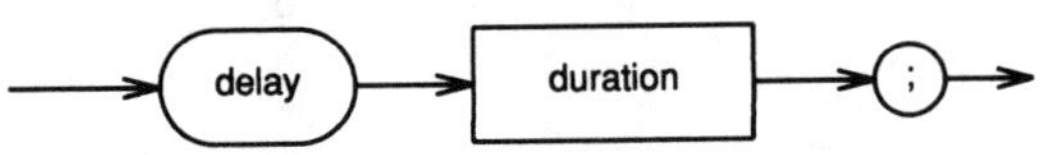

<entry call>

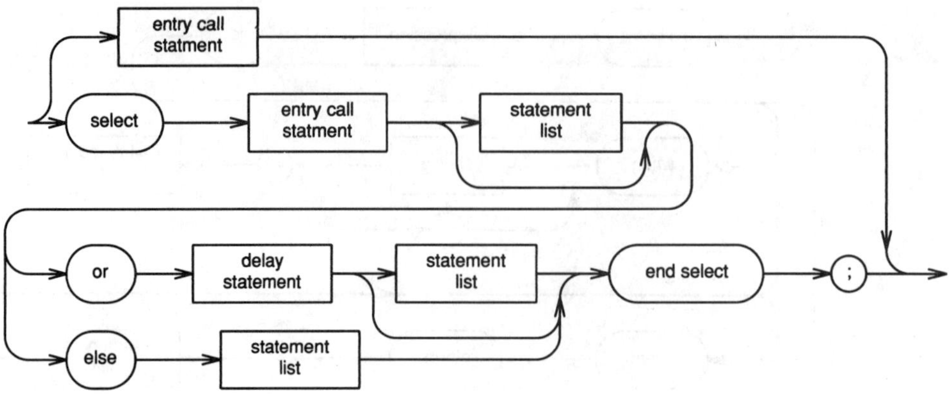

<entry call statment>

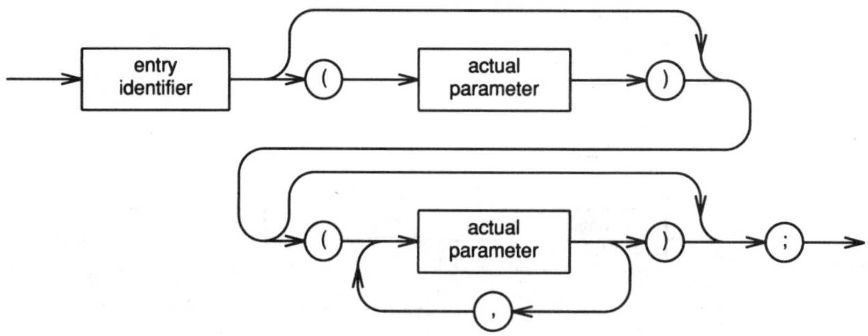

<exit statement>

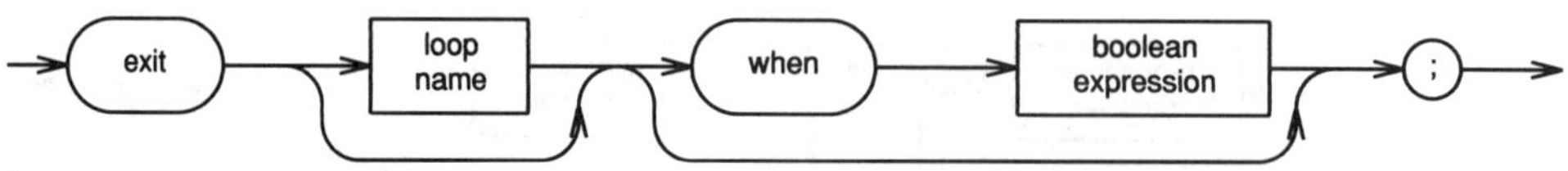

<goto statement>

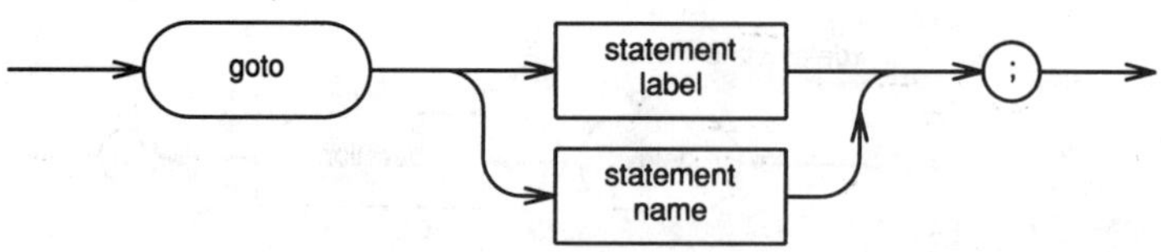

<if statement>

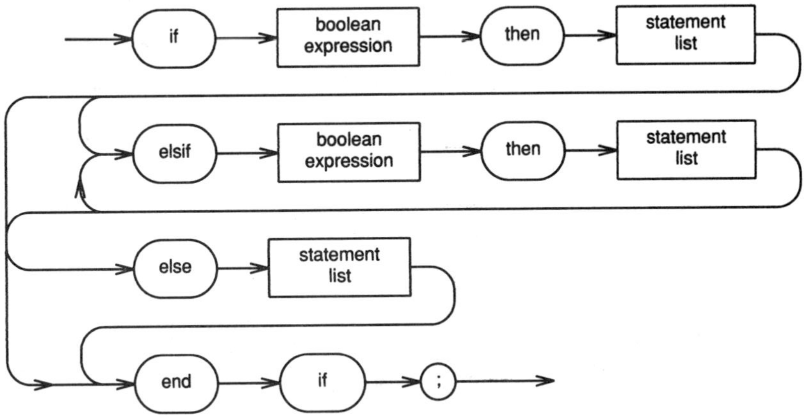

<loop statement>

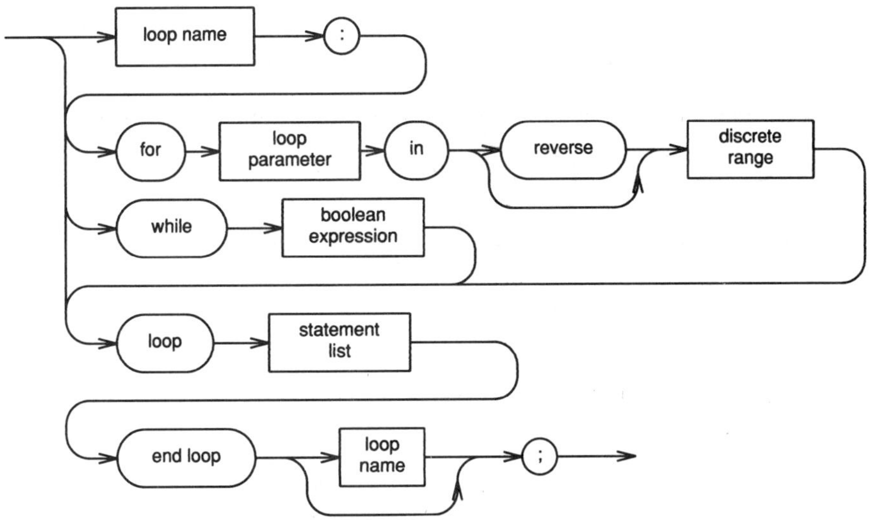

<null statement>

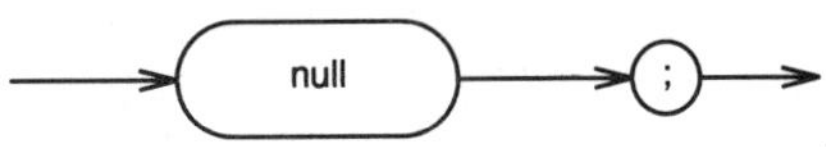

<raise statement>

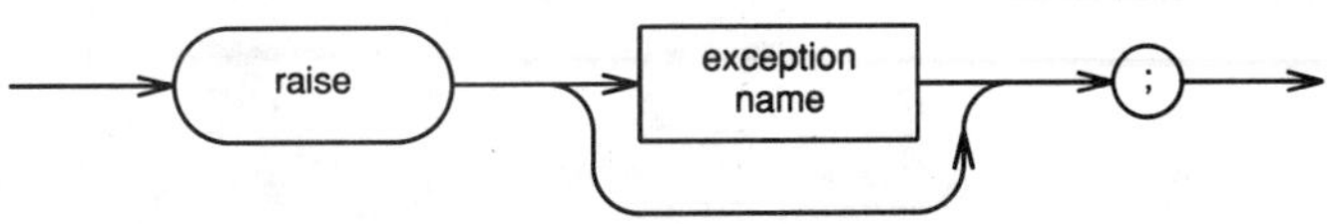

<return statement>

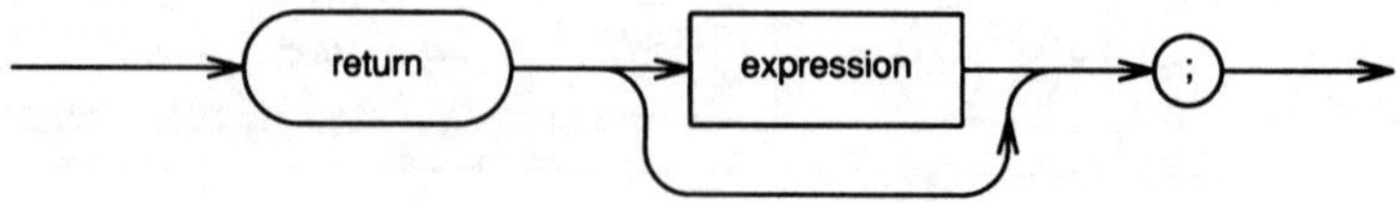

<selective wait statement>

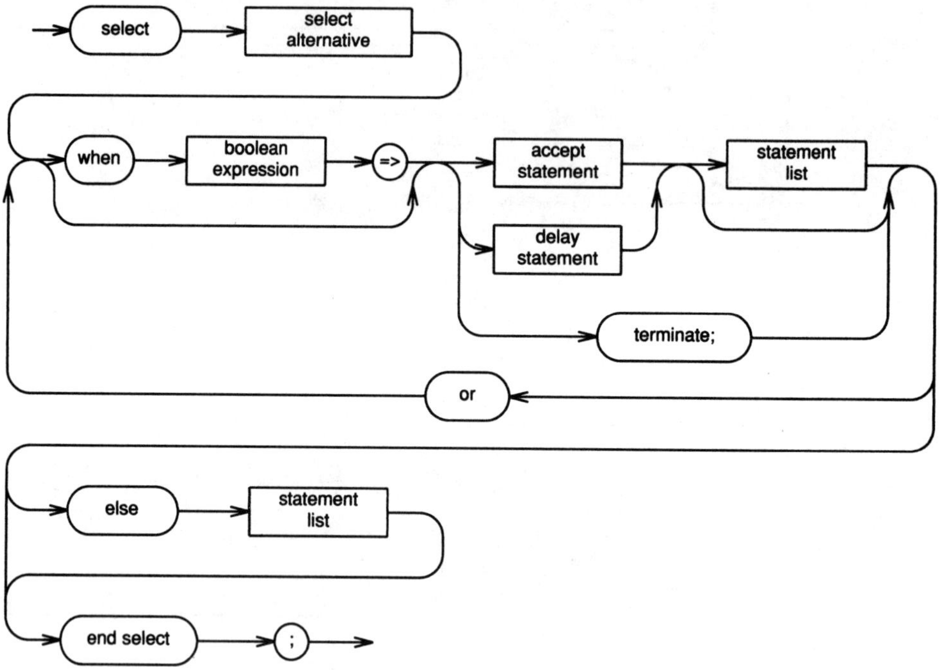

A.6 OTHER

<exception part>

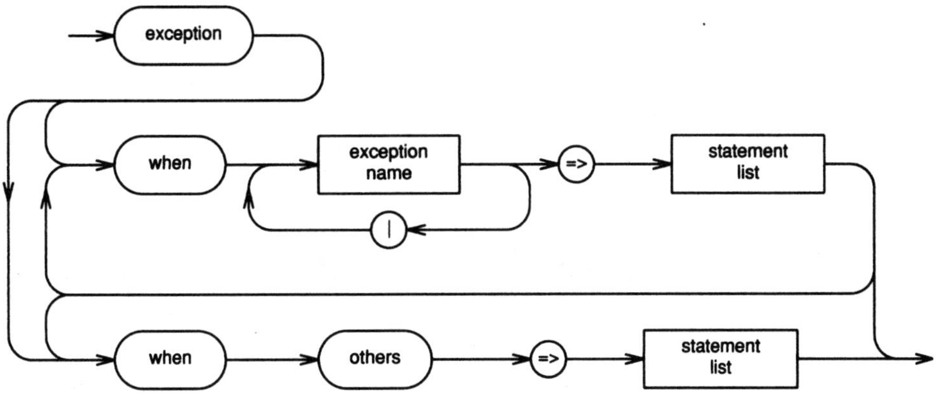

Appendix B

Reserved and Predefined Words

B.1 RESERVED WORDS

```
abort      declare    generic    of         select
abs        delay      goto       or         separate
accept     delta                 others     subtype
access     digits     if         out
all        do         in                    task
and                   is         package    terminate
array                            pragma     then
at         else                  private    type
           elsif      limited    procedure
           end        loop
begin      entry                 raise      use
body       exception             range
           exit       mod        record     when
                                 rem        while
                      new        renames    with
case       for        not        return
constant   function   null       reverse    xor
```

B.2 PREDEFINED IDENTIFIERS

ASCII	INTEGER	CONSTRAINT_ERROR
BOOLEAN	NATURAL	NUMERIC_ERROR
CHARACTER	POSITIVE	PROGRAM_ERROR
FALSE	STRING	STORAGE_ERROR
FLOAT	TRUE	TASKING_ERROR

B.3 PREDEFINED LIBRARY UNITS

CALENDAR	DIRECT_IO
MACHINE_CODE	LOW_LEVEL_IO
SYSTEM	IO_EXCEPTIONS
UNCHECKED_DEALLOCATION	SEQUENTIAL_IO
UNCHECKED_CONVERSION	TEXT_IO

B.4 ATTRIBUTES

ADDRESS	FIRST	MACHINE_OVERFLOWS	SAFE_SMALL
AFT	FIRST_BIT	MACHINE_RADIX	SIZE
BASE	FORE	MACHINE_ROUNDS	SMALL
CALLABLE	IMAGE	MANTISSA	STORAGE_SIZE
CONSTRAINED	LARGE	POS	SUCC
COUNT	LAST	POSITION	TERMINATED
DELTA	LAST_BIT	PRED	VAL
DIGITS	LENGTH	RANGE	VALUE
EMAX	MACHINE_EMAX	SAFE_EMAX	WIDTH
EPSILON	MACHINE_EMIN	SAFE_LARGE	

Appendix C

Predefined Packages

This appendix lists the declarations of the predefined Ada packages mentioned in the text. It also lists the definition of the predefined type **CHARACTER**.

```
package CALENDAR is
  type TIME is private;
  subtype YEAR_NUMBER  is INTEGER  range 1901 .. 2099;
  subtype MONTH_NUMBER is INTEGER  range 1 .. 12;
  subtype DAY_NUMBER   is INTEGER  range 1 .. 31;
  subtype DAY_DURATION is DURATION range 0.0 .. 86_400.0;
  function CLOCK return TIME;
  function YEAR    (DATE : TIME) return YEAR_NUMBER;
  function MONTH   (DATE : TIME) return MONTH_NUMBER;
  function DAY     (DATE : TIME) return DAY_NUMBER;
  function SECONDS (DATE : TIME) return DAY_DURATION;
  procedure SPLIT (DATE    : in  TIME;
                   YEAR    : out YEAR_NUMBER;
                   MONTH   : out MONTH_NUMBER;
                   DAY     : out DAY_NUMBER;
                   SECONDS : out DAY_DURATION);
  function TIME_OF (YEAR   : YEAR_NUMBER;
                   MONTH   : MONTH_NUMBER;
                   DAY     : DAY_NUMBER;
                   SECONDS : DAY_DURATION := 0.0) return TIME;
  function "+"  (LEFT : TIME;     RIGHT : DURATION) return TIME;
  function "+"  (LEFT : DURATION; RIGHT : TIME)     return TIME;
  function "-"  (LEFT : TIME;     RIGHT : DURATION) return TIME;
```

```
  function "-"  (LEFT : TIME;     RIGHT : TIME)     return DURATION;
  function "<"  (LEFT, RIGHT : TIME) return BOOLEAN;
  function "<=" (LEFT, RIGHT : TIME) return BOOLEAN;
  function ">"  (LEFT, RIGHT : TIME) return BOOLEAN;
  function ">=" (LEFT, RIGHT : TIME) return BOOLEAN;
  TIME_ERROR : exception;  --  can be raised by TIME_OF, "+", and "-"
private
  -- implementation-dependent
end;
```

```
with IO_EXCEPTIONS;
generic
  type ELEMENT_TYPE is private;
package SEQUENTIAL_IO is
  type FILE_TYPE is limited private;
  type FILE_MODE is (IN_FILE, OUT_FILE);
  -- File management
  procedure CREATE(FILE : in out FILE_TYPE;
                   MODE : in FILE_MODE := OUT_FILE;
                   NAME : in STRING := "";
                   FORM : in STRING := "");
  procedure OPEN   (FILE : in out FILE_TYPE;
                   MODE : in FILE_MODE;
                   NAME : in STRING;
                   FORM : in STRING := "");
  procedure CLOSE  (FILE : in out FILE_TYPE);
  procedure DELETE(FILE : in out FILE_TYPE);
  procedure RESET  (FILE : in out FILE_TYPE; MODE : in FILE_MODE);
  procedure RESET  (FILE : in out FILE_TYPE);
  function MODE    (FILE : in FILE_TYPE) return FILE_MODE;
  function NAME    (FILE : in FILE_TYPE) return STRING;
  function FORM    (FILE : in FILE_TYPE) return STRING;
  function IS_OPEN(FILE : in FILE_TYPE) return BOOLEAN;
  -- Input and output operations
  procedure READ   (FILE : in FILE_TYPE; ITEM : out ELEMENT_TYPE);
  procedure WRITE  (FILE : in FILE_TYPE; ITEM : in ELEMENT_TYPE);
  function END_OF_FILE(FILE : in FILE_TYPE) return BOOLEAN;
  -- Exceptions
  STATUS_ERROR : exception renames IO_EXCEPTIONS.STATUS_ERROR;
  MODE_ERROR   : exception renames IO_EXCEPTIONS.MODE_ERROR;
  NAME_ERROR   : exception renames IO_EXCEPTIONS.NAME_ERROR;
  USE_ERROR    : exception renames IO_EXCEPTIONS.USE_ERROR;
  DEVICE_ERROR : exception renames IO_EXCEPTIONS.DEVICE_ERROR;
  END_ERROR    : exception renames IO_EXCEPTIONS.END_ERROR;
  DATA_ERROR   : exception renames IO_EXCEPTIONS.DATA_ERROR;
private
  -- implementation-dependent
end SEQUENTIAL_IO;
```

```
with IO_EXCEPTIONS;
generic
  type ELEMENT_TYPE is private;
package DIRECT_IO is
  type FILE_TYPE is limited private;
  type    FILE_MODE is (IN_FILE, INOUT_FILE, OUT_FILE);
  type    COUNT     is range 0 .. IMPLEMENTATION_DEFINED;
  subtype POSITIVE_COUNT is COUNT range 1 .. COUNT'LAST;
  -- File management
  procedure CREATE(FILE : in out FILE_TYPE;
                   MODE : in FILE_MODE := INOUT_FILE;
                   NAME : in STRING := "";
                   FORM : in STRING := "");
  procedure OPEN  (FILE : in out FILE_TYPE;
                   MODE : in FILE_MODE;
                   NAME : in STRING;
                   FORM : in STRING := "");
  procedure CLOSE (FILE : in out FILE_TYPE);
  procedure DELETE(FILE : in out FILE_TYPE);
  procedure RESET (FILE : in out FILE_TYPE; MODE : in FILE_MODE);
  procedure RESET (FILE : in out FILE_TYPE);
  function MODE   (FILE : in FILE_TYPE) return FILE_MODE;
  function NAME   (FILE : in FILE_TYPE) return STRING;
  function FORM   (FILE : in FILE_TYPE) return STRING;
  function IS_OPEN(FILE : in FILE_TYPE) return BOOLEAN;
  -- Input and output operations
  procedure READ (FILE : in FILE_TYPE; ITEM : out ELEMENT_TYPE; FROM : POSITIVE_COUNT);
  procedure READ (FILE : in FILE_TYPE; ITEM : out ELEMENT_TYPE);
  procedure WRITE(FILE : in FILE_TYPE; ITEM : in  ELEMENT_TYPE; TO : POSITIVE_COUNT);
  procedure WRITE(FILE : in FILE_TYPE; ITEM : in ELEMENT_TYPE);
  procedure SET_INDEX(FILE : in FILE_TYPE; TO : in POSITIVE_COUNT);
  function INDEX(FILE : in FILE_TYPE) return POSITIVE_COUNT;
  function SIZE (FILE : in FILE_TYPE) return COUNT;
  function END_OF_FILE(FILE : in FILE_TYPE) return BOOLEAN;
  -- Exceptions
  STATUS_ERROR : exception renames IO_EXCEPTIONS.STATUS_ERROR;
  MODE_ERROR   : exception renames IO_EXCEPTIONS.MODE_ERROR;
  NAME_ERROR   : exception renames IO_EXCEPTIONS.NAME_ERROR;
  USE_ERROR    : exception renames IO_EXCEPTIONS.USE_ERROR;
  DEVICE_ERROR : exception renames IO_EXCEPTIONS.DEVICE_ERROR;
  END_ERROR    : exception renames IO_EXCEPTIONS.END_ERROR;
  DATA_ERROR   : exception renames IO_EXCEPTIONS.DATA_ERROR;
private
  -- implementation-dependent
end DIRECT_IO;
```

```
with IO_EXCEPTIONS;
package TEXT_IO is
  type FILE_TYPE is limited private;
  type FILE_MODE is (IN_FILE, OUT_FILE);
  type COUNT is range 0 .. IMPLEMENTATION_DEFINED;
  subtype POSITIVE_COUNT is COUNT range 1 .. COUNT'LAST;
  UNBOUNDED : constant COUNT := 0; -- line and page length
  subtype FIELD       is INTEGER range 0 .. IMPLEMENTATION_DEFINED;
  subtype NUMBER_BASE is INTEGER range 2 .. 16;
  type TYPE_SET is (LOWER_CASE, UPPER_CASE);
  -- File Management
  procedure CREATE (FILE : in out FILE_TYPE;
                    MODE : in FILE_MODE := OUT_FILE;
                    NAME : in STRING    := "";
                    FORM : in STRING    := "");
  procedure OPEN   (FILE : in out FILE_TYPE;
                    MODE : in FILE_MODE;
                    NAME : in STRING;
                    FORM : in STRING := "");
  procedure CLOSE  (FILE : in out FILE_TYPE);
  procedure DELETE (FILE : in out FILE_TYPE);
  procedure RESET  (FILE : in out FILE_TYPE; MODE : in FILE_MODE);
  procedure RESET  (FILE : in out FILE_TYPE);
  function  MODE   (FILE : in FILE_TYPE) return FILE_MODE;
  function  NAME   (FILE : in FILE_TYPE) return STRING;
  function  FORM   (FILE : in FILE_TYPE) return STRING;
  function  IS_OPEN(FILE : in FILE_TYPE) return BOOLEAN;
  -- Control of default input and output files
  procedure SET_INPUT (FILE : in FILE_TYPE);
  procedure SET_OUTPUT(FILE : in FILE_TYPE);
  function STANDARD_INPUT  return FILE_TYPE;
  function STANDARD_OUTPUT return FILE_TYPE;
  function CURRENT_INPUT   return FILE_TYPE;
  function CURRENT_OUTPUT  return FILE_TYPE;
  -- Specification of line and page lengths
  procedure SET_LINE_LENGTH(FILE : in FILE_TYPE; TO : in COUNT);
  procedure SET_LINE_LENGTH(TO : in COUNT);
  procedure SET_PAGE_LENGTH(FILE : in FILE_TYPE; TO : in COUNT);
  procedure SET_PAGE_LENGTH(TO : in COUNT);
  function  LINE_LENGTH(FILE : in FILE_TYPE) return COUNT;
  function  LINE_LENGTH return COUNT;
  function  PAGE_LENGTH(FILE : in FILE_TYPE) return COUNT;
  function  PAGE_LENGTH return COUNT;
  -- Column, Line, and Page Control
  procedure NEW_LINE   (FILE : in FILE_TYPE; SPACING : in POSITIVE_COUNT := 1);
  procedure NEW_LINE   (SPACING : in POSITIVE_COUNT := 1);
  procedure SKIP_LINE  (FILE : in FILE_TYPE; SPACING : in POSITIVE_COUNT := 1);
  procedure SKIP_LINE  (SPACING : in POSITIVE_COUNT := 1);
```

```
function  END_OF_LINE(FILE : in FILE_TYPE) return BOOLEAN;
function  END_OF_LINE return BOOLEAN;
procedure NEW_PAGE   (FILE : in FILE_TYPE);
procedure NEW_PAGE;
procedure SKIP_PAGE  (FILE : in FILE_TYPE);
procedure SKIP_PAGE;
function  END_OF_PAGE(FILE : in FILE_TYPE) return BOOLEAN;
function  END_OF_PAGE return BOOLEAN;
function  END_OF_FILE(FILE : in FILE_TYPE) return BOOLEAN;
function  END_OF_FILE return BOOLEAN;
procedure SET_COL (FILE : in FILE_TYPE; TO : in POSITIVE_COUNT);
procedure SET_COL (TO   : in POSITIVE_COUNT);
procedure SET_LINE(FILE : in FILE_TYPE; TO : in POSITIVE_COUNT);
procedure SET_LINE(TO   : in POSITIVE_COUNT);
function COL (FILE : in FILE_TYPE) return POSITIVE_COUNT;
function COL  return POSITIVE_COUNT;
function LINE(FILE : in FILE_TYPE) return POSITIVE_COUNT;
function LINE return POSITIVE_COUNT;
function PAGE(FILE : in FILE_TYPE) return POSITIVE_COUNT;
function PAGE return POSITIVE_COUNT;
-- Character Input-Output
procedure GET(FILE : in  FILE_TYPE; ITEM : out CHARACTER);
procedure GET(ITEM : out CHARACTER);
procedure PUT(FILE : in  FILE_TYPE; ITEM : in CHARACTER);
procedure PUT(ITEM : in  CHARACTER);
-- String Input-Output
procedure GET(FILE : in  FILE_TYPE; ITEM : out STRING);
procedure GET(ITEM : out STRING);
procedure PUT(FILE : in  FILE_TYPE; ITEM : in STRING);
procedure PUT(ITEM : in  STRING);
procedure GET_LINE(FILE : in  FILE_TYPE; ITEM : out STRING; LAST : out NATURAL);
procedure GET_LINE(ITEM : out STRING; LAST : out NATURAL);
procedure PUT_LINE(FILE : in  FILE_TYPE; ITEM : in STRING);
procedure PUT_LINE(ITEM : in  STRING);
-- Generic package for Input-Output of Integer Types
generic
  type NUM is range <>;
package INTEGER_IO is
  DEFAULT_WIDTH : FIELD := NUM'WIDTH;
  DEFAULT_BASE  : NUMBER_BASE := 10;
  procedure GET(FILE : in  FILE_TYPE; ITEM : out NUM; WIDTH : in FIELD := 0);
  procedure GET(ITEM : out NUM; WIDTH : in FIELD := 0);
  procedure PUT(FILE  : in FILE_TYPE;
                ITEM  : in NUM;
                WIDTH : in FIELD := DEFAULT_WIDTH;
                BASE  : in NUMBER_BASE := DEFAULT_BASE);
  procedure PUT(ITEM  : in NUM;
                WIDTH : in FIELD := DEFAULT_WIDTH;
```

```
                  BASE   : in NUMBER_BASE := DEFAULT_BASE);
   procedure GET(FROM : in  STRING; ITEM : out NUM; LAST : out POSITIVE);
   procedure PUT(TO   : out STRING;
                 ITEM : in NUM;
                 BASE : in NUMBER_BASE := DEFAULT_BASE);
end INTEGER_IO;
-- Generic packages for Input-Output of Real Types
generic
  type NUM is digits <>;
package FLOAT_IO is
  DEFAULT_FORE : FIELD := 2;
  DEFAULT_AFT  : FIELD := NUM'DIGITS-1;
  DEFAULT_EXP  : FIELD := 3;
  procedure GET(FILE : in FILE_TYPE; ITEM : out NUM; WIDTH : in FIELD := 0);
  procedure GET(ITEM : out NUM; WIDTH : in FIELD := 0);
  procedure PUT(FILE : in FILE_TYPE;
                ITEM : in NUM;
                FORE : in FIELD := DEFAULT_FORE;
                AFT  : in FIELD := DEFAULT_AFT;
                EXP  : in FIELD := DEFAULT_EXP);
  procedure PUT(ITEM : in NUM;
                FORE : in FIELD := DEFAULT_FORE;
                AFT  : in FIELD := DEFAULT_AFT;
                EXP  : in FIELD := DEFAULT_EXP);
  procedure GET(FROM : in STRING; ITEM : out NUM; LAST : out POSITIVE);
  procedure PUT(TO   : out STRING;
                ITEM : in NUM;
                AFT  : in FIELD := DEFAULT_AFT;
                EXP  : in FIELD := DEFAULT_EXP);
end FLOAT_IO;
generic
  type NUM is delta <>;
package FIXED_IO is
  DEFAULT_FORE : FIELD := NUM'FORE;
  DEFAULT_AFT  : FIELD := NUM'AFT;
  DEFAULT_EXP  : FIELD := 0;
  procedure GET(FILE : in FILE_TYPE; ITEM : out NUM; WIDTH : in FIELD := 0);
  procedure GET(ITEM : out NUM; WIDTH : in FIELD := 0);
  procedure PUT(FILE : in FILE_TYPE;
                ITEM : in NUM;
                FORE : in FIELD := DEFAULT_FORE;
                AFT  : in FIELD := DEFAULT_AFT;
                EXP  : in FIELD := DEFAULT_EXP);
  procedure PUT(ITEM : in NUM;
                FORE : in FIELD := DEFAULT_FORE;
                AFT  : in FIELD := DEFAULT_AFT;
                EXP  : in FIELD := DEFAULT_EXP);
  procedure GET(FROM : in  STRING; ITEM : out NUM; LAST : out POSITIVE);
```

```
    procedure PUT(TO   : out STRING;
                  ITEM : in NUM;
                  AFT  : in FIELD := DEFAULT_AFT;
                  EXP  : in FIELD := DEFAULT_EXP);
  end FIXED_IO;
  -- Generic package for Input-Output of Enumeration Types
  generic
    type ENUM is (<>);
  package ENUMERATION_IO is
    DEFAULT_WIDTH   : FIELD := 0;
    DEFAULT_SETTING : TYPE_SET := UPPER_CASE;
    procedure GET(FILE  : in FILE_TYPE; ITEM : out ENUM);
    procedure GET(ITEM  : out ENUM);
    procedure PUT(FILE  : in FILE_TYPE;
                  ITEM  : in ENUM;
                  WIDTH : in FIELD    := DEFAULT_WIDTH;
                  SET   : in TYPE_SET := DEFAULT_SETTING);
    procedure PUT(ITEM  : in ENUM;
                  WIDTH : in FIELD    := DEFAULT_WIDTH;
                  SET   : in TYPE_SET := DEFAULT_SETTING);
    procedure GET(FROM : in  STRING; ITEM : out ENUM; LAST : out POSITIVE);
    procedure PUT(TO   : out STRING;
                  ITEM : in  ENUM;
                  SET  : in  TYPE_SET := DEFAULT_SETTING);
  end ENUMERATION_IO;
  -- Exceptions
  STATUS_ERROR : exception renames IO_EXCEPTIONS.STATUS_ERROR;
  MODE_ERROR   : exception renames IO_EXCEPTIONS.MODE_ERROR;
  NAME_ERROR   : exception renames IO_EXCEPTIONS.NAME_ERROR;
  USE_ERROR    : exception renames IO_EXCEPTIONS.USE_ERROR;
  DEVICE_ERROR : exception renames IO_EXCEPTIONS.DEVICE_ERROR;
  END_ERROR    : exception renames IO_EXCEPTIONS.END_ERROR;
  DATA_ERROR   : exception renames IO_EXCEPTIONS.DATA_ERROR;
  LAYOUT_ERROR : exception renames IO_EXCEPTIONS.LAYOUT_ERROR;
private
  -- implementation-dependent
end TEXT_IO;
```

The initial 32 values in the type **CHARACTER** and the last value (shown as lower case identifiers) are not truly identifiers. Instead they are available only as identifiers defined "within" the predefined package **ASCII**. For example, the character **nul** is available as **ASCII.NUL**.

```
type CHARACTER is
  (nul,  soh,  stx,  etx,      eot,  enq,  ack,  bel,
   bs,   ht,   lf,   vt,       ff,   cr,   so,   si,
   dle,  dc1,  dc2,  dc3,      dc4,  nak,  syn,  etb,
   can,  em,   sub,  esc,      fs,   gs,   rs,   us,
   ' ',  '!',  '"',  '#',      '$',  '%',  '&',  ''',
   '(',  ')',  '*',  '+',      ',',  '-',  '.',  '/',
   '0',  '1',  '2',  '3',      '4',  '5',  '6',  '7',
   '8',  '9',  ':',  ';',      '<',  '=',  '>',  '?',
   '@',  'A',  'B',  'C',      'D',  'E',  'F',  'G',
   'H',  'I',  'J',  'K',      'L',  'M',  'N',  'O',
   'P',  'Q',  'R',  'S',      'T',  'U',  'V',  'W',
   'X',  'Y',  'Z',  '[',      '\',  ']',  '^',  '_',
   '`',  'a',  'b',  'c',      'd',  'e',  'f',  'g',
   'h',  'i',  'j',  'k',      'l',  'm',  'n',  'o',
   'p',  'q',  'r',  's',      't',  'u',  'v',  'w',
   'x',  'y',  'z',  '{',      '|',  '}',  '~',  del);
```

```
package ASCII is
  -- Control characters:
  NUL      : constant CHARACTER := NUL;  SOH       : constant CHARACTER := SOH;
  STX      : constant CHARACTER := STX;  ETX       : constant CHARACTER := ETX;
  EOT      : constant CHARACTER := EOT;  ENQ       : constant CHARACTER := ENQ;
  ACK      : constant CHARACTER := ACK;  BEL       : constant CHARACTER := BEL;
  BS       : constant CHARACTER := BS;   HT        : constant CHARACTER := HT;
  LF       : constant CHARACTER := LF;   VT        : constant CHARACTER := VT;
  FF       : constant CHARACTER := FF;   CR        : constant CHARACTER := CR;
  SO       : constant CHARACTER := SO;   SI        : constant CHARACTER := SI;
  DLE      : constant CHARACTER := DLE;  DC1       : constant CHARACTER := DC1;
  DC2      : constant CHARACTER := DC2;  DC3       : constant CHARACTER := DC3;
  DC4      : constant CHARACTER := DC4;  NAK       : constant CHARACTER := NAK;
  SYN      : constant CHARACTER := SYN;  ETB       : constant CHARACTER := ETB;
  CAN      : constant CHARACTER := CAN;  EM        : constant CHARACTER := EM;
  SUB      : constant CHARACTER := SUB;  ESC       : constant CHARACTER := ESC;
  FS       : constant CHARACTER := FS;   GS        : constant CHARACTER := GS;
  RS       : constant CHARACTER := RS;   US        : constant CHARACTER := US;
  DEL      : constant CHARACTER := DEL;
  -- Other characters:
  EXCLAM   : constant CHARACTER := '!';  QUOTATION : constant CHARACTER := '"';
  SHARP    : constant CHARACTER := '#';  DOLLAR    : constant CHARACTER := '$';
  PERCENT  : constant CHARACTER := '%';  AMPERSAND : constant CHARACTER := '&';
  COLON    : constant CHARACTER := ':';  SEMICOLON : constant CHARACTER := ';';
  QUERY    : constant CHARACTER := '?';  AT_SIGN   : constant CHARACTER := '@';
```

```
  L_BRACKET: constant CHARACTER := '[';   BACK_SLASH: constant CHARACTER := '\';
  R_BRACKET: constant CHARACTER := ']';   CIRCUMFLEX: constant CHARACTER := '^';
  UNDERLINE: constant CHARACTER := '_';   GRAVE     : constant CHARACTER := '`';
  L_BRACE  : constant CHARACTER := '{';   BAR       : constant CHARACTER := '|';
  R_BRACE  : constant CHARACTER := '}';   TILDE     : constant CHARACTER := '~';
  -- Lower case letters:
  LC_A: constant CHARACTER := 'a';
  ...
  LC_Z: constant CHARACTER := 'z';
end ASCII;
```

Appendix D

Packages

This appendix contains the declarations of the **Lines**, **Simple_IO**, **Robot**, and **Robots** packages used in the text. It also contains the bodies of the **Lines** and **Simple_IO** packages. The bodies of the **Robot** and **Robots** packages are found in the instructor's manual for this text.

D.1 THE LINES PACKAGE

A description of this package is found in sections 3.11, 4.10, 6.4.1, and 12.9 of the text.

```
package Lines is
-- Purpose: To provide something close to a variable length array of characters.
--  In fact each line is a record and has a maximum size, but can
--   store any number of characters up to that size.
--  Overloadings: these are designed to allow the use of STRING literals as
--   though they were line literals. The subprograms can operate on STRING
--   variables as well.

  -- The fundamental type is Super_Line. Objects of this type can have any
  --  maximum size.
  -- Super_Line is not limited private because we wish the user to be able
  --  to have out parameters of this type and its Normal_Line subtype.

  subtype Line_Size is NATURAL;
  type Super_Line(Size: Line_Size) is private;

  --  The most commonly used subtype is Normal_Line. Objects of
```

```
--   this type can have up to 96 characters.

Normal_Size: constant Line_Size := 96;
subtype Normal_Line is Super_Line(Normal_Size);

-- Characters in a line are indexed (numbered) from 1 through the number of
--   characters. Accessing and changing often uses an index to indicate
--   where in a line the access or change is to occur

subtype Index is NATURAL;

-- Indexing characters or locations not within the current length of a line
--   results in Illegal_Lines_Index being raised.

Illegal_Lines_Index: EXCEPTION;

function Length (Source: Super_Line) return Line_Size;
-- Purpose: Determine how many characters are currently in the line.

-- Comparison routines for Super_Lines and STRINGS. Comparison is
--   lexicographical.
function "<="(Left, Right: Super_Line) return BOOLEAN;
function ">="(Left, Right: Super_Line) return BOOLEAN;
function "<" (Left, Right: Super_Line) return BOOLEAN;
function ">" (Left, Right: Super_Line) return BOOLEAN;

function "<="(Left: STRING; Right: Super_Line) return BOOLEAN;
function ">="(Left: STRING; Right: Super_Line) return BOOLEAN;
function "<" (Left: STRING; Right: Super_Line) return BOOLEAN;
function ">" (Left: STRING; Right: Super_Line) return BOOLEAN;

function "<="(Left: Super_Line; Right: STRING) return BOOLEAN;
function ">="(Left: Super_Line; Right: STRING) return BOOLEAN;
function "<" (Left: Super_Line; Right: STRING) return BOOLEAN;
function ">" (Left: Super_Line; Right: STRING) return BOOLEAN;

function Equals(Left,             Right: Super_Line) return BOOLEAN;
function Equals(Left: Super_Line; Right: STRING)     return BOOLEAN;
function Equals(Left: STRING;     Right: Super_Line) return BOOLEAN;
-- Note: Since Super_Line is not limited "=" cannot be overloaded.

function Image(Source: in Super_Line) return STRING;
-- Purpose: Produce a STRING from a Line. The length of the STRING is the
--   number of characters currently in the line.

function Location(Fragment: in Super_Line; Source: in Super_Line;
                  Start: in Index := 1) return Index;
function Location(Fragment: in STRING; Source: in Super_Line;
                  Start: in Index := 1) return Index;
function Location(Fragment: in STRING; Source: in STRING;
                  Start: in Index := 1) return Index;
function Location(Fragment: in Super_Line; Source: in STRING;
                  Start: in Index := 1) return Index;
-- Purpose: return the starting location (index) of a fragment in a line (or
```

```
--   string)
--  Fragment: the substring we are trying to locate.
--  Start: ignore the front of the line and start looking beginning at this
--   index.
--  Returns 0 if the Fragment is not found under the given conditions.
--  The default values cause a search for the first occurrence in the line.

procedure Change(Source: in out Super_Line; Position: Index;
                 Alteration: CHARACTER);
-- Purpose: Change a character in a line.
--  Position: the index of the character to be changed.
--  Alteration: the character is to be changed to this value.
-- Illegal_Lines_Index raised if Position is out of range of Source.

procedure Delete(A_Line: in out Super_Line; Start: Index;
                 Amount_Removed: Line_Size);
-- Purpose: Delete characters from a line.
--  Start: the index of the first character to be deleted.
--  Amount_Removed: the number of characters to be deleted.

procedure Insert(Destination: in out Super_Line; Insertion: Super_Line;
                 Location:Line_Size);
procedure Insert(Destination: in out Super_Line; Insertion: STRING;
                 Location: Line_Size);
procedure Insert(Destination: in out Super_Line; Insertion: CHARACTER;
                 Location: Line_Size);
-- Purpose: insert characters into a line.
--  Destination: characters will be inserted into this line.
--  Insertion: the thing to be inserted.
--  Location: where in Destination the insertion is to occur. For example
--   an insertion at location 3 causes the insertion to be placed starting
--   at location 3 and the remaining characters in Destination to be moved
--   back to accommodate the insertion.
-- Illegal_Lines_Index raised if the Location is out range of Destination,
--  or the resulting Super_Line exceeds the constraint on the Destination
--  Super_Line.

procedure Append(Destination: in out Super_Line; Addition: Super_Line);
procedure Append(Destination: in out Super_Line; Addition: STRING);
procedure Append(Destination: in out Super_Line; Addition: CHARACTER);
-- Purpose: catenate onto a line.
--  Destination: the line to receive the catenation.
--  Addition: the value to be catenated onto Destination.
-- Illegal_Lines_Index raised if the resulting Super_Line exceeds the
--  constraints on the Destination Super_Line.

procedure Assign(Destination: out Super_Line; Source: Super_Line);
procedure Assign(Destination: out Super_Line; Source: STRING);
procedure Assign(Destination: out Super_Line; Source: CHARACTER);
-- Purpose: assign a new value to a line. The old value is replaced.
--  Destination: the line that gets a new value.
```

```
-- Source: the new value.
-- Illegal_Lines_Index raised if Source is too long for the constraint on
-- Destination.
-- Note: although assignment (:=) is possible between to objects whose base
-- type is Super_Line, a constraint error will result unless they have
-- identical Line_Size discriminants.

function A_Character(Source: Super_Line; Position: Index) return CHARACTER;
-- Purpose: return a character from a line.
-- Source: the line from which to obtain the character.
-- Position: the index of the character to return.
-- Illegal_Lines_Index raised if Position is not within the current size of
-- Source.

function Extract(Source: Super_Line; Start: Index;
                 Count: Line_Size) return Super_Line;
-- Purpose: extract a portion of a line. A copy is made, the source of the
-- extraction is not changed.
-- Source: the extraction is taken from this line.
-- Start: the subline extracted starts at this index in Source.
-- Count: the number of characters in the extracted subline.
-- Illegal_Lines_Index raised if Start or Count causes any piece of the
-- extraction to fall outside the current size of Source.

private
  type Super_Line(Size: Line_Size) is
    record
      Length: Line_Size := 0;
      Data: STRING(1..Size);
    end record;
end Lines;

package body Lines is

  function Length(Source: Super_Line) return Line_Size is
  -- Purpose: return the length of Source by getting it out of the Length
  -- component.
  begin
    return Source.Length;
  end Length;

  -- The comparison routines.
  -- Purpose: Lexicographically compare two Super_Lines (or a Super_Line and
  -- a STRING). All these use slice comparisons on the data components of the
  -- Super_Lines.

  function "<="(Left, Right: Super_Line) return BOOLEAN is
  begin
    return Left.Data(1..Left.Length) <= Right.Data(1..Right.Length);
  end "<=";

  function ">="(Left, Right: Super_Line) return BOOLEAN is
```

```
begin
  return Left.Data(1..Left.Length) >= Right.Data(1..Right.Length);
end ">=";

function "<"(Left, Right: Super_Line) return BOOLEAN is
begin
  return Left.Data(1..Left.Length) < Right.Data(1..Right.Length);
end "<";

function ">"(Left, Right: Super_Line) return BOOLEAN is
begin
  return Left.Data(1..Left.Length) > Right.Data(1..Right.Length);
end ">";

function "<="(Left: STRING; Right: Super_Line) return BOOLEAN is
begin
  return Left <= Right.Data(1..Right.Length);
end "<=";

function ">="(Left: STRING; Right: Super_Line) return BOOLEAN is
begin
  return Left >= Right.Data(1..Right.Length);
end ">=";

function "<"(Left: STRING; Right: Super_Line) return BOOLEAN is
begin
  return Left < Right.Data(1..Right.Length);
end "<";

function ">"(Left: STRING; Right: Super_Line) return BOOLEAN is
begin
  return Left > Right.Data(1..Right.Length);
end ">";

function "<="(Left: Super_Line; Right: STRING) return BOOLEAN is
begin
  return Left.Data(1..Left.Length) > Right;
end "<=";

function ">="(Left: Super_Line; Right: STRING) return BOOLEAN is
begin
  return Left.Data(1..Left.Length) >= Right;
end ">=";

function "<"(Left: Super_Line; Right: STRING) return BOOLEAN is
begin
  return Left.Data(1..Left.Length) < Right;
end "<";

function ">"(Left: Super_Line; Right: STRING) return BOOLEAN is
begin
  return Left.Data(1..Left.Length) > Right;
end ">";
```

```
function Equals(Left, Right: Super_line) return BOOLEAN is
begin
  return Left.Data(1..Left.Length) = Right.Data(1..Right.Length);
end Equals;

function Equals(Left: Super_Line; Right: STRING) return BOOLEAN is
begin
  return Left.Data(1..Left.Length) = Right;
end Equals;

function Equals(Left: STRING; Right: Super_Line) return BOOLEAN is
begin
  return Left = Right.Data(1..Right.Length);
end Equals;

function Image(Source: in Super_Line) return STRING is
-- Purpose: return a STRING corresponding to the current contents of source
--  by returning the appropriate slice from the Data component.
begin
  return Source.Data(1..Source.Length);
end Image;

procedure Change(Source: in out Super_Line; Position: Index;
                 Alteration: CHARACTER) is
-- Purpose: change the character at the indicated Position to the character
--  given in Alteration.
-- The index of the character to be changed must be within the current
--  contents of Source.
begin
  if Position not in 1..Source.LENGTH then
    raise Illegal_Lines_Index;
  end if;
  Source.Data(Position) := Alteration;
end Change;

-- Deletes Amount_Removed characters from A_Line starting at Start.
procedure Delete(A_Line: in out Super_Line; Start: Index;
                 Amount_Removed: Line_Size) is
  New_Length: INTEGER := A_Line.Length - Amount_Removed;
begin
  if Amount_Removed > A_Line.Length-Start + 1 then
    raise Illegal_Lines_Index;
  end if;
  A_Line.Data(Start..New_Length) :=
    A_line.Data(Start + Amount_Removed..A_Line.Length);
  A_Line.Length := New_Length;
end Delete;

-- Location: Overloaded for lines and strings.
-- Purpose: return the location of the Which_Occurrence'th occurrence of
--  Fragment in Source. The search starts at the Start position in
```

```
--  Source.  Returns 0 if the Fragment is not found under the given
--  conditions.
-- Notes:
--  exceptions never are raised.
--  The empty string or line is always found at Start, even if Start
--  is not within the length of Source.

function Location(Fragment: in STRING; Source: in STRING;
                  Start: in Index := 1)
                  return Index is
  subtype Search_Range is
          INTEGER range Start..(Source'LENGTH - Fragment'LENGTH) + 1;
  -- If the Fragment is to be found, it must be found in this range.
  Position: Index := Start;

begin
  loop
    exit when Position not in Search_Range;
    if Source(Position..(Position + Fragment'LENGTH) - 1) = Fragment then
      return Position;
    end if;
    Position := Position + 1;
  end loop;
  return 0;
end Location;

function Location(Fragment: in STRING; Source: in Super_Line;
                  Start: in Index := 1) return Index is
begin
  return Location(Fragment, Source.Data(1..Source.Length), Start);
end Location;

function Location(Fragment: in Super_Line; Source: in Super_Line;
                  Start: in Index := 1) return Index is
begin
  return Location(Fragment.Data(1..Fragment.Length),
                  Source.Data(1..Source.Length), Start);
end Location;

function Location(Fragment: in Super_Line; Source: in STRING;
                  Start: in Index := 1) return Index is
begin
  return Location(Fragment.Data(1..Fragment.Length), Source, Start);
end Location;

-- Insert: Inserts into a line.
--  Overloaded to insert lines, strings or characters.
-- Inserts the given Insertion into Destination at the indicated Location in
--  Destination.
-- Illegal_Lines_Index raised if the Location is out of the range of
--  Destination, or the resulting Super_Line exceeds the maximum that can
```

```
-- be stored in Destination.

procedure Insert(Destination: in out Super_Line; Insertion: STRING;
                 Location: Line_Size) is
  New_Length: constant INTEGER := Destination.Length + Insertion'LENGTH;
begin
  if Location not in 1..Destination.LENGTH + 1 or
     New_Length not in 0..Destination.Size then
    raise Illegal_Lines_Index;
  end if;
  Destination.Data(Location..New_Length) :=
    Insertion & Destination.Data(Location..Destination.Length);
  Destination.Length := New_Length;
end Insert;

procedure Insert(Destination: in out Super_Line; Insertion: Super_Line;
                 Location: Line_Size) is
begin
  Insert(Destination, Insertion.Data(1..Insertion.Length), Location);
end Insert;

procedure Insert(Destination: in out Super_Line; Insertion: CHARACTER;
                 Location: Line_Size) is
begin
  Insert(Destination, CHARACTER'IMAGE(Insertion)(2..2), Location);
end Insert;

-- procedure Append: add to the back of a line.
--  Overloaded to append lines, strings or characters.
-- Catenates Addition to Destination.
-- Illegal_Lines_Index raised if the resulting Super_Line exceeds the
-- constraints on the given Super_Line.

procedure Append(Destination: in out Super_Line; Addition: STRING) is
begin
  Insert(Destination, Addition, Length(Destination) + 1);
end Append;

procedure Append(Destination: in out Super_Line; Addition: Super_Line) is
begin
  Insert(Destination, Addition.Data(1..Addition.Length),
         Length(Destination) + 1);
end Append;

procedure Append(Destination: in out Super_Line; Addition: CHARACTER) is
begin
  Insert(Destination, CHARACTER'IMAGE(Addition)(2..2),
         Length(Destination) + 1);
end Append;

function Extract(Source: Super_Line; Start: Index;
                 Count: Line_Size) return Super_Line is
```

```
  Temp_Line: Super_Line(Source.Size);
-- Purpose: extract a portion of a line.
--  Returns the fragment of Source that starts at Start and continues for
--  Count characters.
-- Illegal_Lines_Index raised if any portion of the extraction falls outside
--  the range of Source

begin
  if Start+Count-1 > Source.Length then
    raise Illegal_Lines_Index;
  end if;
  Temp_Line.Length := Count;
  Temp_Line.Data(1..Count) := Source.Data(Start..Start + Count - 1);
  return Temp_Line;
end Extract;

function A_Character(Source: Super_Line;  Position: Index)
                    return CHARACTER is
-- Purpose: return the character found at Position of Source.
-- Illegal_Lines_Index raised if Position is out of the range of Source.
begin
  if Position not in 1..Source.Length then
    raise Illegal_Lines_Index;
  end if;
  return Source.Data(Position);
end A_Character;

-- procedure Assign: assign the given Source to Destination.
--  Overloaded so source may be string, character or line.
-- Assigns the given Source to Destination.
-- Illegal_Lines_Index is raised if the length of Source is too long
--  for the constraint on Destination.
procedure Assign(Destination: out Super_Line; Source: STRING) is
begin
  Destination.Data(1..Source'LENGTH) := Source;
  Destination.Length := Source'LENGTH;
exception
  when CONSTRAINT_ERROR =>
    raise Illegal_Lines_Index;
end Assign;

procedure Assign(Destination: out Super_Line; Source: CHARACTER) is
begin
  Destination.Data(1) := Source;
  Destination.Length := 1;
exception
  when CONSTRAINT_ERROR =>
    raise Illegal_Lines_Index;
end Assign;

procedure Assign(Destination: out Super_Line; Source: Super_Line) is
```

```
  begin
    Destination.Data(1..Source.Length) := Source.Data(1..Source.Length);
    Destination.Length := Source.Length;
  exception
    when CONSTRAINT_ERROR =>
      raise Illegal_Lines_Index;
  end Assign;

end Lines;
```

D.2 THE SIMPLE_IO PACKAGE

A description of this package is found in sections 1.15 and 2.10 of the text. Brief mentions also occur in sections 6.9 (**FLOAT**) and 12.8 (overloading).

```
with Lines;  with IO_EXCEPTIONS;
package Simple_IO is
-- Purpose: provide simplified input and output handling.
--  This is achieved by overloading the identifiers Read and Write.

-- Output
  procedure Write(Value: in STRING);
  procedure Write(Value: in CHARACTER);
  procedure Write(Value: in INTEGER);
  procedure Write(Value: in FLOAT);
  procedure Write(Value: in Lines.Super_Line);
  -- Purpose: print the Value.
  --  Writes at the end of the current line. Does not move to a new line.

  procedure New_Line;
  -- Purpose: End the current output line and move to the start of a new line.

--Input
  procedure Read(Variable: out CHARACTER);
  procedure Read(Variable: out INTEGER);
  procedure Read(Variable: out FLOAT);
  procedure Read(Variable: out Lines.Super_Line);
  -- Purpose: Read a value into a variable.
  --  Reads of INTEGER, FLOAT and Lines.Normal_Line work on a one value
  --   per line basis; that is, you can correct typographical errors
  --   before pressing the line terminator key (normally <RETURN>).
  --  For numeric input (INTEGER and FLOAT), any characters on the
  --   line after the value are discarded.
  --  Lines.Normal_Line input includes all characters on the line.
  --  Reads of CHARACTER read a single character. Multiple Reads can be
  --   used to read several characters on the same line.

  procedure Await_User;
  -- Purpose: Pause for the user.
  --  Accepts and ignores any keys typed up to the next <Return>.

  function End_Of_Line return BOOLEAN;
  -- Purpose: detect end of an input line.
  --  Return TRUE if we are at the end of a line of input. Always FALSE unless
  --  the most recently read value was of type CHARACTER.

  function End_Of_Input return BOOLEAN;
  -- Purpose: detect the end of input.
  --  Return TRUE if we are at the end of all input.

-- Handling input errors
```

```
  procedure Set_Read_Tries(Tries: in POSITIVE);
  -- The Tries parameter determines what happens when a data
  --  error (see below) occurs during subsequent calls to Read.
  --  When the Read procedure is given input with no data
  --  errors, it returns the value specified by that input.
  --  The first Tries-1 times a data error occurs in a single call
  --  to Read, the following message is written on its own line:
  --     "Badly formed input.  Please try again."
  --  and the Read procedure accepts input again.
  --  If a data error is found on the Tries attempt, the
  --  Data_Error exception is raised.  A "data error" occurs
  --  when the characters being read do not represent a value of
  --  the required type; e.g., "L23" while reading an INTEGER.
  -- The number of Tries is initially set to 3.

  Data_Error: exception renames IO_EXCEPTIONS.DATA_ERROR;

end Simple_IO;


with TEXT_IO;
package body Simple_IO is
-- Purpose: provide simplified input and output handling.
--  Implemented by calls to TEXT_IO.
-- The only TEXT_IO items used are
--  DATA_ERROR, NEW_LINE, SKIP_LINE, END_OF_LINE, END_OF_FILE;
--  For CHARACTER: GET and PUT;
--  For FLOAT: GET and PUT;
--  For INTEGER: GET (we STRING PUT the IMAGE);
--  For STRING: GET_LINE, PUT;

  package Float_IO is new TEXT_IO.FLOAT_IO(FLOAT);
  package Integer_IO is new TEXT_IO.INTEGER_IO(INTEGER);

-- Error handling
  Max_Tries: POSITIVE := 3;
  -- The number of times the user can make a mistake on input before DATA_ERROR
  --  is raised.

  procedure Set_Read_Tries(Tries: in POSITIVE) is
  -- Purpose: modify the number of times the user can make a mistake on input
  --  before DATA_ERROR is raised.
  begin
    Max_Tries := Tries;
  end Set_Read_Tries;

  procedure Flush_To_End_Of_Line is
  -- Purpose: ignore anything left in this line of input.
  --  Used by Error_Cleanup, Await_User and by the integer and float reads.
  begin
    TEXT_IO.SKIP_LINE;
  end Flush_To_End_Of_Line;
```

```
  procedure Error_Cleanup is
  -- Purpose: an error has occurred, ignore anything left in this line of input.
  begin
    Flush_To_End_Of_Line;
    New_Line;
  end Error_Cleanup;

  procedure Error_Message is
  -- Purpose: an error has occurred, inform the user.
  begin
    Write("Badly formed input.  Please try again.");
    New_Line;
  end Error_Message;

-- Output routines

  procedure Write(Value: in STRING) is
  begin
    TEXT_IO.PUT(Value);
  end Write;

  procedure Write(Value: in CHARACTER) is
  begin
    TEXT_IO.PUT(Value);
  end Write;

  procedure Write(Value: in INTEGER) is
  begin
    TEXT_IO.PUT(INTEGER'IMAGE(Value));
  end Write;

  procedure Write(Value: in FLOAT) is
  -- Format is ?d.dddddE%dd where '?' is ' ' or '-', d is a digit,
  --  and '%' is '+' or '-'.  For example, 0.0 is written "0.00000E+00"
  begin
    FLOAT_IO.PUT(Value, FORE => 2, AFT => 5, EXP => 3);
  end Write;

  procedure Write(Value: in Lines.Super_Line) is
  begin
    TEXT_IO.PUT(Lines.Image(Value));
  end Write;

  procedure New_Line is
  begin
    TEXT_IO.NEW_LINE;
  end New_Line;

-- Input routines

  procedure Read(Variable: out CHARACTER) is
  begin
    TEXT_IO.GET(Variable);
```

```
end Read;

procedure Read(Variable: out INTEGER) is
begin
  for I in 1..Max_Tries loop
    begin
      Integer_IO.GET(Variable);
      Flush_To_End_Of_Line;
      return;
    exception
      when TEXT_IO.DATA_ERROR =>
        Error_Cleanup;
        if I < Max_Tries then
          Error_Message;
        else
          raise Data_Error;
        end if;
    end;
  end loop;
end Read;

procedure Read(Variable: out FLOAT) is
begin
  for I in 1..Max_Tries loop
    begin
      Float_IO.GET(Variable);
      Flush_To_End_Of_Line;
      return;
    exception
      when TEXT_IO.DATA_ERROR =>
        Error_Cleanup;
        if I < Max_Tries then
          Error_Message;
        else
          raise Data_Error;
        end if;
    end;
  end loop;
end Read;

procedure Read(Variable: out Lines.Super_Line) is
  A_String: STRING(1..Variable.Size);
  Size: NATURAL;
begin
  TEXT_IO.GET_LINE(A_String, Size);
  Lines.Assign(Variable, A_String(1..Size));
end Read;

procedure Await_User is
begin
```

```
    Flush_To_End_Of_Line;
  end Await_User;

  function End_Of_Line return BOOLEAN is
  -- Purpose: detect end of line. Good for CHARACTER reads.
  begin
    return TEXT_IO.END_OF_LINE;
  end End_Of_Line;

  function End_Of_Input return BOOLEAN is
  -- Purpose: detect end of input.
  begin
    return TEXT_IO.END_OF_FILE;
  end End_Of_Input;

end Simple_IO;
```

D.3 THE ROBOT PACKAGE

A description of this package is found in sections 1.16, 4.9, and 7.8.1.

```
with Lines; with Robots;
package Robot is
-- Purpose: provide an educational tool.
-- With the Robot package, a program may control one predefined
--  Robot within the Robot world.  The world is made up of a grid of 20 by 20
--  "squares" on the screen.  On the screen, the Robot takes up a two-character
--  "square," consisting of a character for the Robot's symbol and a character
--  indicating the Robot's current direction.
-- The Robot can move, turn, pick items up one at a time, put them down, and
--  look.
-- The Robot can also leave a trail when moving and turning.
-- Items are stacked on squares in the order that they were put down. The Robot
--  can only pick up the item that is on the top of the stack.
--
-- A text window is provided on the right side of the screen. Input and output
--  should be handled using the procedures supplied by the package that avoid
--  interfering with the screen display. The capabilities supplied are similar
--  to those supplied by Simple_IO. The window does not "scroll" but it does
--  "wrap." After the window is full of text, window I/O continues back up at
--  the top, overwriting what was there before.
--
-- Initialize_World may be called to set up a world for the Robot. If it is
--  not the world is initialized to an empty world. The Robot always begins
--  facing to the right edge of the screen.
--
-- Symbols used in Robot package:
--
-- A            The Robot
-- a..z         Items.  Only the top item on a given square shows up if
--                top item is shown.
-- *            Wall and world boundaries.  The Robot cannot move into these.
-- + , - . /    5 paint colors.

  Empty_World: constant STRING(1..1) := " ";
  -- A special value for Initialize_World when the world is to be empty of
  --  walls and items.

  subtype Item_Range is Robots.Item_Range;
  -- a-z represent items in the Robot world

 -- Movement and direction control.

  procedure Move(Distance: in INTEGER);
  -- Purpose: move the Robot in the direction it is facing.
  --  Distance: the number of squares to move.  A negative Distance causes the
  --  Robot to move backwards.
```

```
   -- Path_Blocked will be raised when the next square is occupied by something
   --  which prevents the Robot from entering it.

   Path_Blocked: exception renames Robots.Path_Blocked;
   -- Raised by Move when the Robot can't move into square.

   type Turns is (Right, Left);
   -- The directions which the Robot can turn.

   procedure Turn(Amount: in Turns);
   -- Purpose: Change the direction the Robot is facing.

-- Paint Control
   -- If there are items in a square, the paint will be hidden under the items.

   subtype Paint_Char is CHARACTER range '+'..'/';
   -- The legal characters for the Robot to paint.
   --                        +  ,  -  .  /

   procedure Set_Paint(New_Paint: in Paint_Char);
   -- Purpose: Set the paint color.

   procedure Paint_On;
   -- Purpose: Start leaving paint. When the Robot leaves a square or turns
   --  in a square, paint will be left. This paint will replace any paint
   --  already there.

   procedure Paint_Off;
   -- Purpose: Stop leaving paint. The Robot will not leave (or erase) paint
   --  when it moves or turns.

   type Look_Dir is (Here, Ahead);
   -- Where the Robot can look.

   function Look(Where: in Look_Dir) return CHARACTER;
   -- Purpose: Examine a square. You can examine the one the Robot occupies or
   --  the one directly in front of the Robot. The character displayed on the
   --  screen is the value Look returns.

-- Item Handling
   function Hands_Full return Boolean;
   -- Purpose: returns true if the Robot is already carrying an item.

   procedure Pick_Up;
   -- Purpose: pick up the top item in the square occupied by the Robot.
   --  Already_Holding_Item is raised if the Robot is already holding an item.
   --  Need_Item is raised if there is no item to pick up.

   Already_Holding_Item: exception renames Robots.Already_Holding_Item;
   -- Raised by Pick_Up if the Robot is already holding an item.

   Need_Item: exception renames Robots.Need_Item;
   -- Raised by Pick_Up if there is no item to pick up.

   procedure Put_Down;
```

```
  -- Purpose: Drop the item the Robot is holding in the square occupied by the
  --  Robot. The item dropped goes onto the top of the stack of items in the
  --  square. Not_Holding_Item is raised if the Robot is not holding an item to
  --  drop.

  Not_Holding_Item: exception renames Robots.Not_Holding_Item;
  -- Raised by Put_Down when the Robot is not carrying anything to drop.

-- Input and Output
  -- Supplies the same procedures as Simple_IO (except no FLOAT).
  --  All I/O occurs in a text window to the right of the Robot's world.
  --  Initially, window I/O begins at the top and progresses down the screen.
  --  When reaching the bottom of this window, text will wrap around to
  --  the top of the screen, overwriting what was previously there.
  --  Long lines wrap around (within the window).

  procedure New_Line renames Robots.New_Line;
  procedure Read(Variable: out CHARACTER) renames Robots.Read;
  procedure Read(Variable: out Lines.Super_Line) renames Robots.Read;
  procedure Read(Variable: out INTEGER) renames Robots.Read;
  procedure Write(Value: in CHARACTER) renames Robots.Write;
  procedure Write(Value: in Lines.Super_Line) renames Robots.Write;
  procedure Write(Value: in STRING) renames Robots.Write;
  procedure Write(Value: in INTEGER) renames Robots.Write;
  function End_Of_Line return BOOLEAN renames Robots.End_Of_Line;

-- Set up

  procedure Initialize_World(WorldFile: in STRING)
                                    renames Robots.Initialize_World;
  -- Purpose: Set up a world with walls and objects. The file encodes
  --  a description of this world. (see Load World format description)

  Initialize_World_Error: exception renames Robots.Initialize_World_Error;
  -- The format of the initialization file was incorrect.

-- Clean up

  procedure Exit_World renames Robots.Exit_World;
  -- Purpose: Robot needs to seize control of the screen I/O. This restores
  --  control of the screen to normal mode.

-- Speed Control
  --  Each Robot action takes time. You can set the amount of time.

  function Current_Delay return DURATION renames Robots.Current_Delay;
  -- Purpose: returns the amount of time an action takes.

  procedure Set_Delay(New_Delay: in DURATION) renames Robots.Set_Delay;
  -- Purpose: set the amount of time an action takes.

end Robot;
```

D.4 THE ROBOTS PACKAGE

This package is an extension of the **Robot** package that allows multiple robots, so the descriptions for that package apply. The description of the additional capabilities is found in section 11.10.

```
with Lines;
package Robots is
-- Written (Winter '86) by: Timo Bruck, Jennifer Durand, Maurice Hermeyer
-- Modified (Spring '86) by: Timo Bruck
-- Modified (Fall '86-Spr 87) by: Teri Tracey
-- Modified (Wtr '88) by: Mark Torres

-- Purpose: provide an educational tool appropriate for tasking assignments.
--  This package "extends" the Robot package to allow more than one Robot.
--  In fact, the Robot package is largely implemented by calls to this package.
-- With the Robots package, a program may control up to 26 Robots within the
--  Robot world.  The world is made up of a grid of 20 by 20 "squares" on the
--  screen.  On the screen, the Robot takes up a two-character "square," a
--  rectangle consisting of a character for the Robot's name and a character
--  for the Robot's current direction.
-- Each Robot can move horizontally and vertically, turn, pick items up
--  one at a time and put them down, and look.
-- Each Robot can also leave a trail of when moving and turning.
-- Items are stacked on squares in the order that they were put down. The Robot
--  can only pick up the item that's on the top of the stack.

-- Robots are created by declaring objects of type Robot. All Robots should
--  be declared before calling Initialize_World. When tasking is used, the
--  Robots can move at the same time.  The Robots package supports tasking by
--  making procedures that update the world "atomic events".
-- Although Robots can be declared locally, we do not recommend it. Ada's
--  mechanisms allow us to detect the elaboration of a variable, but not
--  its expiration.

-- A text window is provided on the right side of the screen. Text is
--  output to the window with Write.  Read is used for input.  This window
--  extends from the right edge of the Robot world to the right edge of the
--  terminal screen, and down as far as the bottom edge of the Robot world.
--  The window does not "scroll" but it does "wrap."  After the window is full
--  of text, window I/O continues back up at the top, overwriting what was
--  there before.
--
-- Initialize_World can be called to set up a world for the Robot. If it is
--  not the world is initialized to an empty world.
--
-- Symbols used in Robots package:
--
-- A..Z           Robots. Only one Robot allowed per square at a time.
```

```
-- a..z           Items.  Only the top item on a given square shows up if
--                  more than one is present.
-- *              Wall and world boundaries.  The Robot cannot move into walls.
-- =              Window.  Robots may look and pass items into windows
-- + , - . /      5 paint colors.

  type Robot is limited private;
  -- Each Robot object declared creates a Robot within the world.
  --  When a Robot is declared a screen symbol will be supplied.
  --  This symbol (A..Z) will be different for each Robot so that to
  --  distinguish them. Symbols are assigned alphabetically in the order of
  --  Robot declaration. The Robot will be initially assigned a default
  --  location in the world. This location can be changed by Initialize_World.

  Too_Many_Robots: exception;
  -- raised if more than 26 Robots are declared.

  Empty_World: constant STRING (1..1) := " ";
  -- A special value for Initialize_World when the world is to be empty of
  --  walls and items.

  subtype Item_Range is CHARACTER range 'a'..'z';
  -- The legal items.

-- Movement and direction control.

  procedure Move(TheRobot: in Robot; Distance: in INTEGER);
  -- Purpose: move the Robot in the direction it is facing.
  --  Distance: the number of squares to move. A negative Distance causes the
  --  Robot to move backward.
  -- Path_Blocked will be raised when the next square is occupied by a wall
  --  window or other Robot.

  Path_Blocked: exception;
  -- raised by Move when the next square cannot be entered.

  type Turns is (Right, Left);
  -- The directions a Robot can turn.

  procedure Turn(TheRobot: in Robot; Amount: in Turns);
  -- Purpose: Change the direction the Robot is facing.

-- Paint control.

  subtype Paint_Char is CHARACTER range '+'..'/';
  -- The legal paint characters.

  procedure Set_Paint(TheRobot: in Robot; New_Paint: in Paint_Char);
  -- Purpose: change the paint color for this Robot.

  procedure Paint_On(TheRobot: in Robot);
  -- Purpose: Start leaving paint. When this Robot leaves a square or turns
  --  in a square, paint will be left. This paint will replace any paint
  --  already there.
```

```
   procedure Paint_Off(TheRobot: in Robot);
   -- Purpose: Stop leaving paint. This Robot will not leave (or erase) paint
   --  when it moves or turns.
   -- Looking.

   type Look_Dir is (Here, Ahead);
   -- Where the Robot can look.

   function Look(TheRobot: in Robot; Where: in Look_Dir) return CHARACTER;
   -- Purpose: Examine a square. You can examine the one the Robot occupies or
   --  the one directly ahead of the Robot.

-- Item handling.

   function Hands_Full(TheRobot: in Robot) return Boolean;
   -- Purpose: returns true if the Robot is already carrying an item.

   procedure Pick_Up(TheRobot: in Robot);
   -- Purpose: Pick up the top item in the square occupied by the Robot.
   --  Already_Holding_Item is raised if the Robot is already holding an item.
   --  Need_Item is raised if there is no item to pick up.

   procedure Put_Down(TheRobot: in Robot);
   -- Purpose: Drop the item the Robot is carrying into the square occupied
   --  by the Robot. The item goes to the top of the stack of items in that
   --  square. Not_Holding_Item is raised if the Robot is not holding an item
   --  to drop.

   procedure Give_Item(TheRobot: in Robot);
   -- Purpose: transfer an item from the giving Robot to the receiving Robot.
   --  The receiving Robot must be directly in front of the giving Robot or
   --  directly across from the giving Robot with a window between the two
   --  Robots. The receiving Robot has absolutely no say in the matter.
   -- No_Receiving_Robot is raised if there is no Robot in the proper position.
   -- Already_Holding_Item is raised if the receiving Robot is already carrying
   --  an item.
   -- Not_Holding_Item is raised if the giving Robot is not carrying anything.

   No_Receiving_Robot: exception;
   -- raised by Give_Item when there is no Robot appropriately positioned
   --  to receive the item.

   Already_Holding_Item: exception;
   -- raised by Pick_Up when the Robot is already holding an item.
   -- raised by Give_Item when the target of the give is already holding an item.

   Not_Holding_Item: exception;
   -- raised by Drop when the Robot is not holding an item.

   Need_Item: exception;
   -- raised by Pick_Up when there is no item in the square to pick up.

   -- Input and Output
```

```
  procedure New_Line;
  procedure Read(Variable: out CHARACTER);
  procedure Read(Variable: out Lines.Super_Line);
  procedure Read(Variable: out INTEGER);
  procedure Write(Value: in CHARACTER);
  procedure Write(Value: in Lines.Super_Line);
  procedure Write(Value: in STRING);
  procedure Write(Value: in INTEGER);
  function End_Of_Line return BOOLEAN;
  -- Purpose: input and output. Supplies procedures similar to Simple_IO
  --  Initially, window I/O begins at the top of the text window to the
  --  right of the Robot's world. When reaching the bottom of this window
  --  text will wrap around to the top of screen, overwriting what was
  --  previously there.
  -- If the Super_Line in Write is longer than the text window, it will
  --  wrap to the next line remaining within the text window.
  -- If a non-printable character is read or written a '?' will appear on the
  --  screen.
  -- Read will also input a Normal_Line limited in length to one less than the
  --  width of the text window.

-- Set up.

  procedure Initialize_World(World_File: in STRING);
  -- Purpose: Set up a world with walls and objects. Position the Robots.
  --  This file encodes a description of this world. (See load world
  --  format description.)

  Initialize_World_Error: exception;
  -- raised by Initialize_World if the World_File is not in the correct
  --  format, the wrong Robots placed or incompatible items are placed
  --  in the same square. Before raising this exception Initialize_World
  --  issues an error message to the screen.

-- Clean up.

  procedure Exit_World;
  -- Purpose: return control of the screen to normal.

-- Speed control.
  --  Each Robot action takes time. You can set the amount of time.

  function Current_Delay return DURATION;
  -- Purpose: returns the amount of time an action takes.

  procedure Set_Delay(New_Delay: in DURATION);
  -- Purpose: set the amount of time an action takes.

private
  function Init_Robot return CHARACTER;

  type Robot is
    record
```

```
      Name: CHARACTER := Init_Robot;
    end record;
end Robots;
```

Appendix E

Glossary

Abstraction — The act of clarifying by removing detail. For example, showing the design of a program by showing only the relationships between the subprograms, without showing what the subprograms do.

Access object — An object containing information which permits access to another data object. Most useful when dealing with dynamically allocated information. Also called an address or pointer.

Actual parameter — The value passed to a subprogram from the calling subprogram. Each actual parameter is paired with a *formal parameter* which is used within the called subprogram.

Aggregate — A structure which represents a value of a nonscalar data type. Permits assignment of an entire array or record from a literal.

Algorithm — A sequence of instructions guaranteed to solve a problem. Usually used to refer to previously tested general-purpose subprograms.

Array — A data structure which corresponds to a repetition of objects of a single type. The *components* are accessed by specifying which is intended with an *index*.

Attribute — An operation associated with a *type* or an *object* which provides information about an object or objects of that type, other than the value. Examples are **`IMAGE`** (generates a string version of the value), and **`FIRST`** (the first value in the range of the type).

Base type — The original type from which a type is derived. If a type is derived from another type (either as a subtype or a derived type), then it inherits the base type.

Italics indicate cross-references to other entries in the glossary.

Based literal — A numeric literal which includes an indication of the base in which the literal is to be interpreted. For example, prefixing a numeric literal with **2#** indicates that it should be interpreted in base 2.

Basic declarative item — Any declaration except a *body*. This distinction is made because within any declarative part, all basic declarative items precede all bodies.

Binary search — Search of an ordered list based on dividing the list in half with each value checked. Since the list is ordered, checking the middle item determines whether the desired item is in the first half or the second half. The search is repeated on the appropriate half until the desired item is found. This is a very fast search technique when items are in an array.

Binary — A base 2 number. Each binary digit (called a *bit*) is either 0 or 1.

Body — The portion of a package, subprogram, or task which contains the implementation. Usually separate from the *specification*.

BOOLEAN — Calculation with TRUE and FALSE as the only values.

Bounds — The end points designated for a subtype, for schema, or array index. For example, if we define **subtype Mon is INTEGER 1..12**, 1 and 12 are the bounds of the subtype.

Call — To invoke a subprogram; that is, to start the subprogram executing and wait for it to complete.

Comment — Information added to the source of a program which is intended to inform the human reader and is ignored by the *translator*. Comments do not affect the execution of a subprogram, but are necessary for proper enhancement and correction.

Compiler — See *translator*.

Compilation unit — A declaration which is not nested inside another declaration. It may be a *specification* or a *body*. See also *library unit*.

Components — The objects which make up a portion of a nonscalar object. An *array* is a list of components of the same type, while a *record* is a collection of components which may be of different types. Components are sometimes called fields.

Conform — To match. In Ada this usually means to match closely, not necessarily to match exactly. How close a match is necessary depends on the specific instance.

Constant — An object, the value of which cannot be changed after the object is elaborated. Constants are useful as objects whose value is guaranteed not to change (making them useful in defensive programming).

Constraint — In Ada, the restrictions imposed on an object or subtype. In general, the restrictions which are used to guarantee the validity of operations.

Context clause — A clause at the beginning of a *compilation unit* which indicates which *library units* are made use of within the compilation unit. This clause makes the library units available for use. A use clause may be included in the context clause.

Critical region — A portion of a program which must not run at the same time as some other portions of the program, in order to guarantee correctness. For example, if two parts of the program both update the same global variable, these two parts constitute critical regions and must not execute at the same time.

Declaration — Text which declares something. Declarations include both specifications and bodies. This is a very general term.

Declarative region — For definition of *scope*, programs are divided into declarative regions. These are from the beginning to the end of a declaration. Items declared in a declarative region are not accessible outside that region.

Default value — The value assigned if no initial value is given. For instance, if a parameter of mode `in` is declared with a default value, and no actual parameter is associated with it in a call, the parameter takes the default value for the duration of the call.

Direct visibility — An identifier without a prefix may be used to designate an entity. See also *visibility by selection.*

Discrete — Types for which it is possible to designate a specific predecessor or successor for each value. These include the integer and enumeration types.

Discriminant — A component of a record which is indicated as part of the declaration of the record.

Disk — See *secondary memory.*

Divide and conquer — A problem solving technique based on dividing the problem into smaller parts and solving the parts.

Documentation — Information about a program intended to describe the program either to the user or the future programmers who may work with the program. This information may either be separate from the program or comments in the program.

Elaboration — The execution of declarations before the associated body is executed. This includes allocation of memory for objects and assignment of initial values.

Enumeration types — Types for which the programmer has listed (enumerated) the values. Character types are special cases of enumeration types.

Erroneous — Improper, but not necessarily a problem which the translator will detect. For instance, assuming that the value of a parameter of mode `in out` will not be copied to the actual parameter until the procedure completes.

Exceptions — Indications that an error or unusual situation has occurred. Ada permits the explicit declaration and raising of exceptions.

Exclusive OR — A *Boolean* operation. (X exclusive or Y) is true if and only if either X is true or Y is true, but not both.

Execute — To follow a sequence of instructions. To run a program or subprogram.

Exponent — The part of a formula or numeric literal indicating what power of the base is to multiply the mantissa. For instance, in `1.0e5`, the 5 is an exponent. The value of this literal is 10,000 or 1.0×10^5.

Extended scope — Those parts of a program in which an identifier may be used, but outside of the *immediate scope* of the identifier. For example, identifiers defined in the specification of a package are available in subprograms which list the package name in a context clause.

File — Collection of related information in secondary memory.

Fixed point — Real numbers in which the same number of digits is always stored to the right of the decimal point.

Floating point — Real numbers in which the same number of digits of precision is always represented. The decimal point "floats" as the size of the number increases or decreases.

Formal parameter — The identifier associated with a parameter within the subprogram. Depending on the mode, the initial value may be taken from the actual parameter, and/or the final value may be copied back to the actual parameter. If it is of mode `in` the formal parameter is used as if it were a constant with the value passed from the *actual parameter*. If it is of mode `in out` it is used as if it were a variable. If it is of mode `out` values can be assigned to it which will be copied to the actual parameter. The formal parameter can also be thought of as a way to access the actual parameter.

Function — A subprogram which returns a value. Can be used in an expression.

Guard — A restriction on a statement list which permits the list to be executed only if the guard is true. Used in Ada to restrict application of clauses in a selective wait statement. Used more generally in some other programming languages.

Hardware — The physical portion of a computer system.

High level language — A computer programming language which is designed to be easy for a human to read, even if it is difficult to translate into a form which the hardware can execute. What is meant by the "level" of a language is a point of disagreement among computer professionals, but a higher level language should be easier to read and require that the programmer specify fewer details.

Identifier — A name used to identify an object or operation. In Ada, this is a simple name without any selectors or discriminants.

Immediate scope — The scope of an identifier which extends from the point at which the identifier is declared to the end of the declarative region. See also *extended scope*.

Index — The indicator of which component in an array is desired.

Initialize — To give an object a value before the object is used. Ada provides a means of giving an object an initial value when the object is elaborated. If a value is used from a variable which is not initialized, the value will be meaningless.

Interrupt — As a verb, to stop something prematurely. Used in computer science as a noun meaning an action which interrupts normal processing. Often, the interrupt is processed, and normal processing is permitted to continue.

Invoke — See *call*.

Iterate — To repeat. A program is said to be iterative if it repeats some operation. In Ada, iteration is controlled by the various forms of the loop statement.

Library unit — The specification for a package, subprogram, or generic which is not nested inside any other declaration. These may be referred to in a *context clause*.

Machine code — The binary form of the low level language which instructs the computer. When this language is represented symbolically, it is called assembly language.

Main memory — The part of the computer which stores the program and its information while the program is executing. This is a temporary storage device only. Also called RAM (Random Access Memory) or core, because of the technologies used to implement it.

Mantissa — The formal name for the fractional part of a scientific notation or floating point number. For example, when the number 1/4 is represented in floating point notation as 1.0×2^{-2} the 1.0 is the mantissa.

Memory — The part of the computer which stores programs and information. Often divided into *main memory* and *secondary memory*. Also called storage.

Named association — Actual parameters can be associated with the *formal parameters* by either *positional association* or named association. In named association, the name of the formal parameter is explicitly given in the designation of the actual parameter.

Object — Something which can hold a value. In Ada, these are variables and constants. Sometimes, this term is also considered to include parameters. In Ada, a task is also an object.

Overflow — When performing calculations on a computer, the magnitude of the results is limited by the method used to represent the numbers. Overflow is the condition which occurs when the result of a calculation is too large to be represented with the method used.

Overloaded — When a name is used for more than one purpose, it is said to be overloaded. In Ada, several subprograms can have the same name, but different parameter types. In this case, the translator will determine which subprogram is appropriate for the particular use.

Package — As a verb, to put things into a container. In Ada, structure into which objects and subprograms may be assembled. The package acts to associate the parts, and to store them together in the software library. Moreover, packages can be used to assist in programming techniques such as abstract data types, object oriented programming, and information hiding.

Parameters — The objects used in passing values when a subprogram is called. See *actual parameters* and *formal parameters*. The values are passed from the caller to the subprogram or from the subprogram to the caller.

Parameter mode — There are three parameter modes in Ada, corresponding to different restrictions on what can be done with the formal parameters in a subprogram. Parameters of mode **`in`** act as constants within the subprogram (they receive values into the subprogram). Parameters of mode **`out`** can have values assigned to them, but no value can be obtained from them within the subprogram (they transfer values out of a procedure). Parameters of mode **`in out`** transfer information both ways.

Positional association — Parameters may be passed via either positional association or *named association*. When parameters are passed via positional association, the first actual parameter is paired with the first formal parameter, the second with the second, etc. Thus, the pairing of parameters is implicit.

Pragma — An instruction in the program source to control the operation of the translator. Most do not directly effect the correctness of the resulting program, but merely suggest how the translator should behave in terms of optimization (making the program more efficient), making listings, etc.

Precedence — The order in which operations in an expression are carried out. For instance, multiplication has precedence over addition. This means that unless parentheses are used to control the order of evaluation, multiplications will be performed before addition. Thus, the value of the expression $2 + 3 \times 5$, is 17.

Processor — The portion of the computer hardware which actually carries out computations. Sometimes called the CPU, for Central Processing Unit.

Record — A collection of objects which may be of different types. The *components* are each named by a designator (a name which includes the name of the record object, a period, and the name of the specific object within the record).

Recursive — A subprogram is recursive if part of its processing could cause it to be called. The simplest form of recursion, direct recursion, is when a subprogram calls itself (one or more times) to perform part of its operations.

Reserved words — Those identifiers which have special meanings in a language. A program may not define meanings for these identifiers. In Ada, these are identifiers such as **`if`**, **`raise`**, and **`function`**.

Scalar types — The integer, floating point, fixed point, and enumeration types. Objects of these types are normally thought of as a single piece (even though they are composed of bits). Compound objects (arrays and records) are treated as collections of components.

Scope — The part of a program in which a particular entity can be referred to by the identifier associated with it. A prefix for this identifier (see *visibility by selection*) may be required.

Secondary memory — The part of the computer which stores programs and information permanently. This memory is slow to access, and information is usually read into main memory before being used. Also called disk, because of the technology normally used to implement it. (Note: Tape drives and other backup media are often referred to as tertiary memory.)

Semantic — Dealing with the meaning of something, rather than its form.

Software — The portion of a computer system which is represented as information, but which contains instructions for problem solution. Software is made up of programs. The software is executed by the *hardware*.

Specification — The portion of a package, subprogram, or task which indicates how to interface with (or call) it. Often referred to as the declaration, although for conciseness, the Ada grammar distinguishes between the two.

Subprogram — Either a function or procedure. A term not commonly used by languages other than Ada.

Surface semantics — What something seems to mean when read without careful study. Good programming style includes ensuring that the surface semantics of each piece of a computer program corresponds with the actual meaning (deep semantics) of that piece.

Synchronization — To bring things together in time. In some computer programs, several portions of the program (called tasks in Ada) can operate at the same time. Some operations must wait for others to complete. This coordination of when things are performed is called synchronization.

Syntax — The legal form of a language. Analogous to the grammar of a natural language. The syntax of Ada defines what is legal in Ada.

Tools — Any reusable pieces of a program which are written to be used by other parts of the program. In Ada, tools are often placed in packages.

Translator — The utility program which translates a program into a form which can be executed by a computer. Also called a compiler.

Type — An indication of the kind of information which can be stored in an object. Also used to indicate the kind of information a value represents, or the kind of value a parameter can pass. Ada is a strongly typed language. This means that values of different types cannot be mixed, and that the type of a value must conform to the type of the parameter with which it is used.

Type mark — The name of a type or subtype. Used in describing the syntax of Ada declarations and statements.

Underflow — When performing calculations on a computer, the precision of the results is limited by the method used to represent the numbers. Underflow is the condition which occurs when the result of a calculation is too small or too close to zero to be represented with the method used.

Variable — An object which can hold a data value. The value can be changed by assigning a new value to the variable (variables vary). (Contrast this with *constants* which can hold a value but whose value cannot be changed after the constant is elaborated.)

Visibility by selection — An entity can be designated by using an extended name from anywhere in its scope. In some cases, the entity can be designated by just its identifier (see *direct visibility*), otherwise, we say it has visibility by selection (indicating use of the extended name, including a selector).

Index

Q

R

S

T

U

V

W